HARVARD STUDIES IN EAST ASIAN LAW 7

The Internal Organization of Ch'ing Bureaucracy

The Internal Organization of Ch'ing Bureaucracy

Legal, Normative, and Communication Aspects

Thomas A. Metzger

Harvard University Press
Cambridge, Massachusetts
1973

Library of Congress Catalog Card Number 72-96632
SBN 674–45825–7
Printed in the United States of America

For my parents

Abbreviations

CFTL *Ch'in-ting ch'ung-hsiu liu-pu ch'u-fen tse-li* (1887)
HCCSWP *Huang-ch'ao ching-shih wen-pien*
HPTL *Ch'in-ting hu-pu tse-li* (1851)
LHYFC *Liang-huai yen-fa-chih* (1806)
TCHT *Ta-Ch'ing hui-tien* (1899)
TCHTSL *Ta-Ch'ing hui-tien shih-li* (1899)
TCLL *Ta-Ch'ing lü-li* (1870)
TLti *Hsüeh Yün-sheng, Tu-li ts'un-i*
TWI *T'ao Wen-i kung ch'üan-chi*
TYCS *Ch'in-ting hu-pu ts'ao-yün ch'üan-shu* (1845)
TYT *T'ao Yün-t'ing hsien-sheng tsou-shu*

Acknowledgments

My debt to Professors Robert N. Bellah, John K. Fairbank, Kwang-Ching Liu, and Lien-sheng Yang could not be greater. Their historical interests and intellectual standards have determined to a large extent whatever scholarly outlook I may have, and they guided me in the writing of this book, especially during the earlier stages.

Friend, teacher, and intellectual ally, Professor Hao Chang has for more than a decade aided me in my attempts to obtain some insights into Chinese history. My debt to him also is immense.

Professor Benjamin I. Schwartz's long-standing emphasis on intellectual history as an aspect of political action has had a basic influence on my study. Both he and Professor Albert M. Craig read the draft manuscript, and a number of my revisions are attempts to correct shortcomings they pointed out. I am greatly indebted to them also for many long and fruitful discussions about subjects connected to my study.

Many other defects in my work were pointed out by Professor Jerome A. Cohen, Dr. Fu-mei Chang Chen, and Mr. R. Randle Edwards, members of the East Asian Law Program of the Harvard Law School, and I am most grateful to them for their invaluable criticisms. Professor Cohen's continuous moral support was a major factor making revision and publication possible.

Other scholars also gave me their views on problems in this study, particularly Professor Heng Chang, Dr. Ai-li S. Chin, Professor Randall Collins, Professor Jack D. Douglas, Dr. Achilles Fang, Mr. Horst Huber, Professor Harold L. Kahn, Professor John C. Pelzel, Professor Marius Hendrikus van der Valk, Professor John Watt, Mrs. Mi Chu Wiens, and Mr. Edward A. Winkler.

Any student of the Ch'ing period depends greatly on classic studies by scholars such as Derk Bodde, T'ung-tsu Ch'ü, Ping-ti Ho, Kung-ch'üan Hsiao, and E-tu Zen Zun. Although I may sometimes reach conclusions differing from theirs, I am most fortunate to have the opportunity to try to follow in their footsteps.

Like so many students, I have had the privilege of working in that sinological paradise called the Harvard-Yenching Library, first during the directorship of Dr. Alfred K'aiming Ch'iu, then during that of Dr. Eugene W. Wu. My debt to these two distinguished scholars is great. I also benefited from the inexhaustible expertise and helpfulness of other members of their staff, especially Mr. Toshiyuki Aoki, Mr. Lawrence A. Edsall, Mr. Shigeharu Isobe, Mr. Kai-hsien Liu, Mr. George E. Potter, and Mr. Zunvair Yue. I am especially indebted to Mr. Yue for generously using his profound scholarship to help me solve a number of textual problems.

Mrs. Edward B. Shannon and Mrs. John A. Janowicz deserve much thanks for long hours of expert work in typing this study.

I am deeply grateful for financial aid to the Foreign Area Fellowship Program; the East Asian Research Center, Harvard University; and the East Asian Law Program, Harvard Law School.

Suzanne White Metzger, my wife at the time, helped me in various important ways, particularly proofreading, and I am most grateful to her.

Contents

Introduction

This study describes some organizational aspects of bureaucracy in China under the Ch'ing dynasty (1644–1912): some of the norms or political culture of the bureaucrats; the making of laws and the communicating of them within the bureaucracy; and those laws which constituted the main negative sanctions eliciting effort from the bureaucrats in the routine performance of their duties. These aspects can be called "internal" because they largely concerned conditions of cooperation between the bureaucrats and the emperor rather than bureaucratic activities directly affecting the social world outside the bureaucracy.

Description of these internal aspects is worthwhile because, although inherently interesting and significant, they have hitherto been neglected. An eminent anthropologist has recently stated that "the study of the Chinese family is a never-ending enterprise,"[1] and surely the same can be said for imperial China's bureaucracy, which was a multifaceted institution every bit as real, human, and important as the family.[2] Moreover, Ch'ing bureaucracy occupies a historically pivotal position, being the base line of China's process of political modernization.

The internal aspects of Ch'ing bureaucracy deserve description also because they affected the power of the bureaucracy. Unlike the primary tasks of bureaucracy, such as tax collection or maintenance of law and order, internal activities were not the raison d'être of bureaucracy. Yet the efficiency with which the bureaucracy performed its primary tasks depended to a considerable extent on its internal conditions of cooperation.

1. This is Maurice Freedman's comment on page xiii of Margery Wolf, *The House of Lim* (New York: Appleton-Century-Crofts, 1968).

2. For the study of Ch'ing bureaucracy, the leading general reference works are Ma Feng-ch'en, *Ch'ing-tai hsing-cheng chih-tu yen-chiu ts'an-k'ao shu-mu* (Annotated bibliography for research into the administrative institutions of the Ch'ing dynasty; Peking, n.d.); John K. Fairbank, *Ch'ing Documents* (Cambridge, Mass., 1965); *Chung-kuo ts'ung-shu tsung-lu* (Index to China's collections of varied writings; Peking, 1959–1962); and A. W. Hummel, *Eminent Chinese of the Ch'ing Period* (Washington, 1943). Standard accounts of China's state and society in the Ch'ing period are those in Chapter 9 of E. O. Reischauer and J. K. Fairbank, *East Asia—the Great Tradition* (Boston, 1958, 1960), in Chapters 2 and 5 of J. K. Fairbank, E. O. Reischauer, and A. M. Craig, *East Asia—the Modern Transformation* (Boston, 1965), and in I. C. Y. Hsü, *The Rise of Modern China* (New York, 1970), chaps. 3 and 4.

And efficiency was a major aspect of power: the more efficiently the bureaucracy performed its primary tasks, the greater its power relative to its own society and foreign ones.

That internal conditions affected the efficiency and power of the bureaucracy is a proposition that can be supported in a number of ways. It accords with that prominent outlook in imperial China whereby proper *li-cheng* (management of governmental personnel) was regarded as the foundation of effective and good government. It is backed by much evidence in this book. It accords with propositions put forward in the modern literature on organizations and political systems, which has identified such internal factors as "auxiliary" or "adjective" activities, or as "system maintenance and adaptation functions."[3] And it accords with our common sense.

Thinking about the bureaucracy's power, we are led to put forward some propositions that hover between the status of a heuristic device and an obvious truth: the bureaucracy both enjoyed functional forces stretching its power and suffered from dysfunctional forces shrinking its power. Moreover, the contest between these forces was close and tense.

In reading the literature on Ch'ing bureaucracy, one is often impressed by the energy and ingenuity with which deviants figured and carried out an endless variety of illegal practices, and one receives the impression that, having set up its procedures, the bureaucracy only spasmodically and lazily set out to counter the efforts of the deviants. I would argue, though, that the bureaucracy did not just use the economic and coercive power easily available to it but rather reached out for less easily accessible forms of power, struggling to stretch its organizational capabilities.

True, the Ch'ing bureaucracy often suffered from a shortage of organizational resources, such as a shortage of funds or a shortage of trusted leadership personnel. This shortage was caused by a variety of factors, notably the weakness of society-wide ties of solidarity and the resulting shortage of political support, which in turn inhibited the state's efforts to concentrate economic resources in its hands and use economic rewards to implement its goals. This shortage of organizational re-

3. J. M. Pfiffner and F. P. Sherwood, *Administrative Organization* (Englewood Cliffs, N. J., 1960), pp. 125–127. G. A. Almond and G. B. Powell, Jr., *Comparative Politics—A Developmental Approach* (Boston, 1966), pp. 29–30.

sources, moreover, was often accompanied by an inflation of organizational ambitions. Total control over the whole society was a fundamental political ideal in China which persisted even as organizational problems were aggravated by the great growth in population during the Ming and Ch'ing periods.

There is not the slightest reason to play down the vast flood of deviant acts. Yet conformist acts were numerous also. Attracting less attention and taken for granted to a large extent, they may or may not have constituted a "silent majority," but to a large extent they were consciously elicited through strenuous organizational efforts. Understanding Ch'ing bureaucracy, I would suggest, largely means understanding the conditions of this busy contest between functional and dysfunctional forces.

Once the contest between functional and dysfunctional forces is viewed as a close one, the need for detailed description becomes obvious, and one cannot be content with the macroscopic generalizations so often found in discussions of historical bureaucracies. Baseball can be used as an analogy. If we want to know why a major league team can beat a college team, some remarks about professional and college players as general types of players are perhaps sufficient. But if we want to understand the contest between two top major league teams, detailed information about the idiosyncrasies of the players is needed. This point is particularly relevant for the study of political norms and ideology. Description of these in terms of general, nomothetic categories like rationalization, differentiation, or secularization fails plausibly to express their meaning for the actors involved and sometimes has involved substantively mistaken generalizations. To a large extent, political norms *are* political thought and so need to be described in the idiosyncratic manner used to study intellectual history.

In this book, therefore, I aim to describe some of the internal aspects of Ch'ing bureaucratic organization, suggesting that they involved a close contest between functional and dysfunctional forces affecting the amount of power wielded by the bureaucracy, and that to understand this contest, detailed description is necessary.

Any study of Ch'ing bureaucracy has not only to present facts but also to discuss them in a manner that is consecutive and makes sense in terms of modern perspectives. Yet available theoretical perspectives do not form an integrated whole and to a large extent are not directly useful for sorting out the historical data at hand. Therefore, while struggling to collect the data accurately, the student also has to concoct his own theoretical framework, as much as possible taking over intact categories that already are well established. This process of data collection and eclectic theory building is obviously a collective enterprise aimed at the day when all the data are in and a single, neat, and comprehensive interpretation of Ch'ing bureaucracy is possible.

At this point it may be useful to present more fully the particular analytical scheme underlying this study. My scheme is only intended to facilitate thought about some features of China's imperial bureaucracy regarding which available data are particularly abundant, not to account for all its features. Although eclectic, it leans toward the Weberian wing of modern social and political thought which stresses "values," rather than the Marxist wing which stresses "interests,"[4] and it obviously displays the influence of a number of leading contemporary scholars such as Talcott Parsons, Gabriel A. Almond, G. Bingham Powell, Jr., S. N. Eisenstadt, and Amitai Etzioni. After presenting it, I will briefly consider some other partly supplementary, partly competitive approaches.

I describe certain elements of Ch'ing bureaucracy and its environment either in a simply descriptive way or in terms of certain criteria commonly found in the modern literature on political systems, bureaucracies, and organizations, notably differentiation or specialization, centralization, coordination, flexibility, and universalism. Using such criteria, I consider whether various elements of the bureaucracy or relations between these elements had a functional or a dysfunctional effect in terms of realizing the indigenously recognized goals of the bureaucracy.

4. For this distinction, see S. M. Lipset, *Political Man* (Garden City, N. Y., 1963), p. xx. Yet Reinhard Bendix' interpretation of Max Weber has also led to an approach stressing the interplay of interests rather than shared values. Theoretically, the problem seems to boil down to the elusive issue of relative importance. In Reinhard Bendix, ed., *State and Society* (Boston, 1968), pp. 42–67, Randall Collins attacks the Parsonian stress on the role of values in the political process. Yet at the very least we have to admit that the ebb and flow of political power is conditioned by the psychological-social-cultural context of values, not just by the interplay of interests, in that this context directly affects organizational efficiency, which in turn affects the ebb and flow of power.

As a list of the elements of the bureaucracy and its environment, I use people, the sense of legitimate authority, interests, capabilities, roles, tasks, constraints (including sanctions), and situational factors. Other concepts basic in the study of bureaucracy—such as decision-making, the formulation of policy and goals, communication, control, law, power, and political culture—are here subsumed under these primary categories.

The bureaucracy thus consists of people with certain interests who act in the name of authority and carry out tasks. Tasks are decisions and actions to carry out procedures, whether or not conceptualized as rules and formalized in writing. I regard law as rules backed by sanctions, which are discussed below. The various levels of involvement in tasks can lead to distinctions between advisory, executive, and supervisory authority, as the experience of Ch'ing China shows.

Substantively, tasks can be put into three groups. First, there was top leadership, the ultimate determination of policy and goals, which was carried out not only at the capital by the emperor and a mixture of palace, noble, and bureaucratic personnel, but also, often enough, by high regional officials. In top leadership, executive authority was often in the hands only of the emperor, but at least advisory authority was possessed by others. Largely because of the lack of a formalized representative organ sharing the authority of top leadership with the emperor, modern scholars regard the Ch'ing state as an autocracy.

Second, there were the tasks of internal organization, carried out both by capital and regional units, such as personnel management, internal management of finances, and the maintenance of discipline.

Communication was an integral part of all tasks, but it can also be seen especially as an internal task, involving the whole flow of laws, other commands, suggestions, and reports through which the bureaucrats were coordinated.

One problem in the flow of communication is that of preparing, transmitting, and mentally digesting large volumes of information.[5] The latter problems were major ones in the Ch'ing bureaucracy, especially since there were large organizational complexes, such as the salt monopoly, which involved numerous commands and laws. How laws were communicated within the bureaucracy is the subject of Chapter II. Effectively diffusing

5. See Almond and Powell, p. 172, 178. On law, see III, 1, note 3.

information was as vital an aspect of communication as was obtaining and, at times, withholding information (that is, secrecy).

Third, there were the primary tasks of the bureaucracy, again carried out both at the capital and regionally. These were the raison d'être of the bureaucracy, its output relative to the emperor, the domestic society, and foreign societies. Besides palace services and foreign affairs, primary tasks consisted of economic and cultural affairs along with that whole largely coercive complex of adjudicative, police, and military activities. Economic, cultural, and coercive activities made up the substance of "local government."

With the exception of adjudicative activities, my categorization of tasks does not make explicit the differentiation between the legislative, executive, and judicial branches. This is because in the case of Ch'ing bureaucracy, legislative and executive activities (or, better, "rule making" and "rule applying" activities) to a large extent were intertwined and so simply were part of the tasks of various units in the bureaucracy. For instance, a highly placed office with the task of personnel management both applied personnel regulations and helped make them.

Chapter III describes the formal structure of the rule making process. Yet this chapter also involves the problem of internal communication. Categorization of commands was a way of making communication clearer, and the categorization of Ch'ing laws was the result of the procedures of law making.

People carrying out tasks were placed in officially defined roles with varying levels of status and degrees of formalization or regularity. Two major points should be kept in mind about roles.

First, one should note the distinctions between officials, nonofficials working in the bureaucracy, and outside groups working with the bureaucracy. The last two categories accounted for most members of the bureaucracy's various organizational complexes.

Officials can be defined as roles with both formal and high status; nonofficials working in the bureaucracy had none or only one of these two aspects of status. Thus there were roles with formal and low status, such as clerks and soldiers. There were roles with informal and high status, such as private secretaries and the friends of officials informally offering advice. Then there were roles with informal and low status, such as the servants of officials.

Outside groups working with or co-opted onto the bureaucracy included high-status outside groups, such as rich merchants, gentry, or tribal military allies, and low-status outside groups, such as the traders and boatmen of the salt monopoly.

The second point concerns the nature of the formal, high-status roles, that is, officials. There was here a spectrum of regularity defined in terms of the nature of the official job, the status of the occupant, and the nature of the appointment of the occupant to the job. This is discussed in Chapter IV. One of the major lines of variation in the history of China's bureaucracy lies in the bureaucracy's use of outside groups and of nonofficials working within it, as well as in the varying degrees of regularity with which officials' roles were defined.

We have thus seen that people with interests filled roles and carried out tasks. These involved the application of sanctions, some formal, some informal. In discussing sanctions, I basically follow Etzioni, distinguishing between normative or status sanctions (for example, bestowal or withdrawal of an honorary title), remunerative sanctions (for example, bestowal or withdrawal of a commercial privilege or salary), and coercive or physical sanctions (for example, military action, imprisonment).[6] Officials carrying out tasks of top leadership, internal tasks, or primary tasks all could invoke sanctions (partly formal, partly informal) to elicit cooperation from other persons working in the bureaucracy and clients outside the bureaucracy.

Conversely, these officials were themselves subject to sanctions and other constraints in carrying out their tasks. Bureaucratic action involved a peculiarly complicated relation between tasks and constraints. Every role—even that of the emperor, I would argue—was both a producer and a consumer of constraints. Incoming constraints limited the power of a role, while outgoing constraints manifested it. To the extent that outgoing constraints flowing from a single capital role dominated a task, we say that performance of that task was centralized. Some variations in the patterns of centralization are discussed in Chapters III and IV. The flow of formal constraints constituted the bureaucracy's hierarchy of authority.

While all tasks involved constraints, basically defining the interrelations between tasks, constraints, and roles can itself be seen as a crucial internal task—that of discipline and per-

6. Amitai Etzioni, *A Comparative Analysis of Complex Organizations* (New York, 1961).

sonnel management. The disciplinary sanctions used in the civil bureaucracy are the subject of Chapter IV.

To a large extent, constraints consisted of laws and other formal commands, but laws also played a large part in the definition of roles and tasks. It will be seen that while my study looks at law largely as an aspect of internal organization, virtually all other studies of Chinese law have focused on law as part of the primary task of adjudication, whereby the state sought to settle conflicts and stop deviance in the domestic society.[7]

Finally, the people who filled roles and carried out tasks in terms of sanctions and other constraints did so with certain personal capabilities. The question of capabilities overlaps that of interests. It divides mainly into cognitive (and physical) skills and aspects of morale. Officials had to be skillful and also of high morale in order to perform their tasks well and so avoid negative sanctions and enjoy positive ones. Capabilities could be developed by personnel policies such as those relative to training programs and job experience, but they also involved the political culture or norms of the bureaucrats, those affective and cognitive orientations shared as a common cultural heritage even by persons with conflicting interests. My first chapter and much of my fourth deal with cognitive and affective aspects of the officials' political culture. I ask, for instance, to what extent this political culture was universalistic, to what extent it legitimated flexibility in the performance of tasks and the making of laws, and to what extent it promoted a bureaucratically viable ethic of responsibility.

We should also note the relation between tasks or procedures and political culture. To the extent that procedures had meaning relative to the political culture, we can speak of their normative characteristics. For instance, a procedure of disciplining

7. See J. A. Cohen, "New Developments in Western Studies of Chinese Law: A Symposium Introduction," in *Journal of Asian Studies*, 27.3:475–483 (May 1968). See Chapter III, note 3, and Chapter IV, note 4, for the literature on the relevant features of Chinese law. The third note in Chapter III also explains my use of Weber's definition of law. For my understanding of legal scholars' approach to the problem of internal bureaucratic regulations in general, I am much indebted to an unpublished paper of Richard F. Pfeffer, "Some Sociological Perspectives on the Chinese Communist Legal System." See also Lon L. Fuller, *The Morality of Law* (New Haven, 1964).

officials by inflicting sanctions which varied according to performance rather than status had the normative characteristic of "fairness" (*kung, p'ing*) in the eyes of Ch'ing officials, or "universalism," as we would call it.

The bureaucracy and attached groups thus consisted of people with interests and capabilities filling officially defined roles. These roles carried with them sanctions and other constraints, which formed partly hierarchical patterns of authority. The occupants of these roles, communicating with each other, carried out top leadership tasks, internal tasks, and primary tasks, all undertaken in an environment consisting of clients and situational factors.

The power of the bureaucracy waxed and waned depending on the behavior of members, clients, and hostile groups, and on the impact of situational factors. Conflicts between policies and the interests of members and clients led to many deviant acts, reducing the power of the bureaucracy. However, the other features of the bureaucracy also affected the contraction or expansion of its power. It is with some of these that I am concerned, especially the officials' capabilities and the internal patterns of negative sanctions and communication.

In terms of my scheme, other approaches to Ch'ing bureaucracy have usually described political culture in general terms rather than in detail; have stressed the interplay of interests; and have focused on top leadership, the formalized hierarchy of constraints, and primary tasks, paying less attention to internal tasks, internal sanctions, and internal problems of communication. To a large extent, these studies supplement rather than contradict my approach, but they can be criticized on one or more of the following grounds: they neglect some factors important in the contraction and expansion of power; they put too much weight on one or another factor; and they misunderstand one or another factor.

The first point applies to a large amount of writing which has focused on the fact that the Ch'ing was a Confucian autocracy and on the abuses or dysfunctional characteristics allegedly associated with this fact. In this viewpoint, illustrated by Hsieh Pao Chao's still important book on Ch'ing government, there is a convergence between two great normative traditions of political thought, whereby governments are described largely in terms of their success or failure in reaching certain ideals. In the case of Western political thought, the ideal is usually democracy. In the case of Chinese political thought, the ideal is usually the Confucian one of benevolent rule. In both traditions, the analyst fills the important function of exposing dysfunctional or immoral practices and pointing the way toward improvement. The emphasis on democracy or political participation, moreover, leads naturally to discussion of perhaps the most important aspect of any political system: the basic arrangements through which political interests interact, what Almond and Powell call the "conversion functions."

This approach, however, interested in cure rather than praise, largely takes for granted (if it does not deny) the functional aspects of the bureaucracy, and, preoccupied with the flow of interests between the state and the society around it, focuses on primary tasks and neglects internal ones. Therefore it has not led to a balanced picture of functional and dysfunctional forces.

This stress on the dysfunctional aspects of Ch'ing bureaucracy—its particularism, corruption, lack of specialization, administrative rigidity, contempt for commerce, and so on—has also been taken over in much of the literature discussing the Ch'ing failure to modernize in the face of the Western impact. Again, if we are to have a rounded understanding of this failure, we should try to take into account the bureaucracy's functional as well as its dysfunctional aspects.

Some recent studies have turned away from this focus on dysfunctional factors, rather being interested in describing more precisely the flow of power within the imperial bureaucracy. Silas H. L. Wu's outstanding book on the palace memorial system in early Ch'ing times focuses, in my terms, on the communication and decision making aspects of top leadership in Ch'ing times. Publication of a number of important doctoral dissertations with a common methodology has recently been sponsored by the Political Science Research Institute of National Chengchi University in Taiwan, notably Chou Tao-chi's study of the prime office (*tsai-hsiang*) in Han and T'ang times, Wang Shou-nan's study of the T'ang regional commanders (*fan-chen*), and Fu Tsung-mao's study of the Ch'ing Grand Council. All these Chengchi studies have been influenced by the approach of the senior historian and political scientist Sa Meng-wu, who has stressed that the study of imperial China's government requires scholarship grounded in disciplines such as law and political science.

Generally speaking, these studies postulate that groups and individuals have a strong desire for power and ask to what extent this desire was expressed in certain high offices. The amount of power wielded by an office is seen as stemming mainly from personnel conditions (for example, length of tenure); the formal relationship of this office to political tasks (for example, participating in court conferences, memorializing, issuing orders); the substantive tasks handled by this office (for example, finance, adjudication); and the relations between this office and competitive centers of power.

The Chengchi scholars imaginatively utilize data in the primary sources and have stressed the use of statistics, as illustrated by Wang Shou-nan's demonstration that most of the T'ang regional commanders (*fan-chen*) most of the time were effectively controlled by the capital. They emphasize structure more than process but take into account historical development, situational peculiarities, and the political skills of leading statesmen. While their approach tends to be analytical, they also raise normative questions reflecting the concerns of both traditional and modern political thought, such as the issue of the proper ways of regionally distributing power. Rejecting old-fashioned descriptions of Chinese government, which tended merely to echo the vague categories found in the primary sources, they have boldly yet inductively devised categories of analysis allowing a conceptualization of the flow of power making sense to modern minds.

Their contributions, therefore, along with that of Silas H. L. Wu, have brought our understanding of the imperial bureaucracy to a new level of clarity and specificity, but all these studies focus on only some political aspects, dealing mainly with what I call "top leadership." By themselves, therefore, they cannot fully explain the organizational activities through which this leadership exerted its power within both the bureaucracy and the society-at-large.

For instance, Professor Wu rightly cites Karl Deutsch to insist on the close connection between a leader's mastery of the channels of communication and his capacity to control the behavior of his subordinates.[8] Unless the leader is informed about a situation, he can hardly act to control it. Yet we should em-

8. S. H. L. Wu, *Communication and Imperial Control in China* (Cambridge, Mass., 1970), p. 117.

phasize that once the leader is informed, a lot still remains to be done. After all, he may be perfectly informed about a situation that is out of control. To bring it back under control, he usually has to apply sanctions, the resources for which may or may not be available to him. Even then, his subordinates will be unable to implement his goals unless they have adequate morale and skills.

Another approach to the imperial bureaucracy has been the Marxist one, which focuses on the question of interests, especially on the class or societal basis of interests. This approach is obviously a valuable one, but to the extent that it is pitted against the Weberian stress on values, it is incomplete. My scheme stresses the ultimately Weberian notion of "political culture" as a major factor affecting the organizational capability of the bureaucracy, and I agree with Almond and Powell that the nature of political culture is to a large extent distinct from the question of interests.[9]

Just how distinct is a major problem, and, needless to say, the boundary is blurred. Barrington Moore, Jr., one of the most skillful exponents of what can be called the Marxist approach, has recently stated that culture has to be understood in terms of the process of "transmitting" it. This point is not controversial, but what are the methods of transmission? According to Moore, "To maintain and transmit a value system, human beings are punched, bullied, sent to jail, thrown into concentration camps, cajoled, bribed, made into heroes, encouraged to read newspapers, stood up against a wall and shot, and sometimes even taught sociology."[10]

This is all true, but actually very few of these activities take place in the average family, where children imbibe a great deal of culture through the processes of socialization. At another pole, the creative efforts of leading thinkers cannot be easily derived from the interplay of political interests and situations, and their influence on behavior seems often to persist through long periods of history during which situations vary again and again. Moore's focus is largely on those ideas adults argue over in times of political turmoil rather than on those ideas and attitudes which are widely shared in a society, which condition

9. Almond and Powell, pp. 42–72.

10. Barrington Moore, Jr., *Social Origins of Dictatorship and Democracy—Lord and Peasant in the Making of the Modern World* (Boston: Beacon Press, 1966), p. 486.

the efficiency of routine organizational cooperation, and which affect the capacity of a society to meet various challenges such as the problems of modernization.

At the same time, Moore seems to be saying that social form is more important than intellectual content, that the power of a group depends more on its capacity to punch and bully people than on the particular ideas it happens to put forward. Yet it is a cliché to say that ideas are "dangerous," that is, involve concrete political power. If not, why do so many political groups in so many countries fear and try to eliminate the free discussion by intellectuals of even highly specialized subjects? It would be interesting to try to persuade Chairman Mao that because the discussion of such subjects never has any significant behavioral and political effects outside the ivory tower, he need have no qualms about removing restrictions on it. The power of the pen is often more respected by those who wield the sword than it is by many social scientists and historians. Clearly, power depends on the efficacy of normative as well as coercive and remunerative sanctions; the efficacy of normative sanctions depends largely on what people believe; and the beliefs of people are partly shaped by intellectual currents. All in all, an eclectic approach to the problem of political causation is needed. As Parsons says, "*any* processual outcome results from the operation of plural factors . . . *no* claim that social change is 'determined' by economic interests, ideas, personalities of particular individuals, geographical conditions, and so on, is acceptable. *All* such single-factor theories belong to the kindergarten stage of social science's development [italics in original]." [11]

Like Marxism, the theory of despotism in its various forms neglects political culture and other bureaucratic features included in my scheme, but it is particularly vulnerable because of its exaggerated emphasis on the ruler's use of arbitrary, coercive sanctions. As I will seek to demonstrate, these sanctions were only one among the constraints the ruler used, and probably not the main one. He rather played on the whole range of available sanctions—coercive, remunerative, and normative—frequently shifting tactics to find the right combination of sanctions for the particular problem. Moreover these various kinds of sanctions tended to be intertwined. The emperor's use of

11. T. Parsons, *Societies: Evolutionary and Comparative Perspectives* (Englewood Cliffs, 1966), p. 113.

normative sanctions was colored by the threat of violence, and his use of terroristic violence was usually accompanied by outbursts of moral indignation aimed at achieving normative justification in the minds of the elite. Besides thus playing on a blurred spectrum of sanctions, the Ch'ing emperors tended to see that regularity and law, even to the point of limiting their own scope of arbitrary decision, were needed to make the use of sanctions more effective. Moreover, to the extent that the theory of despotism is linked to the concept of "total power," it overlooks the contest between functional and dysfunctional forces according to which the state's power waxed and waned.[12]

S. N. Eisenstadt takes full account of the general variety of policies and sanctions used by the ruler and develops an admirably eclectic position on the question of interests versus values, making clear that both shape the orientations of the various groups interacting in the political process. However, he analyzes political values in nomothetic terms, and his substantive views about imperial China's political values are open to objections raised below (IV, 5). Furthermore, in explaining the bureaucrats' "political orientation and patterns of activity," he stresses the bureaucracy's "social position within the society," particularly the bureaucrats' pattern of interests relative to the ruler's policies and to the interests of the "major social strata."[13] In thus emphasizing the bureaucracy's relations with the society

12. The concept of "total power" has been emphasized in K. A. Wittfogel, *Oriental Despotism* (New Haven, 1959) and E. Balazs, *Chinese Civilization and Bureaucracy* (New Haven, 1964); see, e.g., pages 10–11 in the latter. Eisenstadt has shown that this concept fails to account for the dependence of the ruler on various groups and is not precise enough for systematic analysis of historical societies. See S. N. Eisenstadt, *The Political Systems of Empires* (London, 1963), pp. 363–365, and his review of Wittfogel's book in *Journal of Asian Studies*, 17:435–446 (1957–1958). Another challenge to the thesis of the despotic character of the political system of imperial China is that of Ch'ien Mu, who sees important limitations on the arbitrary power of the emperor, at least through the middle of the T'ang period and to some extent until the Ming. See Ch'ien Mu, *Kuo-shih ta-kang* (A basic outline of our national history; Shanghai, 1948), I, xi–xiii, xxiii. I argue that such limitations, especially respect for law, existed also in the Ch'ing period (see Chapter II, section 4). Yen Fu's argument against Montesquieu's view of China as despotism also is significant. See B. Schwartz, *In Search of Wealth and Power* (Cambridge, Mass., Harvard University Press, 1964), pp. 160–162.

13. Eisenstadt, *Political Systems of Empires*, p. 293.

around it, Eisenstadt is not necessarily implying that the bureaucracy's internal organizational arrangements were only derivative or symptomatic phenomena, but he says little about these arrangements, by implication assigning them little weight as an independent factor shaping the bureaucrats' behavior. I believe, however, that they were themselves an important area of policy and had a significant bearing on whether the ruler's other policies could be successfully implemented.

Talcott Parsons' interpretation of the society and bureaucracy of imperial China is within the Weberian camp.[14] Parsons focuses on political culture or rather, in his terms, on values and norms. He sees imperial China as dominated by an amalgam of Confucian values and particularistic kinship norms. On the one hand, the elite as vehicles of Confucian values dominated the management of the bureaucracy and reduced the ruler to a mainly ritualistic role. On the other hand, the amalgam of Confucianism and particularism allowed only slight development of universalistic orientations and thus inhibited the development of differentiated political and economic institutions.

Although presented in terms of an extremely useful analytical framework, this view is open to question on two grounds. First, within the bureaucracy, the culture and norms of the elite, as I have maintained, were indeed important, but bureaucratic behavior was the result not only of culture and normative sanctions but also of coercive and remunerative sanctions, other constraints, the nature of the tasks assigned to the officials, the problems encountered in implementing these tasks, and so on. Overemphasizing culture, Parsons also overemphasizes the power of the cultural elite. Being bureaucratic subordinates in the full sense of the word, the elite as officials were subject to severe constraints, and the ruler's role was not "primarily ritual," since he personally and actively wielded immense power.

Second, apart from the place of the elite's culture in the bureaucracy, there is the question of the nature of this culture. Parsons' description errs in neglecting its eclectic and universalistic aspects.

Another approach requiring discussion is that of Almond and Powell. At the risk of oversimplification, I would sum up their view of political systems as involving four dimensions. First, there is the society's generally accepted "political culture" or

14. Parsons, *Societies*, pp. 71–77.

value system. Second, the political system as a specific concrete entity has to maintain itself internally, notably by recruiting and placing its personnel ("system maintenance and adaptation functions"). Third, this entity interacts in terms of interests with the rest of the society, thus carrying out its rule-making (legislative), rule-adjudicating (judicial), and rule-applying (executive) functions ("conversion functions"). Fourth, in this interaction with the rest of the society, the political system displays "capabilities" of various kinds and degrees, such as the capability to regulate social behavior or to distribute scarce resources. Given these four universal dimensions, political systems vary in certain ways, especially in terms of the "secularization" of their culture; the differentiation and autonomy of their rule-making, rule-adjudicating, and rule-applying functions; and the extent of their capabilities. Such lines of variation yield a typology of political systems. This includes the category of the "traditional, centralized bureaucratic system," into which Ch'ing China fits rather well.[15]

In these terms, my approach neglects the question of conversion functions and focuses on political culture and system maintenance and adaptation functions. I believe that, at least in the case of Ch'ing China, a detailed understanding of these two areas is required in order to understand "capabilities." The capabilities or organizational capacity of the Ch'ing state is a major empirical question and to a large extent involved the efficiency with which officials performed their tasks. This efficiency in turn depended to a large extent on the officials' political culture, constraints, and patterns of communication, which are the subject of this book. Also, as indicated above, I take a more idiosyncratic approach to political culture than Almond and Powell do.

Thus far, the major work done by political scientists on Ch'ing political culture has been that of Lucian W. Pye and Richard H. Solomon. My objections to their view of the "authoritarian" character of this political culture are raised below (IV, 5).

Finally I should try to deal with the objection voiced by some scholars that, whatever its particular sociological pedigree, any analysis focusing on organizational and ideological patterns is in danger of becoming ahistorical and of failing to come to

15. See, e.g., Almond and Powell, pp. 28–30, 217.

grips with factors more responsible for determining the flow of power and policy, such as the "human realities" involved in the unfolding of a particular sequence of events. After years when words like "system" and "interdisciplinary" produced an unhealthy sense of awe, it is heartening that historians now are bluntly insisting that a detailed grasp of the sequence of conscious efforts involved is needed to understand any social process. Nevertheless, since conscious political activity often takes place in terms of a relatively unchanging grammar of organizational and attitudinal elements, systematic discussion of any such grammar is needed to help us understand the activities of particular actors. As the historian struggles to find that proper mix of patterns and particularities which can bring a historical phenomenon to life, there is no a priori way to downgrade or upgrade either of these two aspects of existence. The only a priori rule is to deal with important facts about which our understanding so far has remained vague and incomplete. After all, relatively static circumstances are not necessarily less interesting, complex, significant, or human than salient developments. The historian's job is not to avoid discussing them but only to avoid subsuming them under either the clichés of his profession or nomothetic, Procrustian models borrowed from other disciplines.

Having discussed the topics and analytical framework of this study, I should conclude with a word about my sources. Because of the vast number of Ch'ing documents, an analysis balanced by exhaustive research is beyond the scope of this study. Rather I seek to make various arguments which can either be elaborated on or refuted by further research. Still, I have tried to achieve a fairly rounded picture by using not only compilations of law, which represent the less dynamic aspects of administration, but also sources reflecting the more dynamic executive process, especially memorials written by the Nanking governor-general, T'ao Chu (1779–1839), from 1831 to 1834. From internal evidence and the fact that these memorials average out to about one document every five days, it is clear that these memorials do reflect the situational tempo at T'ao Chu's office.[16]

We should also raise the question how much of the behavioral situation within the bureaucracy is revealed in published formal documents. First, it is obvious that the documents themselves

16. See I, 1, note 7.

were part of the behavioral situation in that they constituted some of the channels of communication. In this they largely differ from the writings of indigenous historians or propaganda dispatches. How information was presented in the documents is itself an organizational fact, apart from the question of these documents' reference to a reality outside themselves.

Second, there is no doubt that a large sector of such reality is authentically represented in the documents. Because of the abundance of documents, it is often possible to rely not only on casual remarks or remarks made against self-interest but also to cross-check or make deductions based on an almost complete grasp of the bottlenecks in a particular situation. Since much activity in the traditional society was highly visible and subject to competitive reporting in the memorials of different officials, lying had limits.

Furthermore, the fact that the Ch'ing bureaucracy suffered from what may be called overlegality, from literal and tedious adherence to all sorts of formal requirements creating mountains of red tape, shows that in some areas realization of formal laws was all too prevalent. Unless this tendency existed, how can one explain the complaints of Ch'ing officials that their capacity to act effectively was being stifled by their obligations to observe too many detailed regulations and that local magistrates were unable to attend to the wants of the people because so much of their time was used up studying regulations which they had to observe under pain of sanction? After all, putting laws into effect is often easy when observance is in the interest of powerful persons and involves no large practical difficulties.

Third, it is true that much reality was outside the written sources, especially informal behavior. However, there was no wall separating the formal and informal aspects of organization. Whether a specific law or procedure described in formal documents was carried out is one question. Whether the general norms implied by this law were part of the behavioral situation is a different question. Without doubt they often were. It is inconceivable that a legal system which grew over many centuries could have remained insulated from the norms of the behavioral situation. Moreover, the great and continuous effort in the Ch'ing period to publish up-to-date books of law reflected the desire of officials to close the gap between formalized rules and practice.

CHAPTER I The Normative Background of Law Making: Administrative Flexibility

1. Introduction

Law or rule making, the making and excising of precedents and laws, was a continuous and basic process of the Ch'ing state. The regular flow of governmental decisions on all levels yielded a much smaller but still continuous flow of cases which were compiled as regulations. Over a period of about fourteen years, 1825–1839, the Board of Civil Officials accumulated "more than 380 items" which it felt ought to be entered into its regulations. This was a large body of new law, although it was very small relative to the total number of cases handled by the Board during this time, some 800,000.[1] At least from the middle of the eighteenth century, this situation was typical of the government in general, and the institution of revising books of law every five or ten years was familiar in the various fields of penal and administrative law.[2]

The frequency and importance of Ch'ing law making are one illustration of the Ch'ing state's flexibility. Probably flexibility can be found in any organization, however "tradition-bound,"[3]

1. *Ch'in-ting li-pu tse-li* (Imperially endorsed regulations of the board of civil officials; 1843), prefatory memorials: 1–2b. Asking in 1839 for imperial permission to compile this book, the Board stated that it "annually takes charge of a total of more than 57,000 *kao-an* (cases)." The 380 items had accumulated since the last edition, completed in 1824. This rate of business was no doubt one of the highest of any board since it seems that only the Board of Revenue was as busy as the Board of Civil Officials. For instance, these two boards were the only ones assigned two days instead of one out of the regular ten-day schedule for presenting routine memorials at court. See *Rikubu seigo chukai* (Annotated terms of the six boards; Kyoto, 1940), p. 6.

2. See I, 6.

3. S. N. Eisenstadt, *Essays on Comparative Institutions* (New York, 1965), p. 191. On administrative flexibility in practice, see Thomas Metzger, "The Organizational Capabilities of the Ch'ing State in the Field of Commerce," in W. E. Willmott, ed., *Economic Organization in Chinese Society* (Stanford, 1972).

and some rigidity or fixation on ideals located in the past can be found in even the most modern organizations. Therefore, variations between organizations in terms of flexibility should perhaps be seen as variations in the mix between tendencies to flexibility and to rigidity. Yet sinologists have often been content to view the imperial Chinese state as dominated by an "atmosphere of routine, traditionalism, and immobility" without asking how the latter atmosphere was mixed with the tendencies toward flexibility.[4] There has even been a tendency to think of the Ch'ing state as simply "rigid." While the bureaucrats lazily sat on their power, we are sometimes told, people of all ranks busily and dynamically went about violating the laws. What is sometimes overlooked is that the laws would not have been enforced even to the extent that they were, were it not that the bureaucrats also were busy, continuously and flexibly making adjustments in response to the tendencies toward deviancy. It is this busy activity on both sides—the legal and the illegal—which constituted the life of Ch'ing bureaucracy.

In this chapter we look at the question of Ch'ing flexibility mainly on the level of values and norms rather than practice. According to Talcott Parsons:

> The main point of reference for analyzing the structure of [an organization] is its value pattern . . . [which] guides the activities of participant individuals. . . In the most general sense the values of the organization legitimize its existence as a system. But more specifically they legitimize the main functional patterns of operation which are necessary to implement [the goals of the organization] under typical conditions of the concrete situation. Hence, besides legitimation of the organization's goal and its primacy over other interests, there will be legitimation of relatively specific subgoals and the operative procedures necessary for their attainment.[5]

What, then, were the ideas and attitudes legitimating the flexibility of the Ch'ing bureaucracy's "operative procedures"?

4. Etienne Balazs, *Chinese Civilization and Bureaucracy* (New Haven, 1964), p. 11.

5. Amitai Etzioni, *A Sociological Reader on Complex Organizations* (New York, 1969), pp. 35–36.

One may go a step further and ask about the depth or intensity of the legitimation. Was flexibility merely accepted as a necessary evil or was there a moral commitment to it? Presumably the greater the moral commitment, the more the "hustle," energy, and intelligence devoted in practice to actions involving flexibility.

I argue in this chapter that there was a pervasive moral commitment to flexibility. Ch'ing officials had a strong feeling that frequent criticism and changes of the state's procedures were right and meaningful. This feeling was a normative bridge between their ultimate beliefs and their concrete administrative practice. It simultaneously was rooted in their basic view of man, society, and the state and legitimated their routine involvements with administrative adjustments, including law making. Because this feeling was derived directly from fundamental beliefs and was interwoven with a network of connected ideas and attitudes, it gave normative meaning to a wide range of complex organizational behavior.

At the heart of this feeling was a perception combined with a doubt. Many Ch'ing officials perceived the world as partly bad, but they had doubts about just what parts of it were bad and just how to go about improving it. On the one hand, the idea of the badness of the world promoted a sense of moral obligation to improve society. On the other hand, doubt about the specific object and means of improvement gave validity to a varied spectrum of alternative policies and changes. History itself was seen as a record of such varied changes, some more controversial than others, and the present was seen as another opportunity in history to improve society. By making and changing laws in the present, the state seized this opportunity. Moreover while these perceptions and evaluations of the present and of history supported notions of flexible change, certain famous terms in the classics supported the notion of change in a more metaphysical way, suggesting that it was in accord with the way of the sages and with the ultimate, underlying reality of things, both natural and human. Most important were the term *pien* (to transform), found in the *Classic of Changes,* and the idea of *wei-hsin* (dynastic renewal, reform), found in the *Book of Odes*. All these dynamic ideas, however, had to compete with, or better, were interwoven with a variety of ideas stressing continuity and changelessness. We can confidently infer from Ch'ing documents that a subtle mix of these static and dynamic ideas constituted a widespread outlook in Ch'ing times legitimating administrative flexibility.

To describe this outlook, we must deal not only with statements made in Ch'ing times but also with some of those views and events of earlier periods which formed such a large part of the Ch'ing consciousness. As an organization, the Ch'ing bureaucracy had the distinctive characteristic of being staffed to a large extent by history-minded intellectuals, although nonintellectuals who regarded scholars as pedantic and impractical also played a role.[6] The intellectual outlook of these Ch'ing personnel partly clashed with and certainly complicated their organizational norms. Moreover, their intellectual outlook not only consisted of the main points of the classics but also was shaped by many of the other prominent or respected writings that had accumulated over the course of Chinese history. They faced their daily organizational tasks while intellectually looking down an ever-lengthening corridor of history and discussion.

The norms they thus derived from history were in part complex and ambivalent attitudes rather than ideas forming a consistent doctrine. Especially because they were intellectuals, the

6. *Huang-ch'ao ching-shih wen-pien* (Our august dynasty's writings on statecraft; Taipei, 1964), 2:10 [hereafter, *HCCSWP*]. Here Ch'en Hung-mou (1696–1771) refers to such nonintellectuals, persons who criticized "scholars" as impractical. Possibly he partly had in mind the many Manchu officials without great education. Taking a position well within the Confucian spectrum, Ch'en Hung-mou urged that scholars apply their learning to current affairs. From a somewhat different perspective, the K'ang-hsi emperor in 1709 made the same point. He complained about high officials who had classical learning but were unable to make contributions of practical value at the policy conferences in the capital: "what books have they read? what have they studied?" he scornfully asked. See Fu Tsung-mao, *Ch'ing-tai chün-chi-ch'u tsu-chih chi chih-chang chih yen-chiu* (A study of the functions and organization of the grand council of the Ch'ing dynasty; Taipei, 1967), p. 90. The role of relatively uneducated but possibly practical-minded Manchu officials deserves more study. In the winter of 1722–23 the Yung-cheng emperor referred to high officials who were unable to write. (In order to maintain secrecy, he ordered them to report to him verbally rather than have a subordinate write a memorial for them.) See *ibid.*, p. 109. Of course the distinction between officials with and without a literary education took various forms in Chinese history. In the Han period, officials with classical learning sometimes looked down on officials who had risen from the lowest ranks and had only practical training. Chinese bureaucrats were not always "literati."

doubts and ambivalences found or implied in the intellectual materials they studied entered into the realm of values affecting their behavior. Our task is to take into account some of the connections between intellectual history on the one hand and the widely established values or ideology shaping bureaucratic behavior on the other. It is unreasonable to recognize the complexities in the former and then see the latter as simple and consistent. I have increasingly come to feel that if one asks about a particular Ch'ing political value, the answer lies in dissecting an ambivalent attitude consisting of a variety of prominent, partly contradictory statements made over the centuries and all eliciting widespread respect in the Ch'ing period. No doubt this characteristic of ambivalence is typical of value systems in other societies as well.

Certainly the outlook described here was more typical of Ch'ing scholars committed to the political process than of those more interested in purely ethical or artistic questions. We cannot even be certain that this outlook was fully typical of the former group. But many famous ideas were widely accepted as true, and many phrases and ideas in Ch'ing documents were conventional and noncontroversial; the norms and attitudes found in this conventional material almost by definition had general significance.

One of our main sources is the memorials of T'ao Chu (1779–1839), written in the 1830's when he was Nanking governor-general. The material used here mainly consists of some 275 items (each item consisting of either a memorial or a memorial-postscript written by T'ao Chu alone or with another official, often accompanied by the emperor's reply or another relevant document), totaling about 1000 Chinese-style pages (2,000 Western-style ones), chronologically arranged, and written over only a three-year period (the first memorial of the T'ao Chu in this group was sent off by him on January 29, 1831; the last, on February 8, 1834). T'ao Chu no doubt wrote other memorials also during this period, not to mention other forms of official and private correspondence. Nevertheless these items, dealing extensively with all sorts of administrative issues and crowded into such a small period of time (averaging about one every five days), give us a rounded picture of T'ao Chu's day-by-day administrative activities and ideas in 1831–1834. T'ao Chu admittedly was an exceptionally vigorous statesman connected to the nineteenth-century *ching-shih* (statecraft) movement, which stressed flexibility and practicality in dealing with administration, but many of his ideas and linguistic expressions were conventional.[7]

For the sake of convenience, I have also taken some materials from the book *Huang-ch'ao ching-shih wen-pien* (Our august dynasty's writings on statecraft), which was first published in 1827 by scholars who were part of the statecraft movement. Yet this movement hardly introduced a practical concern with administration into the Ch'ing political scene. After all, many of the pieces in *Huang-ch'ao ching-shih wen-pien* are seventeenth- and eighteenth-century memorials, and their practical tone is the same which one can find in many governmental documents. Moreover, a good number of the authors included in this book were prominent members of schools largely differ-

7. For T'ao Chu's biography, see A. W. Hummel, ed., *Eminent Chinese of the Ch'ing Period* (Washington, D. C., 1943), I:282. T'ao Chu became acting Nanking governor-general on July 24, 1830; he was appointed to the post on a regular basis on October 11, 1830; on February 14, 1831, he heard officially of the emperor's order authorizing that he, as Nanking governor-general, take over the office heading the affairs of the Liang-huai zone of the salt monopoly (*yen-cheng*); and on April 22, 1839, T'ao retired from the office of Nanking governor-general. (Lin Tse-hsü [1785–1850], as governor of Kiangsu, took over the post of Nanking governor-general a few times on a temporary basis, e.g., 1835, 1836). See *Ch'ing-shih* (History of the Ch'ing dynasty; Taipei, 1961), IV:2949, IV: 2954, and *T'ao Yün-t'ing hsien-sheng tsou-shu* (The memorials of the master T'ao Chu; preface of about 1840), 31:3 [hereafter, *TYT*]. Possibly T'ao's name should be pronounced "T'aó Shù," especially since some Yangchow merchants, according to T'ao, once attacked him by making a pun on the word *t'aó-shù* (peach tree); see TYT, 42:31b. The group of T'ao's memorials over three years beginning January 29, 1831, just before T'ao officially became head of Liang-huai, is found in *TYT* 30:45–52:46. The main themes in these memorials are salt affairs, grain tribute affairs, personnel questions such as appointments to office, and relief matters such as tax postponements. The other collection of T'ao Chu's memorials, *T'ao Wen-i kung ch'üan-chi* (The complete writings of the master T'ao Chu; preface of 1840) [hereafter, *TWI*] also contains T'ao's memorials after February 1834, but since this collection arranges the memorials topically (but chronologically under each topic), it is awkward to use if one wants to look at T'ao's administration in a wholistic, chronological manner. I have used *TWI* to follow T'ao Chu's salt policy from the spring of 1834 to 1839, there being some thirty-five memorials or memorial postcripts in *TWI* on salt affairs for this period. See *TWI*, 15:43–18:67b.

ing from the *ching-shih* outlook.[8] The contribution of the nineteenth-century *ching-shih* movement was mainly to lift practical concerns out of the mundane sphere of ordinary administration into that of intellectually prominent writing, thereby increasing interest in reform.

8. For instance, there are selections from Li Chung-fu (ca. 1680) and Lu Shih-i (1611–1672), both of whom were prominent in the struggle to save Ming or Sung neo-Confucianism, and there are selections from Tuan Yü-ts'ai (1735–1815), Ling T'ing-k'an (1757–1809), Lu Wen-ch'ao (1717–1796), Wang Ming-sheng (1772–1798), Ch'ien Ta-hsin (1728–1804), Wang Chung (1744–1794), Chi Yün (1724–1805), Wang Ch'ang (1725–1806), Pi Yüan (1730–1797), and Juan Yüan (1764–1849)—all prominent in the school of empirical research or the overlapping one of Han learning. Moreover, although elements of Legalism and a strong interest in reform appeared in the thought of some nineteenth-century *ching-shih* intellectuals, *HCCSWP* by no means stands for a particular approach to administration. Rather, it is a symposium full of divergent opinions; for instance, the famous views of Ku Yen-wu are both criticized and abundantly represented. Going back to the Taoist classic *Chuang-tzu,* the term *ching-shih* was vague and essentially noncontroversial, broad enough to embrace at least all those six poles of thought discussed in this chapter. For an outline of the main Ch'ing schools of thought, see Liang Ch'i-ch'ao, *Intellectual Trends in the Ch'ing Period,* translated by Immanuel C. Y. Hsü (Cambridge, Mass., Harvard University Press, 1959). For identification of scholars' intellectual affiliation, I have used *ibid.,* pp. 22–24. To find their writings in *HCCSWP,* see the third volume of *Keisei bumpen sō-mokuroku* (General index to editions of writings on statecraft; published in 1956 by *Kindai Chūgoku kenkyū iinkai*). On the publication of *HCCSWP,* see Hummel, I:282.

2. The Fixed Order: The State as Partly Good

A variety of cosmological, ethical, and practical considerations supported the official Ch'ing notion of the immutable foundations of the Ch'ing state. Yet this notion was closely, even paradoxically connected to ideas casting doubt on the moral validity of basic Ch'ing institutions and so implying the propriety of some change.

This notion of unchanging foundations is illustrated by the statement in the 1764 edition of *Ta-Ch'ing hui-tien* (Collected statutes of the great Ch'ing dynasty) that the contents of the latter book "must [deal with] long-lasting, permanent institutions."[1] Interestingly, this notion of immutability was more prominent in Ming and Ch'ing thought than in the Legalist or Confucian thought of Chou times. Yet aspects of both Legalism and Confucianism in Chou times contributed to it.

One aspect was the cosmological consideration that laws should be based on nature, which in turn has unchanging as well as changing aspects. In the *Kuan-tzu,* an eclectic, semi-Legalist book written perhaps around 300 B.C., flexibility is stressed, but the need for a quality of *ch'ang* (unchanging) order in the state is mentioned many times. While this quality of *ch'ang* seems sometimes to be recommended just on its practical merits, it clearly is also connected to the idea that government should be based on the unchanging principles found in the nature of heaven and earth, the seasons, living things, and other natural phenomena: the *ch'ang-tao* (unchanging true way) is simultaneously the foundation of "the myriad things" and the principle of government. The *Kuan-tzu* says that the law emanates from the *tao* (true way) and that policies should be based only on those names for things which are actually inherent in the nature of things. Perhaps overenthusiastically equating this viewpoint with Western natural law, Liang Ch'i-ch'ao found comparable ideas in the classics *Shih-ching, I-ching,* and *Meng-tzu.* With their stress on the need for *kung* (fairness) as opposed to *ssu* (partiality) in administration, the *Kuan-tzu* and other Legalist writings use as a model nature's impartiality and unchangingness. The point made in the *Kuan-tzu* is that only after understanding the unchanging, natural

1. *Ta-Ch'ing hui-tien* (Collected statutes of the great dynasty; 1764), *fan-li.*

basis of law can the ruler use and adjust laws to realize his own interests.[2] (Yet the need to change laws could be derived as readily from cosmology as the notion of unchangingness.)[3] In the same vein, a prominent, official Ming formulation identified the state's unchanging foundations with a "heavenly principle" transcending merely man-made regulations.[4]

Also already in Chou times, long-lastingness or unchangeability in laws was regarded as desirable because it promoted trust. This idea is found both in *Kuan-tzu* and in the largely Confucian work *Hsün-tzu*.[5]

Besides trust, practical advantages, and the model of nature, the Confucian moral notion of the *tao* (true way) involved unchangingness. As an early Sung scholar said, "The way of Yao, Shun, Yü, T'ang, Wen, Wu, Chou, and Confucius is an unchanging way constantly realized over ten thousand generations."[6] Logically speaking, to the extent that the state embodied an unchanging way and accorded with the models of an inherently immutable past, it had to be unchanging to some extent.

This sort of Confucian interest in unchanging laws came to clash with the prominent Legalist stress on adjusting laws to accord with changing current conditions. In the *Discourses on Salt and Iron*, written about 75 B.C., the Legalist-oriented de-

2. Liang Ch'i-ch'ao *Kuan-tzu-chuan* (A biography of Kuan-tzu; Taipei, 1963), pp. 25, 27–28, 33. *Kuan-tzu* (Ssu-pu ts'ung-k'an), 18:3b, 6:4, 13:3a–b, 13:4b–5, 15:4, 15:7, 6:2, 10:9b–10, 10:11, 10:12–13. Hsiao Kung-ch'üan, *Chung-kuo cheng-chih ssu-hsiang-shih* (A history of China's political thought; Taipei, 1966), II:201–202.

3. For an example, see T'ao Hsi-sheng, *Chung-kuo cheng-chih ssu-hsiang-shih* (A history of political thought in China; Taipei, 1964), IV:48, 71. Wang An-shih (d. 1086) cited the cycles of natural change as a justification for his "new laws," while Ssu-ma Kuang (d. 1086) refuted this justification by arguing that the cosmos does not change: "The sun and the moon stay the same."

4. *Ta-Ming hui-tien* (Collected statutes of the great Ming dynasty; 1587 edition; Taipei, 1963), I:1.

5. See *Hsün-tzu*, p. 135, in *Chu-tzu chi-ch'eng* (A complete collection of the works of the ancient scholars; Peking, 1959), Vol. II. *Kuan-tzu's* view is cited in Hsiao Kung-ch'üan, II: 201. Han Fei warned that too frequent basic changes in the laws (*pien-fa*) brought hardship to the people; see *Han Fei-tzu* (Ssu-pu ts'ung-k'an), 6:5b.

6. Cited in T'ao, IV:42. This is a statement by the early Sung thinker Shih Chieh, who in this context is refuting Taoism and Buddhism.

fenders of the imperial policies favored numerous, complex laws continuously adjusted to current conditions, while their Confucian critics desired simple laws, few in number, and in accord with "the true way which has been unchanging for a hundred generations."[7] This preference for unchanging laws is also illustrated by Chu Hsi's (1130–1200) view that in the period of the Three Dynasties, institutions "were handed down over the ages, and conditions did not come to anything like the current manner of destroying in the evening what has been established in the morning."[8]

The central Chinese ideas of political unity and uniformity of institutions also implied immutability. While the Early Han ideal of *ta-i-t'ung* (the great rule of all by one king) was Confucian, unification and the concentration of power in the emperor were also Legalist goals. Similarly, the ideal of uniformity in institutions such as weights and measures as well as in ideology and in the form of writing was pursued by the Legalist-inspired Ch'in dynasty but also is consistent with Confucian thought, especially that of Hsün-tzu.[9] All these notions of uniformity seem connected to the important, widespread Chou assumption that human nature was universally the same, although there was controversy over the character of this identical nature.

The idea of an unchanging order also fell in with the notion that the social-political order had certain fundamental roots (*pen*), in contrast to less essential aspects (*mo*). This notion of *pen* is found already in the partly pre-Confucian classic *Shu-ching* (Book of history),[10] and the distinction between *pen* and *mo* was used by both Confucians and Legalists at least by Han times. The state needed a proper foundation, which implicitly was unchanging. In ruling, one set up the foundation and then worried about the details; one did not just confront problems as they arose. Going back at least to *Hsün-tzu*, the idea that the purity of a stream depended on the purity of its source was important; a bad foundation would lead to a chain reaction of

7. Huan K'uan, *Yen-t'ieh-lun chiao-chu cha-chi* (Discourses on salt and iron with two sets of notes; Taipei, 1962), pp. 342, 361, 364.

8. Cited in T'ao, IV: 122.

9. Hsün-tzu wanted to "unify institutions." Cited in T'ao Hsi-sheng, I: 184. See *Hsün-tzu*, p. 88.

10. James Legge, tr., *The Chinese Classics* (Hong Kong, 1960), III: 158 (*The Shoo King*).

bad effects. The emphasis on *pen* also carried echoes of ancestor worship, since it involved the idea of reverence for and the desire to identify with the beginning of things and of oneself. One's ancestors were one's *pen* (origin, ultimate basis), according to the classic *Li-chi*, which described the meaning of a certain sacrifice as *pao-pen fan-shih* (recompensing those who are one's origin for the blessings received from them and returning to one's beginning).

The similar image of *fan-pen* (returning to the basic foundation) is connected to that of the source of a stream by a Confucian spokesman in the *Discourses on Salt and Iron* (first century B.C.):

> Now if one desires to realize the true way of peacefully settling the people and enriching the state, the answer lies in returning to the basic foundation [of government]. When the basic foundation is established, then the true way arises. If one follows the principles of heaven and the ways of advantage naturally present in the earth, then without effort one will be successful. But if one does not seek to make better the source of a stream and just attends to its flow, one lacks the basic foundation with which to control matters. [In that case], even if one uses up all of one's spirit, energy, and ideas, government will show no improvement.[11]

Another factor favoring fixity may have been reverence for the laws established by the imperial ancestor who had founded the dynasty. This respect, however, varied from dynasty to dynasty. In the Early Han, for instance, there was a movement involving Tung Chung-shu (second century B.C.) to *kai-chih* (revise institutions) long after the reign of the founder, and it was never seriously challenged by the argument that *kai-chih*

11. *Yen-t'ieh-lun*, p. 90; *Hsün-tzu*, p. 154. However, Hsün-tzu here was talking not about laws but about the idea that the ruler's loving the people was the necessary beginning of all political success. On the *Li-chi*, see *Shih-san-ching chu-shu* (Shanghai, 1935), II:1453. See also *ibid.*, II:1449. Tung Chung-shu (ca. 179–104 B.C.) emphasized the need for the sage ruler to derive his governmental order from the "origin" of all things, Tung's formulation being more lavishly metaphysical than that cited above from the *Yen-t'ieh-lun*. See Chan Wing-tsit, tr., *A Source Book in Chinese Philosophy* (Princeton, N.J., 1963), pp. 284–285, 271.

would be disrespectful to him.[12] When Yang Yen (d. 781) proposed his major fiscal reform, critics at the time opposed it on the grounds that "one may not lightly change the laws of [the first two emperors] Kao-tsu and T'ai-tsung." Even after the reform was carried out, such criticism long continued, but Ma Tuan-lin (thirteenth century) refuted it, arguing that although Yang Yen's reform (*pien-fa*) did overturn the laws of the T'ang founders, it met the needs of the times.[13] In the Sung, Ssu-ma Kuang (d. 1086) criticized Wang An-shih (d. 1086) for overturning inherited laws, but this was just one among many criticisms.[14]

In the Ming, respect for the institutions of the founder was perhaps as strong as in any dynasty. It prevented revision of the *lü* (penal statutes) after his death.[15] In Ming salt monopoly affairs, the need to respect the *tsu-chih* (institutions of the imperial ancestors) was a prominent emphasis with no parallel in Ch'ing salt monopoly affairs, but it was complemented by the idea that only the broad outlines, not the details, of Ming T'ai-tsu's salt monopoly procedures need be adhered to.[16]

12. This movement is vividly described in T'ao, II:65–86. Admittedly, T'ao, II:30, gives the story of the fidelity of Ts'ao Shen, prime minister of the second Han emperor, to the institutions of the founder and of his prime minister, Hsiao Ho. But Ts'ao Shen felt these original institutions should be followed because of the superior ability of the founding emperor and of Hsiao Ho, not simply because whatever the founder had created should be respected. Ts'ao Shen suggested to his emperor that they could not match the ability of their respective predecessors.

13. Ma Tuan-lin, *Wen-hsien t'ung-k'ao* (Shanghai, 1901), 3:2a–b. See also Liu Shao-fu, *Chung-kuo ching-chi ssu-hsiang-shih* (A history of Chinese economic thought; Taichung, 1960), p. 217.

14. Cited in T'ao, IV:70 and Hsiao, IV:484. See also Sa Meng-wu, *Chung-kuo she-hui cheng-chih-shih* (A social and political history of China; Taipei, 1965–66), IV:28.

15. Ch'en Ku-yüan, *Chung-kuo fa-chih-shih* (A history of China's legal institutions; Shanghai, 1944), pp. 105, 133.

16. When Yüan Shih-chen carried out a major reform of the Liang-huai zone of the salt monopoly (the first proposals were made to the emperor in late 1616), a major theme in his arguments was "to restore the institutions of the [founding] ancestor." The fact that the "restored" system involved elements different from the system of T'ai-tsu did not look like a contradiction to him. He stated that "at times there must be adjustments to meet new conditions (*pien-t'ung*), but in the last analysis the institutions [of the founder] may not be changed." See the memorial (p. 198) presented by the Ministry

The Ch'ing problem was complicated by the fact that founding and then installing the dynasty in China had taken a succession of three emperors. Under the third one it was explicitly recognized that the earlier laws of the dynasty had been suitable for the simpler, "uncorrupted" society beyond the Great Wall but were not adequate for the more complicated conditions in China. Overriding any sense of fidelity to original dynastic institutions, this consideration led the Ch'ing in 1646 to put out a penal code largely following Ming laws.[17] Moreover, revisions of the *lü* (penal statutes) carried out in 1725–1727 show that later emperors could change some of the most basic laws. Yet an early Ch'ing writer held that it was a common and disastrous tendency for a dynasty's original laws to be changed by statesmen in the later part of the dynasty.[18]

The idea of the unchanging order was also reflected in prominent concepts of law and government in the Ch'ing period. Although the law actually was dynamic enough to allow conceptualization of it as an ongoing process of adjustments, the traditional image of the law was that of an essentially unchanging structure with minor alterations taking place at its periphery. Although the history of Ch'ing governmental institutions involved many marked developments, the image of the government's history was that of an inherited set of institutions adjusted from time to time. A Ch'ing official in 1693 held that the Ch'ing salt monopoly system was *hsiang-fan* (the reverse) of the Ming, but it eventually was more proper to apply the classical idea that the institutions of the preceding dynasty had been taken over with only minor adjustments.[19]

---

of Revenue in late 1616, which consisted of a report written by Yüan Shih-chen as a lower member of the Ministry, in *Huang-Ming ching-shih wen-pien* (The august Ming dynasty's writings on statecraft; a photographic copy published at Taipei in 1964 of an edition printed around 1635), XXIX: 185–346.

17. *Ta-Ch'ing lü-li* (Penal statutes and regulations of the great Ch'ing dynasty; 1870), *ts'e* one, preface of Shun-chih emperor [hereafter, *TCLL*].

18. *HCCSWP*, 15:6. The writer is Yang Sheng-wu, a *chin-shih* of 1713. All biographical information on contributors to *HCCSWP* is taken either from Hummel or from the introductory material in *HCCSWP*.

19. The *hsian-fan* statement is from *Liang-huai yen-fa-chih* (Salt laws gazetteer of the Liang-huai zone; 1693 edition reprinted at Taipei, 1966), I:22. An example of the more conventional view of

This emphasis on continuity clearly has some connection to a number of images noted above, such as the "roots" of a tree, the "source of a stream," and ancestors as "one's beginning." All these concepts served to divide reality into more and less essential modes of existence, a division seen also in the old distinction between *t'i* (essential structure, substance) and *yung* (modes of dealing practically with current situations, function), and the still older theme of *nei* (inner) and *wai* (outer).

Whichever of these concepts is primordial, they all cluster around the idea that if men are to *ying shih-chih-pien* (respond to and deal with the changing world of events), they need to base their actions on some stable point of reference. Because events inherently throw the human spirit off balance, some internal, spiritual mechanism maintaining balance is needed. Since this characterization of events was seldom if ever challenged by traditional thinkers, the quest for inner stabilization remained a central moral and metaphysical problem for them. Applied to politics, this outlook was expressed as a desire for a fixed order underlying the flux of routine administration.[20]

---

the development of the salt monopoly is in *Ch'ing-shih* (History of the Ch'ing dynasty; Taipei, 1961), II:1496. The wording here, as in so many similar institutional accounts, is almost identical with the view of change in the Three Dynasties given in *Lun-yü.* See Legge, *Chinese Classics,* I:153–154 (*Confucian Analects*). Similarly the change from *chün min chiao-tui* (delivery by the people to the military) to *kuan-shou kuan-tui* (collection and delivery by officials) was an important change made in 1652 in the structure of the grain tribute system; see *Ch'in-ting hu-pu ts'ao-yün ch'üan-shu* (The board of revenue's imperially endorsed complete book on the grain tribute; 1845), 9:1 [hereafter, *TYCS*]. But the *Ch'ing shih* (II:1480) again stresses continuity with Ming grain tribute institutions. Similarly, as we note below in "Fixity Versus Flexibility," Hsüeh Yün-sheng, perhaps the leading Ch'ing legal expert, and the *Ch'ing-shih* do not bother to describe a major *lü* (penal statute) change with vital organizational effects. Neither did Hsüeh Yün-sheng make clear the development from Ming through Ch'ing of the basic question of the redemption of heavy criminal sentences by officials (see IV, 3, c). The point here is that although China was perhaps not such a developmental society as those in Western Europe, it had more development than some Ch'ing intellectuals wished to emphasize.

20. On the origin of the *t'i-yung* formulation in the third century A.D., see Chan Wing-tsit, tr., *A Source Book in Chinese Philosophy,* p. 791. For an example of *ying shih-chih-pien,* see *Hsün-tzu,* p. 151. A locus classicus of the *nei-wai* distinction in its moral-ontological sense is the twenty-fifth chapter of the *Doctrine of the Mean.*

Once established, this fixed order limited both the executive process and that of law making. Generally in accord with this order, the executive process yielded a similarly conditioned field of cases available for codification. Proposing a controversial executive action, an official was more likely to win approval if he could quote a precedent.[21] Similarly, editors making substantive judgments as they selected cases for inclusion in compilations of laws could not easily excise older laws in effect regarded as part of the fixed order. There was always a conservative resistance to "lightly changing old regulations."[22] If a law had been recently changed, a suggestion to change it again could be met with the rebuke that it was inherently wrong to change laws frequently. An idea going back to Chou times was that "If the proposed change is not ten times better than the current laws, don't change them; if current institutions aren't ten times worse than the proposed change, then don't make it."[23] This indiscriminate conservatism can be contrasted to the selective conservatism of a Ku Yen-wu (1613–1682), which was based on the assumption that the past contained the greatest political achievements rather than on the emphasis on preserving the current status quo: "Not to grasp the intention of one's predecessors in their establishing of a law and thus lightly to advise changing it have always provoked disorder and produced trouble."[24]

Yet, as shown even by these expressions of conservatism, the fixed order could be legitimately changed. Although the claim could be officially made that this order was a virtually unadulterated expression of "Heavenly" principles, such a claim must

21. In administrative practice, there was direct application of regulations; somewhat doubtful proposals backed by the adducing of analogous precedents; and, occasionally, relatively new ideas advanced without any clear precedents.

22. For an example, see Wang Ch'ing-yün, *Shih-ch'ü yü-chi,* 5:13b. The emperor in 1814 used this phrase in denouncing the suggestion of an official to adopt paper money. Another use of the phrase is in *HCCSWP*, 22:3; the writer is Wang Hui-tsu (1731–1807).

23. J. J. L. Duyvendak, *The Book of Lord Shang* (London, A. Probsthain, 1928), p. 172. This idea had the distinction of being advanced by the opponents of Lord Shang. (See also the biography of Lord Shang in the *Shih-chi.*) An example of its expression in the Ch'ing can be seen in *HCCSWP*, 18:12. The writer is Ch'en Tsu-fan, a *chin-shih* of 1723.

24. *HCCSWP*, 19:1b.

have been a polite way of putting things, not a realistic way. This distinction between statements intended to sound well and realistic statements is of course crucial in studying Chinese values. For instance, it was sometimes appropriate in memorials to say that the emperor's virtue or benevolence was equal to or even superior to that of the greatest sage rulers of antiquity. But in an essay on political problems, a scholar could state, say, that so long as the contemporaneous society contained so many economically parasitical groups, there was bound to be economic misery: "even if there were a *shang-sheng* (sage of the highest virtue or from the oldest antiquity) [on the throne], what could he do?"[25] Such a casual remark, presupposing without fear of controversy or legal prosecution that the current emperor was not a sage, reflects a basic feeling of the scholars about the contemporaneous emperor. By contrast the continuous references to the emperor in memorials as a *sheng* (sage) are less representative of what the scholars actually felt about the nature of the emperor, even though the awe and fear felt by an official when addressing the emperor may well have made the term "sage" fully meaningful at that moment.

It was obvious to Ch'ing scholars that virtually the whole formal system of offices, which comprised much of the image of the fixed order, had roots in the frequently despised, Legalist-influenced Ch'in dynasty and had been repeatedly and basically altered throughout history. The common opinion of scholars was that this order, in, say, Ming or Ch'ing times, was a mixture containing both "remnants" of the sage institutions of antiquity and a number of subsequent historical innovations, including many particularly controversial ones such as the examination system, the prefecture-district system, the system of private, unregulated landownership, and the prime office or cabinet (*tsai-hsiang*) as a weakened organ (III, 2). This is not to deny, though, that efforts were sometimes made to interpret later, problematic changes as realizations of the principles underlying the ancient sage institutions. For instance, although it was known that the six boards had developed not out of the six ministries described in the classic *Chou-li* but out of certain originally minor suboffices of the Han government, as the T'ang

25. The remark about *shang-sheng* was made by Yün Ching (1757–1817) in *HCCSWP*, 11:4. For a similar remark about some forces being too strong even for a sage ruler to control, see Su Tung-p'o's (1036–1101) view cited in T'ao, IV:75.

historian Tu Yu had shown, it was sometimes held that there was an essential similarity between the six boards and the six ministries, and that the six boards realized an ideal, comprehensive differentiation of administrative affairs.[26]

Even very old and fundamental laws could be controversial and qualified in practice. A major law on *hui-pi* (avoidance) good in 1764 held that "officials in the provinces" could not serve in their families' original province or province of current legal residence;[27] but until an edict of 1787, the salt yard supervisors (*ch'ang-ta-shih*) could.[28] The purpose of the avoidance laws was not only to prevent corruption but also to promote the officials' ability to carry out harsh policies, which they might find difficult to apply to those close to them. But these laws clashed with their deep feeling of attachment to their native

26. The abortive attempt of the Northern Chou (557–580) dynasty to restore the six ministries of the *Chou-li* came to an end with the reforms of the founder of the Sui, but, according to Tu Yu, the great T'ang expert on institutional history, the Sui was using the Chou principle of the six ministries in the way it reorganized the six boards and their relation to other capital offices; Sa, II:318; III:60. When the *T'ang-liu-tien* (Six divisions of administration of the T'ang dynasty) was put out under the orders of Emperor Hsüan-tsung (712–755), the actual six boards of the T'ang government were consciously viewed as parallel to the six divisions of administration in the *Chou-li*. Yen Keng-wang has convincingly argued that the *T'ang-liu-tien* was an awkward attempt to compile actual T'ang laws in terms of a format suggesting a parallel between T'ang government and the *Chou-li*'s six ministries, an attempt hanging on the slender reed of the analogy between the six boards and the six ministries. See Yen Keng-wang, "*Lüeh-lun T'ang-liu-tien chih hsing-chih yü shih-hsing wen-t'i* (On problems concerning the nature and the realization in practice of the *Six Divisions of Administration of the T'ang Dynasty*)," in *Bulletin of the Institute of History and Philology, Academia Sinica*, 24:69–76 (1953). When the first Ming emperor put the six boards directly under him, he said he was restoring the Chou principle of the six ministries; cited in Sa, IV:325. See also *HCCSWP*, 1:15, for the view that the organization of administrative affairs according to the categories of the six boards was comprehensive, and that the six boards of the Ch'ing were in essence identical with the six ministries of the *Chou-li*. The writer is Lu Shou-ming, a *chin-shih* of 1652.

27. *Ta-Ch'ing hui-tien* (1764), 5:17.

28. *Ta-Ch'ing hui-tien shih-li* (Precedents and regulations supplementary to the collected statutes of the great Ch'ing dynasty; 1899), 47: *pen-chi chieh-jang hui-pi:* Ch'ien-lung 52 and Kuang-hsü 12 [hereafter, *TCHTSL*]. See also *Liang-huai yen-fa-chih* (1904), 2:12a–b.

place and with their moral obligation not to travel far from aged parents. The argument was made that if a man were honest, he would be honest wherever he was stationed.[29] Although some implied that avoidance should be largely abolished, the usual proposal was a compromise reducing the maximum distance an official would have to travel in order to reach his post. The burden of travel expenses, ignorance of language and customs in distant places, and many other disadvantages were adduced.[30] Moreover, the Han dynasty, often admired in Ch'ing times for the superiority of its system of personnel management, to some extent had not practiced avoidance, as Ch'ing officials pointed out, and many other cases of natives serving as officials were cited relative to subsequent dynasties, including the Ch'ing.[31] A particularly neat point made by one Ch'ing scholar was that, after all, in the Chou period "men of Ch'i held office in Ch'i."[32]

Thus partly controversial, the fixed order also lacked clear definition in the sense that its boundaries and contents were never specified. Neither was it denoted by any one, precise word. Rather there was a variety of words which differed in terms of whether they stressed the idea of law or just that of basic institutions, and whether they referred more to governmental administration or to the social order as a whole. In the proper context, all the following words could connote immutability: *t'i-chih* (fundamental social order), *tien-chang* (statutes and regulations), *fa-chih* or *chih-fa* (laws and fundamental order), *chang-ch'eng* (regulations, as in *i-tai chih chang-ch'eng* [a dynasty's regulations]), *t'i-yao* (essential structure), *ting-chih* (fixed order), *chih-tu* or *tu-chih* (fundamental order and standards), and *cheng-t'i* (fundamental structure of administration). There were many other connected expressions: "Heaven

29. *HCCSWP*, 17:11b. The writer is T'ao Cheng-ching, a *chin-shih* of 1730.

30. See the views of Wang Hsin-ching, who was a fairly old man by 1736. His attack on avoidance in *HCCSWP*, 17:9b–10, which is outstandingly comprehensive, includes the unqualified suggestion that the contemporaneous practice of appointing natives to positions in the court should be extended to at least some provincial and civil posts. Ku Yen-wu's argument, in *HCCSWP*, 17:3b–4b, is for reducing the maximum distance between one's native place and for appointing natives to at least some posts.

31. On Han avoidance, see Appendix II.

32. *HCCSWP*, 17:10. The writer is Wang Hsin-ching.

and earth's natural way of attaining profits is to make compensating adjustments between surpluses and deficits, and the *pu-i chih ching* (unchanging standard) of the state is to reduce what there is too much of in order to increase what there is too little of."[33]

Moreover, these words, although linked to the idea of immutability, also connoted change, as can be seen from the fact that they could also be used to cover the ephemeral, instrumental side of administration (*yung* as well as *t'i*). For instance, in private writing one finds *tien* (fundamental statute, institution) used for extremely minor and local kinds of procedure, as when Pao Shih-ch'en (1775–1855) says that "opening passage at the [North] Bridge is the great *tien* of the new annual salt shipment [of the Liang-huai zone of the salt monopoly.]"[34] *Tien* could also be used in reference to ordinary office records (as in *tien-ts'e*). *Cheng-t'i* (structure of administration) could be used to cover various governmental procedures. A writer of the earlier part of the Ch'ing speaks of a Ming order that officials at the capital should be selected so that their talents suit the *cheng-t'i* of the post to which they are appointed. *Cheng-t'i* here refers to the administrative affairs peculiar to the post and requiring special skill, not just to a few basic laws.[35] *Chang-ch'eng* often denoted the most minor sort of regulations. *Fa-chih* (laws and fundamental institutions) could be quite comfortably used to denote exactly those salt monopoly regulations which were changed or added over time.[36] Such a minor matter as the establishment of government-regulated weight measures for salt at Liang-huai could be called a *ting-chih* (fixed system).[37] The idea of *t'i-chih* could be used to cover such an ephemeral matter as the number of pots allowed per household for the boiling of salt.[38] In this context of the administrative and instrumental side of government, the idea of fixity really connoted the de-

33. *Liang-huai yen-fa-chih* (reprint of a work completed in 1806; Yangchow, 1870), preface: 1 [hereafter, *LHYFC*].

34. Pao Shih-ch'en, *An-wu ssu-chung* (1846), 5: 10b.

35. *HCCSWP*, 17: 1b–2b.

36. *LHYFC*, *fan-li*: 1.

37. *TYT*, 30: 54b. *Ssu-ch'uan yen-fa-chih* (Salt laws gazetteer of the Szechwan zone; completed about 1883), prefatory memorials: 1 states that salt gazetteers are needed to help observance of the *ting-chih*, which clearly means here the total system of regulations, not just the most basic laws.

38. *TWI*, 18: 13.

mand for undeviating compliance with whatever had been authoritatively established, rather than the idea that what had been thus established could not be changed by the appropriate authority.

Furthermore, there was a certain sophistication about the idea of fixity. To say of a certain body of laws that they should "last forever" could be proper even though it was plain that future revisions would be necessary. In 1882, as Szechwan governor-general, Ting Pao-chen (1820–1886) said in a memorial that it was necessary to publish a salt gazetteer for Szechwan. His recent reform of the Szechwan zone of the salt monopoly had been successful, he said, but now, to prevent changes for the worse, it was necessary to provide Szechwan with a salt gazetteer containing "fixed rules for the future which will not be changed."[39] Yet Ting would certainly have agreed that there would be future occasions requiring the state to *pien-t'ung* (make some adjustments to meet changing conditions).

Sophistication about fixity was connected to the practice of making exceptions to otherwise fixed laws. Such exceptions could be thought of as "violating the laws" (*wei-li*) or as the emperor's "bestowing of extraordinary favors" (*ko-wai shih-en*). Such exceptions were not uncommon in making appointments to offices, since the best man often did not exactly meet the appointive requirements for a specific office.[40] An edict of 1806

39. *Ssu-ch'uan yen-fa-chih,* prefatory memorials: 1b. See I, 2, note 16 for Yüan Shih-chen's similar idea of relative fixity.

40. *TYT*, 51:37–38, is a memorial postscript successfully asking that the Kiangning provincial treasurer, just promoted to vice-president of the Board of Punishments, be allowed to retain his old post until a current emergency requiring his experienced leadership is over. *TYT*, 31:47–53, is an important memorial, with the Board of Civil Officials' reply, asking for a rearrangement of appointment channels so as to get more competent yard supervisors (*ch'ang-ta-shih*). In *TYT*, 33:12–14b, T'ao has just read in the *Peking Gazette* that a particularly effective military official under him is to be transferred to Chihli and asks that the man be reordered to stay in Kiangnan; also he asks that the forthcoming promotions of two other valuable naval officers be restricted to Kiangsu—all three requests were granted as extraordinary favors not to be adduced in the future as precedents. In *TYT*, 33:34–38, T'ao Chu again elicits an imperial assent to an act which may not be adduced as a precedent in the future. Another military official is to be transferred to a Kiangsi post who has had long experience with grain tribute affairs in the Yangchow-Huai-an areas. T'ao argues that "at Kiangsi they would

deplored the fact that governors and governors-general lately had come to take for granted that such deviant recommendations would be finally approved by the emperor as an imperial "favor" over the Board of Civil Officials' rejection. Nevertheless, the emperor did not contemplate abolishing such recommendations violating the regulations. He only ordered that when such deviant recommendations were approved, the official making them should in some cases be liable to administrative sanctions should his protégé commit a serious offense.[41]

Administrative necessity sometimes even led the emperor to exempt some officials from the duty of mourning for their parents by temporarily retiring from office and returning to their home residence. In an edict of 1735, the emperor said that this practice had become widely accepted; he tried to restrict this deviant practice of *tsai-jen shou-chih* (fulfillment of mourning obligations while holding office) to a minimum of instances where the official involved was truly irreplaceable.[42] (This practice is outside the shortening or suspension of mourning in many instances for Manchu or Mongol bannermen and imperial astronomers and physicians.)[43] Since mourning obligations were such basic moral norms, it is significant that even they were open to exceptions.

---

only get an ordinary battalion official but grain tribute affairs would in turn be short of one man who can really be put to use." Recognizing that his request "violates regulations," T'ao asks that the man be permitted to continue his career in Kiangsu grain tribute affairs. See also *TYT*, 48:13–14b.

41. *Ch'in-ting ch'ung-hsiu liu-pu ch'u-fen tse-li* (Imperially endorsed and revised regulations on administrative punishment for affairs categorized according to the six boards; 1887), 4:17–19 [hereafter, *CFTL*].

42. *TCHTSL*, 139: see under Yung-cheng 13. See also *CFTL*, 13: 20a–b. When the Ming prime minister Chang Chü-cheng did not "hurry" to his father's funeral and instead stayed at his post, strong but ineffective opposition was voiced, while an extremist follower of Wang Yang-ming's ideas supported Chang; T'ao, IV:235. Ho Ping-ti feels that such exceptional cases of great officials not leaving their posts to mourn increased in number from T'ang to Ch'ing times. See Ho Ping-ti, *Chung-kuo hui-kuan shih-lun* (A historical discussion of *Landsmannschaften* in China; Taipei, 1966), p. 2.

43. These conditions are discussed in connection with the question of paying salaries to such persons in *Ch'in-ting hu-pu tse-li* (Imperially endorsed regulations of the board of revenue; 1851), 72:41a–b [hereafter, *HPTL*]. As a rule, Manchus and Mongols left office to mourn for only one hundred days; *Ta-Ch'ing hui-tien* (1899), 11:16b.

Exceptions were more readily made in matters of purely instrumental significance, such as tax collection deadlines, than in matters of serious political or moral significance. In times of emergency, local relief regulations, say, could be deliberately suspended to speed action.[44]

Arguments rejecting proposals on the ground that they violated the *ting-chih* (fixed system of the state) often had to be reinforced by practical considerations. A good example is a memorial presented by the Board of Revenue to the emperor in 1830 advising against a plan temporarily to commute the grain tribute into silver payments. The Board countered practical arguments for this plan with its own practical arguments, although it also did state that the grain tribute was a "*ting-chih* which cannot be changed."[45]

44. See, e.g., *TYT*, 34:28. Relief was given out in this case without the usual checking of the people to prevent double helpings. Similar suspensions of routine procedure were sometimes carried out in the salt monopoly in order, say, to move some salt quickly in the face of a flood.

45. *Chung-kuo chin-tai ching-chi ssu-hsiang yü ching-chi cheng-ts'e tzu-liao hsüan-chi* (Selected materials on China's economic thought and economic policy in modern times; Peking, 1959), II: 472–473.

3. The Political Order as a Historical Process Continuing in the Present

Partly good, partly bad, partly controversial, the contemporaneous political order had been created through, and was still part of, an on-going historical process containing good, bad, and controversial changes. Maintaining and improving the state in the present required continuing efforts to make the most of the opportunities existing in the current historical situation. In the bureaucratic documents, such efforts were conceived of as largely secular in character, depending on human persistence, inventiveness, and moral drive rather than on supernatural forces. Yet aside from a continuous stream of minor adjustments, there were doubt and controversy over what particular policy steps would be proper and effective in the present situation, just as there were doubt and controversy over the value of various policy moves made in the past.

To put it another way, the contemporaneous political order was looked on as part of an old, on-going struggle between good and bad forces. This struggle was conceptualized variously. A common Confucian version was that of a two-pronged attack by scholar-officials on the attitude of the emperor and on the behavior of the common people. A constant effort was needed to carry out *feng-hua* (transformation of the morals and customs of the people). The famous subjective idealist Lu Chiu-yüan (1139–1192) saw history in terms of a struggle between *li* (principle) and *shih* (unprincipled forces); good rule depended on the dominance of *li*.[1]

True, the bad forces were often viewed as dominant in history. The source of badness could be linked to economic conflict, as in Hsün-tzu's focus on the explosive combination of man's limitless desire for material satisfaction and the scarcity of economic resources. Conflict could also be explained not so much in terms of the scarcity but of the unequal distribution of economic resources, a notion with roots in the *Lun-yü*.[2] Either

1. Cited in T'ao, IV:128–129.

2. Ch'ien Wei-ch'eng (1720–1772) held that the strength of material desires in human nature blocked any attempt to make a fairer distribution of economic resources, and that this unjustified disparity was the source of conflict; *HCCSWP*, 7:2a–b. Confucius' stress on the dangers of such disparity is in Legge, *Chinese Classics*, I:308 (*Confucian Analects*). This is the passage where Confucius warns

way, man's desire for immediate economic gain was viewed as rushing down the road of history, "like water running downhill," eroding or threatening the sage institutions. This desire helped lead to the rise of economically parasitic groups, which could even be viewed as the primary cause of society's troubles.[3] Connected to this view was the one that improper intellectual currents could arise which would release in officials the same corrupt drive for material gain.

The idea of institutional change as caused by man's bad material desires is illustrated by a view of Sun Ting-ch'en (1819–1859). He saw the original sage order as corroded mainly by three changes: Lord Shang's replacement in the Chou period of the well-field system with that of private land ownership; Yang Yen's (d. 781 A.D.) changeover from the *tsu-yung-tiao* tax system to the two-tax system, which was viewed as marking the switch to taxation in money; and the increasing use in Ming times of silver as money.[4]

---

against *pu-chün* (inequality, unjustified disparity), but Legge's translation is at best problematic. "Inequality" here is often understood as referring to unjustified disparity in the distribution of wealth in society. See L. S. Yang, *Les aspects économiques des travaux publics dans la Chine impériale* (Collège de France, 1964), p. 60.

3. In *HCCSWP*, 11:4a–b, Yün Ching (1757-1817) quotes Han Yü's (768–824) view that the economy had been upset after early Chou times by the gradual rise of two nonproductive classes, Taoist and Buddhist monks or priests. Yün Ching enumerated a total of fourteen kinds of groups, including the three economically productive ones of farmers, merchants, and artisans. Yün also held that the Three Dynasties were distinguished not by the absence of such extra nonproductive groups but rather by the presence of policies which reduced their numbers and increased those of the farmers, craftsmen, and merchants. (Han Yü's view is in his essay *Yüan-tao.*)

4. *Chung-kuo chin-tai ching-chi ssu-hsiang yü ching-chi cheng-ts'e tzu-liao hsüan-chi,* II:366–367. The single-whip tax reform also, in Ming times, was denounced as a bad *pien-fa;* T'ao, IV:205. Also see Ku Yen-wu, *Jih-chih-lu chi-shih* (Hupei, 1872), 11:15–26b. Ku Yen-wu was against silver money mainly because, generally condemning tax payments in money instead of in kind, he saw tax payments in silver as still worse than tax payments in copper cash. Tax payments in money were unnatural, since farmers did not grow money and should deliver as taxes what they naturally produced. If they had to sell their crops to pay taxes, moreover, they suffered from commercial exploitation. One reason silver was worse than copper cash was that an extra charge had to be collected for melting down into ingots all the small bits of silver paid in. This argument for taxing in terms

Nevertheless, such notions of history as a worsening linear process were not necessarily dominant. Admittedly, only the most daring spirits, such as Wang Fu-chih (1619–1692), might question whether the base line of history, back in the Three Dynasties, had really been better than the present.[5] But some good change was implied by prominent cyclical views, notably Tsou Yen's (fourth century B.C.), not to mention a few positive linear views, such as the theory in the *Kung-yang Commentary* (possibly written around 150 B.C.), which held that history moved progressively through three stages, the last being one of complete peace and unity.[6]

Even if this view of linear, long-range progress remained peripheral, there were well-established ideas indicating that moments of relative progress had occurred at various times.

---

of what the tax-payer directly produces can be traced back at least to Han Confucians, as in *Yen-t'ieh-lun*, p. 4.

5. Arguing that overly harsh criticism of the present based on an exaggerated notion of the goodness of the past opens the door to the harsh policies of Legalism, Wang Fu-chih says that if one could actually observe the people in the time of Yao and Shun and of the Hsia and Shang dynasties, one would find the same mixture of human qualities and faults as exists in the current society. See Ch'ien Mu, *Chung-kuo chin-san-pai-nien hsüeh-shu-shih* (A history of Chinese thought during the last three centuries; Shanghai, 1937), p. 117. A similar point was made when Ku Yen-wu, despite his admiration for the T'ang, suggested that the moral character of T'ang officials was not necessarily much higher than that of contemporaneous officials. (His point was that if the system of decentralized appointments to office could operate without great corruption in the T'ang period, why should its enactment lead to corruption in his own time?) See *HCCSWP*, 17:4.

6. In Fung Yu-lan, *Chung-kuo che-hsüeh-shih-pu* (Supplement to a history of Chinese philosophy; Shanghai, 1936), pp. 82–92, there is a useful discussion of philosophies of history in the Ch'in and Han periods. Tsou Yen's theory was that all natural and human events were governed by a cycle of five elements. Each element rose to a position of dominance and then declined, giving way to the next. Since a dynasty was based on an element, it too rose and fell with the rising and falling of the corresponding element. Tung Chung-shu had a similar cyclical notion of history, but his cycle consisted of three rather than five units. In both these theories, the unit which rises and falls is a single dynasty. In another cycle approach, illustrated by the thought of Chang Chü-cheng (1525–1582), the unit rather is a group of dynasties. See T'ao Hsi-sheng, IV:231–232, and Wm. Theodore de Bary *et al.*, *Self and Society in Ming Thought* (New York, Columbia University Press, 1970), pp. 375–378.

Above all, even if the ideal society was unreachable, there were intermediate levels of achievement attainment of which was often felt to be practical. The belief in these intermediate levels was a major factor inspiring political effort. For instance, Confucius had strongly praised the controversial statesman Kuan Chung, indicating that his policies had saved Chinese civilization from descending to the level of the barbarians.[7] Confucians must often have felt that Han rule was an improvement over the chaotic conditions in the days of Confucius himself. At least the Han had realized Mencius' goal of unity and had granted the Confucian school a monopolistic position of orthodoxy. Institutional descriptions could imply either morally neutral or progressive linear change. Tu Yu's (d. 812 A.D.) description of the genesis and development of the six boards from Han to Sui times at least involved no adverse value judgment.[8] Su Tung-p'o (1036–1101) held that the development from the Three Dynasties' military system, whereby farmers served as soldiers, to the subsequent system of occupational differentiation between farmers and soldiers was irreversible. Even if a sage arose he could not restore the earlier system, since everyone found the later one convenient.[9] Liu Tsung-yüan (773–819 A.D.) held that the transition from feudalism to the prefecture-district system was a good thing;[10] Chu Hsi held that it was partially good.[11]

Another linear development was in the field of personnel appointment. The Sui dynasty was generally regarded as hav-

7. Legge, *Confucian Classics*, I:281–283 (*Confucian Analects*). Confucius also had reservations about Kuan Chung, apparently being irked by his arrogance. See *ibid.*, I:278–279, 162–163. Interestingly, it was more or less this aspect of Kuan Chung which appealed to Mencius, who admired Kuan Chung's pride in his relations with Duke Huan while, contrary to Confucius, looking down on Kuan Chung's policies. See *ibid.*, II:180–181, 214–215 (*The Works of Mencius*).

8. Tu Yu, *T'ung-tien* (Chekiang, 1896), 22:16–17b.

9. Cited in T'ao, IV:78.

10. *Liu Ho-tung ch'üan-chi* (The complete works of Liu Tsung-yüan; Shanghai, 1935), pp. 31–35.

11. T'ao, IV:121–122. Chu Hsi criticized the fact that under feudalism, unqualified persons often held office and caused great harm. See Professor L. S. Yang's illuminating discussion of the controversy over feudalism versus bureaucracy in his article in C. O. Hucker, ed., *Chinese Government in Ming Times: Seven Studies* (Stanford, Calif., 1969).

ing set up that system whereby all officials staffing district and prefecture government offices were appointed centrally, through the Board of Civil Officials. Previously, each of the heads of regional offices had often had the right personally to choose and appoint many of his subordinates. Citing Confucius, Ku Yen-wu suggested that the latter system of decentralized appointments was better, mainly because the best appointments were those made on the basis of personal knowledge of the candidate,[12] but Chao I (1727–1814) refuted Ku, arguing that decentralized appointments reduced the authority of the emperor and led to corruption and the danger of faction.[13]

The ancient contrast between rude simplicity and elaborate refinement (*chih* and *wen*) yielded a prevalent concept of development. Such development could be considered a decline, as with the cyclical notion of history held by Chang Chü-cheng (1525–1582), the Ming prime minister, whereby there was a degenerating movement from simplicity to refinement.[14] We can, however, see a progressive view in the following remark made by the editors of the *Ta-Ch'ing hui-tien* (Collected statutes of the great Ch'ing dynasty) in 1748: "ever since antiquity, arranging and fixing the fundamental institutions and rules of moral propriety have always been [a process] taking long stretches of time before it was completed; what later times have in detail is what the past had in outline."[15] The editors of the Ch'ang-lu salt gazetteer (1726) note in passing: "The nature of events is necessarily such that there is a beginning in the footsteps of which later happenings follow and increasingly blossom."[16] The same point is made in a famous essay on the history of literature. Here the goodness of increasing elaboration is expressed unmistakably. Moreover, by comparing literary

12. *HCCSWP*, 17:4. Ku was following Confucius; see Legge, *Chinese Classics*, I:263 (*Confucian Analects*).

13. *HCCSWP*, 18:6–7b.

14. See I, 3, note 6. For some classical references to the *chih-wen* dichotomy, see Legge, *Chinese Classics*, I:190, 254–255 (*Confucian Analects*).

15. See prefactory memorial dated Ch'ien-lung 13/5/28 of Chang T'ing-yü in *Ta-Ch'ing hui-tien tse-li* (Precedents and regulations supplementary to the collected statutes of the Great Ch'ing dynasty; 1764).

16. *Hsin-hsiu Ch'ang-lu yen-fa-chih* (Newly revised salt laws gazetteer of the Ch'ang-lu zone; 1726), *li-yen*.

development to the growth of ice out of water, the writer connotes Hsün-tzu's famous description of the learning process. Historical development, he almost suggests, is positive just as learning is, at least in the case of literature.[17] Finally, as L. S. Yang has shown, men sometimes compared a later dynasty favorably to previous dynasties.[18]

Success in the present depended on strenuous effort and flexible action on the part of officials. A key value here, basic equally in Confucian ethics and Ch'ing bureaucratic communication, was the notion of *li* (effort), that is, self-propelled effort, effort arising out of an individual's own decision or free will. For Confucius, being virtuous depended on expending *li* (effort) in order to improve one's character and behavior. Confucius also had the connected idea of all-out striving, of unreservedly summoning all one's energies in order to fulfill one's obligations. This idea became an ethical cliché (*chieh-ch'i-li*) and can be connected to Confucius' notion of the pursuit of virtue as a "heavy" "burden of responsibility" (*jen chung*) which the individual carries over a long road ending only with death.[19] "Effort" was needed to lift this "heavy" burden, we may say.

True, in philosophic discourse one could weigh the value of *wu-wei* (nonaction) against that of *jen-li* (human effort). In Ch'ing bureaucratic thought, however, the desirability of "human effort" was taken for granted, and the philosophical problem of *jen-li* was converted, so to speak, into the administrative problem of *li* (effort, exertion in the performance of duties). This *li* was a pervasive bureaucratic value, as can be seen from endless references to it in a large variety of phrases such as *pu-li* (not to exert oneself) and *ch'u-li* (to put out effort). Whether a particular official exerted himself was a major point in many discussions of particular personnel questions such as a specific promotion, and how to encourage officials in general to exert themselves was a major point of the broader personnel

17. The writer is Hsiao T'ung (501–531). See his *Wen-hsüan* (Selected pieces of literature; Ssu-pu pei-yao), *hsü*:1. See also *Hsün-tzu*, p. 1.

18. Lien-sheng Yang, "*Ch'ao-tai-chien-te pi-sai* (Dynastic comparison and dynastic competition)," in *Ch'ing-chu Li Chi hsien-sheng ch'i-shih-sui lun-wen-chi* [Symposium in honor of Dr. Li Chi on his seventieth birthday; Taipei, 1965], pp. 139–148.

19. Legge, *Chinese Classics*, I:188, 167, 222–223, 210–211 (*Confucian Analects*).

policy discussions.[20] To a large extent, the vast Ch'ing realm of legislation punishing minor official shortcomings (see IV) can be viewed as consciously designed to elicit strenuous effort from officials. Posts were both officially and informally compared in terms of difficulty.[21] Because some posts were regarded

20. See, e.g., *TYT*, 49:46–52, a memorial postscript by T'ao Chu and the advice to the emperor by the Boards of Revenue and Civil Officials on the proposals in the postscript—all of which occurred in the winter of 1833–34. The problem was to elicit more effort from officials in the provinces in apprehending salt smugglers. Since beginning his reform of the Liang-huai zone in 1831, T'ao Chu had had success in largely stopping the smuggling of empty grain tribute boats returning south and in reducing the influx of salt from the Ch'ang-lu zone into the Huai-pei subzone. But smuggling was still rampant in the crucial markets of Hunan, Hupei, and Kiangsi. In these areas, however, an unsuccessful experiment from 1814 to 1818 had shown that pressure could not be put on the district magistrates by holding them responsible for a fixed quota of sales, market fluctuations making such local quotas unrealistic. Therefore in those provinces, for salt sale deficits, only the salt taotais received administrative punishment through the annual *k'ao-ch'eng* (examination of results), and local magistrates lacked the incentive to police vigorously. T'ao Chu's idea was that, although fixed quotas were impractical, local magistrates should still be impeached for signs of laxness in policing and that there should be a law rewarding local magistrates for outstanding success in policing. The Board of Revenue approved these measures, but the Board of Civil Officials pointed out that these measures were provided for in laws already existing and that, while it was important to put pressure on the magistrates, it was also necessary to pressure the officers and soldiers at the green standard battalions and guardposts. The emperor approved the latter advice. For an early reference to *li* in the sense of exertion in the performance of one's tasks, see *Yen-t'ieh-lun*, p. 247.

21. I have not seen the official classifications in any book of laws such as *Ta-Ch'ing hui-tien* (Collected statutes of the great Ch'ing dynasty; 1899) [hereafter, *TCHT*]. They can be found in memorials dealing with appointments or in *Ta-Ch'ing chin-shen ch'üan-shu* (Complete book [of current information on] officials of the great Ch'ing dynasty; published every quarter of a year during much of the dynasty). In *Ta-Ch'ing chin-shen ch'üan-shu*, posts such as prefect or district magistrate are each given a primary categorization of *tsui-yao* (post with an extremely heavy burden of administration), *yao-ch'üeh* (post with a heavy burden of administration), *chung-ch'üeh* (post with a medium burden of administration), or *chien-ch'üeh* (post with little administration). Under this description, a further descriptive phrase often is added using two or more of the four categories of *nan* (difficult), *fan* (complicated and busy), *ch'ung* (strategically located in terms of communications and commerce),

as especially trying, service in them was sometimes shunned. When in 1837 the second highest Liang-huai salt official (*yen-yün-shih*) killed himself, his immediate superior, T'ao Chu, claimed that his depressed mood had been caused by illness, which in turn had stemmed from the strains of his office. His predecessor also had become ill because of these strains, T'ao claimed.[22] When T'ao in 1838 was trying to fill this post, he pointed out that there was a shortage of candidates not only because there was a lack of officials with sufficient experience in salt affairs or with a willingness to learn about them, but also because many officials regarded the post as unattractive and dangerous.[23]

Another point related to this focus on human effort is that references to supernatural forces are rare in Ch'ing bureaucratic documents, even when the problem at hand was explaining and dealing with a major crisis such as the Yangtze delta flood of 1831.[24] Apparently, as Balazs suggests, administration had

---

and *p'i* (exhausting). The latter four categories were introduced around 1730 according to Cheng Ching-i, P'eng Shih, *Fa-lü ta-tz'u-shu* (Large dictionary on law; Shanghai, 1936), II: 1953. In *HCCSWP*, 17: 10b–11, T'ao Cheng-ching, a *chin-shih* of 1730, states that the categorization of a post in terms of one or more of the four categories *ch'ung, nan, fan,* and *p'i* was determined by the governors and governors-general. T'ao also says that because administrative conditions were more difficult in the south than in the north, a southern post with the same rating of difficulty as a northern one was actually more difficult. For a discussion of the historical antecedents of this rating system, see *HCCSWP*, 18: 4a–b.

22. *TWI*, 18: 21a–b. Around 1890 some capital officials used the term *leng-shu* (cold office) to refer to the post of censor, meaning by this that this post carried with it a relatively great risk of receiving administrative punishments. See Chang Te-ch'ang, *Ch'ing-chi i-ko ching-kuan-te sheng huo* (The life of a capital official in late Ch'ing times; Hong Kong, 1970), p. 21. The term *leng-shu* is reminiscent of the "cold families" and "cold official posts" in the period of the Six Dynasties, but in the latter context "cold" refers to low status.

23. *TWI*, 18: 43a–b.

24. This flood began around July 1, 1831. A month or so earlier, there had been a threat of flood which had receded. The content of T'ao's memorials dealing with these problems was overwhelmingly practical in nature, with almost no reference to supernatural causation or aid; relief measures, rather, were the state's major concern. However, T'ao and other officials did pay visits to the temples of the relevant spirits, and when the first threat of flood receded, T'ao asked the emperor to add some phrases to the official titles of these spirits

become more secularized over the centuries.[25]

Yet even when political actions were perceived as intertwined with the "harmony of Heaven," this connection was often viewed as a moral imperative calling for more administrative effort, not only religious observances such as prayer. This is evident from the Ch'ing institution of amnesties, since the punishment of innocents and lack of compassion in the handling of punishments (not, interestingly, lack of success in punishing the guilty) were questions regarded as major points of intersection between the administrative and cosmological processes —perhaps some of the few still taken very seriously in Ch'ing times. True, amnesties were often justified on purely ethical grounds (as a prime manifestation of "benevolent rule"), but an apparently complete list of Ch'ing amnesties from about 1625 to about 1885 has some 45 amnesties (perhaps a third of the total) explicitly justified as a way of restoring the proper natural order (usually by bringing about rain). For instance, in about 1792 the Ch'ien-lung emperor thought that there might be a causal connection between a drought in the capital area and excessive harshness in putting down piracy in the Taiwan area.

"in order to recompense the spiritual protection and follow popular feeling." On the latter, see *TYT*, 34:1b, 3. T'ao first mentions this flood in a memorial sent off July 16, 1831. See *TYT*, 34:10a–b. Sometime after June 20, 1831, heavy, continuous rains began to descend on much of the lower Yangtze valley, leading, among other things, to the Kaoyu flood and various impeachments, discussed below (IV, 4, d). T'ao sent off a number of memorials on this flood, such as *TYT*, 34:12–16, 17–20, 21–23, 24–26, and 27–34. No statistics are given about the number of people killed or otherwise affected (unlike some other cases), but the disruption was great. A memorial on relief policy implies that an 1820 drought and an 1823 flood in Kiangsu were comparable disasters; see *TYT*, 34:18b.

25. Balazs, *Chinese Civilization and Bureaucracy*, p. 140. Another aspect of secularization was the dependence on concrete, rationalistic arguments when weighing opposite interests even when one of them was affected by the slightly supernatural aura of the emperor's personal involvement. For instance, the grain tribute had such an aura, but in 1833 when there was a clash between the interests of the grain tribute and the Huai-nan branch of the salt monopoly, the Nanking governor-general used cold figures to show that grain tribute interests were not more important than salt monopoly interests; he claimed that the grain tribute's quota of "more than four million bushels" was not worth more than the "seven or eight million" taels of Liang-

The key issue here, however, is that amnesties were not just a ritualistic exercise in compassion. Rather their point typically was to eliminate miscarriages of the law by means of an intensive effort to apply the law properly and to re-examine all cases which involved even "the slightest doubt," as an edict of 1737 put it.[26] In other words, to avoid upsetting nature's extremely delicate nervous mechanism, not only ritual propriety but also extreme care in practical administration were required. The fearful sanction here eliciting administrative effort was nature's violent response. Nervousness about natural disasters thus reinforced the Confucian sense of obligation to help the people, and beliefs about supernatural kinds of causation stimulated secular efforts. Pan Ku's criticism of the yin-yang school of cosmology—that it "neglected human affairs and depended on ghosts and spirits"—could not be fairly leveled at this Ch'ing outlook.[27]

---

huai revenue and involved great expenses for the state. See *TYT*, 50:4b–5.

26. *TCHTSL*, 729, 730, 731. The Ch'ien-lung passage is in 730: Ch'ien-lung 57. Strictly speaking this case was not an amnesty but a shift to a more lenient policy of law enforcement.

27. Pan Ku, *Han-shu pu-chu* (The history of the Former Han dynasty, with added explanations [by Wang Hsien-ch'ien]; Peking, 1959), V:3152.

4. Minor Adjustments

To a large extent, the efforts of officials lacked any creative dimension and were regarded merely as a process of diligent work to carry out prefixed obligations, either in the positive sense of implementing orders or in the negative sense of eliminating forces opposing the desires of the government. Officials were to *shih-li feng-hsing* (carry out orders energetically) and *li-ch'u chi-hsi* (energetically do away with accumulated bad practices). The idea of *ching-li* or *pan-li* or *ching-pan* (to manage, direct), frequently used to describe the leadership activities of officials, often connoted an uncreative, practical implementation of regulations. A typical conceptualization of administration was a two-fold sequence whereby a set of procedures was set up (*li-fa*) with care and thoroughness and then was carried out and supervised (*tu-pan*) with vigor.

But officials often had to figure out how to apply old regulations or devise new ones. The distinction between regulations and methods of application is reflected in the administrative literature, since many publications were exclusively concerned with regulations, while others focused rather on the range of possible combinations of actions to meet given problems. For an official, knowing what he would be held responsible for was very different from knowing how to find the right combination of means to meet these responsibilities.

Fairly routine adaptations and adjustments were often conceptualized as and legitimated by the idea of *pien-t'ung* (to make some adjustments to meet changing conditions), an idea with its locus classicus in the *Classic of Changes*.[1] Another important dynamic idea found in this classic was that of balancing affairs by "reducing that which is in excess and increasing that which suffers from deficiency."[2] The immediate application of this idea to legitimate specialized fiscal adjustments is illustrated below in the case of *jung-hsiao* (selling salt by shifting shipments to where the market is better). Originally associated with the arch-Legalist Lord Shang, the idea of *pien-fa* (reform, basic change in laws) was used only rarely in routine administrative documents, but it was far from taboo.

For instance, in 1820 the Nanking and Hu-kuang governors-general agreed to change the system of salt wholesaling at

1. *Chou-i chu-shu* (Ssu-pu pei-yao), 8:1b.
2. *Ibid.*, 2:19.

Hankow. Instead of selling in turn, the salt boats would all be allowed to sell freely whenever they arrived. But just at that time, 413 loaded salt boats were already waiting in the harbor; some had been waiting for more than half a year. Fearing irregularities and a drop in prices, the Hu-kuang governor-general warned: "If we order sales to begin on an unrestricted basis, possibly the *pien-fa* (reform) will be too sudden." Therefore he proposed that these boats sell in stages, the ones which had been waiting longest selling first, and so on. After the 413 boats had sold their cargoes, the system of free sale could generally be followed. By this gradual transition from one system to another, the emperor approvingly answered, the state would happily avoid "first suffering the disadvantages of *pien-fa* (reform) in order to do away with bad practices."[3]

Minor adjustments often involved a concept of substitution in which underlying general principles were explicitly or implicitly adduced as superseding certain regulations. For instance, in the salt monopoly the practice of *jung-hsiao* (selling salt by shifting shipments to where the market is better) complemented that of fixed regional sales quotas. It often involved *tai-hsiao* (to sell at place x on behalf of the quota of sales at y). In 1839 the head of the Liang-huai zone of the salt monopoly, T'ao Chu, obtained imperial permission to sell in the markets of the Huai-pei subzone salt normally assigned to markets of the Huai-nan subzone. Although this move had precedents and was a form of *jung-hsiao*, the shift in markets was especially great, and the Board of Revenue held that "In the handling of master-licenses for shipping salt, there are always fixed boundaries [for the markets]; *jung-hsiao* is definitely not a regular form of management." The zone head, however, argued that above the prefixed programs of fiscal management were the general needs of state finance: "I humbly find that although the Liang-huai [zone] is divided into southern and northern [subzones], the tax revenues [from them] identically are matters of finance (*tu-chih*). [Thus] whenever [in one subzone] the merchants' resources are exhausted and sales are bad, one cannot but make adjustments and draw from surpluses to make up deficits so that there may be no shortage in the funds of the state."[4]

3. *Liang-huai yen-fa-chih* (1904), 3:3a–b.

4. *TWI*, 18:59; 18:63b. Actually *i-chu*, the term here used for "draw from surpluses to make up deficits," is from the *Classic of Poetry* rather than the *Classic of Changes*.

This principle of "drawing from surpluses to make up deficits" was also used to legitimate another somewhat controversial but common device of state fiscal administration, that of *tien* (making advances) from one account to another. Going back to another classic, the *Rites of Chou,* the alternative principle of rigidly connecting a particular source of revenue to a particular expenditure still dominated much state finance in the Ch'ing period.[5] However, problems caused by disjunctions between the flow of revenue and the urgency of expenditures were routinely met through advances.

The principle of substitution was basic in the field of personnel management. For instance, if no regularly established office was adequate for a task, an official could be specially commissioned to do it. If an office were vacated before the new appointee could arrive, it could be temporarily filled on an "acting" (*shu*) basis by someone else. If a high official had to leave his seat of administration, he could handle important documents by having them sent to his *hsing-shu* (mobile or temporary office) and empower a subordinate at his original office to handle routine documents by *tai-ch'ai tai-hsing* (breaking open the seals of communications and acting on behalf of his superior).[6]

In 1830, approving a major canal-dredging project in the Changchow area, the emperor specified that on its conclusion, the Nanking governor-general and lower officials should personally inspect it, but in 1833, announcing its completion, the Nanking governor-general explained that this inspection had been carried out instead by two lower officials, since he had been busy at the time in northern Kiangsu supervising problems of transport on the grand canal. (This excuse was contested by no one.)[7]

Besides substitution, another major theme in applying regulations was that of implementing complex goals by devising policies with double effects. The emperor was frequently assured that if *x* were done, then regarding, say, local government and salt affairs, *chün-yu pi-i* (both would benefit). One example was the practice of *i-kung tai-chen* (providing employment as

5. For this principle in Chou times, see Hu Chi-ch'uang, *Chung-kuo ching-chi ssu-hsiang-shih* (A history of Chinese economic thought; Shanghai, 1962–), I:47. For *tien,* see II, 3 below.

6. *TYT,* 47:34b; 50:9b.

7. *TYT,* 48:15–16b.

a substitute for relief). If people were hired to work, say, on dikes, then "both water control and the people's livelihood would benefit."[8] Similarly, the regulation of water flow in canals had to take into account the needs both of agriculture and transportation. *I-chü liang-te* or *i-chü liang-pien* (two birds with one stone), the saying went in official documents.

The most general and pervasive theme regarding such double effects involved the duality of the state and the people and the problem of devising policies balancing the interests of both elements. This was expressed by a large number of general clichés such as *kuo-chi min-sheng* (meet the economic needs of both the state and the people) and *yü-k'o pien-min* (make the flow of taxes abundant and bring about advantageous conditions for the people). Innumerable other expressions also reflected this theme, such as *k'o-shih liang-hsüan* (taxes and the people's consumption needs were both left unfulfilled), a phrase describing a particular breakdown in the salt monopoly. The idea of "establishing a balance between ruler and people, superior and inferior, so that both profit rather than receive injury" was given as the raison d'être of salt monopoly regulations by an eighteenth-century editor.[9]

How to combine different means to pursue one goal was another problem. For instance, if there was a shortage of grain in a province, a governor-general could devise a policy combining at least six different measures: cancellation or postponement of land taxes; holding back or rerouting of grain tribute boats originally heading north for the capital area; "normal" sales by government granaries; official grain shipments with government funds; suspension of customs taxes in order further to attract private grain merchants to the shortage area; and commanding or exhorting local well-to-do persons to sell their stores of grain at normal prices and to make relief contributions.

In making adjustments, officials were expected to be flexible. A conventional way of praising an official was: "When one views his normal handling of affairs, *yu-t'i yu-yung* (one sees

8. *TYT*, 46:37; 45:27b. On *i-kung tai-chen* as an institution going back at least to Sung times, see L. S. Yang, "Economic Justification for Spending—an Uncommon Idea in Traditional China," *Harvard Journal of Asiatic Studies*, 20:47 (1957).

9. *Hsin-hsiu Ch'ang-lu yen-fa-chih* (Newly revised salt laws gazetteer of the Ch'ang-lu zone; preface of 1726), 8:1.

in him understanding of the fundamental order and a sense for the means to be used in meeting changing circumstances)."[10] The same thought could be expressed as *yu-shou yu-wei* (there is a sense for the maintenance of the fundamental moral order and a capacity for action). An official dominated by the inertia of old ways could be criticized as *yin-hsün* (following old practices without interest in improvements).

Flexibility was furthered also by a certain spirit of unrestrained inventiveness with which Ch'ing officials often approached difficult problems, notably those of economic administration. Respect for tradition was complemented by respect for ingenious and novel policies, and Ch'ing officials often were on guard against the charge that they were unreceptive to new proposals because they held *ch'eng-chien* (closed viewpoints).[11] Ch'ing officials, after all, were guided not only by the norm of the models of antiquity but also by the norms of what they considered to be the natural way for men to act. A novel procedure could be justified on the grounds that it would succeed because men would find it natural and profitable to follow it.[12] Furthermore, sometimes infected by the euphoric idea that difficult problems could be neatly solved forever by simple solutions, Ch'ing officials also sometimes believed that by learning from the mistakes of previous dynasties, they could devise effective solutions to problems previously incurable.[13]

10. *TYT*, 31:13b.

11. *TYT*, 37:49b. This was a memorial in early 1832 in which T'ao Chu protested that he was not guilty of holding a "closed viewpoint" when he rejected again the proposal to collect the main salt taxes from the salt makers or wholesalers at the production yards instead of from the interregional shippers, as was done currently. T'ao Chu had already rejected this idea a year before (*TYT*, 30:45–47); it sounded like an easy way to solve the policing problem, but it was impractical. *Ch'eng-chien* was not a rare term in Ch'ing bureaucratic documents. *Yin-hsün* could also refer to the Taoist virtue of "letting events follow their own course spontaneously."

12. The idea of basing one's policy on "that which the people find profitable" (*li*) can be found in the Analects. See Legge, *Chinese Classics*, I:352 (*Confucian Analects*).

13. *Chung-kuo chin-tai ching-shi ssu-hsiang yü ching-chi cheng-ts'e tzu-liao hsüan-chi*, II:336–337. Wang Liu (1776–1843), the zealous proponent of paper money, raised the problem of how paper money could be expected to work when it had failed in the Sung, Chin, Yüan, and Ming periods. His answer was that officials then had lacked the experience which had since accumulated, and he specifies the safe-

This tendency indeed was connected to a common practice of making stupidly impractical and sweepingly radical proposals —a tendency well suited to the arrogant ignorance typical of some censors. In 1833, for instance, T'ao Chu, the Nanking governor-general, presented a lengthy memorial to the emperor to demonstrate the utter senselessness of a censor's (Hsü Kuang-chin, later the famous governor-general of Kwangtung and Kwangsi) proposal to distribute much of the enormous Liang-huai salt quota through coercive sales rather than through the market, a proposal as wildly impractical as Wang An-shih's scheme of state-managed rural credit, to which T'ao Chu correctly compared it.[14] As T'ao Chu put it, this censor's information largely came from *chü-wai ch'uan-wen* (rumors circulating among those outside the center of affairs). It was indeed a major feature of the Ch'ing political landscape, of the Ch'ing system of political rhetoric, that officials holding down responsible executive positions periodically had to refute bizarre suggestions coming from such outside officials lacking a practical perspective.

Stupidly impractical suggestions could originate not only from such detached observers but also from offices with competitive interests. A good example is the proposal made by the director-general of the grain tribute in 1833 that would have permitted the boat hands of empty grain tribute boats returning south to buy Ch'ang-lu salt in the Peking area and sell it in the Yangtze Valley area, that is, in the Huai-nan markets.[15]

For years, as was well known, it was just exactly the smuggling by these boat hands of Ch'ang-lu salt into Huai-nan which had been a prime factor wrecking Huai-nan, and it was only since 1831 that Huai-nan had been set back on its feet most especially through a striking success in policing this traffic out

guards which previous dynasties failed to use. Actually Wang Liu's monetary reasoning is another example of the euphoric radicalism discussed below. See also Yang Lien-sheng, *"Ch'ao-tai-chien-te pi-sai."* Similar to this faith in simple solutions, there was a tendency of historians sometimes to ascribe a change in institutions to a single policy decision, when in truth the change had been a long, complex, crescive one.

14. *TYT*, 49:32–39. Especially see 49:33–34, 38a–b. Sa Meng-wu points out the tendency of some Ming censors to advance impractical and bizarre suggestions in order to make a name for themselves. This tendency was criticized indigenously. Sa, IV:342–343.

15. *TYT*, 50:5b.

of existence. Yet this success had in turn undermined the interests of the grain tribute system by greatly reducing the remuneration of its personnel. Consequently the audacity of the director-general of the grain tribute is understandable in terms of the pressures on his organization. The important point is that such an unrealistic proposal could be made without embarrassment by an official holding one of the most responsible posts in the empire. Indeed this proposal was so extreme that the emperor later remarked that it was impractical and out of accord with the *cheng-t'i* (basic order of administration).[16]

Another impractical idea was that of unifying the transportation facilities of the Liang-huai salt monopoly and the grain tribute system. Since empty grain tribute boats partly took the same route as loaded Liang-huai salt boats (in that they went from Yangchow to various provinces of the Yangtze valley), why should Liang-huai use a separate fleet of boats? Such transportation unification having worked in the Sung period,[17] the idea had persisted,[18] but T'ao Chu rejected it as impractical. He indicated that the salt trading activities of the grain tribute boats would upset the grain tribute schedule and would attract many bandits, with the unseemly result that the very boats used to deliver the emperor's grain would be hotbeds of criminal activity.[19]

Practical or not, daring ideas could be supported by the clever use of precedents. For instance, Wang Liu (1776–1843), the zealous proponent of paper money, argued for this drastic innovation in 1831 by quoting as a precedent the very limited issuing of paper notes carried out for a decade at the very start of the dynasty: "Some say that the *ch'eng-fa* (established laws) of the state cannot be changed . . . [But] using paper notes would exactly be a resumption of the ancestors' system."[20] (Eventually the government did issue some paper notes.)

If there were no precedent at all available, novel suggestions

16. *TYT*, 50:7, 8.

17. Ch'üan Han-sheng, *T'ang Sung ti-kuo yü yün-ho* (The grand canal and the T'ang and Sung empires; Chungking, 1944), p. 102.

18. The important Ming political thinker, Ch'iu Chün, thought it could be made workable in his day. See Ch'iu Chün, *Ta-hsüeh yen-i-pu* (Hainan, 1931), 28:8a–b.

19. *TYT*, 50:4a–b.

20. *Chung-kuo chin-tai ching-chi ssu-hsiang yü ching-chi cheng-ts'e tzu-liao hsüan-chi*, pp. 341–342.

could still be phrased in an acceptable manner. For instance, one aspect of the monetary crisis faced by Wang Liu was the penetration of foreign silver dollars. Far more convenient to use than the native silver money (which circulated only in the form of ingots or pieces and required constant weighing and testing as to purity), these foreign silver dollars had gradually penetrated the southeastern coastal provinces, being used there possibly even more and eventually commanding a higher price than the native silver. This trend was opposed by some officials on the grounds that it aggravated the crisis of the rising price of silver, that it involved the loss abroad of silver of higher purity, and that there was something improper about silver of a lower purity commanding a higher price. As a remedy Lin Tse-hsü in 1833 cogently discussed the advantages of government minting of silver coins. Such a step, however, was without precedent, and Lin Tse-hsü presented it as the idea of some merchants he had consulted. Thus he brought the idea to the emperor's attention by pointing out its merits while emphasizing that he himself would not be so presumptuous as to advocate it.[21] Thus with a little circumlocution a spirit of inventiveness could enter the flow of bureaucratic communication. (Lin's idea, however, was not adopted.)

What was the outer boundary of the bureaucracy's capacity for routine flexible adjustments? Such boundaries are inherently indefinite, but specific problems give us some inkling into their general vicinity. Apart from vested interests, a major obstacle was that the confusing complexity inherent in certain bureaucratic difficulties impeded that process of cognitive understanding and political consultation required to solve them. Therefore searching for the boundary of flexibility forces us to look into the realm of minute technicalities. A good example is the problem of *p'ei-ko* at the Liang-huai zone of the salt monopoly in the 1830's.

Because freight charges were calculated on a per bag rather than a per weight unit basis, and apparently because larger bags used less of the expensive bag material (*p'u*, a kind of rush) per weight unit than smaller bags, Liang-huai merchants in shipping from the production yards to the repacking center of I-cheng preferred to pack more salt into one bag than the 364 catties—actually 400 catties, including special added

21. *Ibid.*, p. 38.

amounts—which comprised the fiscal weight unit (*yin*) according to which taxes were calculated. The amount above these 400 catties could be regarded as either *chia-tai* (smuggled along within some legal unit), *chia-tai* (legally added to carry along), or *p'ei-ko* (calculated as part of another *yin*). Naturally if the extra salt was *p'ei-ko,* the full tax rate for that portion of a *yin* was paid on it, while as *chia-tai* (legally added to carry along), one could pay less taxes on it, as in the instance of the 100 catties added to each bag in the 1831 shipments of salt from the 1829 and 1830 quotas. Therefore, apart from tacit permission to smuggle, merchants preferred a favorable *chia-tai* arrangement, which could also win the backing of officials interested in speeding sales by lowering prices. The trouble was that salt "legally added to carry along" was typically regarded as added from unsold portions of the quotas of past years. This meant that while part of the current year's market was taken up by *chia-tai* salt, the sales figures and revenues flowing in from *chia-tai* did not count toward the current year's quotas, the missing of which led to the impeachment of the salt officials involved.

The problem confronted by T'ao Chu in 1834 was how to avoid impeachment while maximizing sales. He then insisted on the system of *p'ei-ko* in order to make all current sales count toward the current quotas, but the Board of Revenue objected to *p'ei-ko,* since it was concerned less about the category of revenue and the impeachment of salt officials than about the risk of reduced revenues as a whole; the higher tax rates of *p'ei-ko* threatened a reduction in sales by pushing up prices, thus reducing tax revenue. The rules on impeachment, in other words, affected economic policy by complicating the government's basic interest in maximizing revenue with the interest of individual officials in increasing those categories of revenue for which they bore the heaviest personal responsibility. Solution of this complex problem would have required a degree of flexible coordination between disciplinary and economic policies which, it is safe to say, was just beyond the capacity of the government.[22]

22. See *TYT,* 49:34b, 41b, 43b; 51:40–41b; *TWI* 17:7b, 3b; and, esp. *TWI,* 16:19a–b.

5. The Question of Major Improvements

Doubt as to the proper course both inhibited major change and gave plausibility to a range of alternative policies. This element of doubt can be seen first when we take note of the obvious point that in order to support normative propositions, Ch'ing scholar-officials depended not only on the classics but also greatly on other sources of validation. These included reasoning in the sense of statements governed by the standard of logical consistency; analogies from nature; practical arguments about probable effects; examples from later periods of history demonstrating the effectiveness or ineffectiveness of a given policy; and the authority of later scholars commanding respect for their personal attainments.

A view of Yen Jo-ch'ü (1636–1704) illustrates how a solution to a major contemporaneous problem could be advanced in terms of practical arguments rather than in terms of the classics or even the often relevant historical record of the much-admired Han dynasty. Yen was writing about the problems of local magistrates, especially their corruption and inability to promote the popular welfare. He denied that the local magistrate's problems were due to the fact that, in violation of principles proved true in the Han period, his authority and his salary were too small and his length of tenure was too short. The problem rather was that in late Ming times the periodic evaluations of officials had been changed so that the criterion of success in "soothing and caring for" the people had been dropped, and success in tax collection had been adopted as the main standard. Since the local magistrate was anxious to excel on the periodic evaluations, he naturally cared less about matters that did not count in them. Yen Jo-ch'ü held that the above Han principles (not to mention any ideas from the classics) were in practice irrelevant. He explicitly argued that it was not practical to apply them and that, even if they could be applied, the problems of the local magistrate would not be solved unless the late Ming legislation were rectified. Moreover, he said, rectification of this Ming mistake would by itself be an adequate solution. There is evidence, one might add, that Yen's view had some historical basis.[1]

1. *HCCSWP*, 15:4a–b. Yen's view finds some backing in that a late Ming official, Yüan Shih-chen, complained that, in the case of salt smuggling, local magistrates were concerned too much with the

Another source of doubt was connected to the possibility of accurate knowledge of the models of antiquity. The epistemology of the *tao* (true way) was a problem already in Chou times. Although sometimes confident of his knowledge of antiquity, Confucius lamented the lack of written sources and reliable verbal testimony to "corroborate" his views about the first two sage dynasties, the Hsia and the Shang.[2] Hsün-tzu held that because of the great lapse of time, one could not have detailed knowledge about sage institutions earlier than those of the first Chou rulers (*hou-wang*).[3] The great burning of books in 213 B.C. by the Ch'in dynasty, it was widely felt, further aggravated the problem of authentic knowledge of the models of the past. Liu Hsin (first century B.C. and A.D.) could argue that the founders of the Han had been unable to devise proper institutions because they lacked adequate learning authentically inform them of the true way of Confucius.[4] The whole problem in the Early Han of *kai-chih* (revising institutions) shows how Han Confucians were in doubt about how best to remodel their dynasty along Chou lines.[5] Tung Chung-shu sought to resolve

---

immediate interests of the people under them and not enough with the broader interests of the state. Therefore, they did not try hard to stop smugglers from selling their inexpensive salt to the people. This Ming official emphasized that the periodic evaluations (*k'ao-ch'eng*) should be developed so as to make the local magistrates more mindful of the state's interests. In effect, Yen held that this advice had unfortunately been adopted. See *Huang-Ming ching-shih wen-pien,* XXIX:307–314.

2. Legge, *Chinese Classics,* I:153–154, 158 (*Confucian Analects*). See also *ibid.,* I:424 (*The Doctrine of the Mean*). Han Fei brilliantly exposed the inadequacy of the Confucians' knowledge of the sage emperors Yao and Shun; see *Han Fei-tzu,* 15:2a–b; 19:7b.

3. *Hsün-tzu,* pp. 50–53. Certainly by *hou-wang* (later kings) Hsün-tzu had in mind no one earlier than the first Chou rulers, but just whom he had in mind is still not clear; one scholar has argued that he meant a future ideal ruler, possibly a king of Ch'in. Yet Hsün-tzu also idealized the "former kings," failing to apply consistently his view on the "later kings." See Kung Lo-ch'ün, *Meng Hsün i-t'ung* (Differences and similarities in the thought of Mencius and Hsün-tzu; Feng-shan, 1968), pp. 175–180.

4. Cited in T'ao, II:182.

5. Shu-sun T'ung pragmatically mixed some ancient and some Ch'in rituals to give the first Han emperor his own set of ceremonies, but by this Shu-sun T'ung offended a few Confucians who felt that the devising of proper ceremonies should be a gradual matter, awaiting the gradual proof of the dynasty's virtue; see T'ao, II:81. Later,

this problem of revision through his concept of the close relation of Heaven to dynastic affairs, but his concept of Heaven could not clear away all doubt: since Chou times the tendency toward faith in the role of heaven had been complemented by a tendency toward skepticism.[6] Moreover, Han Confucian thought developed no consensus as to the specific content of the policies, notably economic policies, advocated by Confucius and realized by the sage Chou founders.[7] Despite Mencius' and Hsün-tzu's insistence that there was only one true doctrine,[8] and despite Emperor Wu's (140–87 B.C.) establishment of Confucianism as the single orthodox school, a prominent feeling

---

notably in Tung Chung-shu's eyes, it was held that the Han still lacked proper ceremonial forms, and so the problem of *kai-chih* arose. Tung Chung-shu discussed the problem of how a new dynasty could change institutions and yet retain permanent principles. The crux of his answer was that one could combine adherence to the unchanging principles of the past while acting on the changing will of heaven; see T'ao, II:81–83, 107.

6. A locus classicus of the believing attitude was "The Way of Heaven is to bless the good and to punish the bad," in Legge, *Chinese Classics*, III:186 (*The Shoo King*). A *locus classicus* of the skeptical attitude was a statement said to have been made by Tzu-ch'an in 523 B.C.: "The way of Heaven is distant, while the way of man is near," in *ibid.*, V:669, 671 (*The Tso Chuen*). Hsiao, I:107–109, traces this skepticism from Tzu-ch'an through Confucius and Hsün-tzu. The influence of Hsün-tzu, though not necessarily of his skepticism, is held to have been high in the Han period. In *Yen-t'ieh-lun*, p. 251, the Legalist officials in effect follow Hsün-tzu's skepticism when they deny that the course of nature is greatly affected by the quality of government.

7. One need only contrast the activistic policies in the *Chou-li* with the passive economic views of Confucians in *Yen-t'ieh-lun*. For a convenient account of economic policies in the *Chou-li*, see T'ao, II:191–195. Of course both Wang Mang and Wang An-shih used the *Chou-li* to legitimate their interventionist, activistic economic policies. The relation of activism to Confucianism is still a problem today. One modern scholar holds that the Confucian affinity for passive policies (*wu-wei*) began only in the Early Han period; Tseng K'ang-fan, p. 377. Ch'ien Mu holds that Wang An-shih's activism was a regional trait rather than a revival of Legalist principles, and that Wang's basic political principles were in harmony with the mainstream of neo-Confucianism; see Ch'ien Mu, *Kuo-shih ta-kang* (A basic outline of our national history; Shanghai, 1948), II:413–417, 420–424.

8. *Hsün-tzu*, p. 280; T'ao, I:179; Legge, *Chinese Classics*, II:280 (*The Works of Mencius*).

existed that many different Chou schools, including Legalism, had brought out some facet of the truth, a point explicitly made by the great Han historians Ssu-ma T'an and Pan Ku.[9] The intellectual roots of dogmatism and certainty were not necessarily deeper than those of eclecticism and doubt.

The history of Chinese political thought can be seen as involving this partially doubting, open attitude on the question of how to improve the state. Ch'ing officials looked back through the preceding dynasties at a variety of writings proposing various policies of improvement. These policy proposals gradually formed a spectrum of plausible policy alternatives providing a framework, a "definition of the situation," for discussion in the present. This spectrum can be tentatively described in terms of three polarities, yielding six poles and many subissues that could be variously combined to form the political outlook of a particular thinker.

The first polarity consisted of the field of controversy between Legalism and Confucianism. The second was concerned with the question of whether to promote or inhibit commerce. The third we may label radicalism versus moderate realism.

Following T'ao Hsi-sheng, we may say that the most general issue in the conflict between Legalism and Confucianism was not that of tyranny versus respect for the people's interests but rather that of primary dependence on the state's immediate tools of power (especially physical coercion and the manipulation of economic resources) versus primary dependence on the forces of moral solidarity.[10] This latter dichotomy seems to underly many leading issues, among them: should the ruler's interests be emphasized or the people's; should the stress be on material success (*kung-li*) or moral harmony; should the stress be on fear or on moral solidarity (*li*) as the basis of power;

9. Takigawa, K., comp., *Shiki kaichū kōshō* (The records of the historian by Ssu-ma Ch'ien, with collected commentaries and textual notes; Tokyo, 1932–1934), 130:7a–13. Pan Ku, V:3139–3140, 3148–3149, 3152, 3154, 3156, 3158–3159, 3171–3172. Pan Ku's eclecticism here is a profound, catholic one based on the idea that rediscovering the *tao* is a difficult task requiring a blending of all the insights of all the major schools, but Ssu-ma T'an believed that Taoism had already achieved this blending.

10. The distinction between tyranny or "putting primacy on the ruler's interests" and "putting primacy on the people's interests" is emphasized in Hsiao, II:194. T'ao Hsi-sheng's valuable sociological approach is in T'ao, I:188–189, 141.

should warfare or benevolent influence be the basis of foreign policy; should the official be a mere servant of the state or a scholar with moral independence; should the stress be on law and bureaucracy (*chün-hsien*) or on benevolent influence (*te*) and feudalism (*feng-chien*); should the stress be on activistic (*yu-wei*) or more passive (*wu-wei*) economic policies; and should statesmen inventively respond to current conditions or follow an ideal located in the past.

Although the Confucian school through the ages put primacy on the forces of moral solidarity, its fundamentally ambivalent, "yes, but" attitude can be seen both in general notions and specific issues. When we consider as a whole all the statements expressing this ambivalence, we see that they are not a series of disconnected remarks but rather logically cohere to form a basic attitudinal pattern. This consisted of the realization that in order to improve the world, it was practically necessary to combine Confucian ideals with the hard tools of state power, especially in difficult historical periods. The Confucian concept of power can hardly be identified with Mencian idealism. It is important to realize that many leading Confucians sincerely involved in the pursuit of wisdom accepted the use of force on intellectual grounds.

On the most general level, Confucian ambivalence toward the Legalist notion of force can be seen in attitudes expressed on three pivotal issues: the evaluation to be placed on the *pa* (hegemon), on Kuan Chung, and on the state of Ch'in. The *pa* had come to be a symbol of the Legalist pole of reliance on the immediate tools of state power. The so-called "five hegemons" were feudal lords in the Chou period or earlier who successively assumed leadership over other feudal lords in times when the emperor was weak; Duke Huan of Ch'i (seventh century B.C.) was a famous example. Mencius criticized the rule of the hegemon as merely gaining a hollow kind of success based on force (*li*) in contrast to the ultimately more effective policies of true virtue followed by the sage-kings (*wang*).[11] However, Hsün-tzu held that the rule of the hegemon was in an inter-

11. Legge, *Chinese Classics*, II:196–197 (*The Works of Mencius*). Yet one can find some ambivalence even on this issue. In *ibid.*, II: 214–215, Mencius shows that he realizes that the successes of the *pa* are not to be despised. The idea of *pa* was often pejorative for Confucians, as illustrated by the use of *pa* in criticisms of Wang An-shih and Chang Chü-cheng; see T'ao, IV:49, 233.

mediate position; although lacking the highest virtues, the hegemon relied not on *li* (force) but on *hsin* (trust).[12] According to one modern scholar, the classic *Ch'un-ch'iu* expressed Confucius' relative approval of the policies of the hegemon as a realistic compromise with conditions.[13] As illustrated by an edict of the first Han emperor issued in about 196 B.C., there was a tendency in Han times to see the rule of the true king and that of the hegemon not in Mencian terms but rather as two ideals of government, the former admittedly being superior. This attitude can be seen also in Emperor Hsüan's (73–49 B.C.) famous statement that Han institutions were a mixture of those of the hegemon and of the true king.[14]

Tseng K'ang-fan holds that in Sung times, the distinction between the policies of the true king and of the hegemon was blurred when Wang An-shih, Ch'eng Hao (1032–1085), and Chu Hsi saw moral intention rather than the objective content of policies as the basis of this distinction.[15] At the same time, the more "utilitarian" or less idealistic Sung thinkers tended to defend the idea of rule by the hegemon. Li Kou (1009–1059) showed how the moral distinction between the hegemon and the true king could be dissolved. He said that the achievements of a hegemon like Duke Huan were admirable, and that in its proper meaning the term "hegemon" did not refer to morally impure policies but only to a type of position in the political hierarchy. Ssu-ma Kuang similarly said that the moral difference between the policies of the true king and those of the hegemon was only one of degree. Ch'en Liang (1143–1194), Hou

12. *Hsün-tzu,* pp. 131–133, 194. In *HCCSWP,* 1:6a–b, Wang Chin (1725–1792), a little like Hsün-tzu, distinguishes three main gradations of attitudes on the part of the ruler: the ruler identifies his interests with those of the people, like a parent with his child's; second, a ruler has concern for the people similar to the concern a stranger might have to help find someone a place to rest and sleep; third, the ruler treats the people the way one stranger carries on a commercial exchange with another. Wang Chin differs from Hsün-tzu in his extremely low regard for the intermediate attitude. Even if a stranger is much more able than a relative, Wang argues, he cannot help a person as much as that relative can because he lacks "the feeling in his heart of belonging [to that person]."

13. Hsiao, I:69–71.

14. Pan Ku, I:86, 288.

15. Tseng K'ang-fan, *Chung-kuo cheng-chih ssu-hsiang-shih,* p. 362.

Wai-lu points out, held that there was no "essential distinction" between the hegemon and the true king.[16]

There was a Confucian tradition of admiration for Kuan Chung, who, as prime minister of Duke Huan of Ch'i, had followed policies later associated with Legalism, thereby making the Duke a hegemon. This tradition of admiration, although somewhat interrupted by Mencius, can be traced from Confucius himself through Hsün-tzu, Chia I (second century B.C.), and the Confucians of the *Salt and Iron Discourses*.[17] Kuan Chung, an eighteenth-century writer held, was the point of transition from the way of the *wang* (true king); return to the latter, therefore, meant first returning to the policies of Kuan Chung.[18] When late Ch'ing writers sometimes referred favorably to Kuan Chung, therefore, they were not simply being impelled by Western influences to oppose the Confucian tradition.

Even the much-despised Ch'in state, which unified China in 221 B.C. and was closely associated with Legalism, attracted some admiration. Hsün-tzu traveled to Ch'in in about 266 B.C. and partly admired its government. This visit was an important occasion in the history of Chinese political thought which has not received the attention it deserves. Like his attitude toward Kuan Chung and the hegemon, Hsün-tzu's view of Ch'in was connected to his major interest in the problem of the middle range of political success. He was fascinated by the phenomenon of power that is at once very great, very near ultimate suc-

16. *Ibid.*, p. 371, Hsiao, IV:483. Hou Wai-lu *et al.*, *Chung-kuo ssu-hsiang t'ung-shih* (A general history of Chinese thought; Peking, 1957–1960), IV:725. The context of the hegemon issue in Sung times is illuminated in Hsia Chün-yü's article on Sung attitudes toward Mencius, found in his *Sung-hsüeh kai-yao* (Essentials of Sung thought; Shanghai, 1937), pp. 56–79.

17. On Confucius' and Mencius' views, see I, 3, note 7. Hsün-tzu's opinion of Kuan Chung is cited in W. A. Rickett, *Kuan-tzu* (Hong Kong, 1965), p. 11; see *Hsün-tzu,* pp. 97, 67. For Chia I's adoption of a basic principle in the *Kuan-tzu*, see T'ao, II:71. In the *Salt and Iron Discourses,* which, written around 75 B.C., purports to be an account of a court conference which had occurred a few years earlier, Confucians as well as Legalists at times adduce the alleged words or actions of Kuan Chung to support their positions; see, e.g., *Yen-t'ieh-lun,* pp. 248, 301, 343, 72. At this time, apparently, doubt had not yet arisen as to whether Kuan Chung was the author of *Kuan-tzu.*

18. *HCCSWP,* 11:2b–3. The writer is Jen Ch'i-yün, a *chin-shih* of 1733. For another favorable reference to Kuan-tzu's ideas, see *HCCSWP,* 21:1–2b. The writer is Chang Hui-yen (1761–1802).

cess, and yet unstable. He saw Ch'in as possessing that kind of power. In his eyes, Ch'in not only had the superficial aspects of power such as great territory; it also had basic institutions and customs so excellent that they were the same as those "of old." If Ch'in now appointed as officials "true gentlemen" (*chün-tzu*) governing according to Confucian principles, it could easily rule the world, but if it failed to do so, its success would be short-lived.[19] The rule of Ch'in, therefore, was seen not as an abominable aberration but as a major step in the right direction.

In describing the history of *li* (rules of moral propriety, rituals), Ssu-ma Ch'ien also praised Ch'in, although elsewhere he viewed Ch'in negatively. He said that after the Chou dynasty declined, the *li* were not well observed, and Confucius had little success in reviving them. When Ch'in unified the empire, however, it reviewed the ceremonial practices in the various states it had conquered and "selected the good ones. Although its *li* were not the same as the sage institutions, its emphasis on honoring the ruler and curbing the officials, as well as the awesome gravity of its court ceremonies, accorded with the institutions handed down from the past."[20]

There sometimes was partial admiration for Lord Shang's reforms in Ch'in, as with Li Kou, Wang An-shih, and Su Tung-p'o in the Sung period.[21] Even Chu Hsi saw some advantages in Lord Shang's land reform.[22]

Although regarded as having leanings toward Legalism by

19. *Hsün-tzu*, pp. 200–203. This passage on Ch'in is partly translated in Derk Bodde, *China's First Unifier* (Hong Kong, Hong Kong University Press, 1967), pp. 8–10. This translation is not flawless: "are people who follow precedent obediently" involves a mispunctuation. The sentence should read: "Standing in great awe of the officials, they are obedient. They truly are like the people of old." Also, see discussion in Chiang Shang-hsien, *Hsün-tzu ssu-hsiang t'i-hsi* (The structure of Hsün-tzu's thought; Tainan, 1966), pp. 188–190, 10. For other opinions of Hsün-tzu on Ch'in, see *Hsün-tzu*, pp. 181, 186, respectively translated in Burton Watson, tr., *Hsün-tzu* (New York, 1969), pp. 61–62, 70–71.

20. Takigawa Kametarō, 23:4. This passage has also been adduced in Tu K'uei-ying, *Chung-kuo li-tai cheng-chih fu-hao* (The political symbols of China over successive dynasties; National Chengchi University, 1963), p. 167.

21. For Wang An-shih's view, see T'ao, IV:56–57. For Su Tung-p'o's, see Sa, IV:27. For Li Kou's, see Tseng K'ang-fan, p. 371.

22. I follow T'ao Hsi-sheng's explanation in T'ao, IV:124.

scholars like Ch'eng Chin-fang (1718–1784) and Huang Ju-ch'eng (1799–1837), Ku Yen-wu (1613–1682) nevertheless stood in the mainstream of the Confucian tradition. Therefore his admiration for the moral concerns of the first emperor of the Ch'in dynasty, Ch'in-shih-huang (221–210 B.C.), is extremely significant. Ch'in-shih-huang, Ku said, erected stone inscriptions mostly to glorify his achievements as the unifier of the empire. Therefore the fact that he used his stone tablet at Kuei-chi also to condemn the licentious practices peculiar to that area showed how concerned he was about the morals of the people:

> This being the case, although Ch'in put too much emphasis on punishments, its basic aim of guarding the people [against immoral tendencies] and rectifying their customs cannot be distinguished from that of the Three Kings [the sage-kings who respectively founded the Hsia, Shang, and Chou dynasties]. When the Han dynasty arose, it inherited Ch'in laws, and many of these laws have continued in use until today. When those so-called scholars whom the world admires discuss the Ch'in, they regard its laws as those of a morally depraved state headed for destruction. They indeed have not deeply studied the matter.[23]

Notably in the Ch'ing period, Confucians often admired the Han dynasty in full awareness that so many Han institutions, even the name for the office of emperor, had been inherited from the Ch'in. Some Confucians especially were ambivalent about the Han emperor Wu; he had made their school the orthodox one but also had pursued activist military and economic

23. See second section of *chüan* 13 in Ku Yen-wu's *Jih-chih-lu*. Ku's comments here on the Ch'in inscription are also quoted in Takigawa Kametarō, *Shiki*, 6:64 as well as in Sun K'ai (Chieh ?), *Ch'in hui-yao* (Collection of essentials regarding the Ch'in dynasty; Taipei, 1956), p. 175. Compiled by Sun during the period of intense interest in reform following the Boxer Rebellion, the latter book reflected the increasingly explicit admiration of Legalism emerging at the time and was first published in 1905. Huang Ju-ch'eng's view on Ku's Legalistic leanings is expressed in his note on the passage above in *Jih-chih-lu*, and Ch'eng Chin-fang's view is cited in our text below. On Chang Hsüeh-ch'eng's (1738–1801) admiration of some aspects of the Ch'in dynasty, see D. S. Nivison, *The Life and Thought of Chang Hsüeh-ch'eng* (Stanford, Calif., 1966), pp. 61–62, 167.

policies. The modern Chinese movement of open admiration for Legalism, going back at least to Liang Ch'i-ch'ao, has roots in what can be called a fundamental Confucian ambivalence.

On a more specific level, views mixing Confucian and Legalist poles were common. While Legalists tended to favor the interests of the ruler, and Confucians, those of the people, the idea of finding a mean between these two interests became a cliché, as in the slogan *kuo-chi min-sheng* (promote both state finances and the livelihood of the people). A modern scholar gives Wang An-shih credit for emphasizing this middle way, but it can be traced back to Han, if not Chou, times.[24]

24. Huang Nai-lung, *Wang An-shih pien-fa-te ts'ai-ching cheng-ts'e shu-p'ing* (An evaluation of the fiscal and economic policies in Wang An-shih's reforms; Taichung, 1968), pp. 77–78. This compromise notion of favoring both the state and the people perhaps was linked to the idea, existing already in Chou times, of establishing relations of mutual regard and consideration between superiors and inferiors, each "yielding" (*jang*) to the other. Hsün-tzu stressed that the economic welfare of the common people was the necessary foundation of the state's fiscal strength, but he went further than either Confucius or Mencius in explicitly confirming as valid the state's need for wealth. He aimed for a society in which "both those in superior positions and their inferiors will be wealthy" (*Hsün-tzu*, p. 126). The rather Legalist book *Kuan-tzu*, written perhaps around 300 B.C., combines an emphasis on the ruler's interests with the idea of devising policies which accord with the preferences of the people (*shun-min*); see Hsiao, II:194–197. In the *Han Fei-tzu*, the key notion of *chung-pao* (corruption and satiation in the intermediate positions of society) is presented. Han Fei was referring to corrupt officials who grew rich while the people starved and the state's treasuries were empty. See *Han Fei-tzu* (Ssu-pu ts'ung-k'an), 14:2. The implication is that both the state and the people are legitimate interests. In later times other allegedly corrupt groups, such as exploitative merchants and landowners, also were regarded as occupying such an intermediate position, and this sandwich notion, whereby society was corrupted by its middle layers, became widely accepted. This notion contrasts with some Legalist and Confucian views as to the social location of evil to the extent that Confucians stressed the badness of the rulers, while Legalists stressed the badness of the people and the barbarians. One should add that even in the harshly Legalist thought of *Shang-chün-shu*, written around 300 B.C., the ruler is advised that laws will be ineffective unless when designing them he takes into account the people's feelings; see *Shang-chün-shu* (Ssu-pu pei-yao), 3:3. Phraseology pairing *kuo* (state) and *min* (people) in the cliché manner of later times can be found at least as early as the defense of government policies in the *Discourses on Salt and Iron*, which was written in the first century B.C., e.g., "In

A similar example is the question of adjusting to the present versus following the models of the past. In the Han work *Salt and Iron Discourses*, there is a polarization of opinion, the Legalists stressing adjustment to the present, the Confucians, following the past.[25] Similarly, Wang An-shih spoke of making policies by *i-ku chun-chin* (taking the standards of the past to regulate the present).[26] Yet this position was not necessarily the sole Confucian outlook. Rather there was an important tension between this idea and that of modulating between the ideals of the past and the needs of the present.

Even apart from ambiguities in the idea of *i-ku chun-chin* (for example, should the general principles or specific institutions of the ancient sages be followed),[27] three other formulas can be found in the official Ming or Ch'ing literature. The first is *cho-ku chun-chin* (regulate the present by taking careful account of the models of the past). In some contexts, however, this phrase has a more progressive meaning: "take careful account of the models of the past and make your standards meet the needs of the present."[28] Unambiguously meaning the latter is *tsun ku-fa cho shih-i* (respectfully follow the models and laws of the past while carefully taking into consideration the needs of the present). This phrase was used by a Ming

---

enriching the state, why must one necessarily adopt the policy of taking farming as basic? In providing the people with enough, why must one necessarily adopt the well-field system?" Cited in T'ao, II:161.

25. The Legalist side, however, sometimes leans toward some compromise between following the past and adjusting to the present; see *Yen-t'ieh-lun*, pp. 363, 334–335.

26. Cited in Huang Nai-lung, p. 49. Wang also stressed adjustment to present needs.

27. See *Lü-shih ch'un-ch'iu* (Ssu-pu ts'ung-k'an), 15:20b for the view that one should take as a model not the established laws of the former kings but the principles by which the former kings made their laws. The principle, in turn, is man, and man is understood by understanding one's own "self." Therefore following one's own convictions is the true way to imitate the former kings. In Wang Yang-ming's view (cited in T'ao, IV:218), one should emulate the ancient model rulers' ability to act out of their own sense of what is moral instead of looking for standards outside themselves.

28. For an example in the former sense, see *Liang-huai yen-fa-chih* (1693 edition, reprinted in Taipei, 1966), I:2. For an example in the latter sense, see *Liang-che yen-fa-chih* (Salt gazetteer of the Liang-che zone; edition of 1792, reprinted in Taipei, 1966), I:49.

emperor around 1502 to describe the outlook of the Ming founder.[29] (An almost identical phrase is *chun-ku cho-chin.*) Most innovative in spirit is the phrase used in 1684 by the K'ang-hsi emperor to describe the approach of his three dynastic predecessors: *chun-chin cho-ku* (draw your standards from the needs of the present while taking carefully into account the models of the past).[30]

This outlook had good Confucian credentials. Confucius said: "If a man keeps cherishing his old knowledge, so as to be continually acquiring new, he may be a teacher of others."[31] Hsün-tzu said: "Therefore those who are good at discussing matters of the past necessarily corroborate [the validity of past ideas] by reference to things in the present."[32] Common by Han times was the ideal of the rounded scholar who "has mastered the learning of the past and the present."[33] Ou-yang Hsiu said: "Scholars should not only learn from the past; [their ideas] must also be realizable in the present." Admittedly, when Ou-yang Hsiu wrote this, he felt that many scholars of his day were paying attention only to the past.[34]

More involved considerations led to what we can call a general Confucian ambivalence toward some other problems, such as that of the status of the official relative to the ruler (notably the propriety of punishing officials),[35] activist economic poli-

29. *Ta-Ming hui-tien,* I:1.

30. *Ta-Ch'ing hui-tien* (1690), *ts'e* 1, 1684 prefatory edict.

31. Legge, *Chinese Classics,* I:149 (*Confucian Analects*). Chang Chih-tung used this phrase and others from the classics in 1898 when arguing that the latter legitimated flexibility. See Ssu-yü Teng and John K. Fairbank, *China's Response to the West* (Cambridge, Mass., Harvard University Press, 1954), p. 171.

32. *Hsün-tzu,* p. 293. See also T'ao, I:183–184. *Shang-chün-shu,* 3:3, says: "Therefore the sage's way of governing a state is neither to take the past as a model nor to follow the present." (*Shang-chün-shu* goes on to say that the right path is to make laws which take into account current conditions.) For the meaning of *hsiu-chin* in this passage, I have followed Duyvendak, *Book of Lord Shang,* p. 238.

33. T'ao, II:40.

34. Tseng K'ang-fan, p. 371. Complaints about scholars being preoccupied with the past at the expense of the present were not uncommon. For a Ch'ing example, see *HCCSWP,* 2:10 (Ch'en Hung-mou's view).

35. See IV, 2.

cies,[36] and the use of warfare in dealing with barbarians.[37]

The second polarity was that of promoting commerce versus inhibiting commerce. It is now increasingly recognized that orthodox Confucians did not have a basically negative view of commerce. The mainstream view since Chou times rather was that commerce and merchants had both desirable and undesirable forms. Thinkers varied in terms of whether they stressed the desirable or undesirable dimensions. This line of variation, however, seems to have been logically independent of the Confucian-Legalist dichotomy. The Legalist books *Shang-chün-shu* and *Han Fei-tzu* wanted to inhibit commerce, but the semi-Legalist book *Kuan-tzu* and the Han Legalist officials described in *Yen-t'ieh-lun* wanted to promote it. Similarly, *Mencius* and *Hsün-tzu* were more favorable to commerce than the Confucian spokesmen in *Yen-t'ieh-lun*. In Ch'ing times, both poles on the commerce question were expressed, and innumerable statements favoring commerce can be found in Ch'ing bureaucratic documents. (Of course, European mercantilism in the eighteenth century was even more concerned with the importance of commerce.)[38]

The third polarity, similarly crosscutting the other two, was that of radicalism versus realism. The heart of what we venture to call radicalism was the euphoric idea that good government is easy if the ruler will simply adopt the right policies. This idea was common in Chou times, the writings of which often contain some prescription for easy and full political success. For instance, *Mencius* says: "If the ruler is benevolent, everyone will be benevolent."[39] *The Book of Lord Shang* states that if the ruler is "a man of his word, the officials will not dare to commit any depravity."[40]

Realism, on the other hand, focused on the difficulty of putting into effect even good policies. Although mostly stressing the ease with which good policies can succeed, *Han Fei-tzu*

36. See T. Metzger, "The State and Commerce in Imperial China," in *Asian and African Studies* (Annual of the Israel Oriental Society), 6 (1970), 35–37.

37. See discussion of L. S. Yang in J. K. Fairbank, ed., *The Chinese World Order* (Cambridge, Mass., 1968), pp. 24–27.

38. See Metzger, "The State and Commerce in Imperial China."

39. Legge, *Chinese Classics*, II: 320 (*The Works of Mencius*).

40. Duyvendak, *Book of Lord Shang*, p. 176.

does state that every law involves some difficulty.[41] Similar realism can be found in the view, held by Legalist officials in the *Salt and Iron Discourses*, written around 75 B.C., that many officials had such bad characters that good influences could not reform them.[42] Reforms like Wang Mang's and Wang An-shih's provoked criticism from the standpoint of realism. Su Tung-p'o said that there were developments in society which even a *pao-chün* (tyrannically cruel ruler) or *sheng-jen* (sage) could not control.[43] Yeh Shih (d. 1223) said that the state's power was inhibited by largeness of territory and further reduced by that great increase in private commerce beginning in T'ang times; Wang An-shih had failed because the state inherently lacked the power to recover control over the flow of commercial wealth.[44] In the eighteenth century the charge of impractical radicalism was leveled at the Confucians Ku Yen-wu and Huang Tsung-hsi (1610–1695). Ch'eng Chin-fang said that many of Ku Yen-wu's administrative ideas, such as restoring taxes-in-kind and the equal-field system, were impractical, and that Ku was close to Legalism in his advocacy of "harsh" methods to cure the ills of his day. Ch'eng charged that Huang Tsung-hsi showed himself "unable to grasp changing circumstances and to adjust to current conditions" in his insistence that the empire could not be properly governed without the restoration of feudalism and the well-field system.[45]

When T'ao Chu was Nanking governor-general, his memorials virtually always had a sober, realistic tone focused on the seriousness of the government's practical difficulties. In urging the emperor to accept his modestly designed proposals, he typically avoided euphoric claims for them and merely argued that if they were adopted, "there would gradually be a [favorable] turning point." When the emperor wanted to know whether T'ao *ch'üeh-yu pa-wo* (definitely had his problems under full control), T'ao refused to say that he did, pointing out that success in the Liang-huai salt monopoly partly depended on factors outside his control, such as market conditions in provinces outside

41. *Han Fei-tzu*, 18:6. (The text here mistakenly omits a negative. It should read: "In the world there are no laws free of difficulties and achievements without harmful aspects.")
42. *Yen-t'ieh-lun*, pp. 242–243.
43. T'ao, IV:75.
44. T'ao, IV:133, 148–151.
45. *HCCSWP*, 2:2a–b, 11a–b.

his territorial jurisdiction. In a spirit of practical realism, he tried to limit his responsibility to what was practically within his control.

Yet radical, euphoric ideas were still expressed within the Ch'ing bureaucracy, such as the salt proposal of 1833 made by the censor Hsü Kuang-chin. He held that if local magistrates "really exerted themselves to carry out orders" relative to catching smugglers, then even in bad markets sales would be easy. Hsü also believed that coercive distribution of salt could to a large extent replace the market system. Although T'ao clearly showed the impracticality of this view, such radical proposals were not always denounced by the emperor as *wang-yen* (speaking irresponsibly).[46] Euphoric, unrealistic proposals were perhaps more characteristic of censors than of those who held difficult executive responsibilities.

The "realistic" emphasis on difficulty and the "radical" emphasis on ease can each be correlated with other political views and approaches. Of course, I do not mean that all these correlations always existed but only that there was some tendency toward them.

The radical view held that basic improvements could be made quickly; the realistic, only gradually.[47] The radical view aimed for total control over the society; the realistic, for partial control. Lu Shih-i (1611–1672) pointed out that in the small feudal states to which the institutions in the classic *Chou-li* applied, *mi* (tight) control was proper, but that in the large empire of

46. *CFTL,* 9:31a–b. This is a regulation punishing an official with a one-subgrade demotion plus transfer if he "memorializes irresponsibly," bringing about changes which later prove impractical and must be remedied. This article equates this offense with that of censors who memorialize irresponsibly. The latter offense is given in *CFTL,* 4:37. On T'ao Chu's salt policy, see Metzger, "Organizational Capabilities of the Ch'ing State in the Field of Commerce."

47. Gradualism was explicitly stressed in Sung times as a point against Wang An-shih's reforms. Su Tung-p'o stated that "If [governmental] matters are handled in a gradual way, then the people will not be alarmed." This is cited in T'ao, IV:78. Lu Chiu-yüan also emphasized the need for acting "gradually"; see T'ao, IV:130. See also Sa, IV:29–30, and Ch'ien Mu, *Kuo-shih ta-kang,* II:426–428. Ou-yang Hsiu (1007–1072) emphasized gradualism, as shown in J. T. C. Liu, *Ou-yang Hsiu* (Stanford, Calif.: Stanford University Press, 1967), pp. 114–117.

his day, *shu* (loose) control was proper. If local officials are chosen well, then even the detailed economic and administrative systems of Wang An-shih can be realized in a large empire, but generally such systems can work only in a small feudal state.[48] A radical work like *Kuan-tzu* saw law and state organization as totally penetrating social behavior; the people's customary practices (*su*) grew out of their obedience to laws properly issued by the ruler.[49] A "realistic" thinker like Su Tung-p'o, on the other hand, saw a reverse relation between "customs" and laws. Popular tendencies were sometimes so strong that neither a "sage" nor a "cruelly tyrannical ruler" could reverse them, with the result that "laws and institutions follow changes in customs."[50] By implication, the radical view conceived of direct control of the people by the state, while the fact that groups like the gentry and merchants mediated between the state and the people in Ch'ing times was recognized in the moderate view.

The radical view focused more on large-scale reforms in the society-at-large, while the realistic view, especially after Sung times, focused more on bureaucratically internal reforms, notably the recruitment of better officials.[51]

The radical view leaned toward the Chou ideal whereby the scholar acted through the top of the bureaucracy; he became the ruler's prime minister and then proceeded to reform the whole society. The realistic view leaned to the idea of initiating reform on a local basis, through a low official position, or with regard to only a single institution. An early example is Chang Heng-ch'ü's (1020–1077) plan of establishing the well-field system throughout the empire by first setting it up on land owned by himself.[52] Such views were certainly encouraged by

48. *HCCSWP*, 11:11a–b.

49. *Kuan-tzu*, 10:12a–b; 5:5b. Liang Ch'i-ch'ao, *Kuan-tzu-chuan*, p. 32.

50. T'ao, IV:75.

51. Lu Shih-i's view in *HCCSWP*, 11:11a–b, illustrates this focus on "selecting good prefects and district magistrates and making demotions, dismissals, and promotions according to clear and proper standards." In *Kuo-shih ta-kang*, II:570–572, Ch'ien Mu holds that after the failure of Fan Chung-yen's and Wang An-shih's reforms, scholars increasingly felt that a prerequisite for reform of society was to improve education, the outlook of the ruler, and the caliber of officials.

52. T'ao, IV:92.

the weakening of the *tsai-hsiang* (prime office, cabinet) after 1380 (see III, 2).

The radical view, following the main lines of Chou thought, stressed either fear or moral solidarity (or both) as the basic way of eliciting obedience from the people. The realistic view tended rather to stress remunerative, material incentives. For instance, a major line of discussion in Ch'ing salt monopoly affairs was whether lowering the price of legal salt or intensifying policing was the best way of increasing legal sales. Famous Chou and Han political ideas often revolved around the question of coercion versus moral solidarity. Thus an underlying blurred spectrum of so much Chinese political philosophy moved from the pole of hard force to that of soft, moral appeal: *hsing* (criminal punishments), *fa* (laws), *tien* (institutions), *li* (rules of moral propriety), and *jen* (benevolence). By contrast, Ch'ing administrative discussions often put the pole of soft, normative persuasion in the background and revolved around the questions of coercion versus remunerative incentives. Eliciting legal behavior by making it economically advantageous was a much more explicit and important idea by Ch'ing times than it was in Chou thought.

The radical view often was monocausal, while the realistic was multicausal. Official discussions of personnel questions in Ch'ing times often took for granted that enforcing disciplinary controls and raising the morale of officials both were important. But it was seen that tight disciplinary controls tended to reduce both the morale and the effectiveness of officials. While Han Fei had envisioned a corps of officials both perfectly disciplined and effective, it is clear that some Ch'ing officials felt they were grappling with a contradiction between discipline and effectiveness (see IV, 3, c).

Similarly, "radical" administrators could believe that a single change in procedure might completely solve all the problems of a complex institution, while realists saw the need for changes on many fronts. For instance, in the 1830's, T'ao Chu improved sales in the Huai-nan branch of the salt monopoly by lowering the price of legal salt, intensifying policing, changing shipping procedures so as to tighten control, and changing the administrative structure so as to reduce corruption. Simultaneously he repeatedly had to refute as impractical the radical, simplistic idea that only one change in procedure was needed to solve all problems, namely collecting all taxes before the salt left the production yards. If all taxes had already been collected, what else was there to worry about? Proponents of this idea overlooked many practical difficulties, T'ao had to point out, such as the fact that the yards, occupying more than 1,000 square miles, could not be policed with complete effectiveness. Practical arguments often carried weight in Ch'ing times, but so did euphoric, simplistic ideas.

Radicalism tended to discuss administrative problems in terms of general principles; realism, in terms of organizational details.

Radicalism sometimes was linked to a "fundamentalist" stress on the validity of the classics, while realism drew on a larger variety of the sources of validation mentioned above, especially history.[53]

Some might object that realism in the above sense "naturally" arises as common sense within any bureaucracy, but one can just as well argue that the spread of realistic, eclectic attitudes is an intellectual achievement which cannot be taken for granted, and which makes bureaucratic action more effective. Certainly much Ch'ing bureaucratic thought was realistic rather than radical; favored facilitating commerce rather than inhibiting it; and took a complex, eclectic position on the question of state power versus moral solidarity. Major changes away from this mixture were not easy to bring about, but neither did the heritage of political ideas lead to a static approach to administration. Rather, constant criticism of procedures and a flow of varied adjustments were routine. An innovating official had to shoulder the burden of proof and was likely to suffer a cross fire of skepticism and criticism as he initiated his changes, but as soon as he was successful, he could enjoy a smug "I told you so" while his prestige soared. "Criticism from the people perversely arose every which way," wrote the Nanking governor-general in a memorial of 1833, as he complacently recited all

53. For "fundamentalism" in Sung Neo-Confucianism, see Wm. Theodore de Bary's view in D. S. Nivison and A. F. Wright, eds., *Confucianism in Action* (Stanford, Calif., Stanford University Press, 1959), pp. 35–36. Ch'ien Mu's account of Northern Sung thought also shows the strong tendency then to believe that current problems could be solved through direct application of principles in the classics. See Ch'ien Mu, *Chung-kuo chin-san-pai-nien hsüeh-shu-shih*, pp. 2–6.

the early objections to his now successful and consciously unprecedented Huai-pei salt reform.[54]

54. *TYT,* 46:18. This concept of Ch'ing ideology as continuing, varying efforts to define effective responses to situational changes in terms of the above three polarities perhaps helps explain the relative swiftness of the first Ch'ing intellectual responses to the problem of Western power. Officials with an orthodox scholarly background like Li Hung-chang could fairly quickly perceive the need for new policies strengthening the state's military power because such a perception required little more than a shift within the inherited framework of policy alternatives. Of course along some indefinite boundary this framework became inadequate as thinkers gradually realized that a more far-reaching transformation was needed.

6. Fixity versus Flexibility

The conflict between the ideological need for a fixed order and the need to adapt to changing circumstances was consciously conceptualized. For instance, Jen Yüan-hsiang, writing obviously during the earlier part of the Ch'ing period, touched on this conflict relative to the procedure of appointment to office:

> At the present time, with regard to the system for selecting officials for appointment, we ought to seek uniformity of practice in order to fix the institutions of a dynasty, and we ought to make some suitable changes in order to obtain success in getting the right men. Why? With all dynasties, after several generations respectful maintenance of the established order is valued while the disorder of numerous changes is not. [But] today we can actually create new procedures even though maintaining what is established; it is just the time to seek uniformity [by finding the proper institutions]. In all periods of formless beginning, men use all sorts of procedures to bring the empire to order, lacking the leisure to determine whether or not their procedures are the most proper. [But] today even though creating, we can maintain past procedures; it is just the time to make suitable changes according to new conditions.[1]

The problems of *ch'eng-shu* (completely established books) also reflects this conflict between the ideological need for a fixed order and the practical need to adjust to changing circumstances. Although the term *ch'eng-shu* could be used loosely for any book of state regulations,[2] it was also used in a more solemn sense to refer to a book of laws which really was to be regarded as completed and thus not subject to significant revision. This sense was close to that of *ch'eng-hsien* (completely established laws).

We can contrast the latter sense of *ch'eng-shu* with the practice of regularly issuing *hsin-ting chih shu* (newly fixed books). In an edict of 1742, the Ch'ien-lung emperor took for granted that revisions of the regulations of the six boards were desirable at certain intervals in the form of "newly fixed books,"[3] and

1. *HCCSWP*, 17:1.
2. *LHYFC*, tsou-che:4. *CFTL*, prefatory memorials:3.
3. *CFTL*, 14:3.

beginning around this time, there apparently was an increase in the number of types and editions of books of law. It was in 1747 that the emperor finally authorized the compilation of the third edition of the *Ta-Ch'ing hui-tien,* after rejecting earlier requests to do so on the grounds that the *kuo-chia ting-chih* (fixed order of the state) precluded such frequent changes.[4] Then in the next year, 1748, the emperor approved the novel idea of preparing a volume complementary to the *Ta-Ch'ing hui-tien,* initiating the first of three editions of *Precedents and regulations supplementary to the collected statutes of the great Ch'ing dynasty.* There was a similar tendency in the case of the penal code, since it was only after its third edition, that of 1740, that its system of regular and frequent revision was gradually set up. The Ch'ien-lung emperor's outlook promoted revision, as the *Ch'ing-shih* (The history of the Ch'ing dynasty) points out.[5]

In contrast to this spirit of flexibility, an important edict of 1830 partly interrupted the flow of revisions and reflected the continuing influence of the ideal of *ch'eng-shu.* In this edict the Tao-kuang emperor agreed with the protest of a censor (Wang Wei-ch'ing) that "With regard to revising the regulations of the six boards, there should be the rule of 'He followed the ancient regulations' [Book of Odes].[6] When a change is needed, it ought to be done by memorializing with a *chuan-che* (a separate memorial dealing exclusively with the subject at hand) . . . It is originally expected that the laws issued for each office are handed down to last forever." A regulation of the eighteenth century calling for revision of board regulations once every ten years was thus eliminated. (It must be granted that several practical reasons, not only the ideal of keeping the laws unchanged, were advanced in favor of this move. For instance, when the rule of issuing revisions once every ten years was in force, there often were delays of several years before the new editions were actually compiled and distributed. Such delays

4. *Ta-Ch'ing hui-tien tse-li* (1764), prefatory edict of Ch'ien-lung 12/1/6.

5. *Ibid.,* prefatory memorial of Ch'ien-lung 13/5/28. See discussion in III, 5. *Ch'ing-shih-kao hsing-fa-chih chu-chieh* (The monograph on penal law of the draft history of the Ch'ing dynasty, annotated; Peking, 1957), p. 23; *Ch'ing-shih,* III:1735.

6. Bernhard Karlgren, *The Book of Odes* (Stockholm, 1950), poem #205.

aggravated the corrupt manipulation of the law, because they created uncertainty as to what the law was.)[7]

The pressing need for revisions, however, could not be stilled by this edict. There was a loophole, first of all, in the system of making revisions by *chuan-che*, since such revisions could apparently be stretched to resemble regular revisions. Thus the Board of Civil Officials in 1832 and 1836 presented such *chuan-che*, but each time apparently included a *number* of regulations for imperial endorsement. The format used was that of attaching to the *chuan-che* a standard kind of list which could be routinely attached to all sorts of memorials and was called a *ch'ing-tan* (clear list).[8] A number of regulations could conveniently be presented in this list.

More significant, however, is the fact that various boards successfully argued for new revisions in the face of the decision made in 1830. By 1839 the Board of Civil Officials had found that the above practice of *chuan-che* was inadequate. In an 1839 memorial it pointed out that "annually it handled a total of more than 57,000 *kao-an* (cases)," and that of all the cases handled since the last revised edition of its regulations (that of 1824), there were "more than 380 items" which "ought to be entered into the *li* (regulations)." Pointing out that the emperor in his 1830 edict had "lodged the idea of 'He followed the ancient regulations' amidst the process of making adjustments according to circumstances," the Board stated that a revision was nevertheless needed in order to avoid confusion and corruption. The result was the 1843 edition of the *Li-pu tse-li*.[9]

The Board of Revenue responded similarly to the edict of 1830. Strangely, it put out an edition in 1831 (perhaps this

7. Wang Wei-ch'ing's memorial and the responding edict are referred to in several post-1830 books of law. One of the fullest quotations is in *Li-pu tse-li* (1843), prefatory memorials: 1–2. Also *Hu-pu tse-li* (1838), prefatory memorials: 1b–2.; *CFTL*, prefatory memorials: 4–5.

8. *CFTL*, prefatory memorials: 3–5. These memorials relate more to the compilation of the *Regulations of the Board of Civil Officials* than just to those on administrative punishment. This is clear from the first memorial, which obviously belongs with the 1843 edition of the former regulations, since it refers to an 1824 edition as the last previous one. There was an 1824 edition of the Board's regulations as a whole, but the last edition of the regulations on administrative punishment was that of 1828.

9. *Ch'in-ting li-pu tse-li*, prefatory memorials: 1–2b.

had been started before 1830). Then in 1837 the Board argued in a memorial that the number of new cases necessitated a revision, and the result was the 1838 *hsiao-hsiu* (minor revision). This was followed by a full-scale edition in 1851. It is important to note that demands such as these for revisions almost certainly reflected actual administrative needs rather than some ulterior purpose. Revision to some extent was financed privately by the officials of the office involved and so was not a pretext for dipping into government funds. Admittedly, however, revision was often an occasion for eliciting administrative honors from the emperor for some of the editorial personnel, though not usually for the highest ones.[10] There also were instances where revisions were put out merely to accord with a prefixed schedule.[11]

The history of the Ch'ing penal code also reflects the conflict between the ideal of "He followed the ancient regulations" and that of "making adjustments according to the circumstances of the times."[12] Here the forces against flexibility and revision were particularly strong, because there was not only the temptation to regard the whole code—*lü* (statutes) and *li* (regulations)—as a *ch'eng-shu* but also the idea that the *lü* in particular, as the most basic penal laws, should not be changed.[13] This prominent belief in the immutability of the *lü* went back to the order of the founder of the Ming dynasty to his successors not to change the *lü* as he had fixed them. This belief in Ming times sometimes even was linked to opposition to any develop-

10. *Ibid.*, prefatory memorials: 1b–2 has a denunciation by the emperor of the use of compilations as a pretext to get administrative honors for clerks.

11. *Ch'in-ting hu-pu ts'ao-yün ch'üan-shu, tsou-che:* 1. A censor in 1812 said that the editions of this book then coming out once every ten years were merely copied from the previous editions, and he felt they were unreliable.

12. On the Ch'ing penal code, see Appendix III.

13. "The *lü* are completed laws which once fixed do not change," says a 1736 memorial beginning preparations for the third edition of the code and written nine years after the issuing of the second edition, which had a number of *lü* changes; see *Ta-Ch'ing lü-li t'ung-k'ao, tsou-shu*:3. Possibly this notion was emphasized after the second edition, yet it was also alive before the second edition. For instance, in 1689 the Board of Punishments stated: "The text of the *lü* are a completed book transmitted from the past; the *li* are fixed after deliberation according to the circumstances of the time"; see *Ta-Ch'ing lü-li t'ung-k'ao, tsou-shu*:12b.

ment of a supplementary body of more flexible *li*.[14] It continued to exist despite the fact that both the Ming and Ch'ing penal codes include a *lü* (statute) explicitly treating a certain judicial problem regarding newly promulgated *lü* (if in a particular case the crime occurred before but the trial after the promulgation of a new *lü*, should the old *lü* apply?)[15]

In the Ch'ing period the *lü* were altered. In particular, the second edition of the code, that of 1725, involved significant revision of the *lü*, reducing their number from 457 to 436.[16] Some of these *lü* changes had only minor technical significance, such as the elimination of a term denoting an abolished Ming office or procedure, but at least one change was of major significance, since it greatly reduced the authority of higher officials to punish lower officials without first memorializing the emperor.[17] Furthermore, the third edition of the code, that of 1740, added many annotations in small type to the *lü* text.[18]

It seems clear that because Ch'ing officials preferred to stress the continuity between the Ming and Ch'ing periods and the immutability of the *lü*, they glossed over in their minds what significant *lü* changes there were. For instance, the late Ch'ing legal expert, Hsüeh Yün-sheng, in discussing the above *lü* change of 1725 which greatly affected the procedure for the punishment of officials, fails to specify the change and to point out its significance. On the contrary, despite the fundamental revision of this *lü*, he merely states: "This *lü* follows the Ming *lü*; it was edited at the beginning of the [Ch'ing] dynasty and in 1725 and was revised in 1740."[19] Similarly, this major change is not mentioned by the *Ch'ing-shih* in its list of the Yung-cheng *lü* changes.[20]

Moreover the spirit of the Yung-cheng revision needs to be carefully evaluated. For instance, the Yung-cheng emperor re-

14. Ch'en Ku-yüan, *Chung-kuo fa-chih-shih* (A history of China's legal institutions; Shanghai, 1944), p. 136.

15. *Ming-lü*, 1:96b; *TCLL*, 5:51.

16. *TCLL*, *fan-li:* 1.

17. See IV, 4, c.

18. Many examples of this can be specified in *Hsüeh Yün-sheng, Tu-li ts'un-i* (Questions on reading the penal regulations; 1905) [hereafter *TLti*] where Hsüeh Yün-sheng gives the dates of various changes in the *lü*.

19. *TLti*, 1:48. *Ta-Ch'ing lü-li t'ung-k'ao* gives the full text of the older *lü*; see 4:56–57b.

20. *Ch'ing-shih*, III:1734.

tained the basic *lü* on *pa-i* (eight conditions for consideration) only reluctantly. In an edict of 1728 he said that the special judicial privileges which this *lü* accorded to the highest political elite had never been used in the Ch'ing dynasty, and that they conflicted with the goal of fair and equal treatment. Misconduct by this elite, he said, should not only be punished but also was particularly reprehensible, since they were supposed to be a model to the people and gentry. His preference was to do away with this *lü* and to handle any excusable offenses by this elite through special imperial acts as suited the occasion. He retained this *lü* because "If we wholly excise it, perhaps people would not understand that [it had been removed because] being out of accord with principle, it hurt the law." (The idea that *lü* are unchangeable laws was not even mentioned.) However, in retaining it, he also issued an edict so that the empire would understand the moral reservation he attached to it. Since this edict was prominently reprinted, it should perhaps be regarded as a well-known qualification of this *lü*.[21]

Nevertheless, we can agree that on the whole the flexibility of the penal code stemmed not from *lü* revisions but from the character of the *li*. (We do not consider here the changes made in the code during the last decade of the Ch'ing dynasty under Western influence.)[22]

The *li* added flexibility, first of all, because they were explicitly designed as supplementary articles adapting the more general *lü* to varying and more specific circumstances. Second, at least in the later Ch'ing period, there was an explicit principle whereby in finding the law, the *li* had primacy over the *lü* in case of conflict.[23] This principle in itself greatly mitigated the

21. *TCHTSL*, 725: see Yung-cheng 6 edict under *pa-i*. *Ta-Ch'ing lü-li t'ung-k'ao*, 4:6–7b. *TLti*, 1:37–38b.

22. Hsiao I-shan, *Ch'ing-tai t'ung-shih*, IV, 1444–1454.

23. *TCHT*, 54:1b–2 says: "Those who sentence ought to take the revised penal regulations (*li*) as the standard; they should not stick blindly to the text of the statutes (*lü*)." Moreover the regulations for the Boards of War and Civil Officials determining the hierarchy of priority in searching legal texts for the appropriate article of *ch'u-fen* law give the *li* a preferred position over the *lü*. See *TCHTSL*, 85: Ch'ien-lung 5; *TCHT*, 11:4a–b; *CFTL*, 1:3b; *TCHT*, 48:1b. The precedence of the *li* over the *lü* can also be illustrated in other ways. In *TLti*, 14:2b–3 Hsüeh Yün-sheng points out that a particular *li* conflicts with its *lü*, a fact obviously not jeopardizing the validity of the *li*.

effects of any rigidity in the *lü*. Finally, the *li* introduced flexibility as the principle of frequently publishing and editing them became better established.

It is mainly in the emergence of this latter principle regarding the *li* that one can see a significant conflict with the idea of the code as a *ch'eng-shu* (although this conflict can also be seen in the alterations of the *lü* text). This conflict became most explicit relative to the decision of 1689 to put out a second edition of the code, since this idea was at first rejected by the Board of Punishments, it seems clear, to a large extent on the explicit grounds that the code was a *ch'eng-shu*. The schedule of the code's revision as a whole also suggests that the idea of the code as a *ch'eng-shu* gave way only gradually.

The chronology of the code's revisions breaks down into four periods: 1644–1740, 1741–1767, 1768–1853, and 1854–1910. From 1644 to 1740, neither the principle of regularly publishing *ta-hsiu* (major revisions) (there were only three editions, 1646, 1727, and 1740) nor that of regularly printing *hsiao-hsiu* (minor revisions) (there was only one, that of 1679) was established. Significantly, during this first period when revision was relatively problematic, the *Lü-li-kuan* (Bureau for compiling the penal code), in charge of revision, was not under the Board of Punishments; it was an independent bureau in which a variety of important officials held positions. It was put under the Board of Punishments in about 1742, just as revision of the code became more frequent and routinized. During the second period, 1741–1767, the principle of regularly printing *hsiao-hsiu* existed (there were five editions, 1743, 1746, 1751, 1756, and 1761) but still not that of regularly issuing *ta-hsiu* (there was none). Beginning with the 1768 *ta-hsiu* and until the 1853 *ta-hsiu*, regular and frequent revision of both *ta-hsiu* and *hsiao-hsiu* was completely institutionalized. The five-ten pattern—*ta-hsiu* and *hsiao-hsiu* coming out alternately about every five years—was clearly in operation from 1768 to 1790 and was roughly followed until the 1853 edition, although there are some questions in this regard.[24] The political difficulties of the late Ch'ing period interrupted this schedule. There were still a total revision of the code put out in 1870 and an edition revised under Western influence and promulgated in 1910.

The major point here is that of the twenty-eight *ta-hsiu* and

24. See Appendix III.

hsiao-hsiu put out during the two and a half centuries of Ch'ing rule, twenty-three were issued during the middle century, 1743–1853. The principle that the penal code should be a *ch'eng-shu,* explicitly voiced around 1689, thus was ignored during much of the Ch'ing period as excisions and revisions of the *li* proceeded rather regularly. The will to carry out revision in a flexible way, resisting the ideal of the *ch'eng-shu,* seems to have been strongest during the period of greatest political stability. Since this spirit of flexibility involved the idea that the *li* not only supplemented but also overrode the *lü,* it was in strong contrast to that early Ch'ing viewpoint which was hostile even to the notion of a developing body of supplementary *li.* We may say that the combination of unchanging laws and flexible laws in one code neatly synthesized the Confucian and Legalist attitudes toward the changeability of the laws.

7. Conclusion

Basic changes in Ch'ing administration were impeded by a variety of factors, such as vested interests, "realistic" conservatism, an ideological emphasis on a fixed order, and the Confucian syndrome of belief in the fundamental role of moral solidarity and in the classical learning through which the principles of this solidarity could be derived and through which the ethical qualities of leadership needed to stimulate this solidarity could be developed in individual scholars. Without some major attack on these deeply rooted factors, far-reaching changes would have been difficult if not impossible.

Yet there also were norms favoring administrative flexibility, and these were not just limited to the Legalist emphasis on adjusting to the present and to a few loci classici in the classics indicating in a general way that change was metaphysically meaningful and in accord with the ways of the sages.

These norms, rather, were at least as deeply rooted in Confucian thought as the norms favoring fixity. They were based on a feeling that much of the world was bad and on a sense of uncertainty as to the nature of the various trends in the world and the best ways of effecting improvements. A paradoxical aspect of this outlook was that the sense of badness and uncertainty applied equally to the objects and the agents of reform, which indeed were partly identical. Doubt and criticism were leveled equally at the process of education in the basic moral-political ideals; at the products of this education, that is, the scholar-officials; at the government which they operated; at the emperor himself (though not directly); and at the society-at-large. It was a matter of pulling oneself up by one's bootstraps. The general nature of the desirable moral order was obvious, but the entire process of seeking to specify and effect it was full of doubt.

The heart of the political process was thus perceived as an intersection where good and bad mingled in a partly unclear fashion. Because good and bad were continually being mixed, and because what was good and what was bad were partly unclear, it was easy for Ch'ing officials to have ambivalent attitudes toward various policies and to switch between different policies. In particular, there were arguments both for and against fixity, and arguments both for and against change.

Many Confucian officials felt that they themselves were

riveted into this moral intersection, and they saw themselves as seeking to improve both themselves and the world around them. Trying to inject morality into a base world, Confucians simultaneously disdained and seriously dealt with law, administrative details, and economic and fiscal considerations. Deriving charisma from their knowledge of the Three Dynasties, they simultaneously were ashamed of and accepted as necessary their position as bureaucratic subordinates subject to disciplinary punishments (see IV, 2). Working in a realm between good and evil, they were conscious of the question of medium quality and often saw medium quality as a reasonable goal, as with Hsün-tzu's idea of the *pa* (hegemon) as a form of rule lying between the best and the worst; Han Fei's idea that most emperors were of "medium" quality; the common idea that most officials were neither *hsien* (superior) nor *pu-hsiao* (bad) but rather *chung-ts'ai* (persons of medium quality and talent); and the prominent tendency to classify policies as best, medium, and worst.

It was because they felt themselves to be operating at this moral intersection that so many Ch'ing officials were capable of complex organizational behavior. Because they had this profound feeling of badness within and without and this attitude of uncertainty as to the best policies and organizational forms, they could feel morally comfortable working within a complex organizational structure of which they partly disapproved. At least to prevent further deterioration, they felt they had to act strenuously. Because they were partly doubtful as to what should be preserved and what should be changed, they were ready to act flexibly. Because of this they also could oscillate between various policy alternatives such as those we have tried to describe above in terms of three polarities. Also because of this doubt, they could oscillate between a more static and a more flexible policy toward the revision of the laws.

Ch'ing Confucians indeed were weighed down by their consciousness of their history, but because their outlook was fundamentally critical, they transcended what Max Weber called "traditional" values.[1] We cannot simply say that Ch'ing officials felt themselves to be operating in a doubt-free "moral order" where harmony was basically realized through the *te* (virtue)

1. Max Weber, *The Theory of Social and Economic Organization* (Glencoe, Ill., 1947), pp. 115, 130, 328, 341.

of an emperor who reconciled the cosmic and social orders.[2] Such *te* was implicit or latent in the political order, but it was not easily available directly to solve the various concrete problems with which Ch'ing officials often had to grapple. Although it was pleasant for Ch'ing officials to write of their society purely in terms of "harmony," they actually felt themselves to be poised between harmony and chaos. Although they repeatedly referred to the spotless moral virtues of the emperor, they realized that each of them had to summon his own nervous and moral resources in order to make up for the shortage of *te* (virtue) in the world. In virtually all periods Confucians perceived the society around them as corrupted and in tension with ideals almost beyond the possibility of implementation. While this perception was a source of anguish to them, it impresses us as a "definition of the situation" facilitating work in a complex organization.[3]

2. Robert Redfield, *The Primitive World and its Transformations* (Ithaca, N.Y., Great Seal Books, 1953), pp. 61–63.

3. For W. I. Thomas' term "definition of the situation" and associated theories, see Talcott Parsons *et al.*, eds., *Theories of Society* (New York, The Free Press of Glencoe, Inc., 1961), II:685–744.

CHAPTER II The Communication of the Laws

1. Introduction

While laws or commands cannot be effectively implemented unless they are flexibly adjusted to meet changing circumstances, they also need to be efficiently communicated. In this chapter we will mainly look at two aspects of communication. First, there is the question of clarity of content. This includes the problem of the criteria of clarity consciously expressed and that of the clarity of the expressions used in the bureaucratic language. Second, there is the question of the physical transmission of the laws through compilation, publication, and distribution. We will also ask how much attention officials paid to the laws distributed to them.

Thus, overall, we look at problems of content, transmission of content, and reception of content. Throughout we will follow the premise that in all these matters there was enough uniformity in the bureaucracy for us to generalize after gathering a fair number of examples. Obviously one cannot engage in an endless pursuit of examples. The reader will have to judge whether the character and quantity of the examples justify the conclusions. In this respect the relative lack of originality and creativity in Ch'ing administrative practices is a boon to modern researchers. Certainly many of the remarks about criteria of communication found in prefatory memorials and "principles of compilation" sections are so typical that they have a routinized and merely ritualistic air about them.[1]

1. For instance, the prefatory memorials for the many editions of the penal code—found in the first *ts'e* of *TCLL*—mostly echo each other relative to the need to eliminate inconsistency or redundancy. These editorial ideals, as found in these memorials, are much the same as those found in the prefatory memorials of many or most books of laws. In this chapter we present a sampling of the typical and the more interesting formulations.

2. Criteria of Clarity

Our own common sense suggests that the following criteria of clarity are important: consistency; order (nonarbitrariness) in presentation (that is, efficiency of categorization); exhaustiveness, as in being up-to-date or in gathering into one place all relevant laws; avoidance of ambiguity; relevance; and avoidance of redundancy. Also worth considering is the problem of visual clarity in presentation, that is, clear paragraphing and headings.

Several of these standards are involved in the major problem of overlapping in presentation, a problem that bedevils anyone, whether a Ch'ing official or a modern historian, trying to explain a complicated pattern lacking any inherent order of logical, chronological, or causal priority, as is so often the case with social or governmental institutions. Overlapping may be a virtue if it leads to exhaustiveness of presentation. More often, however, the same subject will be treated in two different presentations neither of which is exhaustive. Overlapping may also involve inefficient categorization or even lead to inconsistencies. It is a major hurdle for understanding.

Yet all these problems of communication are not merely peculiar to Western habits of understanding. When information is voluminous, complex, and partly boring, efficient communication involves certain universal problems, even though the emphasis will vary culture by culture. Some of the above criteria were favorite targets of the Ch'ing compilers of law books, but there was a lack of sustained effort in the matter of efficient categorization and, especially, in meeting the problems of overlapping and exhaustiveness.

One favorite target was inconsistency (*ch'üan pu ho-fu, wei-ho,* etc.), as compilers sought to *i-i kuan-t'ung* (have ideas fall into a coherent pattern). Avoiding redundancy (*tz'u-i ch'ung-fu*) was also a common focus of attention, as was the idea of relevancy. Ch'ing bureaucratic documents often stick to one subject which is clear from the opening sentences. A law put out in 1645 on memorials forbade *to-k'ai t'iao-k'uan* (introduction of too many items) and, requiring that memorials be accompanied by summaries, forbade *ts'en-tz'u i-t'ung* (discrepancies) between the memorial and its summary.[1]

When editions of the penal code were put out, laws *wu-she*

1. *TCHTSL,* 13: Shun-chih 2.

(lacking connection) with the penal code were weeded out. By eliminating the latter, Ch'ing legal compilers sought to reduce *fan-so* (troublesome excessiveness of content). At least one article was removed from the penal code when it was noticed that it did not belong there because it lacked any specification of a sentence.[2] Close to this was the emphasis on *ming-hsi* (clarity) and the fairly common ideal of *chien-ming* (conciseness and clarity).[3] The 1851 edition of the *Regulations of the Board of Revenue* says: "What is valued in the writing of an article is *wen-chien i-kai* (succinctness and comprehensiveness). Articles in previous editions of the Board of Revenue regulations sometimes have as many as several tens of characters each. When such a text is so involved and redundant, it is hard to *pao-chü* (grasp its meaning)."

With regard to visual clarity, this same book says: "Regulations in previous editions completely lacked section headings. The titles of regulations were scattered through the volumes, and it was easy to overlook something when looking up a matter. Now to facilitate perusal we have added a heading for each section."[4] The smudging of characters in old printing blocks was another problem of visual clarity, leading to the replacement of some of the printing blocks for the sixth edition

2. See III, 4, for a discussion of the criteria by which materials were selected for inclusion in the penal code. In *TCHTSL*, *chüan* 763, there is a penal *t'iao-li* introduced in 1725 which only specified procedures, rates, and quotas handled by the Kansu governor relative to the tea monopoly. In 1740 this was taken out and put into the *Regulations of the Board of Revenue* on the explicit grounds that it specified no sentence.

3. Conciseness can be connected to the problems of excessive red tape or excessively complicated bureaucratic procedures. In his 1831 Liang-huai salt reform, for instance, T'ao Chu sought to "eliminate excessive documents," his target being (according to his count) the eleven permits or receipts which Huai-nan merchants needed to ship salt and the twelve salt offices involved; see *TYT*, 30:52a–b. The cumbrousness and complexity of this procedure had been criticized some years before in Li Ch'eng, *Huai-ts'o pei-yao* (Essentials of Liang-huai salt affairs; foreword written in 1823), 3:4a–b. Simplicity was desired here not so much to avoid confusion per se as to reduce squeeze.

4. *HPTL*, *fan-li*: 1b–2. See also *Ch'in-ting hu-pu ts'ao-yün ch'üan-shu* (1845), *tsou-che*: 2, for the ideal of "succinctness of text and a comprehensive presentation of the matter."

of the code, that of 1790.[5] One visual failure, however, was the habit of heading each article of law in a list only by *i* (one) instead of numbering the list. Such numbering, facilitating reference, was partly adopted in Ch'ing bureaucratic papers only in the later nineteenth century, obviously following Western examples (although there were Chinese precedents).[6]

Exhaustiveness in the sense of being up-to-date was much emphasized. Compilers sometimes took pains to insert the most recent executive commands into a book until the last moment of publication, and they often were meticulous in giving the cutoff date for their material, so that the reader would know that all executive decisions or laws effected after a certain month or year were outside the compilation.[7] Completeness was also emphasized in the sense that pains were taken to avoid omissions of material belonging to the same formally defined category (*pu-chih t'o-lou*).

There was far less effort to meet the problem of exhaustiveness in the sense of pulling together all material with a practical relation to a particular administrative activity, whether or not this material was part of the same formally defined category. This also involved the problem of overlapping content in different compilations and that of efficiency in categorization.

5. *TCLL, tsou-shu:* 40b–41b. The fourth (1768) and fifth (1779) editions of the code (*ta-hsiu*) had been printed with blocks prepared in 1741, changes being made by adding to or altering the original blocks. Thus many characters in the old blocks came to be unclear, and, for the 1790 edition, many new blocks were prepared.

6. *Ta-Ch'ing lü-li t'ung-k'ao* in some instances numbers the *li* under each *lü*. See, e.g., 4:5–30b.

7. For instance, in *LHYFC, fan-li:* 5, the editors of this book state that the work on this revised edition began on December 28, 1802, and ended in July of 1805 (actually, the sixth moon), final editing taking several more months, and the last bureaucratic documents used being those available in August 1805 (actually, the intercalary sixth moon). A similar concern was that with giving cutoff dates in making reports on a temporal flow of some item of fiscal importance. For instance, T'ao Chu sent off a memorial on October 1, 1831, saying that in August (actually, the seventh moon) salt sales at Hankow of salt shipped in by the Yangchow merchants ranged from 40,000 to 120,000 packets a day except for August 20, when there was bad weather, and that "from February 23 [1831] until September 5 [1831], total sales [at Hankow] were more than 16,567,000 packets, equaling a little more than 355,900 *yin*." See *TYT*, 35:42. See also *TYT*, 49:41b. *TCHT, fan-li:* 1b, is a good example of concern with cutoff dates in compilations.

Generally speaking, whether presenting a definition, list, or discussion, Ch'ing writers often fell into the trap of open-endedness, that is, partial coverage without any explicit reference to relevant but omitted items. Yet paradoxically, this weakness existed side by side with an emphasis on understanding large and complex administrative situations as a whole and in detail; on rationalistically weighing the multiple practical effects of particular policies; and on locating the strategic variable.[8] One feels that policy discussions benefited more than compilations of law from this stress on coherence and thoroughness. For one thing, comprehensive understanding of some institutions was more difficult than much policy analysis. Japanese researchers in the early twentieth century noted that Ch'ing officials typically understood only that limited part of the regulations on promotion and appointment with which they were personally familiar.[9] The problem of pulling together in one discussion the specialized knowledge of a number of people was a continuing challenge.

The problems of overlapping were, however, faced in a small way. For instance, the above edition of *Regulations of the Board of Revenue* notes that *i tzu ch'ien-hun* (confusion is easily aroused) when one matter is interpreted differently under two different headings, and that it is *nan i chien-yüeh* (hard to look up) a matter when it is scattered under several different headings.[10]

Hsüeh Yün-sheng (d. 1901), who was hailed by members of the Board of Punishments as the day's leading specialist on penal law, and who was an official in this board for about twenty years,[11] wrote *Tu-li ts'un-i* (Questions on reading the

8. *TYT*, 50:1–7 is a good example of a thorough review of the multiple effects of a proposed policy, since T'ao Chu was very anxious to refute a proposal of the grain tribute governor-general, who wanted to allow empty grain tribute boats to carry Ch'ang-lu salt into the Yangtze valley.

9. *Shinkoku gyōseihō* (Administrative laws of the Ch'ing state; Kobe and Tokyo, 1905–1911), I:350. Translated in *Ch'ing-kuo hsing-cheng fa* (Administrative laws of the Ch'ing state; Shanghai, 1906), 3:2:2:43.

10. *HPTL, fan-li*: 1b–2.

11. His biography is, e.g., in *Ch'ing-shih lieh-chuan* (Biographies of persons from the Ch'ing period; Taipei, 1962), 61:18–21b; see also *TLti, tsou-shu*: 1a–b. A *chin-shih* of 1856, he was a departmental official (*ssu-kuan*) at the Board of Punishments from 1869 to 1872,

penal regulations), in which he paid considerable attention not only to overlapping within the penal code but also between the penal code and other compilations. In discussing a penal regulation on the illegal sale of tea to foreigners, for instance, he notes not only that this regulation should be incorporated with another penal regulation but also that two regulations in the *Regulations of the Board of Revenue* should be put in with it.[12] He pointed to the problem of overlapping in his "Remarks on Principles of Compilation":

> The regulations of all boards are books of laws. Some stand in a relation of mutual clarification with the penal regulations, while others obviously differ from the latter. I have now included several tens of them, in some cases to make up deficiencies in the penal regulations, in some cases to rectify mistakes in the latter. By checking all these books, the desirable and undesirable aspects of a matter may be clarified.[13]

As can be seen from a study of salt monopoly law, however, Hsüeh Yün-sheng did not go very far in explicating the interrelations between the articles of law dealing with this institution.

Efforts in categorization were similarly halfhearted. The notion of categories and subcategories was common at least in terms of book subdivisions, as in section headings such as *kang*

---

rising very quickly to the top departmental rank (*lang-chung*). Leaving when his term was up, he began a varied official career in the provinces in 1873, and in 1879 returned to the Board as vice-president. He stayed with the Board until 1897, becoming a president in the winter of 1893–94. His leaving took the form of an impeachment demoting him to a post in the Imperial Clan Court, from which he retired in 1898. In the winter of 1900–01 he again was made president of the Board of Punishments, dying in office in 1901. Hsüeh was also a trainee (*o-wai ssu-yüan*) at the Board from 1856 to 1869. On *o-wai ssu-yüan,* see II, 4. While on the Board, Hsüeh also was involved in a sequence of nonlegal matters, as in the case of a long memorial on military organization and finance presented in 1885. Again, this involvement of officials in important affairs or missions outside the prescribed responsibilities of their posts was a common feature of Ch'ing bureaucratic organization.

12. *TLti,* 15:29a–b. In *TLti,* 15:14b–15b, Hsüeh similarly suggests putting together two *li* dealing with the same problem.

13. *TLti, li-yen.*

and *mu,* or *chüan, mu,* and *t'iao.* Also fairly common was the practice of establishing the distinguishing feature of a category. Some prefatory memorials to the penal code put forward the idea of "relevant to sentencing" as a criterion of content, and this in fact is rather adequate. The "principles of compilation" in the first two editions of *Ta-Ch'ing hui-tien* helpfully point out that in these books, "categories are distinguished according to the governmental matters involved, and within each category items are entered year by year." Yet this formula fails to note that the primary criterion of categorization in these books is not governmental matters (for example, salt laws) but office (for example, Board of Revenue). (The two criteria of categorization given are those on the second and, usually, the fourth levels of subdivision.)[14]

Similarly, as we shall see, Ch'ing precedents and laws in practice did fall into four formal categories, but these were never put together in a single list, and they involved serious ambiguities. The situation in the substantive categorization of the law was still worse, since the reader was faced to a large extent with innumerable chapter headings and book titles.

Yet one redeeming feature, and an important one, was a fairly common effort to put some sort of commonsense order or logic into such lists of administrative topics. This feature was part of a broader tendency in Ch'ing bureaucratic communication, namely to try to achieve neatness of presentation. The kind of helter-skelter discussion sometimes found in historical writing can also be found in memorials, but the following example is typical, illustrating skill in explaining a problem with a complex mixture of spatial, temporal, and institutional elements.

In 1833 the Nanking governor-general had to present the emperor with an overview of Kiangsu maritime defense arrangements. He divided this overview into three parts: the first part describes the geographical extent of Kiangsu's maritime responsibilities and concludes with "These are the circumstances in general regarding the maritime boundaries in four directions"; the second part describes the military units involved, their facilities, and the geographical division of responsibility between them, concluding with "These are the circumstances in general regarding the maritime areas, forts, lookouts (?), and war boats of the battalions under the said two brigades"; and

14. III, 4.

the third part describes the schedules and methods of the naval patrols, concluding with "These are the circumstances in general of the said two brigades' going to sea and patrolling." Only after this overview of the naval apparatus as it has already been set up does the governor-general go into the question of further measures.[15]

Many memorials follow the sequence: description of a current institution; its problems; how these conflict with the imperial will; a proposed solution.

The problem of a sense-making arrangement of topics was sometimes explicitly discussed. One example is the explanation given by the editors of the 1726 edition of the *Salt Laws Gazetteer of the Ch'ang-lu Zone* for this book's sequence of chapters. The first two chapters were not tightly connected: that on imperial commands came first out of respect for the emperor, and the second chapter, that on "successive changes," came second just because the question of historical development was regarded as important. The order of the next eight chapters, however, did represent a coherently unfolding conceptualization of an awkwardly multifaceted complex of administrative activity. This administrative whole is essentially broken down into the questions of its territorial basis; its structure, consisting of its offices and private personnel like merchants; the laws and procedures to be carried out by this structure; and the successes and failures of the particular officials in this structure. After these eight chapters, the five final chapters deal with affective, cultural topics not immediately relevant to administration, such as "Literature." Admittedly, my explanation may be a little more articulate than that of the editors, but only a little. For instance, the editors explain that "Once offices are established and official duties differentiated, the vile and the pure among official talents can be distinguished; by looking at the remonstrances and proposals of officials, one can decide who is superior and who is corrupt among those deliberating on state affairs. One may put next the chapters on 'biographies of officials' and 'memorials' in order to study these questions."[16]

15. *TYT*, 52:13–18b.

16. *Hsin-hsiu Ch'ang-lu yen-fa-chih, li-yen*:1–2. A similar explanation of the sequence of chapters is given in *Liang-huai yen-fa-chih* (1693, reprinted at Taipei in 1966), I:35–37. The form of such explanations is reminiscent of the way scholars sometimes sought to explain how all the various parts of a properly ordered society

Even where such explicit discussion of sequence of presentation is missing, one often finds some implicit sense of ordered presentation. For instance, we can see a meaningful sequence in the list of chapters under "Board of Revenue" in the 1899 *Ta-Ch'ing hui-tien shih-li* (Precedents and regulations supplementary to the collected statutes of the great Ch'ing dynasty). A primary focus on the empire's main sources of wealth (the land and population) and its system for managing its property (treasuries, granaries) is followed by sections on inflow (taxes) and outflow (salaries, tax remissions). Similarly in the same book's section on the Board of Civil Officials, there is a natural order in the topics. The section begins with the raison d'être of the Board, the offices to be filled throughout the civil bureaucracy and the system of official grades; then come sections on how the offices are filled (the methods of appointment, promotion, and transfer); then come sections on the responsibilities and sanctions faced by those who fill the offices (the *ch'u-fen-li*); and miscellaneous matters are put at the rear.

Such examples suggest that the systematic approach to administration for which the Yung-cheng emperor is famous was not entirely peculiar to him. Although in a partly different vein, the following quotation from a 1729 edict of his is relevant:

> With regard to the *tao* (true way) of managing administrative affairs: the energy and intelligence of men in all cases depends on their concentrating their efforts on a single matter. If they do so, then the results, clear and proper in all details, will achieve a reasonable order. However if their efforts are confused and unconcentrated, then the results

---

fitted in with each other according to some sort of sense-making order: after men had learned feed, clothe, and house themselves, they had to learn how to establish proper relations in the family, and after this a political hierarchy was set up, which then had to be enforced through laws and *li* (rules of moral propriety), and so on. A conceptual attempt is made to impose on the complexity of society an order which is not only normative but also cognitively coherent. Possibly this philosophic interest in devising neat expositions of the genesis and structure of society as a harmonious whole unconsciously was a model for attempts to communicate the administrative order in a coherent fashion. An interesting example of this philosophic interest is Li Kou's first essay on *li* (rules of moral propriety), in *Li Kan-chiang hsien-sheng ch'üan-chi* (The complete writings of Li Kou; 1893), 1:1b–4.

will be a welter of unresolved details with many unreasonable aspects. As We have managed the affairs of the government over the past several years, We have always gathered together Our energy and spirit and concentrated Our efforts. If We peruse a memorial, then We peruse only that memorial and don't think of other matters. If We deal with a problem, then We deal only with that problem and don't shift our attention to other problems. Therefore Our intention and determination are completely clear, and the coherence of Our actions is manifest. When one administrative problem is disposed of, then in a natural way one turns to the next and manages it.[17]

17. *Pa-ch'ao sheng-hsün* (The instructions of the ruling sage over eight reigns; latest preface is that of 1856), Yung-cheng, 7:5.

3. Clarity of Language

Ch'ing bureaucratic communication was also facilitated by the nature of the bureaucratic language. The language of official salt documents or of T'ao Chu's memorials, for instance, is generally of a pedestrian, practical, straightforward nature, allowing little room for misunderstanding. Particularly in the case of regulations (rather than memorials), the writing is simple and monotonously conventional. This straightforward style possibly was not so typical in all periods. Ray Huang states: "In the numerous official documents written by Ming bureaucrats we rarely find a writer tackling his problem with businesslike directness. Instead, we find that official memoranda, even on fiscal matters, are developed into lengthy essays in which the key issues are subordinated to ethical considerations."[1]

Such a generalization could never be made with regard to Ch'ing administrative documents, especially fiscal ones, which generally include few moralisms and are practical and to the point. If then there was a change from Ming to Ch'ing times in the style of bureaucratic communication, it perhaps was due to the practicality of the early Ch'ing rulers and to their impatience with classical erudition used for its own sake. Their attitude could well have led officials to change their writing style. As early as 1645 it was imperially ordered that memorials (*t'i-pen* and *tsou-pen*) should not exceed three hundred characters except in the case of those dealing with fiscal and criminal matters; yet even the latter were to avoid "redundancy and needless length."[2] This focus on providing information efficiently was still more important in the case of the secret and

1. Hucker, *Chinese Government in Ming Times*, p. 74. I also was struck by the great length and the large amount of rhetoric and redundancy in the ten-point salt reform memorial prepared by Yüan Shih-chen in the *Hu-pu* in 1616. It totals about 161 Western-style pages, in contrast to the 30 Western-style pages of the 1831 salt reform memorial presented by T'ao Chu and others. The latter document was an attempt to communicate a plan tersely enough so that the emperor and others could read it conveniently, while Yüan Shih-chen's memorial was a piece designed to persuade and make a rhetorical impression. Yet businesslike Ming memorials can also be found. For Yüan's and T'ao's memorials, see, respectively, *Huang-Ming ching-shih wen-pien*, XXIX:185–346, and *TYT*, 30:45–60.

2. *TCHTSL*, 13: Shun-chih 2.

semisecret palace memorials. In the winter of 1722–23, the Yung-cheng emperor instructed certain officials writing palace memorials: "just make your point. Skill or awkwardness in composition and handwriting are not the main thing."[3]

Yet however straightforward, Ch'ing bureaucratic writing was not so precisely standardized as it could have been. Whether the margin of free expression was broader than with other bureaucracies is hard to say. Perhaps it was, because Ch'ing bureaucrats, sharing so much information, could indulge in a certain freedom of expression without danger of misunderstanding. It seems to me almost beyond argument that when Ch'ing bureaucrats expressed themselves loosely, they usually did so deliberately, not out of confusion, and that they could be precise in the appropriate situations.

A good example in the salt monopoly is the frequently vague references to the price of salt in Hankow, a crucial issue because of the important policy of controlling it. Because this price was often referred to in a general way, the reader might wonder which transaction the price referred to. When the head of the Liang-huai salt monopoly zone chose to, however, he spoke of the *mei-pao ti-an shou-chia* (the price per packet received when the salt is sold upon arrival at the port of [Hankow]).[4] This unambiguously denoted the wholesale price received by the merchants shipping salt into Hankow. One may add that in this case the price, the official weight of the packet, the particular weight unit actually used, and the quality and weight units of the silver in which the price was quoted probably all were clear to the government. Because the Hankow wholesale price was highly visible and subject to competitive reporting, that of the salt and the provincial officials, lying in memorials about it was not practical. The weight of the packet was officially fixed at eight catties and four ounces, including the wrapping material. The packet was packed and inspected at a single station (I-cheng) under official supervision involving the use of standardized measures. It is likely that a determined

3. *Ta-Ch'ing li-ch'ao shih-lu* (The veritable records of the successive reigns of the great Ch'ing dynasty; Tokyo, 1937–38), Yung-cheng, 1:30b–31. Cited in Fu Tsung-mao, *chün-chi-ch'u*, p. 109. This question should be connected to that of the lack of classical learning or of interest in classical learning on the part of at least some Manchus in the government. See I, 1, note 6.

4. *TYT*, 52:31a–b.

official like T'ao Chu could enforce adherence to these measures. As given in memorials, the Hankow price was a translation from local silver values into *k'u-p'ing wen-yin*, that is, silver regarded as pure by local standards and weighed according to the local version of the standard *liang* (ounce) of the Board of Revenue.[5]

It is true that officials were sometimes criticized for over-abbreviating references, for taking too much knowledge for granted. Yet when a matter was something "known to everyone" (for example, the costs of the Yangchow transport merchants),[6] loose references to it were clear. Moreover, the fact that many activities were visible to numerous inquisitive spectators was a check against the temptation to lie in memorials, and one can find some indigenous recognition of this check.[7] Such spectators were often motivated to speak up because they often had competitive interests, as in the case of offices with competitive official responsibilities, official cliques, farmers with little sympathy for rich merchants, natives eager to spy on outsider communities, and so on. In other words, social conflict tended to increase the truthfulness of memorials.

The question of "numeracy" is also relevant. Some modern scholars feel that Ch'ing bureaucrats habitually lacked interest in exactitude when discussing quantities. It is plain, however,

5. Pao Shih-ch'en, *An-wu ssu-chung* (1846), 5:18a–b; 5:21b. *LHYFC*, 23:18b; 11:19.

6. In 1788 the problem was raised that, if the wholesale price of salt at Hankow and Nanchang was fixed not by fairly rigid laws but according to current conditions, how could the people in those provinces be notified in advance what the proper price was supposed to be? The Liang-huai salt commissioner's answer was that the costs of the merchants and their margin of profit could be calculated and the resulting proper price communicated once every three months to the Hu-kuang and Kiangsi authorities. These calculations were possible because, according to the salt commissioner, the fluctuations in the costs of the transport merchants were "known to everyone." "Since it is difficult for the [production] yard officials and the transport merchants to report falsely [these costs], the local officials indeed can easily examine the matter." *LHYFC*, 24:24a–b. For another example of visibility see *TWI*, 18:47–48. Here T'ao Chu argues that it would be impossible to store smuggled salt in the houses of merchant associations at Shanghai, because no one violating the law would dare to do so in such a crowded area, "a place where things are known and heard by everyone."

7. *TWI*, 16:7b. T'ao here argues that he would be a fool to lie in a memorial about a financial item which was common knowledge.

that whether or not the norm of exactitude was observed usually depended on context: in broad policy discussions it often was not; in formal financial accounts it regularly was. This was the distinction between *tsung-shu* (totals given in round figures) and *hsi-shu* (breakdowns given in detailed figures). As the Nanking governor-general said in 1834, defending his rough and incomplete presentation of fiscal data in a particular instance, "The proper style of presentation (*t'i-ts'ai*) of memorials and of records indeed involves a distinction between presentation in outline and in detail."[8] This distinction involved the prevailing ethic, according to which the distasteful aspect of economic affairs was by no means large fiscal problems but rather small, trifling figures, concern with which was undignified (*Chu-tzu chi-li i yü cheng-t'i fei i* [calculating profits down to trifling sums is indeed unsuitable relative to the proper order of administration]).[9] Because of the Confucian influence, it was morally precarious for the state to be too concerned with fiscal matters. Although the image of the state's *li-ts'ai* (administering fiscal affairs) was acceptable, this image tended to blur into the deplorable one of *chü-lien* (immorally heavy taxation). Perhaps concern with fractions tended to connote *chü-lien*, although we could also interpret it as expressing the major Confucian value of frugality (*chieh-yung*). At any rate, fractions often were relegated to *ch'ing-tan* (clear lists) accompanying memorials, but they could be put in memorials.

Some of this is illustrated by the state expenditure made in 1830 to buy and ship Huai-pei salt. In January 1831, referring to it in a discussion of policy, the Nanking governor-general roughly stated it to have been "140,000 taels."[10] In a "clear list" some months later, however, he formally gave it as "148,657.487 taels."[11] To give another example, a Liang-huai debt owed in the 1830's to the Office of the Imperial Household (*Nei-wu-fu*) was listed as "964,007.82 taels" in a detailed explanation of this debt made in a memorial by the head of Liang-

8. *TWI*, 16:7b–8b.

9. *TYT*, 49:37b. Admittedly what T'ao Chu had in mind here was the calculation of profits involved if officials themselves would carry out the management of salt shipments and sales. But the point can be taken more broadly.

10. *TYT*, 30:58b.

11. *TYT*, 32:42.

huai,[12] while the emperor in an edict disposing of the problem simply spoke of "more than 964,000 taels."[13]

These examples are representative. In virtually all fiscal "clear lists" that I have seen, the figures are given down to several decimal points. This form of detailed presentation was preferred by the government for the explicit reason that it forced officials to handle figures more precisely.[14] It is another question how efficiently fiscal statistics were kept. There is no doubt that there was a range of bureaucratic behavior here which was partly a function of the quality and intentions of the leadership, and that, at least in those fiscal affairs which were the active concern of the Board of Revenue, maintaining accurate records was recognized to be an important administrative virtue. Furthermore, when such affairs were highly "visible," corruption was difficult and often not worthwhile. Even in the years of mismanagement and fiscal juggling before its 1831 reform, the Liang-huai zone of the salt monopoly kept records on the amount of salt officially sold and the amount of taxes formally collected which were regarded as reliable. When controversy arose in 1835 as to whether the 1831 reform had been a success, the head of Liang-huai, although charging his predecessors with bad fiscal practices, explicitly recognized that their records of sales and taxes were accurate and used them to refute his critics.[15]

While the prevailing ethic encouraged the use of round figures in memorials, looseness or freedom of expression in the bureaucratic language was also promoted by the fact that legal requirements and strong conventions specifically dictated phraseology only to a limited extent. Such dictates, many of which were backed by the threat of administrative punishments such as salary fines, can perhaps be put into three classes.

First, there were some prohibitions, of which the most im-

12. *TYT*, 33:25a–b.

13. *TYT*, 38:29b. Also see *TYT*, 32:39b and 31:36b. Certain financial obligations are listed as "a bit more than 4,990,734 taels" in the latter place, "4,990,734.374 taels" in the former.

14. *LHYFC*, 24:30b–31 is a case where the Board of Revenue asked the head of the Liang-huai zone of the salt monopoly to give the Hankow and Nanchang wholesale salt prices down to all decimals in his reports on salt prices made four times a year. Here the fractions had substantive importance.

15. *TWI*, 16:3b.

portant was that against writing the current emperor's personal name or those of the dynasty's deceased emperors (although using different characters with the same pronunciation was not supposed to be punished).[16]

Second, there were certain requirements as to proper form. For instance, characters referring to the state, the emperor, or some aspect of the dynasty had to be elevated a set number of spaces above the text proper;[17] there were certain set phrases, notably those opening and closing a memorial, such as the opening "*tsou wei* [or *t'i wei*] . . . *shih* (I memorialize with regard to . . . [the so-and-so] matters)"; requirements were made regarding certain references, as when, in 1724, the emperor ordered that officials stop referring loosely to a recent regulation as "a new regulation" and rather give its year of promulgation;[18] there was sensitivity about improper grammar or style;[19] overabbreviation of the names of offices, places, or persons, writing characters with the wrong strokes, and adding in words between the regular columns of characters were sometimes punished.[20]

Third, careless mistakes in meaning were taken seriously.

16. *TLti,* 8:9; *TCLL,* 7:8a–b; P.-L.-F. Philastre, *Le Code Annamite* (Taipei, 1957), I:329. (In all these citations from the penal code, our discussion is based only on the Chinese texts, and Philastre is cited only for reference purposes.) I do not include here punishments for the use of words held to be treasonous or insulting to the dynasty. Such punishments might well be criminal. For instance, around 1712, the K'ang-hsi emperor ordered the execution of a historian and some of his friends for using nonofficial reign titles in writing about the time when certain Ming princes were opposing the Manchus; L. C. Goodrich, *The Literary Inquisition of Ch'ien-lung* (Baltimore, Md., 1935), p. 20. However on the basis of both the latter book and Wu Che-fu, *Ch'ing-tai chin-hui shu-mu yen-chiu* (A study of the movement to ban and burn books during the Ch'ing dynasty; Taipei, 1969), one may conclude that none of the documents in any way condemned during the course of the Ch'ing literary inquisition was a Ch'ing memorial (some Ming memorials were included).

17. *TCHT,* 69:13, specifies with regard to a number of terms how many spaces were required. Some words not directly pertaining to the dynasty, such as "Heaven," also were elevated.

18. *CFTL,* 9:10.

19. *CFTL,* 33:1a–b. This regulation seems relevant to memorials but actually applies explicitly only to the official compilations of books of cases or laws. It punishes "mistakes in *wen-li* (principles of composition)."

20. *CFTL,* 9:1a–b.

For instance, to write in a memorial "10 bushels" when one should have written "1,000 bushels" was punished by a fine of one year's regular salary (*feng*), if the mistake had "harmed affairs."[21]

While legal and conventional prescriptions were few in number, freedom of expression in bureaucratic writing was also promoted by the major fact that many parts of the bureaucratic structure lacked any single technical term and so could be denoted with a certain freedom of expression. It may be suspected that within the concept of "technical term" there are the seeds of a lively controversy, but possibly when we speak of a "technical term," we mean not only that the term denotes a technically specific phenomenon but also that the term has a certain air of prescription and necessary propriety resulting either from law or convention. "President Nixon's administration" is not a technical term, although it denotes a technically specific phenomenon. A term loses its air of prescription or technicality, we may say, when it is "made up" on the spot by a writer or when it exists as one in a series of alternate and equally proper expressions. In Ch'ing bureaucratic communication, the denoting of a technically specific aspect of the bureaucracy often was only in terms of such a series of alternate words of roughly equal propriety, sometimes even involving a certain amount of "made-up-mess." This manner of denotation may well have been due to the lack of a legal tradition emphasizing scrupulous attention to wording. The basic point, perhaps, is the obvious one that the manner of denoting bureaucratically technical phenomena was often affected by that flexibility of expression so common in the classical Chinese language.

Obviously a range of words seeming to denote the same phenomenon or similar phenomena often did involve technical distinctions. The words denoting exit from office are a good example. Voluntary retirement could be referred to either as *kao-t'ui* (to announce retirement from office), *hsiu-chih* (to retire from office), or *k'ai-ch'üeh* (to vacate a post). (Voluntary retirement, making way for candidates who had long waited for a post, was often welcomed, but there was no absolute right to retire; officials' requests for retirement were sometimes denied by the emperor.)[22] *Kao-chia* (to announce a leave of absence)

21. *TLti,* 8:9; *TCLL,* 7:8a–b; Philastre, I:329.

22. For an example, see Fu Tsung-mao, *chün-chi-ch'u,* p. 222.

referred to temporary retirement such as *ping-chia* (sick leave), which officials suddenly required sometimes when faced with some impossible deadline. *Hsiu-chih* (to be retired from office) also could denote forced retirement, as did *le-ling hsiu-chih* (to be forcibly retired from office); the latter was carried out, say, for a senile official who refused to *kao-t'ui*. *K'ai-ch'üeh* (to vacate a post) could also denote a process of removal carried out for some failing but lacking the full character of punishment. *Ch'e-jen* (to remove from office) was similar. The distinction between these two is hard to find. *Ch'e-jen* seems to have been the standard term for that sort of removal carried out at the discretion of a superior official such as a governor-general (see IV, 3, c). (Removal from office usually required imperial approval.) *Ko-chih* (dismissal from office) was a specific kind of punishment within the standard scale of administrative punishments. *Li-jen* (to leave office) was usually used as a descriptive phrase to make clear whether a sentence such as demotion with transfer involved actually leaving office (*li-jen*) or retention of official duties (*liu-jen*) on a probationary basis.

But there are no such technical distinctions made in the wide range of terms for the records kept by a government office. Neither, among all these terms, was there one which was the most standard, although these records were an entirely formalized bureaucratic unit, their maintenance subject to regulations.[23] There were at least nine often interchangeable terms: *an-tu, wen-chüan, tang-an, tang-ts'e, wen-ts'e, chüan-tu, ts'e, chüan-an*, and *an-chüan*.[24] The only technical distinction which

23. See, e.g., *CFTL*, 8:1a–b. Particularly important were storing the records with care, checking them for completeness when the office came under a new official, and avoiding illicit changes in them by clerks.

24. In examples such as these, there is little point in listing all the passages in which such terms can be found. Having seen these terms repeatedly in various contexts, I argue that the differences between them do not correspond to technical differences in the unit of bureaucratic significance denoted. The differences in the words, however, sometimes—by no means always—involved differences in subtle connotations without bureaucratically technical significance or with some linguistic significance. For instance, some words were perhaps better suited to specific rather than general references. Whether such words differed in being fashionable at different times is a problem not fully met here. However, in a situation where persons

could be made here is that all these terms are different from *wen-shu*, a generic word for orders, reports, or letters sent from one office to another. After it was filed, a *wen-shu* became part of the *tang-an*.

Indeed it seems clear that often when the language contained two or more well-established single-character terms for the phenomenon, the Ch'ing bureaucratic style of writing, often requiring a two-character term, could combine with some freedom these various single characters, or, if only one single-character term were available, could combine that one character fairly freely with various more neutral characters. This is illustrated by the terminology regarding one of the major devices of financial administration providing flexibility. This was the diversion to expenditure *y* of funds originally assigned to expenditure *x*. This diversion was regarded as an advance which had to be paid back (without interest) so that eventually the full amount

---

often enjoyed using old words and where many old regulations and documents remained currently valid, it was hard for technical words to go entirely out of fashion. For instance, in the Ming penal code (*Ming-lü chi-chieh fu-li*, 1:11–12) and in the corresponding Ch'ing statute (*TCLL*, 4:16), one finds *ch'ü-ch'u* (to sentence according to the distinctions involved in the case). I have never seen this word in any other Ch'ing document, the standard phrase to cover the broad meaning here being *fen-pieh i-ch'u chih-tsui* (making the proper distinctions, advise on administrative punishment and/or apply a criminal sentence). Yet it is hard to say that any word in the Ch'ing penal code was out of fashion. Similarly (see text below), *ch'e-chih* (to pull out), a term denoting a phase of salt monopoly inspection, did not go out of fashion although the editors of the 1806 salt gazetteer replaced it with *ch'e-yen* (to pull out and inspect) in the case of a title heading, and I-chen did not go directly out of fashion although the Kiangsu district in question was officially renamed I-cheng in the early eighteenth century. On the other hand, some words did go out of fashion with the arrival of a new dynasty. For instance, in Ming times *chi-lu* (to record) was used to refer to a process of recording offenses, a usage replaced in the Ch'ing period by that of *chi-lu* as "commendation." See II, 3, note 64. *Chieh-hsien-jen pieh-hsü* (to be separated from one's current post and appointed to another according to the proper order of appointment), a form of punishment, was used in the Ming code where the Ch'ing code uses *tiao-yung* (to transfer); similarly, the former uses *pa-chih* (to dismiss from office) where the latter uses *ko-chih* (to dismiss from office). See *Ming-lü chi-chieh*, 1:20b, and *TCLL*, 4:18–19. For Ming examples of the loose use of interchangeable technical terms, see Metzger, "Organizational Capabilities," p. 22.

originally due for expenditure x would be met. This diversion of funds was conceptualized, so to speak, both from the front and the back: the term *tien* (to advance) denoted the moving to y of funds originally assigned to x; *chan* (to seize) denoted the taking of these funds away from expenditure x to meet expenditure y (repayment back to x was *kuei-pu*).[25]

While *tien-chan* denoted this diversion as conceptualized from both front and back, *tien* and *chan* could each be combined with a more neutral character to form the often needed two-character term. In *chieh-tien, tien-yung, tien-fa, chan-yung,* and *chan-ai,* the other character does not add any technical meaning. The other character or characters, however, could also be chosen to add a distinctive though secondary meaning, as in *shih-tien* (truly and actually to advance) and *no-i tien-yung* or *no-tien* (to advance under illegal or difficult conditions). *Chan-chuan no-tien* really had the latter meaning, although strictly speaking it added the idea of the same item's being diverted two or more times. The second character could also be chosen to add a distinctive technical meaning as in *tien-chih* (to advance for the purpose of expenditures by the office in question) and *tien-chieh* (to advance for the purpose of delivering the advance to another office).[26]

25. An example of the *tien* method is as follows. Between October 28, 1829, and March 10, 1830, the Liang-huai office used salt tax revenue received by it to "advance" items totaling 1,239,-453.076 taels (*TYT*, 32:40a–b). These advances are itemized in a *ch'ing-tan* (clear list) reproduced in *TYT*, 32:42–43b. The first part of this list gives the expenditures for which the advances were made; the second part, the expenditures originally intended and temporarily postponed. For instance, 161,120 taels were "seized" (*chan*) which were originally due to be paid from Liang-huai revenue to the Office of the Imperial Household and other capital and provincial offices as interest on capital which these various offices had deposited at Liang-huai. Thus these offices currently had a claim on Liang-huai revenue totaling this amount relative to this specific item. This sum was fluidly mixed with other similar "seizures," and the total "seized" was then used to meet a variety of new expenses deemed more urgent, for instance, 148,657.487 taels to buy and ship some Huai-pei salt. Naturally the funds "seized" total the same as the sums advanced, i.e., 1,239,453.076 taels. T'ao Chu at this time was dealing with the question of postponing repayment of these advances or, perhaps better, "deferred claims."

26. Just as *fa* and *yung* are general words added rather interchangeably to the technically specific *tien* to denote the same fiscal phenomenon, so either *chiang* (to send down) or *fa* (to issue)

There is a similar mixture of technical and not-so-technical terms denoting impeachment, that is, the indicting and/or convicting of an official for committing any offense, often an administrative offense under the *ch'u-fen tse-li* (regulations on administrative punishment). The general and technical term for this impeachment was *ts'an*. According to the *Collected Statutes of the Great Ch'ing Dynasty*, there were three technically different phrases used in calling for impeachment, depending on whether the punishment was to be soft, standard, or harsh relative to that particular offense. For soft punishment, *ch'a-i* (examine and advise) was used; for standard punishment, the very common *i-ch'u* (advise on administrative punishment); and for severe punishment, *yen-chia i-ch'u* (advise on severe administrative punishment).[27]

In official communications referring to impeachment, however, terms other than these three technical ones were also often used. *Ts'an-ch'u, ts'an-ho, ts'an-ch'eng, ts'an-pan, chiu-ts'an, ch'a-ts'an,* and *chiu-ts'an* probably did not cover the mild *ch'a-i* and rather were only synonyms for *i-ch'u*. The same interpretation applies to *chih-ming ts'an-tsou, chieh-ts'an, chih-ts'an,* and *t'i-ts'an,* but these four had a slightly different linguistic aspect in that they were also especially suitable in sentences where the agent calling for punishment was specified. Furthermore, *t'i-ts'an* made explicit the legal requirement that a memorial calling for *ts'an* was to be in the form of a *t'i-pen*, not a *tsou-che*.[28]

Ts'ung-yen ts'an-pan, yen-hsing ts'an-pan, yen-ts'an ch'eng-pan, yen-ts'an chiu-pan, and *yen-chia ts'an-ch'u* were synonyms for *yen-chia i-ch'u,* as was *chih-ming yen-ts'an*. The latter, like *chih-ming ts'an-tsou,* makes explicit the requirement of naming the culprit to the throne, a superfluous point since any *ts'an* had

---

could be added to *pan* (to promulgate) in order to form *pan-chiang* and *pan-fa,* which equally denote the technically specific phenomenon of promulgating laws, i.e., issuing them for application. There was also no one proper term for entering an item into the *tse-li* (precedents and regulations of capital offices). Equally proper and "technical" were *tsuan-ju tse-li* (entering the case into the *tse-li*), *kung-tsuan wei-li* (respectfully compiling the article as a *tse-li*), *kung-tsuan ch'eng-li* (respectfully compiling the article as an established *tse-li*), and *tsuan wei ting-li* (compiling the article as a fixed *tse-li*).

27. *TCHT,* 11:5a–b. *Ta-Ch'ing hui-tien* (1818), 8:5a–b.
28. *CFTL,* 9:9.

to go through the emperor. Other variations could almost be made up to suit the writer's fancy: for example, *ts'an-ch'e shih-ch'eng* (remove from office through impeachment, warning officials by the use of punishment).[29]

There was a similar range of words for "arresting" and "trying." Variously combined, *na, pu, ch'i,* and *huo* can be found used with equal propriety to denote the forcible seizure or arrest of a common criminal. However, when an official was to be arrested, a more polite range of words, similar to our "pick up," was used. In this context, the idea of putting a person under physical control could be expressed with equal propriety by either *t'ui* (to pull), *t'i* (to pull out), *ch'ü* (to take), or *kou* (to hook).[30] The idea of carrying out a judicial investigation was complicated by the fact that there could be two kinds of inquiries: criminal trials, and disciplinary inquiries whereby officials were questioned by their superiors, who could make recommendations as to whether or not an administrative sanction such as demotion should be applied.[31] The words frequently used to denote the process of holding an inquiry can be put in a spectrum beginning with maximum connotation of a criminal trial and ending with the idea of mere questioning or investigating: *shen, wen, hsün, yen,* and *ch'a.* Thus "to arrest and try criminally" could be equally expressed by *t'i-wen, ch'ü-wen, kou-wen, t'ui-wen,* or *t'i-hsün.* "To hold a criminal trial" could be equally expressed by *shen-hsün, shen-pan, shen-li,* and so on. At the same time *shen, wen,* and *hsün* could be used for merely disciplinary inquiries. Officials ordered to attend these, however, were not "arrested" but "summoned," an idea usually denoted by *ch'uan.*[32] Thus we have *ch'uan-wen* or *ch'uan-hsün* (to summon to an inquiry), and *ch'a-hsün* (to carry out an inquiry), or *yen-chieh* (to carry out an inquiry to its resolution). Just as with the process of impeachment, it is obvious that the formation of all these words was a somewhat open-ended

29. *TYT*, 30:55.

30. Basic passages illustrating these terms are *Ming-lü chi-chieh fu-li,* 1:11–13, and *TCLL,* 4:14–17.

31. See IV, 4, d.

32. The basic distinction between *ch'uan* and arresting is in *TCLL,* 4:16. Here it is pointed out that imperial permission is needed to "arrest" an official but not "to summon and question him if the matter is minor."

process alternative to the possibility of denoting strictly technical matters with a few, strictly used words.

The large number of generic terms for memorials is obvious.[33] Cancellation of a tax could be written either *huo, chüan, chüan-mien, huo-mien* or *huo-ch'u.* A temporary remission of a tax could be written *huan, chüan-huan* or, presumably, *huo-huan.* In *ti-huan, ti,* a nontechnical word, adds the idea that collection will stretch over two or more years.[34]

A good example of the way that the bureaucratic language might require a two-character term rather than a single-character term is the phrase *tai-cheng chüan-huan ch'ien-liang* (collecting temporarily remitted taxes along with current ones).[35] (*Tai-cheng huan ch'ien-liang* would be linguistically awkward.) Similarly, depending on linguistic context, either *ts'e* or *ts'e-chi* was used for certain reports sent to the Board of Revenue on salt taxes collected,[36] and in the salt monopoly "master license"[37] could be written either *yin, yin-mu,* or, less commonly, *yen-yin.* The word order of technical phrases could sometimes be reversed as in *tai-tsui liu-jen* and *liu-jen tai-tsui* (retention of official duties while carrying along one's guilt).

33. Note *tsou-chang, tsou-shu, shu-chang,* which were commonly used as nouns, and the typically verbal *t'iao-tsou, tsou-ch'en, chü-tsou,* and *tsou-ming.* The somewhat historical and ad hoc manner with which such a term might be chosen in a particular case is illustrated by the choice of *tsou-shu* for the title of *TYT.* The editor states, in *fan-li*: 1b, that: "In examining documents on state affairs written by men of the past, one finds that sometimes they are called *tsou-i,* sometimes *tsou-kao* [*i* denotes deliberation and advising the emperor on state affairs; *kao* refers to the draft version of memorials, or rather to the draft version as a way of referring to the memorial itself.] Now in the case of the master's memorials we are compiling together *che-tzu* and *t'i-pen* [the two technically distinct types of memorials; see below, p. 419]. Therefore we give them the general title of *tsou-shu.*" The use of *tsou-ts'an* (to memorialize calling for impeachment) shows the generic quality of *tsou* (to memorialize), since by law a *t'i-pen*-type memorial, not a *tsou-che* was required, at least for the final processing of the impeachment; *CFTL,* 9:9. *Chü-t'i* (to memorialize), however, seems to have been restricted to *t'i-pen*-type memorials. *Pen-chang* was a technical term covering both *t'i-pen* and *tsou-pen* or *tsou-che.*

34. *TYT,* 32:38a–b.

35. *HPTL,* 30:6.

36. *HPTL,* 30:6b–7.

37. This was the one license which was received from and returned to the Board of Revenue.

What was *the* technically appropriate title of that clearly delimited unit of law which we justifiably call the Ch'ing penal code? From the beginning of the dynasty until about 1740, *Ta-Ch'ing lü* (Penal statutes of the great Ch'ing dynasty) was used, while at the same time the first two editions of the code (1646 and 1725) bore the title *Ta-Ch'ing lü chi-chieh fu-li* (The penal statutes of the great Ch'ing dynasty, collected and annotated, with the penal regulations included). Only with the third edition of the total code, that of 1740, did *lü-li* become established as part of the name for the code, a Ming term thus being revived.[38] Still, although the complete name was usually *Ta-Ch'ing lü-li,* it was technically quite proper in some contexts to use *Hsing-pu lü-li* (Penal statutes and regulations of the board of punishments),[39] *Lü-li ch'üan-shu* (Complete book of penal statutes and regulations),[40] or *Hsing-pu lü-li ch'üan-shu.*[41] There was really no one technically proper title. This is a striking example of the tendency to carry on the most formal kinds of procedures without maximally standardized language.

An interesting case is that of *ch'e-chih* (to pull out [a salt bag as a sample]), which was an important salt monopoly term going back at least to Sung times and denoting inspection of salt bags to detect overweight packing, usually that inspection carried out at the major checkpoints near the production areas just before the salt finally went on its way to its consumption areas. The editors of the 1806 edition of *The Salt Laws Gazetteer of the Liang-huai Zone,* the official manual for that branch of the salt monopoly, criticized the term *ch'e-chih* for redundancy (*ch'e* and *chih* equally mean "to pull out"); they decided instead to use *ch'e-yen* (to pull out and inspect), pointing to usage in the recent Chekiang salt gazetteer as precedent and arguing that the officials in charge of both the Huai-nan and the Huai-pei *so* (stations) had *yen* in their titles (their titles being *p'i-yen so ta-shih* [inspection station supervisor]).[42] This editorial

38. *Ta Ming hui-tien,* III: 2239. *Lü-li* is here used as a heading in *Ta-Ming hui-tien* for all the chapters presenting the penal code, but it does not seem to have been used otherwise as the title of the code or of a book containing the code.

39. *Chung-kuo chin-tai ching-chi ssu-hsiang yü ching-chi cheng-ts'e tzu-liao hsüan-chi,* p. 39. This is a memorial by Lin Tse-hsü (1785–1850).

40. This usage was common in prefatory memorials of the code.

41. *Ta-Ch'ing hui-tien* (1764), *fan-li.*

42. *LHYFC, fan-li*:3.

change, also followed in the next edition of the gazetteer, perhaps indicates a feeling that these important inspections deserved a single, correct name, but subsequent official communications sometimes revert to *ch'e-chih*.[43]

To take another example of a conscious search for the technically more proper term, the same editors replaced the section heading *k'o-ju* (tax intake) with *k'o-ch'eng* (rates of taxes on goods):

> In the old gazetteers there is a "tax intake" section. In the matter of taxes, however, there is no principle of intake without expenditure. Still more, if one were to write together as one term *ch'u-na* (expenditures and intake), the meanings to some extent would not supplement each other. We respectfully note: in the *Penal Statutes and Regulations of the Great Ch'ing Dynasty*, all taxes on merchants and tea and salt taxes are referred to in a general sense as *k'o-ch'eng* (rates of taxes on goods), and the penal salt law articles all are included under this heading. Now in compliance with this, we have replaced the previous gazetteers' term "tax intake" [with "rates of taxes on goods"].[44]

(Although *ch'u-na* was frowned on by the compilers as a title, it was in use at the time in discussions of government finance.)[45]

These examples point up the general fact that governmental terminology was not always frozen in orthodox patterns. *Pien-chung hai-chih* (delivery of supplies at the frontier, issuing of salt at the coast)[46] was sometimes used in Ch'ing times for the Ming grain-salt exchange system, the standard term for which is *k'ai-chung-fa* (system of supply deliveries through listed regulations).[47] A similar instance is the precise but unusual way

43. Writing a few decades after the publication of this gazetteer, T'ao Chu as head of Liang-huai used either *ch'e-chih* (e.g., *TYT*, 30:47b) or *ch'e-yen* (e.g., *TYT*, 48:13).

44. *LHYFC*, *fan-li*:3b.

45. *TWI*, 15:45; 16:3b.

46. See, e.g., *LHYFC*, 31:7b; *Liang-huai yen-fa-chih* (1893), I:11.

47. The meaning of *k'ai-chung-fa* is thoroughly discussed in Fujii Hiroshi, "*Kaiju no imi oyobi kigen* (The meaning and origin of kaiju)," in *Katō hakuse kanreki kinens Tōyōshi shusetsu* (Collected articles on Oriental history in honor of Dr. Katō's sixty-first birthday;

that the Nanking governor-general in 1806 designated the system of salt distribution then in effect at Liang-huai, calling it *kang-shih chih fa*.[48] The standard term was *kang-fa, kang* here being an ambiguous term the main thrust of which was to denote the system of shipment used to transport salt to that class of markets distant from the production areas. The unusual term *kang-shih chih fa* was a neater and more comprehensive way of labeling the Liang-huai system because the term *shih* (to consume) not only covered the other major class of Liang-huai markets, the *shih-an,* those fairly near the production areas, but also was a term apparently peculiar to Liang-huai in this context.[49]

Conversely, single technical words could have two or more meanings. In most of these cases, I would argue, ambiguity was either absent, fairly harmless, or useful and deliberate. Of course there is no shortage of words with two meanings but without ambiguity once seen in context, as with the English word "fly," which can mean either a certain kind of insect or a certain kind of action in baseball.[50] Fairly harmless ambiguity is illustrated by *lü-ling, shih-li,* and *t'iao.* In Ch'ing times, *lü-ling* could be used in the most general sense to refer to any kind of fully established regulations of capital offices;[51] more nar-

---

Tokyo, 1941), pp. 677–700. Fujii shows how *chung* was used during Sung times in various terms denoting various economic transactions where merchants delivered supplies to the capital or to troops at the frontier in return for licenses or vouchers good for money or some monopoly privilege.

48. *LHYFC, hsü*:1b.

49. On the *kang-fa*'s origin, see Metzger, "Organizational Capabilities," pp. 21–24.

50. A good example of a word with two meanings but lacking ambiguity in practice is *ts'an-yin* (leftover master licenses). In both the tea and salt monopolies "leftover master licenses" could refer either to the master license held by a merchant and normally due to be turned in to the government after sale of shipment, or to master licenses still held by the government because they had not been issued to merchants during a certain time period. Context seldom if ever fails to indicate which meaning is involved. There is hardly more risk of ambiguity here than in the use of *ti-pen,* which might denote, e.g., either long-term loans of working capital such as those made by the government to Yunnan copper miners or the primary or original manuscript of a book such as a compilation of government regulations.

51. *HPTL, tsou-che*:1b.

rowly to regulations specifying punishments (that is, the penal code and the punishment-of-officials regulations);[52] and still more narrowly to the penal code alone.[53] *Shih-li* usually denoted regulations or precedents distinguished, on the one hand, from the most fundamental statutes of the empire and, on the other hand, from mere *ch'eng-an*, which were executive cases used as precedents or regulations but lacking the full formal status of a *li*. Yet one finds *shih-li* used to designate not only some penal *ch'eng-an* but also the penal *lü* themselves! Thus the *lü* are classed as *shih-li* pertaining to the Board of Punishments in the two editions of *Ta-Ch'ing hui-tien shih-li* (Precedents and regulations supplementary to the collected statutes of the great Ch'ing dynasty). *Shih-li* therefore can cover the whole spectrum of penal law, although it is not often thought of that way. It is even arguable that *shih-li* overlaps the meaning of *tien* (statute), despite the fact that *tien* emphatically denotes not supplementary laws but the most general and fundamental laws, both penal and otherwise. Thus in the first two editions of *Ta-Ch'ing hui-tien* (Collected statutes of the great Ch'ing dynasty), *shih-li* is used as a generic term covering at least all dated imperial decisions in those volumes.[54] Admittedly these two editions were later officially criticized for including both *tien* and *shih-li*, and the format was changed.[55]

The use of *t'iao* (article) in the penal code is another example. The section of the code under the heading of *k'o-ch'eng* (rates of taxes on commercial goods) is presented as consisting of eight *t'iao* (articles) of *lü* (penal statutes), of which three are on the salt monopoly. The first of these three articles, however, consists of eleven separately paragraphed statements of law, each an independent complex of meaning—properly speaking, eleven subcategories of that *t'iao* (article). But Ch'ing compilers did not use another term for these subcategories. Rather they speak of the thirteen penal *t'iao* (articles) on the salt monopoly, using *t'iao* for each of the eleven subcategories

52. *LHYFC*, 38:1; 39:1.

53. *TCLL*, 7:1. See version in *CFTL*, 14:3–4, for proof that *lü-ling* here means *lü-li*. In the equivalent passage of the Ming penal code, *lü-ling* is an abbreviation for two books, *Ta-Ming-lü* and *Ta-Ming-ling*; *Ming-lü chi-chieh*, 3:1a–b.

54. See *fan-li* in editions of 1690 and 1732.

55. See III, 5.

of the first article as well as each of the other two articles.[56]

Words specifying aspects of legal authority such as jurisdiction and lines of bureaucratic subordination are often loosely used, sometimes deliberately so. For instance, *hsia* (to have authority over) is one of two words (the other is *shu* [to be under the authority of]) most frequently used in a technical way to denote the condition of being under the jurisdiction of an office (whether that condition characterizes people, a territorial area, or another office). Yet little effort was made to reserve this important word for technically precise expression, and it could be used in official documents to denote the vaguer condition of in some way falling under the responsibility of an office. For instance, although the Liang-huai salt commissioner (*yen-cheng*) explicitly lacked territorial jurisdiction over the areas where Liang-huai salt was sold, an imperial decree could state: "The territory under the authority (*hsia*) of Liang-huai is extremely vast. The military and civil officials often do not regard arresting salt smugglers and prohibiting corrupt practices as their concern and do not respond quickly to the salt commissioner."[57]

Another official description of the functions of the Liang-huai salt commissioner says that he "*t'ung-hsia* (controls) supervision over the sale of the legal salt quotas in the prefectures, districts, and departments of Kiangnan, Kiangsi, Hu-kuang, and Honan."[58] This is misleading. Facilitating such sale and combating smuggling were the responsibility of the regular provincial administration, some members of which were subject to administrative punishment if the quotas were not sold. The salt

56. *LHYFC*, 38:1.

57. *LHYFC*, 32:11b. The salt commissioner of Liang-huai "lacks the responsibility of control over territory; military and civil officials are both not under him." See *TYT*, 31:3. Admittedly the former and latter statements are separated by a century, but it is clear that the jurisdiction of the salt commissioner had not changed. At the very least, he had no territorial jurisdiction in Liang-huai provinces such as Hunan or Kiangsi. Actually the territorial authority even of the Nanking governor-general over provinces such as Kiangsi involved problems since his power was diluted by geographical distance. Thus we find that sometimes, when he was Nanking governor-general, T'ao Chu would not simply send an order to his supposed subordinate, the Kiangsi governor, but would ask the emperor to send the latter an edict. See, e.g., 31:11b–12; 42:7b–8.

58. *LHYFC*, 32:12b–13.

commissioner was indeed responsible for the Liang-huai quota as a whole, and he consequently had to act in coordination with the provincial officials. Yet as a rule he had no authority over any of them.[59] A military post (a first captain, in this case heading a Green Standard battalion) could officially be described as "having jurisdiction (*kuan-hsia*) over the districts and departments of Ssu-chou, Hsü-i, and T'ien-ch'ang," but it did not have jurisdiction in the sense that the local magistrates did.[60]

Yet such ambiguities were not due to any dysfunctional confusion. On the contrary, ambiguity in jurisdictional questions often served conscious governmental aims. The fact that leadership was often set up on a joint basis or with ill-designed lines of authority does not mean that the Ch'ing were unaware of the values of *chuan-tse* (assigning responsibility to a single office or official). Rather, they weighed the advantages of *chuan-tse* against those of setting up offices to check each other, a tendency particularly prominent from Sung times on.[61] Perhaps the classic instance of the interplay of these two principles in Ch'ing times is that of the six boards, where the regular joint leadership in each board of two presidents and four vice-presidents was sometimes put under the unifying authority of a single official such as a grand secretary through the device of supradirection.[62]

59. An exception was the arrangement worked out by T'ao Chu in 1831 whereby the annual efficiency report (*k'ao-ch'eng*) on the Hupei salt taotai, who supervised the central salt junction of Hankow, was put partly in the hands of the Nanking governor-general (T'ao Chu); see *TYT*, 30:57b.

60. *TYT*, 49:28.

61. Yen Keng-wang, *Chung-kuo ti-fang hsing-cheng chih-tu-shih* (History of the regional and local administration in China; Taipei, 1961–), part one, I, introd., p. 13, states that the splitting up of the highest regional authority into partly overlapping jurisdictions lacking any clear hierarchy of subordination to a large extent was begun in the Sung period and continued thereafter. Sa Meng-wu, IV:102, also stresses the Sung focus on mutual checks and control over officials. The idea that the Sung increased the use of mutual checks in its table of organization is at least an important hypothesis.

62. *Shinkoku gyōseihō*, I: 339–340. Translated in *Ch'ing-kuo hsing-cheng-fa*, 3:2:2:27–28. A common term for such supradirection was *kuan-li shih-wu* (to direct affairs). Also common were *chien-pu-wu* or *chien-kuan pu-wu* (to direct the affairs of a board as an added responsibility). *Ibid.*, 2:4:4:196, has a valuable quota-

In discussing the role of unclear expressions one must emphasize the major case of ambiguities arising not from lack of skill or interest in finding a clear term but from the obstacles to clarity inherent in the matter denoted, obstacles often arising from the conflict between local variations in practice and the need for some sort of uniform conceptualization. Tax terms (for example, *ti-ting*) are notorious examples.

Finally one can point to terms the meaning of which are not immediately obvious to modern scholars but which were constantly used with an obvious meaning in official documents even if no one ever bothered to define them explicitly. When definitions were made, they often were incomplete or imprecise, apparently because there was a lag between passive and active understanding, between intuitive grasp and comprehensive articulation. Some examples of this can be taken from *Liu-pu ch'eng-yü chu-chieh* (The terminology of the six boards, annotated), a popular dictionary used in the Ch'ing government. It was compiled in the late nineteenth century on the basis of earlier, similar works going back to the late seventeenth century and has been admirably translated into English by Professor E-tu Zen Sun.[63]

For instance *Liu-pu ch'eng-yü chu-chieh* gives an unhelpful definition of the common term *chi-lu* as "putting down an official's achievements in a register in order to have a record of them." A *chi-lu* is a commendation formulated in terms of the

---

tion from Chao I (1727–1814), *Yen-p'u tsa-chi,* describing how power in a board could be concentrated in the hands of such a high official given supradirection: a department director (*lang-chung*) trusted by him could have more power than a president. Chao I also notes that, even without such supradirection, power could be concentrated in the hands of one of the board's head officials. The practice of giving such supradirection to a high imperial noble had ceased because in such instances the concentration of power became too great. Possibly the origin of this Ch'ing practice was in 1631, when the Manchus, still outside the Great Wall, set up their version of the six boards. Each board had three presidents, a Manchu, a Chinese, and a Mongol, and over each board was put a still higher official, a high Manchu noble with the title "directing the affairs of the so-and-so board." See Fu Tsung-mao, *chün-chi-ch'u,* p. 28.

63. E-tu Zen Sun, *Ch'ing Administrative Terms* (Cambridge, Mass., 1961), xiii–xxiv. *Liu-pu ch'eng-yü chu-chieh* is reprinted in Chinese as *Rikubu seigo chūkai* (Terminology of the six boards, annotated; Kyoto, 1940), a version edited by Naitō Kenkichi.

process of recording it. Thus *chi-lu erh tz'u* (recorded two times) means "two commendations." Furthermore it is a commendation with formally specified values relative to other sanctions.[64]

Another unenlightening definition in the above manual is "the punishment which is due" for *ch'u-fen* (administrative punishment).[65] Although *ch'u-fen* by itself does simply mean "punishment,"[66] it was consistently used by Ch'ing bureaucrats to refer to a limited class of punishments, those administered through the Boards of War and of Civil Officials to officials, rather than to the criminal punishments administered under the Board of Punishments. *K'ao-ch'eng* (examination of results) is explained by the manual as "examination by superior officials of their subordinates' handling of affairs to see whether or not there has been success [relative to specified responsibilities]," but everyone knew that this annual examination above all involved determining whether the official should receive either an administrative punishment or an administrative reward.[67] The fact that *k'ao-ch'eng* was annual in contrast to the triannual evaluations (*ta-chi* and *ching-ch'a*) could also have been noted in such a manual. The manual says that *hsiu-chih* (retirement) was carried out for officials who were "old and

64. *Rikubu,* p. 12; *TCHT,* 11:2b–3. Four "ordinary" *chi-lu* or two *chi-lu* for military merit were equivalent to one added subgrade and under certain conditions could be used to cancel off a demotion of one subgrade. In Ming times (*Ming-lü chi-chieh,* 1:19, 1:20b), *chi-lu* (to record) denoted part of the process of maintaining a record of some of an official's offenses, this record being used every nine years as a factor in promoting or demoting him. This usage for *chi-lu* did not exist in the Ch'ing period. See II, 3, note 24.

65. *Rikubu,* p. 15.

66. Although *ch'u-fen* was often used as a verb, as in *chao-lü ch'u-fen* (to carry out administrative punishment according to the penal code), it could also be used as a gerund, as in the sentence: *I chiang kai-yüan-teng ying-te ch'u-fen tsou-shang* (We should memorialize on the administrative punishments which the said officials ought to receive). I am indebted to Professor John Watt for pointing out its use in reference to the punishment of officials in an imperial order of 751; see *T'ang-hui-yao* (Collected essentials of the T'ang dynasty; Shanghai, 1935), 69:1217. As is the case today, *ch'u-fen* by T'ang or Sung times also had the meaning "to dispose of, to handle." See, e.g., *Wen-hsien t'ung-k'ao* (Shanghai, 1901), 58:1.

67. *Rikubu,* p. 14.

no longer of use,"[68] but it could also be carried out for officials in ill health.[69] Furthermore the manual does not mention that such retirement could be either forced (*le-ling hsiu-chih*) or voluntary (*kao-t'ui*).[70] Still another example is the explanation of *ya-cheng* as collecting taxes "in advance."[71] Even if this were the meaning sometimes, *ya-cheng* could also mean the opposite, namely, collecting taxes originally due in the past.[72] *K'ai-ch'üeh* (to vacate a post) is described by the manual only as a procedure carried out if an official were guilty of a minor offense not deserving more severe disciplinary action,[73] but the term was not necessarily opprobrious, since an official could ask to *k'ai-ch'üeh*, say, on account of illness.[74]

Yin-chien (to bring in an official for an imperial audience) is explained purely as a procedure for officials about to be appointed or promoted to an office,[75] but such audiences were held for various reasons, for example, at the triannual capital inspection to determine if an official should receive an administrative honor, continue in office, or be retired.[76] *Ching-ch'a* (capital inspection) is defined as a triannual inspection for "civil officials at the capital city,"[77] but it also applied to all governors and governors-general. Admittedly, the latter officials also had the honorary titles of certain offices in the capital, but since they were fundamentally regarded as *feng-chiang ta-li* (great regional officials), a word of explanation might have been in order. Mistakes based on ignorance are much rarer, such as the manual's definition of the penal *ming-li* as "the title of the regulation or precedent" (*ming-li* means "general principles" or, better, "principles of sentencing").[78] Nor can such

68. *Ibid.*, p. 17.
69. *CFTL*, 6:16. *Ch'ing-shih*, II:1338.
70. *TCHT*, 11:2.
71. *Rikubu*, p. 41.
72. *Ch'in-ting hu-pu ts'ao-yün ch'üan-shu*, 3:1b; *TYT*, 32:38b. These are clear instances of *ya-cheng* as collecting taxes originally due in the past.
73. *Rikubu*, p. 135.
74. *TYT*, 41:4; 47:40.
75. *Rikubu*, p. 14.
76. *CFTL*, 5:1b–2.
77. *Rikubu*, p. 15. A similar definition is found in *TCHT*, 11:8.
78. *Rikubu*, p. 103. The correct contemporaneous meaning of the term is explained in the code itself (*TCLL*, 4:1): "*Ming* refers to the sentences given according to the five punishments; *li* refers to the principles of the five punishments." Since the topic of this section

neglect of the art of definition be ascribed to any fear of redundancy or of stating the obvious. As shown again and again in memorials, the idea was thoroughly established that full presentation of a subject required leisurely reiteration of elementary and obvious points. The emperor received at least ten memorials a year from the head of the Liang-huai salt monopoly zone informing him at length that the territory of Liang-huai was vast and its tax quota enormous. Rather, there was no urgent feeling that definitions had to be precise and comprehensive.

The more prominent and well-known the bureaucratic phenomenon, the less need there was to denote it with a term or phrase clear in itself. A complicated and major tax adjustment in a locality, widely understood because of its deep effects, might be denoted in an abbreviated fashion by a term in itself utterly devoid of any clear meaning to anyone except a person knowing the facts of the case. Such knowledge was part of official gossip, and there was no need or desire to spell it out.

For instance on June 5, 1831, T'ao Chu, the Nanking governor-general, memorialized that the 200,000 taels of government funds needed then for financing Huai-pei salt shipments should be taken from the "taxes collected along with current taxes from the added catties of the master licenses left over from the 1829 *kang* (total annual Liang-huai shipment using master licenses)." [79] No other explanation was given in this memorial.

The reference was to a tax arrangement which had been approved by the emperor probably in early April. To lower the salt merchants' expenses, T'ao had proposed that in making their shipments of the 1831 *kang*, they be allowed to add 136 catties of untaxed and partly taxed salt to the standard amount of 364 catties per bag: while 36 catties of this 136 were un-

---

of the code is essentially the whole range of adjustments made in applying sentences, the title "principles of sentencing" is appropriate. This definition goes back at least to the T'ang code; see *T'ang-lü shu-i* (The T'ang dynasty penal statutes with commentary; 1891), I:9b. *Ibid.*, I:9, gives a history of the term *ming-li* repeated in Cheng Ching-i and P'eng Shih, *Fa-lü ta-tz'u shu* (Large dictionary on the law; Shanghai, 1936), I:436–437. The Wei dynasty (220–264) established the term *hsing-ming* (the names of the criminal punishments); the succeeding Chin dynasty (265–419) established a complementary category, *fa-li* (the principles of the laws); and the Northern Ch'i dynasty (550–577) joined the terms to produce *ming-li.*

79. *TYT*, 32:51a–b.

taxed, the remaining 100 catties were regarded as coming from the unsold salt quotas of the bad years of 1830 and 1829 and, exempted from some three-fourths of the current tax schedule, were subject only to the "regular tax." It was from this "regular tax" on the 100 catties added to each of the 1831 *kang* salt bags as salt unsold in 1829 and 1830 that T'ao financed some of the Huai-pei salt shipments in 1831.[80]

In the salt monopoly there also were abbreviated expressions denoting arrangements the complexity of which arose from chronological complications in the collection of taxes or tax debts or from lack of congruence between the physical size of the salt bags and the fiscal weight unit on which taxes were paid.[81] As the bureaucratic need for prefixed and ordered procedure clashed with the vicissitudes of economic conditions, complex arrangements and difficult terminology were bound to arise.

Complex mechanical procedures, as in the field of water control, also led to difficult and abbreviated terminology. Phenomena suffering from fiscal or mechanical complexity differ from those suffering from the complexity of spatial or temporal variation in that terms denoting the former usually had a clear meaning, however baffling at first glance, while terms such as *ti-ting* (tax levied in terms of land and ting), denoted inherently confusing patterns with an indefinite range of variation.[82]

Without greatly lengthening this list of examples, it would be impossible to determine definitely that the above instances typically and exhaustively reflect the nature of the bureaucratic language. Nevertheless it is possible confidently to hypothesize that when the bureaucratic language failed to denote a technical phenomenon consistently with one or two standardized, precise terms, the meanings of which were either obvious or explained in reference works, this failure did not usually lead to a lack of clarity in the minds of Ch'ing officials. Beyond any doubt it can be said that the many terms for "impeachment" involved no confusion whatsoever, and that the Ch'ing compiler who gave the miserable definition of *chi-lu* (commendation) knew perfectly well what a *chi-lu* was.

80. *TYT*, 31:22b–23; 32:47a–b.

81. The term *p'ei-ko,* discussed in I, 5, is a good example.

82. On the meaning of ting, see Ping-ti Ho, *Studies on the Population of China* (Cambridge, Mass., Harvard University Press, 1959), pp. 24–35.

Rather, the large amount of information held in common by the members of the bureaucracy—combined no doubt with the fact that pressures were not great to absorb other kinds of information also—made it possible for bureaucrats to communicate clearly without trying intensively to express themselves with maximum precision and explicitness.

There was, then, a significant margin of loose or free expression in the bureaucratic language which was connected to the paucity of legal or conventional prescriptions specifically dictating phraseology, to a tendency partly to avoid the establishment of "no-alternative" technical terms, and to a tendency to write in an abbreviated or loose fashion about matters assumed to be obvious. However, although some terms were ambiguous, and although a few institutions or practices were so complicated or confused that they precluded clear denotation, clarity of expression was by far the rule, not the exception.

4. Compilation and Distribution

With such habits of expression, the editors of law books and other administrative manuals often tried to bring the virtues of clarity, succinctness, directness of meaning, consistency, and, to some extent, visual clarity to their compilations. They were interested in including all matters belonging under a formal category and excluding those that did not, as well as in making this material up to date. Moreover, they often sought to arrange a complex of topics in some meaningful sequence. However they were inefficient in categorization and in avoiding the confusions of overlapping between compilations by pulling together all information having practical bearing on a topic.

The editors of some legal compilations—such as the penal code and probably all *tse-li* (fully established precedents and regulations of capital offices)—possibly made some minor substantive changes in the law. In choosing between old and new articles which contradicted each other, editors of the penal code described themselves as weighing the conflict and then deciding on a solution.[1] They acted on their own discretion but subject to imperial approval. Nevertheless it is clear that specialized technical experience with a body of law, not legislative judgment, was the main quality by which compilers were judged. Remarks on the need for editorial personnel with specialized knowledge are common in the prefatory memorials of compilations.

There was an interesting but characteristic episode in connection with the 1734 and 1742 editions of the *Regulations of the Board of Civil Officials.* The 1734 edition, perhaps the origin of this book, was compiled by the *Lü-li-kuan* (Bureau for the compilation of the penal code), which at that time was an independent bureau supposed to check all laws related to punishments and was unoccupied with a penal code revision (the second edition had been finished in 1727; the third [1740] was begun around 1736).[2] In 1738, after a censor pointed out the need for another edition of the regulations of the Board of Civil Officials, two Manchu and two Chinese department directors (the officials directly under the presidents and vice-presi-

1. See, e.g., *TCLL, tsou-shu*:34b; 25b.

2. *Ta-Ch'ing lü-li t'ung-k'ao, tsou-shu*:28–32 has a 1736 memorial calling for a new edition of the penal code.

dents) were selected from the Board of Civil Officials to help at the *Lü-li-kuan* in supervising this new revision. But the next year, 1739, the emperor took the matter entirely out of the hands of the *Lü-li-kuan* and put the Board of Civil Officials in full charge. This was done because "[as became clear] after examination of the past cases had begun, the ins and outs of the Board of Civil Officials' system of monthly appointment were very numerous and the articles on administrative punishments such as demotion and salary fines were very confusing; the officials commissioned by the *Lü-li-kuan* as compilers had had no experience before then with the affairs of the Board of Civil Officials and were unable to have a complete grasp of them."[3]

Such episodes indicate that there was some effort to put out compilations which could be *hsin-shou* (relied on).[4] This is not to argue, though, that efficient communication of the laws necessarily depended on frequent and efficient compilation and publication of books of laws. There can be little doubt that the system for the regular and frequent revision of the penal code, which was set up during the second half of the eighteenth century, facilitated some aspects of the judicial procedure. On the other hand, office records seem to have been adequate for many aspects of administrative law. No revision of *The Salt Laws Gazetteer of the Liang-huai Salt Monopoly Zone* was put out after the 1748 edition until that of 1806. Yet this zone flourished during this gap in publication.

Let us now look at the procedures of compilation and publication. After describing them, we can ask what happened to law books once they were published.

Procedure for all compilations generally shared a certain rhythm. First, as cases accumulated, a decision was taken to make a compilation to prevent confusion and abuses. Second, it was necessary to set up an editorial staff, finance the project, and establish a deadline for conclusion of the work. Finally, a "yellow copy" was presented to the emperor for imperial endorsement, and then the compilation was printed and distributed.

3. Ma Feng-ch'en, pp. 53–54.

4. *The Complete Book on the Grain Tribute* had been on a schedule of one revision every ten years since 1734 when in 1812 a censor memorialized that because the recent revisions had merely been copied from the previous ones, he feared that they had many mistakes and were untrustworthy. *TYCS, tsou-che*: 1.

At each stage, though, there were variables. The decision to compile varied in terms of the stimulus behind it, its frequency, and the mix of *ta-hsiu* (total revisions) and *hsiao-hsiu* (minor revisions, that is, compilations of the batch of regulations created since the previous edition).

The decision to compile could be an automatic one in accord with a prefixed schedule, or it could be based on a new and general policy decision. For instance, the *Regulations of the Board of Revenue* (1776) were compiled in response to a memorial criticizing lack of compilation at a number of the capital's major offices,[5] and the *Liang-huai Salt Laws Gazetteer* (1728) was compiled in response to a Board of Revenue memorial of 1724 asking that most or all salt zones have gazetteers.[6] Finally it could be based on the expressed need of the particular office hampered by the lack of an adequate compilation.

For instance the stimulus for the 1806 edition of the *Liang-huai Salt Laws Gazetteer* came from the Liang-huai *yün-shih* (salt controller), who, immediately subordinate to the head of Liang-huai, was in charge of day-to-day operations in that zone. The Board of Revenue had "ordered" the head of Liang-huai, the salt commissioner, to make copies of various executive communications and regulations ("*t'i-pen* memorials, communications with equal offices, board replies, and original cases") which had accumulated since the publication of the 1748 gazetteer and send them to the Board of Revenue. After the salt commissioner had ordered the salt controller to do this, the latter

5. *HPTL, tsou-che*: 1. The term used here, *pu-yüan*, was a loose, general term, *yüan* denoting not just the three offices which all had *yüan* in their names. For instance, in *TYT*, 32:54b–55, *yüan* clearly includes the Office of the Imperial Household; in *TCHTSL, chüan* 52, a section is called *ko-pu-yüan t'ang-chu-shih* (secretaries of head officials at the *pu-yüan*), and the first article deals with such secretaries at the Office for Keeping a Diary of the Emperor's Movements; *TCHTSL, chüan* 88, has a section called *pu-yüan shih-chien hsien-ch'i* (deadlines for the *pu-yüan* in the handling of public business), and this section seems to have broad reference to various capital offices; in *TCHTSL, chüan* 121, there is a section called *pu-yüan ch'eng-shen shih-chien* (trials held by one or more *pu-yüan*), and this deals also at least with the Court of Judicature and Revision. *Pu-yüan* therefore can be translated as "boards and various other capital offices."

6. *Ssu-ch'uan yen-fa-chih, tsou-shu*: 3a–b.

reported back to him that a new edition of the gazetteer was needed because so many regulations had changed since the last. Thereupon the salt commissioner obtained the Board of Revenue's approval of a new edition and then memorialized the emperor for approval of his organizational plans.[7]

Frequency of revision, as we have seen, varied considerably. In the late eighteenth century a rule was established calling for revision of the *tse-li* of various offices once every ten years, but this rule was abolished by an edict of 1830. There was considerable revision of the penal code in the middle of the dynasty, but little during the beginning and last parts; whether this pattern characterized the flow of law books as a whole is not yet clear.[8] For many of the administrative manuals put out in the provinces, revision was particularly irregular. The editions of the *Liang-huai Salt Laws Gazetteer,* for instance, were put out in 1693, 1728, 1748, 1806, and 1904.

An editorial staff, generally speaking, was headed by one or more directors, often called *tsung-ts'ai* or *chien-tsuan.* Successively ranked under this post often were *t'i-tiao-kuan* (supervisors), *tsung-tsuan* (head compilers), and *tsuan-hsiu* (compilers). Checking (*chiao-tui*) could be part of the function of either a head compiler or a compiler, or officials especially in charge of checking could be appointed. Finally there were *kung-shih* (clerks). Sometimes one also finds head clerks called *ching-shou* or *ching-ch'eng.*[9] Copying was a typical task for a clerk.

The supervisors must have carried out most of the day-to-day tasks of editorial leadership, but the directors could be important. In late 1850, just before the second deadline for completion of what became the 1851 edition of the *Regulations of the Board of Revenue,* a new president and vice-president took up their posts at the Board of Revenue and thus in effect became directors. Partly to allow these directors more time to

7. *LHYFC, tsou-che*:4. This is a slightly unusual reference to an "order" from a board to a provincial official. On major matters, the board sent orders by asking the emperor to issue an edict or rescript. For another example, see *HCCSWP,* 20:18. By "head of Liang-huai," I mean the *yen-cheng* (salt commissioner), not the Nanking governor-general, who then had the responsibility of supradirection (*kuan-li*) over the *yen-cheng.* See II, 3, note 62 and I, 1, note 7.

8. See I, 6.

9. *TYCS, tsou-che*:6a–b; 4b.

review the material, the Board was granted an extension of four Chinese months on its deadline.[10] Similarly, as another compilation of the Board of Revenue (the 1845 edition of the *Complete Book on the Grain Tribute*) was being finished, the part just written up was sent daily by the supervisors to the directors so that the latter could "carefully check it."[11]

For the most important compilations, the members of the editorial staff could be recruited from a number of offices. This tendency in the early Ch'ing period—before about 1732, when the Grand Council was formally established—may be connected to two factors. First, as discussed in detail by Fu Tsung-mao, in this early time much important policy discussion was handled by variously composed consultative groups, each formed out of a variety of offices. In this way the same high Manchu nobles could repeatedly participate in major policy discussions on a variety of subjects, instead of being restricted to the affairs of a particular office. Fu Tsung-mao, basing his position not on systematically gathered statistics but on his broadly-based impression as to the frequency with which various consultative mechanisms are mentioned in early Ch'ing document, holds that four of these groups, all of them excluding the Grand Secretariat, were the "paths most frequently taken to obtain deliberation on governmental affairs before the establishment of the Grand Council."[12] One can say that this system of consultative groups partly filled the function of the *tsai-hsiang* (prime office, cabinet) and partly had the character of *t'ing-i* (court conferences). Yet at least it seems clear that the Grand Secretariat by itself was not the emperor's predominant consultative organ. By setting up the Grand Council for both consultation and secret communication with other officials, the Yung-cheng emperor largely bypassed this system of consultative groups and thus reduced the power of high Manchu nobles.

Second, in the particular case of the penal code, revision in this early period was both rare and an important policy problem.[13] Thus like other such problems, it was largely handled in this early period through consultation between a variety of

10. *HPTL, tsou-che*: 10b.
11. *TYCS, tsou-che*: 4b–5.
12. Fu Tsung-mao, *chün-chi-ch'u*, pp. 92, 81–82; see also I, 1, note 7.
13. On early controversy over the revision of the penal code, see I, 6 and Appendix III.

high offices. Only around 1736, when it became more routine, was the function of revision handed over purely to the Board of Punishments.[14]

This pattern of broad consultation in the early compilations of the penal code is obvious. When the regent Dorgon, in 1644, ordered work to begin on the first Ch'ing code, he put it in the hands of *fa-ssu-kuan* (officials at the offices of law) and the *t'ing-ch'en* (court officials).[15] These "officials at the offices of law" (this term here seems to refer to the Board of Punishments) were "broadly to seek out and collect views entertained at the court."[16] After they had finished their work, the emperor ordered the Grand Secretariat to check their draft and publish it. This the Grand Secretariat did largely by working with the Board of Punishments.[17]

14. The *Lü-li-kuan* (Office for the compilation of the penal code) was placed under the Board of Punishments in 1742 according to *Shinkoku Gyōseihō*, I:20, translated in *Ch'ing-kuo hsing-cheng-fa*, 1:2:1:23. *Ch'ing-shih*, III: 1735, says that the *Lü-li-kuan* was changed from an independent bureau to one under the Board of Punishments in connection with the decision to put out *hsiao-hsiu* regularly, a decision which had two phases: 1736, when the schedule was fixed at one *hsiao-hsiu* every three years; and 1746, when one every five years was decided on. After this, the *Lü-li-kuan* essentially ceased being concerned with the regulations of offices other than the Board of Punishments. *Shinkoku Gyōseihō*, I:20, also says the *Lü-li-kuan* was set up in 1645, but no documents I have seen on the 1646 edition mention it. Probably it was set up later. I am indebted to Mrs. Fu-mei Chang Chen for consultation on this point.

15. See *Ta-Ch'ing li-ch'ao shih-lu* (The veritable records of the successive reigns of the great Ch'ing dynasty; Tokyo, 1937–38), *Shun-chih* 7:3–4b, and *Ch'ing-shih*, III:1733. The former document itself uses the term *fa-ssu* (offices handling laws) with a number of meanings. Here it seems mainly to indicate the Board of Punishments, but maybe the Censorate and the Court of Judicature and Revision also participated. That the Board was the main organ is indicated also by the memorial in *Ta-Ch'ing lü-li t'ung-k'ao, tsou-shu*:1. We know that the first step of revision was in the hands of the *fa-ssu;* the second, of the Grand Secretariat. In this memorial the latter describes its role and begins by stating that a draft was sent by the Board of Punishments to the Grand Secretariat. This action, I infer, was not part of the second step but, rather, was the transition from the first step to the second step. If so, then the *fa-ssu* handling the first step was essentially the Board of Punishments.

16. *Ta-Ch'ing lü-li t'ung-k'ao, yüan-hsü*:1.

17. Some grand secretaries described this process in a memorial; this is a memorial by Kang-lin and others found, e.g., in *Ta-Ch'ing lü-li t'ung-k'ao, tsou-shu*:1.

When the emperor around 1689 was in doubt as to whether to revise the penal code, he ordered that "the Nine Ministries [that is, the Six Boards, the Censorate, the Court of Judicature and Revision, and the Transmission Office[18]], the Six Sections of the Censorate for the Scrutiny of Capital Officials, and the circuit censors confer and memorialize on this matter."[19] Besides adjudicative questions, this particular group often was called together in early Ch'ing times to discuss questions such as the government's structure of offices and the examination system, but not fiscal or military affairs.[20] It should be noted that because the circuit censors had to spend much time in the capital to carry out many if not most of their surveillance duties, they could conveniently participate in such conferences.[21] A similarly broad range of officials participated in the preparation of the second edition of the code, that of 1725–1727, but this time they were formed into a distinct bureau, the *Lü-li-kuan* (Bureau for the compilation of the penal code).[22] Not until

18. *TCHT*, 69:1a–b. Fu Tsung-mao, *chün-chi-ch'u*, p. 84. See also *TCHT*, 69:13, 16. This definition of the "Nine Ministries" is that of the "Great Nine Ministries." In Ch'ing times, inherited from the Ming, there also was a concept of the "Minor Nine Ministries." These excluded the Six Boards and included offices like the Courts of Sacrificial Worship, of Imperial Stud, and of Banqueting; however, there is a little controversy as to the composition of the Minor Nine Ministries, as we can see by comparing the lists in W. F. Mayers, *The Chinese Government* (Shanghai, 1878), p. 24, and in Juan K'uei-sheng, *Ch'a-yü k'o-hua*, 7:1. This work can be found in the collection *Pi-chi hsiao-shuo ta-kuan* (Shanghai; published after 1911). Juan was an eighteenth-century official. Meetings of the Great Nine Ministries may have varied a little in composition. In *TCHTSL*, 95: Yung-cheng 7, we find the three "courts" listed above and the Imperial Clan Court as "henceforth" authorized only to listen to the discussions of the Nine Ministries and secretly to memorialize should they want to put forward a view different from that of the Nine Ministries. Possibly the "henceforth" means that previously these four offices did participate fully in the discussions.

19. *Ta-Ch'ing lü-li t'ung-k'ao, tsou-shu*:2.

20. Fu tsung-mao, *chün-chi-ch'u*, p. 93. Actually Fu holds that the above grouping of offices advised on "adjudicative cases" but not "legal institutions." Our example, however, perhaps falls better under the latter.

21. For their capital-focused duties, see *TCHT*, 69:8–11b.

22. The forty-two-man staff of this bureau at this time is listed in the first volume of the code's second edition, *Ta-Ch'ing lü chi-chieh fu-li* (1725–1727).

about 1736, as we have noted, was the *Lü-li-kuan* put under the Board of Punishments and henceforth staffed just with the members of that board.

Such internal staffing, with or without formation of a distinct editorial suboffice, was common. Broadly political participation was thus sacrificed for specialized experience. In some cases (see the case of the Yunnan Department of the Board of Revenue below), the compilation of a specialized book could even be put largely in the hands of the matching specialized subbureau of a capital office.

To give an example of internal staffing: all officials listed as involved in the preparation of the 1851 edition of the *Regulations of the Board of Revenue* were or had been Board of Revenue officials. Altogether, seventy-one such officials were listed on the editorial staff, but the number active at any one time was considerably less, since this list included the names both of officials who had departed in the course of compilation and of those who had replaced them, as well as of officials called in as temporary replacements. Naturally, the higher editorial positions were occupied by the higher members of the Board. Thus presidents and vice-presidents of the Board served as directors of the editorial staff; the next board ranks down, department directors and assistant department directors, served as supervisors on the editorial staff; and so on. Below this staff were thirty-two clerks selected from among the Board's regular complement of clerks to work solely on the compilation. Two of these clerks were especially welcome because they had had experience on the previous edition of the regulations (1838). Moreover, a good deal of work must have been contributed by some of the numerous candidates for office attached on a training basis to the Board as *o-wai ssu-yüan* (departmental officials outside the regular quota of officials), many or all of them receiving a partial salary. In 1850 there were about 148 of them. No distinct bureau for compilation was established in this instance.[23] The editorial staff of the 1838 edition of the *Regulations of the Board of Revenue* was similarly formed, as was that of the 1845 edition of the *Complete Book on the Grain Tribute*. In both cases, one of the directors of the editorial staff was P'an Shih-en, a grand secretary who had the added respon-

23. *HPTL, tsou-che*:2b–3, 5, 12. See any 1850 edition of *Ta-Ch'ing chin-shen ch'üan-shu* for *o-wai ssu-yüan*.

sibility of supradirection (*kuan-li*) of the Board's affairs for some fifteen years during his term on the Grand Secretariat, 1833–1850.[24]

On the other hand, in the case of the 1806 edition of the *Liang-huai Salt Laws Gazetteer*, only the director and the supervisor were regular Liang-huai officials. The head of the Liang-huai salt monopoly filled most of the editorial positions from the pool of lower-ranking officials on probationary status waiting for a Liang-huai salt post. There were then more than sixty of these at Liang-huai, from whom the salt commissioner chose those whose "status is based on having passed an examination, who write well, and who clearly understand salt affairs."[25] Three head salt merchants were given positions on the editorial staff, and the clerks apparently were hired from the outside.[26]

We have seen that the editorial staff of officials and clerks for the 1851 edition of the *Regulations of the Board of Revenue* numbered some sixty or more, besides the "departmental officials outside the regular quota of officials." Much editorial work was needed, especially when the records of many years had to be sorted through or sent for from various offices. For the 1806 *Liang-huai Salt Laws Gazetteer*, the records of more than fifty years had to be covered, and therefore the salt commissioner feared that "items such as stipends" for those compiling, checking, and copying would require "several tens of thousands" of taels.

The government often had to make no overt outlay to pay editorial personnel, however. Even more, out of a sense of duty or through the hope of receiving some honor, some editorial personnel could be induced to contribute not only their labor but also funds. In the above case of the 1806 *Liang-huai Salt Laws Gazetteer*, the probationary officials put on the editorial staff themselves contributed funds as well as work. Their incentive was the hope that if they finished their work satisfactorily and on time, they would be given preference in appointments to posts.[27] The officials at the Board of Punishments compiling a new edition of the penal code often personally

24. On supradirection, see II, 3, note 62.

25. *LHYFC, tsou-che*:4b.

26. See prefatory memorials and list of editors at beginning of *LHYFC*.

27. *LHYFC, tsou-che*:4b–5b.

financed printing of a *ts'ao-pen* (draft copy), which was circulated in advance of the regular copy.[28] In the case of the 1845 edition of the *Complete Book of the Grain Tribute,* the clerks met their own compiling expenses and received some sort of administrative reward directly from the Board, but the six head clerks received imperially conferred administrative honors (*i-hsü*) possibly involving appointment to office. Later, the head clerks and clerks took charge of printing with the explicit hope of receiving an appointment to office if they did their work efficiently.[29] Although an administrative reward such as a commendation or honorary office title could sometimes be given to anyone from a supervisor (*t'i-tiao-kuan*) down,[30] it was usual that the directors would "not dare" to ask for any administrative rewards for officials on the editorial staff.

So far, we have seen that the government could provide the economic basis of editorial work through the pure use of noneconomic honors, such as *i-hsü* (to advise on an administrative reward), which elicited work; through invisible economic outlays, such as diverting the energies of personnel already on its payroll from other work to editorial work, or making available certain appointments to office as a reward for editorial work; and through private financial contributions from the editorial staff. Also, the government sometimes could get contributions from outside groups such as salt merchants, as was the case with the *Liang-huai Salt Laws Gazetteer* of 1806.[31] Finally, there were outlays from government treasuries or storehouses.

Except for circulating a draft version, government funds clearly were used to print the penal code. For some law books, funds were obtained from the recipient office. For instance, in the case of the 1851 edition of the *Regulations of the Board of Revenue,* a distinction was made between expenses for preparing the printing blocks and expenses for paper and labor in using the printing blocks to turn out individual copies. The former were met out of the annual *fan-yin* (expense money) sent to the Board by the provinces. Expenses for turning out individual copies were met by the *Yin-k'u,* the Board's main treasury, but most of the offices in the provinces receiving copies

28. See, e.g., *TCLL, tsou-shu*:57b.
29. *TYCS, tsou-che*:6a–b, 7b.
30. *CFTL,* 33:2.
31. *LHYFC,* tsou-che:4b–5.

had to reimburse the *Yin-k'u* within one or two years.[32] When up to 3,000 taels was to be spent by the government for the printing of the 1845 edition of the *Complete Book on the Grain Tribute*, offices receiving a copy were to make up this outlay. For this book, the Board's *Yen-liao-k'u* (Dyes and paper storehouse) provided the paper.[33] When the Board of Civil Officials put out an edition of *Regulations on Administrative Punishment* in 1828, it paid for the printing of editions for higher offices but was paid in the case of lower regional offices by the latter.[34]

It seems clear that once compilations reached the stage of preparing the printing blocks, the expense of turning out individual copies—paper, ink, labor,—was small enough to facilitate adequate distribution to offices but not small enough to allow any extravagant surplus of copies or to allow a low price relative to the means of the average private purchaser.

To take again as an example the 1845 edition of the *Complete Book on the Grain Tribute*, when compilation began in 1828, paper was allocated from the *Yen-liao-k'u* and 3,000 taels were issued for printing expenses. But this sum had been entirely used up by 1845 when the Board had finished its draft. It seems clear that at this time the whole printing process still lay ahead: even if some parts had been printed, the Board still had to prepare the yellow copy for the emperor, buy more printing blocks, pay for their preparation through engraving or typesetting, and meet the other expenses of printing.

Five Chinese months were planned for these tasks. More than 700 copies were to be printed. Each copy consisted of 92 *chüan* (chapters) and 46 *ts'e* (volumes); copies were to be sent to offices in some half-dozen provinces. Yet all these expenses lying ahead required only 1,600 taels (exclusive of paper), little more than 2 taels per copy. This figure is probably realistic, because this sum was personally donated by the editorial officials, and it is not likely that they would have reported their contribution as less than it was.[35]

When the 1851 edition of the *Regulations of the Board of*

32. *HPTL, tsou-che*:11b–12. The *fan-yin* probably is the item mentioned in *HPTL*, 74:15.

33. *TYCS, tsou-che*: 2b.

34. *Ch'in-ting hsin-tsuan liu-pu ch'u-fen tse-li* (1828), *tzu-wen*: 1–2.

35. *TYCS, tsou-che*:2b, 6b–7.

Revenue was coming out, the Board pointed out that in the past, 12 taels were counted per copy to meet the costs of paper and of printing each individual copy, but that this sum had proved to exceed the actual expenses.[36] In 1828, 6.848 taels was charged by the Board of Civil Officials for the cost of printing one copy of *Regulations on Administrative Punishment.*[37] Certainly this was not a great sum by governmental standards, but the case of this book illustrates that the government sought to avoid printing too many copies: quotas (up to 60 copies) were set up for each province, but extra copies could be requested. By private standards, 6 taels was definitely a large sum; from Lin Tse-hsü's estimate in 1839, we know that 6 taels was a sixth of the sum required to maintain one person of the higher classes fairly comfortably for one year. Data from the last half of the nineteenth century indicate that law books were expensive relative to many other books (for instance, a particular edition of the *Classic of Poetry* cost 3 taels in 1875, but many books were cheaper). Many officials could easily afford to buy some expensive books annually, but many struggling candidates for office could not.[38]

Besides setting up a staff and arranging finances, compilers, following a widespread Ch'ing bureaucratic habit, established a fixed time limit for the project. The limit in the eighteenth century for a penal code *hsiao-hsiu* (compilation of the new batch of regulations) was set at ten Chinese months.[39] For the 1768 *ta-hsiu* (total revision), this limit was increased to fourteen Chinese months, and the work of revision was finished on time, although the last section of the *huang-ts'e* (yellow copy) of the revised regulations was presented to the throne a couple of Chinese months after the deadline. Other work such as translating the Chinese text into Manchu and the final printing was not included in the time limit.[40]

Lateness, as a censor complained in 1830, was all too common, and time extensions were often granted. The Board of Revenue had a one-year limit to prepare its 1838 *hsiao-hsiu* but then received another four Chinese months for further checking

36. *HPTL, tsou-che*:11b–12.
37. *Ch'in-ting hsin-tsuan liu-pu ch'u-fen tse-li* (1828), *tzu-wen*:2.
38. *Chung-kuo chin-tai ching-chi ssu-hsiang . . .*, p. 45. Chang Te-ch'ang, pp. 106–107, p. 156. On officials' incomes, see IV, 3, c.
39. *TCLL, tsou-shu*:23.
40. *TCLL, tsou-shu*:26–29.

before presenting the yellow copy to the throne.[41] The two-year limit granted for the *Liang-huai Salt Laws Gazetteer* of 1806 could not be met, according to the salt commissioner, who was the editorial director, not only because of the time required to go through over fifty years of complex records but also because of time spent in gathering information from offices spread out in the six provinces to which Liang-huai salt was shipped. When the salt commissioner asked the Board of Revenue for a time extension, he was turned down. He then continued work for more than a year without any authorized time extension, and when he finally memorialized about the delay, he requested a few more months for "minute rechecking" to catch "omissions and mistakes." Because of the delay, he cancelled his intention of asking for administrative awards for those probationary officials who had donated their funds and services to the project.[42]

The many delays involved in preparing the *Regulations of the Board of Revenue* of 1851 suggest still more vividly some of the pressures faced by editors. This edition turned out to be a *ta-hsiu* of 72 *ts'e* (volumes), in contrast to the 6 volumes of the 1838 *hsiao-hsiu*. This may not have been the original intention, however, because at first the editors requested merely the same time limit of one year and the same quota of twenty-two compiling clerks which had been established for the 1838 *hsiao-hsiu*.[43]

Beginning work on August 14, 1848, they memorialized on September 20, 1849, that the deadline could not be met mainly because of the great number of records and the need to fix discrepancies between some treasury regulations and current practice. Finding that precedents (*ch'eng-an*) on *ta-hsiu* time extensions varied from about half a year to a year, they asked for another year and ten more compiling clerks.[44]

On September 10, 1850, a second time extension of four Chinese months was granted. The trouble this time was that earlier in 1850, Wang Ch'ing-yün (1798–1862), the famous compiler of the fiscal essay *Shih-ch'ü yü-chi* and then in the Supervisorate of Imperial Instruction, had memorialized asking

41. *Ch'in-ting hu-pu tse-li* (1838), *tsou-shu*:4a–b. *Ch'in-ting li-pu tse-li* (1843), *yüan-tsou*:1b.

42. *LHYFC*, *tsou-che*:5–7.

43. *HPTL*, *tsou-che*:2b–3.

44. *HPTL*, *tsou-che*:4–5.

that cases not found in the established regulations but possibly useful for analogizing or quoting as precedents be sorted through to separate out redundant and mistaken ones. Besides this added task, a new president and vice-president had just been appointed to the Board and needed time to go over the regulations.[45]

On about January 28, 1851, a third time extension of forty days was granted. Work had been completed and the yellow copy prepared within the second extension, but on December 31, 1850, an edict had been sent to the Grand Secretariat ordering that a stop be put to certain corrupt practices at the Board of Revenue's treasury. This had led to a change in Board regulations which still had to be entered into the yellow copy. (This episode illustrates the emphasis on being current.) The yellow copy was finally presented for imperial endorsement on March 13, 1851, and, despite the delays, the thirty-two compiling clerks received administrative rewards.[46]

Establishing deadlines was not always scrupulously carried out, however. Imperial permission to compile the 1845 edition of the *Complete Book of the Grain Tribute* was given in 1829 with the understanding that establishment of a deadline was to be postponed until all copies of relevant records from offices such as the director-general of the grain tribute and the *ts'ang-ch'ang shih-lang* (granary superintendents in the capital area) had been sent to the Board of Revenue. It seems, however, that a deadline never was set until the last minute. When, ten years later, a censor memorialized that the book was still unfinished, the Board explained that it had been forced to wait for various offices adequately to report on their records. Moreover, the more time needed, the greater the turnover in the compiling staff, creating further delays. Finally in 1844 the heads of the Board decided that compilation had to be promptly finished, and, selecting officials experienced in grain tribute matters from that subbureau in the Board specializing in these matters (the Yunnan Department), the heads ordered them to finish the job. By early 1845 compilation had been completed, and a time limit of five Chinese months was then set for preparing the yellow copy, printing, and distribution.[47]

45. *HPTL, tsou-che*:6b. For Wang Ch'ing-yün, see Hummel, II: 813–814.
46. *HPTL, tsou-che*:8b–12b.
47. *TYCS, tsou-che*:2b–4b; 6b–7.

Once a yellow copy was completed, procedures varied a little with regard to receiving an imperial endorsement, printing, and distributing. Another office might be asked to check the compilation before imperial endorsement was given. In the case of the *Liang-huai Salt Laws Gazetteer* of 1806, a "secondary copy" was sent to the Board of Revenue "according to precedent."[48] When the emperor in 1882 ordered the Board of Revenue to check a secondary copy of the new *Szechwan Salt Laws Gazetteer* later sent to it by the Szechwan governor-general, the Board took more than four months before memorializing in reply. Excusing the delay on the grounds that so many old cases had had to be examined, the Board rejected the margin of freedom used by the gazetteer in giving the number of salt wells. Since this number constantly varied as new wells were opened and old ones gave out, the gazetteer editors had tried to give themselves a margin of flexibility through indefiniteness about the tax status of a small number of wells. The Board, however, insisted that the tax status of every well be clarified.[49]

A regular problem with the penal code was that offices needed the revised regulations as soon as they were imperially endorsed and could not wait a year until publication by one of the "halls" in the palace area (*Wu-ying-tien*). The procedure for the 1779 total revision was as follows. On January 11, 1777, the Board of Punishments memorialized to begin the edition with a time limit of twelve Chinese months and on the same day received the emperor's approval. (It was common for capital offices to receive imperial replies the same day they memorialized.) The Board then began to prepare a unified, up-to-date text of the *t'iao-li* (penal regulations), combining the text in the last totally revised code, that of 1768, with all subsequent material, that is, the regulations put out in the 1772 *hsiao-hsiu* (edition of the new batch of regulations) and selected post-1772 imperial commands.

This was done in such a way as to permit maximum use of the old printing blocks. If only a few characters had to be added or excised in the old regulation, the change was merely explained in a note at the foot of the old regulation. If there was a change in the severity of punishment or some other difference between the old and the new regulation, both the old and the

48. *LHYFC, tsou-che*: 8a–b.
49. *Ssu-ch'uan yen-fa-chih, tsou-shu*: 5b–6.

new regulation were printed in full, and above each in yellow characters was written either "revised" or "added" (probably "canceled" was also used). Of course some entirely novel regulations also were added. All this was in the Chinese language, not Manchu.

Missing the deadline by only a few months, the Board memorialized on March 11, 1778, that editing was completed, and that it was presenting the yellow copy of revised regulations in Chinese to the throne. When this was imperially endorsed, the Board itself printed a *ts'ao-pen* (draft copy) of the revised regulations in Chinese for distribution to offices at and outside the capital. At the same time, the Board had to translate the endorsed revised regulations into Manchu and prepare for the emperor's perusal a yellow copy with both Manchu and Chinese texts.

After this latter text was imperially endorsed, the Board for the first time prepared a complete version of the code, one including the *lü* (statutes). This also was in both Chinese and Manchu and was finished on April 19, 1779, some time after the yellow copy of regulations in Chinese had first been endorsed. Only then was a *yang-pen* (model copy) of the code prepared and sent for printing to the *Wu-ying-tien*. This model copy was in both Chinese and Manchu, but many copies printed by the *Wu-ying-tien* must have been only in Chinese.[50] Probably, if new and relevant imperial executive decisions appeared before printing at the *Wu-ying-tien* began, they could still be worked into the text.

Another example of the need to rush publication is the *Regulations of the Board of Revenue* of 1851. This example also shows that imperial endorsement could take five or more months. The Board had presented a yellow copy to the emperor on March 13, 1851, and was still waiting for imperial endorsement when it received requests for the new regulations from a number of capital offices. Therefore on August 23, 1851, the Board requested and received the emperor's permission to print copies on the basis of its own *ti-pen* (basic or original manuscript) without waiting for the imperial endorsement of the yellow copy.[51]

Whether a law took effect the day that the emperor approved

50. *TCLL, tsou-shu*:32–38.
51. *HPTL, tsou-che*:13–14.

it, the day that it was formally communicated to the office involved, or on a date explicitly set forth for that particular law is a complicated question. A *lü* (penal statute) inherited from the Ming period states: "In all cases *lü* begin [to take effect] the day on which they are promulgated." Commenting on this, Hsüeh Yün-sheng states: "As for the penal regulations (*t'iao-li*), in some instances a proposal is made [and imperially accepted] as to what year they will begin; in some instances after the text arrives [at the yamen in question] the month and day on which it will take effect is determined, and it is carried out from that date on."[52]

Presumably the day on which the text of a penal regulation arrived at the office of a governor or governor-general was often the day on which it took effect for all practical purposes in a particular province. On the other hand, there is evidence that officials could feel that a law had been changed before they received a copy of the new law. Thus officials who knew that a certain new book of regulations had already been imperially endorsed and printed but who had not yet received a copy could argue that the old laws had been changed and be confused as to what the law currently was.[53]

In penal law, officials also had other timing problems: there were degrees of promulgation (a precedent might merely have been approved by the emperor or might already have been "entered" into the penal code); and there was the problem of choosing between the date of an offense or the date of the trial as the criterion of applicability.[54] Interestingly, in the case of administrative orders, a sense of urgency on the part of an official in the field apparently could lead him to act on a proposal sent to the emperor without waiting for the emperor's explicit approval.[55] However, I have not found such an example of

52. *TLti,* 5:43.

53. *Ch'in-ting li-pu tse-li* (1843), *yüan-tsou*:1b.

54. If the offense was committed before a new *t'iao-li* (penal regulation) was "fixed" (i.e., formally promulgated) while the trial was held after promulgation, the old regulation applied unless (a) the new regulation specified a lighter sentence, or (b) the new regulation included specification of the date on which it was to take effect, and this date preceded sentencing. See *TCLL,* 5:51; *TLti,* 5:43; Philastre, I:275. This law illustrates a significant *lü* amendment in the third rather than the second edition of the code.

55. *TYT,* 43:10–13 is an example. The Nanking governor-general and the director-general of the Kiang-nan waterways in late 1832

jumping the gun in the case of administrative *regulations.*

As for circulation, revisions of the penal code were normally supposed to go to all offices trying cases (*wen-hsing ya-men*).[56] We have seen that more than 700 copies of the 1845 edition of the *Complete Book of the Grain Tribute* were planned. Regarding the previous edition of this book, that finished in 1812, there is a list of offices which were to be issued one copy each. Copies were too expensive to be lavishly distributed to offices with only a slight need for them. Not all officials connected to the Peking and Tungchow granaries received them, but the director-general of the grain tribute and any censor charged with checking the grain tribute got copies. In all provinces with grain tribute quotas, copies were issued to the governor-general, governor, provincial treasurer, grain taotai, and prefectural, district, and departmental magistrates.[57]

The list of offices which received copies of the *Regulations of the Board of Revenue* (1851) was extensive: most or all impor-

---

had received two edicts ordering them to undertake a certain dredging project at this opportune moment when the waterways in question were practically dry. They memorialized within a few days that they would act promptly, asking the emperor to order the Board of Revenue to transfer to them 400,000 taels for this purpose, the emperor having already stated that this sum was the maximum permissible. Also they said in their memorial that, rather than wait for the arrival of these 400,000 taels, they "did not dare stick blindly [to regulations]" and would begin work immediately by advancing funds originally assigned to other purposes. All this was concurred in later by the Board of Revenue and the emperor. The one point here is that while they knew that the emperor approved the project and the sum of 400,000 taels, they began work before learning specifically that the emperor also approved transferring the specific funds to them from other offices. These transfers were necessary because, as they stated, the treasury of the waterway administration lacked the money. Confident that the emperor would back the project although it required funds from other offices, they moved ahead by transferring funds on their own responsibility in advance of the emperor's reply.

56. See, e.g., *TCLL*, *tsou-shu*:45.

57. *TYCS*, *tsou-che*:1b. Among the offices over the Peking and Tungchow granaries, only the granary superintendents and the *tso-liang-t'ing* (granary supervisors) were included, not the officials (*ts'ang-ch'ang chien-tu*) over the individual granaries (although they each supervised some eighty 10,000-*shih* bins or more) nor the *ch'a-ts'ang yü-shih* (granary censors). The latter two kinds of officials were explicitly singled out as not due to receive copies.

tant yamen at the capital, including such unlikely offices as the Bureau for Compilation of the Veritable Records, the Imperial Household, and the lieutenant generals of the eight banners; and governors-general, governors, Tartar generals, the governor of Peking, heads of salt zones, customs heads, provincial treasurers, provincial judges, taotais, prefects, departmental and district magistrates, offices heading subprefectures (or at least independent *t'ing*), and *wei* and *so*, the military units which were used to ship the grain tribute.[58]

In the case of the 1828 edition of the *Regulations on Administrative Punishment*, copies appear to have been initially distributed to all capital offices (including the lieutenant generals of the eight banners), and in the provinces to governors-general, governors, heads of salt zones, provincial directors of education, provincial judges, and provincial treasurers. The Board of Civil Officials itself paid for these copies. Offices of taotai or less which needed copies had to furnish 6.848 taels per copy. Quotas of copies were set up for the provinces, but extra copies could be requested. Provinces with many offices—including Shansi, Honan, and Shensi—had quotas of sixty copies each; provinces with fewer offices—including Hunan—had quotas of thirty copies each. In the past, the stimulus for distribution had partly been with the recipient offices, but this time the emperor ordered that the latter must quickly ask for copies. Offices in the provinces of taotai or less were given a three-month deadline, beginning with notification that the new edition had been imperially endorsed, to send officials to the Board of Civil Officials to obtain copies.[59]

In a few cases, besides editions published by the state, compilations were published by private bookstores. Two late nineteenth-century private editions—one of the penal code,[60] the other of the regulations on administrative punishment—state that government editions of their respective units of law were adequately circulated to offices but not easily accessible to private individuals. The editors of the latter, whose book was published in 1887, also state that while editions of the penal code put out by capital bookstores kept up with revisions issued by the state, private editions of the regulations on administra-

58. *HPTL*, *tsou-che*: 11b; 13b–14.

59. *Ch'in-ting hsin-tsuan li-pu ch'u-fen tse-li* (1828), *tzu-wen*: 1–2.

60. *Shinkoku gyōseihō*, I: 21. Also in *Ch'ing-kuo hsing-cheng-fa*, 1:2:2:24–25.

tive punishment had become out of date. According to them, "The state's books of laws are distributed to large and small offices where they are diligently kept and respectfully followed. But they cannot be taken along and studied constantly at will by expectant officials and travelers of uncertain whereabouts. Therefore bookstore editions are widely used. However when they are not revised for a long time, mistakes are passed along to the point that remote and rude places which hear little of the outside world still use old regulations, which is enough to mislead men and ruin affairs."[61]

Referring to the careful study of books of laws by expectant officials, this passage is one hint that these books were not only adequately distributed but also carefully used. T'ung-tsu Ch'ü has shown that a "thorough" understanding of the penal code was beyond most officials, even one who "studied law intensively for a period of eight months . . ."[62] However, eight months is not a long time, and one must take into account degrees of thoroughness. Wang Hui-tsu (1731–1807), himself famous as a private secretary specializing primarily in judicial matters, said that a local magistrate's grasp of the code need not be so thorough as that of a private secretary, but that it was both feasible and vital for a local magistrate to grasp the essentials of those parts of the code involved in cases heard before him. These essentials, Wang held, could be grasped "in some months" by a magistrate who studied an article or two whenever he had some spare time.[63]

There were a *lü* (penal statute) and a *tse-li* (regulation) identically holding that if an official could not explain any part of the penal code when he was examined by his superior at the end of the year, he was fined one Chinese month's salary. In an edict of 1742, the Ch'ien-lung emperor refers to a proposal by the Board of Civil Officials to eliminate this requirement:

> [The Board] says that "officials at the capital and outside all have to manage the affairs connected to their own offices. The items of the penal code are very many, and so it is hard to hold all sorts of officials responsible for understanding them all thoroughly. Henceforth the regulation on officials

61. *CFTL, hsü*:1–2.

62. Ch'ü T'ung-tsu, *Local Government in China under the Ch'ing* (Cambridge, Mass., 1962), pp. 127, 280.

63. *HCCSWP*, 22:4.

> thoroughly understanding the *lü-li*, with the Board of Civil Officials receiving a report and keeping a record on the matter, should be eliminated. We should only retain the article requiring clerks to grasp the whole code." We think that the *lü-li* are pertinent to administration. Take an official at a board's department. If it is said that he is unable completely to understand the *lü-li* classified relative to each of the six boards, that is permissible. But if he is utterly ignorant of how to manage matters relative to the *lü-li* of his own department in his own board and can only delegate them to a clerk, is this right?[64]

It was recognized that a good grasp of the regulations took experience. A regulation held:

> In the case of preparing drafts of joint memorials at the six boards or certain capital offices, care must be taken to hand the matter over to an official who has been at the subbureau in question for many years and is skilled in the *lü-li* (penal code) and to order him to manage it. When an official has first been appointed to the office he ought to be ordered to undertake this matter only after a year, when he is somewhat versed in the affairs of his board. If perhaps he has not yet been there a year but actually is able to manage the matter without error, then he can be assigned to it, but only by the office's head officials; only then can he be permitted to manage it completely. If a particular department puts in charge an unskilled official who has just been appointed to the board and a mistake occurs, the Chinese and the Manchu department directors are to be fined one year's salary.[65]

The skill with which officials used regulations is of course connected to the whole problem of career specialization. Some scholars have exaggerated the "amateurism" of "Confucian bureaucrats." Amateurism was partly a problem, but respect for specialized bureaucratic knowledge was deeply rooted. A

64. *TLti*, 8:1; *TCLL*, 7:1; Philastre, I:321; *CFTL*, 14:3a–b.
65. *CFTL*, 14:11. It is reasonable to suppose that in this article *lü-li* could be loosely interpreted as *lü-ling* to refer to regulations generally.

systematic discussion of this question is beyond our scope, but some basic points should be made.

On the level of ideology, I argued in the first chapter that Ch'ing bureaucratic values included not only distinctly Confucian ideas but also Legalist ones, as well as an attitude of bureaucratic realism. Moreover, while Confucius' statement that "The true gentleman is not a utensil" undoubtedly inhibited the tendency to specialization, the principle of long tenure in a single post, put forward in the classic *Book of History*, was used at times to legitimate specialization.[66] Various examples of a conscious emphasis on specialized experience have been given in this chapter, such as the above law requiring that certain board matters be handled only by experienced officials; the large role, in the preparation of the *Complete Book of the Grain Tribute* (1845), of that subbureau in the Board of Revenue specializing in grain tribute affairs; the Liang-huai salt commissioner's emphasis on recruiting persons with knowledge of salt affairs for compilation of the *Salt Laws Gazetteer of the Liang-huai Zone* (1806); and the decision in 1739 to shift compilation of the *Regulations of the Board of Civil Officials* out of the *Lü-li-kuan* (Bureau for the compilation of the penal code) into the hands of the Board of Civil Officials, because personnel in the latter office had more knowledge about the matters in question. Such examples are commonplace in Ch'ing documents, as any student of them can testify.

A second aspect of specialization was the actual stress on training. In 1850 the Board of Punishments had about 167 *o-wai ssu-yüan* (departmental officials outside the regular quota of officials) attached to it; the Board of Revenue, about 148; the Board of Works, about 93; the Board of War, about 62; the Board of Civil Officials, about 50; the Board of Rites, about 37.[67] Many of these *o-wai ssu-yüan* were *chin-shih,* and many or all of them had been *fen-fa* (respectively dispatched) to the boards for training purposes with a possibility of subsequent appointment at the board where they had been trained. This institution of *fen-fa* has roots at least as far back as Ming times.[68] While a three-month term apparently was common in early Ch'ing

66. Legge, *Chinese Classics,* I:150 (*Confucian Analects*); *ibid.,* III:50 (*The Shoo King*); *HCSWP,* 17:2.

67. See the fall 1850 issue of *Ta-Ch'ing chin-shen ch'üan-shu,* discussed in II, 4, note 75.

68. Ch'ien Mu, *Kuo-shih ta-kang,* II:489–492.

times, nineteenth-century sources refer to three years at one board. Teaching methods clearly involved questioning, testing, and the delegation of minor responsibilities.[69]

A third aspect was the search for persons with specialized experience to fill certain offices. Officials were often brought by the laws of avoidance into localities unfamiliar to them, but they could stay there long enough to acquire familiarity. In 1831 T'ao Chu stressed that the post of Hsüchow prefect was difficult and required an able man familiar with the area; he recommended someone who had already been stationed in Kiangsu for some five years and was experienced in policing and in hurrying along grain tribute boats—matters vital at Hsüchow.

In 1838, the Liang-huai salt controller was leaving to mourn the death of a parent, and T'ao Chu was ordered to recommend and guarantee one of his subordinates for the post. T'ao then complained that among the taotais and prefects under him, although not a few were able, none was experienced in salt affairs, and there was a tendency to shun this salt post as a dangerous one, the monopoly then being in difficulty. T'ao mentioned a Kiangsi prefect who had been Kiangsi salt taotai on an acting basis, but T'ao Chu felt that his experience still was too narrow, even though Kiangsi was a Liang-huai market. Next, T'ao thought of an able official who had been in charge of the entire complicated process of salt repacking and shipment at I-cheng—indeed a pivotal aspect of Liang-huai—but unfortuately he had just been appointed to another post outside Liang-huai. The head of the Huai-pei salt production yards (also part of Liang-huai) was T'ao Chu's next thought, since this man, who eventually did become Liang-huai salt controller, had proved his worth in successfully administering the new ticket system of the Huai-pei salt monopoly. However, the jump from this job to that of salt controller was regarded as too great, and the ticket system still needed his experienced hand. T'ao finally recommended a man distinguished partly for experience in salt affairs gained at the Shantung Department of the Board of Revenue, that department which specialized in the salt affairs of the whole empire.[70]

69. *HCCSWP*, 17:12–14; *HPTL*, 72:27; *TCHT*, 7:6a–b.

70. *TYT*, 31:28a–b; *TWI*, 18:43b–44. About 25% of all promotions from provincial treasurer to governor in 1796–1908 were intraprovincial, according to Wei Hsiu-mei.

A fourth aspect of specialization was the practice of keeping an official for a long time within the same board or even within the same department of a board. An early Ch'ing writer praised the Ming for adopting this practice around 1570. He said that this practice had been dropped in later Ming times but resumed in early Ch'ing times.[71] Li Fu (1675–1750), an acting vice-president of the Board of Civil Officials around 1723, memorialized around 1740 asking that departmental officials be promoted within the same department; if they proved excellent as a head of a department, they could continue for a long time in that position while being given the salary and honorary title of a vice-president or president.[72]

In fact there existed a large quota of departmental posts in the capital which were supposed to be filled by officials transferred within the same office or even department. At the Board of Civil Officials, neither the Department of Grants nor the Record Department had any posts in this quota, but in the crucial Department of Selections, which handled appointments and transfers, eleven of the seventeen posts were in this quota, and in the equally crucial Department for the Scrutiny of Merits, which handled the mild disciplinary punishments of civil officials (*ch'u-fen*), seven of the eleven.[73]

This does not mean, admittedly, that these seven posts in the Department for the Scrutiny of Merits always in practice could be filled this way. Taking a random sample of some 132 persons who had careers in the Department for the Scrutiny of Merits from 1846 through 1894, we can determine a minimum of seventeen careers on this staff involving one or more promotions to the upper from the lower of the three regular rungs of the Department. One example is that of Lin Shih-chün: by 1835 he was a "beyond the quota" trainee at the Board; by 1838

71. *HCCSWP*, 17:1, 2. Jen Yüan-hsiang here refers to a Ming law enacted just a couple of years before Chang Chü-cheng's term as chief grand secretary (1572–1582), during which Chang also, at least in one reform proposal, stressed that the path of effective administration was "specialization in one's duties." See Shen Ming-chang, *Ming-tai cheng-chih-shih* (A political history of the Ming dynasty; 1967), p. 195. In parts of the Ming, there was a striking emphasis on long tenure. Besides Parsons' statistics, see T'ao Hsi-sheng and Shen Jen-yüan, *Ming Ch'ing cheng-chih chih-tu* (Ming and Ch'ing governmental institutions; Taipei, 1967), pp. 200–201.

72. *HCCSWP*, 15:9.

73. *TCHT*, 8:3–5b.

he was on the lowest regular rung of the Department for the Scrutiny of Merits (*chu-shih*); by 1846 he had become one of the four department directors (*lang-chung*); and he stayed in this position at least through 1857.

Lin Shih-chün's career was outstanding. Yet there were other cases, such as that of Hsüeh Yün-sheng, who, beginning in 1869, spent about twenty years at the Board of Punishments.[74] Moreover this sample of 132 officials shows that a good number of them were in the Department long enough to acquire considerable specialized knowledge. Because the data involve some methodological problems, I have used them with a conservative bias. Apart from any time spent as a "beyond-the-quota" official on a training basis, a little more than 24 percent of these 132 careers on the regular staff of the Department lasted four years or more, and almost 50 percent lasted two years or more. (A little more than 50 percent lasted only about one year.) More specifically, 69 officials had careers on this staff lasting about one year; 21, two years; 10, three years; 6, four years; 9, five years; 7, six years; 3, seven years; 1, eight years; 1, nine years; and 5, ten, fourteen, sixteen, nineteen, and twenty years, respectively.[75]

74. On Hsüeh, see II, 2, note 11. Also note Li Tz'u-ming's career in IV, 3, c.

75. I have obtained these data mostly from *Ta-Ch'ing chin-shen ch'üan-shu* (Complete book of persons with governmental status of the great Ch'ing dynasty), a periodical which came out as a rule four times a year with information, culled from sources like the *Peking Gazette,* about the names of those filling regular posts as well as of others with governmental affiliations, such as the *o-wai* (beyond the quota) personnel. In a few cases I have also used data from a similar periodical, *Chüeh-chih ch'üan-shu* (Complete book of persons with official rank). Both kinds of books are at the Harvard-Yenching Library. There are enough data in them to answer many questions about career paths in the Ch'ing bureaucracy. In some cases issues for consecutive years are not at this library. I have used one issue for each of the following 33 years: 1846w, 1850f, 1851su, 1852f, 1854w, 1855f, 1856su, 1857sp, 1859w, 1861, 1864f, 1866su, 1867su, 1868w, 1870su, 1871su, 1872sp, 1873f, 1874su, 1876su, 1877sp, 1878su, 1879f, 1884f, 1885su, 1886su, 1888f, 1889f, 1890f, 1891su, 1892su, 1893su, and 1894f. For one name, Lin Shih-chün, I have also used issues of 1835sp, 1838sp, 1840f, and 1842f. The letters after the dates indicate whether the issue in question was that of spring, summer, fall, or winter. The temporal irregularities lead to certain biases which seem to balance out on the conservative side. For instance, the 1846 issue yields seven one-year careers;

Data about other posts similarly indicate that long tenure in a post was a common Ch'ing phenomenon, although it was also common for tenure to be so brief as to preclude the possibility of developing specialized experience. Average tenure (sometimes discontinuous) as a member of the Grand Council was six and a half years, and many members served ten years or more (see IV, 1). Average tenure in the post of local magistrate appears to have been some two years or more, and terms of five to ten years were far from rare (see IV, 3, c, Table 1).

Admittedly, long tenure does not necessarily indicate expertise. A Mongol, Pai-ying, who retired in about 1872 with some twenty years of service in the Department for the Scrutiny of Merits, may or may not have held his post as a sinecure. It is also relevant to note that of the eleven posts, only four were reserved for Han Chinese (one was for a Mongol, six, for Manchus). Yet even if many Manchus lacked classical erudition, they may well have been expertly practical in Department affairs. Another major point is that in a department consisting of a number of officials cooperatively and on a full-time basis specializing in just one kind of public business—namely administration of the laws on disciplinary punishments for civil officials—learning conditions were superior to those in the office of a local magistrate, where one official with one private secretary had to handle legal cases while also being caught up in a variety of other public business.

One significant piece of evidence suggests that widespread familiarity with the penal code existed at least on a superficial level among officials: no simple and fully explicit system of article headings was developed to make references to the code. Not only was there no unmistakably clear numbering system which, say, would have allowed one to speak of *li* Number 5 under *lü* Number 251, but officials did not even bother to quote the article titles used in the code. For instance, *shih-ch'a ch'in-*

---

without doubt I could have seen that some of these careers were longer if I had had the issues for 1845, 1847, 1848, and 1849. On the other hand, some of these careers may have lasted only a few months. I also assume that if a name is in, say, the 1861 and 1864 issues (and in no others), the individual spent a total of three years in the Department. Although he might have been absent in 1862 and 1863, such cases of discontinuous careers were rare (I found one). In a couple of dubious cases (e.g., the name was printed unclearly), I have made a few other insignificant assumptions.

tao (lack of vigilance leading to fraudulent appropriation or robbery) refers to a *lü* whose title in the code is given as *ch'ien-liang hu-hsiang chüeh-ch'a* (officials and other personnel attached to granaries and treasuries are mutually to watch each other). It is true, however, that commentators sometimes took pains to explain what *li* was referred to in various references mentioning a *li* vaguely.

This informal method of identifying penal articles cannot be ascribed to a general lack of interest in the problem of reference. For instance, edicts responding to the points made in a memorial typically quote the memorial at length if not in full in order to avoid any misunderstanding as to which document and issues are involved. The casualness used in memorials to refer to articles in the penal code indicates that such references were clear and that officials knew the code well enough to dispense with a fuller system of reference.

Although we are far from a full understanding balancing negative and positive factors, the importance of written laws as authoritative guides for Ch'ing administrative action is clear. Just for the sake of illustration, two positive examples can be given.

First, in 1831 T'ao Chu, Nanking governor-general, was struggling to stop the illegal flow of salt from the Peking area into the excellent Yangtze market areas. This illegal salt was carried by grain tribute boats returning from the Peking area to the Yangtze valley in order to pick up their next loads of tribute grain. Such boats were on an urgent schedule, and their crews often resisted inspection for illegal salt by warning inspectors not to be responsible for delaying the grain tribute. Even more, they scared off inspectors by citing a regulation saying: "When the tribute boats reach the Yangtze river, it is not permitted to obstruct them and thus disrupt shipments through delays." T'ao Chu, however, insisted that inspection on the Yangtze was proper. He pointed out in a memorial with which the emperor fully agreed:

> I humbly find in the regulations of the grain tribute: "Imperial order of 1765: As for grain tribute boats smuggling salt, when they are in the south, places such as Yangchow, Icheng, Kuachow, and subprefectures for examining grain shipments are all to commission military and civil officials with the exclusive purpose of inspecting the boats." This is

adequate to see that after the boats are on the Yangtze river, they still ought to be strictly inspected.[76]

The second example illustrates the adducing of Ming law in the early Ch'ing period as an authoritative way of properly setting up Ch'ing administration. The issue concerned salt and tax quotas at the Liang-huai zone of the salt monopoly. A particular group of markets altogether had a salt quota of 12,428 *yin* (units of salt) and a tax quota due on these *yin* of a bit more than 50,913 taels. The question was whether these figures were merely part of the total regular Liang-huai salt and tax quotas or whether they were outside the latter.

In a memorial of 1658, the Board of Revenue indicated that they were outside. This meant that they had not been paid since the beginning of the dynasty in 1644, because the Liang-huai officials had been delivering merely the regular Liang-huai totals. The emperor suspected corruption on their part, but the Board sought no punitive action. It sought merely to demonstrate that added quotas were due and should henceforth be paid.

The regional officials at Liang-huai at first insisted that there were no added quotas, referring to a "book on salt laws published at the end of the Ming dynasty" for corroboration. The Board asked, what book? The Liang-huai head referred to "the ten-point memorial presented by the Board of Revenue in 1616 at the end of the Ming and currently included in *Shu-li ch'eng-pien* (Writings on putting order into salt affairs)," and said that "chapter three, page 11" of the latter showed that the amounts in question were inside the regular Liang-huai totals. The Board then closed the discussion by replying that "generally in all salt affairs, the *Yen-fa-k'ao* (Study of salt laws) is the correct basis," and that "chapter two, page 123" of the latter stated that the figures in question were outside the regular Liang-huai totals.[77]

This was a somewhat arbitrary decision. The passage cited by the Liang-huai head[78] admittedly was only part of a memo-

76. *TYT*, 32:33. T'ao Chu seems to have been paraphrasing a regulation in *TYCS*, 83:18b, although his format indicates a direct quotation.

77. *LHYFC*, 7:4–6.

78. It is found in *Huang-Ming Ching-shih wen-pien*, 29:335, which reprints an edition different from that used by the Liang-huai

rial of the Ming Board of Revenue the proposals of which were to a large extent not realized. In the passage involved, however, the Ming Board of Revenue was referring to a record of salt laws which it regarded as authoritative. At any rate, the Ming *Yen-fa-k'ao* was often relied on in early Ch'ing times, and there also are enough references to Ch'ing salt gazetteers in Ch'ing documents for us to view these gazetteers as the authoritative handbooks of the salt monopoly. For instance, in 1835 the Nanking governor-general defended his system of physically packing in each salt bag more than that weight unit which served as the official unit for fiscal purposes and then adding the proportionate amount of taxes on that bag, a system called *p'ei-ko.* He memorialized: "This is indeed an old Liang-huai salt zone regulation of our dynasty for the last two hundred years, a regulation entered into the salt gazetteers and the records of the Board of Revenue. It is not a change your minister brought about, a term he created."[79]

Emphasis on observing administrative laws had at least four dimensions. First, administrative law was a way of resolving bureaucratically internal disputes, such as that above between the Board of Revenue and the head of Liang-huai, in a neutral, conciliatory way. Second, by insisting on the letter of the law, an official could demonstrate his dedication to the interests of the emperor. Third, organizational efficiency demanded at least some observance of law. And fourth, law was regarded as both a check on and a tool of the emperor's power. Going back at least to early books like *Kuan-tzu,* there was an idea that the law checked the arbitrariness of the ruler, and even in Ch'ing times, the *ch'ao* (court) was viewed officially as following the law.[80] On the other hand, the ruler used law to realize his wishes. Even more, since respect for law was in his interest, giving the law primacy over his own commands was a way for

---

head. In the latter, the passage is in *chüan* 3, p. 11, while in ours, it is in *chüan* 3, p. 15.

79. *TWI,* 16:19b. See also *TWI,* 16:31; *TYT,* 40:17b; 52:32; *LHYFC,* 21:13, 16b, 17, 24b. See III, 5. For *p'ei-ko,* see p. 60.

80. See Introduction, note 12. Besides *Kuan-tzu's* famous principle that both ruler and subjects should follow the law, the explicit concept of law as a check on the ruler's arbitrariness also existed. See *Huai-nan-tzu* (Ssu-pu pei-yao), 9:13. Also cited in Yang Hung-lieh, *Chung-kuo fa-lü ssu-hsiang-shih* (A history of Chinese legal thought; Taipei, 1964), II:93.

the ruler or despot to increase his *overall* power. Both respect for law and a cunning appreciation of it are reflected in the following fascinating edict issued in 1724 by the Yung-cheng emperor to the grand secretaries and the Nine Ministries:

> Previously, with regard to the matter of the lieutenant whose term of office was up, a matter memorialized on by the Board of War, We did not inquire into the *ting-li* (fixed regulations) and sent down an edict containing a mistake. At that time the grand councillors ought immediately to have set forth the issue in detail and so prevented Us from making a mistake. Now fortunately We have understood the fixed regulations before the edict was promulgated. If We had understood the matter too late, there would have been no alternative but to recall the already-issued edict and change the procedure. This would have greatly harmed the *cheng-t'i* (proper order of administration). Our late father was on the throne for more than sixty years. He was thoroughly skilled in all the various affairs of administration. But We lived for many years on Our estate. Although there this nothing We do not understand about the conditions of the world and about what is desirable and undesirable in the realms of both true principle and practical affairs, We cannot, because of Our brief experience, be compared with Our departed father in Our knowledge of those affairs of state involving the fixed regulations. The responsibility for coming to Our aid by rectifying Our mistakes is thus definitely yours. We have repeatedly sent down edicts stating that the ruler and his ministers in their relationship are like one body. Even when the ruler cannot accept the views of his subordinates, they still ought to devote themselves with all their hearts to him, presenting their views without reservation. Not to mention the fact that since We have ascended the throne, We have vigorously warned against the corrupt habit of obsequiously agreeing with whatever We say. Diligently and sincerely aid Our person through correcting Us—that is what We expect of you. [As Tzu-kung, the disciple of Confucius, said:] "The faults of the true gentleman are like the eclipses of the sun and moon. When he has a fault, men all see it. When he corrects it, men all look up to him." In Our character there is no reluctance to correct Our faults. If We Ourselves know We are wrong, then even in the great

court full of people We clearly explain the matter and correct it. We have never tried to hide or gloss over Our faults. Now with regard to the edict We sent down about the lieutenant whose term of office was up—you are completely familiar with the *ch'eng-li* (established regulations) and have had long experience in the handling of state affairs. You can hardly have failed to know that We happened to make a mistake. Yet as always you took the attitude of either obsequiously agreeing with Us or saying nothing. Whether We are right or wrong, you let Us act without speaking up—what a small-minded way to serve Us! Hereafter you should all deeply regret your past error and ponder the great principle that ruler and ministers are like one body. With utmost sincerity and utmost effort to think about the problems at hand, humbly assist Us in realizing Our innermost intentions.[81]

In this edict, the Yung-cheng emperor hardly views law as a check on his own power, but he does genuinely view it as an independently existing body of institutions with which his decisions should accord. He feels that he as emperor has not himself created these institutions but rather must learn about them, and that these institutions are a standard relative to which at least some of his actions can be objectively judged as either right or wrong. Partly because the ruler and his officials share a desire to maintain these institutions, they are like "one body." This edict in effect elucidates the meaning of the statement in the *Ta-Ch'ing hui-tien* (Collected statutes of the great Ch'ing

81. Cited in a different context by Fu Tsung-mao, p. 116. Found in *Ch'ing shih-lu,* Yung-cheng, 24:18–19b. I am indebted to Mr. Zunvair Yue for help in translating some parts of this edict. The Tzu-kung statement is in Legge, *Chinese Classics,* I:346 (*Confucian Analects*). The emperor's version involves a few minor alterations. The emperor's desire here that officials review his orders to discover any mistakes is reminiscent of the procedure called *feng-po* (to seal and return [an imperial order], rejecting it as improper or impractical). More prominent in Han, T'ang, and Sung times, this procedure was at least formally retained by the Ming and Ch'ing governments. *TCHTSL, chüan* 1014, has a section called *feng-po,* the one law in it stating that imperial rescripts were to be sent back by the Censorate if they involved matters "which cannot be conveniently carried out."

dynasty) that these statutes consist of "The duties of offices, what the court and the people respectfully follow."[82]

The question of the ruler's respect for law should also be connected to the notion of *li* (precedent). Phrasing laws as precedents seems to have facilitated legitimation. While various moral reservations were traditionally attached to the concept of law in China, the idea that the ruler and his subjects all should respect precedent seems to have been largely unproblematic. On the one hand, the Confucian mind favored *jen-chih* (governing by relying on men of virtue) over *fa-chih* (governing by relying on laws), but the idea of precedent connoted the approved Confucian processes of following the past and of adducing historical examples in order to guide conduct. On the other hand, while law in the sense of *fa* or *ling* was essentially an order descending from the ruler, the idea of precedent also connoted a standard which could respectfully be adduced as something the emperor should follow. It is true that officials were careful to adduce suitable precedents when making a request from the emperor, but it is also true that one rarely finds the emperor turning down a request backed by precedent. (What Ch'ing emperor would have dared to turn down a request to remit taxes for a flood-stricken district?)

One might say that according to the political logic of the time, the emperor was to some extent bound to respect previous imperial decisions, and the delegated authority of officials in a sense consisted of the responsibility to choose which of these decisions the emperor would be held to. The emperor, in other words, stood ready to honor the prospective and legislative dimension of previous imperial decisions; by contradicting them he would be casting doubt on the authority of the dynasty rather than demonstrating his own power. To put it in a psychological way, the emperor was an authority figure who with routine graciousness and the kindness of a sage was willing to grant requests if they were proper. On the one hand, the official took a supplicatory attitude; on the other, the emperor graciously dispensed "favors" to those supplicating. By showing that his requests accorded with *li* (precedent), the official really was proving that he was acting in accord with *li* (rules of moral propriety) and therefore could impose on the emperor's gra-

82. This is from the *fan-li* of the 1763 edition, reproduced in *Shinkoku gyōseikō,* I:9, and *Ch'ing-kuo hsing-cheng-fa,* 1:2:1:9.

ciousness without fear or shame. Such psychological or cultural elements centered around the institution of *li* (precedent) militated against the arbitrary use of the emperor's "absolute" power. To the extent that the laws were regarded as precedents, both the emperor and his officials could more comfortably feel bound by them.

5. Conclusion

We may thus anchor our discussion of the communication of the laws in the proposition that considerable attention was paid by officials to the meaning of written laws. We have argued that although many laws were communicated only through office records, compilation and publication also played an important role. However, to what extent the amount of compilation kept up with the need is not clear. There was bound to be a huge gap between publication and the bureaucracy's output of cases as a whole. Editorial and secretarial services could be obtained to a large extent without any visible government outlay, since they could be elicited merely by appealing to the career incentives of officials, clerks, and persons with a marginal official status. Yet they still required a large diversion of administrative man-hours and drew upon the limited reservoir of the bureaucratic elite's willingness to work.

All these conditions limited the amount of compilation. Consequently the needs of officials for easy access to information were not always met. In particular, one may argue, publication was a way of asserting centralized policy over local official interests. Although the emperor could always order officials to print and publicly display individual edicts, comprehensive publication of regulations and tax rates in books, as in the case of the salt monopoly, better enabled the public to hold officials to the wishes of the capital.[1] This was explicitly recognized, but there seems to have been a serious lag in the publication of local administrative regulations. On the other hand, although

1. The use of *t'eng-huang*, yellow posters displaying imperial commands, was common as a way of holding officials to the imperial will by widely informing common people, soldiers, etc. as to what this will was. This was done, for instance, if the emperor ordered a tax remission in a district or salary advances to the soldiers of a particular unit. See *TYT*, 37:45; 45:32b; 47:47b. Failure immediately to print and display the *t'eng-huang* when the emperor so ordered was punished by a one year's salary fine. If, after a natural disaster had struck an area and the emperor remitted taxes, a local official received a *t'eng-huang* and failed to post it, the punishment depended on the length of his delay. He was dismissed from office if the delay was one month or more. See *CFTL*, 33:3. There was enough literacy and gossip in the society to make these *t'eng-huang* an effective means of communication. *TWI*, 16:11, and *TYT*, 35:46b show that at the Liang-huai salt zone the shipment merchants' tax rates were annually posted. See also Appendix III.

there partly was a gap between publication and the output of cases, the gap between publication and distribution was much smaller. Once the printing blocks had been set up, the cost of paper and labor was low enough to ensure distribution of copies to all offices involved but high enough to impede wide distribution to private individuals. The sinologist today can generally assume that the Ch'ing administrative handbook he is studying was adequately distributed to offices in its day.

Law compilation staffs were often recruited from the personnel within the office charged with routine administration of the laws in question, but especially in the first Ch'ing century, the desire for consultation with a broad range of important officials led to the establishment of some compilation offices staffed with personnel from a variety of offices. Guided by an administrative ideology which stressed flexibility as well as respect for tradition, compilers made some substantive changes in the law but mainly focused on editorial problems of presentation. Although some compilations were criticized at the time as mere copies of past editions, the work of compilation often proceeded under the pressure of deadlines and of an emphasis on careful attention to detail, reliability, and being up to date. Specialized familiarity with the laws in question was widely recognized as indispensable for compilation as well as administration, and officials with specialized experience were rather common in Ch'ing times. In general, law books were written in a straightforward style full of fairly loose but still clear expressions. The compilers were weak, however, in the categorization of contents and in pulling together various sources to examine a particular problem exhaustively.

The question of categorization is, of course, one aspect of the question of the clarity of laws. At the same time, categorization is the result of procedures—the formal procedures of law making which are the subject of the next chapter.

CHAPTER III The Formal Structure of the Law-making Process

1. Introduction

Ch'ing law making was a process of decision making carried out by the emperor and a large variety of offices in the bureaucracy, not by a separate legislative organ. It should be noted that we here think of law making in broad terms as all those formal processes by which the laws or precedents of the state were established or excised.[1] Apart from the laws of the state, it has been held that Ch'ing China's overall legal framework consisted of reasoning or analogizing in the application of the laws, scholarly commentaries on law, and customary law.[2]

The state's law making process can be divided into basic and derivative law making. Basic law making consisted, first, of the establishment of some of the laws of the previous dynasty as the laws of the current one. This process of inheritance could be carried out in a de facto manner or through an explicit command, typically a command of the emperor endorsing a new book of laws which incorporated material from the previous dynasty.

Second, basic law making consisted of all other commands of the emperor that had the explicit character of law in that they were phrased as a rule, not just as a particular command referring to a single occasion.

The third type of basic law making was the use of previous imperial commands (whether rules or just particular decisions directed at one occasion) as analogies or precedents to support a new proposal. According to an implicit principle, all commands of the emperor could thus be used as precedents or analogies with two qualifications: some imperial commands had priority over others, and some contained a phrase or term ex-

1. See Almond and Powell, pp. 128–142.

2. *Shinkoku gyōseihō,* I:37–40, translated in *Ch'ing-kuo hsing-cheng-fa,* 1:3:44–46.

plicitly precluding their use as precedents. However the latter in fact could sometimes be used as precedents. Officials or nobles with the authority to memorialize could draw on the accumulated stock of imperial commands to find a precedent or analogy supporting their current proposal; they thus sought, often successfully, to elicit an imperial command endorsing their current proposal.

Fourth, officials on their own authority could issue commands which had the character of law in that they were phrased as a rule.

By derivative law making I refer to imperial commands giving certain laws or precedents a special status (such as priority in the finding of the law) relative to other laws or precedents. This process nearly always involved compilation and publication of the laws or precedents in question by either a regular administrative office, a subbureau of the latter specializing in such compilation, or, more rarely, an independent office set up especially for compilation. Closely connected to promulgation, publication in the case of derivative law making should be distinguished from the publication of laws and precedents merely to facilitate communication or to satisfy scholarly interest. At the same time, many laws and precedents were not published at all and existed only as office records or publicly posted notices.

Three major features of this system can be singled out. First, the executive and law making processes were partly identical. Some of the continuous output of executive commands by the emperor and by officials simultaneously was a flow of laws, precedents, or potential precedents. (Of course we here regard both judicial and administrative decisions as part of the executive process.)

Second, law making had formal aspects that were much the same irrespective of the substantive area of law involved. Although specialized offices, notably the six boards, were involved in many of the decisions creating laws within the sphere of their substantive specialty, laws in all substantive areas often involved the decisions of the same multifunctional organs such as emperor and governor-general. Moreover, whatever the substantive content, identical terminology was used formally to categorize both commands and laws. Thus nearly all of the fundamental Ch'ing categories of law have only a formal nature and cut across all substantive lines; only *lü* (penal statute) among the fundamental categories of law is substantively distinctive. (Naturally the most general words for law cut across all substantive lines, such as *fa* [law], *ch'eng-fa* [established laws], *kung-ling chih shu* [books of laws], *lü-ling* [laws], and *chin-ling* [prohibitions and laws].)[3] Finally, the formal unity

3. *Kung-ling* has two meanings going back to Han times, that of educational regulations and that of regulations on the selection for office of meritorious persons; see T. Morohashi, *Dai Kan-Wa jiten* (Great Chinese-Japanese dictionary; Tokyo, 1955–1960), II:1450. In more recent times, however, *kung-ling* also is just a general word for "laws"; see, e.g., *TLti, li-yen*:10. The most general meaning of *lü-ling* in Ch'ing times is illustrated in *HPTL, tsou-che*:1b, a passage where the term is used with particular reference to administrative regulations; see also II, 3, above. *Chin-ling* in modern times has the meaning of an injunction (Cheng Ching-i and P'eng Shih, II:1668), and in Ch'ing times it could be used to cover penal law. However it could also be used as a broad generic term for laws, as can be seen in the table of contents of *Ssu-ch'uan yen-fa-chih*, a late nineteenth-century work, where *chin-ling* covers excerpts from the Board of Revenue regulations, the penal code, and regulations on the punishment of officials. The locus classicus of the concept of *ling* seems to be in the *Kuan-tzu*, where the meaning of *ling* often connotes performance, in contrast to that of *chin* (prohibition). In the case of prohibitions, the ruler desires that something be stopped. In the case of *ling* (orders, laws), the ruler desires that something be carried out; see *Kuan-tzu*, 6:1b. This meaning of *ling* is reflected in the subsequent tendency to use *ling* to denote administrative laws, as was the case notably in the T'ang period. Then in the Ch'ing period, as discussed in III, 2, note 9, *ling* was partly redefined to have a formal rather than a substantive meaning. Apart from the fact that the Ch'ing general terms for law cover administrative as well as penal laws, one should note that both these types of Ch'ing law fall under the modern definition of law as commands which are issued and enforced by some group such as a state and which apply to a general class of occasions. This definition follows Max Rheinstein, tr., *Max Weber on Law in Economy and Society* (Cambridge, Mass., 1954), pp. lxvii–lxx, 13–14. Weber did not focus on the distinction between laws and an executive command applying to a single occasion and good only for a short time (such as an order to appoint a particular official to a particular post), but the distinction does not conflict with his discussion. Ch'ing articles of administrative law often do not themselves specify sanctions, but they were backed by sanctions, as is evident from other articles specifying punishment for violation of a specific administrative regulation; from the catchall article punishing officials for "doing what ought not to be done" (*CFTL*, 1:4a–b; *TLti*, 44:40; *TCLL*, 34:24; Philastre, II:571–572); and from the laws punishing violations of *ling* and *chih-shu*, which, as explained in III, 2, note 9,

of the different substantive fields of law can be seen in the fact that all the kinds of laws could be discussed as a unit, as in the references to the regulations of the *pu-yüan* (six boards and various other capital offices),[4] and in the fact that the formalized technique of adducing and analogizing from precedents was common to all branches of the law.

The third feature of the law making system was its complex relationship to the process of publication. It has been noted that laws sometimes were not published at all; sometimes were published only to facilitate administrative communication or to satisfy some scholarly interest; and sometimes were published as part of the process of derivative law making. It should also be noted that the format of books of laws often had only a loose relation to categories of law. A book devoted to one category of law might nevertheless contain stray paragraphs from other categories. Administrative manuals prepared for multifunctional offices anyway had a mixture of categories and sometimes even material of a nonadministrative nature. Furthermore, the styles of law compilation and historical writing were undifferentiated to some extent; editors had some freedom in deciding on format; and the private and public aspects of a book—notably in terms of sponsorship and financing—sometimes overlapped or were blurred. All these factors promoted variety in formats.

Given these three features, we can discuss the formal aspects of Ch'ing law making in terms of three phases: the issuing of

---

together cover all imperially issued commands and laws, whatever their substantive content. Nevertheless, nearly all scholarly interest in traditional Chinese law has been restricted to the penal law. As a result there has been a neglect not only of the substantive and normative character of administrative law and of the somewhat intermediate category of the law on the administrative punishment of officials but also of the fact that penal law was one part of a broader institutional framework with several unifying characteristics. One of the few works with a bit of information on the history of Chinese administrative law is Ch'en Ku-yüan, *Chung-kuo fa-chih-shih* (A history of China's legal institutions; Shanghai, 1944), and an outline of Ch'ing administrative law can be found in *Shinkoku gyōseihō*, I:1–14; I:22–38, translated in *Ch'ing-kuo hsing-cheng-fa* (Administrative laws of the Ch'ing state; Shanghai, 1906), 1:1:1:1–1:2:1:16 and 1:2:2:25–1:3:1:44. As a whole, this book deals with the formal structure of the government, while we focus on the formal structure of law making only.

4. On *pu-yüan*, see II, 4, note 5.

commands, which was part of the routine executive process; the drawing of distinctions between or the sorting out of commands, a process whereby some executive commands were identified as laws or precedents, and laws and precedents in turn were formally and substantively categorized; and the ways in which commands were published. It should be noted that the distinctions applied to contemporaneously produced commands also were applied to laws and precedents inherited from the Ming dynasty.

2. The Executive Process

Ch'ing executive commands consisted either of commands issued by a superior on his own initiative or of a superior's decision regarding a proposal or problem presented by a subordinate. In either case, the superior could be either the emperor or an official.

A major characteristic of the Ch'ing system was the lack of great *official* executive authority within the capital. Although the six boards had a slightly ambiguous position and could issue orders to provincial offices in minor matters, they basically—like the various advisory councils, the Grand Secretariat and the Grand Council—were only "staff" offices advising the emperor on which orders to issue.[1]

To put the question of executive power at the capital into perspective, one should raise the issue of the *tsai-hsiang* (prime office, cabinet), a term denoting that official or group of officials at the capital occupying some sort of regularized position immediately below the emperor and helping him direct the government. While the institution of the *tsai-hsiang* goes back to Chou times or earlier, the word *tsai-hsiang* itself was a generic term used at least since Han times to denote the prime office or cabinet, the structure and official designations of which frequently changed. For instance, the T'ang historian Tu Yu explained that at one point the Han *san-kung* (three dukes) were the *tsai-hsiang;* in Ch'ing times a view was informally held that a grand secretary who also was a member of the Grand Council was part of the "genuine *tsai-hsiang.*"

The nature of the *tsai-hsiang* was a central ideological and political problem. The original conception of the *tsai-hsiang* was that of a lofty office taking overall charge of the empire on behalf of the emperor. This concept can be seen in Ssu-ma Ch'ien's *Shih-chi.*[2] It also accorded with much Chou political thought which saw the ruler as entrusting his government to

1. On orders emanating from the six boards, see II, 4, note 7, and III, 2, note 12.

2. Chou Tao-chi, *Han T'ang tsai-hsiang chih-tu* (The institution of the prime office in the Han and T'ang dynasties; Taipei, 1964), pp. 1–18, 695. *Ch'ing-shih-kao* (Draft history of the Ch'ing dynasty; 1942), II:1176. For the Sung *tsai-hsiang,* see Chou Tao-chi's contribution in *Sung-shih yen-chiu-chi* (Collection of studies on Sung history; Taipei, 1966), III:245–263.

a skilled statesman; the thrust of much Confucian and Legalist ideology was to make the *tsai-hsiang* the fulcrum of political improvement. Following this conception of the office, critics like Wang Tseng (978–1038) (actually a Sung prime minister) saw a great shrinkage in the authority of the *tsai-hsiang* by their time, or, even more, as with Huang Tsung-hsi (1610–1695), elimination of any office deserving the name *tsai-hsiang*.[3] In a key document of 1779, the Ch'ien-lung emperor also saw such a shrinkage, but he approved of it. His careful formulation of the problem was at the opposite pole of the traditional ideal.[4]

The emperor was offended that Yin Chia-ch'üan (1711–1781) had written that the Ch'ing grand secretaries constituted the *tsai-hsiang*.[5] The emperor said that they did not and should not. The ancient *tsai-hsiang*, the emperor said, "grasped the reins of power and took charge of administrative affairs," but in the Ch'ing dynasty, these "handles of governmental power" are grasped by the emperor, while the grand secretaries merely "hear the emperor's will and write up the rescript." The emperor should grasp these "handles" for several reasons. If the emperor "reveres Heaven, loves the people, and is diligent in administrative affairs," then there is no reason to give the "handles" to his ministers. If he does hand them over, then the relation between ruler and minister becomes distorted: the emperor becomes incongruously insignificant, while the ministers outrageously come to feel that responsibility for the empire is solely theirs, that there is no ruler above them to whom they should submit. Moreover, the "handles" of power can be correctly used only by the emperor; if he is incapable, then even a brilliant minister cannot save the empire.

It is clear that in historical fact, the Han, T'ang, and Sung prime office tended to grasp the "handles" of power more firmly than did the Ming or Ch'ing. For instance, Han prime ministers

3. Chou Tao-chi, pp. 691–695. It may be noted that Sa Meng-wu, I:215–216 says that the great power of the prime office in Han times was in accord with the ideas of Han Fei. But this view admittedly is problematic.

4. This edict is cited in Fu Tsung-mao, pp. 519–520 and is found in Wang Hsien-ch'ien, ed., *Tung-hua ch'üan-lu* (Peking, 1887), 93:11–12. Ch'ien Mu, *Chung-kuo chin-san-pai-nien hsüeh-shu-shih,* I, introd., p. 2, cites a similar statement made by the Ch'ien-lung emperor in a prose piece.

5. Actually, Yin is stated to have said *hsiang-kuo,* a synonym for *tsai-hsiang.*

had the formal authority to execute an official guilty of an especially grave crime without first memorializing the emperor. Bureaucratic communication with the emperor in Han times was channeled to a large extent through the prime office, in contrast to the wide diffusion of the responsibility directly to memorialize the emperor in the Ch'ing period. Still in Sung times, the emperor's orders were generally transmitted through the prime office. When Ning-tsung (1195–1224) sent orders bypassing it, his officials criticized the practice. By contrast, many Ch'ing emperors regularly had two-way, secret communications with officials bypassing any third office or organ, and this practice apparently was never openly criticized. It is also clear that in the Han, T'ang and Sung cases, the prime office on its own initiative laid proposals before the emperor; it did not just advise him on how to respond to proposals made by other offices, as tended to be the case in Ch'ing times.

In Ch'ing times the prime office was essentially a secretarial and advisory organ with no discretion of its own to issue significant executive commands. Whether the prime office in earlier dynasties had such discretion is an interesting question. In general, whatever the period, the decisions of the prime office had to be approved by the emperor, but some of these decisions were broad enough to serve in effect as a significant delegation of executive discretion. An instance of such delegation is the use in T'ang and early Sung times of the *t'ang-t'ieh* (document of the hall for administrative affairs) and, in Sung times, of *cha-tzu* (orders). *T'ang-t'ieh* were issued by the T'ang and early Sung prime office and, it was said, were often regarded as more important than the emperor's own orders. *Cha-tzu* replaced *t'ang-t'ieh* in early Sung times, and the second Sung emperor (976–997) ordered that the prime office issue no *cha-tzu* without first obtaining imperial consent through a memorial. This latter change implies that previously *cha-tzu,* and certainly the *t'ang-t'ieh,* too, had been issued directly at the discretion of the prime office.[6] An episode of about 1043 also shows that the

6. On the power of the Han prime office to execute officials, see Chou Tao-chi, *Han-T'ang tsai-hsiang chih-tu,* pp. 126–127. On the strong tendency in Han and T'ang times for memorials from lower officials to pass through the prime office, see *ibid.,* pp. 10, 93 (n.6), 87, 395–402; Yen Keng-wang, *Chung-kuo ti-fang hsing-cheng chih-tu shih,* part one, I:98, II:266, 269–270. On *t'ang-t'ieh,* see Fang Hao, *Sung-shih* (History of the Sung dynasty; Taipei, 1966), I:33, 38–39.

prime office had executive discretion. When Wang Lun rebelled, the Sung government forbade that the reports of the rebellion being sent by its officials to the capital be made public. Ou-yang Hsiu memorialized protesting this policy of secrecy and indicated that this policy could have been decided on and put into effect without the emperor's own specific command. He said: "I am not clear as to whether this policy stems from an order of the emperor (*sheng-chih*) or is merely due to the desires of the great ministers in the prime office and the Bureau of Military Affairs." [7]

In the gradual weakening of the prime office, the Sung is usually but perhaps unfairly regarded as a pivotal period. Although the Sung government displayed unusual organizational vigor at least in the field of economic regulation and monopolies, there is general agreement among scholars that a pronounced trend began in Sung times toward a greater diffusion of authority in the bureaucracy; the authority of individual offices, including the *tsai-hsiang*, was variously constricted, as control over officials in contrast to their effectiveness became a greater consideration. In particular the Sung laid great stress on a powerful Censorate as a check on the prime office and often, though far from always, kept the prime office and the Bureau of Military Affairs in separate hands. As the emperor Shen-tsung (1068–1085) said, the "handle of military power" would thus stay out of the hands of the prime office, while the

---

An excellent discussion on communication bypassing the prime office in Sung times is in Chu Ch'uan-yü, *Sung-tai hsin-wen-shih* (A history of the flow of news in the Sung dynasty; Taipei, 1967), pp. 273–278, 286. Often called *nei-p'i* (inner court instructions) in Sung times, imperial orders not going through the prime office were not subject to the possibility of *feng-po* (to seal and return [an imperial order], rejecting it as improper or impractical). Such orders were used, Chu says, only to a limited extent in T'ang times, and their use greatly increased in Sung times. However even in Sung times their use was repeatedly and vehemently criticized as undermining proper procedures, whereby imperial decisions were to be reached only through consultation with the appropriate offices. At times officials even refused to carry out the orders in *nei-p'i*, apparently feeling that *nei-p'i* lacked full legal efficacy. In both T'ang and Sung times, the institution of secret memorials going directly to the emperor existed, but apparently was less developed than in Ch'ing times.

7. Chu Ch'uan-yü, pp. 292, 285.

latter and the Bureau of Military Affairs would "mutually support and exert control on each other."[8] (Yet from about 1205, the head of the Bureau regularly was a member of the prime office.) Naturally a major event in the decline of the prime office was its abolition in 1380, although a new form of the prime office developed thereafter.

Yet it is not certain that any power lost by the prime office was completely absorbed by any increasingly despotic emperor; some of it may have slid into the hands of regional offices. The emergence of the offices of governor and governor-general in Ming times may perhaps be viewed in this light. Any notion of increasing despotism in Ming and Ch'ing times should be balanced against the fact that "appellate" decision making, with many decisions being proposed by the governors and governors-general, was a major part of the executive process in those periods. In other words, power is not only the power of ultimate decision but also the power of making proposals, and we seem to see a long-term tendency in Chinese history for the latter kind of power to be diffused from the prime office in the capital to high regional offices. Moreover the tendency toward constricting the authority of offices seems to have been accompanied with a growing proliferation of administrative regulations allowing capital offices tightly to supervise regional ones, and this apparent increase in the amount of law in turn may well have narrowed the emperor's own scope of action.

The Ch'ing emperor's executive authority was wielded through *chih-shu* (imperial pronouncements) and *ling* (imperial orders). *Chih-shu* essentially denotes independently issued imperial commands; *ling,* proposals of officials or nobles approved by the emperor. Modern sociologists also distinguish between these two kinds of executive decisions and sometimes call proposals approved by a superior "appellate cases."[9] A generic term, *chih-*

8. Sa, IV:115.

9. Barnard, pp. 190–191. These definitions of *ling* and *chih-shu* come from two *lü* (penal statutes) on the violation of *ling* and *chih-shu.* The one on *ling* reads: "Anyone who violates a *ling* is to receive fifty strokes of the light bamboo." The official explanation of this *lü* reads: "This refers to instances where there are prohibitions in *ling* for which the penal code does not specify a punishment. If one deliberately violates a *chao* (proclamation) or rescript, one is guilty of violating a *chih-shu* (imperial pronouncement); if one deliberately violates a *tsou-chun* or *shih-li,* one is guilty of violating a *ling.*" See *TLti,* 44:39; *TCLL,* 34:23; Philastre, II:571.

shu usually took the form of *yü* (edicts). *Ling*, that is, appellate cases, usually took the form of *chih* (rescripts) and/or *chu-p'i* (vermilion comments) which were issued in response to a "memorial."

The making or delivering of a statement by a subject to the emperor was called *tsou* (to memorialize). The right or, more exactly, the responsibility (*tse*) to memorialize was widely diffused. While high nobles and almost all important military and civil offices at the capital could memorialize, the right to memorialize was held in the provinces not only by the highest military and civil officials but also by some of their subordinates.[10] This tended to produce skips in the chain of command, reminiscent of Chu Hsi's view that in regional administration some subordinates should have the right to memorialize over the heads of their superiors in order to keep the latter in check.[11] However in an edict of 1730, the Yung-cheng emperor showed himself sensitive to the threat this posed to the authority of superiors. He wanted to have access to information from lower-ranking officials without thereby inflating their power at the expense of their superiors' authority over them. Therefore he ordered that even if he approved a proposal sent to him by a lower official, the latter could not put it into effect until it had been reported to his superior and had passed through regular channels.[12]

As explained below, *shih-li* and *tsou-chun* in effect cover *all* proposals in memorials approved by the emperor (all imperial "appellate cases"). Complementing this definition of *ling*, the penal statute on violating *chih-shu* points out that it does not apply in those "instances where it is a matter of carrying out a *tsou-chun*." "The words of the son of heaven are called *chih*. *Shu* refers to writing them down. Examples of *chih-shu* are proclamations, pardons, edicts, and imperial commands." "Anyone who, receiving a *chih-shu*, intentionally violates it by not carrying out that which it requires is to receive one hundred strokes of the heavy bamboo." See *TLti*, 8:2; *TCLL*, 7:3; Philastre, I:322–323. See also Appendix IV.

10. See Appendix V.

11. Cited in T'ao Hsi-sheng, IV:123.

12. *Pa-ch'ao sheng-hsün*, Yung-cheng, 7:25–27b. I first saw this important memorial as used in Silas Wu, "Memorial Systems," pp. 46–48. From this edict it seems clear that these skips in the chain of command occurred only in the case of the *tsou-che* (palace memorial) system, not in that of the older, somewhat more regular memorial system (*tsou-pen* and *t'i-pen*). In insisting that all decisions to act generally pass through the older system, the emperor was trying to preserve the chain of command. Another significant

To some extent, nonofficials also could memorialize. For instance, when the K'ang-hsi emperor was on a tour in the south in early 1689, a group of Liang-huai salt merchants met his entourage and presented a memorial to him asking that they be relieved of assuming responsibility for a large dredging project. This memorial, interestingly, is written in a flowery style full of redundancies, very different from the more businesslike manner of most memorials from Ch'ing officials.[13] If the merchants had written as directly and tersely as officials often did, their memorial would have seemed impudent. Yet the more usual procedure would have been for the merchants to petition the official over them, who then would have memorialized the emperor on their behalf.

Vermilion comments were often used together with a rescript when the emperor responded to a memorial. In this context, the main difference between them was that the vermilion comment was addressed directly to the memorializing official, while the rescript was addressed to the Grand Council or Grand Secretariat, which in turn relayed it to the memorializing official. (The words "vermilion comment" were also used to head any comment inserted by the emperor alongside any particular passage in the memorial.)

Responding to a proposal in a memorial, therefore, the emperor might simply address a vermilion comment to the memorializing official reading: *I-i ch'in-tz'u* (Let action accord with your advice). More commonly, the emperor's vermilion comment would read only: *Ling yu chih ch'in tz'u* (Apart from this there is a rescript). Then, usually on the same day that he had received the vermilion comment, the official would receive a rescript relayed by either the Grand Council or Grand Secre-

---

aspect of this memorial is its conceptualization of the relation between the six boards and the highest regional officials such as the governors-general. In major matters, no action can normally be taken by the governors-general until a board has advised on it. Therefore the emperor insisted that when a palace memorial proposal already approved by him was then sent up through regular channels via the boards, his words approving the proposal must be omitted. Otherwise, it is clear, the right of the boards to advise before action is taken would be violated. This edict also refers to the boards' "deciding on" (*ting-to*) proposals sent to them by the governors-general.

13. *Liang-huai yen-fa-chih* (1693), II:1113–1119.

tariat. In such a rescript, the critical words signifying the emperor's executive decision often were: *Chao chao-so-ch'ing hsing* (Let action proceed according to what has been requested).

Before sending down such a rescript, the emperor would often send a vermilion comment to a third party, usually the capital office concerned with the affairs under consideration, asking the latter to memorialize giving advice. Often, it should be added, there was no practical difference between a vermilion comment giving approval and an approving rescript, since the latter might merely echo the points made by the memorializer. On the other hand, when sending down a rescript, the emperor could add to his approval a warning to act with care or orders to take certain further precautions. In the *Ch'ing shih-lu* (Veritable records of the Ch'ing dynasty), a chronicle with many imperial executive commands, the issuing of such affirmative rescripts or vermilion comments is usually indicated by the chronicler's expression *ts'ung chih* (The emperor followed the suggestion presented to him).

Analogously an official could independently send down an order (often called *cha*), or, having received a *hsiang* (report) from a subordinate official proposing something, approve the proposal by writing a *p'i* (comment) on it such as *chun ch'i so ch'ing* (what is requested is authorized). Officials apparently always stamped their orders with their office seal.[14] An official executive command addressed to the people-at-large could be

14. *CFTL,* 10:2 requires that any office stamp with its seal any document it is sending to any other office, and this obviously includes orders. Besides *CFTL, chüan* 10, seals are discussed in *TCHT, chüan* 34 and *TCHTSL, chüan* 321–323. According to the law, seals varied in terms of what office handled their manufacture, their names, the material used, the design of their knobs, the type of script used, their sizes, and the office to which they were assigned. One finds *yin* or *yin-hsin* sometimes used broadly to cover two basic types of metal seals cast by the Board of Rites and respectively called *yin-hsin* and *kuan-fang.* Casting was usually done on an "auspicious" day chosen by the Imperial Board of Astronomy. Certain wooden seals made under the supervision of provincial treasurers and issued to certain very low regional officials (*tso-tsa*) were called either *ch'ien-chi* or *ch'o-chi,* but *ch'ien-chi* was also used for some metal seals. See also *HCCSWP,* 18:16b, where the Kiangsi governor in 1731 says that in the case of all districts, "all office records and papers must be authenticated by being stamped with the office seal." He was referring to confusion caused by identically stamped records in different districts with the same name.

described as *ch'u-shih hsiao-yü* or *kao-yü* (to make an order publicly known).[15]

Because imperial "appellate cases" are found so often in compilations, it is important to be clear about their terminology. The problem lies with the titles used by compilers to name and categorize these decisions. In many instances, imperial "appellate cases" were put into compilations with no information beyond these titles regarding the form of the proposal and the nature of the superior's response, but there is little discussion of these titles in either primary or secondary sources. Their meaning was taken for granted.

The first problem is the significance of *chun* (authorize, approve), which is part of all these "appellate" titles.[16] Equivalent in Ch'ing minds to *yün-hsing* (authorize),[17] *chun* denotes not a command but only a permission to do something if one wishes to do it. (The antipode of *chun* was *po* [to reject].) How then are we to know whether the innumerable decisions with *chun* in their titles were necessarily supposed to be carried out? If they were merely authorized possibilities of action, the likelihood that they reflect actual governmental practice is diminished. (Whether they were actually enforced is yet another problem.)

The answer is that *chun* in this context strongly tended to have the authoritative character of a command. This is clear, first of all, from the inherent nature of the documents. Subordinates sent up proposals because they needed a decision on how to proceed, not because they merely wanted another alternative of action, and superiors did not take the time to study and approve a proposal in order to be told later that it was not carried out after all. Furthermore the idea of "authorization" fitted in with the nature of "appellate" decision making. Although the emperor's personal authority touched so many bureaucratic decisions, his role often did not even go so far as weighing alternative proposals. Especially in provincial affairs, it was the responsibility of officials to weigh alternatives and to present the emperor with decisive proposals already worthy of

15. *Shinkoku gyōseihō*, I:28; *Ch'ing-kuo hsing-cheng-fa*, 1:2:5:32–33.

16. The use of this appellate terminology—*t'i-chun*, *tsou-chun*, and *i-chun*—was current in the Ming period, as can be seen from *Ta-Ming hui-tien*.

17. See, e.g., *LHYFC*, *fan-li*: 1b.

receiving imperial validation. On this level, the emperor usually supervised rather than took part in executive decisions, and the idea of "authorization," we may say, fitted this role.

Second, *chun* in a vast number of instances covered approved proposals in which the phrase of approval originally used by the superior *was* an imperative. This applies most obviously to the emperor, who, although often asked to *fu-chun* (graciously authorize), seldom himself used *chun;* instead, he used the imperative *chao* (let), as in the above examples (or occasionally *chao-chun*).[18]

Finally the authoritative character of imperially approved proposals is clear from a *lü* (penal statute) which provides for the beating of anyone violating such approved proposals. The punishment was fifty strokes of the light bamboo. (There was also a *lü* providing for 100 strokes of the heavy bamboo for anyone violating an independently issued imperial order such as an edict. For officials, both these punishments were commuted into administrative sanctions.)[19]

Nevertheless, there was a margin of ambiguity between the concept of an authorization and an order, and it was taken for granted that this ambiguity would be resolved through the common sense of the subordinate. In 1831, as water rose dangerously in the grand canal, officials at the spot twice jointly asked the governor-general to open two sluice gates. In a memorial the latter described his two responses respectively as "I naturally ordered (*ch'ih*) them quickly to manage the matter in a satisfactory way," and "with all speed I ordered (*ch'ih*) them at once to open each gate in succession."[20] Yet in another memorial the governor-general refers to the time "when they received the authorization (*p'i*) to open the gates . . . "[21] By the time the "order" or "authorization" had been received, the embankment had burst, and in this new situation the local magistrate decided after all not to open at least three of the gates, although urged to do so by his colleagues. Although he was later impeached in connection with the break, he was not

18. *TYT*, 31:6b, illustrates *chao-chun*. In *TWI*, 17:30, the emperor warned that if T'ao Chu again asked for a certain postponement, "he definitely will be unable respectfully to elicit *yün-chun* (authorization)."

19. See Appendix IV.

20. *TYT*, 35:11b–12. This case is discussed in IV, 4, d.

21. *TYT*, 35:16.

accused of disobeying orders. Clearly the authoritative character of the governor-general's communication was partly a function of the common sense of the officials dealing with changing circumstances on the spot. If the "authorization" had arrived before the break, presumably they would have had to open the gates.

In fixing the title of an approved proposal, *chun* was added to a word denoting the nature of the proposal. Thus *hsiang-chun* denotes approval by an official of a proposal in a *hsiang* (report) sent up by a subordinate. On the imperial level, there were four major types: *tsou-chun, t'i-chun, fu-chun,* and *i-chun.*

Definitions of the last three are given identically in the first two editions (1690, 1732) of *Ta-Ch'ing hui-tien,* but at least two of these definitions are inadequate.[22] The *Ta-Ch'ing hui-tien's* definition of *t'i-chun* is an approval of a proposal in a "*t'i-pen*-type memorial presented by one or more of the boards or other major capital offices." This is incomplete, since there are also plenty of *t'i-chun* (also contemporaneous with the above editions) consisting of memorials presented by provincial officials such as governor-general.[23]

Rather it is safe to define both *t'i-chun* and *tsou-chun* as "imperially approved proposal in a memorial." A *t'i-chun* is an approval of a proposal in a *t'i-pen,* the type of memorial used on the whole for routine matters, and a *tsou-chun* is an authorization of a proposal in a *tsou-pen* or in a *tsou-che* memorial, which generally were used for more important matters.[24] *Fu-chun* is an "imperially approved reply." Here the above compilations want to limit the term to replies proposed to the emperor by one or more capital offices (*pu-yüan*) in answer to a

22. See *fan-li* in those editions.

23. *LHYFC, chüan* 7, has many examples of *t'i-chun* formed from memorials sent by the Liang-huai salt censor. In 7:10 there is an example for 1666; in 7:18b, there is an example of a *t'i-chun* formed in 1733 from the memorial of the Hu-kuang governor-general and one or more other officials. My discussion here as a whole differs from that in S. H. L. Wu, *Communication and Imperial Control in China* (Cambridge, Mass., 1970), pp. 32–33. Professor Wu's definitions of *t'i-chun* and *i-chun* follow those in the first two editions of *Ta-Ch'ing hui-tien* without taking into account actual practice. His definition of *pu-yüan* is too narrow (see II, 4, note 5), and I disagree with his translation of *fu-chun.* I have followed Wu, p. 12, for the meaning of *pei-le.*

24. After 1748 *tsou-pen* were no longer used. See Appendix I.

proposal emanating from a governor, governor-general, circuit censor, or the Six Sections of the Office for Scrutiny of Metropolitan Officials. Probably some *fu-chun* also involved replies to other offices.

Finally *i-chun* or *i-ting* (imperially approved proposal), we are told, were formed from proposals made by conferences (*hui-i*), the members of which were some or all of the following: *i-cheng-wang* (princes with the authority to deliberate on governmental affairs), *ta-ch'en* (great ministers with the authority to deliberate on governmental affairs), *pei-le* (princes of the third rank), the Nine Ministries, the Supervisorate of Imperial Instruction, the Six Sections of the Censorate for the Scrutiny of Metropolitan Officials, and the circuit censors.

This formulation clearly refers to the system of conferences so prominent during the first century or so of the dynasty (see II, 4). However, the scope of *i-chun*, at least in later periods, was broader. If one or more offices were asked *i-tsou* (to advise in a memorial), they presented their advice in the form of a palace memorial (*tsou-che*) or routine memorial (*t'i-pen*), and, if approved, this advice could be classed as an *i-chun*.

An *i-tsou*, as we can see from an 1833 example,[25] could come from a high provincial office, but usually it came from a capital office. For instance, in advising the emperor on administrative punishments, the Board of Civil Officials, according to an edict of 1817, used a *tsou-che* if the impeachment had been initiated by the emperor, and a *t'i-pen* if the impeachment had emanated from an official. Either way, this memorial could be referred to as *i-tsou* (to advise in a memorial).[26]

One may adduce two clear-cut cases of *tsou-che* which, after their proposals were approved by the emperor, were classed as an *i-ting*, that is, *i-chun*. In early 1831, the Nanking governor-general presented a *tsou-che* jointly with a president and a vice-president of the Board of Revenue, who had been commissioned by the emperor to travel to Kiangsu to confer with T'ao Chu on the problems of the Liang-huai zone of the salt monopoly. This *tsou-che* contained a fifteen-point reform program for Liang-huai, which the emperor shortly approved in a rescript.[27] When many years later a brief version of this reform program was

25. *TWI*, 18:11b, refers to an *i-tsou* from the governor or governor-general of Kwangtung. See *TYT*, 35:7b, for a more typical case.
26. *CFTL*, 1:11a–b.
27. *TYT*, 30:45–60.

entered into the last edition of *Ta-Ch'ing hui-tien shih-li* (1899), it was entered as an *i-ting*.[28] Possibly it was not classed as a *tsou-chun* because the *tsou-che* was the result of consultations between three great ministers.

When in 1832 T'ao Chu presented a *tsou-che* proposing the Huai-pei ticket reform, he included the ticket regulations in a *ch'ing-tan* (clear list) attached to the *tsou-che*. The emperor approved his plan with a vermilion comment,[29] and the next year, referring to this imperial executive order, the Board of Revenue called it a *tsou-chun*.[30] However when a version of these ticket regulations was entered in the *Ta-Ch'ing hui-tien shih-li* (1899), they were classed as an *i-chun*.[31] Apparently the reason is that in the latter version, the ticket regulations included an adjustment made in 1833, which was a proposal presented in a *tsou-che* by T'ao Chu but approved in a rescript by the emperor only after the Board of Revenue had obeyed the order "quickly to deliberate on what to advise and to memorialize." (This adjustment allowed the salt traders to sell in another market if the one to which their shipment had been assigned was currently not a good one.)[32]

28. *TCHTSL*, 223:Tao-kuang 10.
29. *TYT*, 40:16–25b.
30. *TYT*, 46:26a–b.
31. *TCHTSL*, 223:Tao-kuang 12.
32. *TYT*, 46:21–29b.

3. Formal Categorization

Before considering the transition from executive commands to law, we should first note that the Ch'ing concept of law involved a distinction between precedents on the one hand and regulations or rules on the other. This distinction does not accord with the Western one, which is grounded in difference of origin: especially in the Anglo-Saxon tradition, "precedents" refer to judge-made law, "regulations" to laws produced by the executive and, sometimes, the legislative branch. The Ch'ing distinction rather hinged on a difference in the form of the norms. Regulations, as in the unambiguous modern term *pan-shih kuei-t'iao* (regulations on the basis of which matters are managed), were norms authorizing action in a direct, obvious way. Precedents were norms authorizing action in a less direct way; action was authorized through the process of pointing to identical or similar acts in the past as justification. The *K'ang-hsi Dictionary* (preface of 1716) defines *li* (precedent, regulation) as *pi* (to compare) and *lei* (to be of the same category as something else), while the modern dictionary *Tz'u-hai* is still clearer: "It means a standard which can be applied through comparison." In the Ch'ing context, the idea of precedent is relevant where there was doubt as to the relation between legal norms and practice; precedents were "adduced" (*yüan*) to remove doubt as to the legal propriety of a proposed action. Regulations on the other hand were legal norms (such as tax collection deadlines) which applied directly (they were not "adduced") to practice without any element of doubt.

A correlated difference was that regulations not only possessed general significance but also were phrased in a general way. They did not deal with the fate of Mr. Smith but with "anyone who." Ch'ing regulations often begin with or imply the idea of *fan* (in all cases of). Precedents, on the other hand, could be executive commands with general or prospective significance but formulated to deal only with a specific occasion. For instance the abolition of the institution of head salt merchants at the Liang-huai zone of the salt monopoly in 1831 was regarded as a precedent (*shih-li*) and thus suggested the propriety of similar moves in the future, but it was phrased simply as a decision regarding a particular problem.[1] Of course the

1. *TCHTSL*, 223:Tao-kuang 10.

line between precedents and regulations could be blurred. An early Ch'ing imperial executive decision to collect certain originally remitted salt taxes in effect assumed the force of a regulation saying that in all cases these salt taxes cannot be remitted (see below).

Presumably in most societies the phenomenon of precedent—of the very fact of past happening—is a source of legitimation, but the concept of precedent seems to have played an unusually large role in the Ch'ing legal system. This may be due to the development of the term *li* (precedent) as a major legal category, which occurred only in the course of the Ming and Ch'ing periods,[2] and to the common habit of compiling administrative regulations in an annalistic, chronological format, a habit which became a conscious problem in the Ch'ing period.[3] Moreover, as we noted in the previous chapter, the system of laws seems to have been ideologically more appealing to the extent that it took the form of precedents.

A significant problem is the distinction between the nature of precedents in administrative laws and in laws specifying sanctions, although this distinction seems never to have been discussed by Ch'ing writers. Precedents in penal law or in the connected regulations on administrative punishment had bind-

2. The practice of adducing precedents—notably from the classic *Ch'un-ch'iu*—existed already in the Early Han period. As a legal category, *li* emerges first in the Chin period (265–420) with the term *fa-li.* In the T'ang period the term *li* was applied to norms adduced when the *shih* (ordinances) lacked an appropriate article. In the Ming period the emphasis on not changing the penal *lü* because they had been fixed by the founding emperor led to the need for some more flexible category of law, which was filled by the publication of many editions of *li.* These remarks follow Ch'en Ku-yüan, pp. 132–138. See also T'ao, II:152–156. Sa Meng-wu, IV:143–144, cites interesting material about the use of *li* in the Sung period. One official around 1162 deplored the fact that in the appointment and transfer of officials, *fa* (laws) were being displaced by "so-called *li* (precedents, regulations)" manipulated by clerks. Such *li* apparently had arisen when the Sung government, after being pushed south, found itself without its archives, and governmental decisions had to be made on an ad hoc basis, yielding such *li.* By 1162, attempts were being made to codify these *li* in order to reduce irregularities. Yet around 1163–1190 this process of "establishing laws on the basis of precedents" was denounced by an official, much as this sort of "legislation from below," to coin a phrase, was occasionally resisted in Ming and Ch'ing times.

3. See III, 5, below.

ing effect. Law finders were guided by the criterion of maximum conformity with the appropriate article of law, and regulations on finding the law specified the priority according to which different categories of law or precedents were to be searched. The law finder's duty was to choose the appropriate article or precedent in the proper category of law.

In administrative laws, some precedents could have binding effect to the extent that they took on the full force of a regulation. However, in making administrative proposals, officials were often guided not only by the criterion of maximum conformity with the appropriate article of law but also by the goal of doing what was most practical. Although they could act entirely without precedents, it was more usual for them to choose between precedents depending on what was most practical. Administrative precedents, we may say, had less binding effect than those in the field of sanction specification. On the other hand, the adducing of administrative precedents was a more formal process than mere commonsense respect for past experience. These points deserve some illustration.

Two good examples of administrative precedents which acquired the full force of a regulation are the law restricting remission of the taxes paid by long-distance shippers (*yün-shang*) in the salt monopoly, and the law providing for relief grants for salt makers hurt by natural disasters and remission of their main tax. The first of these covered a large amount of taxes and had major practical effects. It is also interesting because it illustrates how administrative law could combine a tendency toward impractical rigidity with various compromise arrangements allowing a degree of flexibility.

In contrast to the flexible Ch'ing system of canceling and postponing land taxes in response to fluctuating harvests, this law inhibited flexible adjustment of salt taxes to fluctuating market conditions. By requiring payment of some taxes on salt never sold, it created a vicious circle in times of bad sales, as tax debts created by bad sales had to be paid by merchants still shipping, raising their prices and thus creating more tax debts as sales declined still more. Because of its disruptive effects, the government would probably have had to discard this precedent except that its establishment was followed by a long period of exceptionally good salt sales, which resulted in a manageable tax debt burden.

On the other hand, tax debts involved no interest payments,

and T'ao Chu's unqualified statement that this law precluded both cancellation and postponement was an exaggeration.[4] First, when salt shipments were canceled because of bad sales, part of the taxes originally due on them were canceled also.[5] And, when the salt shipments were staggered over immediately subsequent years rather than canceled, again part of the taxes originally due on them were canceled. This system was also a way of "postponing" taxes. Finally, when salt tax debts did accumulate, extraordinary adjustments were possible involving at least de facto cancellation, as shown by adjustments at the Liang-huai zone in 1822, 1828, 1829, and 1831, whereby repayment of debts totaling about 50 million taels was either postponed for many years or in effect canceled, an enormous sum by the fiscal standards of the day.[6]

As we can see from the Ming Board of Revenue's Liang-huai salt reform proposals made in 1616, Ming policy also stressed collecting salt tax debts, but such collection was based on practical considerations rather than on a definite precedent automatically adding payments for tax debts to the current tax schedule, and it was looked on as analogous to the collection of land tax debts.[7] The Ch'ing precedent distinguishing the treatment of salt tax debts from that of land tax debts grew in a somewhat roundabout fashion out of a series of events beginning in 1675.

In 1675, because of the disruption caused by Wu San-kuei's rebellion (1673–1681), the salt and the salt tax quotas for seven Hunan prefectures were canceled. As peace was restored, salt shipments to four of these prefectures were resumed in 1678, and shipments to the other three, in 1679. Then around 1691 some merchants started a vigorous campaign to ship some of those quotas canceled in 1675, 1676, 1677, and 1678. At least three Liang-huai salt commissioners opposed their demands, largely on the grounds that the added salt would lead to a glut in the market. By late 1693, however, the merchants had won a favorable decision, and in about 1695 they successfully requested to ship all the remaining canceled quotas.[8]

4. *TYT*, 42:4b.

5. *TWI*, 17:31b. Saeki Tomi, *Shindai ensei no kenkyū* (A study of the salt administration of the Ch'ing dynasty; Kyoto, 1956), p. 222. This device of cancellation was called *ch'ung-hsiao.*

6. Metzger, "Organizational Capabilities," p. 41.

7. *Huang-Ming ching-shih wen-pien*, 29:342–346.

8. This account is from *chüan* 7 and 19 of *LHYFC*.

Possibly their success involved an unpublished agreement to preclude future tax cancellations. At any rate, Wang Shou-chi, a nineteenth-century official with much specialized experience in salt affairs, said:

> During the rebellion of Wu San-kuei, prefectures [in Hunan] such as Heng-chou and Yung-chou were all occupied by the rebels, and salt shipments stopped. After these areas were recovered, not only were the old quotas resumed, but eventually merchants a number of times petitioned at the capital to ship all the amounts which had been canceled, first paying the taxes. Therefore these amounts were authorized. The salt tax precedent precluding cancellation probably originated with this episode. The merchants' request was due to the fact that just then sales were good and three-fold profits could be obtained.[9]

Thus a precedent acquired the full force of a regulation, but in this case the law seems never to have been written down in any book of laws. Rather it was just referred to in memorials, and its content was manifested only in practice. By contrast, the precedent for relief measures relative to salt makers hurt by natural disasters gradually emerged and then was fully articulated as a detailed regulation found in salt gazetteers. It is understandable that the government was happier to publicize this compassionate law than the harsh law above.

Although the Ming dynasty had had various relief measures for salt makers hurt by natural disasters (flooding from the sea was a major problem), it had left behind no definite regulations on relief. In the first seventy years or so of the Ch'ing period, the Liang-huai salt makers' main tax (*che-chia*) was remitted a few times, but only for exceptional reasons, such as the flight of all salt makers from a particular production yard; there was no regulation allowing for routine relief grants of government funds or grain similar to those made to farmers. Thus a censor's proposal in 1665 to give the salt makers relief grants and a tax cancellation was advised against by the Board of Revenue. This advice was connected to the idea that the land tax and the salt makers' tax were not comparable.

However in 1724 there was a major flood affecting many yards, drowning 49,558 persons. This unusually great disaster

9. Wang Shou-chi, pp. 30b–31.

nudged the process of legislation. The emperor decreed cancellation rather than postponement of the salt makers' tax, and the granting rather than the loaning of state funds for relief. Shortly after, a special granary was set up largely for salt makers, ready to issue grain in time of disaster as well as to sell it in order to level prices. The fact of this granary apparently strengthened the suggestion that relief measures relative to salt makers and farmers should be handled in a similar way. After this, officials began to adduce the regulations on canceling the land tax in order to obtain cancellations of the salt makers' tax (*che-chia*). A third legislative nudge seems to have come from the custom of bestowing favors on the people in honor of the ascension of a new emperor. At any rate, it was in 1736, the year that the Ch'ien-lung emperor ascended the throne, that cancellations of the *che-chia* were completely regularized. They were formulated on the model of the relief regulations for farmers and called for automatic cancellation of the *che-chia*, the percentage canceled depending on the extent of the natural disaster.[10]

At the pole opposite to such precedents or regulations with binding effect, one finds administrative proposals made with little or no reference to precedents. For instance, in 1833, stressing the difficulty of carrying out the Huai-pei salt reform, the governor-general of Nanking explained that "Huai-pei ticket salt is of the nature of *ch'uang-chü chang-ch'eng* (initially inaugurated regulations); there is a total lack of anything to go by."[11] (Actually there already were some similar arrangements in Shantung and Chekiang, but T'ao Chu was basically right.)

Commonly, however, officials facing an administrative problem, although careful to move within the limits of the given field of precedents and laws, chose a policy on practical grounds and then found the precedents to back it, or at least part of it. A typical example is a memorial of T'ao Chu presented in 1831 to deal with the problem of bringing grain into flood-stricken Kiangsu.[12] Four steps were proposed in this memorial: using government funds to buy grain in Honan, Hunan, Hupei, and Szechwan; loaning to Shanghai maritime merchants government funds with which to buy grain in Kuantung (southern Manchuria), which would be sold at "normal" prices (or used

10. *LHYFC*, 41:3–4b; 41:8–10.
11. *TYT*, 46:18.
12. *TYT*, 34:17–19.

for military rations) in Kiangsu; canceling customs taxes on grain boats coming to Kiangsu; and canceling customs taxes on grain tribute boats returning by the grand canal from the Peking area after delivering the grain tribute and on their way shipping grain from Shantung and Honan to Kiangsu.

T'ao Chu adduced two *ch'eng-an* (established cases) and one *ting-li* (fully established precedent) in arguing for these steps. The two *ch'eng-an* were occasions in 1814 and 1823 when Kiangsu had been hit by floods and government funds had been used to buy grain in Hunan, Hupei, Szechwan, and Kiangsi for the use in Kiangsu of civilians and soldiers. T'ao Chu's proposal to buy grain in Honan, Hupei, Hunan, and Szechwan was felt to accord with these two cases, even though the latter had involved no purchases in Honan. Practical reasons were given to explain the choice of Honan.

No case or regulation was adduced to support the idea of loaning funds to the Shanghai maritime merchants. This idea might have been regarded as an insignificant innovation or as a technical variation on the 1814 and 1823 cases, like the Honan purchases.

The proposal to cancel customs taxes on private grain boats accorded with a *ting-li* which exactly provided for this sort of action as a relief measure for disaster-stricken areas. (This precedent, it is clear, had originated as a *fu-chun* of 1737 and was also regarded as a *shih-li.*)[13] Furthermore T'ao Chu pointed to the fact that this precedent had been followed in 1820 and 1823.

Finally, the proposal to cancel commercial taxes also for grain tribute boats was a sensitive one, since commercial restrictions regarding this traffic were a continuing problem. T'ao Chu on the one hand justified this step by analogy, indicating that it was "in accord with" the above regulation on canceling customs taxes. On the other hand, he proposed it as an extraordinary measure which would not in turn become a precedent. (The emperor approved all points in this proposal.)

This example shows how administrative policy was devised partly on the basis of adducing precedents and partly through practical considerations. It would be wrong to say, however, that the adducing of administrative precedents in memorials

13. Compare the relevant Ch'ien-lung 2 entry in *chüan* 239 of *TCHTSL* with *TYT*, 34:18a–b.

was a mere appeal to the wisdom of the past. Naturally such commonsense use of precedents was also made. For instance the official editors of the 1806 *Liang-huai Salt Laws Gazetteer* "adduced the precedent of the new Chekiang [salt laws] gazetteer" to change the name of a certain inspection procedure. This precedent was quoted in the *fan-li* (principles of compilation) to reassure readers as to the propriety of the change.[14]

Adducing precedents in memorials had a more formal character. First, it was done not only to demonstrate propriety or efficacy but also to elicit imperial approval. It was the formally proper method of asking the emperor for a decision even in relatively minor matters of a purely practical nature. Second it was subject to laws of procedure, such as the law that in adducing precedents, *tse-li* have precedence over *ch'eng-an,* or the law that certain imperial executive commands may not be adduced as precedents (see below). Third, one may argue that administrative precedents did have some binding effect. Fourth, Ch'ing officials themselves regarded the adducing of precedents as a single procedure common to all substantive fields.

A troop movement in the winter of 1832–33 illustrates how the adducing of precedents was integral to the formal procedure of making proposals to the emperor, even when there was no sensitive issue and the issues were simple and practical.[15] When 1,500 soldiers were dispatched from Szechwan to Taiwan to put down disturbances, the decision as to what route they were to travel from Szechwan to the coast might have been taken by considering simply what route was shortest, quickest, and most convenient, but the discussion took the form of citing *ch'eng-an* (established cases).

The Szechwan governor-general had asked the Nanking governor-general what route was more convenient. Discussing this in a memorial to the emperor, the Nanking governor-general pointed out that when troops had been sent from Szechwan to Taiwan to quell another disturbance in 1787, there had first been an imperial edict designating a route passing through Kiangsu and Chekiang. Then the Chekiang governor had memorialized that it would be shorter to turn south from the Yangtze into Kiangsi, passing from Kiangsi through Chekiang and then into Fukien. This the emperor had approved, but then

14. *LHYFC, fan-li*:3.
15. *TYT,* 44:30–34.

the Kiangsi governor suggested a still shorter route passing directly from Kiangsi into Fukien, and this rerevised plan had also been approved by the emperor. When a similar occasion had arisen in 1806, the Szechwan troops again had passed directly from the Yangtze through Kiangsi into Fukien. Pointing out that this route saved more than 1,700 *li* compared to "making a detour through Anhui, Kiangsu, and Chekiang," the Nanking governor-general said: "This time [1832–33] the matter should naturally be handled according to [these] *ch'eng-an* (established cases)." The emperor expressed approval without raising any further questions.

The issue here is that the Nanking governor-general did not merely point to the 1787 and 1806 expeditions as proof that the Kiangsi-Fukien route was better but in both cases focused also on the fact of imperial approval of this route, noting the imperial decisions of 1787 and quoting from the edict of 1806. The fact that the emperor had approved the shorter route was as relevant to the 1832–33 decision as was the fact that the route had in fact proved to be shorter and more efficient.

Having looked into the distinction between precedents and regulations, we can now turn to the question of the process of categorization whereby various types of executive commands became precedents or regulations. However, three more preliminary points should be made. First, it must be stressed that, with one qualification, we are here dealing with formal categories which were applied by Ch'ing officials to all the substantively different fields of law such as criminal and administrative laws. Second, as the discussion will make clear, our categorization adds a degree of articulation to the indigenous outlook but basically accords with indigenously used distinctions. Third, official executive commands, as well as imperial ones, were sometimes used as some form of law, but it seems that the great bulk of the more prominent laws were imperial executive commands. My study of the salt monopoly shows that even many minor decisions were taken in the form of imperial appellate cases.

Executive communication included executive decisions; executive decisions included executive commands; executive commands with no prospective or general significance can be distinguished from those possessing such significance; and, finally, the latter sort of commands fall into different categories of law. Some Ch'ing terms, however, blur over some of these distinctions. A notable example is the term *an* (case), which covers nearly all the above categories and thus bridges the executive and law-making processes. *An* included all the various forms of executive commands described above, such as *yü* (edicts), *tsou-chun, t'i-chun, fu-chun,* and *i-chun.* The latter forms of commands could be used as laws in any substantive field, whether penal or administrative, as we can see from a glance at the *Ta-Ch'ing hui-tien shih-li* (Regulations and precedents supplementary to the collected statutes of the great Ch'ing dynasty), in which all these formal titles are used to designate the various laws contained therein. Thus commands with all these formal titles could be placed in any of the four formal categories of law: precedents, administrative rules, fully established regulations and precedents of capital offices, and basic statutes.

In one sense, *an* denotes any bureaucratic paper or file on a specific matter, whether or not involving an imperial or official executive command. At this pole *an* almost merges with the idea of office business in general. Handling *an-chien* (cases) was almost the same as managing *shih-chien* (affairs),[16] except that *an-chien* means that the matter at hand is represented by one or more bureaucratic papers. This meaning is really part of *tang-an* and other such terms denoting simply "office records."

In another sense, *an* covers those records consisting of commands without prospective or general significance, for instance, a case applying a precedent of tax remission to a particular flood-stricken district for a particular year. The term *ch'eng-an* (completed case) could also be used for such commands when these involved some matter which had been fully carried out, such as a routine trial of a criminal.

These *an* were distinguished in various ways from *an* used as laws or precedents. If an imperial command had the form of a *t'e-chih* (special rescript), it could not be adduced as a precedent. When officials tried to adduce *t'e-chih* as precedents, they were refuted on the explicit grounds that *t'e-chih* could not be so adduced.[17] It was more common, however, for the emperor directly to state in his approving rescript that his approval was good for only one occasion and was not to be used as a precedent, as in the statement "Authorization this time of your request is an extraordinary favor bestowed by Us. The act may

16. For this usage of *an-chien,* see *CFTL,* 14:25.
17. *LHYFC,* 15:7, 13b.

be done once but not again. In the future do not quote [this favor] as a precedent."[18]

In point of fact, however, cases thus removed from the realm of precedents might still be referred to later. An official could argue that although case *x* was not to be adduced as a precedent, it was desirable on practical grounds to repeat the action involved. For instance, in 1822, 1823, 1827, 1828, 1829, and 1831, there had been deficiencies in the grain supplies due to soldiers in Kiangsu on account of natural disasters hurting harvests in the areas from which these supplies were normally collected. Each time, to make up the deficiency, grain tribute grain due to be shipped up to Peking had been held back and issued to the soldiers. Yet these actions had partly been legally problematic, because in the 1827 case, the emperor had ordered that this case be treated as an exception not fit for use as a precedent; the emperor had stated that the correct procedure in such an emergency was rather for the government to buy grain.

Then in the winter of 1831–32, the Nanking governor-general and other responsible officials again faced the problem of such a deficiency and again asked the emperor to permit the holding back of some of the grain tribute. In an advice which the emperor accepted, the Board of Revenue unqualifiedly confirmed the legality of this proposal, although it objected to some of the details of the fiscal arrangement involved. Strong practical reasons were advanced in this instance for taking this legally problematic course. First, the preferred procedure, buying grain, would have been too expensive, since buying large amounts in bad years raised prices, and probably much grain would have had to be shipped in from afar. Second, the other legally unproblematic procedure, using grain in government granaries, was impractical because the amounts in these granaries not only were insufficient but also were needed for other purposes.[19]

Besides explicit statements precluding future use as precedents, commands not used as laws also were identified through common sense. They were regarded as *ch'ung-fu* (redundant). Around 1850 the famous expert on government finance, Wang Ch'ing-yün, memorialized that such redundant cases (and "mis-

18. *TYT*, 33:38. See also *TYT*, 33:36; 34:18b–19; 48:14b; and *TYCS*, 9:6b.
19. *TYT*, 37:11–20b, esp. 37:13–15, 17.

taken ones," that is, superseded ones) should be separated from those useful for analogizing or quoting as precedents.[20]

It is worth adding, though, that these redundant cases were rhetorically useful as demonstrating the wisdom of a precedent through the fact that action based on it had been taken more than once; memorialists sometimes quoted more than one precedent for the same action. No doubt publication of redundant cases, as in some salt gazetteers, was partly to facilitate such rhetoric.

In still another sense, *an* referred to our first formal category of law, precedents. These *an* were regarded as precedents in that they were available for *yüan-wei-li* (adducing as precedents) or for *pi-chao* (analogizing) in the finding of the law, activities common to all the substantive fields of law. Such *an* formed a category emphatically distinguished from another category of law, the *tse-li* (fully established precedents or regulations of capital offices), which generally had priority over these *an* in the finding of the law. Such *an* could also be called *ch'eng-an* (established cases) and, sometimes, *chang-ch'eng* (rules).[21]

The same set of names—*an, ch'eng-an,* and *chang-ch'eng*—was used also to denote our second category of law, administrative rules. Although often set up through an imperial executive decision, these rules were too numerous and locally peculiar to find a place in the *tse-li.* To take an example, when the Board of Revenue compiled the 1845 edition of the *Ts'ao-yün ch'üan-shu* (Complete book of the grain tribute), it asked the offices of the director-general of the grain tribute and the *ts'ang-ch'ang*

20. *HPTL, tsou-che*: 10b.

21. The use of *chang-ch'eng* to cover both administrative regulations and regulations on the administrative punishment of officials is illustrated by the 1872 edition of *Ch'in-ting li-pu chang-ch'eng* (Imperially endorsed rules of the board of civil officials). Since the 1843 edition of that board's *tse-li,* many *chang-ch'eng* had accumulated which were not fit to be compiled as *tse-li* because of their temporary nature but were still needed for quoting. Ma Feng-ch'en, pp. 55–56. In penal law, *chang-ch'eng* is illustrated by *Hsing-pu t'ung-hsing chang-ch'eng* (Generally circulated rules of the board of punishments). It also consisted of *an* which were much referred to but not compiled as *li* for various reasons such as their temporary nature or the fact that they were waiting to be compiled. (An edition put out in 1892 included cases from 1838 through 1892, while an edition published in 1909 brought the collection up through 1908.) On analogizing, see Bodde and Morris, pp. 175–178.

shih-lang (granary superintendents in the capital area) to look over their *chang-ch'eng* (rules), copy out what should be entered in the book, and send it to the Board.[22] The provincial regulations of Kwangtung lay uncompiled in the provincial offices for some two hundred years until the 1846 edition of *Yüeh-tung sheng-li hsin-tsuan* (Newly compiled provincial regulations of Kwangtung) was put out. Its editors referred to these regulations as *wai-pan chang-ch'eng* (rules for handling affairs in the provinces).[23] The use of *an* for "administrative rule" is illustrated by the following statement regarding the problem of fixing production and tax quotas for salt wells in Yunnan: "unless one runs the well on a test basis one or two years, fixing its production quota through comparison [of its rates of productivity], one cannot make a report [on this well and its quota] to the Board of Revenue for the latter to *li an* (set up a case or rule on)."[24]

Our third formal category is the *tse-li* (fully established regulations or precedents of capital offices). One can find instances where *tse-li* denotes administrative precedents or regulations peculiar to offices in the provinces.[25] However, *tse-li* largely referred to certain laws connected to capital offices.

Tse-li typically was used in the titles of administrative regulations, and *t'iao-li* is often associated with the regulations in the penal code. But some penal *t'iao-li* were officially called *tse-li*,[26]

22. *TYCS, tsou-che*:2.

23. *Yüeh-tung sheng-li hsin-tsuan,* prefatory material:2a–b; *fan-li*:1a–b.

24. Wang Shou-chi, pp. 61b–62. The term *chang-ch'eng* was used very loosely. Besides its use to denote our first and second categories of law, it could be used to denote our fourth category, the empire's most basic laws, as in the phrase *i-tai chih chang-ch'eng* (a dynasty's laws). *Chang-ch'eng* also could be used in almost any memorial as a label for a set of regulations or even just proposals. The fifteen points of the 1831 Liang-huai salt reform, for instance, were called *chang-ch'eng,* although some of them, e.g., the abolition of certain fees or taxes, were policy moves rather than regulations and indeed were not entered in the *Regulations of the Board of Revenue. TYT,* 30:50b.

25. In *LHYFC,* 21:12b, we find a 1736 memorial by the salt commissioner (*yen-cheng*) of the Liang-huai zone of the salt monopoly referring to the *tse-li* (administrative regulations) of a salt production yard (*ch'ang*) under him. The article of *tse-li* in question gave certain tax rates.

26. The edition of penal *t'iao-li* put out in 1679 was called *Hsien-hsing tse-li* (*Tse-li* currently in effect); *Ch'ing shih,* III:1733–1734.

and administrative regulations could sometimes be thought of as *t'iao-li*.[27] However, there is perhaps a slight difference in the dictionary meanings of these terms, in that *t'iao-li* strongly denotes "regulation," while *tse-li* perhaps more strongly connotes "precedent."[28] Moreover, *t'iao-li* was more commonly used than *tse-li* for the laws of a provincial office.

Shih-li tends to mean "precedent" and was used more loosely than either *tse-li* or *t'iao-li*. Admittedly, to some extent *tse-li* and *shih-li* were interchangeable, as can be seen in one instance where a writer uses both within the space of two pages to denote the regulations on administrative punishment.[29] However, *shih-li* seems never to have been used in the official title of a capital office's fully established regulations. Moreover, *shih-li* could be used to cover the whole penal code or to cover minor kinds of precedents not entered into any capital office's fully established regulations.[30]

Ting-li (fully established regulations or precedents) was often synonymous with *tse-li*, and in one context *ting-li* is specifically identified with the regulations of capital offices in contrast to the *li* (precedents, regulations) of a particular province. *Tse-li* could also be called *ch'eng-li* (established *li*), but *ch'eng-li* seems to have been looser than *ting-li*, since provincial *li* which were not *tse-li* could be called *ch'eng-li*.[31]

Tse-li of course was used for the regulations on administrative punishment, which were closely connected to the penal code. An eighteenth-century volume of penal *t'iao-li* has the title *Hu-lü tse-li* (Regulations of the penal statutes of the board of revenue section). Ma Feng-ch'en, p. 80.

27. An edict of 1806 which speaks of "clearly fixing the *t'iao-li*" refers to regulations generally, not just the penal *t'iao-li*. *CFTL*, 4:17b. *T'iao-li* could be also used to cover administrative regulations in the provinces. Ma Feng-ch'en, p. 111.

28. Morohashi defines *t'iao-li* as "laws written out article by article" but states that a *tse-li* is a "precedent" arising out of action in accord with cases or laws and held to be a *ting-li* (established regulation or precedent).

29. *HCCSWP*, 15:10b–11.

30. See II, 3.

31. *Yüeh-tung sheng-li hsin-tsuan, fan-li*: 1a–b. Also, in *LHYFC*, 10:18, *ch'eng-li* is used in 1770–71 to denote a precedent regarding administrative matters of a local nature in the provinces. The issue here was that there was no such precedent for a certain district in Kiangsi temporarily to receive salt from one zone of the monopoly instead of from its regular zone.

Many capital offices, not just the six boards, had *tse-li*—for instance the Court of Banqueting and the Court of Sacrificial Worship. A book entitled *tse-li* could also be put out for just one of a capital office's areas of activities, for instance, *Kung-pu chün-ch'i tse-li* (The board of works' regulations on military equipment).[32]

The transition from *an* to *tse-li* was made quickly by important imperial executive commands. A good example is the *chang-ch'eng* (rules) through which the ticket system was set up at the Huai-pei section of the salt monopoly. T'ao Chu, Nanking governor-general and head of that salt section, included these regulations in a *ch'ing-tan* (clear account) which he attached to a memorial sent off on June 2, 1832. On June 24, 1832, Tao Chu received a *chu-p'i* (vermilion comment) from the emperor endorsing the rules with the words: "Properly manage the matter according to [your] advice. The Board of Revenue is to take note."[33]

Possibly these rules were first published in the *Peking Gazette*. This was a publication which was put out regularly and frequently (in some instances, daily) by a government-sponsored, commercially-operated office for the purpose of keeping officials informed of new laws and other publicized governmental matters.[34] From references to it in writings by T'ao Chu and other officials, it seems clear that it was widely read by officials.[35] These regulations also must have been immediately printed on posters displayed publicly in the Huai-pei area for the benefit of the merchants. The government often publicized laws through widely distributed posters, and the tax rates of the Liang-huai zone of the monopoly were regularly posted.[36]

The Huai-pei ticket regulations appeared in an official compilation for the first time when the next edition of the *Regulations of the Board of Revenue* came out in 1838. When compared to the *ch'ing-tan* version, this version of 1838 shows considerable rewriting but only a few additions or omissions of content. For instance, the Board of Revenue did not bother to include the fact that the licenses handed out to merchants under

32. Ma Feng-ch'en, pp. 103, 105.
33. *TYT*, 40:16–25b.
34. See R. S. Britton, *The China Periodical Press 1800–1912* (Shanghai, Kelly and Walsh, 1933), pp. 7–17, and *Rikubu*, p. 1.
35. *TWI*, 16:1; *TYT*, 45:39; 52:23b; *HCCSWP*, 17:1, 17.
36. See II, 5, note 1.

this new system came in sets of three duplicates, each duplicate being routed through different offices and so checkable against the others. Probably this fact was omitted because precisely the decisive characteristic of these licenses was that, in contrast to the type of license they replaced (*yin*), they were handled totally through the regional salt administration and never passed through the Board of Revenue. On the other hand, the 1838 version included a regulation not in the *ch'ing-tan* version because it was an adjustment made in 1833 (a procedure to sell outside one's designated port).[37]

The version of these ticket regulations found in the next edition of the *Regulations of the Board of Revenue,* that of 1851, and that included, purely as a matter of historical interest, in the first subsequent edition of the *Precedents and Regulations Supplementary to the Collected Statutes of the Great Ch'ing Dynasty,* that of 1899, is essentially identical with the 1838 version.[38]

Tse-li were differentiated from *an* in three main ways. First, they were generally more prominent or visible, since they were typically published in books, while *an* often were found only in office records. Admittedly many *an* of various kinds were published, but one has to keep in mind the vast administrative role—still largely invisible to modern researchers—of unpublished office records. The financial accounting system of the Board of Revenue, for instance, partly consisted of periodic and detailed reports to the Board which seldom were published and which are only roughly reflected in the parallel flow of memorials and edicts. Especially in the case of administrative laws, office records were primary, published compilations, derivative and often inadequate. The edict to compile the first *Collected Statutes of the Great Ch'ing Dynasty,* for instance, came only in 1684, forty years after the dynasty's conquest of China, and although much of its material was obtained from already existing books of administration, a great deal came from records of the important offices which were listed by the editors as their sources of information.[39] Office records were regarded as a way of keeping laws on file, and they were supposed to be managed with utmost care to prevent rotting and illicit changes by clerks.

37. *Ch'in-ting hu-pu tse-li* (1838), 6:15–18. For the 1833 adjustment, see *TYT,* 46:24a–b.
38. *HPTL,* 30:12–15; *TCHTSL,* 223:Tao-kuang 12.
39. See *fan-li* of the 1690 edition.

The Yung-cheng emperor called them *i-tai chih tien-ts'e* (a dynasty's records of statutes).[40] Office records naturally included both official and imperial executive commands. When the Nanking governor-general in an 1831 memorial quoted as precedents two official executive decisions made at his Liang-huai salt monopoly zone, the Board of Revenue in an advice to the emperor stated: "As for the 1787 and 1793 cases on postponing tax payments adduced by the said governor-general, according to his statement these matters were managed as *hsiang-chun* (proposal of an official approved by a superior official). Your ministers' board has no way to examine them. He ought to be ordered to make copies of the original cases and send them to our board as proof which can be checked."[41]

Second and closely connected to the fact of publication, *tse-li* usually involved two imperial executive commands: the command originally determining the individual case and the endorsement of a compilation of such cases whereby they were turned into *tse-li*. (The original imperial executive command sometimes included an order to put the command in the *tse-li*.)[42] Admittedly the books into which various *an* were compiled were, in addition, almost invariably endorsed by the emperor, but this endorsement did not change the formal category of law. With the *tse-li*, compilation and publication involved the idea of a transition into a higher category of law, a process of being *ting* (fully established). As the main regulations of capital offices dealing with affairs throughout the empire, the *tse-li* were more important than merely local regulations.

Third, the regulations on finding the law emphatically distinguished the *tse-li* from other formal categories. Generally speaking, the *tse-li* in all substantive fields had priority over all other formal categories of law, not only over *an* but also, at least eventually, over the more important or long-lasting laws such as the penal *lü*.[43] They were indeed the focus of law making

40. *TCHTSL*, 91:Yung-cheng 1.

41. *TYT*, 35:8b–9.

42. *TCHTSL*, 117:Tao-kuang 21.

43. The priority of the penal regulations (*t'iao-li* or *tse-li*) over the *lü* is explicitly formulated in *TCHT*, 54:1b–2: "When deciding a sentence, officials should take the revised *li* as their standard and need not adhere blindly to the penal statutes (*lü*)." In the field of penal law, the priority of *tse-li* or *t'iao-li* over *an* can be seen in the following regulation (*t'iao-li*) of the penal code: "[Officials, except those at the three offices of penal law at the capital,] may only quote

as a practical administrative activity, less susceptible, we may say, than the *tien* and the *lü* to "formalism," what the Ch'ing called *shih-wei-chü-wen* (to regard [an order] as a mere document).

The priority of *tse-li* over *an* in all the substantive areas of law is illustrated by imperial decrees of 1804 and 1811. The 1804 decree stated that the *pu-yüan* (boards and various other capital offices) should act according to the *ting-li* (established regulations). Only where the latter were incomplete could analogies be properly drawn from "old *an* (cases)." Unfortunately the latter currently included directly conflicting cases allowing corrupt manipulation by clerks in the finding of the law. The emperor ordered the *pu-yüan* to add explanatory notes to any of their established regulations which were unclear and to check through any discrepancies among their *an*, deciding which *an* should be discarded and which entered into the *tse-li* at the next revision.

The 1811 decree similarly complained of the tendency at the *pu-yüan* to *she-li yen-an* (disregard established regulations and cite cases). If certain *an* (cases) filled gaps in the *tse-li*, they should be entered into the *tse-li*. If they contradicted the *tse-li*, an explanation of the discrepancy should be entered into a record and the original case should be destroyed unless it had to be kept for future reference. In a decree the same year, the emperor stated that this important work of straightening out the cases and regulations at the capital offices must be entrusted

---

the penal statutes and regulations or precedents proper. It is wholly and severely prohibited that they drag in anything of the nature of *ch'eng-an* (established cases) which have not yet been generally established as *ting-li* (fully established precedents or regulations), with the result that the sentence is too severe or lenient. If the governors-general or governors in handling a penal matter really find an old case which is closely similar [to the matter at hand] and can be adduced as a precedent (*li*), they are permitted to report it in their memorial and append a request that it be established as a *ting-li*, the Board of Punishments then closely examining the matter." *TLti*, 49:92b; *TCLL*, 37:56b–57; Philastre, II:712. At the Board of Civil Officials, the Department for the Scrutiny of Merits, handling *ch'u-fen* law, could propose a regulation based on *ch'eng-an* if the code and the *ch'u-fen tse-li* both lacked either a directly appropriate article (*cheng-t'iao*) or an article from which an analogy could be drawn. See *TCHT*, 11:4a–b; *CFTL*, 1:3b. See the similar situation for military *ch'u-fen* in *TCHT*, 48:1b.

only to persons who had been at the office in question for a long time and were skilled in handling its affairs; otherwise lack of clarity and confusion would result.[44]

While the *tse-li* thus were differentiated from *an* in these three ways, there were two major areas of ambiguity in the relationship between them. Because of these ambiguities and because of the identity of origin of *tse-li* and many *an*—imperial executive commands—any view which drastically separates the categories of *an* and *tse-li* is unacceptable.[45]

The first area of ambiguity involved the extension of the idea of *li* to penal cases which had importance as precedents for a restricted locality or type of activity and which were classified as *shih-li,* although they were not important enough to be entered into the code proper as penal *t'iao-li.* They can be found appended to that text of the penal code entered in *Precedents and Regulations Supplementing the Collected Statutes of the Great Ch'ing Dynasty* and, relative to salt monopoly laws, in such publications as the 1806 edition of *Liang-huai yen-fa-chih* (Liang-huai salt laws gazetteer). The former work having an historical orientation, they are referred to as "precedents established over the years";[46] the latter having much more the character of an administrative manual, the precedents given there are called "precedents currently applicable."[47] On the whole, these salt *shih-li,* more often than the *t'iao-li,* are applicable only to a geographically limited area and deal with matters of limited relevance (such as the relation of Liang-huai merchants to wharfmen). They do not specify a sentence, merely pointing out that if a certain offense occurs, criminal and sometimes also administrative punishment is called for. To determine the specific sentence, an official would then have to refer to the penal code proper.

Another example of the use of *li* to denote regulations outside

44. *TCHTSL,* 85: Chia-ch'ing 9 and 16.

45. See *Shinkoku gyōseihō,* I:37, and *Ch'ing-kuo hsing-cheng-fa,* 1:3:1:43 for such an unacceptable categorization which puts *tse-li* on the side of statutory law and classes *ch'eng-an* together with customary law.

46. These can be found in various of the *chüan* of *TCHTSL* under "Board of Punishments." Those of *chüan* 724, following the *t'iao-li* on redemption, for instance, include valuable data on the development of the dynasty's redemption policy. *Chüan* 763 includes some on salt monopoly penal laws.

47. *LHYFC,* 38:15–27b.

the *tse-li* is some compilations of provincial administrative regulations entitled *sheng-li* (provincial *li*). Also there were at least three editions of a book of general provincial regulations called *T'ung-hsing t'iao-li* (Generally circulated regulations).[48] Usually administrative manuals designed for activities in the provinces were heterogeneous compilations bringing together all sorts of *an* with excerpts from *tse-li*, and they were published as a unit under some nontechnical title such as *shu* (book) or *chih* (gazetteer). As Ma Feng-ch'en's bibliography shows, *li* was seldom used for such books.

The second area of ambiguity involved *ch'eng-an* about to enter the *tse-li*, such as penal *ch'eng-an* which obviously were going to be entered into the penal code but which had been created in the five-year interval before publication of the revised penal *tse-li*. Such *ch'eng-an*, we may presume, could be adduced by provincial officials as soon as they came out, in spite of the fact that provincial officials were by law forbidden to adduce established cases or anything outside the "code proper."

For instance, in 1833, during the interval between the 1830 and 1836 revisions of the penal code, the Kiangsu governor, Lin Tse-hsü, facing the famous crisis of the silver flow out of China, complained in a memorial that while the regulations of the Board of Revenue called for the punishment of merchants who illegally sold silver to foreign merchants, there was no article in the penal code specifying a sentence.[49] The same year a penal *t'iao-li* was promulgated specifying sentences for those who illegally shipped either silver or gold out to sea.[50] No doubt it could be immediately adduced by all officials.

In the closely connected field of administrative punishment handled by the Board of Civil Officials, we have a similar instance of a regulation which was fully established as a *tse-li* in 1841, although there was no published compilation to enter it into until the *tse-li* of 1843. In this instance the emperor was worried about the smuggling of saltpeter, an ingredient of gunpowder during a time of war and domestic unrest. He ordered the Boards of War and Civil Officials to formulate a *ch'u-fen* ([article on] administrative punishment) to apply to civil and military officials guilty of lack of vigilance in stopping the smug-

48. Ma Feng-ch'en, pp. 111–112.

49. *Chung-kuo chin-tai ching-chi ssu-hsiang yü ching-chi cheng-ts'e tzu-liao hsüan-chi*, I:39.

50. *TCHTSL*, 776:1.

gling of saltpeter. When the Boards presented the article to him, he ordered that it be entered into the regulations immediately.[51] There is little doubt it could be immediately adduced.

The distinction between the *tse-li* and our fourth formal category, those laws regarded as the most basic, unchanging, or important, requires only brief discussion. This distinction was stressed by the compilers, but it was of greater ideological than administrative significance. Although this fourth category was regarded as more basic or important than the *tse-li,* the *tse-li* to a large extent had priority over it in the finding of the law.

A clear definition of our fourth category is that given by the compilers of the 1763 edition of *Ta-Ch'ing hui-tien* (Collected statutes of the great Ch'ing dynasty), a book covering the most important laws in all substantive fields: "The *Collected Statutes* are based on the idea of statutes and regulations and of collected essentials of government. What they record must deal with long-lasting and permanent institutions. Now we compile these as the state's great standards and great laws. The duties of offices, what the court and the people respectfully follow—in all instances we draw together the fundamentals and publish them as a completed book."[52]

It was the compilers of this edition who in 1748 carried out the idea of reserving the *Ta-Ch'ing hui-tien* for long-lasting laws and creating a new kind of book, *Ta-Ch'ing hui-tien tse-li,* for short-lived regulations or precedents supplemental to the *tien.* However, the exact dividing line between *tien* and *tse-li* or *shih-li* was never clarified. To a large extent, the *tien* simply gave general statements about matters described more completely in the *shih-li,* and there was much overlapping between these two categories. A good example is penal affairs. The three later editions of *Ta-Ch'ing hui-tien* under the heading "Board of Punishments" discuss basic penal principles and procedures of the code, most of which can be found in the code. The code itself was somewhat ambiguously viewed as *tse-li* and is included *in toto* in the two editions of *Ta-Ch'ing hui-tien shih-li* (its omission from *Ta-Ch'ing hui-tien tse-li* is discussed below).

Since any command or proclamation of the emperor, depend-

51. *TCHTSL,* 117:Tao-kuang 21.

52. This passage from the *fan-li* of the 1763 edition is quoted partly in *Shinkoku gyōseihō,* I:9, and in *Ch'ing-kuo hsing-cheng-fa,* 1:2:1:9–10.

ing essentially on its content, might have the character of a law of utmost importance and fixity, one may also place in this fourth category all such imperial commands lying wholly or partly outside the *tien* and *lü*. In particular the various compilations of *sheng-hsün* (sage instructions) were regarded as important, and one may infer that the *shih-lu* (veritable records), an official, chronological record of the emperor's actions, had a similar character. The "principles of compilation" of the third edition of *Ta-Ch'ing hui-tien* (1763) mention that relevant material in the *shih-lu* kept at the Office of Imperial Historiography was copied out and entered into this edition of the *hui-tien*.

In this fourth category of most important laws, many items were inherited from the Ming. However, a considerable amount of fresh material was introduced during the first century of the dynasty. First a few changes were made in the *lü* when the second and third editions of the penal code were put out (1727, 1740). Second, the third edition of *Ta-Ch'ing hui-tien* (1763) was based largely on material taken from the first two editions (1690, 1733), and the material in these editions to a large extent consisted of Ch'ing imperial executive decisions made over the years. The editors of the 1763 edition did not preclude all further changes in the *tien*, but they did intend that there be very few. Actually, some significant ones still were made. For instance, the 1818 edition introduced a distinction between foreign countries having tributary relations with China and those having merely commercial relations. The latter kind of relations thus received full legal recognition as part of the emperor's basic "unchanging" political order. Putting this distinction into the *tien* may have either signified recognition of the failure of the tributary system or expressed a spirit of "moderate realism" (see I, 5) often present in the history of imperial China's foreign relations. Either way, the editors of this book were trying to keep at least this area of law in touch with a changing reality.[53]

53. *TCHT* (1818), 31:3–4. Fairbank and Teng, *Ch'ing Administration*, pp. 154–159, 174–178. For another *tien* change after 1763, see IV, 3, d, note 12.

4. Substantive Categorization

In defining our four formal categories of precedents and other laws, we have had to make a number of awkward qualifications and discuss various ambiguities. Yet compared to the concepts available for substantive categorization, these formal categories comprised a well-ordered spectrum. Three points should be made about Ch'ing substantive categories. First, contrary to some modern opinions, there were no generic terms to make the fundamental distinction between penal and administrative law. Second, substantive categorization was carried out through a large number of topical headings which, although lacking any architectonic pattern, did essentially segregate penal and administrative laws and did involve some effort to achieve neatness and order of presentation. Third, if we today analyze Ch'ing law in terms of its governmental or political functions, we should add to the two major substantive categories of penal and administrative laws that of the law on administrative punishment, since the content and institutional framework of the latter were distinctive.

The penal code is clearly defined as a substantive category. Prefatory memorials sometimes identify the distinguishing feature of the code's content as follows: "The compilers will minutely check and compile according to their respective categories all those edicts and rescripts received over the past years [since the last edition], memorials from officials at the capital and in the provinces which were approved after an advice, and all *i-chun* (imperially approved proposals) [originating] from the Boards of Civil Officials, Revenue, Rites, War, and Works—all those of the above documents received over the past years [since the last edition] which involve criminal sentences and ought to be compiled as regulations." [1]

Another formula was also used (for instance, in the prefatory memorial of the 1830 edition): "The compilers entered into [the new volume], article by article, all those edicts and rescripts received from the emperor and those memorials approved after an advice and presented by officials at the capital and in the provinces which are relevant to the severity of sentences and which ought to be compiled as *li*, not compiling those which

1. *TCLL, tsou-shu*:25. This is a prefatory memorial of the 1768 edition.

only state legal prohibitions and lack connection to the determination of a sentence."[2]

This reference to the exclusion of articles "which only state legal prohibitions and lack connection to the determination of a sentence" is helpful, because administrative laws are full of such articles calling for *chih-tsui* (sentencing by inflicting a criminal punishment) or *i-ch'u* (advising on administrative punishment) but not giving the specific sentence. The late Ch'ing legal expert Hsüeh Yün-sheng complained that some articles in the code did not belong there because they specified no sentence, and at least one such article was in fact removed explicitly on these grounds.[3] Conversely, officials generally felt that the code should specify sentences for anyone violating the prohibitions contained in administrative regulations. The following example suggests that if someone violated a prohibition for which the code specified no sentence, he could not always be punished. In 1833 Lin Tse-hsü noted: "I find in the regulations of the Board of Revenue: 'Those maritime merchants who illegally deliver silver to barbarian boats for shipping out to sea are to be criminally sentenced according to the penal law.' However the Board of Punishments' penal code only has an article on the criminal sentences for shipping gold and copper cash out to sea and completely lacks any clear text on how to administer criminal sentences in instances where silver has been shipped out to sea, with the disturbing possibility that there is no way to subdue the ambitions of corrupt merchants." (That same year a penal regulation providing sentences relative to silver was promulgated.)[4]

Although the penal code can be regarded as a body of law basically specializing in criminal punishments, this view must be clarified. First, it is useful to keep in mind the broad range of criminal punishments included; no complete list has ever been compiled, apparently. Hsüeh Yün-sheng, commenting on an article specifying the sizes of the cangue, remarks, as though with surprise, that the use of the cangue shows that the notion of the "five punishments" was not exhaustive.[5] If he had looked

2. *TCLL, tsou-shu*: memorial of Tao-kuang 10/11/17.

3. *TCHTSL*, 763:*ch'a-fa*. A *li* here specifying tea monopoly procedures in the Kansu area was taken out of the code of 1740 because it specified no sentence.

4. *Chung-kuo ching-chi ssu-hsiang . . .* , p. 39; *TCHTSL*, 776:1.

5. *TLti*, 1:6.

up the imperial order of 1647 fixing the "five punishments," he would have found a good number of punishments explicitly given as "outside" the five punishments. However, even this list from 1647 is incomplete.[6] Second, the penal code includes articles of an administrative nature which specify no punishment.[7] Third, it includes articles on administrative punishment (*ch'u-fen*) both in the form of commuted criminal sentences and, perhaps less frequently, in the form of articles themselves specifying *ch'u-fen* such as dismissal from office.[8] Fourth, the code includes punishments that are status deprivations but not *ch'u-fen,* such as stripping a degree holder of his rank or forcibly returning a Buddhist or Taoist monk to the lay world. Naturally one also has to keep in mind the variety of principles in the *ming-li* (principles of sentencing) section whereby criminal sentences were commuted or otherwise adjusted. Unlike the connected *ch'u-fen tse-li* (regulations on administrative punishment), the penal code seems to lack any positive sanctions such as administrative honors or promotions.

There was no generic concept complementing *lü-li* to cover administrative regulations, that is, regulations positively specifying operational requirements instead of the sanctions applied to offenders. Describing the famous four T'ang categories of law—*lü* (code), *ling* (statutes), *ko* (regulations), and *shih* (ordinances)—one scholar holds that the *ling* "are purely administrative rules, and contain no sanctions for use against offenders . . . [and that] . . . this rigorous distinction between an entirely penal *Code* and the purely administrative *Statutes* was a post-Han development, and a conscious expression of the Confucian bureaucrats' instinctive distrust of penal law."[9]

This Confucian distrust of penal law, however, went hand in

6. See Appendix III.

7. For instance, there is an article specifying procedures whereby innkeepers were to keep records of all traveling merchants with whom they dealt. It goes on to deal with the question of disposing of property left behind by a traveling merchant who dies. See *TLti,* 17:2; *TCLL,* 15:2b.

8. *TLti,* 15:12b, e.g., prescribes *ko-chih* (dismissal from office) for a salt yard supervisor whose lack of vigilance leads to illegal selling of salt by the salt makers under him. Also found in *TCLL,* 13:7b.

9. Denis C. Twitchett, "The Fragment of the T'ang Ordinances of the Department of Waterways Discovered at Tun-huang," *Asia Major,* 6:23–79 (1957–58), p. 28.

hand with an acceptance of penal law as a necessary tool of government, as Ch'ü T'ung-tsu and others have shown.[10] Even when administrative and penal law were in fact segregated, the motive was practical at least as much as ideological. The thought of sanctions easily mingled with the writing of administrative regulations even if specification of sanctions was not properly included in such regulations. Thus in both Ming and Ch'ing times, writers of administrative regulations did not hesitate to insert general statements calling for criminal or administrative prosecution of offenders, even when specification of sentences was left to the bodies of law distinctly devoted to this subject.

At least after the T'ang period, moreover, this "instinctive distrust of penal law" failed to produce generic concepts rigorously distinguishing between penal and administrative law. Already in the Sung period, according to the modern scholar Ch'en Ku-yüan, the penal *lü* (or rather the penal category of *ch'ih*, which in the Sung period tended to supplant the *lü*) were intermixed with the *ling*.[11] Similarly, the *Ta-Ming-ling*, a body of *ling* theoretically in effect during the whole Ming dynasty, contained penal regulations, such as many or all of the *ming-li* (principles of sentencing) in the Ming *lü*.[12]

In the Ch'ing period, *ling* was no longer a prominent legal category of any sort and never a distinctive category for administrative regulations.[13] As we have seen, in one context it denoted imperial executive commands issued as approvals of proposals made to the emperor in contrast to *chih-shu*, commands independently issued by the emperor. It was occasionally used as a synonym for *tse-li* or simply to denote a form of imperial command, either singly or in compounds such as *yü-ling*.[14] The term *lü-ling*, while common, was never used to denote administrative regulations as a distinct category. On the contrary, it

10. Ch'ü T'ung-tsu, *Law and Society in Traditional China* (Paris and The Hague, 1961), pp. 267–279; Hsiao Kung-ch'üan, *Chung-kuo cheng-chih ssu-hsiang-shih*, I:63.

11. Ch'en Ku-yüan, pp. 110, 117.

12. Naitō Kenkichi, pp. 100–103.

13. This point is also made by Ch'en Ku-yüan, p. 111.

14. *TCHTSL*, 8:*i-hsü i-ch'u*: Ch'ien-lung 55 and Ch'ien-lung 56. This shows how *ling* and *ting-li* could be synonymous. In Ch'ien-lung 55, the emperor sent down a rescript specifying a new procedure and concluding "Let this be a *ling*." The next year, the emperor referred to this *ling* as a *ting-li*. For a similar usage, see *CFTL*, 31:9.

was often a synonym for the penal code, although it could be stretched to include the regulations on administrative punishment or to cover all imperially effected laws, including administrative ones.

We have seen that *tse-li* covered both administrative and penal regulations, although it was usually used for administrative ones. Neither were the *Ta-Ching hui-tien* (Collected statutes of the great Ch'ing dynasty) and its companion volumes of *tse-li* or *shih-li* reserved for administrative regulations, as is held by some scholars.[15] The universality of scope of these volumes stemmed not only from their use of the institution of the six boards as their *t'i-li* (structural principles)[16] but also from the fact that they took as their models the *Chou-li*, a classic of about 300 B.C., and *T'ang liu-tien*, a book officially put out in the eighth century A.D. The *Chou-li* includes the concept of the *liu-tien* (six divisions of administration), one of which is that dealing with punishments (*hsing*), and this concept in turn was the precedent for *T'ang liu-tien*, which accordingly also deals with punishments.[17] Although the six boards, as was well known, had developed not out of the six ministries of the *Chou-li* but out of certain originally minor suboffices of the Han government, it was sometimes held that there was a structural similarity between the six boards and the six ministries.[18]

In accord with this outlook, the penal code (*lü-li*) is presented *in toto* under the "Board of Punishments" section in the last Ming edition of *hui-tien*, that of 1587, and presumably it is also included in the earlier edition.[19] It is also included *in toto* in

15. *Shinkoku gyōseihō*, I:4, 9. Translated in *Ch'ing-kuo hsing-cheng fa*, 1:1:2:4–5, 1:2:1:10. Sybille van der Sprenkel, *Legal Institutions in Manchu China* (London, 1962), pp. 56–58. S. van der Sprenkel also errs here in implying that all the empire's administrative laws were in the various editions of *TCHT* and *TCHTSL*.

16. *Ssu-k'u ch'üan-shu tsung-mu t'i-yao* (Annotated list of works in the complete book of literature from the four categories; Shanghai, 1933), II:1704.

17. Naitō Kenkichi, p. 64; Ch'en Ku-yüan, p. 112.

18. See I, 3.

19. For all practical purposes, there was, besides the 1587 edition, only one previous one, which has a 1510 preface by the Cheng-te emperor, who notes that this book consists of a compilation which had been finished under the previous emperor (who wrote a preface for it dated 1503) and which had been on the verge of being issued when the latter died. Before issuing it, the Cheng-te emperor ordered some minor corrections; see *Ta-Ming hui-tien*, I:4–5. Some decades

the first two editions of *Ta-Ch'ing hui-tien;* its fundamentals are discussed in the last three editions of this book; some aspects of it are found in the first edition of *Ta-Ch'ing hui-tien tse-li,* published in 1763; and it is reproduced *in toto* in the two later editions of this work. While the editorial evolution of these books explains their variations in the presentation of the code, they all were universal compilations and all embraced the penal code at least in principle.

Although Ch'ing terminology lacked a generic term for administrative regulations, the distinction between administrative regulations and regulations on criminal or administrative punishments was carried out to a large extent by the various topical headings under which laws were printed, and these were often listed with some logic of presentation (see II, 2). This method of categorizing the law through topical headings is best illustrated by the various editions of *Ta-Ch'ing hui-tien* and *Ta-Ch'ing hui-tien shih-li* (*tse-li*). The three main criteria of organization used in these volumes are chronology; governmental office (for example, the Board of Revenue); and governmental activity or function (for example, maintenance of population statistics).[20]

The five editions of *hui-tien* and the three editions of supplementary precedents and regulations between them combine these categories in three different ways. Generally, in the original format followed by the first two *hui-tien* and all editions of *shih-li* (*tse-li*), the primary criterion is office; the second, governmental function; the third, a subheading of that function; and the fourth, chronological order. This format is identically described in highly abbreviated form in the "principles of compilation" of the first two editions of *Ta-Ch'ing hui-tien*: "As for the structure of compilation, categories are distinguished according to [governmental] matters, and within each category entries are arranged year by year."

The first change in format was decided on in 1748 by the editors preparing the third edition of *Ta-Ch'ing hui-tien.* As we

---

later a revision was prepared bringing material in the book up to 1549, but this compilation was not publicly issued. *Ibid.*, I:6–8. Chang Ch'i-yün's statement in the preface of *Ta-Ming hui-tien* that the Ming "revised" this book four times is misleading.

20. For "office," one often finds the words *kuan* or *kuan-ssu,* for "function," *shih, chih, chih-chang,* or *kuan-ssu so-shou.*

shall see, they carried out a minor editorial revolution based on the ideas that chronological presentation was appropriate to annalistic history but interfered with the clear presentation of current laws, and that long-lasting laws should be segregated from short-lived ones. Their solution was twofold: first, to put all short-lived laws in a new sort of book, the *Ta-Ch'ing hui-tien tse-li,* which retained the format of the two first *Ta-Ch'ing hui-tien;* and, second, to redo the format of *Ta-Ch'ing hui-tien* by largely eliminating chronological presentation in it.

There still was to come a second but minor change in format. This third edition of *Collected Statutes,* although eliminating chronology in its format, still used the old primary and secondary criteria of office and governmental function, respectively. The fourth and fifth editions of *Collected Statutes,* however, used office also as their secondary criterion.

Thus if we look at the Board of Civil Officials section in the 1899 edition of *Collected Statutes,* the first three sections are entitled "Functions of the Presidents and Vice-presidents," and the remaining sections are given under the titles of the Board's suboffices. For instance, to look up the regulations on administrative punishments, one looks under "Department for the Scrutiny of Merits." On the other hand, in the 1899 edition of *Ta-Ch'ing hui-tien shih-li,* these regulations would be found under their name, *ch'u-fen-li.* In this volume there are twenty functional headings under Board of Civil Officials such as chapters on types of promotions or on administrative sanctions.

Outside of such editorial organization of laws, there was no substantive categorization of laws by Ch'ing writers. Although the *Ta-Ch'ing hui-tien's* categorization suffers from a bewildering excess of topical headings, it had at least more order than those lists of books on governmental affairs which mixed administrative handbooks with compilations having mainly literary or historical interest.[21]

If we now try to categorize Ch'ing law in terms of its actual governmental functions (rather than in terms of the categories of traditional compilers or of modern legal scholars), we may say that by about 1740, Ch'ing law, on the most general level,

21. The *cheng-shu* category of *Ssu-k'u ch'üan-shu tsung-mu t'i-yao* is a typical example. Similar are the bibliographies in works such as *Huang-ch'ao cheng-tien lei-tsuan* (Our august dynasty's statutes of administration compiled by category; Shanghai, 1903) and *Ssu-ch'uan yen-fa chih.*

fell into three substantive categories: penal laws, that is, laws specifying criminal sanctions; laws on administrative punishment, that is, laws applying essentially to officials and specifying noncriminal sanctions such as grade demotions (officials were also subject to penal law); and administrative regulations, which specified not sanctions but administrative or procedural requirements, focusing on the performance requirements of the government. This categorization is not so convenient for the early Ch'ing period because, as we shall see, the category of laws on administrative punishment was not so clearly differentiated then. By 1740 or earlier, these three categories were largely differentiated in practice, although there was no explicit idea that the law should be thus categorized. The *Ta-Ch'ing lü-li* specialized in penal law; chapters and books called *ch'u-fen tse-li* (regulations of administrative punishment) were overwhelmingly restricted to the category of administrative punishment; and most books of *tse-li* (regulations) focused on administrative regulations.

5. The Format of Books of Law

The main factor obscuring these categories is that the relation between them and books of law, although congruent to some extent, was not perfectly one-to-one. Unless this point is thoroughly appreciated, one cannot but be confused by the organization of Ch'ing law. In other words, to understand the latter one must think in terms of three principles: formal categorization of laws, substantive categorization of laws, and book format. The reasons for the considerable variability of book formats can be sought mainly in three areas: the organization of publication; the purpose of publication; and the nature of some of the administrative structures for which books of law were devised.

The intermingling of public and private elements in the organization of publication can be seen as a background factor promoting variability in formats. Publication was regarded as serving the interests of the historian as well as those of the government (see below), and traditionally the activities of the historian often mingled official and private aspects.[1] Moreover, publication of the laws was often privately financed and led. Even when compilation and distribution were arranged entirely through government organs and the compilers worked under the threat of salary fines in case of mistakes in grammar or style, private financing often played a role. Conversely, compilations made essentially through private initiative could still gain imperial endorsement and be regarded as official.

For instance, *Tu-li ts'un-i* (Questions on reading the penal regulations), published privately in 1905 under the empire's new copyright law, was compiled by Hsüeh Yün-sheng, who had written it using "leisure time outside his office duties" during many of the some twenty years that he was an official of the Board of Punishments. He died in 1901, and around the winter of 1903–04, lower officials of that Board, hailing him as the outstanding "specialist" on the law of punishments of the day, petitioned the Board's senior officials to present the volume to the emperor. This was done, and an imperial rescript was issued ordering the officials in charge of code revision to use the volume for reference.[2]

This mixture of private and public impulses, however, was

1. Han Yu-shan, *Elements of Chinese Historiography* (Hollywood, Calif., 1955), p. 8.
2. *TLti, tsou-shu*:1:3.

not the most important cause of format variability. More important was the purpose of publication. Although promulgation was sometimes a goal, especially in the case of the *tse-li*, administrative communication and satisfaction of the general scholarly, historical interest in governmental institutions were two major purposes. This latter historical interest was connected, it would seem, to the self-image of the compilers as historians and to a feeling that publication enhanced the dignity of the governmental unit which was the subject of the book. The interplay of the purposes of administrative communication and historical writing was a major factor in the development of formats.

Admittedly, the needs of administrative communication led to the appearance of books that we can comfortably call "administrative manuals." The *Hu-pu tse-li* (Regulations of the board of revenue), for instance, is made up almost entirely of quotations from bureaucratic documents and reformulations of laws written in a style devoid of any literary values except clarity and terseness. Although Ch'ing compilers regarded such books as the raw material for later historians, they had little immediate value outside the active uses of administration.

Administrative manuals can be identified in terms of three key features: their prefatory memorials and often also their principles of compilation (*fan-li*) explicitly emphasize that they were compiled in order to overcome the administrative confusion created by an overflow of bureaucratic cases and to facilitate the knowledge and observance of the law; they largely consist of chapters pruned of all content except laws "currently in force" (*hsien-hsing*) or cases useful as precedents for current practice; and they were routinely used by officials in office to find the law and carry out the administration of government, as is clear internally and/or from references in other bureaucratic documents. In other words, administrative manuals are not peculiar in the fact that most of their contents consist of bureaucratic documents but in the fact that the bureaucratic documents in them are arranged in the format through which they were understood for the purposes of administration.

Yet these administrative manuals were perceived as books of history. They fell into the broad category of compilations of material about government affairs. The major official bibliography *Ssu-k'u ch'üan-shu tsung-mu* (completed in 1782) places law books in the *cheng-shu* (books on institutions of government) category. This in turn was one of the subcategories of *shih* (history) and thus existed on the same formal level as those three other major subcategories of history: standard histories, annals, and narratives from beginning to end. The broad scope of *cheng-shu* is indicated by the nature of the original progenitor of this category, the famous governmental encyclopedia *T'ung-tien* of the T'ang historian Tu Yu.

Given this perception of administrative manuals as "history," it is not surprising that the very act of compiling past cases was ambiguous. Even though such compilations were administratively needed to look up precedents, their historical character inevitably became pronounced in an intellectual atmosphere where even compilations of laws "currently in force" were bibliographically classed as "history." Moreover, while there was an articulated need for books simply and clearly presenting laws "currently in force" which "should be given credence to and followed," there also was a desire to discuss an institution in a narrative or chronological manner so as to make clear its successive successes and failures (*te-shih*). Practical understanding of laws and understanding of past practice after all were interconnected. The only problem was how to convey both kinds of understanding efficiently through a single process of communication. This problem is illustrated by the editorial evolution of the three editions of *Ta-Ch'ing hui-tien shih-li* (*tse-li*) (1763, 1818, 1899) and the five editions of *Ta-Ch'ing hui-tien* (1690, 1733, 1763, 1818, 1899).

On the one hand, the character of all five editions of the *Ta-Ching hui-tien* as administrative manuals was a corollary of their ideology: communicating the basic laws of the state, they necessarily were supposed to be communicating laws currently in effect. In his 1684 edict issued at the start of the compilation of the first edition, the K'ang-hsi emperor pointed out that "for a dynasty to flourish, there must be a dynasty's laws by which to govern," and he deplored the fact that because the regulations were scattered in office records, it was hard for officials to examine them and for people to be acquainted with them.[3] Although the idea of a book of laws inherently had attractions, communication for the purpose of eliciting compliance was a central reason for publication.

Yet the first two editions of *Ta-Ch'ing hui-tien* had a particu-

3. *Ta-ch'ing hui-tien* (1690), prefatory edict: 1a–b.

larly pronounced historical character because, in contrast to the other three editions, a great part of their content was presented as dated imperial executive decisions grouped according to topic and then chronologically arranged. Currently valid regulations and superseded ones were thus not segregated and had to be distinguished by each official as he read the book. For instance, in 1648, years before either edition was put out, twenty wooden archetypical capacity measures were issued to the provinces, and a little while later, in 1655, these wooden measures were replaced with iron ones. Both the 1690 and 1733 editions of the *Ta-Ch'ing hui-tien* record each of these imperial executive decisions, leaving it to the reader to see that the arrangement of 1655 superseded that of 1648.[4]

It was to overcome the inconvenience of this mixture of content that the editorial reform of 1748 took place. When the emperor in 1747 initiated the compilation of the third edition of the *Ta-Ch'ing hui-tien,* he gave the cue for this reform by stating: "Furthermore, as for regulations carried out in the past which have repeatedly been fixed in detail, naturally one ought to give a correct version of their meaning and present the whole matter in outline. But if original proposals and old ceremonial forms are all recorded, filling up page after page, it only dazzles the eye and, contrary to what one desires, covers up the text proper."[5]

It was only after editorial work was under way, however, that this cue was taken up and that the complementary proposals were made and approved to overhaul the *Ta-Ch'ing hui-tien*'s format and to create a companion volume of supplementary precedents and regulations. These proposals were advanced in midstream since they were made in a memorial presented in 1748 by the Bureau for Compilation of the *Collected Statutes* after a small part of the draft of the newly revised *Ta-Ch'ing hui-tien* had already been delivered to the emperor:

> With regard to annals, the compilers when recording a matter include both the successes and the failures. The *Collected Statutes* [however] are meant to collect and present the great completed order of the laws used for governing,

4. See *ch'üan-liang* (weights and measures) sections under *Hu-pu* (Board of revenue) in the first two editions.

5. *Ta-Ch'ing hui-tien tse-li* (1763), prefatory edict of Ch'ien-lung 12/2/6.

so as to make known what [laws] should be given credence to and followed. The principle of the latter is [thus] very different from that of the annals' recording of events. [Yet] in the previous editions of *Collected Statutes,* whenever a great statute or ceremonial procedure was entered, the compilers necessarily set forth the matter as it was carried out in each reign. Even for each change of an official matter, for each alteration in some small part of the state, the compilers necessarily made a complete year-by-year account. Indeed it was like what the sage's edict described as "If original advices and old ceremonial forms are all recorded, filling page after page, they cover over the text proper." Not to mention the fact that ever since antiquity, fixing the fundamental institutions and ceremonies has always been [a process] using up long stretches of time before it was completed; what later times have in detail is what the past had in outline. If all [this process] is recorded period by period, the outcome necessarily will be that successes and failures will appear in the text as though to be compared to each other. When an official confronting a matter of state consults the text, he then finds that it does not fit the situation or that the statistics in it differ from the figures involved in the actual conditions. While he originally desired to follow the established laws, on the contrary it turns out that the text fails to make clear what should be followed.

Your ministers [therefore] respectfully request to assemble what the previous *Collected Statutes* recorded, obtain material from the records of the various offices, and edit all these items. With regard to all old regulations and new institutions existing from the time this dynasty set up the state until the announcement of completion of the currently revised *Collected Statutes,* we will put together the matter as a whole and prepare it in detail after careful consideration.[6]

The editors thus stripped the *Ta-Ch'ing hui-tien* of its annalistic character in order to make it a more efficient administrative manual. When the 1818 and 1899 editions of the *Ta-Ch'ing hui-tien* came out, the idea of focusing on currently valid laws

6. *Ibid.,* prefatory memorial of Ch'ien-lung 13/5/28, pp. 9–10.

was also directly expressed: "All statutes and ceremonies of the court and of the imperial ancestral temples and all duties of the offices are directly written into the *Statutes* according to what is currently practiced."[7]

The editorial change of 1748, however, did not fully solve the problem of distracting historical content. While largely freeing the *Ta-Ch'ing hui-tien* of purely historical content, the editors viewed this book as concisely presenting only long-lasting laws, the foundation of the state. This greatly reduced the scope and size of the book in comparison with the first two editions, which had had a larger goal of collecting all major laws. These editors therefore still had to face the task of compiling short-lived regulations, or, more specifically, of providing a comprehensive administrative manual for those capital offices still lacking published regulations. They met this problem by inventing a companion volume for *Ta-Ch'ing hui-tien,* namely *Ta-Ch'ing hui-tien tse-li* (Precedents and regulations supplementary to the collected statutes of the great Ch'ing dynasty). However, the format of this book and its two successors was chronological, like that of the first two *Ta-Ch'ing hui-tien,* with the result that the nature of these books again came to hover between the currently practical and the historical. The argument for creating a book of supplementary precedents and regulations was as follows:

> What the *Collected Statutes* record must deal with long-lasting and permanent institutions. As for the *shih-li* (precedents and regulations) of the various offices, there are some which are continually being adjusted and cannot serve as statutes and essentials of government. The most enduring of these take three to five years before they must be adjusted according to circumstances, the less enduring, perhaps one or two years. If no detail is omitted and all matters without exception are entered into the *Collected Statutes,* one indeed fears that printing and circulation will never be completed and that there will be too many alterations of the institutions. . . [Thus the fundamentals should be entered into the *Collected Statutes.*] If there are points which turn out to be incorrect or omissions, matters which still require careful deliberation, the officials can request a rescript to

7. *TCHTSL,* prefatory memorial. See also *Ta-Ch'ing hui-tien shih-li* (1818), prefatory memorial:5.

> decide them. All laws having been mutually adjusted and fixed in the most proper way, they can be handed down to last for ten thousand generations. With regard to setting forth the less important texts and the minor points clearly and in proper order, the Boards of War and Civil Officials each have [books of] regulations (*tse-li*), the Board of Rites is currently compiling a general digest on rites, and the Board of Punishments has for a long time had the penal code. All these can be revised from time to time so as to suit the needs of governing. As for the other offices, which lack *tse-li*, their [regulations] should be handed over [to us], and at [our] bureau we will compile them under their respective categories. In accord with the original advice of the Board of Rites, all [these] offices should be ordered to dispatch to us some officials of superior ability from their suboffices exclusively to take charge of the records of their offices so that mistakes are not passed on. As each chapter of the *Collected Statutes* is completed, it will be supplemented with one chapter of *tse-li*. [These chapters] will then be sent over to their respective offices for checking, and if there are no omissions or mistakes, they will then be presented to the emperor respectfully to await imperial endorsement.[8]

The first edition was probably more immediately useful in administration than its two successors. Perhaps it was because they regarded this book as parallel to board *tse-li* (regulations) that, in 1748, the editors used *tse-li* in its title (*Ta-Ch'ing hui-tien tse-li*). In the next two editions, *shih-li* (regulations, precedents), a broader term less associated than *tse-li* with the idea of current regulations, was used. The editors of these last two editions recognized their historical character by contrasting them to the *Ta-Ch'ing hui-tien*. While the most fundamental laws "were directly written into the *Collected Statutes* according to what is currently practiced, the successive changes and alterations are entered in detail into the *Precedents and Regulations*. Thus the latter are like following the stream to its source; indeed they are like [Confucius'] idea of 'I transmit [the past] and do not create.' "[9]

8. *Ta-Ch'ing hui-tien tse-li* (1763), prefatory edict of Ch'ien-lung 12/2/6, pp. 8–9.
9. See III, 5, note 7.

The more administrative nature of the first edition of these supplementary laws is also suggested by the fact that it does not include the penal code, there being no administrative need to reprint it. The two later editions, however, reproduce the penal code *in toto,* with the historian's touch of including the obsolete, excised penal regulations (which were not printed in the usual editions of the code), including valuable material explaining the changes. Certainly many parts of the last two editions had little administrative value. The sections on the Liang-huai zone of the salt monopoly, for instance, are hopelessly brief and include no material outside the gazetteers and the regulations of the Board of Revenue. Liang-huai salt officials in, say, 1820 relied mainly on office records, the 1806 *Salt Laws Gazetteer of the Liang-huai Zone,* and the latest *Regulations of the Board of Revenue,* and they had little if any occasion to refer to either the recent *Ta-Ch'ing hui-tien* or its companion volume.

Yet the administrative usefulness of these last two editions varied depending on the particular administrative activity. One variable was whether the *shih-li* compilers were able or wanted to keep up with a growing body of law. They were not in the case of salt monopoly regulations but were in the case of the *ch'u-fen tse-li* (regulations on administrative punishment) to a large extent. In the case of the tea monopoly (*ch'a-fa*), a minor governmental activity controlling only a little of the tea trade, the body of laws was so small that apparently no administrative manual specializing in the tea monopoly was ever put out. Coverage of the *ch'a-fa* in the *Ta-Ch'ing hui-tien shih-li* (1899) is about as full as in the *Hu-pu tse-li* (1851) and indeed includes some material arranged not chronologically but as "general rules," supposedly summing up current practice. In the late nineteenth century the leading financial expert Wang Ch'ing-yün referred to the *Ta-Ch'ing hui-tien* as the authoritative source for *ch'a-fa* regulations.[10]

Besides this interplay of historical and administrative purposes, we should, thirdly, take into account the problem of the compilers in devising handbooks adequately depicting their administrative objects. Especially in the case of some regional organizational complexes involving various areas of law, compilers often had to draw on a number of formal and substantive

10. Wang Ch'ing-yün, 5:64b.

types of laws or cases, including both imperial and official commands, and themselves to present administrative information in the form of explanations, lists, and so forth. Their problem was especially acute when dealing with large, complicated organizational networks lacking any clear-cut boundaries. At the same time, even while seeking to communicate the legal structure of such open-ended networks, they still thought of themselves as historians and sought to produce books with a historical character. Salt gazetteers exemplify this strain between historical interests and the need to depict complicated organizational configurations.

The salt monopoly was not made up of a clearly bounded hierarchy of offices similar to a modern corporate organization. It lacked an official name explicitly involving either the idea of a monopoly or some kind of corporate organization. Its regional subdivisions lacked an official generic name. Its legal foundation did not consist of a charter or any clearly delineated body of law but rather of numerous and various laws scattered in various books, office records, and public posters.

Neither did it consist of a head office at the capital with regional branches (although its organization in parts of the Han and T'ang periods resembled such a model). Rather it consisted of some ten regionally defined complexes of governmental and private activity, which we call "zones"; a process of capital-based supervision; and the empire-wide unifying executive authority of the emperor.

The complexity of organization within each zone involved, first, complex lines of horizontal coordination between offices. Generally speaking, there was a hierarchy of officials specializing in salt affairs supervising the production and the shipping off of the salt, but this hierarchy had to coordinate itself with various civil and military officials in the productive and distributive provinces, notably in order to counter smuggling. A secondary but still major problem was horizontal coordination between this salt hierarchy and other salt zones, other provinces, and other organizations such as that specializing in the shipment of grain to the capital.

At the same time, zone officials were controlled by a capital-based apparatus of supervision, but there was no one commissioner in charge of the empire's monopoly, no one office in the capital with comprehensive supervisory authority over the monopoly, nor even any organ at the capital except the emperor which could send orders to a zone (except for minor, routine affairs). Generally, the function of the six boards was to check on the fulfillment of the regulations assigned to them, to be well and broadly informed about all matters relevant to these regulations, and to give often definitive advice to the emperor regarding their whole area of supervision. Usually salt memorials to the emperor from zone heads or heads of the recipient provinces required the advice of the Board of Revenue, but the Board of Civil Officials was also important, and in fact salt affairs were touched on by all six boards' regulations. Like all governmental affairs, salt affairs were also influenced by the Grand Council, the Grand Secretariat, and some other units within that very wide range of offices and title holders at the capital and outside with the authority to memorialize. Admittedly, however great the number of offices allowed to discuss salt affairs, the noise of the discussion usually came from only a few. Finally we should add that the workings of all this bureaucratic machinery involved two main missions: controlling the salt trade and maintaining bureaucratic discipline.

The second area of complexity in the organization of a zone lay in the complex relations between the above bureaucratic machinery as a whole on the one hand and the economic facilities and personnel directly involved in the production and distribution of salt on the other hand. Generally speaking, Ch'ing salt offices depended little either on the device of territorial jurisdiction or that of state ownership of facilities in order to exert their control over the salt trade. Territorial jurisdiction largely remained in the hands of the regular provincial officials, and ownership of facilities largely remained in private hands. Zonal offices impinged on production and distribution mainly by setting up authorized forms of access to various private economic facilities for various private personnel such as saltmakers, porters, packers, boatmen, and merchants; by positive control over their activities, seeing to it that these people carried out their economic and fiscal obligations, pressuring, coordinating, and helping them; and by negative control, preventing them or persons outside the monopoly from smuggling.

Conceptualization of any particular zone as a whole, therefore, involved an open-ended complex of economic facilities, the economic and fiscal obligations of the personnel authorized to use them, the ways in which they were supervised, the zonal executive offices carrying out this supervision, and the Peking-based process of control, consisting essentially of the investigatory and advisory activities of capital-based offices and the emperor's executive authority.

Zonal salt gazetteers had to give an account of these matters because they were administrative manuals. Their prefatory material focuses on the concept of facilitating communication of the administrative system in order to elicit compliance and reads just like the prefatory materials of board regulations; the bulk of their material is currently relevant administrative information unobtainable in any other book; and their use as administrative manuals is illustrated by many passages in memorials which cite information in them in order to find the law. As typically put in a prefatory memorial in the *Newly-revised Ch'ang-lu Salt Laws Gazetteer* of 1726: "I would say that the true reason there are gazetteers for the salt monopoly is to present the laws and administrative institutions and to stop quarrels and litigations. There are maps for the production areas, population figures, different designated sales areas for those with master licenses or local licenses, fixed regulations for tax rates—printing all these facilitates following the law."[11]

At the same time, the compilers of salt gazetteers thought of themselves as historians and sometimes specifically compared salt gazetteers to "local gazetteers," which were regional histories. For instance, in the 1693 edition of the *Salt Laws Gazetteer of the Liang-huai Zone*, a preface written by the just-departed Liang-huai salt controller states: "a city, prefecture, or district tends to have a *chih-shu* (gazetteer), which gives a full account of the social and economic characteristics of the locality, population, taxes, constructions, and the history of successive changes. Thereby later men may act by taking into proper consideration both the models of the past and the needs of the present and may understand what they should take as an example and what they should be warned against. This is indeed important, and how much more so in the case of the salt laws of the Liang-huai zone, which is of the greatest importance both for the state's material needs and for the livelihood of the people!"[12]

Thus designed both to accord with the historian's orientation and to present a complex legal order, the format of many salt

11. *Hsin-hsiu Ch'ang-lu yen-fa-chih,* prefatory memorial. See also II, 4.

12. *Liang-huai yen-fa-chih* (1693), I: 1–2.

gazetteers can be viewed as divided into three parts. The heart of any zone's manual was communication of the administrative order peculiar to the zone. The manual, however, was produced essentially for the use of that hierarchy of specialized salt officials in charge of production and shipment. Consequently it focused on their responsibilities, neglecting the salt responsibilities of officials in the recipient provinces in charge of local wholesaling and retail distribution. The nature of the administrative order was conveyed partly by explanations, maps, tables, and pictures devised by the editors, and partly by the reproduction of official and imperial cases, some of which served as precedents or were even labeled "regulations" (usually *kung-shih, chang-ch'eng,* or *kuei*).

Most of this material was far too particular, detailed, and voluminous to have been drawn up into the *Regulations of the Board of Revenue.* This hardly means, however, that the detailed administration of the zones was outside the powerful influence of that board. On the contrary, zone precedents down to an extremely detailed level were set through imperial cases, that is, through requests made to the emperor by zone heads and granted by him often on the advice of the Board of Revenue. Thus in the *Liang-huai Salt Laws Gazetteer* of 1806 the bulk of the material consists of just such imperial cases, too numerous and too peculiar to the zone to have been entered in the board's regulations. Some official cases—precedents set originally without reference to the emperor—were also included, for instance, one dealing with the detailed procedure of inspection and repacking of salt bags at I-cheng, explaining which entrances of the inspection depot should be used to bring in and take out the bags.[13]

Because the activities of a zone were so complex, hopeless confusion would have resulted from trying to compile the material under the headings of zonal offices rather than function. Chapter organization is, therefore, largely based on the idea of function or types of activities. These varied significantly from zone to zone, largely depending on the size of the zone and on the way producers and distributors were organized. While the Ch'ang-lu gazetteer of 1726 had altogether only three or four chapters dealing with production, shipment, and merchants' taxes, the Liang-huai gazetteer of 1806 has twelve chapters

13. *LHYFC,* 11:21–23.

dealing with "shipment," nine chapters on "taxes," and five chapters on "yard saltmakers." Further designated with various subheadings, these chapters partly deal with very specialized subjects such as "loading at and shipment out of the production yards," "hastening shipments," "diverting shipments to other markets," and "total outlay of shipment merchants."

A second distinct part of salt gazetteers often was reproduction of the relevant sections of various board regulations including the penal code. The above Liang-huai gazetteer uses the generic term *lü-ling* (laws) to list relevant sections from the penal code, certain penal cases significant for Liang-huai but not entered into the penal code, and relevant regulations on administrative punishment. (It omits the Board of Revenue's regulations.) The late Ch'ing *Szechwan Salt Laws Gazetteer* uses a similar generic term, *chin-ling* (prohibitions and laws), under which it reproduces relevant sections from the laws on (civil) administrative punishment, the Board of Revenue's regulations, laws on administrative punishment for members of the Green Standard army, and the penal code. No salt gazetteer I have seen exhaustively quotes all board regulations relative to its zone, but typically the major items were pulled together.

The third part of a typical salt gazetteer consisted of material essentially of extra-administrative significance: various imperial edicts falling outside the scope of the administrative sections and often including items from previous dynasties; other kinds of imperial matters, such as the arrangements made by Liang-huai salt officials to entertain the K'ang-hsi and Ch'ien-lung emperors at Yangchow and Huai-an during the tours they made there; cultural materials such as sections on literature; and various sections of a historical nature.

Paralleling typical chapters in local gazetteers, there were chapters in this third part devoted to topics like biographies or tables of salt officials, biographies of outstanding people living in the area, "successive changes," and historical landmarks or stone inscriptions. But because local gazetteers dealt far more comprehensively with their area and its people, and because they dealt with many activities peculiar to local government and irrelevant to the salt monopoly, they typically had sections not found in salt gazetteers, such as "constellation and territory," "customs," "products," and "post stations." One might also say that, because salt gazetteers focused more than local gazetteers on administrative matters, they made a stronger point of recording in historical sequence memorials and other writings dealing with their administrative problems (the Liang-huai gazetteer of 1806 has two long chapters on "Important discussions of salt affairs from the past until today").

Finally, the historical character of salt gazetteers is evident in the compilers' explicit preoccupation with historical methodology. For instance, in the "General Principles" section, the editors of the *Salt Laws Gazetteer of the Liang-huai Zone* (1806) raised the old and basic question of the use of tables in historical writing.[14] In contrast to previous gazetteers, they said, they had put tables into their editions because tables were part of the proper format of historical writing, to which category, they said, gazetteers belonged.[15] The late nineteenth-century *Szechwan Salt Laws Gazetteer* has a brilliant bibliography called *cheng-yin shu-mu* (list of books used for verification) and stretching back to the classic *Chou-li.* The editors of this book weighed the method of quoting from or wholly presenting original governmental documents against that of devising freshly written accounts based on such documents. On the one hand, they felt that they should include many documents in full. On the other hand, both to avoid troublesome fiscal details and to cover over gaps in the record available, they did provide a good number of freshly written accounts. In this they felt that their format contrasted with that of the Liang-huai and Liang-che salt law gazetteers, which relied far more on original documents.

They also stressed that a gazetteer should make clear the good and bad points of various administrative practices.[16] Again we see how the question of making clear the good and bad points of an institution (*te-shih*) was a major link between the ideals of historical writing and the needs of administrative communication. Yet too much history could also be a danger, as the editors of *Ta-Ch'ing hui-tien* (1748) had indicated. The editors of the *Salt Laws Gazetteer of the Liang-huai Zone* (1806) criticized previous gazetteers for collecting historical information in each section and aimed in their book to restrict such informa-

14. See Lien-sheng Yang, "The Organization of Chinese Official Historiography," in W. G. Beasley and E. G. Pulleyblank, eds., *Historians of China and Japan* (London, 1961), p. 56.
15. *LHYFC, fan-li*:2b.
16. *Ssu-ch'uan yen-fa-chih, fan-li*:2b–3.

tion to two sections set aside especially for historical background.[17]

To some extent, then, the editors of *Ta-Ch'ing hui-tien* (1748) focused more on administrative needs than did some salt gazetteer editors, while the latter were more concerned with the dignity and historical character of their work. While the former rejected an annalistic format and the goal of making clear the good and bad points of laws (*te-shih*), the latter aimed for an administrative manual which would serve as a guide for practice by providing considerable historical background clarifying the good and bad points of different procedures. Because of both the self-image of editors and the objective needs of administration, historical and more purely administrative styles of presentation continued to overlap.

17. *LHYFC, fan-li*:2b.

6. Conclusion

We may now try to sum up the organization of Ch'ing laws. Although our scheme is based only on a sampling of the primary sources, it should at least have heuristic value.

Apart from those laws inherited from previous dynasties, the source of the state's laws was the administrative process itself, which generated executive commands and laws in a formally unified fashion, whatever the particular substantive field of administration. Although substantively distinct areas of law were especially shaped by the memorials of the corresponding specialized offices, the communications from multifunctional organs such as emperor and governor-general fed into all substantively different branches of law.

Some imperial and official executive decisions, whatever their form at origin, were sorted out according to a spectrum of four formal categories of precedents and laws. Although there were some ambiguities between categories, precedents or laws were distinguished in terms of one or both of the following criteria: having priority over other precedents or regulations in the finding of the law, and being considered more important in an ideological sense than other precedents or regulations. The four categories were: cases used as precedents, cases used as administrative rules, the fully established precedents and regulations of capital offices, and the empire's supposedly most important and unchanging laws.

Substantive categorization lacked such a neat spectrum and consisted of a bewildering number of topical headings. There was not even a generic term for "administrative regulations" to balance against *lü-li,* which basically stood for "penal code." Yet in fact *tse-li* usually referred to administrative regulations; topical headings typically segregated penal and administrative laws, and the sequence with which topical headings were presented often had some inherent logic. After about 1740, topical headings also segregated the regulations on administrative punishment, and these may be regarded as a third basic substantive category alongside penal and administrative laws.

Publication of the fully established regulations of capital offices and of the empire's most important and unchanging laws usually was congruent with a clear-cut substantive and formal category. This was so because the substantive categorization of law essentially derived from the functions of capital offices.

When all the fully established regulations of a capital office were put in one book, formal and substantive homogeneity was bound to be the main result, although stray paragraphs from other substantive areas were often inserted.

Many offices in the provinces, however, were multifunctional, administered affairs touching on all three of our main substantive categories, and required detailed regulations which were so locally peculiar and so numerous that they could not be crowded into *tse-li* (even if many of them had been established through imperial executive decisions). The complexity of some such offices was also increased by the "open-ended" nature of their affairs, since the scope of such offices could not be simply identified with either a clearly delimited unit of law, a closed set of offices, or a clearly delimited territorial unit of administration. Administrative manuals for such offices therefore could contain a complex mixture of substantive and formal categories of law. Furthermore, because the idea of compiling books useful for administration was only partly differentiated from that of writing history, material with no directly administrative relevance could also be put into some administrative manuals. Editors had some leeway in designing their formats, and although most books of laws or cases eventually were imperially endorsed, private and public initiatives mingled loosely in the organization of compilation. The kinds of elements which could be put into administrative manuals can be classed under two headings:

I. Information about the current administrative order:
   a. laws and precedents of the various substantive and formal types, as well as commands with no prospective or general significance
   b. other kinds of bureaucratic papers (e.g., *shuo-t'ieh*)
   c. information prepared by the compilers such as maps, lists of officeholders, and explanations of procedure

II. Materials to put the administrative order into perspective:
   a. Past cases or laws with more value as history than as precedents
   b. imperial matters of only general relevance
   c. editorial criticism or comment
   d. historical discussions
   e. cultural items

In surveying the way in which laws were made and communicated, one is struck by two themes central to organizational efficiency: the emphasis on flexibility and the problem of properly channeling a vast flow of information. Flexibility can be seen in many of the norms underlying law making, notably the emphasis on printing revisions at the cost of the ideal of "He followed the old regulations." The quality of freedom or looseness of expression in the bureaucratic language also reflects the stress on flexibility. Most important, there was an open and flexible relationship between the executive process and that of law making. The process of executive command was to a large extent the same as that of legislation, and new executive cases could be easily entered in books of law while obsolete ones were excised. Ideology demanded a class of laws essentially unchanging, but these laws in fact consisted to a large extent of imperial executive decisions issued over the first century of the dynasty and after; they were partly ill defined; and, most explicitly in the field of sanction specification, they were subordinate to the frequently changing *tse-li* in the finding of the law. Finally one can see flexibility in the freedom with which editors of law books could often devise that format most suited to their purposes. All these aspects of flexibility furthered effectiveness in designing and communicating laws. Yet given inadequate clarity in substantive categorization and the complicated mixture of cases and laws pertaining to some branches of administration, efficient communication was often not realized.

CHAPTER IV The Law on the Administrative Punishment of Civil Officials

1. Introduction

The law on the administrative punishment of civil officials was the main system of negative sanctions used by the Ch'ing bureaucracy to control the performance of civil officials. As presented in the books or chapters called *ch'u-fen tse-li* (regulations on administrative punishment), it essentially dealt with the punishment of officeholders for light offenses involving governmental affairs by means of impeachment and of economic and status deprivations. Although little studied, it was a major part of the total system of sanctions, which also included various informal elements and formal rewards, such as administrative honors and promotions.[1]

1. There are brief outlines of *ch'u-fen* law in *Shinkoku gyōseihō,* I:460–469, translated in *Ch'ing-kuo hsing-cheng-fa,* 3:7:1:181–194, and Hsieh Pao Chao, *The Government of China (1644–1911)* (Baltimore, Md., 1925). Neglect of the question of disciplinary sanctions in the traditional Chinese bureaucracy seems to be due partly to the fact that study of this bureaucracy has been influenced by the theory of despotism and by Weber's concept of bureaucracy, both of which neglect the question of sanctions. According to the theory of despotism, the character of the sanctions—their harshness—is obvious. According to Weber's theory of bureaucracy, the question of sanctions is only one among a number of more significant issues and just involves the problem of whether the bureaucrat "is subject to strict and systematic discipline and control in the conduct of the office." See Max Weber, *The Theory of Social and Economic Organization,* tr. A. M. Henderson and T. Parsons (Glencoe, Ill., 1947), p. 334; and Wittfogel, *Oriental Despotism,* pp. 155–156. Eisenstadt's approach also has led only to a few general remarks about bureaucratic discipline. See his *The Political Systems of Empires,* pp. 277–278. Neglect of the question of *ch'u-fen* law is reflected in the remarks of various scholars. Thus one cannot agree with T'ung-tsu Ch'ü's implication that the Ch'ing government did not make a distinction between "punishment for an administrative fault and for a criminal offense." This is an oversimplification; see T'ung-tsu Ch'ü, *Local Government in China under the Ch'ing,* p. 194. D. C. Twitchett

Since this law was a form of organizational control, many of its characteristics can be conveniently summed up in terms of a model of control requirements hypothetically applicable to any organization. As a social unit devoted primarily to the achievement of specific goals, any organization such as a state needs to control its members in such a way that they help to achieve its goals. To be effective, such control tends to require sanctions of a certain type.

First, the sanctions must be regarded as legitimate by the members. Otherwise, application of the sanctions will bring about disruption of the organization instead of eliciting effort from the members. The problem of legitimation can also be viewed as that of maintaining a sense of solidarity within the organization.

Second, the sanctions' scale of severity must accord with the members' success or failure in achieving the organization's goals; otherwise the sanctions will fail to elicit effort in realizing these goals. Therefore the sanctions will have to be "universalistically" correlated to performance rather than "particularistically" to the members' status. This also tends to involve the rationalization of the concept of responsibility. To some extent, the responsibility of an individual member must be rationalistically or realistically limited to those events within his practical control; otherwise the punishing and rewarding of the member will not accord with his failure or success in implementing the goals of the organization in a practical way.

Third, the punishment of members for minor lapses and mistakes must be mild enough so that the members will be willing to risk such mistakes. Otherwise the members will shun those

---

similarly writes that ". . . Chinese law made no very clear distinction between criminal acts and administrative errors, which were very severely punished." See *Bulletin of the School of Oriental and African Studies*, XXVII:3 (1964), p. 651. With some writers, lack of information about *ch'u-fen* law has been part of a basic misunderstanding about the nature of the imperial bureaucracy. Lucian W. Pye writes: "Nowhere in Chinese politics do we have a frank acceptance of the fact that men may be crass and self-centered and that it is only prudent in designing public institutions to insist upon checks and balances and to provide objective rather than subjective restraints on the use of power." This statement would more nearly be correct if "nowhere" were replaced with "everywhere." See L. W. Pye, *The Spirit of Chinese Politics* (Cambridge, Mass., 1968), p. 30.

organizational tasks which inevitably involve the risk of such mistakes.

The mildest punishments are normative-remunerative ones, such as the lowering of one's reputation and of one's chances for increasing rewards in the future. More severe treatment is where mistakes are turned into legal offenses punished by economic or status deprivations. Still more severe, these legal offenses can be regarded as vicious crimes and punished with physical deprivations. The distinctions between these kinds of deprivations may be only a matter of practice, or they may be accompanied by formal differentiation as well. Frequency of the punishments is another dimension of their degree of severity. Frequent application of individually mild sanctions may either increase the severity of the total impact or have an opposite effect, in that the frequency of the sanctions makes them seem usual and thus may reduce their humiliation.

Fourth, the sanctions must be changeable and flexible so that they can be adjusted to elicit maximum response. Thus the sanctions are also problematic, the subject of criticism and possibly intellectual debate.

If the organization is a bureaucracy with many thousands of members, to some extent the system of sanctions must be set up as a centralized and differentiated administrative unit in order to achieve uniformity of application. Various aspects of centralization and differentiation should be kept in mind.

A major kind of differentiation refers to the classic question of "separation of powers," which deals with the autonomy of the adjudicative process relative to the rest of the political system. Besides this, there are various aspects of administrative differentiation. The establishment of specialized offices must be distinguished from the staffing of such offices with persons possessing specialized experience; these two forms of differentiation often did not go together. Then there is specialization of procedure, and specialized procedures may or may not be carried out by specialized offices. *Ch'u-fen* law involved the following basic procedures: surveillance and announcing the offense or suspicion of it; finding a verdict; determining a sentence; applying the sentence; and allowing for the correction of adjudicative mistakes. Determining the sentence involved the question of the systematization of the schedule of sentences. There were also auxiliary procedures like keeping records. There was specialization of communication through the publication of charters or books exclusively devoted to the disciplinary system. Finally, the clients of the procedures (that is, offenders) could be formally differentiated in order to specify the applicability of the procedures.

The question of centralization breaks down into two parts: how much of the procedure was centralized? And what were the dimensions of centralization involved? Various dimensions of centralization could apply to part or all of a particular procedure.

In the imperial bureaucracy many acts were minimally centralized in the sense that all the main officials were centrally appointed, were linked to the emperor through some chain of command, and acted in terms of centrally issued orders. But compared to the extreme of relative decentralization, where such officials enjoyed broad discretion, various factors could intensify centralization.

First, the center itself could carry out the act. We can define the center as the emperor or a high capital office close to him.

Second, the act could be supervised by the center. There were degrees of supervision. Supervision always involved communication of varying regularity, but it could also involve the center's issuing of regulations with which the procedures had to accord; the center's checking into violations of these regulations; the center's formal assignment of responsibility for violations and use of sanctions to prevent violations; and even the center's approval of the act before it was fully carried out. Admittedly at this point the line between supervising and carrying out an act becomes blurred.

Third, the center could affect the act by its high evaluation of it. The center might neither supervise nor carry out the act but still be interested in it, thus influencing those who carried it out.

Abstractly speaking, one could look for extreme centralization, with one central office carrying out all of a procedure, or with the procedure split up between two powerful central offices, each acting as a check on the other. In Chinese history, neither of these possibilities was frequently realized relative to the procedures of bureaucratic discipline.

More frequently found was a pattern of considerable decentralization, with the main centralizing aspects being high evaluation by the center.

Still more frequent was the centralized network pattern. Here, much of the procedure was carried out by a large, open-ended network of centrally appointed officials stationed both in the capital and the provinces; these officials were centrally supervised; and some of the procedure was carried out by the center. This network pattern is illustrated by the Ch'ing salt monopoly and the Ch'ing administration of *ch'u-fen* law.

Finally, however differentiated and centralized, the administration of disciplinary sanctions has to be coordinated with closely connected governmental functions. On the one hand, the system of bureaucratic discipline has to be coordinated with that of criminal justice. On the other hand, it largely overlaps the system of personnel management, since personnel shifts are simultaneously negative or positive sanctions; the method of properly matching personnel with offices in order to maximize performance and minimize the waste of talent and other resources; and a way of meeting the personal preferences of officials regarding their appointments. These questions of coordination, however, can only be touched on briefly in this chapter.

A large bureaucracy's need to control its members, therefore, makes certain normative and administrative requirements on the type of sanctions it uses. These control requirements amount to a kind of "ideal type" in terms of which actual sanction systems can be described. The normative and administrative characteristics of an actual sanction system will correspond or fail to correspond to these abstract control requirements depending on the various concrete elements making up this system. Particularly important among these concrete elements were the rulers' formally established policies; the resulting formalized procedures; and the situational, institutional, cultural, and technological factors conditioning these policies and procedures. Like all political phenomena, the Ch'ing disciplinary system was partly the result of deliberate, free efforts, and partly the result of forces conditioning these efforts.

Our evidence indicates that the formal structure as it existed on paper was in fact a major positive determinant of actual behavior. The rulers' policies especially affected the degree and nature of administrative differentiation and centralization, but they also could affect normative characteristics.

However, optimal control by the rulers over the bureaucrats was limited, in the first place, by certain situational dilemmas of choice involving the indeterminate nature of the future. For instance, stress on effective performance could conflict with control in the narrower sense, since tight controls often reduced discretion, which was needed for effectiveness. Controls in turn tended to conflict partly with feelings of solidarity, which also were needed for effectiveness. Similarly, if a policy of advancement through seniority increased solidarity, it also tended to reduce effectiveness. Such situational dilemmas, in effect, were a major topic of indigenous discussion of *ch'u-fen* law.

Second, the sanction system was institutionally conditioned through the relative lack of differentiation of political system functions. This lack, in turn, reflected the "despotic" quality of the authority of the emperor, who had the legal right arbitrarily to intervene in the adjudicative process, thus possibly disrupting the tendency toward universalism. Yet we have seen that the Ch'ing rulers' desire to maximize their power was compatible with their respect for law in certain fields (see II, 4). Indeed it seems that the Ch'ing emperors were content to stay out of much *ch'u-fen* adjudication, although they frequently made slight adjustments in the sentences to express their displeasure or display their benevolence.

Third, there were basic aspects of the bureaucrats' orientation. This orientation included a tendency toward particularistic ties of solidarity leading to corrupt practices, which interfered with the realization of universalism. But the Ch'ing bureaucrats, as illustrated by their commitment to the examination system, also had a strongly universalistic orientation, and their self-image involved notions of responsibility and attitudes toward punishment which in their minds largely legitimated *ch'u-fen* law.

This orientation as a whole was the result of sociocultural factors outside the rulers' control. But while it influenced policy, it also was somewhat influenced by policy. On the one hand, it influenced the gradual legislative process through which a sanction system with various normative characteristics was created, although the actual legal structure set up was never fully congruent with the orientations of all the bureaucrats, which anyway were not homogeneous. Therefore a process of criticism and discussion filled the gap between legal norms and the values of bureaucrats, and the rulers could take this discussion into account in order to widen or narrow this gap. At the same time, the rulers, by their policies, could influence the inherent tendency in the bureaucrats' orientation to swing between its particularistic and universalistic poles.

Finally, the fourth major factor largely outside the control of the rulers was the relatively low level of the technology of communication. This tended to increase the harshness of the sanctions. If the rulers had enjoyed a quick flow of reliable information about conditions involved in specific adjudicative cases, they might have weighed the excuses of offenders more carefully. Instead, lacking the opportunity conveniently to weigh these excuses against other information, the emperors usually preferred to apply the law rigidly rather than risk losing all control.

Our purpose, therefore, is to see what kind of disciplinary system was produced by these various policy, situational, institutional, cultural, and technological factors, and to see to what extent this system accorded with our ideal control requirements. One major issue in this regard, which can now be conveniently summed up, is the role of despotic terror as a characteristic of the disciplinary system.

Obviously at times the ruler disciplined the bureaucrats not through any mild, universalistic, and rationalistic sanctions but through the use of arbitrary, terroristic, coercive sanctions. Having the legal authority to apply virtually any sanction he wished, the ruler could spontaneously act with extreme severity, especially when he felt that his prestige was at stake. The extreme cruelties of the first Ming ruler,[2] the Ch'ing literary inquisition,[3] and the forced suicide of the diplomat Ch'i-ying in 1858 [4] are well-known examples. Moreover, even when terror was not used, the possibility that the ruler could use it must have colored the sanction system.

Yet Wittfogel and others have given us a one-sided picture of the official's life as "beset with many dangers." Wittfogel cites an unpublished study of officials' offenses in nineteenth-century China, which states that of the cases studied, all apparently taken from the chronicle *Tung-hua-lu*, 22 percent involved severe sentences ranging from corporal punishment to execution, and 42 percent involved dismissal, while the remainder involved lighter penalties such as demotions.[5]

2. See Mote, "The Growth of Chinese Despotism," pp. 1–41.
3. Goodrich, *Literary Inquisition of Ch'ien-lung*.
4. I. C. Y. Hsü, *China's Entrance into the Family of Nations* (Cambridge, Mass., Harvard University Press, 1960), pp. 39–45.
5. Wittfogel, *Oriental Despotism*, p. 338. All officials' offenses, since about 1727, were reported to the emperor, except for very slight

What is overlooked here is that many dismissed officials were reappointed; that the *Tung-hua-lu* includes only a very small proportion of all officials' offenses; that the offenses included in it do not necessarily have a representative character; and that while this sample deals with the percentage of offenses handled criminally, it does not touch on the question of the frequency of criminal offenses.

A different picture, indicating long tenure and the infrequency of severe punishments, is suggested by looking at the 146 men who served on the Grand Council during its whole period of existence, 1729–1910 inclusive (some four to eight men served at any one time).[6] Careers on the Council were probably longer than in many other government posts. Of these 146 men, 44 (30 percent) served about one year or considerably less; 38 (26 percent) served a total of about two to four years; 22 (15 percent) served a total of about five to nine years; and 42 (29 percent) served a total of ten years or more. The 29 percent included many cases of extremely long tenure, the longest being thirty-eight years. Altogether, for these 146 men,

---

ones not even punished with a salary fine of one month. However only the more significant ones were reported in a single memorial exclusively dealing with one offense, and even many of these were not noteworthy enough to enter the chronicles like *Tung-hua-lu.* After all, most of the emperor's routine business never entered these chronicles. The Yung-cheng emperor said he read some thirty or more palace memorials a day (Silas Wu, "The Memorial Systems of the Ch'ing Dynasty," *Journal of Asian Studies,* 27:7–75 [1967], p. 47), and this did not even include *t'i-pen* memorials. Yet *Tung-hua-lu* only occasionally includes more than one or two items per day. I have never seen in *Tung-hua-lu* one of those routine *t'i-pen* memorials which in a single memorial listed a *number* of impeachments resulting from the annual *k'ao-ch'eng* (examination of administrative results). Nor does *Tung-hua-lu* include any of the memorials connected to the fairly noteworthy Kao-yu impeachments discussed below. See *Tung-hua ch'üan-lu, Tao-kuang, chüan* 23 and 24.

6. These dates are from the table in *Ch'ing-shih,* IV:2486–2512. Fu Tsung-mao discusses the problems in dating the beginning of the Grand Council (see Fu Tsung-mao, *chün-chi-ch'u,* pp. 118–126), and his table begins with 1726. Use of his table would have slightly increased our figure for average length of tenure on the Council. For another discussion of the problem of dating the origin of the Grand Council, see Wu, *Communication and Imperial Control in China,* pp. 84–92.

average total tenure was six and a half years (many careers on the Council were continuous, but far from all).

The average length of tenure on the Grand Secretariat was even longer: it has been calculated as eight years and nine months.[7] It is interesting that in the Early Han period (206 B.C.–8 A.D.), when the prime office possibly was more powerful than at any other time, the average term of office in this organ was "slightly more than 4.5 years" in the case of *ch'eng-hsiang* (prime ministers) and only something more than two years in the case of all other officials who served in the prime office during this period as well as during the Eastern Han (25–220). In the case of the prime office in T'ang times (618–907), the 368 men who served in this organ served an average of about four years, some of their careers, however, being discontinuous.[8]

Of the 146 men in the Ch'ing Grand Council, 127 (87 percent) ended their careers on the Grand Council in an honorable fashion, whether through retirement, natural death, transfer to another post without punitive connotation, retirement on account of sickness or old age, or another such reason. Of these 127 men with an honorable final exit, 6 men received an administrative punishment such as demotion or dismissal during their careers on the Council, their careers on the Council continuing after the punishment either immediately or after an interval.

Another 19 men (13 percent) ended their careers on the Council in a punitive, dishonorable way. Of these 19, 11 men left with only administrative punishment, such as demotion, and 8 left receiving punishment of a clearly criminal character, such as execution or a commuted death sentence that was eventually followed by resumption of one's official career. Thus criminal punishment immediately inflicted for actions connected to service on the Grand Council occurred in 8 cases out of 146 (5 percent).[9]

7. Hsieh Pao Chao, *The Government of China,* pp. 74–75. Similar statistics have been collected for the years 1403–1628 during the Ming period, and they similarly indicate that the average Ming grand secretary enjoyed long tenure with a nonviolent, nonpunitive end. These figures have to be weighed against the findings in Mote's article mentioned in IV, 1, note 2. See Y. C. Wang, *Chinese Intellectuals and the West* (Chapel Hill, University of North Carolina Press, 1966), p. 18.

8. Chou Tao-chi, *Han T'ang tsai-hsiang chih-tu,* pp. 248–249, 635–636.

9. See Appendix VI.

True, this low figure must be regarded with reservations. Possibly some men after leaving the Council became involved in scandals retroactively connected to their service on the Council; certainly some men, after leaving the Council, received criminal punishments on account of new troubles not connected to their previous service on the Council. Moreover, we cannot be sure that this 5 percent was typical for service in all offices.

Yet this 5-percent figure is significant. After all, service in constant, personal contact with the emperor should be especially dangerous, according to the theory of despotism, as it indeed was in parts of the Ming period. In this office, the stakes were especially high and the emperor's personal ire was easily aroused, since the emperor sometimes felt that because he had lavished favors on these high, close advisers of his, any bad performance on their part was a particularly horrendous betrayal of his trust in them.

All our evidence suggests that unless a Ch'ing official thus aroused the emperor's ire, made a serious military mistake, or committed a grave crime very different from normal administrative failings, his chances of receiving more than an administrative punishment were minimal if not insignificant. One should also remember that the above 5 percent included not only cases illustrating the application of despotic terror but also cases illustrating the application of justice, as with the forced suicide of the scoundrel Ho-shen in 1799.

Still more, terror was not always regarded in Chinese eyes as despotic, that is, the action of a *pao-chün* (viciously tyrannical ruler). If terror was an effective tool of control, this was partly so because the ruler, the victim, and the audience often shared certain values and felt that they were participating in a meaningful political drama.[10] As we shall see, the need to purge the bureaucracy of corrupt, oppressive officials by executing them, as the terroristic Ming founder had done, was stressed by some leading Confucians like Ku Yen-wu and Chao I. We also should recall that the use of terror fluctuated. For instance, it seems clear that service at the court was safer in Ch'ing times than in Ming.

Terror, then, was an important tool of Ch'ing bureaucratic

10. See an excellent example in Charles Hucker's "Confucianism and the Censorial System," in Nivison and Wright, *Confucianism in Action,* p. 208.

control, but it probably was not the most important. Other sanctions were perhaps more important in making officials do what the emperor wanted. Without normative sanctions, the Ch'ing dynasty would certainly have been less successful. After all, we cannot deny the presence of class interests and ties of solidarity among the political elite. The dynasty would also have been less successful without its great stress on remunerative and status sanctions to control officials in the performance of their routine duties. Rather than terror, it was these relatively mild sanctions, written up in the *ch'u-fen tse-li,* which permeated ordinary bureaucratic life, according to the evidence presented in this chapter.

The importance of these milder sanctions, we can say, was due to the fact that considerable observance of the control requirements listed above was necessary if the bureaucracy were to succeed in pursuing its goals. Yet at the same time, our hypothetical control requirements were far from fully met. If the Ch'ing bureaucracy had turned away from primary reliance on terror, it still had not adopted a system of sanctions as mild as that found in many modern organizations.[11] Rather, its discipline tended to be harsh, discretion-constricting, and rigidly centralized.

While terror still played at least a peripheral role, the main problem was the harsh definition of many shortcomings as legal offenses punished by severe status and remunerative sanctions. This meant that the area of the bureaucrats' discretion was narrowed by the increasing use of law. At the same time, this general narrowing of discretion was accompanied by the narrowing of a particular sort of discretion, that is, the narrowing of the discretion of superior officials in disciplining their subordinates. That is, there was a change in 1725–1727 in the administrative structure of the disciplinary system. This was a shift from a fairly decentralized system to a centralized network pattern (see above).

This tendency toward harsh, centralized discipline, extending the scope of law at the expense of discretion, was a conscious

11. This discussion of sanctions leans on Etzioni, *Comparative Analysis of Complex Organizations.* On the importance of mild sanctions, such as informal changes of attitude or denial of promotion, for efficient performance in many modern organizations, see *ibid.,* p. 202, and James G. March, ed., *Handbook of Organizations* (Chicago, 1965), pp. 13–14.

problem of the day. Whether we should regard it as a case of increasing bureaucratic rationalization or of pathological, dysfunctional, and excessive use of law is a question without an obvious answer. At the same time, however, Ch'ing bureaucracy was not entirely free of another old problem: excessive leniency.

2. Historical Background

The origin of a legitimated system of universalistic, rationalistic, mild, and changeable sanctions applied to officials is connected to Chou Legalism. Despite an ambivalent posture, however, Confucianism in the Chou period and thereafter also supported such sanctions.

Legalist ideas in the *Book of Lord Shang,* written perhaps in the third century B.C., stress the universalistic application of the law, no matter what the status of the offender.[1] This also involved the idea that the ruler exerted control by playing on the whole spectrum of sanctions. As the *Kuan-tzu* states: "allowing someone to live or killing him, enriching or impoverishing him, honoring or debasing him, these six handles are what the ruler grasps."[2] In later times it was a commonplace to say that the best administrative results are obtained if one finds a good man and then subjects him to rewards and punishments.[3] This combination of the idea of sanctions with that of the merit principle can also be found in *Kuan-tzu.*[4]

Moreover the development of three basic institutions for the disciplining of officials has certainly some connection to Chou Legalism: the periodic evaluation of officials, often given the general term *k'ao-chi* (examination of meritorious acts); *ch'u-chih* (demotion or dismissal and promotion); and the surveillance of officials by censors.[5]

1. Ch'ü, *Law and Society in Traditional China,* pp. 241–243.
2. Cited in Hsiao Kung-ch'üan, *Chung-kuo cheng-chih ssu-hsiang-shih,* II:195; *Kuan-tzu,* 15:6. *Kuan-tzu*'s categories correspond to Etzioni's, which are coercive sanctions (such as imprisonment), remunerative sanctions (such as salary fines), and normative sanctions (such as the removal of a symbol of honor). See Etzioni, *Comparative Analysis of Complex Organizations,* pp. 12–13.
3. *TYT,* 42:24, is an example.
4. *Kuan-tzu,* 10:11.
5. The Censorate as an organ for surveillance over bureaucrats was originated by the Legalist-influenced Ch'in dynasty. See C. O. Hucker, "Confucianism and the Censorial System," pp. 187–188. Cho-yun Hsu discusses how in *Chan-kuo* times (463–222 B.C.) a type of "despotic government" became prevalent, which required "a very effective system of supervision to keep the officials in line," including annual reports sent in by various offices and a system of rewarding officials by promotion and punishing them by demotion. Obviously such developments were in accord with Legalism, and the origin of some may have been linked to the famous Shen Pu-hai, generally

It is true that the *Book of Lord Shang* is against mild punishment, holding that "light offenses should be regarded as serious," that sentences should not be canceled off against past merits (a common practice in later times), and that officials who "do not carry out the king's law" should be punished by death, "their punishment being extended to their family for three generations." The *Kuan-tzu* also demands death for anyone who distorts or does not carry out orders.[6] The idea of relying on terror to control officials thus struck some early thinkers as sound.

On the other hand, the Legalist Shen Pu-hai of the fourth century B.C. wanted to control officials by enforcing strict standards of responsibility but without using severe punishments to force officials to act against their inclinations.[7] Later scholars, justifying the lenient treatment of offending officials, preferred to cite a Confucian classic. The *Book of History* says: "Mere mistakes, however great, are treated with indulgence; intentional offenses, however small, are punished." Mention of redemption in the *Book of History* indicates that this mechanism

---

regarded as a precursor of Legalism. Hsiao Kung-ch'üan, *Chung-kuo cheng-chih ssu-hsiang-shih*, II:225–226. Cho-yun Hsu, *Ancient China in Transition* (Stanford, Calif., Stanford University Press, 1965), pp. 92–96.

6. T'ung-tsu Ch'ü, *Law and Society*, p. 242, 266; *Kuan-tzu*, 5:8b. Liang Ch'i-ch'ao, without doubt correctly, points out that in this passage prescribing death for five ways of not following orders exactly, the *Kuan-tzu* in four of these cases has officials specifically in mind. See *Kuan-tzu-chuan*, p. 35.

7. See p. 616 in H. G. Creel, "The *Fa-chia*:'Legalists' or 'Administrators'," in *Ch'ing-chu Tung Tso-pin hsien-sheng liu-shih-sui lun-wen-chi, Chung-yang yen-chiu-so chi-k'an wai-pien ti-ssu-chung,* part 2, Taipei, 1961. In this excellent article Professor Creel goes too far in referring (p. 628) to the "virtual disappearance of the school of Shen Pu-hai from the historical record . . ." After all, the term Shen-Han (Shen Pu-hai and Han Fei) was not uncommonly used to stand for Legalism. For a Ch'ing example, see *HCCSWP*, 2:2b. Shen Pu-hai is commonly mentioned in modern Chinese histories of Chinese political thought since at least Liang Ch'i-ch'ao's. See, e.g., Hsiao, II:229, 242. Hsiao's account of Shen Pu-hai's thought, while brief, does agree with Creel's in identifying Shen Pu-hai as the leading early contributor to the doctrine of controlling officials by *shu* (methods) distinguishing between satisfactory and unsatisfactory performance in office, a doctrine then elaborated in *Han Fei-tzu*. A still fuller account of Shen is in Hou Wai-lu *et al., Chung-kuo ssu-hsiang t'ung-shih* (A general history of Chinese thought; Peking, 1957–1960), I:596–599.

for lightening punishment already existed in pre-Confucian times.[8]

With regard to flexibility, it is significant that while the *Kuan-tzu* stresses that the law must be basically unchangeable in order to retain its effectiveness, it links this notion to a complementary emphasis on the flexibility of the law.[9] Generally speaking, it was the Legalists who urged that laws be flexible and numerous enough to cover all contingencies, while the Confucians favored a small number of unchanging laws simple enough to be easily understood by the people.[10] However it was the Confucian classic, the *Book of History*, which states: "The severity of punishments and fines varies from period to period."[11] This was a famous statement, and it was used in the Ch'ing period to describe the fluctuations of the penal regulations, which occurred often within the space of a few years.[12] In general, disciplinary laws involved those same attitudes toward administrative flexibility discussed in Chapter I.

Turning now to the complicated question of the Confucian legitimation of the disciplinary system, which was certainly fundamental to whatever efficacy it had, I offer an argument differing from the view of a distinguished scholar that "Confucius and his followers trusted to the virtuous example of the ruler to maintain morality and morale in the administration, and they seemed to feel that once a good man had been put in office he should suffer no constraints other than those imposed by his own conscience."[13]

We should first raise again the methodological point made in chapter one about political values in imperial China. A complex, ambivalent outlook, consisting of a number of partly con-

8. Legge, *Chinese Classics*, III:39; III:59 (*The Shoo King*). For a Ch'ing cite, in connection with *ch'u-fen*, of the *Shu-ching* passage on pardoning unintentional faults, see *HCCSWP*, 15:8b. Confucius also urged that rulers "pardon the small faults" of officials; see Legge, *Chinese Classics*, I:262–263 (*Confucian Analects*).

9. Hsiao, II:201–202.

10. This generalization regarding Legalism and Confucianism at least applies to the positions of these two schools as represented in the *Salt and Iron Discourses*. See especially, *Yen-t'ieh-lun*, p. 342, 361. See I, 2.

11. Legge, *Chinese Classics*, III:607 (*The Shoo King*).

12. *TCLL, fan-li*:1.

13. C. O. Hucker, *The Censorial System of Ming China* (Stanford, Calif., 1966), p. 6.

tradictory statements made over the centuries, all widely commanding respect, was frequently the operative value by Ch'ing times regarding a particular issue. And this ambivalence stemmed not so much from the coexistence of distinctly Legalist and distinctly Confucian statements as from the interplay of distinctively Confucian ideas themselves. In the case of the punishment of officials, Confucians, already well before Ch'ing times, were moved both by a charismatic sense of status honor calling for exemption at least from humiliating punishments, and by a variety of ideas and attitudes legitimating officials' punishment. These latter views I label the "probationary ethic." Put together in a single mind, the sense of charisma and the probationary ethic involved some intellectual contradictions but psychologically united to form an ethic of responsibility that made disciplinary sanctions meaningful and acceptable.

What we call charisma can be found, for instance, in the notion of *tsun* (reverently to respect).[14] The basic demand of Confucian thought was that the ruler and others *tsun* (reverently respect) the scholar-officials, or at least the good ones. The strength of Mencius' demand for such respect seemed excessive to some later scholars like Ssu-ma Kuang, but Hsün-tzu's more humble position, which Ssu-ma Kuang approved of, still called for the ruler's *tsun* (reverently respecting) the scholar-official, while the latter in turn *tsun* (reverently respected) the ruler.[15] By contrast, the notion of *tsun-chün i-ch'en* (reverently

14. The concept of charisma used here follows that in Etzioni, *Comparative Analysis of Complex Organizations,* pp. 202–213. Diverging from Weber's outlook, Etzioni defines charisma as "the ability of an actor to exercise diffuse and intense influence over the normative orientations of other actors." He holds that charisma can be found in many bureaucratic positions, not just the top ones, and that, among various sources, it can stem either from an office or from attainments like learning. I further assume that charisma involves a feeling of being an ultimate leader and therefore is not easily compatible with a subservient attitude whereby one readily accepts the right of someone else to punish one and correct one's behavior.

15. Legge, *Chinese Classics,* II:213–214, 392 (*The Works of Mencius*). Also see Chou Tao-chi, p. 704. Ssu-ma Kuang's criticism is cited in Hsiao Kung-ch'üan, IV:482–483. Ssu-ma Kuang especially rejected Mencius' view that nobles who were relatives of a bad ruler could properly dethrone him, and to make his point, Ssu-ma Kuang paraphrased a passage in *Hsün-tzu,* pp. 165–166, mentioning two proper ways of opposing bad policies, in contrast to Mencius' idea

respect the ruler and lower and curb the officials) was to a large extent associated with Legalism.[16]

This Confucian demand for honor had perhaps two major facets. A desire to inject the honor of feudal status into the bureaucratic system was certainly one. It has been acutely pointed out that the advent of a more bureaucratic system in Ch'in and Han times greatly raised the emperor's status, because in the feudal system, many of the political elite enjoyed hereditary status, while in the bureaucratic system, few did except the emperor. The status gap between one who had hereditary power and one who did not was likely to be especially great.[17] Moreover, in the ideal feudal system, as Chu Hsi said,

---

of deposing a bad ruler: resigning from office and *ssu* (arguing against the policies of one's ruler even to the point that the latter executes one). (I am indebted to Dr. Achilles Fang for explaining the latter term to me.) On Hsün-tzu's attitude toward the question of *tsun*, see *Hsün-tzu*, pp. 164, 166, 115. Confucius' similar and prominent idea that the ruler should treat his officials according to *li* (rules of moral propriety) is in Legge, *Chinese Classics*, I:161 (*Confucian Analects*).

16. Ssu-ma Ch'ien praised the Ch'in dynasty for practicing the principle of *tsun-chün i-ch'en*, which he regarded as a norm inherited from the past rather than a Legalist contribution, and as a norm followed by the Han. See Takigawa Kametarō, *Shiki kaichū kōshō*, 23:4, and Sa Meng-wu, I:126. Similarly, in *Po-hu t'ung-te-lun* (Ssu-pu ts'ung-k'an), 4:4b–5, a work attributed to Pan Ku, the virtually identical idea of *tsun-chün pei-ch'en* is advocated and is clearly linked to the feudal problem of rebellious vassals. Yet the Ch'in dynasty is generally regarded as Legalist-inspired, and the Chou Legalist Shen Pu-hai was associated by the Han scholar Liu Hsiang with this same idea of *tsun-chün pei-ch'en ch'ung-shang i-hsia* (reverently respect the ruler and lower the standing of the officials, exhalt superiors and lower and curb inferiors). This quote from Liu Hsiang, cited in Creel, "The *Fa-chia*: 'Legalists' or 'Administrators'," pp. 619–620 (my translation differs slightly from Creel's), is found in the commentary of the Wang Hsien-ch'ien edition of the *Han-shu*, at the beginning of the chapter on Yüan-ti. See also Ch'ien Mu, *Kuo-shih ta-kang*, II:424, for a discussion illustrating how the idea of *tsun-chün pei-ch'en* came to focus on despotically lowering the position of the official rather than prudently safeguarding the position of the ruler. We should keep in mind, though, that this idea sometimes was focused not on the Legalist goal of making the official a humble subordinate but on the more general goal of curbing rebellious ministers or vassals.

17. Ch'ien Mu, *Kuo-shih ta-kang*, I:87, 113.

the emperor fundamentally shared authority with the feudal lords; they did not just act as his agents and at his pleasure.[18] The Confucian demand for higher status and more authority was certainly influenced by this feudal ideal.

At the same time, Confucians often had a self-image which corresponded to what we would call the image of charismatic leadership. The crucial thing about this image was that it partly contradicted the role of a bureaucratic subordinate. Charisma was diffused throughout the bureaucracy instead of being monopolized by the one leader, the emperor. Although often able to fit into the political and occupational hierarchy of their day, Confucians saw themselves as occupying a morally ultimate rather than a subordinate and relative position in their political universe. This basic feeling was in tension with the idea emphasized by the great Han Confucian Tung Chung-shu, whereby the emperor occupied the central, pivotal position between heaven and earth.

This feeling of pride was connected to the nature of their learning, which hopefully put them into contact with the *tao* (the true way) of Confucius and the Duke of Chou and so made them vehicles of sacred truths which the emperor needed if he were to be fully successful. They filled the role of *chün-tzu* (true gentlemen), persons ultimately dedicated to principles of morality transcending the ruler's wishes, and sometimes they even aspired to realize the ultimate moral perfection of a *sheng* (sage), a role which connoted the right to take charge of the empire.

One of the clearest expressions of the *chün-tzu's* moral ultimacy is in *Hsün-tzu,* a work which simultaneously is important for its stress on the authority of the ruler: "Therefore heaven and earth bring forth the true gentleman, and the true gentleman brings order to heaven and earth."[19] Although this passage refers more to moral than cosmological power, it can be linked to the belief, common through much or all of the imperial period, that the avoidance of natural disasters depended on the

18. Cited in T'ao Hsi-sheng, IV:122. Chu Hsi held that "The meaning of feudalism was that the sage did not consider the empire as his own but divided it with his relatives and worthy persons and ruled it together with them."

19. *Hsün-tzu,* p. 104. Watson, trans., *Hsün-tzu,* p. 44. See also *Hsün-tzu,* p. 151. *Chün-tzu* can mean "ruler" but clearly not in these passages.

moral correctness of high officials as well as the emperor.[20] Contrary to the impression of some modern scholars, the magical capacity to establish harmony between cosmic and human affairs was not monopolized by the emperor. Ultimately this glorification of the *chün-tzu* can be seen as rooted in the general Confucian glorification of *jen* (Man). Since Man was often seen as forming a central cosmic triad along with heaven and earth, the *chün-tzu*, who was nothing but Man in the process of perfection, was bound to have remarkable powers, even, in the eyes of some philosophers given over to subjective idealism, the function of serving as the source of all phenomenal change. "The ten thousand transformations flow out of me," said Ch'en Hsien-chang (1428–1500) during an age notorious for its despotic absolutism.[21]

Especially in the earlier dynasties through the Sung period, Confucians often had the career goal of occupying the *tsai-hsiang* (prime office), through which they could decisively influence reform of the whole society. It has been pointed out that the most idealistic Sung schools of thought viewed the prime office, rather than the emperor, as the crucial governmental position and the political fulcrum of change.[22] Similarly, Fan Chung-yen expressed the feeling that he "regarded the empire as his own [moral] responsibility."[23] This proud attitude certainly fluctuated from period to period, and some have deplored

20. In the *Shih-chi* it is stated that one of the duties of a prime minister is to "help the Son of Heaven order the yin and the yang and to bring about the harmonious succession of the four seasons." Takigawa, 56:22. Cited in Chou Tao-chi, *Han-T'ang tsai-hsiang chih-tu*, p. 1. Prime ministers in Han times sometimes took the blame for natural disasters and accordingly resigned from office. See *ibid.*, pp. 251–252. Similarly, the Yung-cheng emperor once blamed Pu-lan-t'ai, then governor of Kiangsi, for causing a drought in Kiangsi. See IV, 3, c.

21. Jung Chao-tsu, *Ming-tai ssu-hsiang-shih* (A history of thought during the Ming dynasty; Taipei, 1969), p. 38.

22. Ch'ien Mu, *Kuo-shih ta-kang*, II:423, points out that the idealistic Lo and Wang An-shih schools of Sung thought "emphasized respect for the prime office," in contrast to the more conservative Shuo and Shu schools, which "emphasized respect for the ruler." The Lo school "sought with its learning to transcend the authority of the ruler." On *tsai-hsiang*, see III, 2, above.

23. Cited in Fang Hao, *Sung-shih* (History of the Sung dynasty; Taipei, 1954), I:104.

its weakening and wavering in the Ch'ing period.[24] Yet the idea that officials should "take the affairs of the empire as their own responsibility" was a cliché even in the Ch'ing period, although it was then used less as an expression of high ambition than as an admonition to unconscientious officials.[25] Similarly it was believed in Ch'ing times that "Whether the empire is in order or disorder is tied up with the condition of *hsüeh-shu* (learning)."[26]

Formed by such elements, the Confucians' sense of honor was expressed in various ways: in the demand of subordinate officials that since they were nevertheless men of learning, they should be treated politely by their superior officials; in the tendency to look down on the vulgar technicalities of administration, which should be left to clerks; and in the contempt for the *neng-li* (capable official), who was good at these technicalities but supposedly lacked the moral qualities of the *hsien-li* (official of superior quality).[27]

It was also this sense of honor which made it difficult for Confucians to accept punishment as officials. The *chün-tzu* (true gentleman), as Confucius himself saw him, made mistakes.[28] However, externally imposed punishments were dis-

24. Ch'ien Mu, *Chung-kuo chin-san-pai-nien hsüeh-shu-shih,* pp. ii–iii.

25. See, e.g., a 1677 memorial in *HCCSWP*, 17:13a–b of the censor Hsü Hsü-ling deploring the laziness of new *chin-shih* who, assigned to an office to watch the workings of government for a while in order to train themselves before assuming official duties, request a vacation after a few days and go home. Hsü unfavorably compares them to the conscientious degree holders of the past who "desired to take the affairs of the empire as their own responsibility."

26. *HCCSWP,* 2:10. See also *ibid.,* 1:13b.

27. For various examples, see *HCCSWP*, 15:3b; 19:9, 4b; Sa Meng-wu, I:350; IV:133.

28. For the *chün-tzu* as liable to have faults, see Legge, *Chinese Classics,* I:141, 302, 346; *HCCSWP,* 21:20b, 17; 15:8b; 22:3. Some of these examples deal specifically with the idea that *kung-tsui* were unavoidable. Evidence of the sense of shame about receiving punishments in the Ch'ing period is the fact that although there was a great development in the publication of the regulations on administrative punishment, this law attracted no commentators, not even the small number attracted by the Ch'ing penal code. This branch of law, in terms of publication and as an institution, formed a clear-cut legal unit, but, as we can still see from the writings of twentieth-century Chinese historians, such as the compilers of the *Ch'ing-shih,* it was respectable or fashionable to write about the punishment of

tinctly shameful. Yet at the same time Confucians were deeply committed to other ideas legitimating their punishments, and so they embraced a complex, ambivalent position.

One point relevant to the Confucian acceptance of punishment is that of the general ambivalence often found in Confucian thought toward Legalist methods (I, 5). Connected to this is what we may call "derivative legitimation": the imperial government, which was generally legitimated, was conceived of as something inherently involving many improper actions. Even if the punishment of officials per se were denounced, therefore, it could still be tolerated as an unavoidable part of the government.

Aside from any such "derivative legitimation," Confucians usually accepted the idea that good government required the dismissal of bad officials, and dismissal through the ages was regarded as one of the main punishments applied to officials. Admittedly, linked to Chou attitudes, there was a famous Han ideal that "The *li* (rules of moral propriety) do not descend to the common people; the *hsing* (criminal punishments) do not reach up to the officials." Chia I, an Early Han scholar, said that this principle had been applied in Chou times.

Clearly, however, it referred only to exemption from humiliating punishments. Sanctions such as termination of one's governmental career under the pressure of public opinion, exile, and forced suicide were in fact inflicted on nobles in the Chou period and apparently were regarded as compatible with the idea of not inflicting *hsing* on them. Moreover, when Chia I urged that *hsing* not be inflicted on officials, he explicitly accepted punishments such as forced suicide as appropriate for them. When Hsün Yüeh (second century A.D.) similarly made the point that the *chün-tzu* (true gentleman) should be controlled by the rules of moral propriety and the *hsiao-jen* (petty

---

officials only very superficially and as an aspect of two well-established subjects, redemption of criminal sentences and the triannual evaluation of officials. *Ch'ing-shih,* II:1338–1341, deals with some administrative punishments in describing the triannual evaluations, and, in II:1740, discusses redemption, but without even mentioning the officials' commutation of criminal into administrative sentences. A similar neglect can be found in Chang Chin-chien, *Chung-kuo wen-kuan chih-tu-shih* (A history of China's civil service; Taipei, 1955), and Hsü Tao-lin, *Chung-kuo fa-chih-shih lun-lüeh* (Outline history of China's legal institutions; Taipei, 1953), pp. 127–129.

person) by criminal punishments, he added that the *chung-jen* (man of medium quality) should be governed by both, and his implication seems to have been that most officials were *chung-jen.*[29]

Other Han views also share this tendency to accept some punishments while trying to win judicial privileges. In one passage of his letter to Jen An, Ssu-ma Ch'ien indicates that sparing the scholar-official humiliation is the meaning of the statement that "The criminal punishments do not reach up to the officials."[30] The classic *Chou-li,* probably written in Early Han times, holds that nobles may properly be punished but should enjoy privileges such as not suffering the punishment of being made a slave and not having to attend their trials personally.[31] The Confucians in the famous court conference of about 83 B.C. strongly agreed with the idea of dismissing bad officials, as indeed Mencius did too.[32]

The idea of dismissing bad officials was intertwined with four overlapping institutions: staffing the government according to the merit principle; the periodic evaluation of officials, that is, *k'ao-chi* (examination of meritorious acts); *ch'u-chih* (demotion or dismissal and promotion); and the surveillance of officials

29. *Li-chi chu-shu* (The *Li-chi* with commentary and subcommentary; Ssu-pu pei-yao), 3:3b. See also James Legge, *The Texts of Confucianism* (Oxford, Eng., 1885), III:90. Besides the *Li-chi,* a work probably of the Han period, this same statement with slightly different wording is found in a memorial of Chia I (second century B.C.). See *Ch'ien-Han-shu* (Ssu-pu pei-yao), 48:18–20b and T'ao, II:72. As one can see from the excellent discussion in Ch'ü T'ung-tsu, *Law and Society in Traditional China,* pp. 172–176, this idea is also put forward in Hsün Yüeh's *Shen-chien* (Ssu-pu ts'ung-k'an), 1:4b–5, and in *Po-hu t'ung-te-lun* (Ssu-pu ts'ung-k'an), 8:18a–b; the latter work is ascribed to Pan Ku of the Later Han. Close to Chia I's approach is also the view in Wang Su's *K'ung-tzu chia-yü* (Ssu-pu ts'ung-k'an), 7:8b–9b. Hsün-tzu also held that control over the governing class should be through the rules of moral propriety, while laws should be applied to the governed. See *Hsün-tzu* (Ssu-pu ts'ung-k'an), 6:4b; cited in T'ao, I:182. A passage in Legge, *Chinese Classics,* II:291 (*The Works of Mencius*) suggests that Mencius too associated criminal punishments more with the governed than with the ruling class.

30. *Ch'ien-Han-shu,* 62:15b–16.

31. T'ao, II:195–196; *Chou-li* (Ssu-pu ts'ung-k'an), 9:32–33; 9:13b–14b.

32. *Yen-t'ieh-lun,* p. 240. Legge, *Chinese Classics,* II:164 (*The Works of Mencius*).

by censors. As indicated above, the origin of this complex of institutions clearly was connected to Legalism. However, this complex was largely in accord with Confucianism as well. Both the Confucian concern for the people and the Legalist concern for realizing the ruler's will meant that such bureaucratic mechanisms to control officials were necessary. This was especially true with the increasing size and complexity of Chinese government. In a bureaucracy of many thousands there must have been a euphoric ring to Mencius' claim: "Therefore if the ruler acts with benevolence, everyone else will; if the ruler acts with righteousness, everyone else will."[33]

The extent to which these basic bureaucratic mechanisms accorded with indubitably Confucian thought is not always fully appreciated. Although Mencius perhaps wavered on the matter, a locus classicus of the merit principle is his ideal of "important positions are held by persons of superior quality and offices are filled by able persons."[34] Mencius praised two institutions perhaps connected to that of the periodic evalutions (*k'ao-chi*): imperial inspection tours (*hsün-shou*), and reports to the emperor by feudal lords on the discharge of their duties (*shu-chih*).[35] Another basic passage, in the classic *Book of History*, speaks of the disciplining of officials by the sage emperor Shun, mentioning *k'ao-chi* and *ch'u-chih*: "Every three years there was an examination of merits, and after three examinations the undeserving were demoted or dismissed and the deserving promoted." This passage was well-known: the section on *k'ao-chi*

33. Legge, *Chinese Classics*, II:320 (*The Works of Mencius*).

34. Sa Meng-wu (e.g., Sa, I:62) constantly refers to this phrase as the basic formulation of the principle of bureaucracy in the Chou period. It is found in Legge, *Chinese Classics*, II:197 (*The Works of Mencius*). See also *ibid.*, p. 199. However, in the light of the difficult passage (*ibid.*, p. 165) about "causing the low to overstep the honorable, and distant to overstep [the ruler's] near relatives," it seems that Mencius had an ambivalent attitude toward the merit principle. Confucius also adopted the merit principle; see Legge, *Chinese Classics*, I:262–263 (*Confucian Analects*).

35. Legge, *Chinese Classics*, II:159 (*The Works of Mencius*). Yen Keng-wang says that the "feudal" institutions of *shu-chih* and *hsün-shou* were the historical background of the system of periodic evaluation developed in the *Chan-kuo* period as states became more centralized. Yen Keng-wang, *Chung-kuo ti-fang hsing-cheng chih-tu-shih: chüan-shang: Ch'in Han ti-fang hsing-cheng chih-tu* (A history of regional and local administration in China—part one: the Ch'in and Han periods; Taipei, 1961), II:257.

in *The History of the Ch'ing Dynasty* begins: "The system of an examination of merits once every three years first appeared with the emperors Yao and Shun."[36] The great Han Confucian Tung Chung-shu, as well as a work ascribed to the famous Han historian Pan Ku, thoroughly endorsed both *k'ao-chi* and *ch'u-chih*.[37]

A forceful argument favoring disciplinary controls over bureaucrats was made by Liu Tsung-yüan (773–819). Arguing that the district-prefecture system was superior to feudal rule, he criticized feudal rule precisely because its system of hereditary officials precluded effective discipline and thus prevented good government.[38] In the Sung period Su Tung-p'o stressed the punishment of officials and even went so far as to say that Shang Yang's and Han Fei's use of punishments in principle, though not in practice, was in accord with the policy of the sage-emperor Yao.[39] An early Ch'ing writer, tracing *k'ao-chi* back to the sage emperors Yao and Shun, stated: "surveillance of officials is the basic means of making the people content and peaceful." Other Ch'ing examples of this view can be adduced.[40] Certainly there was nothing exceptional about a Confucian like Ku Yen-wu who, although he had reservations about surveillance, greatly admired the Han surveillance office of circuit inspector (*tz'u-shih*), even though it had developed out of a Ch'in office, and said it was like the Ming and Ch'ing office of circuit censor.[41] Chao I praised the surveillance system of early

36. Legge, *Chinese Classics*, III:50, 37–39 (*The Shoo King*); *Ch'ing-shih*, II:1338.

37. Cited in Teng Ssu-yü, *Chung-kuo k'ao-shih chih-tu-shih* (A history of China's examination system; Taipei, 1967), p. 3.

38. *Liu Ho-tung ch'üan-chi* (Shanghai, 1931), pp. 31–34.

39. Cited in Sa, IV:27.

40. *HCCSWP*, 1:15b. The writer in Lu Shou-ming, a *chin-shih* of 1652. For the same point by other writers in this collection, see *ibid.*, 20:2b; 11:4a–b.

41. Ku Yen-wu praises the office of regional censor in *HCCSWP*, 19:1–2. His doubts are in *HCCSWP*, 18:5b–6. Here he develops a favorite theme of his that good government is based on close personal understandings, not impersonal procedures. Praising the personal contact established by some Han emperors with their prefects, Ku argued not that surveillance was bad but that impersonal procedures of surveillance compared unfavorably with such personal contact as a way of eliciting good performance from provincial officials. See also Ku's views on the Ch'in dynasty in I, 5.

Ming times, connecting the Ming decline to the decay of this system.[42]

The basic point here is that it is hard if not impossible to find any prominent Confucian in any period arguing against *k'ao-chi* (examination of meritorious acts) and *ch'u-chih* (demotion or dismissal and promotion), and these two institutions, covering the whole range of regular disciplinary punishments, were a sufficient basis for the Ch'ing dynasty's *ch'u-fen tse-li* (regulations on administrative punishment).

There was even some Confucian backing for the harsh and humiliating punishment of bad officials. Here love for the people (*ai min*) and disgust with bad officials hurting the people fully pushed aside the sense of status honor.

It was explicitly his "love" of the people which led Hai Jui (1514–1587) to urge restoration of the Ming founder's cruel punishments for corrupt officials.[43] Chao I was full of praise for this emperor's use of the death penalty for corrupt officials.[44] In his essay strongly urging harsh criminal punishments for corrupt officials, Ku Yen-wu criticizes the switch to leniency in the punishment of corrupt officials during the reign of the Hsüan-te emperor (1426–1435). Ku Yen-wu even approved of an emperor of the Chin dynasty (1115–1234) who ordered that the sons of an official executed for financial corruption be excluded from officialdom: the sons of "shameless persons without a sense of integrity," Ku held, "necessarily will be without integrity and purity of character." Ku approved of this emperor's view that the crimes of officials were worse than those of the common people, because the latter at least had the excuse of being driven to crime by economic pressures.[45] A complementary point made by the Yung-cheng emperor in the eighteenth century was that officials' crimes were worse because officials had a responsibility to act as models for the people (see below). Admittedly, Ku Yen-wu subsequently was criticized for the Legalist-like harshness of the methods he advocated.[46] In urging the harsh punishment of corrupt officials, Ku Yen-wu adduced a story about Tzu-ch'an, a prime minister of Cheng in the sixth century B.C. whose

42. *HCCSWP*, 19:3.
43. T'ao, IV:235–239.
44. *HCCSWP*, 19:2b–3.
45. *HCCSWP*, 19:4a–b.
46. *HCCSWP*, 2:2b. See also Derk Bodde and Clarence Morris, *Law in Imperial China* (Cambridge, Mass., 1967), p. 35.

policies partly were close to Legalist ideas: "Tzu-ch'an asked Jan-ming how to govern. Jan-ming answered: 'Regard the people as your children. If you see someone who is not benevolent [toward them], execute him just as a hawk drives off birds.' For this reason executing the unbenevolent is how one treats the people as one's children."[47]

We can therefore say that the Confucian attitude virtually always called for the disciplining of bad officials through punishments like dismissal but wavered on whether or not humiliating punishments should be used. This wavering is connected to the fact that the law did actually swing back and forth between leniency and harshness. According to Ku Yen-wu, in both the Han and the T'ang periods there was a commendable if not always complete tendency to execute officials guilty of *tsang-tsui* (the crime of illegally taking wealth), and in both the Sung and the Ming periods there was a deplorable switch to leniency in mid-dynasty. In the case of both switches, the ancient formula was adduced that "the criminal punishments do not reach up to the officials." One might infer here a mid-dynasty lack of self-confidence among these rulers, leading them to give in to elite interests at the expense of societal ones.[48] Ku's view of Ming leniency is corroborated by the Ming penal code (at least as far back as 1587), whereby officials and other gentry could generally redeem any sentence except execution.

In Ch'ing times, the pendulum swung back toward harshness, as the rulers gradually tightened the conditions for the redemption of criminal sentences. In 1655 the basic principle was introduced of not permitting redemption if the crime involved corruption such as the illegal taking of wealth. In 1801 the Chia-ch'ing emperor eliminated any routine redemption by officials and other gentry of sentences of penal servitude or up. However officials could still petition to have the Board of Punishments advise the emperor on whether to allow redemption,

47. *HCCSWP*, 19:2b. Unable to find the origin of this passage, I am not sure whether the last sentence is added by Ku himself. Tzu-ch'an was admired by Confucius, but he is held to have been the first statesman to have made the laws public, and for this act, according to the *Tso-chuan*, he was criticized in terms that would be regarded by us as Confucian. See Legge, *Chinese Classics*, I:178, 278 (*Confucian Analects*); V:609–610 (*The Ch'un Ts'ew with The Tso Chuen*).

48. *HCCSWP*, 19:3b–4.

and the practice of redemption apparently continued to some extent (see below).

Admittedly, one should take into account not only how the law was written (*li-fa*) but also how it was applied (*yung-fa*). Sometimes there was a tendency to balance harsh laws with mild application and vice versa. From the complaints of one Ch'ing writer, for instance, it is clear that imperial pardons for officials convicted of illegally taking wealth (for example, embezzlement) frequently saved them from the harsh sentences prescribed for this offense; he advocated a milder law more strictly enforced.[49] Besides the use of pardons, one must take into account failures to enforce the law (Ch'ing officials recognized that laws on their financial corruption were not fully enforced) and the tendency of judges to give or not give officials the benefit of the doubt in cases, such as judicial mistakes, where the question of intention greatly affected the seriousness of the sentences.

Let us now look a little further into the strong feelings that scholars like Ku Yen-wu directed at bad officials. One can perhaps detect here echoes of Hsün-tzu's theory of the originally bad nature of man and Han Fei's apparently linked idea that because of the shortage of good men, the state had to employ many mediocre officials, who could then be controlled through punishments and rewards.[50] Besides inherent mediocrity, it was sometimes felt that scholars could be corrupted by bad intellectual currents, and that the difficulty of pursuing moral standards increased as one rose in the government and came to enjoy wealth and power.[51]

Thus side by side with the charismatic ideal of the *chün-tzu* (true gentleman), there was the clearly widespread belief that most officials were merely *chung-jen* or *chung-ts'ai* (men of medium ability), whose morality depended on their outer, economic circumstances, rather than their inner spiritual strength.

49. *HCCSWP*, 19:3a–b. The writer is Ch'u Fang-ch'ing, a *chin-shih* of 1667.

50. Jui Ho-cheng, *Hsi-Han yü-shih chih-tu* (The system of the censorate in the Western Han dynasty; Taipei, 1964), pp. 1–3.

51. On the gradual corruption of scholars who had pure principles when in low circumstances, which they lost when rising in the world, see Hai Jui in T'ao, IV:238–239. See also *HCCSWP*, 16:7b, and the linked idea in Legge, *Chinese Classics*, II:265 (*The Works of Mencius*). These examples are very similar to Lord Acton's idea that power corrupts.

The man above average, Wang An-shih said, was good even when enduring bad material conditions; conversely, the man below average was bad even when enjoying good material conditions; but the men of average ability, who constituted the vast majority of all officials, were good when enjoying good material conditions and bad when suffering from bad material conditions.[52] Ku Yen-wu's comments about the *ts'ai-li* (talented official) are similar: whether the *ts'ai-li* followed the path of corruption or of good service did not depend on his inner character. On the contrary, most such "talented officials" were corrupt persons, but they would serve well if the government restrained them by laws and made use of their talent.[53]

Chün-tzu or *chung-ts'ai*? Whether the elite had an inner spiritual core of morality or were contemptibly controlled through outer circumstances was a central doubt in the Confucian value system. Moreover, this doubt must have been not only directed at other officials but also directed at oneself and thus internalized as self-doubt. This point is somewhat involved and hard to document, but it serves as a reasonable explanation for certain Ch'ing administrative practices and terms.

The main issue here is the normative implications of the fact that, at least in Ch'ing times, officials who had fully acquired the status of a criminal often later fully resumed their status as officials. In Ch'ing times, such bouncing back into office was supposed to be blocked by two laws, but they involved loopholes or ambiguities. First, officials could be dismissed from office with the injunction "never to be appointed [again]" and then be reappointed through an imperial "favor." Second, an article based on the idea of excluding "morally deficient" officials held that even with a pardon, an official guilty of any offense with a corrupt character ("private offenses," see below) could not return to office; the pardon applied only to punish-

52. Cited in Sa, IV:152, and Sung Hsi, *Sung-shih yen-chiu lun-ts'ung* (Studies in Sung history; Taipei, 1962), p. 4. For an example of the view that most officials are *chung-ts'ai* as held in the Ch'ing period, see the memorial of about 1799 written by Wang Chih-i in *HCCSWP*, 16:4. See also Sa, I:267, for a Han use of *chung-ts'ai*.

53. *HCCSWP*, 19:4b. The common people too could be regarded as sliding between a moral and an immoral status depending on outer circumstances. For instance, a Ch'ing view held that by changing salt monopoly procedures so that smuggling would be impossible or unprofitable, "smugglers will be transformed into good people."

ments beyond his dismissal. However, this article was criticized by Hsüeh Yün-sheng as unclear and too severe,[54] and in fact some officials dismissed on account of "private offenses" were reappointed even without a pardon.[55] Neither was an official necessarily barred from reappointment if he received a sentence of penal servitude or even actually served it. Sentences of penal servitude or more could sometimes be redeemed by a money payment, and reappointment could follow after such sentences had been either redeemed or served (see below). Thus sometimes nothing but a money payment, an act which had no moral significance in Confucian ethics, functioned as the line between criminal and official status.

This is also illustrated by the Ch'ing law on the juggling of state finances (that is, the use of state funds for genuine state purposes but not for the specifically authorized ones). If one was convicted of juggling more than 10,000 but less than 20,000 taels and could pay the sum back in one year, one was returned to office; if one could not pay it back, one was criminally sentenced to serve as a soldier at a nearby frontier.[56] Similarly, if an official in charge of a granary or treasury used its contents to make a private loan, his act was regarded as the same as theft of government goods by the person in charge of them.[57] Thus his punishment could go as high as detention for beheading, which was eventually commuted to the special sentence of "imprisonment for life" (*yung-yüan chien-chin*).[58] If he could return the sum in about one year, however, he was restored to office. The law was similar if he falsely reported taxes as paid that were unpaid.[59]

This is not to say that there was no ideal of disassociating those of official and criminal status. The classic *Li-chi* says that "One who has received *hsing* (criminal punishment) shall not be at the ruler's side." Judging from the commentaries, the idea here was not only to preserve the physical safety of the

54. *TLti*, 2:47–49b; *TCLL*, 4:36a–b. On amnesties, see also *TLti*, 2:31a–b, 1:56, and 2:45; *TCHT*, 56:17b–18; *TCHTSL*, *chüan* 729–731. Public offenses were routinely included in regular amnesties, and private offenses could be pardoned, but at least the worst private offenses were excluded from regular amnesties.

55. See, e.g., *CFTL*, 2:66.

56. *TLti*, 14:2b; *TCLL*, 12:3a–b.

57. *TLti*, 13:39; *TCLL*, 11:22.

58. *TLti*, 25:58b–59; *TCLL*, 23:26–27.

59. *TLti*, 13:40a–b; *TCLL*, 12:22–23.

ruler by keeping him away from dangerously embittered persons but also to dissociate completely scholar-officials from criminals: "If a *shih* (scholar-official) happens to meet one who has received punishment on the road, he does not speak with him."[60]

This outlook might well have become fully institutionalized, leading to a rigid exclusion of anyone with a taint of criminality from officialdom. After all, how could someone with a criminal background carry out the official's function of diffusing moral influence throughout society? At the very least there could have been a consistent system of laws excluding criminals from office in theory, even if violated in practice; such laws would have partly satisfied any ideological need to dissociate criminal and official status.

That a strong normative impulse in this direction existed is indicated by Ku Yen-wu's approval of a Chin case barring from office the sons of an official executed for corruption, and by Ku's explanation that "the sons of greedy and shameless persons without a sense of integrity necessarily will lack integrity and purity of character."[61] But this impulse had to compete with the feeling of officials like Hsüeh Yün-sheng that officials convicted of serious crimes of corruption should eventually be allowed back into office, "so as to manifest the idea that it is unbearable to cast them aside for their whole lives . . ."[62] Even Ku Yen-wu himself, as we have seen, believed that *ts'ai-li* (talented officials), although usually of corrupt character, could function well in the bureaucracy if properly used.

If, then, there was no rigid moral line drawn between official and criminal status, we can infer that there was a feeling that the honor of officials was partly compatible with criminal activity. This feeling can be explained in terms of the internalization of the *chung-ts'ai* (man of medium ability) image. I, a *chung-ts'ai* with no solid inner core of morality, am liable to commit criminal acts when under material pressures of one sort or another. Contrary to Mencius' ideal, my integrity depends on material conditions, and I am happy openly to accept

60. *Li-chi chu-shu* (Ssu-pu pei-yao), 3:3b–5. The subcommentary cited here is by K'ung Ying-ta of the seventh century A.D., who here is citing *Po-hu t'ung-te-lun* as found in *ch'üeh-wen*:8b of the edition of *Po-hu t'ung-te-lun* in *Pao-ching-t'ang ts'ung-shu* (Peking, 1923). See also *Yen-t'ieh-lun*, pp. 353–354.

61. *HCCSWP*, 19:4b.

62. *TLti*, 2:49b.

a regular supplementary salary called *yang-lien* ([payments] to nourish integrity; a Ch'ing institution with roots probably going back at least to Sung times). Thus I am a potential criminal morally similar to the convicted criminals whom I welcome back into my status group after they have served their criminal sentences. Yet if I am a potential criminal, I am not a *chün-tzu* (true gentleman), and I am ashamed of myself. Ashamed of myself, I accept humiliating punishments as morally appropriate to me, and I welcome the opportunity to expiate my wrongs.

Together with the intellectually articulated view that good government required the dismissal or even execution of bad officials, this diffuse inner feeling of shame legitimated the punishment of officials. This sense of shame can be seen as linked through the idea of the officials' mediocrity to Hsün-tzu's notion of the originally bad nature of man. All these ideas and attitudes together can be labeled the officials' "probationary ethic."[63]

They gave meaning to the frequently used Ch'ing disciplinary sentence of *ko-chih tai-tsui liu-jen* (dismissal from office with retention of duties while carrying along one's guilt). An official who was being punished, it was often said, was "exerting himself to expiate his guilt" (*hsiao-li shu-tsui*); thus he was "renewing himself" (*tzu-hsin*).[64] Impeaching oneself (which often

63. I do not in this book use "guilt" or "shame" in the technical senses developed by social scientists. As Eberhard points out, it is generally agreed that virtually all cultures use both "guilt" and "shame" as socialization mechanisms, the only question being which of the two in the particular culture is more important; see Eberhard, *Guilt and Sin in Traditional China* (Berkeley, Calif., 1967), pp. 2–3. In this context another relevant work is L. W. Pye, *The Spirit of Chinese Politics*. Although confused about the nature of personality and of organizational behavior in imperial China, Pye, correctly I believe, stresses that childhood socialization in imperial China promoted not only particularistic but also organizationally viable behavior. Pye's account of socialization seems to be sound and can be tentatively regarded as providing a psychological basis for my "probationary ethic"; see chap. vi in Pye's work, esp. pp. 95, 97, and 105, where he discusses the interrelated factors of an internalized sense of shame, the felt need for externally imposed authority and rules, and the desire to perform well according to these rules in order to win approbation. In IV, 5, I offer a critique of R. A. Solomon's views, which largely applies also to Pye's.

64. On *tzu-hsin*, see, e.g., *TCHTSL*, 86:*kuan-yüan k'ai-fu*:Ch'ien-lung 35. *Tzu-hsin* was also used in connection with amnesties for criminals; see *TCHTSL*, 729:*ch'ang-she so-pu-yüan*:*li-nien shih-li*:

led to a lighter penalty or no penalty) was a much-emphasized practice and, as a form of confession, seems to have involved this moral notion of expiation. Although the hope of success and promotion played a vital role, the character of the officials was such that holding the fear of failure very close to them was organizationally productive (although they complained of it). Above all, it seems likely that without this attitude they could not have endured a disciplinary system which punished them sharply for mere mistakes or even shortcomings beyond their control. Without it, they could not have accepted a system of law which turned unavoidable shortcomings into legal offenses denoted with the same terminology applied to crimes (such as *fan* and *tsui*).

The capacity to feel shame (*ch'ih*) was of course a major Confucian virtue and inseparable from moral aspiration. Thus one can speak here of a dialectical, partly unstable relationship in the minds of many of the Confucian elite between the probationary ethic and the sense of charisma. The man of learning simultaneously was proud of what learning and virtue he had and ashamed of his failure to perfect his learning and virtue. Pride and shame tended to be connected, since without awareness of one's shameful shortcomings, one could not proudly overcome them. The feelings of pride and shame together promoted that sense of responsibility which was needed if disciplinary sanctions were to be effective. In contrast to the materialistic Legalist view that sanctions worked because men feared pain and desired pleasure, one Ch'ing writer said: "Only when officials have morale and integrity can they be made use of. Such officials, when rewarded, appreciate why they are being encouraged, and, when punished, appreciate why they are being chastised." [65]

This perception was certainly a common one. Chou Kao, a *chü-jen* of 1783 who rose to be a prefect, deplored the lack of *hsin* (a sense of trust) in the Ch'ing bureaucracy and said: "When a sense of trust is not present, the process of punishing

Ch'ung-te 7. Here the emperor says: "in all instances we now release you from your punishment. May you correct your faults and renew yourselves."

65. *HCCSWP*, 15:2b. I have been unable to trace the writer, Lu Hsi-chin, but this piece, like virtually all others in *HCCSWP*, must have been written in the Ch'ing period.

and encouraging officials will be ineffective for lack of a proper basis."[66]

Without motivational commitment, men would shrink from the unpleasantness and emotional strain of bureaucratic work, which often involved the need, as the cliché had it, to *chin-hsin so-shih jen-lao jen-yüan* (exhaustively devote one's spirit and energy to the matters for which one is responsible and endure the hardship, toil, and hatred of others that come with holding office). The central type of deviancy here was *t'ui-hsieh* (shirking responsibility). Whether one "shirked responsibility" or "exhaustively devoted one's spirit and energy to the matters for which one was responsible" could on the whole not be determined merely by external sanctions. Ch'ing bureaucratic documents have endless warnings against "shirking responsibilities."

Officials who could not be "made use of" because they "shirked responsibilities" were a real problem. Within about two months during the winter of 1832–33, T'ao Chu, the Nanking governor-general, had to deal with three such cases of deliberate insubordination and irresponsibility; these cases are also significant as illustrating the relatively small role of fear in the bureaucracy. These three officials were not afraid of their exalted superior, the governor-general. Unable to call on their motivational commitment, their superiors had no means to make them perform.

The first case involved official discipline at the Huai-pei subzone of the salt monopoly during 1832, which was then in a sensitive period of reorganization, that is, the establishment of the ticket system. It was T'ao's view that being so distant from its superior office at Yangchow, the Huai-pei administrative center at Haichow had to be headed by an official with great ability. T'ao therefore in early 1832 had gone outside regular channels to assign Tsou Hsi-ch'un, an official just dismissed from the post of Huai-an-Yangchow taotai for a "public offense" (see below), to direct the regular Huai-pei officials; Tsou was merely "commissioned" to perform this task and lacked a regular post. The need for Tsou became especially evident at the end of 1832 when T'ao impeached one of the leading regular salt officials at Haichow, the Haichow branch head, Shan Chuang-t'u.

According to T'ao Chu, Shan, a low and direct subordinate of his, had openly and repeatedly criticized the new ticket sys-

66. *HCCSWP*, 16:6. See IV, 3, c.

tem then being established by T'ao and had without authorization left his post and stayed at Yangchow for several weeks, using the excuse that he had to supervise the administrative business of Huai-pei merchants at Yangchow. When Shan's immediate superior, a high official, repeatedly ordered him back to Haichow, he refused to go, claiming he needed leave on account of sickness. Moreover he had taken his seal of office with him, which was needed at Haichow to transact salt business, and when the Haichow salt production yards happened to suffer a flood, he failed to travel to them to inspect the situation personally. Found guilty of "hurting the management of public affairs and deliberately shirking responsibilities," he was dismissed from office (*ko-chih*). Previously due for "compulsory retirement," Shan may have been an old man exhibiting the obstinate self-confidence of old age.

In the second case, an expectant salt official at Yangchow lost his status as a high priority candidate for office. At first requesting a sick leave and then repeatedly absenting himself from his duties, he was regarded as unconscientious. In the third case, a probationary Liang-huai salt official was dismissed from his position (*ko-chih*). Almost three years previously, he had been commissioned to escort a shipment of Liang-huai revenue silver to Peking. Although he had delivered the silver, he had never returned to Liang-huai to have his mission approved and to hand in the receipt he had received from the Board of Revenue for delivery.[67]

Such, then, were some of the problems and attitudes involved in eliciting disciplined work. In the course of our discussion, we have seen how a legitimated, universalistic, mild, and flexible system of disciplinary sanctions had roots in the Chou period. Rationalization of the concept of responsibility also had a long past. The idea of "turning one's back on public interests to pursue private ones" was commonly applied to officials in Han times,[68] and the distinction between *kung-tsui* (public offenses)

67. *Liang-huai yen-fa-chih* (1904), 4:5b–6; 4:7b–8. On Tsou Hsi-ch'un's appointment, see *TYT*, 38:15–17; 40:16b. Shan Chuang-t'u is not listed as Haichow branch head in the *LHYFC* (1904) tables of officials, presumably because of his disgraceful exit. I am indebted to Mr. Zunvair Yue for seeing the connection between Shan Chuang-t'u's insubordination and possible old age. See IV, 4, d.

68. This standard was part of the "six articles" used by circuit inspectors in appraising prefects during the Early Han. See Sa, I:253–254.

and *ssu-tsui* (private offenses), basic in all major dynasties since the Sui, has been traced back to the Ch'en dynasty (557–589) or earlier.[69] Roughly speaking, public offenses were shortcomings involving governmental affairs and lacking any corrupt self-interest, while private offenses involved corruption (see IV, 3, a). By routinely making this distinction, the government weighed motivation more rationalistically when considering the seriousness of an offense.

We can now turn from the normative side to questions of administrative differentiation and centralization, which have been discussed above in an abstract way (IV, 1).

As we have said, in the history of the disciplinary system one rarely if ever finds extreme centralization, with all the procedures being carried out by one or two capital offices. Either considerable decentralization or the network pattern was far more common. One can see here again the dilemma facing the rulers between tight control and effectiveness. Decentralization possibly promoted the effective management of personnel by regional superiors, whose flexibility was inhibited by the tight controls of the network pattern.[70]

One important point is that, at least outside the capital, the Censorate had no major effect on the centralization of the disciplinary system in any period. First of all, to the extent that it played a role in discipline, the Censorate was often limited to surveillance and the announcing of offenses and did not become greatly involved in the other procedures of discipline. Second, even in the realm of surveillance, offices besides the Censorate often played a major role, especially outside the capital.

The system of periodic evaluations employed by all major

69. Étienne Balazs, tr., *Le traité juridique du "Souei-chou"* (Études sur le société et l'économie de la Chine médiévale; Leiden, 1954), p. 167. Balazs here traces the distinction back to the Ch'en dynasty, but Later Han (25–220) sources refer to the case of an official who was "judged guilty of a public [offense]" for having failed to eliminate certain bandits, while a Chin (265–420) source states that "There are public and private crimes." See Ch'eng Shu-te, *Chiu-ch'ao lü-k'ao* (A study of the penal statutes of nine dynasties; Taipei, 1965), I: 122, and Tai Yen-hui, *T'ang-lü t'ung-lun* (A comprehensive discussion of the T'ang penal code; Taipei, 1965), p. 264.

70. On the earlier history of the administrative aspects, I largely follow Sa Meng-wu, but see also Charles O. Hucker, *The Censorial System of Ming China,* pp. 10–20.

dynasties since the Ch'in was always to a large extent outside the control of the Censorate.[71] At least by Early Han times, a tendency had naturally begun to develop for officials holding regular administrative posts to carry out surveillance over their subordinates. Surveillance and administration, after all, inherently had a tendency to blend into one another. This was especially so in the case of that problematic third or provincial level of regional administration, where surveillance offices could turn into administrative offices, as happened in the case of the Han circuit inspector (*tz'u-shih*), or administrative offices could be assigned the main surveillance functions, as happened in the Sung period.

In the early Han period, besides the Censorate, two offices at the capital also had responsibilities for surveillance.[72] In regional administration, the circuit inspectors (*tz'u-shih*) carried out surveillance only relative to the highest officials, the prefects; the prefects carried out surveillance over all lower regional officials.[73] It is also clear that the Han district magistrates carried out surveillance over their subordinates. Similarly in the T'ang, Sung, Ming, and Ch'ing periods, regular administrative superiors commonly carried out surveillance relative to their subordinates.[74]

It should be remembered that the Ming and Ch'ing circuit censors (*chien-ch'a yü-shih*) were stationed in the capital most of the time. At times even these Censorate posts at the capital were left unfilled, but this was just a symptom of governmental disarray in the late Ming period.[75] Although regular Ming and Ch'ing regional officials often had at least honorary titles as censors, no full-fledged censors in either dynasty seem to have been stationed full time in the provinces. Thus it is hardly surprising that, as our detailed Ch'ing data show, regular Ch'ing administrative superior officials constituted the backbone of regional surveillance. These Ch'ing superiors had the knowledge about and carried the main legal responsibilities for their subordinates, and if a censor impeached one of their subordinates

71. Sa, I:62–64, 277–278; III:124; IV:158, 375.
72. Sa, I:220.
73. Sa, I:254.
74. Sa, III:122–123; IV:158, 120, 157–158, 373.
75. *Ming Ch'ing she-hui ching-chi hsing-t'ai-te yen-chiu* (Studies in the social and economic structure of Ming and Ch'ing times; Shanghai, 1957), comp. Han Ta-ch'eng *et al.* See pp. 84–85.

before they did, they typically were to be impeached for lack of vigilance. A censor in 1800 complained that governors-general and governors were refusing to impeach subordinates for illegal financial deficits. He did not even mention the possibility that such impeachments should be carried out by censors and suggested that they henceforth should be the exclusive responsibility of taotais.[76] At least in the provinces, the Ch'ing Censorate just backstopped surveillance (IV, 4, c and d).

Often the whole procedure for important cases of discipline was decentralized in the sense that centrally appointed officials carried out the act on their own discretion. This tendency toward decentralization was prominent in earlier times and then largely stopped in 1725–1727.

Thus the Han prime office (*tsai-hsiang*) had the right of "first killing, then memorializing" in the case of officials guilty of grave crimes.[77] In Han times, most of the subordinate officials of the prefects and district magistrates were not appointed by the capital but rather by the prefects and district magistrates themselves, respectively. Moreover, the relationship between the latter and their subordinates is said to have preserved some of the characteristics of the feudal ruler-minister (*chün-ch'en*) relationship of Chou times and thus involved a diffuse sort of loyalty and authority.[78] Clearly the prefects and district magistrates took responsibility for the behavior of their subordinates and on their own discretion could punish and reward them, at least by dismissing them and by recommending them for higher office. In the Ming period, if an official's offense was punishable only through a salary fine or redemption, the whole sanction process could be carried out at the discretion of certain superior officials, and much of it could be so carried out also for offenses that were slightly more serious. After 1725–1727, superiors only retained discretion to punish subordinates in minor ways such as issuing demerits, removing their seal of office, and keeping them in custody.

Of course, there also was some centralization in earlier periods, for instance, in the form of centralized supervision involving centrally issued regulations. However, it again seems clear that such supervision was more intense in the Ch'ing

76. *HCCSWP*, 20:10a–b.

77. Chou Tao-chi, pp. 126–127. See also III, 2.

78. Sa, II:39. Yen Keng-wang, *Chung-kuo ti-fang hsing-cheng chih-tu-shih*, part one, II:403–404. See also Appendix II.

period than in many earlier periods. There apparently was a long-term tendency for disciplinary regulations to become more numerous and systematized.

Han experts generally regard the Han government as one in which the authority of regional officials was relatively large, and it is hard to find Han complaints about administration being hamstrung by too many regulations. One example of Han disciplinary regulations is the famous "six articles." The six articles determined what the circuit inspectors should look for when examining the affairs of the prefects and were largely in the form of general, catchall definitions of offenses such as "turning one's back on public interests to pursue private ones."[79]

T'ang circuit censors also had a set of "six articles" telling them what to look for in inspecting regional administration, but eventually they had to apply more than seventy articles. The complaint arose that they could not work effectively because their inspections were hamstrung by too many regulations. The T'ang periodic evaluations were carried out according to a systematized list of criteria of performance.[80] There also was a clear-cut schedule of sentences. In general T'ang officials were punished by criminal sentences which were commuted in one of three ways (listed according to ascending severity): redemption; *kuan-tang* (removal of one or more official ranks as a substitute for criminal punishment); and *ch'u-mien* (temporary dismissal from office). *Kuan-tang* was a form of demotion whereby an official gave up one or more ranks such as an actual post or an honorific title; he was eligible for reappointment to a lower position after a year. *Ch'u-mien*, depending on its degree of severity, kept an official out of office for one to six years and at its worst (*ch'u-ming*) temporarily reduced him to the status of commoner. Fixed rates determined how much criminal punishment was commuted by the surrender of what kind of official status.[81]

79. Sa, I:253–254, 280. A. F. P. Hulsewé, *Remnants of Han Law*, Vol. I (Leiden, 1955), has many examples of the punishment of officials, such as p. 206, 134–135.

80. Sa, III:123, 125–126.

81. Tai Yen-hui, *Chung-kuo fa-chih-shih kai-yao* (Essentials of the history of China's legal institutions; Taipei, 1960), pp. 231–234. For Sui sentences, see Balazs, *Le traité juridique du "Souei-chou,"* pp. 75–76, 166–167, 52. Information clarifying the involved T'ang system can be found in Tai Yen-hui, *T'ang-lü t'ung-lun*, pp. 244–273. In all cases except redemption, an official was put out of office

Yet Ho Wei-ning's discussion of T'ang laws on officials' behavior in the salt monopoly indicates that these laws were very few and general. They were adducible for salt violations but often not written directly and specifically to cover salt violations.[82] By the late Ming period there were regulations specifying punishments for local officials who at the time of the fiscal evaluations (*k'ao-ch'eng*) had failed to sell all the salt quotas assigned to their jurisdictions. However, routine enforcement of these salt *k'ao-ch'eng* was still a problem in 1616.[83] Such regulations were common by Ch'ing times, when salt monopoly *ch'u-fen* regulations were numerous, detailed, and often enforced. The Ch'ing schedule of administrative punishments similarly was more systematized than the Ming.[84]

---

for at least a year and then could be reappointed with a lower rank. It is amazing that such mild sanctions applied, at least theoretically, to an official guilty of even the worst offenses, "the ten abominations." The complexity of the T'ang system largely stemmed from the fact that because official rank was multidimensional (it involved not only the categories of honorary title, noble title, official with actual governmental responsibilities, official without such responsibilities, and officer with command responsibilities, but also gradations within each of these categories), specifying changes in official rank resulting from punishment was not simple.

82. Ho Wei-ning, *Chung-kuo yen-cheng-shih*, I:105–107.

83. *Huang-Ming ching-shih wen-pien*, 29:310–313. The development of the *k'ao-ch'eng* system from Ming to Ch'ing times deserves more study. Ming specialists such as Hucker and Shen Ming-chang do not note the existence in Ming times of any regular annual evaluation such as the *k'ao-ch'eng*.

84. *Ming-lü chi-chieh*, 1:19–23, and the entries *wen-wu-kuan fan kung-tsui* and *wen-wu-kuan fan ssu-tsui* in *chüan* 726 of *TCHTSL*. In the case of public offenses, before 1727 officials' sentences of the light bamboo were redeemed, and no record of the offense was made or at least officially held against them. After 1727, they were commuted into salary fines beginning at a month's fine for a sentence of ten blows and ending at a nine-months' fine for a sentence of fifty blows. If the public offense had a sentence of beating with a heavy bamboo, before 1727 a record of the offense was made, and presumably there also was a redemption fee. At the end of each year, a total account was made of all such offenses and sent to the Board of Civil Officials. Every nine years, when there was a general evaluation, the whole list of these offenses would be considered as one factor determining promotion, demotion, or dismissal. After 1727, if the public offense was punished by blows of the heavy bamboo, these sentences were immediately inflicted according to a scale beginning at a year's salary fine for sixty blows and ending at demotion

The Ch'ing disciplinary system, after 1727, thus was a centralized network pattern. Much of the procedure was carried out by an open-ended network of centrally appointed officials, but these officials were centrally supervised, having under pain of sanction to carry out procedures written down in detailed, centrally issued regulations. Moreover, some of the procedure was centrally carried out.

Along with increasing centralization in 1725–1727, the Ch'ing also increased differentiation. While the various conditions of differentiation are discussed below, we should note here that the Ch'ing not only systematized the schedule of sentences but also increased specialization in communication by collecting most of the articles on administrative shortcomings, which had been scattered in the penal code and under various headings of administrative law, and, apparently for the first time in Chinese history, publishing specialized chapters or books of the laws on administrative discipline. (Later, many editions of such books appeared.)

These moves increased the formal differentiation of the disciplinary sanctions from the criminal law. Although retaining important connections to the latter, the system of administra-

---

by four subgrades and transfer for one hundred blows (the latter sentence could also be one of probationary retention of duties instead of transfer). In the case of private offenses after 1727, there was a similar scale beginning with a two-months' salary fine for a sentence of ten blows of the light bamboo and ending at dismissal from office for a sentence of one hundred blows of the heavy bamboo. Before 1727, in the case of private offenses, if the sentence were forty blows or less of the light bamboo, the sentence was (presumably apart from being redeemed) commuted by making a record of it, which again might lead to status deprivation only nine years later. Only for more serious private offenses did the Ming system call for immediate status deprivations. Here the scale began at transfer to a less desirable post for fifty blows of the light bamboo, passed through a number of such transfers accompanied by increasing demotions in grade, and ended at dismissal from office with no reappointment. Consequently, apart from whether or not permission to sentence came from the capital, only the most serious administrative sentences were inflicted immediately after the offense and presumably reported immediately. In the case of a large range of lighter offenses, status deprivations, if any, were inflicted only at nine-year intervals, and the capital received the records of offenses only once a year. Admittedly, other kinds of reports on offenses may well have been sent more frequently. It should be noted that there were some salary fines in the Ming period also; see *Ming-lü chi-chieh,* 1:11b.

tive punishment now depended less on the principle of the commutation of criminal sentences into administrative ones, since there was a continuous flow of new regulations in which the sanctions were originally phrased as administrative ones. The situation therefore differed from that of T'ang, Sung, and Ming times, when officials were usually punished through sentences originally phrased as criminal sentences and then commuted either into money payments or various sorts of administrative sanctions. The Ch'ing disciplinary sanctions tended to be more clearly integrated into that system of periodic evaluations and personnel shifts run under the supervision of the Board of Civil Officials.

However this was not necessarily a victory for the official sense of honor and instead had the purpose of increasing the efficiency of personnel administration. The late Ch'ing legal expert Hsüeh Yün-sheng thought that the T'ang system of bureaucratic sanctions was milder and thus preferable to the Ch'ing, despite the fact that the T'ang sentences had less formal differentiation than the Ch'ing from the criminal law.[85]

The Ch'ing rulers, therefore, inherited a tradition of disciplinary sanctions with a considerable tendency toward legitimation, universalism, mildness, rationalization, and flexibility. While perhaps decreasing the role of arbitrary terror in the sanction system, they increased the harshness of officials' punishments for grave crimes and displayed interest in the lenient treatment of administrative shortcomings. The Yung-cheng and Ch'ien-lung emperors also increased the differentiation and centralization of the administrative framework, thus possibly increasing uniformity and universalism, and under the Ch'ien-lung emperor there was a little legislation increasing universalism (see below).

We can now look more closely into the Ch'ing system, first inquiring into the question of the differentiation of administrative shortcomings from crimes, the rationality of the concept of responsibility, the mildness of the sanctions, and their universalistic quality.

85. *TLti,* 1:56a–b.

3. The Normative Framework

a. The Distrinction between Administrative Shortcomings and Crimes

The concept of a mere administrative mistake or shortcoming, often called *kung-shih shih-ts'o* (mistakes in public matters) or *yin-shih kua-wu* (to be pressed by circumstances into a transgression), had a complex relation to the concept of a crime. On the one hand, all mistakes and crimes formed one continuum, both terminologically and, we may venture, normatively. On the other hand, it was recognized that bureaucratic performance would suffer unless administrative mistakes were treated with leniency. Consequently a distinction was made not only between light and heavy offenses but also between those light offenses which were mere administrative shortcomings and those which retained some taint of criminal character.

I have argued in the previous section that many officials had a "probationary ethic" according to which the notions of official honor and criminality were not rigorously separated. This argument meshes with the fact that terminologically the concept of a crime and the concept of an administrative mistake, which almost no official could avoid, also were not rigorously distinguished. Thus in the case of both kinds of offenses, action against an official often required impeachment (*ts'an*), and all such cases were referred to with the terms *fan* (to offend against) and *tsui* (offense, guilt). The concept of *yü-tsui* (leftover guilt) also suggests this continuity: if an official had been punished by dismissal from office and still had "leftover guilt," he was given a criminal trial.

Similarly legal compilers did not feel that the penal code and the *Regulations on Administrative Punishment* were two different branches of law. Separate publication was regarded merely as a matter of convenience. The "principles of compilation" of the 1870 edition of the penal code states: "The salary fines, demotions, and dismissals of civil and military officials belong to [the category of] administrative punishments. Some are also entered in the penal code, but in many instances they are missing or incomplete in the latter. In the present day the Boards of Civil Officials and of War have opened compilation bureaus and have made compilations. Each has a specialized book [for administrative punishments]. There is no need that these articles appear in the code mixed in confusedly here and there."[1]

At the same time, there was a prominent distinction between light and heavy offenses. Light offenses were handled under the supervision of the Board of Civil Officials; heavy ones, under that of the Board of Punishments. Light offenses received administrative punishments such as demotion; heavy offenses, criminal punishments such as penal servitude. (Admittedly both criminal and administrative sentences could take the form of money payments—the former when the sentence was redeemed, the latter in the case not only of salary fines but also of restitutive payments, for example, to make up a tax deficit.)[2] Administrative punishments were called *ch'u-fen;* criminal ones, *hsing.*[3] *I-ch'u* (to advise on administrative punishment) was reserved for the Board of Civil Officials' memorial recommending an administrative sentence, and *chih-tsui* (to sentence inflicting criminal punishments) applied purely to the criminal sentences administered under the ultimate supervision of the Board of Punishments. Equally unambiguous was the standard phrase *ko-chih fa-shen* (dismiss from office and dispatch to be tried). This process is also described as: "If after dismissal from office there is leftover guilt, then turn the case over to the Board of Punishments."

The clarity of this distinction had a firm ideological basis involving the ancient idea that "The criminal punishments do not reach up to the officials." Dismissal from office was explicitly regarded as the line of demarcation between those punishments administered by the Board of Civil Officials and those administered by the Board of Punishments and as a legal precondition for subjecting an official to an ordinary trial. This is clear from a proposal, approved by the regent Dorgon, made by

1. *TCLL, fan-li*:2b–3.

2. For the use of such restitutive payments as administrative sentences, see, e.g., *TYT* 49:47b. District magistrates in bad Liang-huai salt monopoly markets such as Anking were ordered to make up any tax losses due to bad sales in their areas, a system stopped in 1793 in favor of the more usual administrative sanctions. It was obviously not practical.

3. An imperial executive order of 1653 uses *ch'u-fen* with regard to criminal punishments administered by the Board of Punishments, but this is a very rare exception. See *li-nien shih-li,* Shun-chih 10, under *chih-kuan yu-fan,* in *chüan* 726 of *TCHTSL.* On the term *ch'u-fen,* see II, note 84.

a censor in a memorial presented at the start of Ch'ing rule in China, in 1644. After urging compilation of the first edition of the Ch'ing penal code, the censor went on:

> The second point is that we should preserve the *kuo-t'i* (state's order and dignity). "The criminal punishments do not reach up to the officials"—this is the ancient idea of treating those of high position with respect. May I request that henceforth when civil officials commit a crime, the case should first be referred to the Board of Civil Officials for it to examine into and advise on. If the official is guilty of a grave crime, it should be necessary to request an imperial rescript dismissing him from office, and only then would his case be sent to the Board of Punishments for trial. The military officials are under the Board of War and should be treated likewise. As for the prefectural, departmental, and district officials in the provinces who are impeached, dismissed, and due to be arrested and tried, order the governors and/or the provincial judges involved immediately to arrest and try them. When they have completed the trial, they should make a report on it to the office of law at the capital [that is, the Board of Punishments]. However until the record of the case is drawn up and the case is reviewed, it is not necessary to keep the official under arrest. Thus the morale of officials will be lifted up and the *kuo-t'i* (state's order and dignity) will be preserved." [4]

The distinction between light and heavy offenses was also marked by obvious but largely implicit criteria of the seriousness of the offense. Offenses receiving administrative punishments typically stemmed from laxness, inefficiency, mild greed, laziness, desire for comfort, cheating to advance one's career, recklessness, ineptness, and the like. Offenses receiving criminal punishments typically involved wicked intent. Although the practical consequences and especially the moral significance of an act affected its degree of seriousness, intent was often the crucial factor. Many lightly punished administrative shortcomings had major practical consequences, while many heavily punished crimes had minor practical consequences.

The role of intent is illustrated by the punishments for magis-

4. *Ta-Ch'ing li-ch'ao shih-lu,* Shun-chih, 7:3b–4b. See IV, 4, d.

trates making wrong judicial judgments: if the mistake was unintentional, the punishment was only an administrative one, but if it was intentional, the magistrate received the criminal sentence he had unjustly inflicted (or the criminal sentence which he had unjustly failed to inflict).[5]

Intent plays a similar role in punishments connected to the maintenance of waterways. Failure to repair or build dikes in time to prevent a flood or to be watchful in maintaining them was punished only by administrative punishments, even if human lives were lost, and if a dike burst on account of rain and bad weather lasting a number of days, conditions regarded as beyond human control (*fei jen-li so chih*), then there was not even an administrative punishment. If, however, officials deliberately destroyed a dike in order to dip into the funds which would then be issued for repairs, this was a criminal act punishable by execution. (However, according to Hsüeh Yün-sheng, this sentence of execution was regarded as too severe and was a dead letter. Presumably the usual sentence was some degree of penal servitude or banishment.)[6]

The role of intent is illustrated also by punishments regarding the handling of funds. Criminal punishments were used not only for theft or embezzlement of government funds but also inflicted on an official who, in charge of such funds, knew of their theft and failed to report it. If he did not know of the crime and merely was guilty of lack of vigilance, however, the punishment was only administrative.[7]

Yet the shielding of another official guilty of juggling or embezzlement was not necessarily punished criminally. A prefect was held responsible for any improper fiscal acts of the local magistrates under him. If he knew that one of his magistrates

5. T'ung-tsu Ch'ü, *Local Government in China under the Ch'ing*, pp. 128–129. Actually if we look at *Hsing-an hui-lan* (Conspectus of penal cases; 1834) comp. Pao Shu-yün *et al.*, 59:35–39b, we find that while the penal code itself provided for criminal sentences even for unintentional adjudicative mistakes, *ch'u-fen* law provided for mere administrative punishments, and, in the cases cited here, was given primacy over the penal code. I am greatly indebted to Mrs. Chen Chang Fu-mei for bringing these valuable cases to my attention. See esp. *Hsing-an hui-lan*, 59:35b–36. See also IV, 3, c, for another formulation of the distinction between light and heavy offenses.

6. *TLti*, 51:3–5; *TCLL*, 39:2b–3b.

7. *TLti*, 14:20; *TCLL*, 12:11.

had juggled or embezzled funds and shielded the magistrate by failing to ask for his impeachment, the prefect had to make up the shortage in case the magistrate could not do so in three years. However, despite this act of shielding, there was no criminal punishment; apart from the possibility of making up the shortage, the only punishment was dismissal from office.

If the prefect was guilty only of lack of vigilance, not shielding, the punishments were somewhat milder. Interestingly, the unvigilant prefect was punished more severely if his magistrate had juggled than if the latter had embezzled (since in the former case but not the latter the prefect might be forced to make up the shortage). This was a quirk of the law and was criticized by Hsüeh Yün-sheng as unfair.[8]

One of the worst crimes was accepting a bribe to apply the law with favoritism.[9] If the sum was as little as 20 taels, the penalty was 60 blows of the heavy bamboo and a year of penal servitude; the punishment rose with the sum to detention for strangling at 80 taels.[10] As a rule, the sentence could be mitigated only by imperial pardon, not the regular procedure of redemption.

Clearly because the intent was regarded as less wicked than in the case of bribery, the treatment was more lenient for officials who stole the contents of the granaries or treasuries they were in charge of. In some instances, if they made up the loss within a certain time limit, their criminal sentence was canceled or reduced. If the sum was as little as 7.5 taels, the punishment was 60 blows of the heavy bamboo and a year of penal servitude. Punishment for 40 taels was five years of penal servitude (a special form of commuted death sentence).[11] As the sums increased, punishment rose through three grade of banishment, and if the sum was 1,000 taels or more, the sentence was detention for beheading. If the sum was paid back within a year, however, all original sentences of penal servitude and banishment were canceled, and the death sentence was commuted. Persons unable to make restitution in one year were given a second year. If at the end of the second year they still had not paid back the sum, sentences of banishment and penal servitude

8. *TLti,* 13:26–27b; *TCLL,* 11:18b–20.

9. *TLti,* 1:15, shows how this crime was typically listed along with the "ten abominations" among the worst crimes.

10. *TLti,* 41:2a–b; *TCLL,* 31:2b–3.

11. *TLti,* 25:52a–b; *TCLL,* 23:24a–b.

were carried out, but persons with a death sentence were imprisoned. If at the end of the third year the prisoner's family had not made up the sum, the death sentence was changed to imprisonment for life.[12]

Besides distinguishing between light and heavy offenses, the law divided light offenses in such a way that administrative mistakes were clearly identified and could be treated with special leniency. However, this was done somewhat indirectly through the distinction between *kung-tsui* (public offenses) and *ssu-tsui* (private offenses).

As Kracke and others have indicated, while this distinction focused on motivation, it also denoted the distinction between governmental and nongovernmental affairs.[13] The latter distinction, following the idea of spatially or temporally distinct spheres of activity, accorded with the loci classici of "public" and "private," as in the *Book of Poetry's* "May it first rain on our public fields, and then on our private,"[14] or Mencius' "And not till the public work is finished, may they presume to attend to their private affairs." This distinction between the public and private spheres of activity can also be found in some later usages. For instance an edict of 1655, referring to the need for a salt tax arrangement convenient both to the state and the consumers, spoke of a system which would *ling kung ssu liang pien* (bring about a situation which would be convenient from the standpoint of public and private needs). Here the *kung* (public) sphere is virtually identical with the *kuo* (state), while the *ssu* (private) sphere is virtually identical with the *min* (people), in other words with a sphere of interests fully legitimated in Confucian eyes. Similarly, in 1728 the Yung-cheng emperor explained how the demand of superior officials for gifts from subordinate officials had led the latter to impose customary fees on the people. He therefore had established the *yang-lien* (payments to nourish integrity) in order to stop this whole

12. *TLti*, 25:58b–59; *TCLL*, 23:26–27.

13. Kracke, *Civil Service in Early Sung China—960–1067* (Cambridge, Mass., 1953), pp. 171–172. T'ung-tsu Ch'ü, *Local Government*, p. 32. Professor Ch'ü's reference to public and private offenses in *Law and Society*, p. 182, is not so clear as in his *Local Government in China under the Ch'ing*. *Shinkoku gyōseihō*, I:465–468, translated in *Ch'ing-kuo hsing-cheng-fa*, 3:7:1:188–190, has a rounded explanation, using the excellent definition in *TCHT*, 11:4.

14. Legge, *Chinese Classics*, IV:381 (*The She King*).

process, "causing public and private needs to have something on which to rely and saving officials from having any anxieties regarding either their superiors or their inferiors."[15]

This distinction, involving the use of *ssu* (private) in a morally neutral or even positive sense, is a sociologically significant one sometimes overlooked by scholars stressing the pejorative connotation of *ssu* (private). However, it lacked important adjudicative use at the time, because whether an offense had been committed in or out of relationship to governmental affairs was not a salient criterion of its seriousness.

The connection of the public-private distinction to the question of intent was legally more significant. While the idea of weighing intention to decide the seriousness of an offense goes back at least to the *Book of History*,[16] credit for first emphasizing this idea is sometimes given to Early Han Confucians such as Tung Chung-shu, who quoted precedents from the *Ch'un-ch'iu* in applying the law, often citing motivation as a factor calling for leniency.[17] However the ethical distinction between *kung* (following the public interest, being fair) as opposed to *ssu* (following selfish interests, being partial) is strongly associated with the universalistic Legalist emphasis on fairness, which especially involved the idea that people will accept the laws without resentment if administration is impartial. This can be seen from use of this distinction in *Shang-chün-shu, Kuan-tzu, Hsün-tzu, Lü-shih ch'un-ch'iu,* Chia I's thought, and *Huai-nan-tzu.* This motivational or ethical distinction between *kung* and *ssu* was further developed in Sung Neo-Confucianism.[18] Yet the distinction between governmental and non-governmental affairs still was pertinent, because the idea of a mistake committed despite good intent was often intertwined with the idea of being driven into such a mistake by the pressure of governmental affairs.

15. Legge, *Chinese Classics,* II:24 (*The Works of Mencius*). *Liang-che yen-fa-chih* (1966), I:65. *Ch'ing-shih-lu,* Yung-cheng, 69:5.

16. Legge, *Chinese Classics,* IV:39, 59 (*The Shoo King*).

17. T'ao, II:152–156; *Yen-t'ieh-lun,* p. 344.

18. For instance, see the following: *Hsün-tzu* (Ssu-pu ts'ung-k'an), 9:1a–b, 9a–b; *Kuan-tzu* (Ssu-pu ts'ung-k'an), 10:11–12; *Shang-chün-shu* (Ssu-pu pei-yao), 3:12–13; T'ao, II:52; T'ao, II:73; *Lü-shih ch'un-ch'iu* (Ssu-pu ts'ung-k'an), 1:9–13. For *kung* and *ssu* in Neo-Confucian ethics, see Ch'ien Mu, *Kuo-shih ta-kang,* II:570–571.

The blurred interplay between these two interpretations is reflected in the definitions of public and private offenses since at least T'ang times. Sometimes the definitions simply are vague, as in the definition of the Ming penal code: " 'Private offenses' means that the matter did not come about through public [activities? considerations?], and that the guilt was incurred on account of private [activities? interests?]."[19] Sometimes, however, the definitions begin with or take for granted the notion of distinct private and governmental spheres of activity and add the qualification that motivation is also a factor. In such definitions two points are emphasized: the concept of a private offense extends to corrupt acts in government, and the concept of a public offense extends to offenses outside the government committed without corrupt intent. This kind of clarification is found in the T'ang code's useful discussion of private offenses[20] as well as the Ming code's definition of public offenses.[21] The *Ta-Ch'ing hui-tien* also is entirely lucid: "[*Kung-tsui*] means that guilt was incurred on account of public matters or that although guilt was incurred through private matters, the offense was unintentional . . . [*Ssu-tsui*] means that guilt was incurred on account of private matters or that even though it was incurred through public matters, the offense was intentional."[22]

Logically these definitions yield a wide range of categories of offenses, but only some of these categories were important in practical terms. First, offenses committed by someone not holding office were in fact seldom "public." For this reason Ch'ing scholars were puzzled by a *lü* (penal statute) determining punishment for a public offense committed before taking office and discovered after: if one did not hold office, how could one commit a public offense? One view was that being implicated through no fault of one's own in the crime of another was the same as a public offense.[23] Yet there also were some clear-cut

19. *Ming-lü chi-chieh,* 1:21. Similarly unhelpful are the definitions in the Ch'ing penal code, *TCLL,* 4:18, 19.

20. Tai Yen-hui, *T'ang-lü t'ung-lun,* pp. 264–265.

21. *Ming-lü chi-chieh,* 1:19.

22. *TCHT,* 11:4. Equally good definitions are in *Ch'in-ting wang-kung ch'u-fen tse-li* (Imperially endorsed regulations on the administrative punishment of princes; not published before 1845), 1:2b.

23. *Shinkoku gyōseihō,* I:466–467, translated in *Ch'ing-kuo hsing-cheng-fa,* 3:7:1:189–190. The *lü* is in *TCLL,* 4:26; Philastre, I:148.

cases of persons not holding office committing public offenses (see IV, 3, c).

Second, distinguishing between private and public offenses in serious crimes had limited practical use, because the main use of this distinction was in handling lighter offenses. Admittedly, there were at least two laws whereby serious crimes were classed as public. First, juggling government funds (*no-i*) was explicitly classed as a "public offense" and, depending on the sum, could be punished by sentences up to detention for beheading.[24] Second, an official making levies on the people's wealth without an order from his superior could be punished criminally (by three years' penal servitude, for example) even if he used the funds only for public purposes. These two laws, however, were exceptional, and Hsüeh Yün-sheng felt that the severity of the sentences for juggling was questionable.[25]

Again, it may be granted that the concept of a public offense as applied to a serious crime was useful to the extent that conviction for any public offense was in principle more readily followed by eventual restoration to office. Yet in fact commission of serious public offenses such as unauthorized tax collection tended to preclude restoration to office, as shown by the law on *chüan-fu* (restoration to office by making financial contributions) (see IV, 3, c).

The category of private offense, therefore, was used especially to specify those light governmental offenses which still had a taint of criminality and so were distinguished from mere administrative shortcomings, to which the concept of public offense usually referred. The rationale of the distinction between these two kinds of light governmental offenses, as given in the *Ta-Ch'ing hui-tien,* was that public offenses were punished "in order to encourage officials in the performance of their duties," while

24. *TLti,* 14:1–4; *TCLL,* 12:2–3b.

25. *TLti,* 41:38; *TCLL,* 31:23. Hsüeh Yün-sheng says that the severe treatment of juggling had been determined on in order to prevent the use of a light article on juggling as a loophole for embezzlers: "However, juggling and embezzling are after all not the same," i.e., it is unfair to treat juggling with the same harshness; see *TLti,* 14:3. The exceptional nature of these two articles is also clear from an important 1801 imperial executive order in which these two articles were singled out as precedents for the proposition that public offenses could be punished criminally. This argument was made in connection with certain 1801 *li* revisions discussed below in IV, 3, c.

private offenses were punished "in order to warn officials not to act corruptly."[26] A saying from the *Book of History* quoted in this context was: "Mere mistakes, however great, are treated with indulgence; intentional offenses, however small, are punished."[27] The organizationally major point was explicitly made by Ch'ing writers, such as the prominent official Li Fu, that lenient punishments for minor shortcomings were necessary if officials were to have confidence in carrying out their duties.[28] As we shall see, various other practical arguments were made on either side of the question of leniency, but most views favored leniency.

It is significant that the treatment of public offenses was more lenient than the treatment of private offenses only if all other things were equal. Some private offenses were punished more mildly than some public ones. Contrary to the *Book of History*, intent was not always decisive. For instance, if a language translator at a board deliberately failed to assume his duties when it was his turn, with the result that the tasks involved were badly performed, he was punished with a fine of one year's salary. This was a private offense.[29]

Typical "public offenses" were lateness in meeting one of the many deadlines and "lack of vigilance" leading to an offense committed by someone else.

The more serious, but still light, governmental offenses classed as "private" can be subdivided into at least five categories. They often were distinguished by a mild selfish interest. If an offense was intentional or inherently grave, however, it could be classed as "private" even if no selfish interest was apparent.

First, there was the interest in material gain. For instance if an official wished to exchange his office seal for a new one (because it had become blurred through use in stamping documents) and his superior demanded a fee for doing it, the superior's offense was a private one punished by dismissal from office. On the other hand, if the official received his new seal and then

26. *TCHT*, 11:4.

27. Legge, *Chinese Classics*, IV:59 (*The Shoo King*). Two Ch'ing documents quoting it are in *CFTL*, 1:5b, and *HCCSWP*, 15:8b.

28. *HCCSWP*, 15:8b. See also *ibid.*, 1:9b; 16:6. See IV, 3, c.

29. *CFTL*, 14:15. See *ibid.*, 14:2, for a stronger but still rather mild punishment for a local magistrate who leaves his post without authorization. This also was a private offense.

carelessly failed to turn in his old one, his offense was a typical public one, punished only by a six months' salary fine.[30]

Second, there was the selfish desire to seek one's personal comfort or pleasure. If an official was ordered through a proposal endorsed by the emperor to be stationed in a rural area and did not go there because of fondness for living in the city, the offense was a private one, and he was dismissed from office.[31] A private offense punished by dismissal was that of officials who, living in cities, entertained guests and amused themselves excessively, with the result that they did not arrive early at their offices and cases accumulated unattended to. A somewhat similar private offense punished also by dismissal was that of provincial judges, provincial treasurers, and taotais who delegated too many matters to their clerks with the result that their clerks acted corruptly on these matters.[32]

Third, there was the selfish interest in cheating in order to escape blame and advance one's career. Because an official escaped blame if a storm sunk his grain tribute boat on the Yangtze River or certain other large stretches of water, there was a temptation for officials who lost their boats on small waterways falsely to report the scene of the disaster. Such a false report was a private offense punished by a demotion of one subgrade plus transfer. (Loss of grain tribute boats on such smaller waterways due to bad weather was a public offense.)[33] Similarly, if an official was traveling outside his jurisdiction for a legitimate reason when an offense occurred in it for which he normally would have been charged with lack of vigilance, he was excused. If he falsely reported that he had been traveling or juggled the dates, his offense was a private one punished at least by a one subgrade demotion and transfer.[34]

Fourth, intentional offenses could be private even without any significant aspect of selfish interest. If a local magistrate "recklessly" used his office seal to stamp his private letter to someone of superior status, or if an assistant magistrate used his own seal to stamp a receipt for the tax on a land sale (this was supposed to be stamped only by the magistrate), these were private

30. *CFTL*, 10:1.
31. *CFTL*, 14:26.
32. *CFTL*, 14:25.
33. *CFTL*, 18:35.
34. *CFTL*, 1:21.

offenses punished by a demotion of one subgrade and transfer.[35]

Fifth, grave ineptitude, even if without a trace of selfish interest or intention, could be classed as private. If a province was thrown into total disorder and its people into misery, the governor-general, governor, and lower officials were dismissed from office, and this offense was a private one. Local magistrates suffered the same penalty for this offense of "lack of skill in soothing the people."[36] Similarly it was held that if among the subordinates of an official there were many failures in the carrying out of duties, the superior was guilty of a private offense and was dismissed from office; the superior had proved unable to be a model of the needed administrative virtues.[37]

All in all, therefore, mild offenses associated with governmental affairs were singled out as a legal category and sorted through to separate the more reprehensible from the more excusable, that is, the private from the public offenses. This process was a fundamental one, but terminologically and normatively all offenses shared a certain moral character. Moreover the distinction between light offenses involving governmental affairs and other light offenses was not made in a completely clear-cut fashion. There was no word or phrase at all—not to mention a single technical term—to denote the category "light offenses involving governmental affairs." In practice it was singled out because it was the focus of the distinction between private and public offenses; yet the theoretical definitions of public and private offenses transcended "light offenses involving governmental affairs." Neither was the notion of an "administrative mistake" congruent with the latter category, since "administrative mistakes" referred only to public offenses involving governmental matters. Besides being the practical focus of the distinction between public and private offenses, "light offenses involving governmental matters" were singled out by being used as the main content of the books or chapters called *ch'u-fen tse-li* (regulations on administrative punishment), which first were published around 1740. However this title also was no terminological improvement, since "administrative punishments" were inflicted also for those light offenses by officials involving nongovernmental matters.

35. *CFTL,* 10:7.
36. *CFTL,* 14:22.
37. *CFTL,* 14:21.

b. Responsibility

While the control requirement of the rationalization of responsibility was met to a large extent, the notion of responsibility applied to Ch'ing bureaucrats had an inherently severe and diffuse character.[1] Responsibility as a liability to punishment was often held by officials not only for their own illicit actions but also for their own minor mistakes, for events beyond their control, and for the actions of other persons.

The first point is illustrated by the fact that although mere administrative mistakes were treated with special leniency, officials were still punished for them. The fact that no wicked intent or even personal weakness was involved was an excuse entitling one to lenient treatment, but not an excuse necessarily to waive all punishment. Moreover in certain instances the mistake was inherently so grave that, however pure the intent, the punishment had to be severe. These mistakes typically involved the emperor's prestige. For instance if one accidentally lost an imperial edict and could not find it in thirty days, the punishment was ninety strokes of the heavy bamboo plus two and a half years of penal servitude.[2]

The 1831 Kaoyu impeachments (see IV, 4, d) illustrate how officials could be held responsible for events recognized to be outside their control, such as dike bursts. We can infer that the reasoning here was partly based on the universally objective fact that whether a situation is within a person's control is often unclear to all concerned. In the Ch'ing period, there was explicit discussion over whether difficulties inherent in a post or lack of ability were more responsible for failure.[3] If officials were given the benefit of the doubt, they would not exert themselves when the situation bordered on being within their control. In the Kaoyu case the governor-general decided to punish the officials involved largely in order to warn other officials, even though he admitted that the Kaoyu officials were not to blame.

Besides this issue of deterrence, hard lines of responsibility were often maintained because of inefficient bookkeeping and

1. This section has been influenced by Professor Yang's views on the concept of responsibility in traditional China as found in Lien-sheng Yang, "Government Control of Urban Merchants" (unpublished).

2. *TCLL*, 7:4a–b; *TLti*, 8:3.

3. *HCCSWP*, 18:10b–11. The writer, Ts'ai Fang-ping, lived in early Ch'ing times.

other lapses in communication, together with the relative lack of solidarity or trust between many officials and the government. The government often lacked precise knowledge about the actual difficulties of an official involved in, say, tax collection. Since it could hardly tailor his responsibilities to his own unverifiable account of what was within his control, it had no choice but to define his responsibility according to some standard reasonable in its own eyes, whether or not the standard conformed to the actual situation. Moreover, such a standard, although adjustable, could not be altered for every recognized change in circumstances. Consequently living with such standards was simply a professional hazard.

When an official failed to meet a standard, the notion that he had "not exerted himself" (*pu-li*) was a conventional fiction. For instance, many districts were notoriously troublesome; although officials assigned to them were held responsible for arresting all criminals in them, it was obvious that the large volume of crimes there was not the fault of the officials. In 1729 the Yung-cheng emperor pointed to the problems officials in such districts had in paying salary fines. Salary fines, before 1729, could multiply because any second or third salary fine levied on top of a current confiscation of one's salary had to be paid within a certain time limit if a large late fine was to be avoided—and the late fines similarly had deadlines. "This regulation is not very satisfactory," the emperor noted. "One can deeply sympathize with the plight of officials at departments or districts with many cases of salary fines and low officials who are poor and for whom it is difficult to pay the fines."[4] In this statement the emperor meant that certain administrative units inevitably saddled their magistrates with salary fines, however much these men exerted themselves. In a memorial of about 1799, the governor of Fukien forcefully argued that because of difficulties inherent in some posts, the number of public offenses for which an official was convicted was not necessarily a reliable guide as to that official's quality. This point was made by others too.[5]

Often the official was held responsible for the actions of the people whom he governed. Officials could also be held responsible for subordinates, protégés, and colleagues within the same

4. *TCHTSL*, 85:*kuan-yüan fa-feng*: Yung-cheng 7.
5. *HCCSWP*, 16:5. See also *ibid.*, 17:11.

office. The concept of collective responsibility involved here was prevalent throughout the society, as illustrated by the pao-chia system, the occasional criminal punishments whereby family members of the criminal were punished together with the criminal, and the common practice whereby the state held one or more merchants responsible for the actions of a large commercial group.[6]

Diffuse in these various ways, however, responsibility was also often restricted by rationalistic considerations and argued about in rationalistic terms. This tendency rationalistically to accept failure without assigning blame can perhaps be connected to the outlook of "moderate realism" (see I, 5). For instance, although the officials in the Kaoyu impeachments of 1831 were punished for the flooding of the grand canal embankment, the original intention of the governor-general was not to punish them, following the law that when such flooding was beyond human control, no one should be punished.

An interesting distinction in scope of responsibility can be seen by comparing the *k'ao-ch'eng* (examination of administrative results) for 1830 Liang-huai salt sales with that for 1831. The 1830 *k'ao-ch'eng* applying to those local magistrates and taotais in the Liang-huai zone with salt quota deficiencies was prepared in early 1832 and called for punishment, even though factors outside the control of these officials, especially the excessively high price of salt, where widely regarded by officials as responsible for bad salt sales in 1830.[7] But when floods disrupted some of the Liang-huai salt monopoly markets in 1831, it was felt that the local magistrates involved had a valid "reason" (*yin*) for the deficiency in the salt sales within their jurisdictions, and they were not punished when the *k'ao-ch'eng* for 1831 was prepared in late 1832.[8] Possibly it was felt that in 1830 more vigorous policing might still have been of some use.

More generally, there was a significant effort to adjust the

6. Collective responsibility was also a principle in private organizations, as illustrated by the Shansi banks, which were prominent in the nineteenth century: the family of the head of a branch office was "taken charge of by the bank" as security for his conduct. See Yang Lien-sheng, *Money and Credit in China* (Cambridge, Mass., Harvard University Press, 1952), pp. 84–85. In *Yen-t'ieh-lun*, pp. 354–355, one finds Confucians opposing collective punishment, but one cannot say all forms of diffuse responsibility were un-Confucian.

7. *TYT*, 38:12–14b.

8. *TYT*, 43:6a–b.

standards of the annual *k'ao-ch'eng* (examination of results) to those matters within human control. For instance in 1814, as a measure to counter the decline in salt monopoly sales, local magistrates in Hunan, Hupei, and Kiangsi were made individually responsible for the sale of a certain quota of salt within their districts or departments. However, in these provinces market conditions fluctuated so much that a district with large sales one year might have small ones the next, traders being allowed to ship wherever the market was best. In these circumstances it was not practical to hold a particular district responsible for a prefixed volume of sales, and in 1818 magistrates were relieved of this responsibility for a particular quota; only the salt taotai was held responsible, since it was meaningful to judge him by the quota of the province as a whole. In other markets of the Liang-huai zone, on the other hand, as we have seen, local magistrates did have an annual salt *k'ao-ch'eng*.[9]

One Ch'ing writer deplored the fact that a local magistrate who had achieved such a high level of peace and order in his jurisdiction that "at night people did not need to shut their doors" was liable to be punished if suddenly a criminal arrived from afar and committed a crime he could not solve.[10] Yen Jo-ch'ü (1636–1704) complained that an official could be held responsible for deficiencies in not only his tax quota but also that of his predecessors.[11] Around 1800 the governor of Fukien, Wang Chih-i, criticized as "unreasonable" the fact that "innocent" officials under him should have to make up out of their own pockets losses due to the misconduct of their predecessors.[12] It was recognized that holding an official responsible for the actions of a man he recommended for office, although a device needed for control, involved a problematic judgment about the ability to predict human behavior.[13]

On the highest levels of policy, the scope of responsibility was subject to discussion. When T'ao Chu was Nanking governor-general in the 1830's, he insisted several times that he could not absolutely guarantee the success of his salt monopoly policy, committing himself only to a hope for gradual improvement. In the winter of 1834–35, for instance, T'ao Chu proposed a

9. *TYT*, 49:47a–b.
10. *HCCSWP*, 15:2.
11. *HCCSWP*, 15:4b.
12. *HCCSWP*, 16:5b.
13. *CFTL*, 1a–b; Sa, IV:145.

major tax adjustment in response to a recent period of bad sales. He wanted to postpone payment of taxes on the current quota (the 1835 *kang*), splitting this quota into ten installments, one of which was to be paid over each of the next ten years. He also offered to pull back by one month every year the deadline for the annual fiscal report until it was back to the proper month; it had been pushed ahead in order to give him more leeway to meet his quotas on time. The Board of Revenue, advising the emperor on this proposal, wondered "whether or not [this plan] offers full security and won't come to a state of existing merely in name." The Board was worried that T'ao Chu's new tax arrangement would also be unfulfilled. Replying, T'ao Chu refused to say that the plan was bound to succeed: "How can I dare still to speak of full security?" His point was that one had to think in relative terms: the plan was justified by past precedents; it was a means for struggling with difficult circumstances; and its success depended on the state of the market in Hunan, Hupei, and Kiangsi, over which, in fact, he had only limited control. (The emperor's decision was a typical compromise. The proposal to pay the current quota over ten years was approved, but T'ao Chu's request to return year by year to the original deadline for the annual fiscal report was rejected; the original deadline had to be met beginning with the next year's quota.)[14]

As a whole, T'ao's tempestuous career as head of Liang-huai illustrates how the political flow of criticism and refutation affected the image of a high official as meeting or failing to meet his responsibilities. Even after initially demanding great fiscal sacrifices from the court, T'ao was unable to design a set of fiscal goals that he could fully meet. Yet he managed to excuse his failures and continue in office by blaming his shortcomings on others, especially his predecessors in office and officials in retail provinces who failed to carry out policing duties efficiently, and by seeking to lower the court's expectations as to his responsibilities. In contrast to the euphoric hope of total success for Liang-huai still entertained by others, he warned the court that gradual improvement in the face of continuing difficulties was the only realistic expectation. The persuasiveness of his argument in the face of repeated hostile criticism from other officials indicates how arguments appeal-

14. *TWI,* 17:17–20.

ing to a spirit of moderate realism could be credibly used to rationalize responsibility. T'ao's self-image as a man fulfilling reasonably limited responsibilities despite the failings of others was largely accepted; he retired honorably and, on his death, was eulogized by the emperor as an exceptional statesman.[15]

The fact that the concept of responsibility had both these diffuse and rationalistic dimensions was reflected in a range of considerations entertained by the Board of Civil Officials when it was asked to determine an administrative sentence. Uninvolved in the process of determining verdicts, the Board often handled the specification of the sentence and was responsible not only for finding the proper article but also for stretching the sentence within certain prefixed margins according to the particular character of the offense, although whatever it proposed had to be approved by the emperor. In weighing circumstances limiting the guilt or responsibility of an offender, the Board, we may say, dealt with two kinds of circumstances: some were an aspect of the offense itself, often just mitigating circumstances; others were an aspect of the degree of responsibility inherent in the offender's official position.

A major example of the former was the possible reduction of a punishment if the offender himself revealed his mistake. This only applied to public offenses, and in some interpretations was restricted to cases of lack of vigilance or to cases where the mistake could be corrected. With higher officials (at the capital, head officials of offices or higher; at the provinces, provincial judges and treasurers or higher), reduction of the sentence depended on the Board's advice and the emperor's decision. With lower officials, the reduction was automatically advised by the Board.[16]

Some other examples are the exemption from punishment of a territorial official for lack of vigilance in those instances where the offense occurred while he was traveling outside his jurisdiction on government business,[17] and the use of a reduced sentence to close the case of a local magistrate who, trying to avoid a sentence by catching a criminal before a certain deadline, had the good fortune of having his criminal caught by another official.[18] If a crime within a certain juris-

15. See Metzger, "Organizational Capabilities."
16. *CFTL*, 1:18a–b; *TCHT*, 11:6; *TLti*, 4:48.
17. *CFTL*, 1:21.
18. *CFTL*, 1:22.

diction was discovered by an official other than the one responsible for this jurisdiction, the official responsible was charged with lack of vigilance but received a reduced sentence if he then caught the criminal.[19] If a head official at a capital office was guilty of lack of vigilance within the first month of his appointment, he was not sentenced.[20]

The editors of the 1869 edition of *Regulations on Administrative Punishment* single out the distinction between being in charge of a governmental function (*ch'eng*) and supervising it (*tu*) as a basic principle parallel in importance to the distinction between private and public offenses.[21] However, the problem of degrees of responsibility inherent in official position was a little broader. First, although the distinction between *ch'eng* and *tu* was the central one, it is necessary to view the problem of the diffusion of responsibility from the primary agent a little more broadly. Second, the way in which the primary agent was held responsible varied because of distinctions in the nature of primary agents.

Regarding the main kind of extension of responsibility, that from the primary agent (*ch'eng*) to the supervising official (*tu*), one must keep in mind the passive-active spectrum of supervision. Supervision could vary from a general responsibility to watch one's subordinates with vigilance to an active supervision over a particular matter, and, finally, to a supervision so active that it blended with the primary activities. Generally, the more active the supervisory role, the more severe the administrative punishments.[22] (It is also worth noting temporary responsibilities of supervision or assistance such as

19. *CFTL*, 1:23.
20. *CFTL*, 1:24.
21. *CFTL*, *hsü*:1.
22. *Ch'u-fen* for salt tax deficits are a good example. Viewed as a hierarchy of equally primary agents, the salt shipment controller, the branch heads (who each were over a number of salt production yards), and the various yard supervisors (who each headed one yard) all received the same administrative punishment for the same percentage of salt tax deficit in the quotas they each were responsible for. However the zone head, i.e., the salt commissioner, had a less severe scale of punishment. For instance, he was dismissed from office only if his deficit reached 70 percent, but officials in the former group were dismissed from office if their deficit reached 60 percent. See *LHYFC*, 39:1–2. (Of course each official was responsible only for the quota of the administrative unit he headed.)

that of provincial officials for official silver or copper shipments passing through their jurisdictions.)

Besides "supervising" offices, which were in the regular chain of command, responsibility might be extended to "directing" offices (often *kuan-li*) and to "examining" (*chi-ch'a*) offices. "Direction" was a special sort of supra-authority common at the capital but also found in the provinces. It was a way of increasing the effectiveness of leadership. For instance a grand secretary might "direct" the affairs of a board in addition to carrying out the duties of his original post. "Examining" was a surveillance activity not directly related to leadership. The "examining" of a primary agent was usually assigned to a censor, but there were exceptions. For instance, the Imperial Patent Office was "examined" by a grand secretary.[23] Admittedly the responsibilities of "examining" or "directing" offices seem not to have routinely involved impeachments, as did those of "supervising" offices.

There was also extension of responsibility from the primary agents in a capital office to some of their colleagues, although in 1782 the emperor denounced a tendency in the Board of Punishments to restrict responsibility for mistakes to one Manchu and one Chinese departmental official (*ssu-kuan*). Thus a distinction was made between those board officials with prime responsibility, such as two departmental officials who had "taken charge of a document," and board officials with lesser responsibility for the same matter, such as other officials from the same department who had signed and affixed their seals to the document.[24]

While responsibility could be extended from the primary agent, the responsibility of the primary agent sometimes was reduced. Here one should connect the problem of legal responsibility to the fact that the Ch'ing bureaucracy had different ways of formally defining primary agents in order flexibly to enlist the efforts of different kinds of people on different occasions. The formal nature of primary agents varied in terms of a spectrum of degrees of regularity. This spectrum involved three variables: the nature of the official job, the status of the man filling it, and the nature of his appointment to it. At one extreme, the job, the occupant's status, and the form of ap-

23. *TCHT*, 7:3a–b; *Shinkoku gyōseihō*, I:339–341, translated in *Ch'ing-kuo hsing-cheng-fa*, 3:2:2:27–30.

24. *CFTL*, 2:10–11b.

pointment all could be of the fullest regularity. At the other extreme, all could be less regular, so to speak. Then there were various in-between combinations. The various mixtures of regularity and irregularity in the bureaucracy's network of primary agents was a major line of variation in the history of the imperial bureaucracy.

We can outline the spectrum of regularity in Ch'ing times in terms of our three variables. First, the official job could be an *o-ch'üeh* (regular post), or it could be a job added to a regular post. Such an added job could be formulated in four ways: as an added function (*chien-kuan*); as an added post (*chien-ch'ung*); as the performance of specified duties in an office-like setting (*hsing-tsou*); or as a certain mission one was commissioned to carry out (*ch'ai-wei*). Persons lacking any regular post also could have an official job in the form of a commission (*ch'ai-wei*) or an assignment to carry out duties in an office without holding a regular post in it (*hsing-tsou*). *Hsing-tsou* was typically the status of the many *chin-shih* and others *fen-fa* (respectively dispatched) to the boards for training purposes. Of course, outside this network of official jobs, there still were friends of high status called on for advice and private secretaries.

Second, some aspects of status can be better seen as inhering in the person rather than the job. For instance, the person could be a full-fledged official who had previously held a regular office; could hold an honorary office title; could be a mere degree holder; or could have status as a candidate for a certain office.

Third, the form of appointment varied in that persons could be appointed to a regular post not only in a regular way but also as short-term replacements (*hu-li*); on an "acting" basis, that is, as longer-term replacements (*shu-li*); or on a probationary basis (*shih-yung*).[25]

Legal responsibility varied to a significant extent in terms of this spectrum of regularity. With jobs added to regular posts there was sometimes a more lenient use of *ch'u-fen*,

25. *TCHT*, 7:3–7 is the basis for much of this discussion of jobs. See *TYT*, 42:2, for a *hu-li* example. On differences of status inhering in the person, see Chang Chung-li, *The Chinese Gentry* (Seattle, Wash., 1955). On private secretaries, see Folsom, *Friends, Guests, and Colleagues: The Mu-Fu System in the Late Ch'ing Period* (Berkeley, Calif., 1968).

clearly on the theory that an official could not devote so much energy to them as he could to his main responsibilities. For instance, an official exclusively in charge of salt affairs was punished more severely for a salt tax deficit than was a provincial official with salt affairs as an added responsibility (*chien-kuan*).[26] In many tax *ch'u-fen*, acting officials (*shu-li*) were not impeached if their deficit appeared less than a month after taking office.[27] Similar allowances were made for officials taking over as a regular assignment a post to which tax deficits were already attached.[28] Indeed, the excuse that one's troubles stemmed from the shortcomings of predecessors was a weighty one, as can be seen from several of T'ao Chu's memorials in the 1830's explaining his salt tax deficits.[29]

26. *CFTL*, 21:1–2.
27. *Ch'u-fen tse-li t'u-yao* (Essentials in tabular form of the regulations on administrative punishment; 1872), 2:5b–6. *CFTL*, 35:37.
28. *CFTL*, 35:38.
29. See, e.g., *TWI*, 16:6b–7.

c. *Leniency*

While the punishment of officials for committing either private or public offenses was thoroughly legitimated, the question of the severity of their punishment, especially in the case of public offenses, was a lively issue in Ch'ing political thought.

The spectrum of formal punishments to which officials were subject can be divided into three groups.

First there was that area of punishment, much narrowed under the Yung-cheng emperor, where superior officials could punish a subordinate on their own discretion without *ts'an* (impeaching) him. Impeachment primarily meant that a memorial was sent to the emperor accusing the alleged offender, but it also often included the notion of carrying out all further adjudicative steps only with the approval of the emperor. In Ming times and until the Yung-cheng emperor changed three *lü* (penal statutes) in 1725–1727, a large part of the process of bureaucratic discipline was handled in a decentralized fashion through the discretion of superior officials who could arrest and to a large extent sentence lower officials without impeaching them. In this category were all cases of the arrest and sentencing of officials in which the sentence was only a salary fine, redemption, or making a record of the offense (*chi-lu*) to be used every nine years at the capital in determining whether the official was to be promoted, demoted, or dismissed. This covered most routine administrative shortcomings (see IV, 4, c and IV, 2, note 84).

A memorial of 1655 shows the desire of the Board of Civil Officials to be better informed about administrative shortcomings not covered by impeachments.[1] After the *lü* changes

1. *HCCSWP*, 17:11b–12. A vice-president of the Board of Civil Officials, Liang Ch'ing-piao, was interested in increasing the role of the merit principle in promotions and demotions at the expense of the seniority principle. He proposed that at the two relevant departments in the Board of Civil Officials—the Department for the Scrutiny of Merits and the Department of Appointments—there be set up two registers: one for recording merits (*chi-kung*) and one for recording faults (*chi-kuo*). The governors and governors-general and heads of capital offices were to make reports to the Board of Civil Officials on the merits and faults of their subordinates, and these reports would be entered in the above registers. Liang specifically stated that the faults to be reported were those not bad enough to require impeachment. The information in the registers was then to be used in deciding on promotions and demotions.

of 1725–1727, administrative shortcomings down to a very minor level had to be handled in a centralized fashion by impeachments, but some superior officials still could inflict a range of sanctions without imperial permission. First they could inflict *chi-kuo* (demerits) and *chi-kung* (merits). This system apparently goes back to the 1655 memorial above. The typical practice was for superiors to count up the merits and demerits of their subordinates "at the end of the year" and to memorialize for an impeachment or an administrative reward if the number of demerits or merits went beyond a certain level. This was the practice, for instance, in handling a local magistrate's record in clearing up robberies and thefts[2] and in handling the record of certain Liang-huai guard-post officials in arresting smugglers and helping to promote legal salt sales. *Chi-ta-kuo* (major demerits) could also be issued. A salt yard official in Kiangsu whose lack of vigilance allowed the illegal cultivation of one to four *mou* of land reserved for reeds (these were needed in salt production) received one "major demerit," and he received a year's salary fine if the amount was five *mou* or more.[3] Officials at the boards or other major capital offices could receive a demerit either through a rescript from the emperor or from the head officials (*t'ang-kuan*) at their offices.[4] In some instances merits and demerits could be cancelled off against each other, just as the higher administrative sanctions could.

Moreover, although superiors could not arrest subordinates without memorializing for imperial permission, they could "summon them for questioning." Governors and governors-general had the authority to remove an official from his post (*ch'e-jen*), remove his seal of office and his grade-signifying button, and "keep him under custody" (*k'an shou*) awaiting judicial inquiry.[5] The governor or governor-general's right to *ch'e-jen* was complemented by the fact that he had the discretion to fill any office up through first-class subprefect on an acting basis without first memorializing (thus he could imme-

2. *CFTL,* 42:50a–b.

3. *LHYFC,* 39:37.

4. *CFTL,* 2:12.

5. *TCHTSL,* 726:*chih-kuan yu-fan*: *li-nien shih-li*: Ch'ien-lung 18; *TYT,* 49:51b; 34:31. *Ch'e-jen* could also be done at the command of the emperor; see *CFTL,* 2:49.

diately replace the offender).[6] During the Kiangsu flood of 1831, for instance, the Nanking governor-general thus removed and replaced the Kaoyu magistrate, impeaching him later.[7] He reported these moves in a memorial but clearly did not wait for imperial action to carry them out, as he would have had to in the infliction of a *ch'u-fen.*

The second group of punishments was made up of the regular administrative punishments requiring the approval of the emperor. The standard scale was that of *fa-feng* (salary fines) (from one month to two years); *chiang-chi liu-jen* (demotion in subgrade with retention of duties) (from one to three subgrades); *tiao-yung* (demotion in subgrade with transfer out of original post) (from one to five subgrades); *ko-chih liu-jen* (dismissal from office with retention of duties); *ko-chih* (dismissal from office); and dismissal from office with the added injunction of *yung pu hsü-yung* (never to be reappointed).[8]

This scale was inefficiently graduated, a not uncommon failing in Ch'ing law.[9] Demotion by five subgrades plus transfer was sometimes regarded as a more severe punishment than dismissal from office with retention of duties and dismissal from office. "Transfer" did not necessarily mean automatic appointment to another post, and dismissal was often followed by being restored to a post (*k'ai-fu*). On the other hand, dismissal from office could be regarded as more severe than demotion by five subgrades with transfer. The latter can be seen from the *Ta-Ch'ing hui-tien*'s statement: "In all cases of administrative punishment, when dismissal from office has been reached, then one stops."[10] The use of this punishment frequently reflects the same view. Heads of salt monopoly zones

6. *TCHT*, 7:6b. *TLti*, 1:56, states that even unimpeached officials could be ordered to the provincial capital by a governor or governor-general, who then commissioned someone else to take over their original post on an acting basis. Presumably this happened when the official was suspected of some misdeed.

7. *TYT*, 34:28b.

8. *TCHT*, 11:1a–b.

9. For another example, see *TLti*, 25:52a–b, 58b, 60. Here the apparently simple idea of reducing a series of punishments each by one degree led to a situation where the "scale of severity was upside down," as Hsüeh Yün-sheng put it, because the original punishments included some of the awkward categories outside the five punishments.

10. *TCHT*, 11:1b–2.

with an original tax deficit of 60 percent still not fully collected after two years were demoted by five subgrades and transferred; if the amount was 70 percent or more, they were dismissed from office.[11]

Besides this standard scale, somewhat different sanctions were also involved in the process of *chan-ts'an* (extended impeachment), which applied to the major matters of tax collection and the catching of criminals. Officials lagging in tax collection could receive the sanction of *t'ing-sheng* (temporary ineligibility for promotion), *chiang-feng* (reduction in salary [without reduction in grade]), and *chiang-chih* (demotion in office title?). (In at least one example, *chiang-chih* involved retention of the duties of one's original post.[12]) Officials lagging in the solution of criminal cases could receive the sanction of *chu-feng* (stoppage of salary) as well as *t'ing-sheng* (temporary ineligibility for promotion).[13] The sanction of forcing officials to make up financial or property losses (*p'ei*) was also used, as when officials had a tax deficit, had misused government funds, or were responsible for the loss or destruction of property such as dikes or grain tribute boats. This punishment had an administrative character, but it could be connected to criminal punishments. At least in the latter case, an official's son or family could also be held liable.[14]

Various other kinds of administrative punishments were devised to suit particular circumstances. For instance, grand councillors, whose job was conceptualized not as a regular post but as performance of certain assigned duties (*hsing-tsou*), were sometimes punished merely by the cancellation of this

11. *LHYFC,* 39:2b.
12. *LHYFC,* 39:1b.
13. *TCHT,* 11:1b–2.
14. For a case of family responsibility in paying an official's debt, see *TLti,* 25:58b–59; *TCLL,* 23:26–27. A regulation in *CFTL,* 28:11, provided for the holding back of an official's *yang-lien* (payment to nourish integrity) as well as his regular salary in some circumstances in order to make up debts that his father or grandfather had incurred through juggling when the latter was an official. An official charged with such a debt on behalf of his father or grandfather was given a deadline to pay it back, and if he had not managed to pay back half when the deadline was up, his grade-signifying button was removed, and the deadline was extended. If he then paid back all but 20 percent or less, he was restored to full official status, and the remainder of the debt was collected by holding back payments on his regular salary and his *yang-lien.*

assignment; whatever regular post they had, such as president of a board, they kept.[15]

At the periphery of this second group of sanctions were some sanctions further refining the process of losing one's status as an official. The issue here was to what extent the status of the dismissed official should be fully reduced to that of the common people (*wei-min*). The exact use of these sanctions in Ch'ing times is hard to determine. Besides being dismissed with the injunction "never to be reappointed," an official could have his name removed (*ch'u-ming*) from the "register of officials," and his title patent (*kao-ch'ih,* generically), as well as those titles of his senior relatives derived from his title patent, could be taken back.[16] Title patents were not withdrawn at least in the case of officials dismissed for public offenses.[17]

We turn now to our third and final group of sanctions, the criminal sentences, which, according to a law of 1644, could not be inflicted on an official until after he had been dismissed from office.[18] Officials could receive virtually any of the regular criminal sentences,[19] but there were some sentences especially connected to officials. For one thing, they could be "dispatched" (*fa-wang*) to serve at a military postal station in cases where a common person would have been given a term of penal servitude, and they could be exiled to Sinkiang where a common person would have been merely banished (banishment [*liu*] was normally to one of the settled provinces [*nei-ti*]). The original point of these sentences was that officials, knowing the law, should be punished for their offenses more severely than the common people.[20] Introduced in the eighteenth century after the subjugation of Sinkiang, the sentence of exile in Sinkiang can be viewed as a variation on a punishment found as early as 1647, banishment beyond the frontier with reduc-

15. See, e.g., *Ch'ing-shih,* IV:2497.

16. On officials' title patents, see *TCHT,* 12:7b–9 and IV, 3, d, below. In *TCHTSL,* 78:*ching-ch'a tung-li*: K'ang-hsi 1, there is an example of the sentence *ko-chih wei-min* (dismissal from office and reduction to the status of the common people) issued for officials judged as "without the strength to act effectively" and "careless in ordinary matters."

17. *TLti,* 2:16; *TCLL,* 4:27; *Ta-Ch'ing lü-li t'ung-k'ao,* 4:97–98; Philastre, I:149–150.

18. See IV, 3, a, and Bodde and Morris, p. 220.

19. See Appendix III.

20. *TLti,* 25:60; *Ch'ing-ch'ao hsü wen-hsien t'ung-k'ao,* III:9955.

tion to the status of commoner. Yet sentences served in Sinkiang sometimes had a form whereby the official was not reduced to the status of a criminal, although the same term, *fa-wang,* was also used for this form. When Lin Tse-hsü received the latter punishment in 1841, he had administrative responsibilities in Sinkiang. According to an imperial order of 1797 (using *p'ai-wang* instead of *fa-wang*), officials dismissed from office and dispatched to Sinkiang were still to receive some salary payments, and after their term was up, they were to have an imperial audience to determine whether or not they should be reappointed to office.[21] The nature of the Sinkiang exile requires clarification. Although it seems to have been a criminal sentence (whatever the quality of life allowed to the convicted person), it is sometimes prescribed in the *ch'u-fen tse-li.*[22]

From the standpoint of the question of leniency, two major questions concerning criminal sentences were those of redemption and of resumption of one's official career after the carrying out of the sentence.

Becoming increasingly severe, the Ch'ing redemption laws seem to have been influenced by those various ideas calling for the harsh treatment of bad officials (see IV, 2). There were other similarly severe laws, such as those requiring officials to serve terms of penal servitude and banishment in Sinkiang; the edict of 1768 precluding the use of administrative honors to "cancel off" administrative punishments given for private offenses; and the laws prohibiting, though not with absolute effect, certain categories of dismissed officials from *chüan-fu* (being restored to office by making a financial contribution) and *chiang-chüan* (being restored to an office lower than one's original one by making a financial contribution). This severe outlook, however, was not without some roots in the Ming period, as we can see from the Ming laws barring "morally deficient" officials from office permanently even if their offense was pardoned.[23]

The increasingly severe Ch'ing redemption policy involved the history of three *li* (penal regulations) in the redemption section of the penal code's *ming-li* (principles of sentencing)

21. *TCHTSL,* 85:*kuan-yüan chiang-ko*:Chia-ch'ing 2.
22. See, e.g., *CFTL,* 37:2b.
note 54.
23. *Ming-lü chi-chieh,* 1:23. On this law, see references in IV, 2,

section. These were *li*(a), inherited from the Ming code, on redemption covering degree holders and officials;[24] *li*(b), introduced in 1725, on the redemption of criminal sentences by officials;[25] and *li*(c), also introduced in 1725, on officials originally ousted from office for some form of illegal taking of wealth and then at their subsequent criminal trial found guilty only of public offenses.[26]

As inherited from the Ming code,[27] *li*(a) covered a wide variety of statuses including officeholders, idle or retired officials, and certain degree holders. It provided an extremely broad scope of redemption for all these statuses, namely the possibility of redeeming all sentences through *tsa-fan ssu-tsui* (death sentences commuted to a term of penal servitude) irrespective of the nature of the offense and depending purely on the offender's capacity to pay.

Li(a) was taken over intact by the first edition of the Ch'ing penal code (1646), but then a more severe policy was adopted, although not without some wavering at first. An imperial order of 1655 precluded redemption for officials guilty of some sort of *tu* (corruption) in office. Yet an imperial order of 1661 failed to exclude officials guilty of "corruption" from the category of those permitted to request redemption of some criminal sentences through the carrying out of construction work. And a similar law in 1680 again failed to exclude these officials.[28] In 1801 an imperial order did, however, state that the K'ang-hsi period (1662–1723) had begun a more severe policy of redemption. In Ming times, this order said, redemption by officials through *tsa-fan ssu-tsui* had depended only on ability to pay, but in the K'ang-hsi period, redemption for the first time was made to depend also on the circumstances of the offense.[29] When *li*(a) was put into the second edition of the

24. *TCLL*, 4:8b. *TLti*, 1:28–30. All the successive Ch'ing versions of all three *li* are in *TCHTSL*, 724:*shu-hsing*.

25. *TCLL*, 4:7a–b. *TLti*, 1:27b–28. The 1725 version includes *both* criminal sentences attached to crimes in office (*yü-tsui*) and criminal sentences due for offenses prosecuted or committed after dismissal. The 1801 and 1824 versions explicitly deal only with the latter offenses but seem implicitly to cover the former as well.

26. *TCLL*, 4:7b–8; *TLti*, 1:24b.

27. *Ming-lü chi-chieh*, 1:2b.

28. *TCHTSL*, 724:*shu-hsing*: *li-nien shih-li*: Shun-chih 12, Shun-chih 18, and K'ang-hsi 19.

29. *Ibid.*, Chia-ch'ing 6.

penal code (1725–1727), it was adjusted to exclude some cases from the right of redemption.

While thus interested in restricting the right of redemption, the Yung-cheng emperor also was interested in centralizing and systematizing the punishment of officeholders in particular. Consequently he took the question of their redemption out of *li*(a). On the one hand, by revising two *lü* he arranged that for any light offense their punishment was covered by a systematic schedule of administrative sanctions.[30] On the other hand, he introduced the new *li*(b) to cover any criminal sentences of penal servitude and above received by officeholders or dismissed officials. This followed the early Ch'ing principle of redemption except for serious offenses. If an official was to receive any criminal sentence through *tsa-fan ssu-tsui,* he could commute it so long as his offense did not involve any illegal taking of wealth for his private profit (*t'an-tsang*). This law explicitly applied to both the offenses committed in office and offenses committed by dismissed officials. Also the Yung-cheng emperor used the lenient principle that these redemptions should follow the inexpensive rates in the table for "those with financial resources" (*yu-li*). For example, 25 taels, roughly the annual income of a low member of the gentry, redeemed a sentence of five years penal servitude.[31]

This same policy is also to be seen in the other *li, li*(c), set up by the Yung-cheng emperor in this connection. This stated that if an official originally dismissed from office for some form of illegal taking of wealth was later found guilty at his criminal trial only of juggling public funds or of unauthorized tax collection, he could redeem any further sentence beyond dismissal.

At this point, however, a kink developed in this early Ch'ing policy of redemption. The Yung-cheng emperor, it seems, was interested in closing a loophole whereby the lighter laws on juggling were applied to officials accused of embezzling. Therefore in 1727 he established a new *li* calling for extremely severe, nonredeemable criminal punishments for officials guilty of juggling large sums.[32] Moreover, there already was a *lü*

30. See IV, 2, note 84.
31. *TCLL,* 2:8–11.
32. This is Hsüeh Yün-sheng's explanation; *TLti,* 14:2b–3. On the establishment of this *li,* I have followed the date in *TCHTSL, chüan* 760.

calling for severe, criminal sentences for officials guilty of unauthorized tax collection, a similar public offense. This produced an unreasonable situation. It was not fair that officials *originally* charged with these public offenses should be punished severely, while officials originally accused of more serious private offenses and *later* charged only with these public offenses should be treated leniently.

Resolution of this unreasonable situation was combined with the Ch'ing dynasty's second major move toward restricting redemption. The Chia-ch'ing emperor in 1801 was struck by this unreasonable situation,[33] and he therefore revised *li*(c) so that the harsher treatment of no redemption was extended to all officials guilty of juggling and unauthorized tax collection, whatever the judicial sequence. At the same time he stiffened other conditions of redemption for certain degree holders and officials by revising *li*(a) and *li*(b). For *chin-shih* and other degree holders, the right of redemption for sentences of penal servitude or above was unequivocally removed. For officeholders, redemption of such sentences was still possible. However, redemption was no longer automatic for all cases except those involving the illegal taking of wealth for private purposes, as had been the case before. Rather it depended on a decision made by the emperor on the merits of the individual case with the advice of the Board of Punishments. (Also the light rate schedule of *yu-li* was dropped in 1801.) It is not surprising, therefore, that, in those cases involving civil officials translated in the study of Bodde and Morris, criminal sentences of penal servitude and up were inflicted without any redemption or mitigation, except for some instances where auxiliary humiliations like tattooing were canceled. Yet there is also evidence that officials in the nineteenth century did redeem sentences of penal servitude and up, such as the regulations on the possibility of being restored to office after such redemption, which were initiated in 1805.[34]

It should be added that the question of the beatings regularly accompanying unredeemed sentences of penal servitude or banishment was problematic. Hsüeh Yün-sheng held that the law was not clear on whether officials could redeem them but

33. This contradiction lay behind the Chia-ch'ing 6 imperial order in *li-nien shih-li* of the *shu-hsing* section in *TCHTSL*, 724.

34. See below and Bodde and Morris, p. 194.

inferred that they apparently could. His reasoning was that the official phrases describing an official's penal servitude or banishment had no references to beating.[35] Yet in some instances these beatings may have been carried out.[36]

Commentators on the penal code reflect this change in the Ch'ing policy on redemption. The *chi-chu* (collected annotations) commentary, obviously describing conditions before 1801, states that officials could redeem sentences through *tsa-fan ssu-tsui* if the circumstances were excusable and the crime was not one of the more serious ones. Clearly referring also to this passage, Hsüeh Yün-sheng states that the *chi-chu's* whole discussion of redemption does not apply to his day (ca. 1900) and complains about the harsh tendency to carry out criminal sentences without qualification.[37]

On the other hand, one cannot yet conclude that there was a one-way tendency toward increasing severity in the Ch'ing period. As we shall see, the Chia-ch'ing emperor in 1820 acted to lighten the punishment for public offenses. More has to be learned about the application of the laws, such as trends to pardon officials convicted of illegally taking wealth and to fail to apply the death sentence to officials guilty of destroying dikes in order to profit illicitly from their repair.[38]

Apart from provisions in the penal code, officials also sometimes could redeem criminal sentences by making extremely large contributions to the state (*chüan-shu*). Various articles were promulgated allowing this practice, going back at least to 1661, but the only one used over a long period of time (according to the *Ch'ing-shih*) was one established in 1734, whereby officials and commoners could redeem even death sentences if their crimes were not of the worst sort. The amount demanded rose with the status of the offender and the seriousness of the sentence. Officials of the third grade or higher sentenced to death had to contribute 12,000 taels, commoners 1,200 taels.[39]

Sometimes after redeeming a sentence, and sometimes even after serving it, officials could resume their official careers. This striking fact is reflected in a law established in 1805 fixing

35. *TLti,* 1:28.
36. Ch'ü, *Local Government in China under the Ch'ing,* p. 282; p. 194; and *Law and Society in Traditional China,* p. 182.
37. *TLti,* 1:14b–16, 56a–b.
38. *TLti,* 51:4; *HCCSWP,* 19:2a–b.
39. *Ch'ing-shih,* III:1739–1740.

the sums which these convicted criminals had to pay in order to *chüan-fu* (be restored to office by making a financial contribution). These sums were given as "added percentages," the base amounts clearly being those determined through the varying complex of laws dealing with the purchase of office; these base sums varied from several hundred to several thousand taels.[40] If after being ousted from office (*ko-chih*), an official received a criminal sentence of blows of the heavy or light bamboo, which he had redeemed, and he wished to *chüan-fu*, he could do so by paying 20 percent or more than the normal contribution (provided that he was not in one of the excluded categories of particularly grave crimes). He paid 30 percent more if he had not yet redeemed the sentence. If he had been sentenced to a short term of penal servitude (*t'u*) which had already been completed, he could similarly be restored to office by paying 50 percent more. If he had received the full term of regular penal servitude (three years) and had completed it, he paid 60 percent more. If the official had been sentenced to banishment or to servitude for life as a soldier and had been allowed to redeem his sentence, he paid 80 percent more. Officials who had completed a term of servitude at a military postal station in Sinkiang paid 60 percent more. Officials who had been exiled to Sinkiang and who had been released paid 100 percent more.[41] Officials who had redeemed a death sentence were ineligible to *chüan-fu*.[42] Officials who merely wanted to have their office title restored without returning to an actual office did not have to contribute any of these extra amounts.

From the standpoint of bureaucratic discipline, the question of leniency relative to public offenses is more important than that relative to serious crimes. This is because impeachments for public offenses were far more numerous, as is clear beyond any reasonable doubt.

For instance, the threat of administrative punishments is constantly mentioned in official documents. The Ch'ing had both an annual evaluation of officials called *k'ao-ch'eng* (exam-

40. See tables beginning on p. 111 in Hsü Ta-ling, *Ch'ing-tai chüan-na chih-tu* (The system of purchasing offices and official titles during the Ch'ing period; Peking, 1950). On the normative implications of such laws, see IV, 2.

41. *CFTL*, 2:73; *TCHTSL*, 87:*kuan-yüan k'ai-fu*:Chia-ch'ing 10.

42. *CFTL*, 2:60. See IV, 5.

ination of administrative results) and a triannual evaluation, and both led to impeachments. Admittedly, in 1723 the Yung-cheng emperor complained that in the provincial part of the triannual evaluations (*ta-chi*) "no more than several tens of men" were singled out each time, either to be impeached or to be rated as "extraordinary" in terms of their merits.[43] Whether or not this situation was remedied, cases such as the 1830 and 1831 Liang-huai *k'ao-ch'eng* (see IV, 3, b) indicate that this annual evaluation did lead to many impeachments for public offenses such as late tax collections. The frequency of impeachments is suggested also by the fact that the need of officials to study the regulations on these punishments was so great that not only were private bookstore editions put out but also special digests with the material ingeniously arranged to speed comprehension. Impeachments were so numerous that many could be presented to the emperor only in *t'i-pen* memorials combining the cases of several persons, individual memorials being reserved only for the more important cases.[44] In about 1799, Wang Chih-i, then governor of Fukien, stated that of the sixty-two posts of district magistrate in Fukien, thirty-nine district magistrates just at that time were enduring the *ch'u-fen* of temporary ineligibility for promotion on account of tax deficits and/or had ten or more cases of *ch'u-fen* against their names involving matters such as uncaught criminals and salt tax deficits. Besides these thirty-nine, others of the 62 had already been dismissed or demoted.[45] The prominent official Li Fu (1675–1750) complained that some local magistrates served only several months before being impeached.[46] Table 1 below indicates that such complaints were justified to a large extent.

How commonplace public offenses were is shown by an 1820 order of the Chia-ch'ing emperor that public offenses be disregarded when weighing the eligibility of officials for certain posts; previously, he said, too many officials had been ineligible for these posts on account of the public offenses in their records.[47] When in the 1830's the Nanking governor-general

43. *TCHTSL*, 80:*ta-chi t'ung-li*:Yung-cheng 1. See also *Pa-ch'ao sheng-shün*, Yung-cheng, 18:3.

44. *CFTL*, 9:4a–b.

45. *HCCSWP*, 16:5. Yet Wei Hsiu-mei shows that perhaps only 9.9% of all provincial treasurer terms in 1796–1908 ended on account of *ch'u-fen*.

46. *HCCSWP*, 15:8b.

47. *CFTL*, 1:1–2.

would recommend someone to the emperor for a particular post, he would routinely note that the man's *ch'u-fen* for public offenses were not to be taken into account in weighing his eligibility and that arrangements should be made that he pay up within a certain deadline whatever salary fines of his were still outstanding.[48] For one document explicitly indicating rarity of private offenses, we can cite a memorial by Li Chih-fang, a *chin-shih* of 1647 who rose to be a grand secretary. He said that the majority of all vacancies filled through the Board of Civil Officials' monthly appointments were caused by dismissals for public offenses, and that dismissals on account of more serious shortcomings were "less than ten or twenty percent." [49]

We should note, however, that the ratio of public to private offenses in impeachments was not necessarily the same as the ratio of public to private offenses committed. This was because not all offenses committed led to impeachments. The censor Chang P'eng-chan in 1800 deplored the failure to impeach officials in many cases of illegal shortages in treasuries. He also said that the overwhelming majority of these shortages were the result of embezzlement (a private offense) rather than juggling (*no-i*), a public offense whereby an official used state funds for genuine state purposes but not for the prescribed ones.[50]

The routineness of public offenses seems to have reduced their humiliation. Any offense linked terminologically to the system of criminal law must have involved humiliation, but public offenses were partly perceived as the kind of fault that even a *chün-tzu* (true gentleman) could not avoid, as Confucius had made clear.[51] Around 1740 the distinguished official Li Fu noted that "No one except a sage can avoid faults," and, ascribing the statement to Fan Chung-yen of the Sung, said that "In being an official, private offenses are out of the question, but public offenses are unavoidable." This seems to have been a cliché.[52] Similarly, the Yung-cheng emperor said: "Now, in the person of an individual there are achievements

48. *TYT*, 39:41b; 44:2b; 31:29; 40:14b–15.
49. *HCCSWP*, 15:11.
50. *HCCSWP*, 20:10a–b.
51. See IV, 2.
52. *HCCSWP*, 15:8.

and there are faults; in the grade of an official, there are reductions and there are additions."[53]

Wang Hui-tsu (1731–1807), a famous private secretray, also said that public offenses were unavoidable: "There is no man of perfect virtue; nor is there one of perfect ability. In the administrative affairs one handles, it is impossible wholly to avoid mistakes." Wang warned magistrates not to scheme to avoid being impeached for a public offense. After a public offense, he said, reappointment was still a strong possibility, but if caught in a private offense like scheming to avoid impeachment for having failed to arrest a criminal, then "one is lost and one's reputation is ruined." Therefore, Wang said, "In comparing two evils, one chooses the lesser."[54] Being impeached for a public offense was a much lesser evil, but it still was an evil, or, perhaps better, an extremely disagreeable event.

The relative lack of humiliation was only one among a variety of factors reducing the severity of the punishments for public offenses. Sentences for public offenses were milder than for comparable private offenses, although, as I have said, a light private offense was punished more lightly than a serious public offense.[55] Amnesties, which came perhaps every ten or twenty years, routinely included public offenses but not necessarily private ones.[56] On those occasions when public offenses were punished with criminal sentences, permission to redeem the sentence was either routine, or, after 1801, more likely (one would assume) than when the offense was private.

One should also take into consideration that relative to officials' offenses, *ch'u-fen* law seems to have had primacy over the penal code. This primacy is indicated in a general way by the regulations on finding the law (see IV, 4, e), but recently attention has been directed to several valuable cases concretely

53. *TCHTSL,* 86:2.

54. *HCCSWP,* 21:20b; 22:3.

55. *TCHT,* 11:4b–5. The explicit principle was that for comparable offenses, the punishment was one degree more severe in the case of private offenses. Actually the gap seems to have been bigger. For instance, if originally the penal code called for seventy blows of the heavy bamboo, the sentence was commuted into "demotion by one subgrade with retention of duties" in the case of public offenses, and "demotion by two subgrades with transfer" in the case of private offenses.

56. *TCLL,* 4:34a–b.

illustrating this primacy. In one of these cases, which was decided in about 1826, a departmental magistrate had unintentionally made a mistaken judicial decision. Although this clearly was just a public offense, the magistrate was sentenced under the penal code to eighty blows of the heavy bamboo and two years penal servitude. The Board of Punishments then pointed out that since the Board of Civil Officials had *ch'u-fen* regulations covering this offense, these regulations, which called for only administrative sanctions, rather than the penal code should be used to determine the sentence. In about 1833, the Board of Punishments said that "in the past" the Board of Civil Officials had handled all "ordinary" cases of officials guilty of committing judicial mistakes; only "grave" cases had been referred to the Board of Punishments. This situation, the Board felt, was proper, and no doubt it continued to exist.

In these cases we find that a clear-cut article in the *ch'u-fen* regulations is preferred over a clear-cut article in the penal code. Not surprisingly, therefore, in 1827 a clear-cut *ch'u-fen* article was preferred over a vague argument seeking to apply to an official's offense a broad law in the penal code, that on violating the emperor's orders (*wei-chih*).

This same case also dealt with a similar borderline issue, and again the decision was in favor of the Board of Civil Officials' *ch'u-fen* procedures. Here the problem was not conflicting articles in the *ch'u-fen* regulations and the penal code, but, rather, a lack of any definitely applicable article in either body of law and also a lack in the impeaching memorial of the clarifying phrase *i-ch'u* (to advise on administrative punishment). The offenses involved typically were "following one's urges and acting absurdly," or "deceitfully refusing to admit responsibility [for some unfortunate occurrence]," and the punishment was dismissal from office (*ko-chih*). Before 1827, the Board of Punishments often referred such cases to the Board of Civil Officials, but in 1827 it resolved to do so always. Unperturbed by the shrinkage in its authority, it reasoned that "after all the dismissal of officials from office is a matter within the spheres of the Boards of Civil Officials and of War."[57]

57. *Hsing-an hui-lan* (Conspectus of penal cases; Taipei, 1968), 8:3715–3718; 9:3806–3808. The former citation was brought to my attention by Dr. Fu-mei Chang Chen; the latter, by Professor R. Randle Edwards. I am much indebted to both of them for this illuminating material.

Besides this tendency to put borderline cases under *ch'u-fen* law, three other important factors led to leniency in the case of public offenses. First, sentences for public offenses could to a large extent be canceled off against previously acquired honors (*ti-hsiao*). Administrative honors such as "added subgrades" and "commendations" were acquired either through some special action (typically a memorial by one's superior describing one's special achievement); automatically, by periodic evaluations according with regulations published in the *ch'u-fen tse-li* (typically such regulations consisted of a scale of negative and positive sanctions correlated to a scale of shortcomings and achievements in tax collection);[58] or through a financial contribution to the state. The latter were called *chüan-na chia-chi* (added subgrades obtained by making a contribution) and *chüan-na chi-lu* (commendations obtained by making a contribution).[59] Honors obtained through military merit were rated higher than ordinary ones. (One honorary added subgrade obtained by military merit could cancel a two-subgrade demotion, but one ordinary honorary added subgrade could cancel only a one-subgrade demotion.)

The scope of this mechanism of canceling off was restricted in the winter of 1768–69. The emperor then was angered by the Board of War. It had advised canceling off a sentence due in the case of a military official who, the emperor held, had committed private offenses. For instance, he had ordered subordinates to buy certain goods and then had delayed making payment for them.

The emperor broadly ordered that henceforth no private offenses be canceled off, while public offenses in general could be. However, the regulation fashioned out of this order referred only to lighter public offenses, those punished with salary fines or demotions. There also were other conditions limiting canceling off in the case of public offenses. Some individual regulations on public offenses explicitly precluded canceling off.[60]

58. See, e.g., *CFTL,* 18:26–27b; 18:42.

59. See, e.g., *CFTL,* 2:31.

60. *CFTL,* 1:5–7. For two apparent instances of *kung-tsui* precluding canceling off, see *CFTL,* 2:61, and *TCHTSL,* 117:Tao-kuang 21. In the former, the offense was lack of vigilance leading to the development of heterodox doctrines in one's jurisdiction; in the latter, lack of vigilance leading to the smuggling of saltpeter. Besides commendations and added subgrades, there were two honors, each regarded as equivalent to one added subgrade: the notation in

Even without such an explicit restriction, canceling off for public offenses was not automatic; it tended to require a decision in each case. Also there was leeway in deciding which offenses were public, which private (see IV, 4, e).

A second major factor, touched on above by Wang Hui-tsu, was the strong possibility of reappointment in the case of public offenses involving transfer or dismissal. Here the feelings of solidarity among officials blended with the state's strong desire to retain the services of effective officials. When an official had been dismissed from office for a public offense, it was common for the emperor to order his governor or governor-general to issue an "evaluation" (*k'ao-yü*) of him and send him to the Board of Civil Officials to be presented at court (*yin-chien*). At the audience, the emperor evaluated his general capacity, age, and vigor, and often reappointed him to his old post. The audience was not necessarily just a formality. As discussed below in "The Determination of the Sentence," these audiences in the case of impeachments connected to the "six rules" could sometimes have the function of reviewing the original sentence. (Officials who had been "demoted and transferred" also typically had audiences before reappointment.)

Restoration to office was regarded as *ko-wai shih-en* (an extraordinary bestowal of a favor), but it was common. For instance, in an edict of 1729 the Yung-cheng emperor explained that when an official is dismissed for an administrative mistake, he fears that the man still has usable talent and so cannot bear to discard him permanently. Consequently he "often" in such a case orders the superior to make out an evaluation and send the man to the capital for an imperial audience to determine the question of reappointment. He was mainly focused here on the problem of such officials who, after being ordered to the capital, received another punishment of dismissal from office. If this second offense also was just another administrative shortcoming, the emperor ordered, the culprit should still have the imperial audience to determine the question of reappointment.[61] Such examples again illustrate the frequency of impeachments for public offenses.

---

one's record of *chi-sheng* (to be promoted as soon as possible) and of *cho-i* (outstanding), the latter being the highest rating in the triannual evaluations of officials in the provinces; *TCHT*, 11:2b–3.

61. *TCHTSL*, 85:*kuan-yüan chiang-ko*:Yung-cheng 7; see also *CFTL*, 2:75a–b.

Similarly, an edict of 1750 dealt with the problem of overburdening officials repeatedly transferred or dismissed from office for public offenses with too many trips to the capital for imperial audiences. "We think that the fact [the said] officials have already received a favor in a forgiving manner shows that their talent is necessarily such that they are still fit to be appointed. If we again order them to travel back and forth, transferring their office and being replaced, the outcome will be to put them in difficult straits in many instances." Henceforth, the emperor ordered, if they had had an imperial audience within three years, it was possible to cancel the new one.[62]

If the emperor did not order an audience, it was still possible for the stimulus to come from the governor or governor-general. If the ousted official had a good reputation and valuable experience in the affairs of the area, the governor or governor-general could memorialize on his behalf that he be allowed to *chüan-fu* (be restored to office by making a contribution to the state). In this case, the official also had to have an audience to let the emperor reach the final decision. It was also possible to *chiang-chüan* (be restored to a lower office by making a financial contribution) or *kai-chüan* (be restored to a different office by making a contribution).[63]

When an official dismissed for a public offense had not been reappointed, he might still be used as a *wei-yüan* (commissioned official), that is, as an official commissioned to carry out a certain task without being given a regular office. One suspects that this flexible, talent-saving device was used a lot. An example given earlier (see IV, 2) shows such a *wei-yüan* put in command of regular officials and taking local responsibility for an important reorganization of the salt monopoly (see IV, 3, d).

In the case of the more severe offenses, public as well as private, reappointment was at least very difficult. This was

62. *TCHTSL*, 85:*kuan-yüan chiang-ko*:Ch'ien-lung 15.

63. For *chiang-chüan*, see *CFTL*, 2:81a–b. It seems clear that the regulations on *chüan-fu* in *CFTL*, 2:60a–b, were largely initiated in 1770. In this year the emperor sent down an edict mentioning that the practice of *chüan-fu* had been discontinued and ought now to be resumed. He ordered regulations drawn up, and the resulting regulations are partly similar to those in *CFTL*, 2:60a–b. For the 1770 edict and regulations, see *TCHTSL*, 86:*kuan-yüan k'ai-fu*: Ch'ien-lung 35.

due both to the Ch'ing emphasis on the harsh treatment of corrupt officials, discussed above, and to an emphasis on barring the return of officials unfit for duty for reasons of health, age, or ineptitude.[64] But even in these areas, there sometimes were loopholes. This is not surprising when we remember that even officials who had served criminal sentences could sometimes be reappointed.

On the one hand, there were laws excluding certain categories of official offenders from the right to be restored to an office by making contributions (*chüan-fu* and *chiang-fu*). These categories were drawn up in a severe way. Some officials dismissed for private offenses could *chüan-fu,* but those with the more serious private or public offenses were excluded. Any official who at dismissal had received the injunction "never to be reappointed" was excluded.[65]

Yet even if the officials with the injunction "never to be reappointed" could not *chüan-fu* or *chiang-chüan,* they could still be restored to office through a recommending memorial from their governor, governor-general, or *t'ang-kuan* (head officials at capital offices). The relevant law on this point merely forbade giving a deceptive account of the ousted official's career in such a memorial.[66] An imperial edict in 1863 insisted that there could be no compromise on the injunction "never to be reappointed." It complained that too many memorials were being presented recommending for office men who had received this injunction or asking that these men be permitted to make contributions with the purpose of being restored to office (*chüan-fu*). Governors and governors-general also were recommending for office retired (*hsiu-chih*) officials who by law were not supposed to return to office, even through making contributions. The emperor ordered that henceforth the governors and governors-general refrain from recommending for office either retired officials or officials dismissed with the injunction against

64. On permanently excluding this latter group under "the six rules," see *TCHT,* 11:2, and IV, 4, c.

65. *CFTL,* 2:66, shows that some persons dismissed for *ssu-tsui* could *chüan-fu.* The categories excluded from *chüan-fu* are in *CFTL,* 2:60a–b. They included a catchall article excluding all those whose offenses involved serious corruption and also serious *kung-tsui* such as making unauthorized levies. *CFTL,* 2:62–63, lists those not allowed to *chiang-chüan.*

66. *TLti,* 7:25; *TCLL,* 6:15.

any future reappointment, and also from asking that these men be allowed to *chüan-fu*.[67] But the pressure to make exceptions in personnel matters, illustrated also in other personnel problems, presumably continued.[68]

Besides the questions of canceling off and of reappointment, there was a principle of being cautious in impeachments relative to minor offenses. This principle was given prominence in the Yung-cheng emperor's criticism of the way Pu-lan-t'ai had conducted affairs as governor of Kiangsi in 1727–1728, especially of four impeachments recommended by Pu-lan-t'ai.[69] Around 1740 the prominent official Li Fu adduced some of this criticism in arguing for reducing the number and severity of punishments for public offenses. He also said that despite the Yung-cheng emperor's criticism, the tendency toward excessive severity on the part of high provincial officials had continued.[70]

This criticism had applied mainly to treatment of minor private offenses, but Li Fu was certainly right in inferring its application to public offenses as well. It was made in response to three memorials presented by Pu-lan-t'ai during his period as Kiangsi governor and in response to Pu-lan-t'ai's defense of his actions when the emperor called him to court to explain himself.

The first memorial, received by the emperor on December 18, 1727, concerned a military official who had falsely reported expenditures for military supplies greater by 20 percent to 60 percent than he had actually made, pocketing the difference. After this officer had been normally shifted to another post, Pu-lan-t'ai had arrived in Kiangsi to assume the position of governor, had then discovered the offense, and had immediately impeached the officer, asking that he be dismissed from his new office (*ko-chih*) and be forced to pay back the amount he

67. *CFTL*, 2:67a–b. The text literally prohibits "carrying out too many" or "indiscriminately carrying out" recommendations for office in the case of those categories of officials, i.e., logically speaking perhaps some recommendations of retired officials or officials dismissed with an injunction against any reappointment might still be permitted. Despite this literal meaning, however, I interpret the essential meaning of this regulation as precluding any such recommendations.

68. See I, 2.

69. *Ch'ing-shih-lu*, Yung-cheng, 63:6–7; 69:5–6; 71:9b–11b; 75: 15–16b.

70. *HCCSWP*, 15:8b.

had pocketed. Yung-cheng, however, changed this sentence to demotion by three subgrades with retention of duties and without having to pay back the amount pocketed.

In the second memorial, received June 19, 1728, Pu-lan-t'ai impeached a subordinate official for having sent a gift to a superior, apparently some time previously. The emperor dismissed the impeachment.

In the third memorial, received August 14, 1728, Pu-lan-t'ai sought the dismissal (*ko-chih*) of a district magistrate charged with improper behavior during a time of drought, such as failing personally to pray for rain, and of the prefect over him, charged with lack of vigilance in detecting this misbehavior and with efforts to conceal it. The emperor instead ordered that if these two officials were not guilty of any other offenses, they come to Peking for an audience to determine appointment to another post.

Then on December 22, 1728, after the Kiangsi provincial treasurer had complained about Pu-lan-t'ai's severity, the emperor called Pu-lan-t'ai to court, was dissatisfied with his explanation, and dismissed him from office (*ko-chih*).

Taken as a whole, the emperor's criticisms stressed two points. First, it was morally necessary to be "fair" (*kung, p'ing*) and to have a sense of the proper fit between offense and punishment. Second, the emperor stressed the practical consequences of finding a mean between excessive severity and excessive leniency. Excessive leniency encouraged more violations, and excessive severity meant that the government lost the services of able, badly needed officials, and that administration could be disrupted. If anything, one should err on the side of leniency, because it was a worse mistake to oust a capable official than mistakenly to recommend a bad official. A bad official was bound to reveal himself, but an ousted good official was lost for good.

Both these practical and moral considerations were especially important relative to minor violations which were old, widespread customs, as in the first two cases. The emperor said that it was not proper to equate such customary if illicit practices with serious financial corruption (*t'an-tsang*), which hurt the "people's livelihood and state finances" and thus had grave consequences. Moreover, when such a minor illicit practice was so widespread, prosecuting everyone guilty would be impractical, while singling out a few offenders would be unfair.

The proper procedure in such instances was to seek to promote future good behavior rather than to punish officials for past misbehavior. By instructing one's subordinates and warning them against future violations, one gave them a chance to "repent, reform, and renew themselves." If they still persisted in carrying out the customary violation involved, one should punish them. Following an old Confucian principle,[71] the emperor thus emphasized that instruction and warning should precede punishment, in effect urging more admonition and less impeachment.

Besides this principle and the general stress on fairness, the emperor condemned particularly unfair kinds of excessive severity. Excessive severity was particularly bad when it involved calling for a heavier punishment than the regulations specified, or if it involved the attempt of superior officials to blame subordinates for their own shortcomings. The emperor viewed in this light Pu-lan-t'ai's impeachment of the district magistrate during a period of drought, since the drought basically indicated the failure of Pu-lan-t'ai himself to establish virtuous rule, which would have elicited a harmonious response from nature.

At his audience in December, Pu-lan-t'ai admitted that he had been excessively severe and explained that his expectation had been that the emperor would reduce the punishments he had recommended; thus, Pu-lan-t'ai meant, the offenders would be moved by receiving a favor from the emperor after first being threatened with severe punishment. The emperor was shocked by this explanation: "As soon as We heard these words, We trembled on account of them and unconsciously began to perspire, the perspiration drenching Our back." The emperor pointed out that he had had no way of knowing that that was Pu-lan-t'ai's intention.

The attitude above of the Yung-cheng emperor to prosecution in the case of widespread practices illustrates how the partial contradiction between considerations of control and effectiveness put a certain upper limit on the quantity of impeachments independent of the quantity of violations. Another similar case occurred around 1830, when prosecution was initiated against clerks at the Board of Revenue who had been carrying out certain corrupt practices since about 1818. At the same time,

71. Legge, *Confucian Classics,* I:353 (*Confucian Analects*).

the Board of Civil Officials impeached for lack of vigilance all the officials who over those roughly twelve years had occupied the posts of president and vice-president at the Board of Revenue. For all of these many officials, most of whom held other posts by 1830, various sentences of demotion in subgrade and transfer were advised. However, the emperor reduced these sentences to allow the officials to carry on with their current duties. His reason was that if so many officials were removed at once, it would be hard to find enough qualified men to fill their posts.[72]

Of course, the question of leniency is always relative. Lenient treatment for public offenses often meant infliction of a salary fine, and these fines could be burdensome. Annual regular salaries for civil officials ranged from 360 taels plus 180 bushels of grain (after 1728) to 31.5 taels. Even if the salary was a small percentage of the official's total income, it was still a large sum in absolute terms: 3 to 5 taels around 1730 (6 to 10 taels around 1830) could supply one person with enough rice for a year. Once one's income is fully committed to expenses, being deprived of even a small fraction of it is highly unpleasant.

Yet on account of a variety of conditions, salary fines often were only a minor economic deprivation. First of all, the deprivational impact of the fines was lessened by two actions of the Yung-cheng emperor. In 1724 he set up a system of "payments to nourish integrity" (*yang-lien*),[73] and these, often dwarfing the regular salaries, never fell in the scope of the fines. For instance, in 1851 the regular salary of a Kiangsu local magistrate was 45 taels; his *yang-lien,* 1,000 to 1,800

72. Wang Hsien-ch'ien, *Tung-hua ch'üan-lu,* Tao-kuang, 24:4b–5b.

73. Hsiao I-shan, I:580–582. The salary and *yang-lien* scales can be found respectively in *HPTL,* 72:19–26 and *HPTL, chüan* 74 and 75. Officials with offices at the capital received a salary in grain on top of the regular salary in money. Both kinds of salary were doubled in 1728 by the Yung-cheng emperor for the presidents and vice-presidents of five boards (not the Board of Rites). This favor was extended to the Board of Rites in 1736. Grand secretaries also came to enjoy this favor. In 1736 this doubling of salary—but only the part in money—was also extended to all other civil officials at the capital. In 1737 this increased part of the salary was included in all salary fines. See *TCHTSL,* 85:*kuan-yüan fa-feng*:Yung-cheng 6, Ch'ien-lung 1, and Ch'ien-lung 2. See the same documents also in *ibid., chüan* 249. See IV, 3, d, and IV, 3, d, note 17.

taels (depending on the particular post). The Kiangsu governor, according to his grade, received 155 taels of regular salary, while his *yang-lien* was 12,000 taels. We should remember, though, that part or all of the *yang-lien* could be held back in some cases of restitution[74] or as a form of compulsory contribution for public needs.[75]

The second act, in 1729, greatly eased the conditions of payment. Generally, salary fines were collected by the holding back of salary payments. Civil officials in the capital received their salaries from the Board of Revenue, which was informed of any salary fines by a suboffice of the Board of Civil Officials, namely the *Chi-feng-t'ing* (Office for examining regular salaries). The Board of Revenue must also have informed the provincial treasurers, who usually paid the salaries and *yang-lien* of civil officials in the provinces out of amounts reserved from the collections of land tax and wastage.[76] Frequently, however, an official received another salary fine while his current salary was already being held back. Before 1729, such a new fine had to be paid in one year or a fine for late payment was added. If the latter were not paid on time, another late fine was added, and so on. The Yung-cheng emperor abolished late fines, thus removing this harsh multiplier effect.[77]

However many salary fines were levied, officials often did not bear any burden beyond the cancellation of their regular salaries.[78] Moreover it was possible to be promoted while owing salary fines. When certain promotions were carried out while the official still owed salary fines, a time limit was placed on the payment of the debt ranging from half a year for 300 taels

74. See *CFTL*, 29:17 and IV, 3, c, note 14. If an official had to make restitution on some item and lacked the property to do so by a certain deadline, he could, until 1802, be kept in office with all his salary and *yang-lien* held back. In 1802, however, the emperor decided that henceforth in such circumstances only half the *yang-lien* and salary would be held back.

75. In a memorial written around 1800, Wang Chih-i, then governor of Fukien, noted that currently 30 percent to 40 percent of the *yang-lien* of Fukien officials was being deducted to meet various governmental expenses, and he opposed a procedure whereby still more would be deducted to make up an unauthorized expenditure for military expenses carried out by previous Fukien officials; see *HCCSWP*, 16:5b.

76. *CFTL*, 26:20a–b; *TCHT*, 11:19b.

77. *TCHTSL*, 85:*kuan-yüan fa-feng*:Yung-cheng 7.

78. *CFTL*, 2:38; *HPTL*, 73:32.

or less to five years for 10,000 taels or more.[79] Before about 1729, salary fine debts were mostly canceled not only when an official retired but also when he was dismissed (*ko-chih*). After that date, if an official retired because of old age, the debts were canceled, but if he was dismissed (*ko-chih*) and was a local magistrate or higher, he paid the debts to the extent that he had received salary payments in the past. If the debts were more than past salary payments, the difference was generally canceled, but not always.[80]

It is true that salary fines came to include all parts of the regular salary paid in money, including the 100% increase granted to all capital officials by 1736. Moreover the grain allotments received by capital officials also were included until about 1786. At this time, however, the emperor ordered that henceforth salary fines apply only to the money portion of salaries. Even in the case of "dismissal with retention of duties," a capital official's grain allotments were to remain unaffected by sanctions.[81]

Better to understand the financial impact of salary fines, we need more information about officials' incomes. Amazingly detailed data gathered by Chang Te-ch'ang from Li Tz'u-ming's (1830–94) diary seem to yield a roughly comprehensive picture of the amounts of money and grain passing through the hands of a low capital official in late Ch'ing times, although more work is needed on how price and monetary fluctuations affected the purchasing power of this money.

Li's income fell into four categories: official income, that is, salary and other income formally attached to his official job; gifts (*k'uei-tseng*); privately earned stipends; and other items like loans.[82] Chang subdivides the first category into the regular

79. *CFTL*, 28:12.

80. *HPTL*, 73:25a–b. In 1729 the emperor referred to a certain law whereby retired or dismissed officials were excused from paying any outstanding salary fines to the extent that these exceeded past salary payments. Thus we may infer that officials sometimes had had to pay *hsü-feng* (empty salary), i.e., regular salary which had been never paid out or even been due in the past but which was owed to the government by the official involved in order to pay off salary fines. See *TCHTSL*, 85:*kuan-yüan fa-feng*:Yung-cheng 7.

81. *TCHTSL*, 249:Ch'ien-lung 51 and Chia-ch'ing 7. See IV, 3, c, note 73 and IV, 3, d, note 17.

82. Many gifts received by capital officials were made by regional officials seeking to build up ties of solidarity useful to their careers.

salary paid in money, grain allotments, *fan-shih-yin* (meal money), *yang-lien*, and *yin-chieh-yin* (guarantee silver). The latter came from a number of funds at the capital, each managed by a group of officials from the same province, Chekiang for example. A native of Chekiang who had bought some form of official status had to be "guaranteed" by capital officials from Chekiang before he could obtain a post. When obtaining their guarantee, he paid in "guarantee silver" to their Chekiang fund, from which monthly payments then were made to men with official jobs at the capital (presumably only Chekiang natives). Men native to other provinces had parallel arrangements.

Because of Li's low status at the Board of Revenue (for many years he was merely a trainee, a "departmental official outside the regular quota of officials"), his official income often included only *yin-chieh-yin* and *yang-lien*. Starting work at the Board in

---

On some pretext such as a common native place, a capital official would invite a regional official visiting the capital to a banquet, at which the latter could fittingly make a present to his host. Although some felt that an official like a censor should be above it, this custom of gift-giving was carried on openly in Li's time with only faint moral disapproval (see Chang Te-ch'ang, p. 63) and no legal sanctions. Yet how this custom was distinguished from the illegal gift-giving subject to *ch'u-fen* or even criminal sanctions is not obvious. A *ch'u-fen* promulgated in about 1679 punished with dismissal and a criminal trial "any governor-general, governor, provincial judge or treasurer, taotai, prefect, departmental or district magistrate who asks a capital official to act in his favor on a particular matter or who presents gifts to a capital official, seeking to flatter him and win his esteem." This law would seem to cover many gifts received by Li, but a *ch'u-fen* promulgated in about 1740, although referring only to capital officials, makes a distinction which could have provided a legal basis for the innocent exchange of gifts between officials. Capital officials who were "close relatives or friends, who had the same native place, or whose families had old ties" would normally be expected to "have social intercourse and offer condolences or congratulations to each other on appropriate occasions." Such social activities, which implicitly involved the exchanging of gifts, "in themselves reflect in no way on one's good name or integrity," this law noted. What was illegal was using such social occasions to "ask [one's relative or friend] to take into account one's personal connection to him by handling a particular piece of public business in a partial way." See *TCHTSL*, 96:*k'uei-sung chu-t'o*:K'ang-hsi 18 and Ch'ien-lung 5. It should be added that the patterns of gift-giving between officials were multidirectional. For instance, the 1679 law noted above also refers to illegal gifts made by capital officials to regional ones.

1863, he began receiving a regular money salary in full only in 1887. Totalling all of his official income received while at the Board in the years 1863–65 and 1871–88 (he was on leave in 1866–70), we get 4,664.43 taels, plus a little grain. Of this, 3,704.54 taels was *yin-chieh-yin* and only 413 taels was regular salary, to which fines might have been applicable. On the other hand, when Li's rank rose and the annual harvest of *yin-chieh-yin* fell, his regular salary could amount to almost half of his official income, as was the case in 1888.

When all of Li's sources of income are considered, the significance of the regular salary declines further. In the years 1863–65 and 1871–88, Li received some 6,066.04 taels in gifts and some 7,822.53 taels in stipends and other items. On the other hand, Li's flow of stipends and gifts largely depended on his political reputation and potential. If he had received a salary fine at the Board (he apparently never did), the money involved would have been a relatively small sum for him before 1886, but any *ch'u-fen* would probably have threatened his basic economic position had it cast any shadow on his political reputation.

It is significant that Li's total known income while at the Board considerably exceeded his total known expenditures: for 1863–65 and 1871–88, his income was some 18,553 taels, his expenditures, some 15,119 taels. These figures, contrary to the usual picture of Ch'ing officials, suggest that Li was not typically under any economic pressure to tread the dangerous path of embezzlement, bribery, or other forms of corruption. Therefore it is possible that illegal forms of income, not noted in his diary, were either insignificant or nonexistent.[83] No doubt in some other official jobs, outright corruption played a larger role.

A variety of conditions, therefore, promoted considerable leniency in the treatment of public offenses. However, the problem of the right degree of leniency often was not solved,

83. Chang's master tables on Li's income and expenditure are in Chang Te-ch'ang, pp. 70–218. Derivative tables in *ibid.*, p. 64 and p. 228 are relevant to our discussion, as is the text in *ibid.*, pp. 46–49 and pp. 55–56. In calculating total income, I have relied on the cash-silver ratios given in *ibid.*, pp. 6–7. Chang's book involves some careless mistakes in the copying and handling of numbers, but checking his master tables against Li's diary would have been too time-consuming a task. I feel reasonably sure that the vast majority of the data has been accurately transcribed.

according to indigenous views. There were important tendencies both to excessive leniency and to excessive severity.

The state's fiscal needs sometimes led to allegedly excessive leniency. Revenue was raised by selling various kinds of administrative advantages, a tendency often criticized by Ch'ing scholars as reducing effectiveness, because it put corrupt or incompetent persons in office. This tendency involved not only the sale of office but also sometimes a reluctance to impeach the buyers. Regulations established in about 1679 required that after a buyer had been in office for three years, he be promoted in case of good performance and impeached in case of bad performance. However, Hsü Yüan-wen, a *chin-shih* of 1659, complained that despite these regulations, no buyer had been impeached so far as he could recall. Some buyers, he said, had held their posts five years without being either impeached or recommended for promotion. Hsü similarly criticized a regulation of his time which allowed officials to buy promotion after three years on a post without any recommendation based on their performance.[84] Lu Lung-chi (1630–1693) also memorialized criticizing such conditions.[85] Clearly, military expenses in these early Ch'ing years put pressure on the government to make discipline more lenient in order to attract buyers.

Yet the statistics in Table 1 are inconclusive on the question of whether buyers or officials with examination degrees enjoyed longer terms of office as local magistrates. The increase in the number of buyers during the middle and later nineteenth century has also been viewed as weakening discipline. That there was an increase of buyers is easy to confirm, but establishing representative statistics is difficult. My figures indicate that only one-third of the local magistrates around 1886 had purchased degrees, but another sample of local and provincial officials in 1895 suggests one-half.[86]

84. *HCCSWP,* 17:16a–b.

85. *HCCSWP,* 17:15a–b.

86. Kwang-Ching Liu, "Nineteenth-century China; The Disintegration of the Old Order and the Impact of the West," in Ho Ping-ti and Tang Tsou, eds., *China in Crisis* (Chicago, 1968), Vol. I, Book 1, p. 115. While Professor Liu suggests that corrupt buyers were protected by the regulations, I would gather that they depended more on lenient policies toward them. Possibly the sinister impact of corrupt buyers has been exaggerated. Some buyers, like Li Tz'u-ming, were gifted scholars who also advanced via the examinations; Chang Tech'ang, pp. 11–22. Moreover one finds that buyers could not fre-

In any case, selling honors, like "commendations" (*chüan-na chi-lu*), which could be used to cancel off sentences for some public offenses, was still another way of putting fiscal considerations above disciplinary ones.

Excessive leniency also sometimes stemmed from an attempt to strengthen ties of solidarity between the bulk of the officials and the state by stressing seniority at the expense of the merit principle. For instance in a memorial of 1655, Liang Ch'ing-piao, then a vice-president of the Board of Civil Offiicials, complained that currently promotions were being made only on the basis of an official's formal standing, with no consideration given to outstanding ability. Liang urged that merit play a greater role in promotions.[87] Chou Chen-yeh, who obtained a low degree in about 1723, similarly pointed out that those promotions of local magistrates handled by the Board of Civil Officials were based purely on the formal standing of the magistrates, with the result that bad and outstanding magistrates were treated alike. To correct this, he urged that governors and govenors-general, rather than the Board, play a greater role in impeaching magistrates and in recommending them for promotion. Explicitly set up in late Ming times to promote fairness, the system of appointments run by the Board placed candidates according to qualifications such as seniority in certain categories, the members of which were each assigned a post through a periodic lottery. Yet however fair, this system often resulted in assigning posts to individuals unsuited to them. By contrast, the alternative system of assigning provincial posts through individual recommendations by governors-general and/or governors was perhaps more open to favoritism but also more likely to lead to effective appointments. Reasonably enough, most of the difficult provincial posts were or came to be filled in the latter way.[88] Generally speaking, the tendency to put emphasis on seniority was linked to the recurrent policy of *t'ing-nien-ko* (ap-

---

quently rise above taotai. In 1796–1908, perhaps only 14% of all provincial treasurers had no more than purchased degrees. See pp. 510–512 in Wei Hsiu-mei, "*Ts'ung-liang-te kuan-ch'a t'an-t'ao Ch'ing-chi pu-cheng-shih-te jen-shih shan-ti hsien-hsiang* (A quantitative study of the personnel flow in the post of provincial treasurer during the late Ch'ing period)," *Bulletin of the Institute of Modern History, Academia Sinica,* 2:505–533 (1971).

87. *HCCSWP,* 17:11b–12.

88. *HCCSWP,* 15:1; *Shinkoku Gyōseihō,* I:377–381, 384–390. Translated in *Ch'ing-kuo hsing-cheng-fa,* 3:2:77–83; 3:2:86–93.

pointing officials on the basis of seniority and merit), which Ku Yen-wu criticized as having little to do with merit and traced back to the Northern Wei period (386–534).[89]

Lu Lung-chi also criticized excessive leniency from another standpoint. He wanted a more rigorous weeding out of incompetent officials as a method of creating more openings for the masses of candidates for office whose morale was sagging as they waited year after year.[90]

When we turn to the problem of excessive severity, we find many Ch'ing complaints revolving around the charge that the state's effectiveness was reduced through the various consequences of excessively numerous and harsh disciplinary regulations. An official reading through the *li-cheng* (management of government personnel) section of *Huang-ch'ao ching-shih wen-pien* (Our august dynasty's writings on statecraft), which was published in 1827, would have found the following six main areas of criticism expressed by various scholars at various times since the beginning of the dynasty.

First, the *ch'u-fen tse-li* led officials, especially local magistrates, to put primacy on following regulations and pleasing superiors instead of caring for the people. Moreover, they had to spend so much time studying these regulations that they lacked time for the people.[91]

Second, there was a waste of good men who were either dismissed or made ineligible for promotion on account of some minor fault. This involved an excessively rapid turnover of officials, with the result that many officials lacked a chance to develop the experience needed to be effective, and that clerks had little fear of an official whom they knew would be gone tomorrow.[92]

Third, overly afraid of committing an offense, officials lacked not only the discretion but also the courage to act. Officials felt badly treated and lost the morale (*ch'i*) needed for effective performance. There was an important concept here of the capacity for independent initiative. For instance, Lu Hsi-chin, a *chin-shih* of 1688 who rose to be a prefect, spoke of the need for an official to *t'e-li tu-hsing* (stand and act on his own):

89. *HCCSWP*, 17:5–6; see also *ibid.*, 16:6.
90. *HCCSWP*, 17:9a–b.
91. *HCCSWP*, 16:1; 15:4a–b, 9b–10b; 16:7.
92. *HCCSWP*, 16:4b–5; 15:2, 4, 8b–9; 16:8b.

> When the forms of official intercourse involve lack of respect, men regard themselves as of little importance. When men regard themselves as of little importance, they feel that they are persons of low and vulgar status. When they feel that they are persons of low and vulgar status, they lack courage in undertaking their responsibilities and steadfastness in maintaining what is proper. If they lack courage in undertaking their responsibilities and steadfastness in maintaining what is proper, then the people will not benefit from their administration.[93]

Fourth, some laws unfairly or unwisely punished officials for acts beyond their control. This has been touched on in connection with the question of the rationalization of responsibility (IV, 3, b).

Fifth, multiplying salary fines added to that economic burden which forced officials to commit acts of financial corruption.[94]

Sixth, the laws were a large, confusing tangle. This confusion made officials uncertain how to act and facilitated the corrupt juggling of the law.[95]

To meet such criticisms, various remedies were suggested and sometimes realized. There was a feeling that there were better ways to evaluate personnel than the strict use of the *ch'u-fen tse-li.* Was it not obvious, after all, whether a man was doing a good job, however many *ch'u-fen* he received? One proposal was to reduce the number of *ch'u-fen* articles.[96] Memorializing around 1740, Li Fu blamed governors-general and governors for excessive severity and suggested that any sentence of dismissal from office or less for a public offense be commuted to probationary retention of the post; however, this plan never took root.[97] Another possibility, suggested by a censor in 1803, was to change the mechanism for canceling off *ch'u-fen* by relying more on the discretion of the governors and governors-general instead of on the advice of the Board of Civil Officials, which applied rules more inflexibly: if a local magistrate was judged

93. *HCCSWP,* 15:3b–4; see also *ibid.,* 15:2b, 8, 9; 16:6. *T'e-li tu-hsing,* also a cliché of modern Chinese liberalism, is found in the writings of Ch'eng I (1033–1108). See Jung Chao-tsu, p. 102. The terms goes back at least to the *Li-chi.*

94. *HCCSWP,* 15:11.

95. *HCCSWP,* 15:9, 11.

96. *HCCSWP,* 15:10b–11.

97. *HCCSWP,* 15:8b.

to be successful by his governor-general, the latter could advise on the canceling off of any *ch'u-fen* for public offenses. The issue of the discretion of the governors-general versus the authority of the Boards was touchy, however.[98] Then in 1820 the Chia-ch'ing emperor expressed great concern over the waste of official talent due to the excessive severity of punishments for public offenses. He ordered that the Boards of War and of Civil Officials cease taking public offenses in a man's record into account when advising on his appointment to certain important provincial posts. For all other promotions, public offenses were to be counted only if they involved temporary ineligibility for promotion due to deficiencies in the regular tax quotas and cases of uncaught criminals.[99]

At the same time, the problem of discipline was only one part of the complex tangle of questions of *li-cheng* (management of governmental personnel), some of which also were dilemmas. We may infer that officials facing this tangle wavered between two attitudes. They felt that even if the problem of discipline could be solved, the state's effectiveness would still be impaired because of other problems of *li-cheng*. Conversely, they perhaps felt that if disciplinary problems could not be solved, maybe there could be compensatory improvements in other areas of *li-cheng*.

For instance, while excessive severity undermined effectiveness, so might the lines of authority connecting offices whenever the principle of *hsiang-chih* (mutual control) displaced that of *chuan-tse* (assigning responsibility exclusively [to one official or office]). Some offices, perhaps on account of the excessive size of the territory under them or the excessive number of assigned functions, were regarded as inherently unequal to their tasks. The office of local magistrate was sometimes criticized in this way. The remedy of adding a vice-magistrate sharing responsibility was considered by the Yung-cheng emperor around 1729 but then rejected, largely because of the difficulty of clearly assigning responsibility in such a system. Splitting up populous, busy districts also involved obstacles such as the difficulty of financing the new city walls, office buildings, schools, granaries, and jails.[100]

98. *HCCSWP,* 16:1; 6:5; 15:8a–b.

99. *CFTL,* 1:1–2.

100. *HCCSWP,* 18:17–18, 13. The post of vice-magistrate considered by Yung-cheng differed from those of the already established

Effectiveness was also impaired when the needs of an office were not properly matched by the qualifications of the occupant.[101] What kind of administrative experience was better training for gifted candidates: direct acquaintance on the district level with the people's problems or acquaintance on the provincial level with the larger issues? Would effectiveness be increased by keeping a good man in a difficult, unpleasant job or by rewarding him with an easy one? A buildup of proper solidarities was impeded not only by severe punishments but also by the inadequate moral education of many officials, their long wait for office followed by an inadequate career path, and the humiliating, demoralizing personal treatment they often recevied from superiors. Finally, officials became demoralized and failed to act legally because of their lack of sufficient legal economic rewards.

Two major complementary themes seem to unite all these considerations about disciplinary punishments and other personnel questions: promoting the capabilities of the officials and freeing the officials from undue constraints. It was necessary that officials in themselves be capable, while outer circumstances be so shaped as to encourage or at least allow the exercise of these capabilities. Both the capacity and the freedom to act were at issue.

In philosophic terms, this general attitude, as I have tried to induce it from numerous documents, can be seen as an eclectic combination of the ancient Confucian ideal of *jen-chih* (governing by relying on good men) with the Legalist ideal of *fa-chih* (governing by relying on laws). However, specification of this problem in terms of the practical issues of the day led to a more complex outlook than either of these two principles originally indicated, if not a qualitatively different one. More was involved than just saying that both laws and the discretion of virtuous officials were needed, since many factors had to be artfully combined. Also, much of the discussion reflected the attitude I labeled "moderate realism" (see I, 5).

Admittedly, in order to think comprehensively about the issues of *li-cheng* (management of governmental personnel), we

---

local subordinate officials in that the assistant local magistrate would not have been formally subordinated to the magistrate. See also *ibid.*, 18:12–15; 15:2a–b; 19:7b; 21:1b.

101. *HCCSWP*, 15:6b; 17:1b.

would need, besides capabilities and constraints, at least one more logically distinct category, the problem of designing the tasks of an office so as to suit the capabilities of the occupant. Even if an official had both the personal capabilities and the freedom to assume significant responsibilities, he could not succeed if too much official business was thrust on him; if he had to meet a tax quota the fulfillment of which depended on the inadequate policing efforts of officials outside his jurisdiction; if he had to supervise a geographically distant office to which he could not travel frequently enough; and so on. Such considerations about tasks are illustrated by the problem of the vice-magistrate noted above. They formed an important issue too, but, for the sake of convenience, we may focus here just on the questions of capabilities and constraints.

Capabilities had two major aspects. First they involved skills, which were promoted by training within the government, long experience in a particular office, and a well-designed career path. Second, they involved the many-faceted question of the attitude, morale, and outer dignity of the officials. We previously discussed this question in terms of what we labeled the officials' "probationary ethic" and their "sense of charisma" (IV, 2). Looking at the same matter now in terms nearer to the vocabulary of the *li-cheng* documents, we would speak of the following diffusely interrelated facets of morale: the prestige needed to elicit respect from subordinates, self-confidence, feelings of solidarity, willingness to shoulder responsibilities, and willingness to refrain from abusing one's power by committing crimes. (The loyalty of officials was usually not openly questioned, but many of the constraints on them were designed to minimize the opportunities for disloyal behavior.) The factors adduced by Ch'ing writers as improving morale included improving education or intellectual currents; minimizing demoralizing experiences such as a long wait for office or humiliating treatment from superiors; pleasing and encouraging officials in matters of tenure and promotion; and adjusting constraints.

While "capabilities" refers to features more connected to the person of the official, "constraints" refers to often distasteful outside pressures. These included the lines of authority imposed on an office, disciplinary and criminal laws, and economic pressure in the form of inadequate salaries.

In seeking to promote capabilities and adjust constraints through its disciplinary and other personnel policies, the state faced three key problems or dilemmas. First, there were the uncertainties of the morale problem. These centered around the elusive distinction between *jen-shih pu-yung* (lack of courage in carrying out responsibilities) and *t'ui-hsieh* (shirking responsibilities). If the state made disciplinary regulations milder, improving morale by emphasizing seniority and reducing the fear of expulsion, would officials then find the "courage" to carry out their responsibilities, or would they then be tempted to "shirk their responsibilities"? Since the question of morale involved a diffuse mixture of desirable and undesirable solidarities, seeking to improve morale through greater leniency was likely to have ambiguous results. Officials sometimes claimed that they could not be effective unless they were "trusted" more, but were they trustworthy? Yet if officials were not trustworthy and were of improper moral stock, prone to abuse their power by spending extravagantly to seek favors from superiors, to entertain themselves, or illegally to help their families, and so on, it was hard for critics to agree on any program to improve the educational and intellectual situation so as to produce officials of better character.

Still more, the morale requirements of different groups could conflict. If the morale and skills of officials were increased by slowing turnover, the morale of gentry waiting for office was improved by hastening turnover, as Lu Lung-chi suggested.

Second, there tended to be some inevitable contradictions between the need to develop capabilities and the need to impose proper constraints. Superior officials had to have enough authority to impose constraints on subordinates, but once they had that much authority, they were likely to abuse it by humiliating or unfairly punishing subordinates, thus undermining their morale and capabilities. Even if fairly applied, the imposition of disciplinary sanctions according to regulations sometimes reduced capabilities, but there were no obvious solutions. As we have noted, reducing the severity of the sanctions could also reduce capabilities, and if one changed the manner of applying sanctions by relying more on the discretion of high officials and less on board regulations, different abuses could arise.

The third key factor impeding the adjustment of constraints was the state's tendency to be or feel short of funds. We have seen how the state's need for funds often led it to sell various administrative advantages, excessively reducing constraints for some corrupt, incompetent officeholders. The state's shortage of funds also was behind the question of inadequate salaries. If salaries were to be increased, where were the funds to come from? Should, for instance, the large salaries of nobles be reduced, should more of the annually uncommitted funds be used for salaries, or should taxes be increased? Outside the Yung-cheng emperor's establishment of the supplementary salaries, it is hard to find a courageous confrontation of this problem. One reason was that the basic Confucian stress on frugality inhibited straightforward calculations about increasing salaries. Indeed, in a time of rising population, when the number of people in the average district was four or five times what it had been in the earlier dynasties, it still was fashionable to try to reduce the size of the bureaucracy. In the winter of 1831–32, the Tao-kuang emperor ordered that an effort be made to find and eliminate unneeded offices and admiringly referred to the fact that approximately 937 offices had been eliminated since about 1720.[102]

The power of the emperor and the state, therefore, could not be maximally extended without properly organizing officials by promoting their capabilities and adjusting their constraints and tasks. Yet this involved problems which often were dilemmas, notably, unreliable shifts in the officials' morale; unavoidable contradictions between the question of capabilities and that of constraints; and the state's fiscal policy and recurrent fiscal crises. Because it was intertwined with this pattern of dilemmas, the problem of leniency in *ch'u-fen* law was hard to solve. Yet the difficult goal of simultaneously disciplining and utilizing competent officials was partly met through an artful combination of punishments and compensatory devices. Table 1 sheds some light on how this combination worked out in practice.[103]

102. Wang Hsien-ch'ien, *Tung-hua ch'üan-lu*, Tao-kuang, 24:15b–16. The emperor said that in about 1720, according to the *Veritable Records*, 335 offices had been eliminated. The other figures referred to by the emperor came from a report prepared by the Board of Civil Officials: in the Yung-cheng period, "more than 250" offices; in the Ch'ien-lung, "more than 330" offices; in the Chia-ch'ing, "more than 20" offices; since 1820, 2 offices. These calculations do not seem to take into account the offices created during this time.

103. All data here is taken from *Ta-Ch'ing chin-shen ch'üan-shu*, issues of winter, Kuang-hsü 12, and of winter, Tao-kuang 13. The names of local officials are given in these books with the date of appointment to their current job. Checks made on suspicious data, notably very long terms of office, resulted in affirmative corroboration

TABLE 1. Local magistrates and time already spent in office currently held

	Winter, 1833–34			Winter, 1886–87		
	Anhui	Kiangsu	Kansu	Anhui	Kiangsu	Shensi
Number of magistrates:						
Total	59	67	58	55	65	79
With examination degrees[a]	38	51	35	26	39	47
	64%	76%	60%	47%	60%	59%
With bought degrees	15	10	7	20	21	28
	26%	15%	12%	36%	32%	36%
Average number of years already spent in current office:						
All magistrates	2	1.9	2.8	4.8	2.9	2.5
With examination degrees	2.3	1.8	3.1	4.6	3.1	2.7
With bought degrees	1.7	2	2.7	4.9	3.6	2.4
Number of magistrates with						
3 yrs. or more in current office	17	19	30	39	26	30
	29%	28%	52%	71%	40%	38%
2 yrs. in current office	7	11	6	4	9	15
	12%	16%	10%	7%	14%	19%
1 yr. in current office	26	20	11	3	17	18
	44%	30%	19%	5%	26%	23%
Less than 1 yr. in current office or data unclear	9	17	11	9	13	16
	15%	25%	19%	16%	20%	20%

[a] Percentages given in these two columns do not add up to 100 because some persons, such as those without degrees, were omitted.

This table shows that the complaints about excessive turnover were justified to a large extent. Even in the apparently anomalous case of Anhui in the winter of 1886–87, where average time already spent in one's current office was a fat 4.8 years, 21 percent of the magistrates were newcomers with only one year or less already spent in their current post. Newcomers were up to 59 percent in Anhui during the winter of 1833–34. In general, given this large number of newcomers, the overall average for years already spent in office was respectable only because these newcomers were statistically balanced by a small group of extremely long-lived old hands: magistrates with five, ten, or even thirteen years in their current post were far from uncommon. Of course, one must remember that a good number of newcomers were not green, since they had had previous experience at another post.

The second point is that alongside these newcomers (both experienced and inexperienced), old hands also made an impressive showing. In two cases, old hands with three years or more of experience numbered more than 50 percent. Old hands with two years or more went as low as 41 percent but usually stayed above 50 percent.

True, such a limited sample does not support any final conclusions. For instance Chang Chung-li's slightly smaller sample yields a finding totally at variance with that produced by mine—namely, that there was a great decline during the nineteenth century in the length of tenure of district magistrates. Yet even his figures show a generous length of tenure before 1800, his lowest being a respectable 2.6-year average for the terms of five magistrates; his highest, 5.5 years for the terms of eleven magistrates.[104]

All in all, then, the application of *ch'u-fen* law still allowed

---

in every case, e.g. by looking up the name and post in earlier issues of this periodical. However the issue for spring, Ch'ien-lung 57 turned up some discrepancies and so was not used. This periodical thus seems to be highly but not perfectly reliable. Therefore I also calculated length of tenure from another source, local gazetteers (see below). For distinguishing between purchased and examination degrees, I followed Ch'ü T'ung-tsu, *Local Government in China under the Ch'ing*, p. 20. This means that my figures for buyers are probably on the high side, since I counted all *kung-sheng* as buyers. In the arithmetical compilation of this table, I also leaned on the conservative side. For instance, many officials given "one year" actually had served one year plus some months.

104. Chang, *The Chinese Gentry*, chap. ii, table 2.

a considerable number of officials to develop some valuable administrative experience even in the post of local magistrate, which was more vulnerable to *ch'u-fen* than most. Many magistrates could finish their terms of office, thus fulfilling a routine requirement for promotion. (To meet this requirement, magistrates had to serve amounts of time varying according to the post; for instance, in some cases three years were enough; in others, six were required.)

The indigenous criticisms of *ch'u-fen* law I read did not prepare me for the fact that so many magistrates held their jobs for three years or more. The moralistic tone of these criticisms inhibited a more balanced account of pros as well as cons.

Averages of time already spent in one's current job are similar to averages of the total time spent in an office. The average magistrate of the department of Su in Anhui altogether spent 2.7 years in that office. This figure is derived from about 65 terms of office in 1666–1742 and 1790–1888. In Suining, a district in Kiangsu, the average magistrate spent two years. This figure is derived from 120 terms of office in 1645–1884.[105]

Unfortunately, it is difficult to corroborate statistically the impressionistic evidence that terms of office were shorter in the more difficult posts, the occupants of which allegedly were showered with *ch'u-fen*. Paradoxically, according to the official ratings of 1792 (Ch'ien-lung 57), Suining, where the average tenure was a short two years, was a post of the very lowest degree of difficulty, while the department of Su, where magistrates managed to stay longer, was a post of the very highest degree of difficulty and importance. There is also an inconclusive result when we compare easy and difficult provinces on this question. In presumably easy Shensi, officials in 1886–87 did less well than in presumably difficult Kiangsu. Yet in the presumably easy Kansu of 1833–34, one does see the relatively long tenure one would expect. The rich statistical materials available regarding such questions deserve more study.[106]

105. *Su chou-chih* (1889), 12:18b–24b; *Sui-ning hsien-chih* (1886), 11:14–24b.

106. According to Kessler's statistics, the average amount of time spent by Ch'ing officials in a particular office of governor or governor-general was somewhat more than two years, a figure comparable to ours for local magistrates. See tables 12 and 13 in L. D. Kessler, "Ethnic Composition of Provincial Leadership During the Ch'ing Dynasty," in *Journal of Asian Studies*, 28.3:489–511 (May 1969). The figures for provincial treasurers in 1796–1908 are similar, according to Wei Hsiu-mei.

d. Universalism

According to our theory of the control requirements, an organization cannot carry out its goals unless it rewards and punishes its members "universalistically," that is, according to their performance, rather than "particularistically," according to their status. This control requirement was met, to a large extent, since the *ch'u-fen tse-li* virtually always correlate severity of punishment only to the seriousness of the offense. In this they significantly contrast with much other traditional Chinese law. As Professor T'ung-tsu Ch'ü has shown, the severity of punishment in many criminal provisions depended both on the seriousness of the offense and the status of the offender.

It is also significant that steps were taken to make administrative punishment more universalistic by countering some of the particularistic or "unfair" elements which inevitably crept in. Apart from variations in the severity of the sentence due to corruption or political considerations, this unfairness had two main aspects: the chances of receiving a *ch'u-fen* and the impact of a sentence relative to the offender's situation as a whole.

Some of the political or personal factors affecting the chances of receiving a *ch'u-fen* are explained in a memorial presented in 1800 by the censor Chang P'eng-chan. Writing during a time of increasing corruption, Chang gave four reasons why governors-general and governors so rarely impeached subordinates for illegal shortages in treasuries or storehouses. First, they were afraid of being themselves consequently impeached for lack of vigilance and forced to make up the shortages. Second, if they had received illegal gifts from the offender or had been otherwise implicated in his wrongdoing, they were afraid that impeaching him would bring to light their own wrongdoing. Third, even if the governor or governor-general himself was free of any wrongdoing, he could not be sure that his immediate subordinates, such as the provincial treasurer and judge, had not been implicated in the offender's wrongdoings. He feared triggering off a major case implicating them. Fourth, once corruption had become widespread and widely accepted, a superior who suddenly singled out an offender could get a reputation for harshness. Chang also indicated that once corruption was widespread, starting prosecution in earnest would decimate the bureaucracy.[1]

1. *HCCSWP*, 20:10a–b.

We have seen that the chances of receiving a *ch'u-fen* sometimes declined in the case of buyers. They also depended on the nature of one's post. Primary agents in the provinces with obligations difficult to fulfill were more exposed to the threat of heavy administrative punishments than provincial officials supervising them, not to mention capital officials whose legal responsibilities often were easily met. Local magistrates in particular bore the brunt of three particularly vexing responsibilities: *chui* (to press persons, often dismissed officials, to pay certain debts such as salary fines or government funds which they had misused or embezzled); *ch'i* (to catch and arrest a particular criminal); and *ts'ui* (to press for the payment of taxes)—all frequent and difficult obligations with deadlines the missing of which led to impeachment. Occupants of high posts could more easily attract the emperor's ire, but, as we have seen, grand councillors received few *ch'u-fen.*[2]

The second aspect of unfairness was that the relative impact of the same administrative sentence sometimes differed on account of aspects of the official's general status or situation unaffected by the sentence. One example of this illustrates how the advantages and disadvantages of various offices could partly cancel each other out. High officials at the capital were generally less exposed to *ch'u-fen* than high officials in the provinces, but the latter typically had much bigger supplementary salaries (*yang-lien*). For instance, officials at the Board of Revenue were free of the tension of trying to meet tax quotas, but governors-general struggled to meet these quotas under threat of impeachment. However, while the two presidents and the four vice-presidents of that board as a group received a *yang-lien* of about 17,200 taels, the Nanking governor-general alone had a *yang-lien* of 18,000 taels.[3]

Also sometimes affecting the relative impact of a *ch'u-fen* was

2. See IV, 1. Described in detail by Chang Te-ch'ang, Li Tz'u-ming's (1830–1894) long service at the Board of Revenue (about 20 years) apparently lacked a single *ch'u-fen.* Among capital posts around 1890, service as a censor was regarded as carrying an especially great risk of receiving a *ch'u-fen.* Capital officials at this time seem generally to have had the opinion that regional posts tended to be more desirable than capital posts because they were more lucrative, even though they might well carry a greater risk of receiving *ch'u-fen.* Chang Te-ch'ang, pp. 21, 55, 20.

3. *HPTL,* 74:15, 31.

possession by the officeholder of an hereditary rank or certain extra salaries. In this case the government did try to counter the "particularistic" tendencies of favoritism relative to high status. To a slight extent, it can even be argued that *ch'u-fen* law favored officials of lower status over those of higher status. For instance, salary fines for higher officials were obviously heavier in absolute terms; from a practical point of view, fines could just as well have consisted of money payments identical in amount for all officials.[4]

There were three main kinds of hereditary ranks (*shih-chüeh* or *shih-chih*). First there were imperial nobles consisting of the imperial house (*tsung-shih*) and its collateral relatives, the Chüeh-lo. Second there were foreign nobles, consisting of the leaders of Mongol and other tribes. Third there were nonimperial nobles. They held one of the nine ranks from *kung* to *en-chi-wei*. These nonimperial noble ranks must be distinguished equally from hereditary military offices (such as many of the captains in the banners); from entrance into government service as a right based on family relationship to an official;[5] and from the honorary titles (*kao-ch'ih*) which each official received automatically according to his grade (and which, beginning with grade seven, yielded derivative titles to an increasing range of relatives). Nonimperial nobles were found most especially in the ranks of the eight banners, but these titles were also bestowed for merit in civilian posts. The general supervision of all nonimperial nobles, whether military or civil, was by the Board of Civil Officials, and all nobles, imperial or not, were

4. The law on reducing punishment for officials revealing their own public offenses in time to allow correction favored lower officials, since their punishment was automatically reduced, while for higher officials, reduction of punishment depended on evaluation of the individual case; see *TCHT*, 11:6. Another law favoring lower officials was that which permitted them to be restored to office by making a financial contribution after committing a public offense leading to transfer or dismissal. Higher officials thus punished for a public offense "according to regulations are not permitted to be restored to their original office"; see *CFTL*, 2:54.

5. "For practically the whole of the Ming-Ch'ing period . . . a son of a first-rank official could enter government service without examination as a fifth-ranking official, and, through a descending scale, a son of a third-rank official received an office of the seventh rank." Ho Ping-ti, *The Ladder of Success in Imperial China* (New York, 1962), p. 149.

paid by the Board of Revenue (general supervision of imperial nobles was by the Imperial Clan Court; of foreign nobles, by the Court of Colonial Affairs).

Salaries for nobles generally dwarfed the regular salaries of officials. True, with their supplementary salaries nonnoble officials sometimes had bigger legal incomes than nobles, but the economic hold of nobles on the Ch'ing state is impressive. Salaries for imperial clansmen began at 10,000 taels and 5,000 bushels of grain annually, the lowest rank getting 110 taels and 55 bushels. Salaries for nonimperial nobles ranged from 7,000 taels and 350 bushels to 45 taels and about 22 bushels.[6]

The basic procedural article for officeholders who were nonimperial nobles was established in 1725. It reflected the principle that if the offense was a light or public one, punishment should be restricted to the noble's office, but that his status as a noble should also be involved if the offense was serious enough. Thus if a nonimperial noble was guilty of an administrative mistake, the punishment applied only to his position as a holder of the office involved. If the offense did not involve the affairs of his office, the punishment was applied to whichever of his statuses was greater. If the offense was serious enough, both his office and hereditary rank were removed.[7] Once thus removed, however, the hereditary rank was given to a descendant of the culprit, unless serious corruption, such as taking a bribe to bend the law, was involved. In such instances the law called for completely extinguishing the noble status of both the culprit and his descendants. If the culprit was not the original winner of the rank, however, it was considered unfair to make the penalty reach back to the original winner by extinguishing the noble status of *his* posterity. In such a case, the noble rank was transferred from the culprit's line of descendants to another line of the original winner's descendants.[8]

6. For salaries of foreign nobles, see *HPTL*, 73:13–14; of imperial nobles, *HPTL*, 72:1–2b; of nonimperial nobles, 72:6–8. For the titles of nonimperial nobles, see H. S. Brunnert and V. V. Hagelstrom, *Present Day Political Organization of China*, tr. A. Beltchenko and E. E. Moran (Recent unidentified Taiwan reprint of copy with 1911 translator's preface), p. 492.

7. *TCHTSL*, 85:*kuan-yüan chiang-ko*:Yung-cheng 3. The same law is given in *TCHT*, 11:6b, and *CFTL*, 2:7a–b. In some instances of offenses in office, it was left open to decide whether or not the hereditary rank would be removed.

8. *TCHT*, 12:5.

Efforts to restrict particularism in the case of imperial nobles were more sluggish but still significant. Although imperial nobles could not normally be stripped of their hereditary rank, it could be lowered and the button signifying it could be removed.[9] Moreover it seems that until 1778, office-holding imperial nobles receiving salary fines lost only their office salaries. In 1723 the Yung-cheng emperor—in a different spirit from that in his 1728 criticism of the *lü* on the "eight conditions for consideration"[10]—sent down a "favor-dispensing proclamation" that any noble, imperial or nonimperial, receiving a salary fine relative to an office he was holding would be fined only according to his office salary.[11] We have seen that nonimperial nobles lost this privilege just two years later (1725).

Not until 1778, however, was there a similar change for imperial nobles. This law of 1778 applied to certain imperial nobles who held posts at the Imperial Clan Court and directed banner affairs, or were in charge of the imperial tombs. It held that if their offense was a private one, the fine applied to their hereditary salary; if a public one, to their office salary.[12]

Then in 1790 a similar step was taken to show "fairness" in the punishment of imperial nobles who also held the office of tartar general or lieutenant-general. The basic rule here was that imperial nobles holding such a military office and receiving a sentence of demotion in subgrade plus transfer could commute the sentence into a salary fine at the rate of two years' office

9. *TCLL,* 4:13; *TCHT,* 1:13–15. That his rank could be lowered is clear from *Ch'in-ting wang-kung ch'u-fen tse-li* (Imperially endorsed regulations on the administrative punishment of princes; published no earlier than 1845), 1:6b.

10. See I, 6.

11. *TCHTSL,* 85:*kuan-yüan fa-feng*:Yung-cheng 1.

12. *TCHTSL,* 85:*kuan-yüan fa-feng*:Ch'ien-lung 43. Because the imperial nobles in charge of the imperial tombs did not have any office outside their noble rank, the arrangement was that if they committed a public offense, the salary of a lieutenant-general of the eight banners would be deducted from the salary attached to their noble rank. This law can also be seen in *CFTL,* 2:5, and *TCHT,* 11:7. This is a good example of an important law entered into the *Ta-Ch'ing hui-tien* after the third edition of 1763. This law is also in *TCHTSL,* 8:*i-hsü i-ch'u*:Ch'ien-lung 43, since this section deals with the Imperial Clan Court which, along with the Boards of War and of Civil Officials, was concerned with the *ch'u-fen* of imperial nobles. See also *TCHT,* 1:14.

salary per subgrade.[13] To show "fairness," the 1790 law provided that if such an imperial noble received such a sentence together with another officer who was not an imperial noble, the rate of commutation should be stiffened to that of four years' office salary per subgrade.[14]

In 1791 the Ch'ien-lung emperor stiffened this provision still more, stating that the 1790 law "tended to shield" the imperial nobles and "was very unfair," because, in contrast to their colleagues, they could retain their posts without a demotion. Henceforth any sentence of demotion and transfer received by such imperial nobles was to be carried out: "Not to mention the fact that the demotion only applies to their grade as an official and has no connection at all to their original hereditary rank!"[15]

Moreover there was an explicit principle that office-holding imperial nobles should receive the same *ch'u-fen* as other officials, apart from adjustments relative to their hereditary position. It is also significant that their administrative sentences were sometimes handled by the Board of War or of Civil Officials, not the Imperial Clan Court. The basic principle was that administrative sentences for princes of the blood of the first six degrees were handled by the Imperial Clan Court, while those for imperial nobles below this rank were handled by a board. However, the boards could also be involved in cases dealing with the highest princes. For instance if such a prince shared responsibility for the same offense with a non-noble official, the memorial advising on the sentence was prepared by the Imperial Clan Court working with the Board of War and/or the Board of Civil Officials; moreover it was the Board involved, not the Court, which "took charge" of the memorial.[16]

Some other adjustments also illustrate the problems in reducing favoritism toward officials of high status. In 1728 the Yung-cheng emperor, anxious that his most important officials receive enough income to relieve them of distracting worries regarding their family finances, doubled the salaries (money and grain) of the president and vice-presidents of five boards (the Board of Rites was excluded) and provided that in case of a salary fine, the income newly added not be affected. This

13. *TCHT*, 1:14.

14. *TCHTSL*, 8:*i-hsü i-ch'u*:Ch'ien-lung 55.

15. *Ibid.*, Chien-lung 56; *TCHTSL*, 85:*kuan-yüan chiang-ko*: Ch'ien-lung 56; *CFTL*, 2:4a–b.

16. *Ch'in-ting wang-kung ch'u-fen tse-li*, 1:5a–b.

placed other capital officials at a disadvantage, which was largely remedied with two steps. First, all other civil salaries at the capital also were increased in 1736, and the added amounts also were excluded from salary fines. Second, in 1737 all the added salaries of all capital civil officials were included in any salary fines.[17]

The problem of favoritism in minor arrangements is illustrated by an episode of 1742–43. Since the smallest kind of administrative honor used for canceling off *ch'u-fen*—one "commendation"—canceled off a fine of a half year's salary, canceling off salary fines of five months or less raised a problem. The practice had been simply to pay them, but in 1742, explicitly to relieve officials of this needless financial burden, the emperor ordered that henceforth in the case of bannermen at capital offices, these small salary fines were to be merely recorded until, added up, they were large enough to be equivalent to one commendation or more. Then in 1743 this privilege was extended also to all Chinese officials at the capital on the grounds that "the affairs of all capital offices are all handled by Manchu and Chinese head officials and department officials working together . . ."; consequently, procedures should be "uniform."[18]

In the winter of 1788–89 the emperor made officials at the Office of the Imperial Household (*Nei-wu-fu*) fully subject to demotions and transfers. Previously, the emperor noted, sentences of demotion and transfer had been changed to salary fines on the grounds that this office had a shortage of personnel. Today, he noted, these grounds were no longer valid since the office was now adequately staffed. The usual practice of capital offices should now be extended to this office also in order to show "fairness."[19]

Besides adjustments to avoid favoritism, sentences were also adjusted where removal of an official from his post would have been disruptive and where the official lacked those aspects of status the removal of which the sentence called for. Mostly

17. *TCHTSL*, 85:*kuan-yüan fa-feng*:Yung-cheng 6 and Ch'ien-lung 1 and 2. Only grand secretaries and presidents and vice-presidents of the six boards had their grain salaries doubled as well as their money salaries. Other capital civil officials only had their money salaries doubled. This is clear also from *HPTL*, 72:25. See IV, 3, c, note 73.

18. *CFTL*, 2:37a–b.

19. *CFTL*, 2:9a–b.

these adjustments also accorded or did not conflict with universalistic criteria.

The two main examples of the former were officials on a military campaign and the hereditary chieftains of tribal areas. Their administrative sentences were typically postponed or reduced, although dismissal was still possible.[20]

One example of the latter was the case of an official without a grade who received a sentence of demotion and transfer. If the demotion was not more than three subgrades and the offense was a public one, he might retain the post by being put on probation for four years. This depended, however, on an advice of the Board of Civil Officials to the emperor and was possible only if his conduct as an official was regarded as above average. Otherwise he was dismissed from office.[21] An edict of 1794 complained about the lack of disciplinary leverage connected to such cases: these low officials, when ordered to catch a criminal, felt little pressure to succeed, since if they failed, they could so often expect to be retained on a probationary basis. The emperor ordered that their salary and supplementary salary (*yang-lien*) be stopped during the probationary period of four years.[22]

A similar problem was that of sentences calling for salary fines in cases where the official lacked a proper salary. The two questions in this respect are the degree of regularity of the official job and the case of officials currently lacking any official job.

As discussed earlier (see IV, 3, b), one may place official jobs in the Ch'ing bureaucracy onto a spectrum of degrees of regularity. Legal responsibility partly varied with this spectrum. So did salary.

True, salaries did come with many of the less regular official jobs. Many persons assigned to work on a training basis at a capital office without holding a regular post in it (*hsing-tsou*) received a partial salary.[23] Less regular official jobs often came with salaries if they involved a position which had been funded and which was not at the same time occupied by someone else. According to a law of about 1768, if in the provinces an official with an expectant (*hou-pu*) or probationary (*shih-yung*) status was appointed on an acting basis (*shu*) to a regular post which

20. *TCHT,* 11:6b–7; *CFTL,* 2:21.
21. *CFTL,* 2:26.
22. *TCHTSL,* 85:*kuan-yüan chiang-ko*:Ch'ien-lung 59.
23. *HPTL,* 72:27a–b, 28b–29. Note Li Tz'u-ming's case in IV, 3, c. As a trainee at a board, Li had *hsing-tsou* status.

then was empty, he received the regular salary attached to that post, and, according to laws of about 1773 and 1793, half of the supplementary salary (*yang-lien*) as well. However, if the post then was occupied by a regular occupant who was merely temporarily absent, this replacement did not receive the regular salary, and, presumably, not the supplementary salary either. Similarly, a law of about 1793 dealt with local magistrates dismissed from office (*ko-chih*) and then commissioned to take charge of another office on an acting basis (*shu*) in the same province where they had been stationed before dismissal. They received half the supplementary salary and, presumably, all of the regular salary attached to their new posts.[24] In all such cases, salary fines presumably were levied in a routine fashion.

Yet what about official jobs not funded on a regular basis? In some cases funding could be arranged from some specially designated source of revenue.[25] A regulation of 1734 referred to about 12,980 taels then available at the Liang-huai salt monopoly zone, and stated that this sum would be partly used to make salary payments to "probationary officials." These clearly were officials commissioned to carry out official jobs lacking any regular basis.[26] Yet even when officials thus commissioned received some payment, it is not clear that these payments were regarded as regular salaries that could be held back to pay fines. Thus there was a law that expectant officials (*hou-pu, hou-hsüan*) who received a salary fine paid it only beginning the day they received an office.[27]

Adjustments also had to be made for officials lacking any official job, since again salary fines were sometimes owed by persons lacking a salary. Civil officials who were temporarily retired to mourn for their parents received no salary during the period of retirement.[28] Moreover, it was unusual for permanently retired officials to receive a salary. Getting it depended on such matters as being old, having high rank, having military merit, and retiring voluntarily. For instance, if an official of the third grade or less voluntarily retired on account of old age or

24. *TCHTSL, chüan* 251:Ch'ien-lung 33; Ch'ien-lung 58. *Ibid., chüan* 263:*shu-jen kuan-yüan yang-lien*:Ch'ien-lung 38.

25. See, e.g., a Tao-kuang 6 case in *TCHTSL, chüan* 263:*shu-jen kuan-yüan yang-lien.*

26. *LHYFC,* 41:61.

27. *CFTL,* 2:15; *TCHT,* 11:6b–7.

28. *HPTL,* 72:43. *Wang-chih* is here a misprint for *chu-chih.*

sickness, was sixty years old or more, and had been not only on a military campaign but also in combat, receiving a wound or otherwise distinguishing himself, the emperor might grant him a full salary on retirement.[29]

An official who had permanently retired because of old age or sickness but was under impeachment for offenses in his last post was exempted from further salary fines. If, however, the sentence was demotion with transfer or dismissal from office and it could not be cancelled off with administrative honors, he was punished by having his grade button and grade-signifying belt replaced or removed or by removal of his office title.[30]

The law was also lenient in dealing with officials who, charged with some deadline, had to leave their post before the deadline arrived. However, the excuse of a sick leave was regarded with suspicion, and officials who left for this reason had a harder time closing their case than those who had left to observe the mourning period for their parents, to support aged parents, or because of some sort of transfer. The latter could close their case without any punishment if they had left less than a month after the deadline had been set. Even if they left later, they still could close it with a maximum fine of one year's salary. If the excuse was a sick leave, however, officials often had to serve some years of probation when resuming office.[31]

29. *HPTL,* 72:44–46.
30. *CFTL,* 2:20.
31. *CFTL,* 2:18a–b. *CFTL,* 2:16a–b.

4. The Administrative Framework

Turning away now from the question of the normative meaning of the disciplinary punishments, we will look at the administrative structure through which they were applied. This structure can be conceptualized as consisting of offices; officials filling these offices; the system of authority and communication linking these offices; the procedures of legislation and administration carried out by these offices; and the clients of these procedures, that is, the persons subject to *ch'u-fen* law.

In describing these aspects, our two main concerns are centralization and differentiation (in some contexts, "specialization" is more appropriate than "differentiation," but the two concepts are theoretically very close). Abstract and historical considerations relevant to these two issues have been discussed (see IV, 1 and 2).

With regard to centralization, we find a centralized network pattern. Many procedures were at least initially in the hands of an open-ended network of offices, namely surveillance, announcing the offense, the finding of verdicts, the determining of many sentences, and procedures for correcting adjudicative mistakes. However, these offices were closely supervised by the center in carrying out these procedures, and the center, in the form of the Department for the Scrutiny of Merits at the Board of Civil Officials, itself carried out some procedures. That is, this department kept records, determined many sentences, and saw to the effecting of sentences. Moreover, like the administration of *ch'u-fen* law, the process of *ch'u-fen* legislation also involved an open-ended network of offices (see III, 1): an open-ended network of offices proposed legislation; a central office (the Board of Civil Officials) often was important in advising on legislation, and the emperor had to approve all legislation.

Differentiation, obviously occurring as a response to the need for effectively uniform application, can be seen along all the various administrative dimensions, but so can nondifferentiation, which was attributable both to conceptual and institutional factors.

The Department for the Scrutiny of Merits was a highly specialized office devoted to *ch'u-fen* adjudication and legislation, but most offices carrying out *ch'u-fen* procedures were not specialized. Although many officials in the Department had specialized training, many did not, not to mention officials outside it (see II, 4).

In the realm of communication, specialized books on *ch'u-fen* law did not form a fully distinct entity. Important articles were not included in the *ch'u-fen* books. For instance, the key, perhaps organic, article of *ch'u-fen* law, *chih-kuan yu-fan* (when officials commit an offense), was in the *ming-li* (principles of sentencing) section of the penal code and seems never to have appeared in any *ch'u-fen* book. The *ch'u-fen* role of the Board of Civil Officials was definitively described in *Ta-Ch'ing hui-tien.* Yet whether this statement was equivalent to some sort of charter for a distinct body of legal activity is problematic.

When we look at that fundamental conceptual triangle of law —offender, offense, and sentence—we do not find the basis for fuller differentiation of *ch'u-fen* law. As we have seen, the notion of an administrative offense remained normatively and terminologically linked to the penal code's concept of crime; there was no generic word denoting "light offenses involving governmental affairs"; and the system of sanctions still consisted in part of the commutation of criminal sentences.

The status of the official offender also was not a salient enough consideration to lead to a distinct body of law. True, *ch'u-fen* law can be seen as partly based on the view that sentences should be adjusted for persons with official status. However, official status, as we shall see, was a concept with somewhat blurred boundaries. Moreover, the basic perception here was not that there should be different branches of law for different social strata but that the law was a unified whole which should be applied with sentence adjustments in response to a variety of conditions distinguishing offenders. This is clear from the nature of the *ming-li* section, in which one finds the key or organic *ch'u-fen* articles. Articles in this section, listed to a large extent in an arbitrary fashion, call for sentence adjustments not only for persons whose outstanding characteristic was their position on the social hierarchy but also for convicts, soldiers, cripples, foreigners in the empire, children, elderly persons, skilled astronomers at the Imperial Board of Astronomy, women, and others. A woman guilty of a crime calling for military exile could not practically serve in the army; therefore her sentence could be adjusted to slavery or imprisonment. Skilled official astronomers were allowed to redeem some sentences of exile because of the urgency of the state's need for their services. The vision of a justly ordered society was one in which considerations of hierarchy were mixed with others such as practicality, propriety, and compassion. One is tempted to suggest that the primary social principle here is the broad one that everyone has his proper place (*fen*), not the narrower one that everyone's proper place is fully defined in vertical, hierarchical terms.

Most important, the sentence adjustments made for officials involved more than the idea that persons of high status should enjoy relatively lenient treatment (see IV, 3, c). First, official status was often seen as a reason not for relatively lenient but for relatively severe punishment. Second, the state's urgent desire to retain and encourage the services of skilled personnel (as in the case of astronomers) was a major reason for many of the sentence adjustments and compensatory devices applied to officials. Other practical considerations behind sentence adjustments for officials have been discussed earlier (see IV, 3, d).

In its conceptual basis, therefore, *ch'u-fen* law developed out of a desire to apply a unified system of law by devising sentence adjustments appropriate to both the peculiar conditions of governmental offenses and the various aspects of the officials' nature and status. Much legislation growing out of these adjustments eventually led to specialized publication, but no ideologically announced, formally distinct body of law emerged. This was probably because the relevant concepts of the offense and the sentence were not fully differentiated and because sentence adjustments stemming from the nature of the official offender were perceived as part of a broad, mixed area of considerations integral to the penal code.

There was specialization in the procedures, notably in the existence of a special sort of disciplinary inquiry distinct from a trial, but announcing a disciplinary offense had the same legal form (impeachment) as announcing a crime. The differentiation of the clients also was not complete in the sense that *ch'u-fen* law applied not only to active officials.

The following description leans on the 1887 edition of the *ch'u-fen tse-li* but is roughly applicable to the whole Ch'ing period, and the major historical changes are discussed. It should be noted that my discussion does not deal with impeachments leading to criminal sentences and focuses on the questions of communication, clients, and procedures. The other aspects of the administrative structure do not require separate discussion.

a. Publication

Increasing specialization in the publication of *ch'u-fen* law was a significant development. Much *ch'u-fen* law was always found in the penal code, but there was a gradual effort to pull together the increasing number of *ch'u-fen* articles, especially those outside the penal code. Separate *ch'u-fen* chapters probably came first, and then separate *ch'u-fen* books appeared, some in tabular form and some merely listing the laws.

While the *ming-li* (principles of sentencing)[1] section of the penal code included articles specifying the basic procedures of administrative punishment, the rest of the code contained not only many articles dealing with specific serious crimes by officials but also many articles dealing with the lighter offenses. Punishments for the latter were specified either as blows of the bamboo, which were routinely commuted into administrative sentences, or directly as administrative sentences. There was no tendency to segregate in separate sections either the lighter official offenses from the heavier, or offenses by officials from those by other people. Rather the main principle of topical division was that of the six boards, and all offenses by persons of all statuses involving the affairs of a particular board were mixed together within the chapters devoted to that board.

Naturally the two chapters under the Board of Civil Officials are devoted to offenses by officials and clerks. Many articles in the first, *chih-chih* (institutions of office), deal with offenses in obtaining and leaving official positions, such as making unauthorized appointments, deceptively memorializing the emperor to grant a noble rank to an official without outstanding merit, deceptively memorializing the emperor to recommend for office an official previously barred permanently from office, and leaving one's post without authorization. Many articles in the other chapter, *kung-shih* (general rules), deal with offenses involving state documents and seals, such as failing the annual examination on understanding the penal code, disobeying or losing an edict, not memorializing when one should, and not properly stamping official communications with one's office seal.

Practically any other chapter of the code, however, also contains articles on official offenses. For instance laws on mistakes or crimes committed by officials with respect to water control works are in the Board of Works' section; offenses in carrying

1. See II, 3, note 78.

out judicial affairs are in the Board of Punishments' section, as are the crimes of bribery and theft; and the misuse of state funds and abuses in tax collection are in the Board of Revenue section.

Articles on *ch'u-fen* were also published outside the penal code since at least the K'ang-hsi period. Clearly such articles were excluded from the penal code, just as were numerous minor criminal precedents (called *shih-li*), because they lacked sufficient general importance. Also, since all *ch'u-fen* were always centrally applied through the Department on the Scrutiny of Merits in the Board of Civil Officials, typically without consultation with the Board of Punishments, and since this department handled administrative rewards as well as punishments, it was natural to publish administrative rewards and punishments in one text. (The penal code seems to lack a single article on administrative rewards.)

Until the middle part of the eighteenth century, however, such articles were scattered throughout the regulations of different boards instead of being collected as a subsection of the regulations of the Board of Civil Officials (and the Board of War). For instance the first two editions of *Ta-Ch'ing hui-tien* (Collected statutes of the great Ch'ing dynasty), completed respectively in 1690 and 1733, present a good number of *ch'u-fen* in the Board of Civil Officials' section entitled "Department for the Scrutiny of Merits." However the *ch'u-fen* here are limited to a few topics such as the periodic evaluations of officials. In both volumes, under the heading of that office, there is a section called *ch'u-fen tsa-li* (miscellaneous regulations on administrative punishment), which begins with the following significant note:

> The administrative punishments related to civil governmental duties are the function of the Department for the Scrutiny of Merits. Relative to each office, entries are classified by subject [in the various sections of this book]. The regulations on administrative punishment are added to the basic articles [in these various sections] in order to facilitate reference. If an official is to be impeached, the matter is referred to the Department for the Scrutiny of Merits, which deliberates on it and replies. As for those articles which involve peculiar circumstances or divergences between regulations or which cannot be completely entered under the

[headings for the various] offices, they are appended here.[2]

In other words, this section on "miscellaneous regulations on administrative punishment" was viewed as a residual category, and *ch'u-fen* law as a whole was not viewed as an editorially distinct entity. Most *ch'u-fen* articles were in fact scattered throughout these books under the headings of the various boards, being appended to administrative articles specifying positive performance requirements. For instance, *ch'u-fen* related to late delivery and other shortcomings in tax collection are in that part of the Board of Revenue section specifying tax collection procedures.[3]

Ta-Ch'ing hui-tien tse-li (1763) (see III, 5) is the earliest book examined by this writer in which *ch'u-fen* articles are pulled together as a distinct subsection of the regulations of the Board of Civil Officials. However, it is possible that the earliest book with this format is the 1742 edition of *Li-pu tse-li* (Regulations of the Board of Civil Officials): it has a section called *ch'u-fen tse-li.* Even though there was at least one earlier edition, that of 1734, it is suggestive that the organizational change made in the preparation of the 1742 edition—whereby the work was taken from the *Lü-li kuan* (Bureau for the preparation of the penal code), which had put out the 1734 edition, and given solely to the Board of Civil Officials—was based partly on the need for specialized knowledge in editing the *ch'u-fen* (see II, 4). Behind this change, one can sense the outlook of the Ch'ien-lung emperor, which, on the whole was favorable to editorial innovation (see I, 6).[4]

During the following century, it is clear, the *ch'u-fen tse-li* continued to come out as a section of the various editions of *Li-pu tse-li.* Editions of the latter were coming out once every ten years by the time of the 1790 edition, a schedule which ceased with an edition apparently put out in 1824, before that 1830 edict which partly interrupted the publication of the boards' *tse-li* in general. In 1832 and 1836 small numbers of revised *tse-li* were promulgated, but the next edition was put out

2. *TCHT* (1690), 12:1; *TCHT* (1733), 18:1.

3. *TCHT* (1733), 33:10.

4. In *Tseng-ting tse-li t'u-yao pien-lan* (The enlarged regulations [on administrative punishment]: essentials in tabular form, a digest to facilitate scrutiny; 1792), the 1790 preface of Shih Chung-yin refers to a 1742 edition of *ch'u-fen tse-li.* Presumably this is the same book as the 1742 *Li-pu tse-li.*

only in 1843; it included the *ch'u-fen tse-li* in full. As with the penal code, the schedule of publication was disrupted during the last half century of the dynasty. An edition came out in 1872, but this did not consist of true *tse-li* (regulations), only various new rules (*chang-ch'eng*) needed for reference. One of the four parts of this book was devoted to *ch'u-fen*.[5]

The initial splitting off of the *ch'u-fen tse-li* to form a separate book may have been the 1776 edition of *Tse-li t'u-yao* (Essentials in table form of the regulations [on administrative punishment]). There were a number of later editions, including that of 1790, compiled by Shih Chung-yin, and that of 1792, compiled by Wang Yin-t'ing and Ch'en Ko-t'ang. The latter was definitely a private effort, and the others almost certainly were too, since such digests were not typically put out by the government.[6]

The 1792 edition, called *Tseng-ting tse-li t'u-yao pien-lan* (Enlarged regulations [on administrative punishment]—essentials in tabular form presented to facilitate scrutiny), has an arrangement which facilitates comprehension and cuts reading time. Heavy lines and spatial arrangements are used to make quickly obvious which pieces of information go together. For instance the middle of one page is taken up from top to bottom with a column headed "Delays by governors-general and/or governors in presenting guaranteed recommendations of candidates for posts under them." Under this heading, the column is split vertically in half. The right-hand side of the column sums up what these high officials are to do; the left-hand side gives the administrative punishments for not doing it, including a highly readable table correlating degrees of lateness to the amounts of the fines.

Since punishment often involved more variables than the degree of the offense, tables often were more complicated. The tables in a similar 1872 edition pay much attention to the question of the public or private nature of the offense and that of the various offices implicated, such as superior offices guilty of lack of vigilance.[7]

5. Ma Feng-ch'en, pp. 53–56; *CFTL, tsou-shu; Li-pu tse-li* (1843), *yüan-tsou*:5b; see I, 6.

6. Information on the 1776 and earlier editions is available in prefatory material in *Tseng-ting tse-li t'u-yao pien-lan.*

7. *Ch'u-fen tse-li t'u-yao* (Essentials in tabular form of the regulations on administrative punishment; 1872).

The earliest separate publication of a straightforward edition that I have seen was issued by the Board of Civil Officials in 1828.[8] Private versions probably also came out by this time. A private version prepared in 1869 by one Shen Chiao-sheng and Sun Mei-shan almost certainly was such a straightforward presentation, not a digest in table form. These compilers stated that they had put out their work because previous bookstore editions of the *ch'u-fen tse-li,* unlike those of the penal code, had not kept up with changes in the law.[9] The first revision after 1869 appeared in 1887. This 1887 edition was semiprivate in that it was endorsed by the emperor and issued by the Board of Civil Officials but actually was compiled outside the Board by one Tu Huan-ch'en. The demand for this book is indicated by the fact that a private publishing firm in Shanghai reprinted it in 1892.

The 1887 edition has sixteen chapters under "Board of Civil Officials," twelve chapters under "Board of Revenue," ten chapters under "Board of Punishments," six chapters under "Board of War," six chapters under "Board of Rites," and two chapters under "Board of Works." Nearly all the book specifies punishments for offenses by provincial and capital officials with regard to the various kinds of activities associated with the various boards, but some chapters also deal with connected provisions of administrative law, including the procedures through which the Board of Civil Officials was to determine and apply administrative sentences.

These procedural rules are found almost entirely in the first two chapters, *kung-shih* (general regulations), and *chiang-fa* (demotions and salary fines). We can discern four main procedural topics: the mechanics of office procedures, such as deadlines; basic rules, such as the hierarchy of priority in searching texts; problems affecting the degree of guilt or responsibility of the offender; and problems in carrying out the sentence. For a Westerner to grasp the concrete interrelations of the various articles, it is perhaps necessary to group them under such categories, but clearly Ch'ing officials could master these procedural articles in that more arbitrary sequence whereby they were entered in these two chapters.

In some instances it is not clear why one article is in "general

8. *Ch'in-ting hsin-tsuan liu-pu ch'u-fen tse-li* (1828).
9. *CFTL, hsü*: 1–2.

rules" instead of "salary fines and demotions." For instance the main laws on canceling off "added subgrades" and "commendations" against salary fines and demotions are in "general rules," but the special problem of canceling off administrative punishments so small that there was no equivalent administrative reward is handled in "demotions and salary fines." In the synoptic explanation of *Ta-Ch'ing hui-tien,* all these questions concerning canceling off are put on one page.[10]

These two chapters also deal to a small extent with matters outside these adjudicative procedures of the Board of Civil Officials. They both deal with some connected procedures of other offices, and "general rules" includes some non-procedural articles specifying punishments, such as eight major laws from the penal code (for example, the punishment for disobeying an edict). Still, these two chapters, in contrast to the rest of the book, clearly specialize in the procedural aspects of the law on administrative punishment. Other chapters, their subject matter fairly obvious from their titles, deal more with substantive and specific offenses by the various capital and provincial offices. For instance, the third chapter, *sheng-hsüan* (promotion and appointment), deals with deadlines and other obligations relative to the filling and vacating of offices, and chapter four, *chü-ho* (recommending and impeaching), deals with obligations in recommending persons to office and in impeaching them.

In sum, then, once the principle was established, in the middle of the eighteenth century, of printing the *ch'u-fen tse-li* as a separate unit, officials, at various times, could find them in the three editions of *Precedents and Regulations Supplementary to the Collected Statutes of the Great Ch'ing Dynasty,* the editions of *Regulations of the Board of Civil Officials,* and specialized books or digests devoted to them. Moreover, various specialized administrative manuals such as salt gazetteers or manuals for the grain tribute often had sections of *ch'u-fen* pertinent to their subject matter. Also the continuing role of the penal code must not be forgotten. For instance, if the *ch'u-fen tse-li* (and clearly also the *t'iao-li* of the penal code) lacked a directly appropriate article, the *lü* were the first text which was to be searched. In case of conflict between the *ch'u-fen tse-li* and the penal code, as with the sections on dike bursts (see IV, 4, d), the *ch'u-fen tse-li* clearly had primacy. In one instance

10. *CFTL,* 1:6–12b; 2:37a–b; *TCHT,* 11:3.

the Ch'ien-lung emperor considered whether to eliminate an article in the *ch'u-fen tse-li* which also happened to be a *lü* (penal statute), but in deciding to retain it he did not even mention that it was a *lü*.[11]

Finally, at least in the middle part of the nineteenth century, publication, whether private or governmental, lagged well behind office records. Yet the large amount of publishing that was done, not to mention the fact that private bookstores felt a demand and that digests were put out ingeniously designed to speed comprehension, indicates that there was a widespread need among officials to understand and apply these regulations carefully. Besides the penal code, few books of law, if any, were privately published. Along with the penal code, the *ch'u-fen tse-li* were one of the very few administrative handbooks overarching the activities of virtually all civil offices and calling for the attention of practically all civil officials, no matter what office they held. As Tu Huan-ch'en said in his preface to the 1887 edition: "If those who undertake to fill an office do not study this book, they will lack the standards which their actions should follow; if those who undertake to assist officials [that is, private secretaries] do not study this book, they will lack [knowledge of the laws they ought] to quote. There is no need to dwell on this point."

Printing *ch'u-fen* as a unit must have increased their impact on administrative action by facilitating study of them. Whether the large amount of attention paid to them diverted officials from the real needs of administration, as some officials claimed, is another question.

11. *TLti*, 8:1. *CFTL*, 14:3a–b. On the primacy of the *tse-li*, see III, 3, note 43, and IV, 3, c, and 4, e.

b. The Status of the Offender

Ch'u-fen law mainly applied to officeholders, sometimes called *hsien-jen-kuan* (officials currently holding office), and virtually any other persons carrying out official jobs, wherever these jobs were located along our spectrum of regularity (see IV, 3, b). However, one can speak of two dimensions of diffuseness of application: persons without an official job but with some connection either to activities of a public nature or to official status sometimes also were affected by some aspects of *ch'u-fen* law. This point, however, should be phrased more precisely. Since *ch'u-fen* law had in fact no strictly defined boundaries, we can only say that certain concepts and legal procedures basic in *ch'u-fen* law were also used in the legal cases of some persons lacking jobs with an official status.

The concept of *kung-tsui* (public offense), so basic in *ch'u-fen* law, was sometimes applied to persons lacking official jobs but having duties of a public nature. Three examples can be given. First, if clerks or other low-status governmental employees committed a public offense punishable by up to a hundred blows of the heavy bamboo, they received the blows and kept their jobs. If the offense was a private one and punishable by sixty heavy bamboo blows or more, they received the blows and also lost their jobs.[1]

Second, if members of Buddhist or Taoist orders committed serious crimes including "all offenses involving illicit taking of wealth or other matters of corrupt self-interest (*ssu-tsui*)," they were to be returned to lay life. However, if they were guilty only of "mistakes involving public matters," they could retain their religious status.[2]

Third, the concept of *kung-tsui* (public offense) was sometimes applied to licensed salt merchants. Such merchants at the Liang-huai zone, after receiving permits to buy salt at the production yards, were given forty-five days to go to the yards and bring the salt back to a certain inspection point (the North Bridge), which was on the way from the yards to the central depot of I-cheng. Arriving late at the North Bridge was called

1. *TCLL,* 4:18–19; Philastre, I:138–139. The word here used for clerks and other low-status governmental employees is *li-tien.* Another example of *li-tien* is in Cheng Ching-i and P'eng Shih, I:438. If a defendant confessed his guilt, *li-tien* were not permitted to write his confession out for him.

2. *TCLL,* 4:7; Philastre, I:113.

wei-hsien kung-tsui (the public offense of violating the time limit). The sentence was some blows of the heavy bamboo, obviously commuted to a fine.[3]

Another example also pertaining to these Liang-huai salt merchants was that of *i-chin kung-tsui* (the public offense of carrying catties of salt beyond the legal limit). According to this law, Huai-nan salt bags going from the production areas to I-cheng were inspected for excess weight. Besides confiscating the excess salt and levying fines, the state convicted the merchant involved under the catchall article in the penal code covering the offense of "doing what ought not to be done." The resulting sentence, calling for beating with the heavy bamboo, was commuted to a fine.

The "public" character of this offense was quite similar to that of the public offenses of officials, since in the salt merchants' case also, the force of circumstances made it difficult to act legally, as was recognized by officials. This was because during the long trip in leaky boats to I-cheng, the salt bags easily changed weight, especially because of variations in dampness. The problem here was the typical disciplinary one of exerting control in a situation where it was hard to distinguish between corrupt motives and the force of circumstances. The Ch'ing had inherited this use of *kung-tsui* from the Ming, and the Board of Revenue (in 1660) viewed it as an effective added deterrent against overpacking salt bags, but it was problematic. Small-scale traders whose total costs per shipment were only some thirty to forty taels found themselves paying fines for this *kung-tsui* of twenty to thirty taels, which were larger than the fines for the much more serious offense of smuggling several thousand catties, and merchants with large shipments paid the same fine as did those with little ones. To correct this felt injustice, a law of 1660 specified a relatively small, absolute sum (four taels) as the fine for any merchants shipping small amounts of salt (fifty *yin* or less) and convicted of the public offense of carrying thirty excess catties or less per *yin*. However, there were other impracticalities as well, and the whole added deterrent of this *kung-tsui* sentence was abolished in about 1677.[4]

3. *LHYFC*, 11:5.

4. A helpful account of this law is in *Liang-huai yen-fa-chih* (1904), 93:11b–12b, but it is frequently referred to in documents of the time found in earlier editions of the same work. See, e.g.,

For the sake of completeness, one should also mention that the reward system or nomenclature connected to *ch'u-fen* law also affected nongentry involved in public affairs. Thus *i-hsü* (to advise on administrative rewards), the standard complement of *i-ch'u* (to advise on administrative punishment), could refer to honors bestowed, say, on merchants or common people who had made financial contributions for relief.[5]

We may now turn to the second dimension of diffuseness: the use of impeachment or administrative sentences in the cases of persons with a loose connection to official status rather than to public duties.[6] This involved considerations of solidarity.

LHYFC, 11:3–7. The inspections involved here were, at first, those at the North Bridge and the Southern Barrier, which were two points between the two major junctions at Taichow and I-cheng. However, in about 1658, the inspection at the Southern Barrier was abolished for reasons not relevant here. As for the fine merchants paid for excess salt, apart from the sentence for *kung-tsui*, it totaled .016 tael per excess catty, including the fine at I-cheng.

5. *TYT*, 45:27b; 48:2.

6. This discussion is based on what might be called the organic *ch'u-fen* articles, found in the *ming-li* section of the penal code. Apart from the question of amnesties (see IV, 1, note 54), the *ming-li* section includes, first of all, seven *lü* largely specializing in the punishment of officials currently holding office. All except the seventh have at least one *li* (penal regulation) attached to them. Proceeding according to their order in the book, we first find the most basic article, "when officials commit an offense," which held that the arresting and sentencing of an official required imperial approval. See *TCLL*, 4:16–17b; Philastre, I:135–137. Immediately following this *lü* are two others, giving the rates for commuting criminal into administrative sentences for public and private offenses, respectively. See *TCLL*, 4:18–19b; Philastre, I:138–141. These *lü* are discussed above (IV, 1, note 84). The four other *lü* are of less general importance: *wu-kuan fan-tsui* (if the offense was committed before taking office), *TCLL*, 4:26a–b, and Philastre, I: 148–149; *ch'u-ming tang-ch'ai* (removing names [from status registers] and having persons carry out labor and other services for the government), *TCLL*, 4:27a–b, and Philastre, I:149–151; *t'ung-liao fan kung-tsui* (if a public offense is committed in affairs carried out jointly by official personnel), *TCLL*, 5:23a–b, and Philastre, I: 225–229; and *kung-shih shih-ts'o* (if there is a mistake in public matters), which deals with officials and clerks who reveal their own offenses, *TCLL*, 5:24a–b, and Philastre, I:229–231. Of the above seven *lü* with their attached *li*, one *li*, which is under *chih-kuan yu-fan*, deals not with officeholders but with persons merely holding certain degrees. Besides these seven *lü*, there are three relevant

As the penal code put it in one connection, an official whose relative was being tried would *t'i-hsü* (pity him, feeling as though in his place).[7]

The extension of the procedures of impeachment to such persons is evident, in the first place, from the relation of the main *lü* relating to officeholders, *chih-kuan yu-fan* (when officials commit an offense), to that called *i-li ch'ü-kuan* (officials who have left office for a valid reason). The former in effect defined what is usually called "impeachment" as that judicial process whereby imperial permission is required to arrest and try an official, and also no sentence can be applied without prior imperial approval. As we know from the 1725 imperial executive order changing it, this *lü* was designed as the basic article for carrying out administrative punishments relative to officeholders (see IV, 4, c).

The other *lü*, *i-li ch'ü-kuan*, extended these privileges regarding arrest, trial, and sentencing to officials who had left office temporarily or permanently in a proper way (for example, retired officials and officials between posts); officials who had left office on account of some trouble and with a demotion but who still retained their grade patent (generically called *kao-ch'ih*); and those relatives of an official who had honorary titles derived from his grade patent. This derivation worked as follows: officials of grade seven and up counted their father, mother, and wife; those of grade three or more added their paternal grandparents, and those of grade one added their paternal great-grandparents.[8] If a woman had been divorced from an official and had not remarried, she evidently lost any legal privileges deriving from his grade, but she derived such privileges from her son, if the latter was an official of grade seven or more.[9]

Under *i-li ch'ü-kuan*, officials' children had no legal privileges. However, virtually the same privileges as those above—arrest,

---

articles in the *shu-hsing* (redemption of criminal punishments) section of the *ming-li*, two of which deal with officials, and one with mere degree holders. These three articles are discussed in IV, 3, c. One should also take into consideration the *pa-i* (eight conditions for consideration) section of the *ming-li*; *TCLL*, 4:10–15, and Philastre, I:127–135. On the *pa-i*, also see Ch'ü, *Law and Society in Traditional China*, pp. 177–179.

7. *TCLL*, 4:16.

8. *TCHT*, 12:7b–8.

9. *TCLL*, 4:25; Philastre, I:145–148.

trial, and sentence all contingent on imperial approval—applied to the children and grandchildren of those officials qualifying under the *pa-i* (eight conditions for consideration). These categories included imperial relatives and officials of special distinction favored by being classed under one of the eight conditions, such as having "merit."

Even if not classed under the eight conditions, officials could extend some legal privileges to their sons and grandsons if they themselves had grade five or four (or above, presumably), and if these descendants of theirs had derived *yin-sheng* (government student through inheritance) titles from them. Arrest of these *yin-sheng* might or might not require impeachment, but they could not be convicted and sentenced without imperial approval.

This same degree of privilege was also extended to maternal grandparents, paternal aunts and uncles, paternal uncles' wives, brothers and sisters, and brothers' children in the case of those persons qualifying under the highest of the eight conditions: certain imperial relatives, high-ranking concubines, husbands of princesses, and officials with "merit."[10]

Retired officials received administrative sentences, although these had to be adjusted. For instance, a grade demotion meant only a replacement or removal of one's grade button. Similarly the sentence of an official's female relative who had an honorary title derived from his grade patent (*ming-fu*) could be carried out through commutation into salary fines, following the rate schedule in the two *lü* "If civil or military officials commit a public offense" and "If civil or military officials commit a private offense." The amount she paid depended on the salary of the official from whom she had derived her title, whether her husband, son, grandson, or great-grandson.[11]

On the other hand, the extension of these judicial privileges to idle and retired officials or such official relatives was not always complete. If an official was guilty of some form of illicit taking of wealth while an official and the offense was found out after he was dismissed from office, he was to be arrested without an impeaching memorial, although he still had the privileges of an official with regard to the commutation of the sentence.[12]

10. *TLti,* 1:45, 49b. See IV, 4, b, note 6, on *pa-i.*

11. *TCHT,* 11:7a–b.

12. *TLti,* 2:14; *TCLL,* 4:26b; Philastre, I:149. The text says: "If while an official he illicitly obtained wealth and the matter was

Apart from officeholders, certain of their relatives, and permanently or temporarily retired officeholders, the procedures of impeachment were used in the treatment of some mere degree holders. While there was a variety of degree holders, the penal code focused on *chin-shih* (metropolitan graduates), *chü-jen* (provincial graduates), and *sheng-yüan* (government students), all of whom had obtained their degrees through examinations; *kung-sheng* (imperial students), whose titles were sometimes purchased;[13] and *chien-sheng* (students of the imperial college), whose titles always were purchased. Generally speaking, adjudicative procedures regarding mere degree holders were carried out by the adjudicative structure used for commoners supplemented by the role of the local director of studies, the provincial director of studies, the special attention of the governor or governor-general, and that of the Board of Rites. While degree holders enjoyed conditions of sentence commutation roughly comparable to that of officials,[14] they also at times enjoyed the privilege of impeachment, but this largely depended on the severity of the offense involved.

If the offense involved a sentence of less than a hundred strokes of the heavy bamboo, there generally was no impeaching memorial. In the case of *chin-shih, chü-jen,* and *kung-sheng,* the magistrate allowed redemption of the sentence. In the case of *sheng-yüan* and *chien-sheng,* there was an alternative procedure: the local magistrate notified the local director of studies, who "warned" the culprit, a process evidently involving beating. Hsüeh Yün-sheng complained that the code was not clear on which of these alternative procedures was used when. At least in the "warning" case, the provincial director of studies was notified. When guilty of such light, redeemable offenses, a *chien-sheng* or a *sheng-yüan* could still lose his de-

---

found out after he was dismissed . . ." The implication is that the dismissal was for some other misdeed. Conversely, if such a crime had been committed before and was discovered after the culprit became an official, he was impeached as an official, but was sentenced as a commoner.

13. To what extent *kung-sheng* refers to a purchased title is not always clear. See Chang, *The Chinese Gentry,* pp. 19, 4–5; and Ch'ü, *Local Government in China under the Ch'ing,* p. 20.

14. See discussion of the Ch'ing developments in redemption practices in IV, 3, c.

gree; this was decided on through consultation with the Board of Rites.

If the offense was one punishable by one hundred heavy bamboo strokes or more, a *chin-shih, chü-jen, kung-sheng, chien-sheng,* or idle official was to lose his rank, and this involved a memorial. The local magistrate through his superiors notified the top provincial authorities, who memorialized to "impeach" (*ts'an*) the guilty degree holder.[15] There are other examples of such impeachments. One regulation, which significantly is in the *ch'u-fen tse-li,* states if military or civil *chin-shih, chü-jen, kung-sheng, chien-sheng,* or *sheng-yüan* (as well as idle or retired officials) refuse to pay their land taxes, the local magistrate is to report the matter through his superiors to the governor and/or governor-general, who in turn are to impeach these offenders, the punishment being removal of title and wearing of the cangue.[16]

15. *TLti,* 1:49b–50b; *TCLL,* 4:16b; *TLti,* 1:28a–b; *TCLL,* 4:8a–b. See also Ch'ü, *Law and Society in Traditional China,* pp. 182–183.

16. *CFTL,* 15:30b–31.

c. The Initiation of Impeachment

In Ming times and until the Yung-cheng emperor changed three *lü* in 1725–1727, a large part of the process of bureaucratic discipline was handled in a decentralized fashion through the discretion of superior officials who could arrest and sentence their subordinates without impeaching them, that is, without memorializing on the offense and receiving imperial approval of the punishment. However the nature of the superior official's discretion was a complicated matter which must be looked at in terms of not only this Ming *lü* on the right to arrest and sentence officials but also the two Ming *lü* on the nature of the sentences;[1] all three *lü* were changed in 1725–1727.

In many instances, arrests could be carried out without requesting imperial permission, unlike the situation after 1727. However, even though sentences in many cases could also be decided without requesting imperial permission, the inherent nature of many of these sentences was such that the actual deprivation took effect only through the action, every nine years, of a capital office. Thus on the one hand, many of these sentences were really effected in a centralized fashion at the capital. On the other hand, the fact that there often was a large time lag between the offense and the final effecting of the sentence, in contrast to the swifter sequence after 1727, suggests looser centralization.

All cases of the arrest and sentencing of officials in which the sentence was only a salary fine, redemption, or making a record of the offense (*chi-lu*) were to be carried out without a memorial. This covered a wide range of offenses, since it covered many or virtually all administrative mistakes—it covered all public offenses punishable by up to a hundred strokes of the heavy bamboo and all private offenses through forty strokes of the light bamboo. Moreover, in the case of redemption or salary fines, the deprivation was directly inflicted without delay by the superior. When, however, the superior made a record of the offense (*chi-lu*)—the punishment for the more serious public offenses and for private offenses through forty strokes of the

1. *Ming-lü chi-chieh*, 1:11–13, 19–23. The Ch'ing changes in these *lü* can be looked up in *chüan* 726 of *TCHTSL* under the titles of the *lü*: *chih-kuan yu-fan*, *wen-wu-kuan fan kung-tsui*, and *wen-wu-kuan fan ssu-tsui*. Changes in the latter two are discussed further in IV, 2, note 84.

heavy bamboo—the deprivation was not immediate. Such records were sent to the capital once a year, and every nine years were considered in determining whether the official was to be promoted, demoted, or dismissed.

Any sentence of transfer or dismissal—these were immediately imposed for more serious private offenses—required imperial approval, but in some instances officials charged with such private offenses could be arrested without imperial approval. Such arrests on official discretion could not be carried out relative to capital officials and higher officials in the provinces, but they could be carried out for officials in the provinces of grade six or less, such as district magistrates, so long as they were made by certain offices such as the Provincial Surveillance Office and that of regional inspector; district magistrates could not be thus arrested by their direct superiors such as the Provincial Administration Office.

The memorial of 1725 reducing this broad scope of discretion stated: "Today if officials commit an ordinary, minor offense and ought to be summoned and questioned, then one summons and questions them. If they ought to be impeached in a *t'i-pen*-type memorial, then such a memorial is presented whether the matter is major or minor. With regard to punishments such as salary fines, in all instances a *t'i-pen*-type memorial is presented to resolve the case."

The new *lü* thus required permission from the emperor to arrest and try any official, but in 1753 a concession was made relative to timing. If the impeached official had a rank lower than that of taotai or prefect, the impeaching superior could arrest and begin to try him on the same day that the impeaching memorial was sent off, without waiting for the emperor's answer.[2] As has been mentioned, some superior officials still had the discretion to issue merits and demerits, which when added up could lead to impeachment and an administrative sentence; to summon an official for questioning; and to "remove" an official from his post, remove his button and his seal of office, "detain" him, and temporarily replace him (IV, 3, c).

As we have noted, the initiation of impeachment was a greatly diffused responsibility, and in the provinces at least, the

2. *TCLL,* 4:16b–17; *TLti,* 1:50b.

Censorate played little more than the role of a backstop.[3] Impeachments were initiated at any time by the offender; by a colleague, superior, or office outside the offender's chain of command such as the Censorate; or by the emperor. Officials who lacked the general right to memorialize reported offenders to their superiors with a request to impeach them. This was the practice, for instance, of prefects who were responsible for supervising the financial management of local magistrates under them.[4] Complaints by commoners or gentry could also stimulate an impeachment.[5] Subordinate officials at times acted to impeach superiors.[6]

A 1750 edict ordered governors and governors-general "generally" to use *t'i-pen*-type memorials in making impeachments. Pointing out that such matters should not be handled secretly, the emperor did not disapprove of the practice of first impeaching in a *che-tsou,* which was secret or semisecret, and then put-

3. See IV, 2. This point about the capital-based role of the Censorate is reinforced by a piece, apparently a memorial, written by Ch'u Fang-ch'ing, a *chin-shih* of 1667. He speaks here of two main lines of authority in the state: one goes through the six boards and the regular provincial offices; the other consists of the circuit censors, the Censorate's Six Sections for the Scrutiny of Metropolitan Officials, and two types of officials abolished by early Ch'ing times. One was a kind of judge (*t'ui-kuan*), and the other, called *hsün-fang* and abolished already under the Shun-chih emperor, was used to check the power of the governors and governors-general. The circuit censors and the Six Sections, in Ch'u's view, check "board officials." See *HCCSWP,* 18:7b–8. Ch'u's view is significant in trying to define two main lines of authority, one of which largely ceased to exist outside the capital after early Ch'ing times when the *hsün-fang* and *t'ui-kuan* were abolished. His view corroborates my strong impression that Ch'ing regional surveillance was largely carried out by regular administrative officials.

4. *TLti,* 13:26; *TCHT,* 11:18b–19.

5. *CFTL,* 4:42 refers to impeached officials whose corruption was "reported" by gentry and commoners.

6. The role of subordinates in impeaching was apparently limited. If one grants that governors-general, governors, and provincial treasurers and judges formed three levels in the chain of command, then it is significant that governors had the duty of impeaching a "corruptly avaricious" governor-general, but provincial treasurers and judges did not have the duty of impeaching either a corruptly avaricious governor-general or such a governor; see *CFTL,* 4:42. On the other hand, as is clear from the discussion of appeal in IV, 4, e, subordinates sometimes could act to impeach superiors. See also III, 2, on the need to protect the authority of superiors.

ting the matter into a *t'i-pen*, but he did generally preclude using only *che-tsou*.[7]

The impeaching memorial was answered by an imperial edict or rescript, a process which could be repeated one or more times until the emperor was satisfied with the facts of the case and the verdict. The emperor then through a rescript (*chih*) sent the case to the Board of Civil Officials for sentencing, or just for general processing if the sentence had already been determined in the communications between the impeacher and the emperor.

The emperor himself initiated impeachments using either a *t'e-chih* (special rescript) or *yü* (edict).[8] The Board of Civil Officials itself had little responsibility for initiating impeachments except with regard to the behavior of its own staff and the various personnel activities throughout the empire which it supervised.

While impeachments could arise almost any time, they also were a part of the annual and triannual evaluations of officials. Such institutions of evaluation went back at least to the Ch'in dynasty.[9] The annual *k'ao-ch'eng* (examination of results) typically involved assessing an official's positive and negative achievements in fiscal matters and accordingly recommending administrative honors or punishments. Salt officials, for instance, were mainly evaluated in terms of the amount of salt sold, the taxes collected, and effectiveness in arresting smugglers. The salt controller, branch heads, and supervisors had the same scale of negative sanctions depending on the percentage of the regular tax uncollected, beginning at temporary stoppage of promotion if less than 10 percent was uncollected and ending at dismissal from office for 60 percent or more. If the quotas of the regular tax and of salt to be sold were all met in time for the annual financial report (*tsou-hsiao*), the number of commendations or added grades depended largely on the size of the quota.[10] We have given examples of some specific *k'ao-*

7. *CFTL*, 9:9. The official impeaching could ask for lenient treatment, using *ch'a-i* instead of *i-ch'u* (see II, 3). See also *TWI*, 18:27b, for an example. He could also call for harsh treatment, using *yen-chia i-ch'u*, but not unless the matter really was serious; see *CFTL*, 1:14a–b.

8. *CFTL*, 1:11a–b. *CFTL*, 1:11b, shows the use of edicts by the emperor as does Wang Ch'ing-yün, 5:13a–b. However *TCHT*, 11:15, lists only *t'e-chih* as the emperor's way of initiating an impeachment.

9. See IV, 2.

10. *LHYFC*, 39:1a–b; 10a–b.

ch'eng carried out by T'ao Chu (see IV, 3, b). Interestingly, besides the *k'ao-ch'eng,* T'ao Chu annually sent the emperor a secret memorial with "evaluations" (*k'ao-yü*) of the higher officials under him. These were rounded evaluations of character and ability based on personal impressions and inquiry, not on quantitative criteria.[11]

Apparently less numerous than those stemming from the *k'ao-cheng* (see IV, 3, c), impeachments also resulted from the triannual examinations. These examinations were divided into a "capital examination" (*ching-ch'a*), which covered not only officials at Peking but also the vice-presidents of the five Sheng-ching boards and all governors, governors-general, and directors-general in the provinces; and the "great accounting" (*ta-chi*), which was for other officials in the provinces. In the course of either examination an official could be placed under one of the *liu-fa* (six rules) and accordingly impeached. If one was judged "careless" or "lacking force of character and incapable," the penalty was dismissal from office (*ko-chih*). If the judgment was "inadequate vigor and talent," the penalty was demotion by two subgrades and transfer. If the judgment was "too old" or "ill," the official was forcibly retired (*hsiu-chih*). If the judgment was "unstable," the penalty was demotion by three subgrades and transfer.[12] At the beginning of the Ch'ing period, there had been "eight rules," the two other categories being "cruel" and "avaricious." The term "six rules" appeared by 1738. It was felt that "cruel" and "avaricious" officials, who obviously were wicked, were not such problematic personnel cases as officials in the other six categories. Therefore in the triannual examinations of later times, officials found to be "cruel" or "avaricious" were impeached separately.[13]

11. *TYT,* 52:7–11.
12. *TCHT,* 11:8–15; *CFTL, chüan* 5 and 6.
13. *TCHTSL, chüan* 80:*ta-chi t'ung-li*:Yung-cheng 4, and Ch'ien lung 3; *TCHT,* 11:14b; Ch'ü, *Local Government in China under the Ch'ing,* pp. 33–35.

d. The Determination of the Verdict

The verdict in the triannual examinations was arrived at through either the evaluation of the emperor or that of superiors, with the emperor giving final approval. The highest provincial and capital officials could be evaluated by the emperor without having an audience. The emperor merely evaluated them after receiving their *lü-li* (curriculum vitae) from the Board of Civil Officials. Capital officials of medium rank would usually also have an imperial audience. The process of evaluation by superiors was carried out for both capital and provincial officials of the lower ranks. Often these superiors consulted with other offices or had their evaluations rechecked by other offices.[1] Mostly, therefore, as with the *k'ao-ch'eng*, determination of the judgment or verdict did not require any sort of hearing.

As illustrated by the 1831 Kaoyu dike bursts or by T'ao Chu's own impeachment in 1832, many other kinds of impeachments could also be carried out without any hearing, because there was no question as to the facts. In 1832 there was a major scandal in northern Kiangsu when some persons criminally destroyed a section of a dike, and T'ao Chu impeached himself for failing to "guard against [this crime] in advance." (His sentence was severe: demotion by four subgrades with retention of official duties.)[2] In the 1831 Kaoyu case, there was some disagreement between T'ao Chu and the director-general of the Kiang-nan waterways as to whether or not the officials involved in the dike bursts should be punished. However, this question hung not on the facts but on disciplinary philosophy. Consequently no hearing was needed, but, when T'ao Chu traveled to the scene of the disaster, he interviewed most of the officials involved. Yet sometimes a sort of disciplinary inquiry, distinct in nature from a criminal trial, was held in order to determine the facts and the question of guilt.

This can be illustrated by the interrogation by the Nanking governor-general T'ao Chu, during the winter of 1832–33, of Wang Ch'üan-chih, magistrate of Ningtu, a department in Kiangsi. Wang, a native of Hunan, was a *chin-shih* of 1805. Among local magistrates, he was one of that relatively small group of extremely long-lived "old hands" (see IV, 3, c, Table 1).

1. *TCHT*, 11:8–15b.
2. *TYT*, 42:17b–18.

He had been Ningtu magistrate for about eight years, since 1824. The reason for his interrogation was that he had initiated a large-scale and futile search for a notorious escaped criminal by making reports to his superiors based on incorrect information. The emperor, questioning Wang's efficiency and motives, had ordered T'ao Chu to examine him.[3]

The old case of this escaped criminal, Chu Mao-li, the famous leader of a rebellious sect, had occurred in Kiangsi in 1814, ten years before Wang Ch'üan-chih had taken office at Ningtu, and Wang would never have had any connection with it but for a few accidental circumstances. First, a few days after he had taken office, an unidentified corpse was found in his jurisdiction. With this corpse there were a forged permit or ticket and a type of badge worn around the waist. At least one of these items was stamped with a seal, but Wang could not determine whether or not this seal was a governmental one. As he later testified at his inquiry, this seal reminded him of a forged document, found in the Chu Mao-li case, which appointed someone to an official post. Since this was just speculation, however, he reported at the time that the corpse had no connection to Chu Mao-li. Nevertheless, he obtained copies of certain documents used by Chu Mao-li and his followers and then determined that they did have similarities to the items found with the corpse. No doubt, he now started to have dreams of glory about helping to capture Chu Mao-li.

His interest must have quickened three years later (1827) when he received a letter that Chu Mao-li was in Anhui, raising trouble together with bandits in Honan and Shantung. However he did not act until the winter of 1832–33, when he received two letters that had circulated through the hands of various local magistrates in Kiangsi. They stated that at Yingchow prefecture in Anhui there had been a criminal case of a bandit sect involving twelve men, and that its leader, Chu Mao-li, had escaped. Wang immediately asked higher officials to order a wide search for Chu. At this time Wang also reported his new interpretation of the 1824 case of the unidentified dead man, linking it to Chu Mao-li. Partly because of evidence that this man had spoken with a Fukien dialect, Wang suspected Fukien as well as Anhui as possible locations of Chu Mao-li.

3. The account of this case here is from two memorials of T'ao Chu: *TYT*, 47:1–5, and *TYT*, 52:22–28.

This search not only proved fruitless but also caused a furor. Cutting across provincial lines, it involved communications between the emperor, the governors of Anhui and Fukien, and the Nanking governor-general. It was soon established that there had been no recent Yingchow case involving a bandit sect led by Chu Mao-li. Rather, some years before, in 1827, there had been a case in that area which had generated a false report of Chu Mao-li's whereabouts. One of the criminals then captured had testified that he had seen Chu Mao-li at the home of a person in the Honan district of Lu-i, but investigation had shown that this Chu Mao-li was an impostor, using his guise to induce persons to kowtow and make gifts of money and grain to him. T'ao Chu, the Nanking governor-general, pointed out that the 1832–33 letters received by Wang, which stated that Chu Mao-li had escaped from Yingchow, must have been based on a misunderstanding of this 1827 case. But T'ao Chu also asked that the Fukien and Kiangsi governors look into the origin of these misleading letters.

By late 1833, as this investigation also failed, the emperor had come to suspect Wang's judgment and motivation in raising the alarm on Chu. Ordering T'ao Chu to investigate Wang, the emperor also wanted to know why Wang had changed his story on the corpse discovered in 1824. Moreover, why had Wang not yet solved the 1824 case? Why, if he were genuinely investigating the problem of Chu Mao-li's whereabouts, had he been unable to solve it?

T'ao Chu requested the Kiangsi governor to commission an official to take over Wang's office on an acting basis and ordered Wang to come quickly to Kiangning (Nanking) for the inquiry. At no time was Wang "arrested." Instead, he was merely ordered to appear, and he himself reported on his arrival at the provincial capital. At a trial, his judge would have been a prefect; instead, he had the privilege of being interrogated personally by the governor-general. (The governor-general being out of town when Wang arrived, he instructed the provincial treasurer to begin the inquiry; later he took it up himself.) On the other hand, Wang was questioned repeatedly in an atmosphere of undisguised suspicion, being asked to explain every point raised by the emperor; he spoke under oath (*shih*), and his testimony was referred to in memorials as *kung*, the same word used for testimonies at criminal trials. Moreover the outcome of the inquiry had a formally judicial character. The governor-general reached his verdict tentatively and presented it in a memorial for the emperor's approval, meanwhile ordering Wang to repair to the capital of Kiangsi to await the emperor's decision. The emperor in turn approved the verdict and sent the case to the Board of Civil Officials for sentencing. Naturally the sentence was reviewed by the emperor.

We can say that a decisive characteristic of such a disciplinary inquiry was that the official defendant had not yet been dismissed from office (*ko-chih*). As we have seen, according to a law of 1644, a criminal trial presupposed dismissal (*ko-chih*), at the very least in the case of capital officials. A common phrase illustrating this principle is *ts'an-ko fa-shen* (impeached, dismissed from office, and sent to be tried). Less punitive-sounding words like *ch'a-hsün* (to carry out an inquiry) were usually used to denote disciplinary inquiries (see II, 3), but *shen* (to hold a trial or inquiry), the usual word denoting criminal trials, also could be used.[4]

Wang was cleared by T'ao Chu and the emperor of everything except "rashness," and the emperor ordered the Board of Civil Officials to sentence him lightly (*ch'a-i*). At the inquiry Wang defended his judgment and motivation in raising the alarm. Although the three letters he had received were not themselves stamped with an official seal, he had put confidence in them because on the outside they had been sealed with a stamp similar to an official one. Moreover around the time he had received them, he had read an edict in the *Peking Gazette* warning of the danger of bandit societies and ordering "local magistrates" to act immediately upon receiving any "information" about them. "My office is that of a local magistrate," T'ao Chu paraphrased him, "and since I had received letters, this was a case of there being information. Therefore I sent reports to all relevant offices asking for an investigation." Wang convinced T'ao Chu that he had not acted to seek merit for himself or to create difficulties for other officials but only out of fear that the bandit would escape. Wang also explained the evidence which had caused him to change his interpretation of the corpse's relation to Chu Mao-li. He protested that he had done his best to solve the case of this corpse, now nine years old, and that he could

4. *TCLL*, 4:17 calls for the use of prefects to hold criminal trials for officials such as local magistrates. *CFTL*, 4:53b, shows how *shen* could be used for inquiries that were not criminal trials. For the 1644 law, see IV, 3, a.

not be expected alone to solve the problem of Chu Mao-li's whereabouts.

T'ao Chu's verdict of "rashness," it is clear, hinged partly on the feeling that since all this furor had been caused, some kind of punishment was due simply as a warning, and partly on the feeling that Wang's judgment had been slightly off in acting on the letters. Yet T'ao also indicated that although Wang could have waited for the reply from the governor of Anhui before acting on the letters (this would have cleared up the misunderstanding that Chu Mao-li had just escaped from Yingchow prefecture), "his action also was not entirely without reason." Possibly the Board of Civil Officials determined the sentence by applying the *lü* provision that an official sending a document with a mistake in it to any superior office except one of the six boards received twenty strokes of the light bamboo, if the mistake had "harmed affairs."[5] Since this was a public offense for which the emperor had ordered an especially lenient sentence, the sentence would have been less than a two months' salary fine. Wang must have returned to his post at Ningtu, since he was still there in the winter of 1833–34.[6]

Wang's resumption of his duties is significant, when we recall that his transgression was not an ordinary one; had created much trouble if not embarrassment for his superiors; and had drawn the emperor's anger directly onto him. This lengthy, tension-ridden episode did not break off Wang's long occupancy of a post officially rated as extremely difficult and important. Moreover it is hard to believe that Wang persuaded T'ao to render a favorable verdict by bribing him, and there is no evidence that Wang and T'ao had some other particularistic tie. On the contrary, if one is inclined to be cynical, one would suppose that T'ao's predominant interest in this extremely visible affair was to build up his own reputation as a fair-minded, virtuous official. Already vulnerable to criticism as his Liang-huai salt reform had offended various interests, T'ao would have hesitated further to endanger his reputation in order to protect a lowly magistrate.

Of course, a basic problem in bureaucratic cooperation is whether doubt engenders suspicion or is countered with a reaffirmation of confidence. In Wang's case, superiors reaffirmed

5. *TCLL,* 7:8a–b.

6. *Ta-Ch'ing chin-shen ch'üan-shu,* issue of winter, Tao-kuang 13, 2:75.

confidence in a subordinate caught in a doubtful situation. Yet we cannot be sure his case was typical. Curiously, the idea was not explicitly expressed that the benefit of the doubt should be given to Wang because he had proved his worth through his long tenure at Ningtu.

Our second example is one where determination of the sentence as well as the verdict was partly handled by the provincial officials, although they still acted under the supervision of the Board of Civil Officials.[7] Nearly all of the impeached officials apparently were interviewed by their governor-general, but there clearly was no "disciplinary inquiry" similar to the one above. This impeachment concerns the bursting of two sections of the eastern bank of the grand canal in northern Kiangsu during the major lower Yangtze flood of 1831. This case again illustrates how administrative rather than criminal punishments were used even in some affairs involving serious consequences.

From mid-June 1831 on, coming just after an earlier threat of flood had receded, rain had begun falling continuously in much of the lower Yangtze valley.[8] Within a few weeks, water draining off from several provinces had swollen the Yangtze, flooding its banks in hundreds of places, and also had raised to a dangerous level those lakes in northwest Kiangsu which bordered and partly merged with the grand canal. Here, therefore, increasing pressure was being put on the canal's eastern bank, the dikes and natural elevations of which protected maturing crops in the low-lying areas to the east. The main problem for the two highest officials responsible—T'ao Chu, the Nanking governor-general, and Chang Ching, the director-general of the Kiang-nan waterways—besides that of relief measures throughout much of Kiangsu, was to avoid flooding of the crops in the northeast without endangering the canal's eastern bank. So long as they were confident that this eastern bank could withstand the pressure of the water, they could refrain from opening its sluice gates to relieve that pressure, and so they could protect the crops. But if the pressure threatened to reach the burst-

7. This account is based on *TYT*, 34:24–26, 27–29, 30–34, 37–40; 35:10–18. For maps, see *Kao-yu hsien-chih* (District gazetteer of Kaoyu; 1815), *t'u*:2b–3; *t'u*:6b–7.

8. *TYT*, 34:1–2, 5b, 10. These passages are the chronologically most pertinent to show the receding of the earlier flood threat and the earliest emergence of the new one.

ing point, they had to act quickly to open the sluice gates: otherwise the bank as well as the crops would be destroyed.[9]

This game failed on July 26, when the water, whipped up by sudden rain and strong winds from the west, flooded over and destroyed two sections of the eastern bank north of the city of Kaoyu: a section perhaps half a mile long (250 to 260 *chang*) at *Ma-p'eng-wan* (Ma-p'eng bend), which was about five miles north of the city (30 *li*), and another section perhaps one-tenth of a mile long (50–60 *chang*) and located almost a mile more farther north (5 *li*).[10] Since the sections of the west dike opposite these breaks had long since fallen to ruin, the east bank here had been exposed unprotected to the force of the lakes to the west.[11]

The breaks flooded much of Hsinghua and Yench'eng districts to the east,[12] and although they had the good effect of lowering the pressure on the rest of the east bank, they also made the canal partly unnavigable just at the time that the empty grain tribute boats were about to return south. Since funds were being diverted to relief and since the fall and winter, when the water was very low, was the best time for repairs, repairs could not be started right away, and plans were made partly to detour the grain tribute boats through the lakes to the west, as had been done in the past, despite the danger of their shallowness.[13]

The law on such breaks held that "When heavy flooding and continuous rain destroy dikes or other embankments and the event was not brought about by human action, there is no sentence."[14] This article tended to favor the officials at Kaoyu. On the other hand, if the desire to impeach predominated, articles were available holding officials responsible for such breaks even if there had been no impropriety such as laxness.

These latter articles were not entirely consistent. In the penal code it was provided that the last repairers were held responsible if the break had occurred within three years of their work, the guarders, if after three years.[15] However in the *ch'u-fen tse-li* published a few years before the Kaoyu break (1828 edition),

9. *TYT*, 34:37b.
10. *TYT*, 34:37–38.
11. *TYT*, 35:12b.
12. *TYT*, 34:28.
13. *TYT*, 34:46b–47.
14. *TLti*, 51:5; *TCLL*, 39:5; Philastre, II:745.
15. *TLti*, 51:3–4; *TCLL*, 39:2b–3b.

an article holds guarders responsible also during the first three years. Another problem was restitution. The above penal code article held that whoever were responsible, they had themselves to pay 40 percent of the cost of repairs; the state paid the rest. This regulation clearly goes back to a 1727 edict ordering more compassionate treatment of officials responsible for a water break but guilty of no improper behavior. Previously, even these officials had had to make full restitution. Yet there was also another article calling for no restitution at all, only administrative sentences.[16] Apparently the latter came to have primacy, since impeachments carried out in this 1831 case made no mention of restitution. At any rate, even though the general Kiangsu emergency at first distracted attention from the question of impeachment, the latter hung nervously in the air, soon provoking mutual recriminations.

In the days before the break, the policy of T'ao Chu and Chang Ching had been not to open the four main sluice gates near Kaoyu in order to protect the crops to the east,[17] and the officials at the spot lacked the authority to do so themselves, although they did have the discretion to act quickly in case an emergency struck suddenly. The two civil officials on the spot were Kuang Ch'ien, the acting Kaoyu departmental magistrate, and Chang Hsin-yüan, the second-class subprefect in charge of *Yang-ho t'ing* (Yang-ho subprefecture), a long, narrow jurisdiction along the canal.[18] The Huai-Yang taotai (not, interestingly, the Yangchow prefect) also had some responsibility. He was stationed at Huai-an and was responsible for affairs of the salt monopoly, grain tribute, and coastal defense.[19] Finally four military officials were involved: two higher ones with only broad responsibilities, a lieutenant colonel and a major; and two lower ones with local responsibilities, a second captain heading the *Yang-ho ying* (Yang-ho battalion), a green standard unit, and a lieutenant in charge of *Yung-an hsün* (Yung-an guardpost), probably a subunit of the latter battalion.

As one can see from the fact of their joint report to the governor-general on the day of the disaster,[20] the departmental

16. *Ch'in-ting hsin-tsuan li-pu ch'u-fen tse-li* (1828), 51:1, 22a–b. On the primacy of the *tse-li* over the penal code, see IV, 4, a.

17. *TYT*, 34:30b.

18. *TYT*, 35:12b.

19. *Ch'ing-shih*, II:1393.

20. *TYT*, 35:11b.

magistrate, the subprefecture head, and the captain exercised their responsibilities partly through the typical process of joint decision making, although the magistrate had the final local authority over the sluice gates. All three officials could report directly to the highest provincial official, bypassing the offices between. The lieutenant clearly was one of those indolent officials without any stern sense of moral responsibility, such as we have described above (IV, 2). In the impeachment, T'ao Chu remarked with disgust that in his tours of the area, the lieutenant had never once been present for an interview.[21]

The main leadership problem was that the time lag involved in communicating with the governor-general—who was tied down by affairs at his flooded provincial capital (Nanking) and traveled to the scene only after July 26[22]—aggravated the natural split of interest between the local magistrate and the other officials. As T'ao Chu later indicated, in such a crisis there was likely to be a conflict of interest between the local magistrate sensitive to the demands of the people below a sluice gate to delay opening it and waterway officials mainly interested in preserving their constructions.[23]

Therefore it is not surprising that on July 24, two days before the disaster, T'ao Chu received a report from the Kaoyu magistrate that although the water was still rising, he would not open the four sluice gates so long as the weather was good and no west wind arose. At this time also, T'ao Chu received a report from the lieutenant colonel, the subprefecture head, and the captain asking to open the gates, and T'ao then permitted them to do so quickly.

Even before T'ao's authorization arrived, however, the various officials came to a meeting of minds. On about July 25, the Kaoyu magistrate, the subprefecture head, and the captain made a joint report to T'ao Chu proposing gradually to open all four sluice gates. Again T'ao Chu issued his permission, but his response still had not arrived and the gates had not been opened by July 26, when suddenly heavy rain began and strong northwestern winds arose and the breaks occurred. After the breaks had occurred, and when the crisis seemed to be enlarging, the officials again came to a meeting of minds, agreeing to open the

21. *TYT*, 35:17b.
22. *TYT*, 34:38b, 27b.
23. *TYT*, 35:13b.

gates without waiting for T'ao's permission. At this moment T'ao Chu's permission did arrive.[24]

Yet the gates still were not opened. Just at this point a large crowd of farmers from the area below the gates assembled in front of the Kaoyu magistrate's yamen—after the warning gong announcing the opening of the gates had been sounded, according to the magistrate. The crowd's effect was to rekindle the magistrate's earlier reluctance not to open the gates. At this point the captain and the subprefecture head argued that unless the gates were opened, the whole eastern bank would collapse, and the city itself would be endangered. The magistrate felt that on the contrary, opening the gates before Ma-p'eng bend was repaired would endanger the city. (Apparently one gate was then opened.)

This conflict shortly led to recriminations. Within the next day or so, in a report to T'ao Chu, the captain and subprefecture head said that because the magistrate favored the interests of the farmers, he had been unwilling to "suppress" the crowd, which they put at "several thousand," and it had not been possible to open the gates. The magistrate in turn, estimating the crowd at a more respectable "several hundred," said he had learned from it that Ma-p'eng bend had collapsed because the subprefecture head had failed to strengthen it in advance and had not made an adequate effort to reinforce it when the emergency struck.[25] At any rate, although the magistrate was shortly removed from office for a general failure to master the emergency,[26] he was right in this instance. The break at Ma-p'eng bend so reduced the water pressure that three of the four gates did not have to be opened.[27]

When T'ao first heard of the breaks, he fully ascribed them to the water conditions and had no thought of blaming the officials.[28] Moreover from the content of his memorials it appears that during this first week he was too preoccupied with the

24. *TYT*, 35:11–12b, 16.

25. *TYT*, 35:12b–13; 34:38. The fact that the crowd allegedly was blaming the subprefecture head for the breaks shows that the latter had occurred *before* that meeting when the Kaoyu magistrate and other officials decided to open the gates just as T'ao Chu's order arrived.

26. *TYT*, 34:28b.

27. *TYT*, 34:31, 38b.

28. *TYT*, 35:12b, 16b.

whole Kiangsu crisis to focus on the Kaoyu situation in particular. Not until August 8, when he inspected the breaks close up, did he seem to concentrate on this situation. Although his doubts about the Kaoyu officials were aroused within a couple of days, he did not send off a memorial mentioning the breaks until about one week after the breaks, August 2, and in this memorial he did not touch on these suspicions, merely referring briefly to the breaks and explaining that "because of the great power of the water and the violence of the wind, against which human resources could hardly avail, the bank gave way."

It is significant also that in his edict responding to this news, the emperor did not express anger over the breaks. He did not blame the lower officials involved for any specific shortcomings. He did not blame the highest regional officials for bringing about natural disasters through any failure to "spread *te* (virtue) and practice *jen* (benevolence)." (We should keep in mind that high officials, not just the emperor, could be held responsible for evoking harmonious responses from nature through their *te*.)[29] His main response, at least at first, was just the conventional one of blaming himself. With regard to the flood generally, he said in a vermilion comment: "How sorrowful are these circumstances! One cannot bear to think of them. Of what are the common people guilty! As always, it results from Our lack of virtue."[30] Chang Ching also took the position that the officials involved were not to be blamed and maintained this position as T'ao Chu came to decide in favor of impeachment. Even after insisting on the impeachments, T'ao Chu admitted that these officials had done their best in reinforcing the bank, that once the water had risen above the marker calling for the opening of the gates, they had responsibly asked to open them, and that the suddenness of the storm was responsible for the failure to open the gates before the break.[31] Because of the weight of these considerations, as well as the emperor's request for further explanations, T'ao Chu had to back up his original impeachment memorial with another and a memorial postscript.

T'ao Chu's suspicions were first aroused one or two days after the breaks when he received a report from the Kaoyu magistrate and one from the captain and subprefecture head reflecting

29. *TYT*, 34:24b–26b. For a Ch'ing example of the responsibility of high officials for natural harmony, see IV, 3, c.

30. *TYT*, 34:27b.

31. *TYT*, 35:16a–b.

their disagreement on whether to open the gates after the breaks had occurred and containing their mutual recriminations, which T'ao Chu especially deplored. In a bureaucracy stressing the principle of leadership through a plurality of officials acting in consensus, this sort of disharmony was a major fault. He did not move to impeach them, however, until after he had arrived at Kaoyu.

Arriving there on August 6, he shortly tried to inspect the breaks but was kept at a distance by the roughness of the water. In a memorial sent off on August 7, still concentrating on the general Kiangsu flood situation, he reviewed the adequacy of various provincial officials in meeting this situation. In this context he stated that he was replacing the Kaoyu magistrate, and in a memorial postscript he mentioned that Chang Ching was preparing some impeachments.

On August 8 the water was calmer, and he managed to inspect the breaks closely. As he indicated, this experience, bringing to mind the great cost of repairs, played a large role in influencing him to make the impeachments; however, his earlier disgust with the officials' mutual recriminations had certainly predisposed him against them. That same day he sent off his impeaching memorial.[32]

His position was legalistically or logically inconsistent in Western eyes. The facts as he himself granted them neatly put those officials under the provision: "When heavy flooding and continuous rain destroy dikes or other embankments and the event is not brought about by human action, there is no sentence." Yet in his original impeachment he accused them of "laxness in the matter of guarding embankments," as well as seeking to shift responsibility off onto others.[33] Later, defending his impeachment, T'ao again brought up the charge of laxness and argued more broadly in terms of disciplinary policy. If the officials were not punished, efforts in water control would generally relax. T'ao also used typical ideas in describing the process of punishment and expiation. Referring to two officials who were to be dismissed from office while retaining their duties on a probationary basis, he said that by repairing the damage they were responsible for, they would expiate their faults. After their work was finished, it would be proper to ask the emperor

32. *TYT*, 34:37, 27b, 28b, 30–31b; 35:16.
33. *TYT*, 34:38.

as a "favor" to restore them to office. Those below rectify themselves, while the emperor above, pleased with their efforts, restores to them their previous high status, not as a reward, but as a favor (*en*).[34]

T'ao Chu thus seemed to be saying that although the officials were not really to blame, they had been lax; they had behaved badly in trying to blame one another; and they should be punished, one might say, whether guilty or not simply as a warning to others. Based on moral grounds and disciplinary policy, this view predominated over the rationalistic arguments freeing the officials of legal guilt, even though these rationalistic arguments were obvious at the time.

It is worth noting that in T'ao Chu this kind of severity went together with a marked interest in the effectiveness of his subordinates and in rewarding successful performance. He emphasized performance criteria such as skill in salt affairs or familiarity with a particular region when making recommendations for appointments.[35] Three times in the first half of 1831 he asked that exceptions be made to personnel regulations so that he could retain or obtain efficient officials. In one of these cases he won the grudging consent of the Board of Civil Officials to a temporary but basic change in regulations allowing him to go outside normal channels to obtain capable yard supervisors, the officials immediately over salt production.[36] Possibly it was routine when he elicited from the emperor many promotions and other rewards for the officials who had seen through the passage north of the grain tribute boats in the spring of 1831.[37] T'ao Chu's severity in the Kaoyu impeachments certainly was not based on any simplistic belief in harsh discipline.

The sentences proposed by T'ao Chu for the head of the subprefecture and the captain were dismissal from office with retention of duties on a probationary basis while they directed repairs.[38] These sentences accord with those in the *ch'u-fen tse-li* (assuming that the break occurred after any three-year guarantee period following repairs). Four other officials, including the Kaoyu magistrate, were referred to the Board of Civil Officials for sentencing. The dismissal from office (*ko-*

34. *TYT*, 35:13b–14, 16b–17.
35. See II, 4.
36. *TYT*, 31:47–53; 32:12–14b; 33:35–38.
37. *TYT*, 33:37a–b.
38. *TYT*, 34:38b; 35:17a–b.

chih) received by the lazy lieutenant seems to be an example of the "stretching" of a sentence in the light of particularly reprehensible aspects. Although the *ch'u-fen tse-li* on such breaks call only for the impeachment of the director-general of the waterways (at the highest rung), T'ao Chu also impeached himself for having been "unable to consider the possibility of disaster and to guard against it in advance." It was on September 22 that T'ao Chu received the rescript approving all his impeachments, including his own.[39]

39. *TYT*, 35:14–15b.

e. The Determination of the Sentence

Once the verdict and perhaps the sentence were approved by the emperor, he ordered the Board to handle the matter, using an edict or a special rescript (*t'e-chih*) if he himself had initiated the impeachment, and a rescript if the impeachment had been initiated through a memorial. The Grand Secretariat then delivered a copy of the case to the Board,[1] where the matter was handled by the Department for the Scrutiny of Merits. Of the four directors of this department, three were Manchu, one was Chinese. The Department officials either came to an agreement and drew up a draft of the memorial, or, if they disagreed, presented their various points of view to the presidents and vice-presidents, who then came to a conclusion.[2]

The Department's task, first of all, was finding the appropriate article and paragraph. To do so, it often had to consider various extenuating circumstances and the degree of responsibility inherent in the offender's office. Such considerations were also relevant to specifying the seriousness of the offense within the limits of the article. The Board not only determined—after 1820 largely through prefixed rules—if the offense was public or private. It also advised the emperor on whether to allow the sentence to be canceled off against administrative honors (since cancelling off was not automatic for public offenses) and whether, given the particulars of the case, the sentence should be stretched either way. Finally the Department had to consider aspects of the case other than the seriousness of the offense which affected the nature of the sentence, such as the noble rank of the offender or the fact that his grade was too low to allow the required demotion.[3]

Whether legalistic and rationalistic criteria or moral and disciplinary ones predominated in the determination of the sentence remains unclear. Certainly it is clear that the way in which the law was written (*li-fa*) was largely influenced by rationalistic and legalistic criteria, but, as the Kaoyu impeachments of 1831 show, moral or disciplinary considerations, not to mention corrupt motives, could influence the application of the law (*yung-fa*).

Possibly the amount of rationalism at the Board has been

1. *CFTL*, 1:11b.
2. *TCHT*, 11:1; *CFTL*, 14:10.
3. These problems are discussed above in IV, 3, b and d.

underestimated. One Ch'ing official, arguing that the determination of the sentence was an arbitrary matter dependent on the desires of the clerks, used as an example the fact that any one of four different articles could be applied to punish lateness.[4] In fact, however, there was a procedural article dealing with this situation and specifying that if two (or more) offenses were committed through one act, the offender was to be punished for that offense with the heaviest penalty.[5]

Still, it is not apparent that there were such definite procedures for all other kinds of conflicts, or that the Board always had the expertise to weigh all the relevant articles. For instance the regulation introduced in 1770 restoring the practice of *chüan-fu* (restoration to office by making a contribution) and defining the categories of officials ineligible to *chüan-fu* stated that all officials retired or dismissed by impeachment at the time of the triannual evaluations were ineligible. Then in 1807 a new regulation was established that any such official "impeached" and forcibly retired on account of sickness who later recovered his health could *chüan-fu* by paying 50 percent above the regular amount.[6] However while both the 1828 and 1887 editions of the *ch'u-fen tse-li* list the 1770 law, they do not include the 1807 amendment, not to mention adding a note to the 1770 law to refer the reader to the 1807 amendment and to explain its current status (the sort of note with which Hsüeh Yün-sheng peppered the penal code).[7]

Similarly the 1887 edition of the *ch'u-fen tse-li* prints without comment a regulation set up in 1723 that any salary fine received by a noble holding an office was to apply to his office

4. *HCCSWP*, 15:10b–11.

5. *TCHT*, 11:2; *CFTL*, 1:16.

6. *TCHTSL*, 86:*kuan-yüan k'ai-fu*:Ch'ien-lung 35. This 1770 law both precluded *chüan-fu* for persons retired at a triannual evaluation and allowed it for persons who voluntarily retired on account of sickness when the sickness arose. This latter provision was explicitly the basis for the 1807 amendment, which is in *TCHTSL*, 87: *kuan-yüan k'ai-fu*:Chia-ch'ing 12. This amendment explicitly was based on the precedent of the 1770 provision permitting *chüan-fu* to persons who had voluntarily retired on account of sickness apart from the triannual examinations. Of course, persons impeached for sickness were guilty not just of being sick but of shirking their responsibility to retire.

7. *CFTL*, 2:60, 62; *Ch'in-ting hsin-tsuan li-pu ch'u-fen tse-li* (1828), 2:49.

salary, rather than his usually much larger hereditary salary.[8] Yet this rule was largely superseded by later laws whereby for many nobles the fine applied to their hereditary salary if the offense was a private one.

Such relationships between different articles, however, must, individually, have had obvious answers. Difficulties could arise only through the sheer multitude of such relationships and conflicts, which could never have been mastered without vigorous expertise. Yet there is strong circumstantial evidence that considerable expertise was developed at the Department, especially the fact that some officials did stay in the Department long enough to develop skill in its affairs (see II, 4). Given this probable background of expertise, one cannot lightly dismiss the universalistic, rationalistic philosophy of the Board whereby "one examines the circumstances of the case and then adduces an article correctly and properly. One takes care that the law is adequate to cover the crime and that the punishment is neither too heavy nor too light. Only then does one achieve fairness in the application of the law."[9]

Besides the question of the Board's rationalism, there was the question of the balance of discretion between the Board and the emperor in the determination of the sentence. From the standpoint of the emperors, the Board at various times had tendencies toward both excessive severity and excessive leniency. The interests of the Board did not necessarily go one way or the other. Neither did the Board have any steady interest in increasing its autonomy by reducing imperial interference. Rather the Board apparently had a desire to avoid responsibility for harsh decisions, while the emperor was sometimes torn between two interests: that in maximizing his immediate authority and that in maximizing his popularity, which, he sometimes felt, depended on procedures which put the burden of severe actions on the Board while making himself appear as the source of leniency. Of course, it was a common idea that the officials should be under disciplinary pressure occasionally relieved by "favors" emanating from the emperor. Again we find the tend-

8. *CFTL*, 2:7b–8.

9. *TCHTSL*, 85:*yin-yung lü-li*:Chia-ch'ing 4. This quote actually is directed at use of the penal code, but it is found in a section devoted to *ch'u-fen* law. The rationalistic word *chi* (to calculate) is often used to denote finding the proper *ch'u-fen*.

ency of the emperor to build his power around the theme that he was the source of blessings or favors.

Admittedly, this problem applied little to the question of which article to adduce, since the hierarchy of priority according to which different categories of law were to be searched was fixed by law. If the *ch'u-fen tse-li* and the penal code's *t'iao-li* yielded no directly appropriate article, the Department for the Scrutiny of Merits was to search for one in the text of the *lü* (penal statutes). If this failed, it was to try to analogize first from the former category, then from the latter. If this too failed, it was to formulate a new article on the basis of cases (*an*) and then send the new article to the presidents and vice-presidents of the Board, who made a final decision and memorialized, asking the emperor to establish this new article as a full-fledged regulation (*li*).[10]

Once the article was chosen, however, the sentence could be stretched either way in order to fix the offense more exactly, and there was a question as to whether the sentence should be canceled off against administrative honors. Stretching, which conformed to prefixed margins, could be done either on the initiative of the emperor or that of the Board: the emperor's rescript could call for "advising on severe administrative punishment" (*yen-chia i-ch'u*) or for "examining and advising [on light] administrative punishment" (*ch'a-i*); and the Board itself could make adjustments either way in "all instances where the matter for which administrative punishment is being considered resembles the text of the regulations but the circumstances of the case are different."[11] However, since at least 1730 the emperors consistently insisted that only they, through a special rescript, could call for a doubling of the sentence.[12]

10. *CFTL*, 1:3b; *TCHT*, 11:4a–b.

11. *CFTL*, 1:17. Strictly speaking, this quote refers only to reducing the sentence, but it obviously applies also to making the sentence more severe. Both types of adjustments are provided for in this article.

12. *TCHTSL*, 85:*yin-yung lü-li*:Yung-cheng 8, Ch'ien-lung 7, Chia-ch'ing 4. In the latter decree, the emperor forbids the board to use the phrases "[This sentence] is not enough to cover the crime" or "determine the sentence severely." He reserves for himself the discretion to make any adjustments beyond what the law specifies. Presumably the emperor was referring to adjustments beyond the legal margin for stretching. See also *TCHT*, 11:5b, for the prohibition against the board's calling for a doubling of the sentence.

In the balance of discretion regarding "canceling off" (*ti-hsiao*) there was an interesting flux. In 1768 the Board's discretion was reduced when the Ch'ien-lung emperor, angry over the Board's advice to cancel off the punishment for an obviously private offense, ordered that henceforth canceling off would be permissible only if the offense were a public one.[13] In 1806, however, the Chia-ch'ing emperor angrily ordered the Board to take fuller responsibilities in deciding whether or not to cancel off a sentence:

> Recently in matters of advising on the administrative punishment of civil or military officials, the Boards of War and of Civil Officials, when the regulations call for demotion and transfer, frequently adduce an article and still at the end of the memorial ask whether or not the punishment should be canceled off, requesting a rescript to decide the matter. Their only intention is that by their having originally suggested both alternatives, any severe decision will be a matter decided by the emperor, and the animosity will be directed at Us. Since We are the ruler of all in the empire, it is natural that We bear the responsibility and the animosity, but what is the idea of these high officials that they must desire to market their favors and fish for fame!

The procedure demanded by this edict was that the Board, by referring to the regulations, would advise definitely either for or against canceling off the sentence, and that the emperor would then possibly make a final adjustment. Above all, a "compromising, undecided" attitude on the part of the Board was denounced, and the Board was "not in an abruptly improper manner to use the phrase 'we request a rescript to decide the matter.'"[14]

Yet this practice clearly had the reverse danger. By giving definite advice, the Board not only shouldered responsibility for unpopular decisions but also enjoyed the rewards of making popular ones, denying the emperor opportunities to take credit for lenient decisions. By 1810 the emperor had enlarged his role, clearly in order to obtain this credit. When the offense was a mild one (that is, when it was "ordinary" or when the offender

13. *CFTL*, 1:5a–b; see IV, 3, c.
14. *TCHTSL*, 86:*kuan-yüan chiang-fa ti-hsiao*:Chia-ch'ing 11.

had himself disclosed it), the Board did not simply advise canceling off. Rather it asked whether or not the emperor permitted canceling off in the case at hand.[15] This was also the procedure called for in an 1817 edict.[16]

On canceling off public offenses, therefore, the Board sometimes definitely advised one way or the other, and sometimes just suggested both possibilities. Another problem was deciding whether or not an offense was public. Here the Board's discretion was severely limited in 1820, when the Chia-ch'ing emperor ordered that the Boards of War and Civil Officials mark all articles to indicate whether they were public or private offenses.[17] Some articles, however, had to remain open, for instance that on failing to report something to one's superior when one should have.[18] Moreover, some public offenses could not be canceled off. Of course, whatever the procedure, the emperor could exercise final discretion, as in 1832 when the Board recommended that T'ao Chu be demoted by three subgrades and transferred, and the emperor as a favor revised this to a four-subgrade demotion with retention of duties.[19]

A special problem was whether the Board had the discretion to raise the question of "canceling off" when the impeachment had emanated from the emperor. The Chia-ch'ing emperor was particularly sensitive and inconsistent about this, but his main idea seems to have been, again, that the Board should not appear more lenient than he. Thus in 1806 he ordered the Board that in such impeachments it should not raise the question of "canceling off" at all, leaving solely to him the privilege of tempering his original ire. Two years later, in 1808, he changed his mind and said that if in such imperial impeachments the offense was a public one, the Board should set forth in its advice "the various points regarding whether or not to authorize canceling off" and "request a rescript" to decide the matter. When in 1809 the Board of War did just this, however, the emperor denounced the action: "This is a case handed over through a special rescript for the Board to advise on administrative punishment. How is it permissible rashly to advise on canceling off

15. *Ibid.*, Chia-ch'ing 15.
16. *CFTL*, 1:11–12.
17. *CFTL*, 1:1–2.
18. *CFTL*, 1:4a–b.
19. *TYT*, 42:17b–18. This is also an example of a public offense for which canceling off was not permitted in a particular instance.

the sentence?" Apparently the situation still was not clear. In 1810 the Board of Civil Officials asked whether or not to cancel off a sentence in the case of an imperial impeachment and was criticized by the emperor.[20]

The imperial desire to put the burden of severity on the boards is also illustrated by the Tao-kuang emperor's 1824 revision of the *li* (regulation) in the penal code on the redemption by officials of sentences of penal servitude or more. The 1801 version of this *li* merely stated that if such an official petitioned for redemption, "The Board of Punishments examines the circumstances and memorializes requesting a rescript giving the decision." The change in 1824 required the Board to advise either for or against redemption. It was "not permitted to make a double request by entering the phrase 'is it proper or not?' into the memorial."[21]

Normally the board had a five-day deadline to memorialize an answer. However twenty days were allowed if the impeachment had not been initiated by the emperor and if the offender's case required a memorial dealing solely with it. Presumably the deadline could be extended when the memorial was a joint one with other offices, since regulations allotted a separate five-day period to each office involved. An edict of 1817 deplored that delays were occurring due to the process of determining whether or not the impeached official had any commendations or added subgrades which could be used to cancel the sentence, but there is no evidence of any serious logjam. Actually the Board had the records of these matters for all civil officials in the empire except those at the Office of the Imperial Household and at the Imperial Clan Court. When it sent a letter to the latter two offices for this information, it included in its letter the phrase "*t'i-pen*-type memorial to be presented according to deadline" in order to hurry the response.[22]

It is worth noting that joint memorials with the Board of Punishments or with the Board of War were often necessary. If a case involved both civil and military officials, the joint memorial was "taken charge of" by the Board of War if the military official had the higher rank, and by the Board of Civil Officials in

20. *TCHTSL*, 86:*kuan-yüan chiang-fa ti-hsiao*:Chia-ch'ing 11, 13, 14, 15.

21. The successive versions of this *li* are in *chüan* 924 of *TCHTSL*. Its final version is in *TCLL*, 4:5a–b, or *TLti*, 1:27b.

22. *CFTL*, 1:11–12b.

the opposite case.[23] If a civil official also held a military office and committed an offense relative to the latter, the matter was usually to be handled by the Board of War alone,[24] although the Board of Civil Officials handled the punishment of governors and governors-general when the condition of the green standard brigades under them was "lax."[25]

According to an edict of about 1817, if the impeachment had been initiated by the emperor, the Board was to use a *che-tsou* in answer, but otherwise it was to use a *t'i-pen*. The reason given was that impeachments emanating from officials were so numerous that using *che-tsou* for them would lead to "an excess of troublesome details," that is, they were better handled through *t'i-pen* because the latter required less individual attention from the emperor.[26] It was still another problem whether the case was to be put by the Board in a "collective *t'i-pen*" (*hui-t'i*), which was presented on one of the two days out of ten assigned to this Board for presenting routine memorials, or whether the Board was to prepare an individual memorial (*chuan-t'i, chuan-an t'i-pen*) and present it on the earliest day possible. Detailed rules on this were based on the principle that the higher the official and the more serious the punishment, the more desirable it was to use individual memorials. Officials of grade three or more all received individual memorials whatever the punishment, and local magistrates still received individual memorials if the punishment was a demotion or a dismissal from office, but not if it was a salary fine.[27] Whatever the kind of memorial, the Board had to identify the article it was adducing either by a full or partial quote, and it had to discuss whether or not the punishment should be canceled off.[28]

What procedures were available for avoiding or correcting adjudicative mistakes? On the one hand, officials initiating impeachments were affected both by laws requiring them to impeach if there was an offense and by laws punishing them if their impeachment was false; moreover the officials finding sentences at the Board were impeached for doing so improperly.

23. *CFTL*, 11:4a–b.
24. *CFTL*, 1:28.
25. *CFTL*, 37:2.
26. *CFTL*, 1:11b.
27. *CFTL*, 9:4a–b. The 10-day schedule for regular memorials is in *Rikubu*, pp. 5–6.
28. *CFTL*, 2:1; 1:11–12; *TCHTSL*, 85:*yin-yung lü-li*:Ch'ien-lung 5.

On the other hand, officials being impeached were affected both by laws allowing them channels of appeal and by laws punishing them if their appeal involved false accusations. In general, this process was a serious attempt to uphold the authority of superiors while avoiding acts of oppression (for example, *yüan-i*) by superiors against their subordinates, a difficult problem in even the most modern organizations. However, the basic fact in this whole process seems to be that an appealer risked a criminal sentence for making a false accusation,[29] while a superior, so long as no corruption could be proved, at worst lost his office. The penalty for "oppression" of subordinates was demotion by three subgrades and transfer, a private offense.[30]

The pressures on the impeachers and on the Board of Civil Officials can be easily summarized. Innumerable articles of law specified the responsibility of officials under pain of sanction to impeach offenders. For instance, if a governor-general was found guilty at a trial of some form of illicit taking of wealth ("being avaricious") and his governor had not impeached him, the latter was demoted by three subgrades and transferred, even if he had the excuse of not having been stationed in the same city. (The same responsibility applied to the governor-general in case the governor was guilty, but the provincial treasurer and provincial judge were not responsible for impeaching the governor or governor-general in these circumstances.) Another law with a broad scope punished superiors in the provinces with administrative sentences if through lack of vigilance they failed to impeach subordinates guilty of avaricious or corrupt behavior. If the corrupt official was a district magistrate, all his superiors through the provincial treasurer and provincial judge were impeached, the punishment being less if the superior was not stationed in the same city and also diminishing as the rank of the superior rose.

This law was reinforced by another which levied a one-year salary fine on a governor or governor-general if, when impeaching a subordinate for corrupt behavior, he failed to list in his memorial the names of those officials who should have but had not impeached the corrupt official. Similarly, if a censor im-

29. *TLti*, 39:36; *TCLL*, 30:24; Philastre, II:406. The basic principle of the law on false accusations was that, up to a certain point, the accuser should receive a punishment more severe than that due for the offense with which he had charged the accused.

30. *CFTL*, 4:53a–b; see also Sa, III:128.

peached an official for corrupt behavior and the charges proved true, then the governor-general and governor were demoted by three subgrades and transferred for having failed to impeach. A salt commissioner and his subordinate, the salt controller, were also punished if a salt official under them was impeached for corrupt or avaricious behavior by, say, a governor or censor.[31]

On the other hand, if a high official impeached for corrupt behavior an official who was really a man of integrity, the impeacher was dismissed from office; if, however, the impeacher had acted on the basis of trumped-up charges made by subordinates, his punishment was slightly less.[32] A governor-general was also dismissed from office if an official he had impeached for a serious matter was cleared at a trial, and it was found that the impeacher had acted out of enmity. If he had not acted out of enmity but only made a mistake, the punishment was considerably less.[33] The article applied here was the same as that punishing a superior for making an impeachment based on a mistake regarding his subordinate's deadlines or some other aspect of the latter's responsibilities. (The punishment varied depending on how severe a sentence had resulted from the mistaken impeachment.)[34]

At the Board of Civil Officials, there was a question whether excessive leniency or excessive severity was the worse offense. An imperial executive order of 1778 held that excessive leniency was worse, since it suggested bribery, while excessive severity could anyway be corrected. Thus punishment was severe if the Board mistakenly canceled off a sentence with administrative honors which had already been used for this purpose before.[35] However the main law on these matters took the other position, that excessive severity was worse. Thus if the Board advised too light an administrative honor or too heavy an administrative sentence, the Department officials in charge of the case received a nine-months' salary fine, the presidents and vice-presidents, a three-months' salary fine. But if the administrative honor was too great or the administrative punishment too lenient, the punishment was less. The penalties were more severe if the Board's

31. *CFTL*, 4:42–43.
32. *CFTL*, 4:47.
33. *CFTL*, 4:49.
34. *CFTL*, 4:44.
35. *TCHTSL*, 86:*kuan-yüan chiang-fa ti-hsiao*:Ch'ien-lung 43.

excessively severe punishment involved adducing an inappropriate article and presenting it in a distorted fashion.[36]

It is clear that with most public offenses, officials had little reason to appeal, because the risks of appealing were outweighed by the fact that they could expect to continue their official careers anyway. Even if they had to leave office on account of dismissal, they were often reappointed. An imperial audience to decide on the possibility of reappointment was often arranged, whether on the initiative of the emperor or of the official's highest superior. It should be kept in mind that imperial audiences were common as part of the procedure of appointment, even in the case of rather low offices.[37]

The late nineteenth-century work *Liu-pu ch'eng-yü chu-chieh* describes the procedure for audiences.[38] One day before the audience, the official (if he was a regional civil official) went to the Board of Civil Officials, which checked that there was no mistake in the matter of how he had acquired eligibility to become an official (*ch'u-shen*) or in his *lü-li* (curriculum vitae). Then it ordered him to practice the court etiquette (that is, the kowtow) and wrote down his *lü-li* on an individual tablet. If the official had been dismissed or demoted and transferred, typically the "evaluation" of him written by his superior would also be presented, together with an "audience memorial" explaining his offenses.[39] Between 3:00 and 5:00 a.m., the official (or a group of such officials) would be led into the palace by a delegation from the Board led by its senior officials. When the emperor ordered that this particular audience begin, the

36. *CFTL,* 1:30; 2:1a–b.

37. I have found no general law in *TCHT* on which kinds of appointments required imperial audiences and which did not. The routineness of such audiences is illustrated by a law in *CFTL,* 2:49. If an official had been removed from office (*ch'e-jen*) and subjected to an inquiry into alleged offenses, and the inquiry revealed no serious offense (none requiring actual demotion or dismissal), he naturally was due for reappointment. This law made the point that in such a case his reappointment was to go through without an imperial audience. The need for this law shows that an imperial audience would otherwise have been routine. This tendency toward face-to-face contact between the head of the bureaucracy and low subordinates is an interesting feature of China's bureaucracy, no doubt reflecting the special emphasis on personal bonds.

38. *Rikubu,* pp. 7–8. Civil officials stationed in the capital were brought into audience by the officials of their own office.

39. On "audience memorials," see, e.g., *CFTL,* 2:52.

senior officials stepped forward and presented the *lü-li* tablets. Then they knelt on either side of the area in front of the throne steps, and their subordinates led forward the subjects of these tablets, who, in a kneeling position, themselves stated their name and age to the emperor. (Even grand councillors usually knelt during an audience.) Even if the official's grade were a low one, further conversation might follow, as in the case of a prefect in 1726, to whom the emperor gave a message to be orally transmitted to his governor-general on arriving at his province.[40] That the *lü-li* could be presented orally by the subject is shown by an episode in 1777. The emperor felt that the rules of avoidance (*hui-pi*) had been violated when a second-class subprefect (*t'ung-p'an*) stationed at Shaohsing presented his *lü-li* at an audience and spoke with a Shaohsing accent. When the emperor asked him for an explanation, he answered that he was not a native of Shaohsing but had lived there when young.[41]

After the audience, the officials were led outside the palace to await any decision. If the emperor appointed one of the officials just presented, this was immediately written on his tablet in red ink, and the tablet was handed to the Board's senior officials. Then the senior officials went outside the palace to the waiting officials who had just been presented and announced the emperor's decision. After this announcement, the audience was considered over.

This procedure was not necessarily just a formality. With regard to officials dismissed or "transferred" for a public offense, there was an explicit tendency to view the audience as an intermediate step where the emperor could weigh the official's qualifications and decide whether or not to reappoint him. In 1776 the emperor said that this audience was routine in the case of regional officials impeached for a public offense and noted an oversight in the procedures whereby this audience was omitted in the case of an official transferred from a regional to a capital office, even when this official's record included *ch'u-fen* calling for demotion. For the sake of "uniformity" and "fairness," he ordered audiences in these cases.[42]

While the audience could be used to decide whether or not to appoint a man, this purpose could sometimes blend into that of weighing whether or not his sentence had been fair. This

40. *HCCSWP*, 20:1b.
41. Cited in Ho Ping-ti, *Chung-kuo hui-kuan shih-lun*, pp. 6–7.
42. *TCHTSL*, 85:*kuan-yüan chiang-ko*:Ch'ien-lung 41.

latter function of the audiences, however, seems to have been restricted to cases where an official had been removed from office on account of those general deficiencies of body or mind listed under the "six rules" (*liu-fa*).[43] The audiences apparently were not a forum for reviewing sentences issued for serious offenses or for the lightest public offenses.

An imperial rescript of 1732 states that the procedure already existed of giving imperial audiences to officials removed from office at the "great accounting," so long as the reason was one of the "six rules." It extended this privilege to officials removed according to the six rules through an impeachment during the interval between the great accountings. A rescript of 1749 makes clear that these audiences could be a means to vindicate the removed official. In this rescript the emperor was searching for a way to remove these officials quickly for the sake of governmental efficiency while at the same time avoiding the danger of unfair treatment by their superiors. His solution was that if an official was to be removed according to the six rules, his superior on the one hand was to memorialize on the removal and on the other hand was forcibly and immediately to retire him. "If perhaps among such officials there are those who are not willing to be discarded and desire to go to the capital for an audience," their governor or governor-general was to arrange that the Board of Civil Officials present them at court. The regulation fashioned out of this rescript provided that such officials, removed for old age, sickness, indolence, laxness, mediocrity, and so forth, not only could petition the governor or governor-general over their post to arrange an audience, but, if he refused and ordered them to return to their native place, they also could petition the governor or governor-general there to arrange an audience. If he also refused, they could then petition the Board itself.[44]

Even an official ousted for a serious private offense still had avenues of appeal, but if he used them, he faced the risk of criminal punishment under the statute for false accusations. A subordinate had the right to memorialize if he were being "oppressed" in a manner out of accord with "the rules of moral propriety" by his superior. This right apparently extended to low officials otherwise not permitted to memorialize.[45] In practice, however, this right seems to have been neglected in favor

43. See IV, 4, c. On audiences, see also IV, 3, c.
44. *CFTL*, 4:51–52; see also *CFTL*, 6:17–18.

of the practice of petitioning various offices. One regulation held that, if an official was being "oppressed" by a superior, he was permitted to report the matter to his governor and/or governor-general, asking them to impeach the accused. If these superiors shielded the accused and refused to act, the accusing official could report the matter to the Six Sections for the Scrutiny of Metropolitan Officials. If these censorial offices found that the story of oppression had substance, they memorialized on the matter and also handed it over to the governor-general and/or governor involved. The latter were then to carry out what we have called a disciplinary inquiry. If the inquiry found the accused guilty, he was impeached, demoted by three subgrades, and transferred. The governor and/or governor-general were punished the same way if an inquiry found that they had shielded the accused.[46]

The danger in charging "oppression" was great, however. One law provided for criminal punishments for an impeached official who "himself knows that there is no way of denying his guilt" and yet tries to remove the evidence before the impeaching memorial arrives at court and falsely accuses his impeachers of making an improper impeachment.[47] Even more, accusations of oppression which were rejected were not easily dismissed as mistakes. The presumption seems to have been that the accuser had acted wickedly rather than out of innocent misunderstanding. An imperial decree of about 1653 stated: "As for cases where in actuality there was no oppression and the impeached official recklessly made a false accusation, then administer a severe criminal sentence."

Especially to control the desire for revenge, certain appeals were not acted on: *li-an pu-hsing* (the case was filed with no action taken). If an impeached official accused his impeacher of some form of corruption not related to his offense, the impeached official was dismissed from office or even criminally prosecuted, and no action was taken against his impeacher whom he had accused of corruption. Because they reflect a strong desire for vindication, such laws suggest that the avenues of appeal were used.[48]

45. *TCLL*, 4:16; Philastre, I:135. See Appendix V.
46. *CFTL*, 4:53a–b.
47. *CFTL*, 4:53b–54.
48. *TCHTSL*, 80:*nei-wai k'ao-ch'a kuan-yüan ch'eng-pien*:Shun-chih 10, and *pei-ho jen-yüan hsieh-ssu pao-fu*:Yung-cheng 12.

5. Conclusion

Ch'u-fen law was a system of bureaucratic disciplinary sanctions shaped by the Ch'ing rulers' policies as well as the situational, institutional, cultural, and technological constraints on these policies and their implementation. We have postulated that if the bureaucracy was to be effective, these sanctions had to have certain normative and administrative characteristics: they had to be legitimated, mild, universalistic, rationalistic, and flexible, and they required an administrative framework sufficiently differentiated and centralized to apply them uniformly.

We have shown that these ideal administrative and normative characteristics were partly realized. This important fact indicates that the Ch'ing bureaucracy was effective not just because it wielded the economic and coercive power more easily available to it but also because it reached out for less easily accessible sources of power, strenuously struggling to stretch its power by controlling its officials in ways designed to increase its effectiveness. In other words, the significant extent to which *ch'u-fen* law realized our hypothetically-defined ideal characteristics reflected this organizational struggle for effectiveness.

Realization of universalism, administrative uniformity, and legitimation, however, were particularly problematic. Universalism and uniformity were inhibited by particularistic ties leading to bribery or favoritism, as well as by the limited extent of administrative centralization, of professionalization in adjudicative activities, and of differentiation between political and judicial activities.

Yet the Yung-cheng emperor increased centralization by reducing the discretion of superior officials in punishing their subordinates, and thus he probably increased uniformity. At the same time, any limitations in centralization partly promoted the universalistic aspect of "fairness" by limiting abuses of power. The Yung-cheng emperor also probably increased uniformity by making the schedule of sanctions more systematic. Uniformity was also furthered by the practice of publishing most of the disciplinary sanctions in specialized chapters or books, a practice which began apparently around 1740. The Ch'ien-lung emperor acted to increase universalism by reducing inequities in the impact of sanctions due to various privileged aspects of the status of imperial nobles. Similar policies were still stronger in the case of nonimperial nobles. There was much official propaganda calling for "fairness" in the application of the sanctions.

Above all, universalism was strikingly realized in the way the law was written, since, in contrast to many laws applied to the population-at-large, the severity of most disciplinary sanctions depended only on the seriousness of the offense, not on the status of the offender. Universalism was also promoted by two sets of forces including strong political interests: one set involving especially the bureaucrats and their outlook; the other, especially the position of the emperor.

On the side of the bureaucrats, there were various forces promoting respect for law: their considerable amount of specialized experience; the usefulness of law as a neutral umpire for settling disputes in a conciliatory way between competitive offices; the officials' competitive tendency to display their respect for the laws as a way of demonstrating their loyalty to the emperor's interests; the inescapable imperatives of organizational efficiency; and the ideologically appealing connotations of respect for *li* (precedent), which was the form of so much Ch'ing law (see II, 4).

The emperor also had reasons for respecting law. As we saw in the case of Yung-cheng, he appreciated that respect for law was a way of extending his overall power even if it constricted his freedom of choice on particular occasions (II, 4). Moreover, his deliberately emphasized awesomeness made it relatively difficult for officials to develop particularistic ties with him; his great wealth often made him unbribable;[1] and he often had an overriding political interest in effective universalistic performance. Because of these factors, the emperor's immense power was often inclined in a universalistic direction, although arbitrary despotism also was a characteristic of his.

These sociological reflections echo that indigenous outlook

1. Clearly under Tz'u-hsi the court's decisions on even low-level personnel cases were often shaped by bribes. See Chang Te-ch'ang, p. 21. The later part of the T'ang dynasty, from about 800 on, is also notorious as a period of bribery and corruption, of which a leading part was gifts made by the military governors to the emperor in order to bring about his acquiescence to their wishes. See Wang Shou-nan, *T'ang-tai fan-chen yü chung-yang cheng-fu kuan-hsi chih yen-chiu,* pp. 250–251. I believe, though, that such periods, when the imperial will was routinely tied in with the particularistic flow of corruption, were exceptional.

whereby the twin foundations of government were the roles of the *chün* (ruler) and the *chün-tzu* (true gentleman), each of which were to be exalted in its own way. From this standpoint we can agree that the emphasis on *tsun-chün* (reverently respect the ruler), even though open to Mencian reservations, was crucial for effective governmental action and was not just an expression of the emperor's dysfunctional desire for excessive power. Particularistic impulses conflicting with organizational aims had to be restrained somehow. If they could not be restrained through an intense, common commitment of all members of the organization to its goals, then they could be restrained by raising the position of the leader as much as possible beyond their reach. All in all, the mixture of political interests, orientations, and procedures inclined toward universalism should be given as much weight as the more commonly emphasized tendencies toward particularism and deviancy.

There was a similar mix of functional and dysfunctional factors determining the level of leniency. Harshness was promoted by the relative lack of trust between the emperor and his bureaucrats, which was aggravated by the fact that the bureaucracy was not just an executive arm but also an arena of politics. In applying the sanctions, therefore, the emperor generally aimed not only to elicit performance but also to maintain his authority. This connection to the problem of maintaining authority over an organization with weak ties of solidarity at times made the sanctions so severe as to endanger performance.

The low level of communication technology also seems to have increased the severity of the sanctions. Because the capital lacked a swift flow of reliable information about changing circumstances allowing it quickly to make and communicate adjustments in the sanctions, it tended to take a posture of inflexible severity rather than lose all control.

Yet these factors did not lead to primary reliance on terror. On the contrary, administrative mistakes were distinguished from crimes and treated with relative leniency. Not only administrative mistakes but also light offenses classed as "private" and involving mild greed, recklessness, cheating, fondness for pleasure and ease, or ineptitude were routinely punished only by remunerative or status sanctions, not physical deprivations. Sentences for administrative mistakes were particularly mild not only in terms of their inherent content but also because their frequency mitigated their humiliation; they could often be canceled off against administrative honors; if the same mistake was dealt with harshly in the penal code and mildly in the *ch'u-fen tse-li,* the latter generally had primacy; if the sentence involved loss of one's office through transfer or dismissal, the chances of reappointment were good; administrative mistakes were favorably treated with regard to amnesties and the question of redemption; and, as expressed by the Yung-cheng emperor, there was a principle that superiors should overlook certain minor failings rather than stick blindly to the letter of the law.

Nevertheless the administrative punishments often constituted a harsh discipline. Emotionally they still must have been tainted by fear of the legally unchecked imperial authority from which they all were directly issued. If the frequency of the sentences reduced humiliation, the fact that one was punished frequently not for avoidable or deliberately wicked actions but for mere shortcomings or mistakes was in itself harsh. One could be punished for the actions of others or occasionally for natural events beyond one's control. This whole disciplinary system, although the hope of success was important, leaned toward the idea that keeping the fear of failure alive in a man's daily thoughts was the best incentive. Demotion and dismissal, rather than denial of promotion, seem to have been the main negative sanctions. Moreover, when the question of an offense arose, the verdict and the sentence were determined not only through rationalistic but also moralistic and disciplinary considerations. Even the mildest salary fines could be a financial burden, and, if one lost one's office and could not be reappointed, one lacked the opportunity to find a comparable position elsewhere. Statistics show that in fact the rate of dismissals and demotions was great, even though, at the same time, a significant number of officials were able to continue in their posts for several years.

The bureaucrats would not have responded positively to such harsh sanctions had they not had deep-seated attitudes according to which such harshness was basically appropriate. I have tried to infer from the nature of the laws and the ideas associated with them a "probationary ethic," although I have presented it only tentatively as an ideal type or explanatory model. I have stressed the contrast between the officials' self-image as charismatic leaders holding ultimate responsibility for the fate of the empire, and the fact that the officials typically found themselves as subordinates in an organization whose social relationships were often shaped by suspicion and humiliation. Consequently, their self-image involved some sense of shame. They were ready to think of themselves as deserving of suspicion and lack of trust. They accepted a disciplinary system which carried the implication that they were not persons of basically upright character. This involved the idea that the morality of most officials depended largely on their financial circumstances and that the commission of a crime merely made manifest character traits previously latent. This belief in turn made normatively acceptable a considerable "bounce back" effect, whereby officials could be restored to office after having been convicted as criminals. The common notion of "expiating" a crime through punishment; the practice of clearing oneself or winning a milder punishment by the process of self-impeachment, which was a sort of confession; the idea of "renewing oneself" through blameless performance following an offense; and the willingness to accept such a strong moralistic and disciplinary element in the system of sanctions—all this has religious overtones and points to the belief in one's unworthiness.

Officials could criticize *ch'u-fen* law as a bad substitute for relations of trust and discretion, but, because of their self-image, they indicted themselves as well as their rulers for this deplorable situation. Certainly a striking aspect of the elite's political culture was their capacity to meet failure as much with self-criticism as with the desire to find a scapegoat. Even while demanding to be trusted more, the officials not only distrusted each other to some extent but also were ashamed of not being trustworthy.

Since this view involves a readiness to be blamed, it can be connected to that diffuse sense of responsibility which so many of the sanctions involved. The feeling of bearing responsibility as an official had two facets equally conducive to administrative effort: it gave the subject a sense of pride and charismatic authority, and it gave him the feeling of painfully bearing a heavy burden and the fear of suffering shame if he let it slip. Charisma being a floating, elusive condition largely dependent on achievement, an individual could seldom feel secure in his possession of it; it had to be repeatedly revalidated. An old saying went that discharging responsibility successfully was "like being freed from a heavy load." A modern popular Chinese writer on morals says that the most miserable thing in the world is not death or poverty but bearing an undischarged responsibility, because the latter resembles a load of several thousand pounds pressing down on one's shoulders.[2]

As some Ch'ing writers indicated, the effectiveness of disciplinary sanctions largely depended on the officials' sense of responsibility and shame. Admittedly some Ch'ing officials held that whether or not one received sanctions had nothing to do with one's actual efforts and moral worth, but we can see in this view not only a partly realistic conclusion but also a psychological defense mechanism. Successfully meeting a tax collection deadline must often have given officials a pleasurable feeling "like being freed from a heavy load." Conversely, when they missed such a deadline, they must often have had a painful feeling aroused by the idea that they had failed to meet a moral responsibility. To relieve this painful feeling, they were grateful for a chance to expiate their wrong by suffering a judicial sentence and then being regarded as "renewed." For this reason, sentences with suggestive titles such as "dismissal from office with retention of duties while carrying along one's guilt" were an appropriate and partly effective means of eliciting effort. This inner moral pressure felt by the officials often made the organizationally crucial difference between "shirking responsibilities" and "exhaustively devoting one's spirit and energy to the matters for which one is responsible." This was the pivotal point where external sanctions and internalized motivations intersected.

The feeling of bearing a heavy responsibility can be connected with Hsün-tzu's view that man's nature is bad and that his desires (*yü*) need to be repressed with rules of moral propriety (*li*). The sense of responsibility, one may argue, could only become heavy through a connection with the idea that there are bad forces at work within one's nature. The heavy burden of a bad nature is projected onto the responsibility. To the extent that one's nature is felt to be good, after all, one has no need to act to vindicate it. But if it is felt to be bad, or if one feels the threat of being rejected by others as bad, then one may feel a need to vindicate oneself by rising to the challenge of responsibility. Moreover, if one is actualizing one's personality through a constant struggle to overcome the feeling of having a bad nature, then punishments are not only accepted but even un-

2. *Ch'eng-yü ku-shih hsüan-chiang* (Kaohsiung, 1967), p. 148.

consciously desired as a transaction integral to this struggle.

These partly unarticulated feelings regarding punishment and responsibility were connected to the explicit tendency of Confucian philosophy to approve of the system of bureaucratic discipline, particularly of surveillance by censors, periodic evaluations of officials, promotions and demotions, and the merit principle. Cruel and humiliating punishments for corrupt officials were also sometimes advocated by Confucians like Ku Yen-wu. Thus breaking through the sense of status honor and elite solidarity, this demand for humiliating punishments perhaps reflected the unconscious feelings of self-blame.

The question of submission to punishment overlaps that of submission to authority. Some light can be shed on this matter by using Erich Fromm's approach, whereby a concrete type of authority pattern is viewed as a gradation between the two categories of "inhibiting authority" and "rational authority."[3] On the one hand, Fromm sees "inhibiting authority" as typical of the master-slave relationship, involving great social distance and based on exploitation of the subordinate. The Ch'ing bureaucratic case is not a pure instance of "inhibiting authority" because of the Chinese notion that all officials, irrespective of rank, were supposed to have the honored status of *chün-tzu* (true gentleman), and because of the consequent emphasis on treating subordinates with politeness, on respecting their advice, on raising their morale and sense of pride, and on controlling them normatively by acting as a model of behavior. As the law on administrative punishment vividly illustrates, superior officials did not merely thrust responsibility on subordinates but shouldered it together with them. Admittedly, the relation between emperor and official was a little closer to the model of the master-slave relationship, though even here one should recall that cliché of imperial rhetoric: "the ruler and his ministers in their relationship are like one body." On the other hand, rational authority for Fromm is typical of the teacher-student relationship, involves less social distance, and is based on helping the subordinate. The Ch'ing case is not a pure instance of this type because of the strong authoritarian elements involved in the probationary ethic. (Interestingly, in Ch'ing times superior officials were sometimes addressed as "teacher" by their immediate

3. Erich Fromm, *Escape from Freedom* (New York, 1941), pp. 164–166. Pfiffner and Sherwood, p. 199.

subordinates, who affected the status of "disciple" relative to them.)[4]

The probationary ethic can be compared to the Protestant ethic to the extent that both are regarded as forms of motivation to carry out organizational work. In both instances there was the organizational problem of inducing an elite class to carry out arduous work barren of immediate gratification. In both cases this was done by injecting this elite with a moral tension more distasteful than the work and so formulated that it could be relieved only through performance of the work. This point of similarity perhaps holds despite differences between these two ethics in terms of the type of work involved, the greater role of external sanctions in the Chinese case, and the possibly greater degree of self-reliance or rationalization in the Protestant attitude. At any rate, we cannot accept Weber's view of the Chinese bureaucrat as seeking self-fulfillment essentially through "ceremonial and ritualistic propriety" and lacking "any tension . . . between ethical demand and human shortcoming . . ."[5] Weber failed to appreciate that if organizational effectiveness is to be attained, organizational leaders, whether entrepreneurs or bureaucrats, have to be motivated by an internalized sense of moral obligation.

I have thus argued that the Ch'ing elite's internalized sense of responsibility promoted the effectiveness of the sanctions applied to them. This sense of responsibility can be seen as an integral part of a broader pattern of political culture. Connected to a feeling of inner badness and shame, the sense of responsibility promoted the desire to improve the world, which also was perceived as containing much badness. At the same time, as I noted in chapter one, there was doubt as to how best to proceed in improving the world, and indeed in improving oneself. This combination of the sense of inner and outer doubt, the sense of inner and outer badness, and the sense of responsibility was crucial for the promotion of flexible and disciplined organizational work. It gave normative support to a focus on bureaucratic effectiveness involving efforts to achieve the various sorts of administrative differentiation, to employ various patterns of centralization, to rationalize responsibility, to ap-

4. *HCCSWP*, 20:8.

5. Max Weber, *The Religion of China* (Glencoe, Ill., 1951), pp. 228, 235.

proach problems with a sense of "moderate realism," to act in a universalistic fashion, and to communicate efficiently.

To put it otherwise, the feelings of badness and doubt, inner and outer, as well as the sense of responsibility, bridged two aspects of the elite's political culture: the more subjective or affective aspect, and the more objective or cognitive aspect. As I have argued, on the subjective side, there was the elite's sense of charisma and the probationary ethic, while on the objective side, there was their consciousness of a spectrum of policy alternatives. These latter I described in Chapter I in terms of three polarities: the Legalist emphasis on the concrete tools of state power versus the Confucian emphasis on the forces of morally expressed solidarity; promotion versus inhibition of commerce; and radical euphoric totalism versus moderate realism. It was in terms of this political culture as a whole, subjective and objective, that the leadership could mobilize organizational efforts which to some extent were both affectively and cognitively adequate.

True, this mobilization often failed, on account of either inner weakness or outer obstacles. But it was exactly these inner and outer obstacles which were realistically confronted in terms of that attitude I have called "moderate realism." With this attitude, the bureaucrats could gradually grapple with difficulties and stretch their organizational resources while retaining their ideals, instead of seeking through a sudden euphoric rush to storm their way immediately to total success or crashing disappointment. The sense of moderate realism, in other words, allowed the officials to pace themselves and encouraged a varied, sustained search for success in devising more effective organizational structures and procedures and in manipulating the sanctions behind them. The Ch'ing dynasty's voluminous record of legislation in the field of administration is a monument to this search.

To see the elite's political culture as a whole, however, we need to connect these functional or positive aspects to the dysfunctional ones. It was the diffuse combination in one outlook of both these functional and dysfunctional aspects which created uncertainties in the elite's morale and commitment to organizational goals. These dysfunctional aspects also can be classed as more subjective and affective or more objective and cognitive.

On the subjective side, along with the probationary ethic and the sense of charisma, there were the elite's particularistic ties and egotistic motivations (see below), which impeded the development of a strong sense of trust and solidarity connected to organizational goals. As we saw in the case of the Ningtu magistrate Wang Ch'üan-chih (IV, 4, d), doubt about an official could be resolved through a reaffirmation of confidence. However, it often led to spiraling suspicion.

On the objective side, we need but recall the ambivalences involved in the elite's consciousness of policy alternatives. Admittedly, I have argued that the elite's outlook supported flexible, universalistic bureaucratic action more than has been indicated in some previous interpretations, which have gone too far in suggesting that Confucian ideas largely failed to legitimate administrative flexibility, specialization, and the punishment of officials. Similarly, I have argued elsewhere that the elite's outlook was more supportive of trade and of governmental commercial action than has been granted in some other interpretations.[6]

Yet on many of these issues, legitimation was still problematic, and the rightfulness of much bureaucratic procedure was thus open to doubt. Doubt in turn easily led to deviancy. A striking example is the tendency in 1616 of some local officials to refuse to cooperate in enforcing the salt monopoly regulations on account of their explicit adherence to Confucian arguments against the monopoly made in the Han work *Discourses on Salt and Iron.*[7] Certainly such a troubled relation between political culture and political action was unique neither to imperial China nor to premodern societies. Yet the feeling in imperial China about the morally dubious character of certain important state activities was strong and seems to have led as often to alienation as to the pursuit of reform.

Moreover, it is not clear that the outlook of "moderate realism," vital for bureaucratic effectiveness, was institutionalized with a sufficiently strong moral foundation. Certainly it was often perceived not as a moral path of political progress but as a form of moral betrayal epitomizing the ancient vice of *hsiang-yüan* (hypocritically following fashionable moral trends of the day). A patient attitude toward partially ethical endeavors leading to partial political success can be seen already in Hsün-tzu's view of the *pa* (hegemon) (see I, 5), but this attitude may have

6. Metzger, "The State and Commerce in Imperial China."
7. *Huang-Ming ching-shih wen-pien,* 29:307–314. See I, note 97.

been overshadowed by the euphoric radicalism associated with Mencian idealism. Although a conservative respect for the status quo is vulnerable to moral objections in many cultures, it is possible that in imperial China "moderate realism" was so to a peculiar extent. It is significant that some students of modern China have been impressed by the difficulties faced by reformers seeking to arouse moral enthusiasm for moderate, gradualistic programs.

All these remarks about the Ch'ing elite's political culture can be conveniently summarized as follows:

	Affective-Subjective	*Cognitive-Objective*
Bureaucratically functional	Probationary ethic Sense of charisma	Spectrum of policy alternatives defined in terms of three polarities
Bureaucratically dysfunctional	Particularism Egotism	

If it is appropriate to look at Ch'ing political culture this way, then we should avoid simply calling it "Confucian," or even "an amalgam of Confucianism and Legalism." Confucian ideas were important, especially because Ch'ing scholars and officials wanted to believe that their principles were derived from the *tao* transmitted by Confucius. But this image they often had of their principles, although an important ideological fact in itself, did not entirely determine the actual character of their principles. What these scholars wanted to be only partly determined what they were. We do them justice by pointing to the complexity of their thought, even though they themselves may well have preferred to be identified with only the highest ideals of Confucianism.

In discussing political culture, there is a danger in relying too much on the dichotomy of universalism-particularism. The problem of a bureaucratically functional orientation was not just that of a contradiction between universalistic and particularistic orientations. For instance, many disciplinary problems met in *ch'u-fen* law stemmed from a conflict between universalistic, bureaucratic rules and the officials' desire for personal gratification, rather than a conflict between universalistic, bureaucratic rules and the officials' particularistic obligations to friends and relatives. The bureaucrat not only was motivated by his obligations to social groups but also was a worried, harried, sometimes emotionally upset individual with a personal desire for pleasure. These egotistic tendencies could hurt all the groups he belonged to and even himself. The major bureaucratic deviancy of "shirking responsibilities" was hardly a way to help one's family. Neither were the offenses of being "cruel" or "careless." In Parsons' terms, the personality of the bureaucrat was a major factor aside from the various social system orientations.

At the same time, the interests of the various groups an official belonged to were not necessarily in conflict, since a successful bureaucratic career helped one's family. A censor in 1800, Chang P'eng-chan, said that officials did not engage in uninhibited corruption to help their families unless they felt that they lacked the possibility of an eminent career and also thought that the chances of prosecution for corruption were slim.

Of course, besides the triangular relation between universalistic, particularistic, and egotistic motivations, one also has to take into account competition between different particularistic needs. The need to establish particularistic ties within the bureaucracy had to be weighed against the need to help one's family: should I buy a present for my superior or my father? Chang P'eng-chan said that spending to please superiors was a major sort of financial pressure leading officials into debt and corruption.[8] Yet the strengthening of particularistic ties within the bureaucracy was not entirely dysfunctional, since it facilitated cooperation with universalistic ends. Obviously the diffuse desire to please superiors was often a motivational mixture in which particularistic, universalistic, and egotistic feelings intermingled. From the standpoint of the effectiveness of the bureaucracy, the distinction between the presence or absence of this desire is as significant as that between its universalistic and particularistic aspects.

A linked problem is the recent mistaken tendency to identify Legalism with universalism, Confucianism with particularism. Ch'ing ideas with universalistic dimensions often had Confucian aspects, as with that whole complex of bureaucratic rules revolving around the merit principle, and with the officials' sense of charisma. At the same time, universalistic attitudes crucial for the functioning of the bureaucracy seem often to have been rooted in the relatively particularistic realms of kinship life and

8. *HCCSWP*, 20:10a–b.

childhood socialization, as we can presume relative to the norms of political authority and the probationary ethic. After all, Confucian thought not only stressed kinship ties but also planted universalistic ethical principles within the family and emphasized that from serving one's father, one learns to serve political superiors.[9] The notion of "serving" (*shih*) certainly played a pivotal ethical role. Carrying out one's occupational tasks with utmost diligence, whether farming or commerce, was also a way of "serving superiors." Capacity to fulfill the whole spectrum of societal obligations, particularistic and universalistic, was supposed to be realized through the process of *hsiu-shen* (self-cultivation), the ultimate lodestar of which, the *tao* (true way), was a unifying principle integrating the whole variety of societal obligations with the cosmos itself. Together with this emphasis on integrating familial and societal obligations, Confucian thought stressed dedication to the *kung* (public) good, a fundamental universalistic value in Chinese thought prominent in Legalism too.

In this light, one can hardly identify Confucian ethics with kinship particularism legitimating the corrupt violation of universalistic bureaucratic rules. Such ethical particularism certainly existed, but it was a one-sided version of Confucianism, just as the despotism of a *pao-chün* (tyrannically cruel ruler) was a one-sided version of Legalism. To make an obvious point, the subject of that ethical process called *hsiu-shen* (self-cultivation) was not the family nor even the lineage but the individual. A major ethical thrust of Confucianism was a call addressed to the male individual to enter the dialogue between *chün* (the ruler) and *chün-tzu* (true gentlemen), through which conflicting societal obligations and drives could be harmoniously resolved. It would indeed be hard to decide whether in Confucian thought this political dialogue is primary and kinship ethics derivative, or vice versa. The role of the official was defined in terms of this dialogue and thus was not externally tacked onto any system of Confucian particularism.

This brings us back to our earlier methodological point: if we are to understand political values and even vaguely weight

9. For instance, connected to the universalistic quality of *jen*, the capacity to judge people on the basis of their qualities rather than on the basis of one's liking or not liking them was regarded as necessary to harmonize relationships within the family. See, e.g., Legge, *Chinese Classics*, I:369 (*The Great Learning*).

or estimate their impact on behavior, we need to discuss them descriptively and idiosyncratically. Interestingly, Max Weber's stress on the relative autonomy of the value sphere has been more widely accepted than his method of describing values idiosyncratically and in terms of their intellectual dimensions, which is illustrated by his study of the Protestant ethic. A recent prominent trend has been to try to categorize values simply by saying that they exhibit more or less of a certain nomothetically formulated quality like universalism, secularization, or differentiation. Few sociologists today share Weber's fascination with the impact of the intellectual process on the value system.

Yet especially in a society like China, where much of the elite consisted of intellectuals, this impact seems important. Some values are not just ideals but rather a process of thought whereby ideals are worried about in terms of the historical problems impeding their realization and the historical efforts made to implement them. The value system thus partly consists of the accumulated images of history centering around this triangular relationship between ideals, problems, and efforts, as well as feelings like sadness, irony, and hope aroused by these images. To say otherwise would be to regard the members of the society or organization being studied as simpletons.

Another way to say this is that if a political value is a blend of ideas, we cannot just identify its behavioral thrust with the single most prominent idea in this blend. From a behavioral standpoint, ideas less prominent in the consciously held opinion of the subject may be as important as the prominent ideas, and the implications emerging from the interplay of all the various ideas may also act as norms. Of course, prominent ideas are behaviorally important too, but their prominence may be due not to their behaviorial importance alone but also to the fact that people like to publicize them and like to think that they express reality, even while behaving according to other norms as well. What is involved here is the complex question of how people perceive the relation between their highest ideals and the norms they feel comfortable living by. This methodological point is, I hope, illustrated by my discussions in Chapter I of attitudes regarding administrative flexibility and of attitudes regarding the punishment of officials (see IV, 2).

The issues at stake here, however, are substantive, not just methodological. Ch'ing political culture is not fully congruent with either those surface appearances visible to sociologists concerned mainly with macroscopic theory or those aspects stressed by indigenous experts and critics who have been guided by a normative preoccupation with the extirpation of obstacles to progress. Largely invisible to the former and insignificant to the latter, a structurally crucial network of attitudes and feelings lies beneath the surface. As this network is examined, we find that Ch'ing political culture differs markedly from the picture currently presented by leading sociologists. One key difference revolves around the issue, basic since Max Weber, of the presence or absence of any dynamic or transformative quality in the dominant Ch'ing ethic.

Max Weber, as mentioned above, saw no such quality, and his position is further developed by S. N. Eisenstadt in the latter's article, "The Protestant Ethic Thesis in an Analytical and Comparative Framework." [10] Eisenstadt stresses particularly that in order to have a potential for the transformation of its society, a religion or ideology has to focus on a normative order which transcends and so is in tension with the established political order, that is, the cultural order has to be differentiated from the actual, present political order.

According to him, this differentiation was not achieved in imperial China (whether in the Ch'ing or earlier periods). In his view, the "cultural symbols" of "Chinese intellectuals and bureaucrats," despite some transcendence "in principle," were "embedded in the existing political structure" to the point that there existed an "ideological identity between the cultural and political orders." Similarly, the elite had no "autonomous, independent status orientations," since the state was "the sole distributor of prestige and honor." Neither had the elite any moral obligation to any groups outside their bureaucracy and their families. The fact that values and elite interests were thus intertwined with the political status quo means that "Chinese culture" had "nontransformative orientations." This helps explain the "ineffectiveness of the initial stages of China's modernization."

Eisenstadt's position is valid to some extent, since Ch'ing political culture probably lacked any strong transformative tendency which could by itself have led to modernization. But the unqualified notion of the "nontransformative orientations

10. N. Eisenstadt, ed., *The Protestant Ethic and Modernization* (New York, 1968), pp. 25–27.

of Chinese culture" is highly problematic. Ch'ing political culture in fact involved dynamic elements which partly resembled that quality Eisenstadt calls "transformative." The important question here is one of degree. Moreover, Eisenstadt's view of "the ideological identity between the cultural and political orders" in imperial China is untenable.

On the contrary, as we have seen, Ch'ing political culture involved a basic set of coherent, abstract, universalistic ideas which transcended the status quo in that according to them, much of both the status quo and the character of the Confucian subject seeking to transcend it was bad. Perceiving this badness, the Confucian subject felt a heavy sense of responsibility to improve his character and reform the world.

Certainly he looked to the state as the organ of reform, but he most emphatically also regarded it as the basic object of reform. Certainly he placed great value on any honors he received from the state, but he had been bred on a classical literature stressing that self-cultivation—the only road to the charismatic status of a "true gentleman" and the potential pathway to sagehood—was a matter largely contingent on his own autonomous efforts. Certainly he felt obligated to his family and his bureaucracy, but there were no higher obligations in Confucianism than the universalistic ones he owed to "the people" (*min*), whose welfare was the proper object of government.

Thus even though government and intellectual life were intertwined to a peculiar degree, there still was a basic tension between political ideals and political reality. Much of the Ch'ing elite perceived the political arena as consisting of three basic parts which had a continuous, tortured interaction: the "people," usually suffering and requiring help; an often corrupt, inefficient complex of power culminating in officialdom and the emperor; and the Confucian scholars, themselves often tainted by this complex but still graced through their learning with the high, flattering mission of realizing the *tao*, reforming this complex, and helping the people.

True, this picture was a "definition of the situation" in terms of which the Confucian elite could comfortably slide between conscientious exertion and self-indulgent corruption. But one cannot say it lacked moral leverage, tension, and dynamism. As I have stressed throughout, this moral tension was the indispensable motivational matrix of routine organizational action in Ch'ing times. Moreover, it was also connected to the propensity of the Ch'ing elite to think in reformist terms, a propensity which certainly facilitated that transformation of Chinese society achieved in this century.

Another recent attempt to analyze traditional China's political culture, Richard H. Solomon's, also fails to recognize differentiation between the moral and political orders.[11] Solomon focuses on the "authoritarian" value of respect for superiors, without relating this value to the Confucian tendency to evaluate superiors according to generalized moral standards. In effect, he accepts at least part of the "probationary ethic" without recognizing the "charismatic" aspect of the traditional culture. Emphasizing the anxious desire of many Chinese individuals to please superiors and thus follow an "external superego," Solomon ignores the fact that a basic goal of *hsiu-shen* (self-cultivation) was to develop an inner equilibrium, Mencius' *pu-tung-hsin* (a mind which cannot be emotionally disturbed by outer forces), thus freeing one from any anxious need for external approbation. To *ying shih chih pien* (respond to and deal with the changing world of events), one needed a stable inner core of emotional poise and moral integrity, which was often perceived as derived from contact with "heaven" itself. Unless all the concern with *hsiu-shen* is to be dismissed as a trite epiphenomenon with no behavioral importance, we have to say that the Confucian personality involved not only respect for superiors but also an inner autonomy based on moral standards differentiated from the current political order. To use David Riesman's concepts somewhat out of context, Solomon sees the traditional political culture as a web of other-directed behavior oriented to the cues of superiors and fails to see how this other-directedness was combined with the inner-directedness of the *chün-tzu* ideal, which was integral to maintaining the *ch'i-chieh* (high morale and integrity) of the bureaucrats.

Despite their differences, Eisenstadt and Solomon agree that according to the basic Confucian outlook, there was no creative tension between the actual political order and political ideals. For Eisenstadt, this lack means a lack of "transformative" orientations; for Solomon, it means an "authoritarian" political culture precluding a tradition of moral autonomy in terms of

11. R. H. Solomon, *Mao's Revolution and the Chinese Political Culture* (Berkeley, Calif., 1971). For a more detailed critique, see my review in *Journal of Asian Studies*, XXXII:1 (Nov., 1972), pp. 101–105.

which one could legitimately challenge those occupying positions of authority.

Their view in turn has a complicated pedigree within Chinese intellectual history itself. Chinese with vastly different ideologies have agreed that traditional Chinese culture lacked any creative tension between political reality and political ideals. On the one hand, denial of any such tension has been a basic tenet of state Confucianism. Thus the K'ang-hsi emperor strongly implied that under his dynasty *tao-t'ung* (the line of transmission of the true way down the ages) had merged with *chih-t'ung* (the line of transmission of imperial authority down the ages). On the other hand, some modern Chinese reformers committed to Westernization have deplored the lack of this tension, charging that Confucian scholars typically let their moral ideals become corruptly entangled in the current political order.[12] Our question is whether either a propagandistic claim or a moralistic polemic can serve as a accurate picture of Ch'ing political culture.

As modern scholars continue to discuss the nature of the traditional political culture, the role it has played in modern times, and the role it ought to play in the future, no question will be more central than that of the behavioral importance which should be ascribed to the Confucian perception of a split between political reality and political ideals. Those who regard this perception as behaviorally important will tend to link the traditional political culture to creative political efforts throughout history and in the present. Conversely, those who say that this perception is of merely intellectual importance will probably view Confucianism as a pathological force blocking or distorting modernization. Certainly more work is needed before a balanced position on this issue can be developed.

Thus it seems clear that we are only on the threshold of understanding Ch'ing political culture and its role in the processes of modernization. At the same time, the question of the elite's political culture must be connected to other factors if we are to move toward a theory of Ch'ing organizational effective-

12. Yin Hai-kuang, *Chung-kuo wen-hua-te chan-wang* (An appraisal of Chinese culture and its prospects; Taipei, 1966), II:608–610. Yin's views, however, especially his later views, involved admiration for the Confucian stress on moral autonomy. Profound works by Fung Yu-lan, T'ang Chün-i, and others have explored the relevance of Confucian thought to modernization.

ness and ineffectiveness. As discussed in the introduction, it is necessary to aim for an analysis of Ch'ing bureaucracy which is both balanced and comprehensive. Besides understanding Ch'ing political culture, we need to avoid exaggerating the importance of one or another facet of the bureaucracy, such as coercive sanctions or class interests, and we need to analyze the relationships between functional and dysfunctional features, instead of just pointing with alarm at dysfunctional or "backward" aspects.

Perhaps one step in this direction is my attempt to discuss the capabilities, constraints, and tasks of officials (see IV, 3, c). The question of the elite's political culture overlaps that of their capabilities. On the subjective-affective side, the elite had a fundamental morale problem affecting their capabilities. We have noted the cultural foundations of this morale problem, but policies within the bureaucracy were important too. How the elite's morale wavered between its functional and dysfunctional poles partly depended on the extent of demoralizing experiences in the bureaucracy, such as constraints regarded as "unfair."

On the objective-cognitive side, the elite's capabilities were enhanced by its cultural awareness of a spectrum of policy alternatives and could be further developed by training programs, long experience in a particular office, and a well-designed career path.

Given such capabilities, officials acted in terms of constraints, which to a large extent were sanctions, especially the remunerative and status deprivations of *ch'u-fen* law. Yet even with their capabilities and constraints, officials still could not be effective unless their tasks were designed in a practical fashion. Proper adjustment of capabilities, constraints, and tasks was a central topic in the indigenous discussion of *li-chih* (administration by official personnel). Such adjustment was hindered especially by uncertainties in the officials' morale, the state's shortages of financial resources, and unavoidable contradictions between capabilities and constraints.

All three of these obstacles were involved in the administration of *ch'u-fen* law. The central problem was whether the constraints of *ch'u-fen* law were so severe and extensive as to inhibit the exercise of capabilities, although in some instances the opposite problem emerged, that of constraints so mild that officials did not feel pressed to exercise their capabilities. Given the uncertainties in the officials' capabilities, especially in their morale, it was hard to adjust constraints properly, and the inevitable contradictions between constraints and capabilities were aggravated.

Often the elite themselves did not take a balanced view of the matter and just singled out the severity of the constraints as the key problem, looking back with nostalgia to the Han dynasty as a time when constraints allegedly were minimal, local officials having a large salary, long tenure, and great discretion. As Chou Kao, a *chü-jen* of 1783 who rose to be a prefect, put it: "[Today] the laws [for local magistrates] are too *mi* (numerous and constricting), and a sense of trust is not realized. When laws are too numerous and constricting, the inhibitions of officials cannot but be many. When a sense of trust is not present, the process of punishing and encouraging officials will be ineffective for lack of a proper basis."[13]

But once trust is down, strict regulations may be one way to keep effectiveness from slipping still further. If administered fairly, moreover, such regulations may elicit some renewal of solidarity. This will be so especially if the bureaucrats not only blame the lack of trust on their rulers but also perceive it as an integral aspect of their own personalities and social relations, as Ch'ing officials apparently did. Therefore, seen as discretion-constricting, *ch'u-fen* law appears largely dysfunctional, but seen as part of an attempt to control an organization with weak ties of solidarity, *ch'u-fen* law appears more functional. The proper mix of law and discretion, in other words, should be evaluated in connection with the conditions of morale and solidarity. Thus as a means of eliciting organizational performance, the extension of law at the expense of informal behavior is not necessarily a form of rationalization. In this area of behavior, the development of both the affective and cognitive aspects of political culture is probably more fruitful than the development of law.

In this book, therefore, I have looked at various facets of the internal organization of Ch'ing bureaucracy, especially at the officials' political culture and capabilities, and at problems in making, communicating, and applying laws, which played such a large role in specifying the constraints and tasks in terms of which the officials exercised their capabilities. A fuller study

13. *HCCSWP*, 16:6.

of Ch'ing bureaucracy would have to go deeper into some of the problems outlined in the introduction.

We may doubt that Ch'ing bureaucracy has left us a legacy of norms and experiences from which the statesmen of today can learn. Study of it, however, should be a step toward a more comprehensive typology of organizations, especially since the literature on organizations has so far been largely concerned with modern organizations in Western countries. With a better understanding of the Ch'ing bureaucracy's organizational capabilities, we will be better able to explain the sequence of successes and failures that made up its history and the heritage of organizational habits with which China responded to the challenges of modernization.

Appendix I

T'ao Chu's Memorials

Virtually all memorials I have used in *TWI* or *TYT* are of that one type called either *tsou-che*, *che-tsou*, or *che-tzu* (palace memorials). Silas Hsiu-liang Wu, in "The Memorial Systems of the Ch'ing Dynasty," *Harvard Journal of Asiatic History*, 27:7–75 (1967), shows that the Ch'ing inherited from the Ming two other kinds of memorials, *tsou-pen* (personal memorials) and *t'i-pen* (routine memorials); added the *tsou-che* in the late seventeenth century; and abolished the *tsou-pen* in 1748. He also shows that many *tsou-che* were semisecret in that they were handled not only by the memorialist and the emperor but also by the Grand Council, and that such semisecret *tsou-che* could be answered either with some secrecy through a letter sent via the Grand Council, or without secrecy, through a rescript or edict passing through the Grand Council and the Grand Secretariat. See also his *Communication and Imperial Control in China*, chs. IV, V, pp. 80–84, and Fu Tsung-mao, *Ch'ing-tai chün-chi-ch'u tsu-chih chi chih-chang chih yen-chiu* (A study of the functions and organization of the grand council of the Ch'ing dynasty; Taipei, 1967), pp. 339–355.

The *tsou-che* in *TYT*, I gather, were virtually all semisecret, and they were answered either publicly or secretly (in *TYT* there are many Grand Council letters called *tzu-chi*). Yet even though secret or semisecret, these documents were all published apparently shortly after T'ao Chu's death in 1839. Thus a further aspect of the secrecy problem is how long the secrecy was supposed to be maintained and how seriously violators were punished. An episode of 1836 casts some light on this; see *Liang-huai yen-fa-chih* (Salt laws gazetteer of the Liang-huai zone; preface of 1904), 4:22b. A censor charged in a memorial that T'ao Chu had "illegally published" some of his (T'ao's) memorials. The emperor answered that, having looked at the publication, he felt that there was nothing wrong with publishing documents that had been openly circulated in the government, but that a high official like T'ao Chu should keep "vermilion comments" (*chu-p'i*) secret. Therefore the emperor ordered that T'ao receive an administrative punishment. I have found no specific article for this offense, but failure to maintain secrecy in the case of memorials and of documents sent from one office to another, in those cases where secrecy was required, was punished mildly, e.g., by a one subgrade demotion; see *CFTL*, 9:34b. Possibly the punishment for publishing *chu-p'i* was more severe, but T'ao of course kept his office and retired a few years later with honor.

Li T'ing-hsi, a prefect under T'ao Chu in 1834 (see *TYT*, 52:11b) and writer of the *TYT fan-li*, states that (*fan-li*: 1b–2b) *TYT* contains both *t'i-pen* and *che-tsou*, and that because the *che-tsou* deal with more important affairs, they are presented ahead of the *t'i-pen*. However I have not found one *t'i-pen* in *TYT*, virtually every memorial in it being called *che-tzu* and beginning *tsou wei* rather than *t'i wei*. (The memorial postscripts are typically called *fu-tsou*, *fu-p'ien*, or *che-p'ien;* there are also many *ch'ing-tan* [clear lists], which were appended to memorials usually to present purely factual matters such as the names of recommended officials or financial statistics, in contrast to the more problematic matters discussed in the memorial proper.) One can only conclude that the chapters originally presenting the *t'i-pen* have been omitted from this edition.

It could be argued that a reading of T'ao Chu's *t'i-pen* would lead to a less dynamic view of his administration. Moreover, T'ao Chu certainly sent many communications to the boards involving those *hsiao-shih* (minor matters) which the boards were authorized to decide without consulting the emperor. (See *TCHT*, 4:1; 13:1; 26:1; 43:1; 53:1; 58:1. Each board had the fundamental directive: "Major matters are to be presented to the emperor; minor ones are to be carried out.") Even so, the number of *che-tsou* shows that nonroutine matters were numerous enough to require communication with the emperor more than once a week.

Appendix II

On Han Avoidance

Following Yen Keng-wang, for each staff of a Han prefecture or district, one has to distinguish between (*a*) the head official, i.e., the district magistrate or prefect; (*b*) certain special assisting officials; and (*c*) other subordinate officials of the prefects and district magistrates. See Yen Keng-wang, *Chung-kuo ti-fang hsing-cheng chih-tu-shih chüan shang: Ch'in Han ti-fang hsing-cheng chih-tu* (A history of regional and local administration in China—part one: the Ch'in and Han periods; Taipei, 1961), I: 102, 218. The data definitely allow the view that group (*c*) officials were appointed by their immediate superiors, i.e., the district magistrates and prefects, respectively, instead of by the capital, and that natives were generally used. The main exception was the three capital area prefectures (*san-fu*), where outsiders could be used. See Yen Keng-wang, I: 68–70, 77, 223; II: 301, 345–383. The situation for the group (*b*) officials was the reverse. They were centrally appointed, and natives were generally not used, but natives could be used at least on the district staffs in the three capital area prefectures. This is clarified by Yen in Ho Ping-ti, *Chung-kuo hui-kuan shih-lun* (An historical discussion of *Landsmannschaften* in China; Taipei, 1966), p. 4. The situation was much the same for district magistrates and prefects. They were centrally appointed and generally were not natives, with the exception of the capital prefecture (Ching-chao) and the capital district (Ch'ang-an), where natives could be used. At the same time, for the group (*a*) posts, there were, mostly before 100 B.C., a few exceptional cases where natives were appointed even outside the capital area, not to mention the large number of natives appointed at the beginning of the Han by the then-powerful feudal lords. See Yen Keng-wang, II: 345–348. These appointments of natives to the posts of district magistrate and prefect in the Han impressed Ch'ing officials such as T'ao Cheng-ching (*HCCSWP*, 17: 11b) and also the modern scholar T'ao Hsi-sheng, who mistakenly says that in the Western Han, prefects "mostly" were natives; T'ao Hsi-sheng, *Chung-kuo cheng-chih ssu-hsiang-shih* (A history of political thought in China; Taipei, 1964), II: 20. Certainly in subsequent periods also there were significant exceptions, encouraging the inference that avoidance was wrong. For some of these, see Ho Ping-ti, *Chung-kuo hui-kuan shih-lun*, pp. 5–6, and Sa Meng-wu, *Chung-kuo she-hui cheng-chih-shih* (A social and political history of China; 1965–1966), IV: 127.

Wang Hsin-ching also refers to some of these exceptions in various dynasties; *HCCSWP*, 17:10. J. B. Parsons notes a striking exception to avoidance in C. O. Hucker, ed., *Chinese Government in Ming Times* (New York, 1969), p. 216.

Yet one might argue that employing natives was as common in the Ch'ing as in the Han. The Han group (*c*) officials, who numbered in the hundreds within each district, to a large extent filled the functions of clerks. Whether in Han or Ch'ing times, therefore, those filling these functions were largely natives, and, quantitatively, natives played a similar role in the district yamen in Han and Ch'ing times. But in the Han period, many more of these native subordinates had the status of officials, and this fact encouraged the idea that avoidance was practiced less in Han times. For an outline of the steps whereby the status of lower-level office workers dropped from that of official to that of clerk, see Miao Ch'üan-chi, *Ming-tai hsü-li* (Clerks in the Ming dynasty; Taipei, 1969), pp. 1–9.

Appendix III

On the Ch'ing Penal Code

I am indebted to Professor Marius Hendrikus van der Valk for invaluable help regarding the penal code. No secondary account has a full discussion of its history, so far as I have found. The *Ch'ing-shih* (History of the Ch'ing dynasty; Taipei, 1961) has a useful synopsis of the first 75 years. See *ibid.*, III:1733–1734, and *Ch'ing-shih-kao hsing-fa-chih chu-chieh* (The monograph on penal law of the draft history of the Ch'ing dynasty, annotated; Peking, 1957), pp. 12–17. This includes the only list I have found of the *lü* changes of the second edition, but this list does not include the three changes discussed in IV, 2. My discussion is based largely on the first *ts'e* of the 1870 edition of the code, which contains the vast majority of prefatory memorials from the beginning of the dynasty up to that point. The first edition of the code, completed in 1646, can be found in the first edition of *Ta-Ch'ing hui-tien* (Collected statutes of the great Ch'ing dynasty; 1690), *hsing-pu* section, or in *Ku-chin t'u-shu chi-ch'eng* (A complete collection of writings, pictures, tables, and maps from the past and present; Shanghai, 1884), *chüan* 40–49 in *hsiang-hsing* section under *ching-chi.* Both of these books were originally published before the second edition of the code came out. This second edition was completed in 1725, issued in 1727 (see *Ch'ing-shih,* III: 1734). It is available at the Harvard-Yenching Library. Both the first and second editions followed the title of the 1610 Ming edition, being called *Ta-Ch'ing lü chi-chieh fu-li* (Penal statutes of the great Ch'ing dynasty, annotated, with the penal regulations included). Although the *Ku-chin t'u-shu chi-ch'eng* uses the title *Ta-Ch'ing-lü* for the first edition, the more proper title can be seen from the 1646 edict prefatory to that edition; see this edict e.g. in *Ta-Ch'ing lü-li t'ung-k'ao* (The penal statutes and regulations of the great Ch'ing dynasty, entirely annotated; 1886), *ts'e* no. 1, pp. 1a–b. The standard term *lü-li* was used first in the title of the third edition. For brief descriptions of the second and third editions, see Ma Feng-ch'en, *Ch'ing-tai hsing-cheng chih-tu yen-chiu ts'an-k'ao shu-mu* (Annotated bibliography for research into the administrative institutions of the Ch'ing dynasty; Peking, 1935), pp. 74–75. *Lü-li,* however, was also used as a title of the chapters presenting the penal code in *Ta-Ming hui-tien* (Collected statutes of the great Ming dynasty; Taipei, 1963), *hsing-pu* sections.

A most important source for the history of the penal code is *TCHTSL*: its Board of Punishments section has the penal code in toto with apparently all revised or excised and obsolete items since the beginning of the dynasty. Often, valuable explanatory quotations are included from the memorials which led to the changes. Also included in this section are *shih-li,* which in this instance are precedents considered too minor to be entered in the code proper, sometimes including a little of the memorial or edict involved.

Valuable explanations relative to the Ch'ing code can sometimes be found in the lavish commentary of *Ming-lü chi-chieh fu-li* (The penal statutes of the Ming dynasty, annotated, with the regulations included; 1908). The late Ch'ing legal expert Shen Chia-pen states in his preface to *TLti* that, besides Hsüeh, the Ch'ing period produced only one expert on the penal code, Wu Tzu-feng, also known as Wu T'an; see *TLti,* p. 2 of Shen Chia-pen's preface. Wu T'an was the compiler of *Ta-Ch'ing lü-li t'ung-k'ao,* which was put out around the end of the eighteenth century. For further information on the code and its editions, see Derk Bodde and Clarence Morris, *Law in Imperial China* (Cambridge, Mass., 1967), pp. 52–75. On *ibid.*, p. 66 the impression is mistakenly conveyed that the penal code revision plan in the early Ch'ien-lung period called for a total revision every three or five years. Actually, the plan then was only to issue periodically the batch of recently accumulated *li* (regulations or substatutes). On the same page, there is also a list of the years during which revisions of the code were put out. This list largely differs from my own, given below, which is based on the code's successive prefatory memorials.

A significant aspect of the history of the code, touched on in the text, is the 1689 decision to put out a second edition, since it seems clear that an especially conservative argument was made that such revision would violate the code's character as a *ch'eng-shu* (completed book). The central document here is one consisting of quotations from or paraphrases of (*a*) the Board of Punishments' memorial rejecting the suggestion of a regional censor, Sheng Fu-sheng, to revise the code; (*b*) Sheng Fu-sheng's original memorial; (*c*) the emperor's reply to the Board of Punishments' rejection, which consisted of an order for advice from the *Chan-shih* (Supervisorate of imperial instruction), the regional censors, the Six Sections of the Censorate for Examining the Six Boards, and the Nine Ministries (see II, 4, note 18); (*d*) the advice given in 1689 to the emperor by these offices, which comprised a typical group consulted on general questions of state; and (*e*) the emperor's approval of this advice, also given in 1689. This document is in *Ta-Ch'ing lü-li t'ung-k'ao, tsou-shu*, 12–14, and *TCLL, tsou-shu*, 5–7.

The *Ch'ing-shih* (III:1733–1734) has a convenient summary of the code's early history. The first edition was completed in 1646. In 1656 a version in Manchu was issued, apparently for the first time. In 1670 the code (here *lü-wen* must refer to the whole code, not just the *lü* proper) was generally revised or corrected. Finally, in 1679 a supplementary book was published consisting of penal regulations and called *hsien-hsing tse-li* (regulations currently in effect).

In his 1689 memorial, Sheng Fu-sheng had the goal of publishing the penal code as one internally consistent volume incorporating the *li* in the 1679 supplement and excising or correcting any obsolete items inherited from the Ming code. This clearly involved changes in the *lü* as well as the *li*, and indeed such changes were made when the next revision came out, that of 1725–1727. He also contemplated revisions in the severity of punishments.

The Board of Punishments rejected the idea of incorporating the successively promulgated *li*, such as those in the 1679 book, into the *lü*, i.e., the *li* section of the original penal code; if this is done, it argued, "Then it will be hard to proclaim the code as complete." Also it rejected the idea of excising obsolete items from the code on the grounds that these might still be needed for analogizing.

On the other hand, the Nine Ministries and other organs agreed with Sheng Fu-sheng that the 1679 *li* should be incorporated into the *li* of the code itself, and that obsolete items in the code should be excised. They also generally approved his emphasis on consistency, asking that steps should be taken to eliminate redundancy between the *li* and the *lü* and inconsistency between the Manchu and Chinese texts.

A problem remains as to whether in 1689 the Board of Punishments was rejecting the idea of altering *Ta-Ch'ing-lü*, that is, *Ta-Ch'ing lü chi-chieh fu-li*, the first edition of the Ch'ing penal code (1646), or just that of altering the *lü* in the narrower sense. Although it expressed itself ambiguously, it was at least strongly hinting that *Ta-Ching lü chi-chieh fu-li* was a *ch'eng-shu* which should not be altered. First of all, we must remember that because the term *lü-li* was not just then in vogue, *lü* might easily have been used as an abbreviation for *Ta-Ch'ing-lü*, i.e. *Ta-Ch'ing lü chi-chieh fu-li*.

Second, there are various other instances where *lü* seems to be used in this broader sense. The *Ch'ing-shih*, III:1733, says the *lü-wen* were revised in 1670 and that in 1679, *t'iao-li* "outside the *ting-lü*" were used to compile *hsien-hsing tse-li*. (See also *Ta-Ch'ing lü-li t'ung-k'ao, tsou-shu*: 10–11.) Similarly, Sheng Fu-sheng spoke of *lü-shu,* obviously meaning the whole code, not just the *lü* (*ibid., tsou-shu*: 12). Also calling the *lü-wen* a *ch'eng-shu* is strange unless one has in mind the whole book, *li* included. One could use *ch'eng-fa* or *ch'eng-hsien* to denote only the *lü* in the narrower sense. We may also note that *lü-hsüeh* typically refers to the study of the penal code as a whole, not just the *lü*.

Third, what the Board was in fact resisting, when it insisted that the *lü-wen* was a *ch'eng-shu,* was incorporating the 1679 *Hsien-hsing tse-li* into the *t'iao-li* of *Ta-Ch'ing-lü chi-chieh fu-li*. (Eliminating obsolete items in the *lü* or *Ta-Ch'ing-lü* was also an issue.) This is virtually demonstrated by the paraphrase of Sheng Fu-sheng's request in *ibid., tsou-shu*: 13b. Moreover, no one would have dreamed of putting *Hsien-hsing tse-li* into the *lü* of the code as opposed to the *li!* And still more, when Sheng Fu-sheng's proposal was reviewed by the Nine Ministries and other organs, they saw it as a question of eliminating redundancy or inconsistency between "the *t'iao-li* of the *lü-wen*" and the *Hsien-hsing tse-li* (*ibid., tsou-shu*: 13a–b). It is this process of entering new *li* into the *t'iao-li* of the code—which later became routine—that both Sheng and the Board referred to as putting new *li* into the *lü* or *ch'eng-lü* (*ibid., tsou-shu*: 12b–13). Therefore, when the Board stated that following Sheng Fu-sheng's idea would make it "hard to proclaim the *lü-wen* as completed," it was referring to *Ta-Ch'ing lü chi-chieh fu-li* as a *ch'eng-shu,* although by implication it was a fortiori against changing the *lü* proper. Moreover, this conservative view accorded with some Ming opinions. Opposition to *li* as a developing body of regulations arising out of individual cases and supplementing or replacing more basic laws can be found already in the Southern Sung period; Sa, IV: 143–144.

After the 1689 decision to print a second edition, a second edition finally came out in 1727, and a third, in 1740. Of the five *hsiao-hsiu* put out respectively in 1743, 1746, 1751, 1756, and 1761, Ma Feng-ch'en (pp. 76–77) has found four at the Peip'ing Library. Only the 1756 edition was missing. Reflecting the recognition that new *li* would now be regularly issued, an enlargement of a *lü* made with the third edition of the code, that of 1740, handled the problem of which *li* applied in the case of an offense committed before but tried after the promulgation of the new *li*. See *TLti,* 5: 43a–b. Then there were a 1768 *ta-hsiu,* a 1772 *hsiao-hsiu,* a 1779 *ta-hsiu,* a 1782 *hsiao-hsiu,* and a 1790 *ta-hsiu*. Irregularities in the time used to prepare the revisions are responsible for the divergences from a pure five-year cycle.

TCLL also has prefatory memorials to subsequent editions of 1796, 1802, 1806, 1810, 1815, 1822, 1826, 1830, 1836, 1841, 1846, 1853, and 1870. These dates all refer to the year in which the Board notified the emperor that the revision had been completed. It is not clear in all cases, however, whether the revision was a major or a minor one. *TCLL, tsou-shu,* p. 42, makes clear that the 1796 edition was a minor revision, the 1802, a major one. Also, from Ma Feng-ch'en, pp. 78–79 we can see that 1815, 1822, and 1853 were all minor ones, since each consists of only one *ts'e* (volume). However, the prefatory memorials beginning with the 1806 edition and through the 1870 edition are virtually identical. They all state that the revision referred to in the particular memorial does not consist only of the new batch of *li* arising since the previous revision but also involves the revision of old *li.* They thus all suggest a *ta-hsiu* (major revision). This is hardly possible. The answer seems to lie in the apparent fact that these revisions were mostly minor revisions which nevertheless also involved some touching up of the old text without large-scale alteration. This was done by inserting new pages and adding some phrases to the old pages explaining the status of some of the old *li.* This procedure is described in the prefatory memorials. The new *li* is added after the old *li* and at the head of each old or new *li* is stamped one of four phrases in yellow: "revised," "combination of two or more articles," "added," or "excised." Further explanations could also be added at the bottom of articles.

In evaluating the efficiency of these revisions, one should keep in mind that certain laws could not be altered because of their great social or moral importance, even though it was clear that they were not enforced. For instance, it was ridiculous to try to punish all consumers who bought illegal salt as well as the smugglers, but one could hardly withdraw the law forbidding people from buying such salt. Similarly (*TLti,* 17:19) while it was impossible to effect the uniformity of weights and measures at the market, the ideological importance of "unifying institutions" precluded withdrawing the law forbidding the use of irregular measures at the market. On the other hand, when such issues were not at stake, excisions were made with some efficiency. For instance (see *TCHTSL,* 762:2b–3b), the second edition of the code (1727) eliminated a *lü* which, referring to *ch'ien-hu* (leaders of battalions) and *po-hu* (leaders of companies) whose soldiers engaged in salt smuggling, called for their punishment by beating and "reduction by half of their salaries." This was eliminated on the grounds that such lack of vigilance was already handled under another article and that the terms *ch'ien-hu* and *po-hu,* as well as the practice of reducing a salary by half, no longer existed. Also a *li* dealing with abuses of the grain-salt exchange system (*k'ai-chung-fa*) was eliminated in 1725 because this system no longer existed.

Some regulations were retained with full knowledge that they worked only sometimes. For instance (*TLti,* 17:2a–b), Hsüeh Yün-sheng notes that a certain regulation was effective only when the pao-chia system worked. (This required inns to keep records on all visiting merchants, these records to be regularly presented to the authorities.)

To what extent were the penal code and other laws effectively communicated to the public outside officialdom? We should keep in mind books such as the 1870 *Sheng-yü shih-liu-t'iao fu-lü i-chieh* (Sagely edicts in sixteen sections with the penal code appended and explained in a simple fashion.) Printed in the late nineteenth century partly through imperial auspices, this book explained edicts using common words and presented the code in a simplified fashion or with simplifying explanations. Its explicit purpose was to familiarize literate persons among the common people and soldiers with these materials in the hope that they would pass on their knowledge to illiterate ones; see Ma Feng-ch'en, p. 26. Printing materials for the common people in a manner "easy to understand" was a concern also, say, in preparing notices about tax obligations; see *TYCS,* 9:13.

It seems likely that any book of laws directly affecting the affairs of both officials and persons outside the government would be accessible to the latter and would partly have the purpose of publicizing the emperor's policies to the people so as to avoid distortion of these policies by officials. This view is supported by the following statement of Ting Pao-chen in an 1882 memorial announcing completion of the *Salt Laws Gazetteer of the Szechwan Zone*: "Szechwan salt affairs are this province's number one major administrative matter. Previously there was no salt gazetteer to be promulgated and respectfully followed, the effects of this lack reaching the point that *officials and merchants* [emphasis added] had no reliable standard to observe and created confusion at will, evils arising in profusion and the monopoly falling into a disorder almost beyond the possibility of recovery. Therefore, I previously memorialized that we compile a salt gazetteer so as to facilitate the observance of the law." See *Ssu-ch'uan yen-fa-chih* (Salt laws gazetteer of the Szechwan zone; about 1883), *tsou-shu*:3.

From this passage one may infer that salt gazetteers were consulted by both merchants and officials when doubts or disputes arose, but, as we have seen (II, 4), such law books were not easily and cheaply available to the general public. More evidence to this effect is available in *Hsin-hsiu Ch'ang-lu yen-fa-chih* (Newly revised salt laws gazetteer of the Ch'ang-lu zone; 1726), 1:1, where the prefatory memorial states that the reason that there are salt gazetteers is "to present the laws and institutions and to stop quarrels and litigations." The latter naturally involved merchants.

It may be noted that there were a wide range of views supporting the publicizing of law. The Legalists stressed publicizing the law and are associated by some modern scholars with the famous events of 536 and 513 B.C., when the states of Cheng and Chin respectively publicized their laws and supposedly were criticized respectively by Shu-hsiang and Confucius. See Ch'ü, T'ung-tsu, *Law and Society in Traditional China* (Paris, 1961), pp. 170–171. Creel, however, shows that laws were often known to the public long before 536 and doubts the authenticity of the passage ascribed to Confucius deploring the publicizing of the law; see H. G. Creel, *The Origins of Statecraft in China, Vol. I, The Western Chou Empire* (Chicago, 1970), p. 162. Be that as it may, later Confucians often believed in the need to make the law clear, simple, and known to the people; see, e.g., Huan K'uan, *Yen-t'ieh-lun chiao-chu cha-chi* (Discourses on salt and iron with two sets of notes; Taipei, 1962), pp. 342–343.

A final point is the large variety of punishments in the code. *TCHTSL*, 723: *Shun-chih* 4, has a useful list, which begins by elaborating on the standard five punishments—beating with the light bamboo, beating with the heavy bamboo, penal servitude, banishment for life, and death—not only by noting the usual subgrades but also by pointing out that for bannermen and the personal slaves of bannermen, a whip was used instead of the light bamboo, and by explaining the cangue as connected to the punishment of beating with a heavy bamboo: the cangue accompanied sentences of beating with the heavy bamboo when the maximum number of strokes nominally allowed in a sentence—one hundred—was considered insufficient. "Beyond the five punishments," this document lists the following punishments, some of which had subcategories: (1) *ch'ien-hsi* (removal), which was a form of banishment for life but milder than the regular banishment (*liu*), because the criminal was sent only 1,000 *li* from his native place, the degrees of *liu* beginning at 2,000 *li;* (2) service for life as a soldier, which was regarded as harsher than *liu,* and which had five degrees, the worst service being in a malarious part of an extremely distant border area; (3) reduction to the status of a commoner and banishment beyond the border—this was later abolished; (4) a penal servitude term of four years, a sort of commuted term of banishment (three years was the normal maximum of penal servitude); (5) a penal servitude term of five years, which was a sort of commuted death sentence; (6) two methods of making execution more severe—the slicing process and displaying the severed head publicly. This list, partly because of its early date, omits the following physical deprivations also in the code: (7) tatooing; (8) mutilation of the corpse of a criminal who dies before punishment; (9) imprisonment and imprisonment for life (*yung-yüan chien-chin*); (10) the punishment of relatives as well as the offender; (11) banishment to Sinkiang, Heilungkiang, or Kirin—connected to this was the problematic sentence applied to officials of temporary or permanent exile in Sinkiang (see IV, 3, c). No doubt this list is not exhaustive. Also the code had penalties of a criminal nature calling for (12) the repayment of certain sums, whether by the offender, his son, or his family, and (13) confiscation of property. *Ch'ing-ch'ao hsü wen-hsien t'ung-k'ao* (A supplement dealing with the Ch'ing dynasty of the comprehensive historical study based on documents and more recent discourses; preface of 1915), III: 9955 is useful on the forms of banishment, and *Ch'ing-shih*, III: 1738–1739 has a fairly good list of punishments. Nearly all these punishments are thoroughly discussed in Bodde and Morris, pp. 66–98.

Appendix IV

On *Ling* and *Chih-shu*

Mentioned in III, 2, note 9, *chih-shu* were defined as commands issued by the emperor, while *ling*, in a complementary way, came to be defined as imperial approvals of proposals made in memorials. These definitions received their final form only in the second edition of the penal code, which was completed in 1725. Two issues were involved in the development of these definitions. First, should violations of imperial appellate cases be punished the same way as violations of independently issued imperial commands? Second, what was *ling* to denote?

At least as early as the Ming period, there was an idea that violations of imperial appellate cases should be treated differently. Thus the commentary to the Ming code quotes a view that imperial orders such as *tsou-chun* arrived at through imperial approval of an official's decision should not be called *chih-shu*, and that it is wrong to try violations of such imperial appellate cases as though they were violations of *chih-shu*. See *Ming-lü chi-chieh fu-li* (The penal statutes of the Ming dynasty, annotated, with the regulations included; 1908), 3:4a–b.

However it seems clear that Ming law lacked any article specifically on violations of imperial appellate cases. Its article on the violation of *ling* had a different function, since *ling* here denoted a specific book, *Ta-Ming-ling*, originally promulgated in 1368 and containing both administrative provisions and punishments; see *Ming-lü chi-chieh*, 26:14b–15, and Naito Kenkichi, *Chūgokū hōsei kōshō* (Studies in Chinese law; Kyoto, 1963), pp. 90–116. This article on *ling* in Ming times thus had much the same function that it had in the T'ang penal code, where, according to Twitchett, it was used to back up with sanctions a body of administrative laws which were called *ling* and which themselves lacked any specification of sanctions; see D. C. Twitchett, "The Fragment of the T'ang Ordinances of the Department of Waterways Discovered in Tun-huang," *Asia Major*, 6:23–79 (1957–58), pp. 28–29. The Ming code's definition of *ling* follows that of the T'ang code verbatim: "This refers to instances where there are prohibitions in *ling* for which the penal code does not specify a punishment"; *Ku-T'ang-lü shu-i* (Ssu-pu ts'ung-k'an), 27:23.

In the Ch'ing period, however, *ling* lacked any such definite reference and as explained above was used loosely in a variety of ways (III, 4). Thus the article on *ling* now offered an opportunity to give full legal articulation to the notion that violations of imperial appellate cases should not be treated as violations of *chih-shu.* This opportunity, however, was seized only in a confused way by the first edition of the Ch'ing code (1646). It is true that this edition did, in its explanation of *chih-shu,* add to the Ming explanation: "Instances where it is a matter of carrying out a *tsou-chun* do not fall under this article." However this point is contradicted in this edition's explanation of the article on *ling,* since here the first edition retains the T'ang and Ming explanations and only adds: "If one intentionally violates a proclamation, rescript, *tsou-chun,* or *shih-li,* one is also guilty of violating a *chih-shu.*" See *Ku-chin t'u-shu chi-ch'eng* (A complete collection of writings, pictures, tables, and maps from the past and the present; Shanghai, 1884), 49:10b and 43:12 in *hsiang-hsing* section under *ching-chi.* This problem was finally solved, however, with the second edition (1725), which rewrote the definition of *ling* to make the term clearly refer to *tsou-chun* and other imperial appellate cases.

The terminology of imperial appellate cases is discussed in III, 2. For the knotty problem of the terminology on independently issued imperial commands, see J. K. Fairbank and Ssu-yü Teng, *Ch'ing Administration: Three Studies* (Cambridge, Mass., 1961), pp. 76–106; *Shinkoku gyōseihō* (Administrative laws of the Ch'ing state; Tokyo, 1905–1911), I:27–28; and *Ch'ing-kuo hsing-cheng-fa* (Administrative laws of the Ch'ing state; Shanghai, 1906), 1:2:3:31–32. Apart from official definitions, there is the problem of how strictly *chih-shu* was used in practice. Derk Bodde and Clarence Morris, *Law in Imperial China* (Cambridge, Mass., 1967), p. 178, indicates broad and loose usage.

Appendix V

On the Right to Memorialize

In Silas Hsiu-liang Wu, "The Memorial Systems of the Ch'ing dynasty," *Harvard Journal of Asiatic Studies*, 27:7–75 (1967), pp. 61–62, there is a list, following *TCHT*, 82:10b–11, of officials qualified to present *tsou-che*-type memorials, and his list serves to indicate the diffuse scattering of this right directly to communicate with the emperor throughout many offices. It should be noted that this *TCHT* passage states that the higher nobles of the *tsung-shih* (imperial house) had the right to memorialize. (On types of nobles, see IV, 3, d.) Just how many of the twelve ranks of the imperial house had the right is not clear. There is evidence that the phrase used, *tsung-shih wang-kung*, covers just the first six. There is also a list of persons qualified to present *tsou-che*-type memorials "by themselves" in *Rikubu seigo chūkai* (Terminology of the six boards, annotated; Kyoto, 1940), pp. 3–4. The text in this book is that of *Liu-pu ch'eng-yü chu-chieh*, a handbook partly prepared in the late Ch'ing period. This list gives the first four grades of the imperial house as qualified as well as the first three grades of non-imperial nobles.

A definitive understanding of who could memorialize is still beyond us. *Rikubu* diverges from the *TCHT* list in that (a) it states that *tsung-ping* (brigade generals in green standard units), provincial treasurers, and provincial judges lack the right to "memorialize by themselves"—*TCHT* says they have it; (b) *Rikubu* omits taotais, while *TCHT* says that taotais, like certain censors, have a partial right to memorialize in that they may present memorials in which they *yen-shih* (discuss state matters). From *Rikubu*, p. 8, we learn that besides *yen-shih* there were two kinds of memorials: *hsieh-en* (expressing thanks for an imperial favor) and *ch'i-ch'ing* (to make a request [from the emperor]). The latter clearly was that main category of executive memorials making specific proposals.

One should also note that all officials had the right to memorialize if they were "being oppressed in a way out of accord with the rules of moral propriety" by their superiors (*TCLL*, 4:16; Philastre, I:135). However low his rank, an official speaking to the emperor at an audience was said to be "memorializing." An official without the full right to memorialize could ask one who had it to memorialize on his behalf (*tai-tsou*). Finally we should keep in mind that the realization of the legal right to memorialize partly depended on changing policies or fashions.

For instance, in 1653 an imperial edict complained that although the head officials at the six boards and some other capital offices included both Manchus and Chinese, only the Manchu officials were presenting memorials; it was ordered that henceforth such head officials at an office work and memorialize together. See *Shinkoku gyōseihō* (Administrative laws of the Ch'ing state; Tokyo, 1905–1911), I:161, and *Ch'ing-kuo hsing-cheng-fa* (Administrative laws of the Ch'ing state; Shanghai, 1906), 2:4:4:195. Similarly, in 1800 the emperor sent down an edict criticizing *t'i-tu* (generals-in-chief of the green standard forces in a province) and *tsung-ping* (brigade generals in green standard forces) for only memorializing on routine matters such as thanks for imperial favors and floods. In the Yung-cheng period (1723–1735), the Chia-ch'ing emperor said, these officials memorialized both on local government and military affairs. Today, they should at least memorialize on the latter, and, even though they now have little if any responsibility for local government, they should also memorialize on the latter if they happen to have some sound information (*TCHTSL*, 577: Chia-ch'ing 5).

On which officials were allowed to present *t'i-pen*, see *TCHTSL*, 1042:5b–6. Generally, the regular right to present *t'i-pen* regarding administrative issues was possessed only by the head officials (*t'ang-kuan*) of capital offices, governors-general, governors, and three ranks of military officers.

Appendix VI

On Calculating Average Length of Tenure in the Grand Council

Calculations as to lengths of careers on the Grand Council were not made by Fu Tsung-mao. Mine are based on the table in *Ch'ing-shih* (History of the Ch'ing dynasty; Taipei, 1961), IV:2486–2512, and that, largely based on *Ch'ing-shih-kao,* in Fu Tsung-mao, *Ch'ing-tai chün-chi-ch'u tsu-chih chi chih-chang chih yen-chiu* (A study of the functions and organization of the grand council of the Ch'ing dynasty; Taipei, 1967), pp. 529–683. To avoid worrying about fractions of a year, I have roughly determined the length of each career (many were continuous, but far from all) by counting the number of times a person is found on those lists which each give all members for a particular year, and then subtracting one year, except in the case of those names found on only one such list. The latter persons may well have served for only a month or two, and I count them as "about one year or considerably less." My conservative bias is reinforced by the fact that if a person appears on two lists, he may well have served for almost two years, but, again, I give him only one year. Also the careers at the very end of the dynasty were abnormally short, being cut off by the abolition of the Grand Council. As a further precaution to prevent undue inflation of my figure for the length of the average career on the Council, I have counted the forty-four men whom I list as serving about 1 year or considerably less as having altogether served only 22 man-years; thus I arrive at a total of 951 man-years on the Council, which, divided by 146, yields 6.5 years as the average length of a career.

On the other hand, I have not subtracted time spent by a grand councillor outside the Council (often outside the capital) on a special mission, after which he often returned to the Council. Since the job of grand councillor was legally not a regular post but simply a condition of *hsing-tsou* (to perform certain administrative functions not defined as a regular office), being ordered to do something else was about equivalent to leaving the Grand Council; one's place there apparently lacked any other residual legal form. However, from a practical point of view, such missions outside the Council, although sometimes taking several months, can be looked at as temporary leaves, and that is how I have regarded them. Fu Tsung-mao, *chün-chi-ch'u,* p. 145, also takes this view.

As for the reasons given in the table of the *Ch'ing-shih* for officials' leaving the Grand Council, there is only one category that is conceivably problematic, namely the words by themselves *mien* or *mien-chih* (participation in imperial audiences as a grand councillor stopped). I have counted these as signifying an honorable departure, following Fu Tsung-mao, *chün-chi-ch'u,* p. 217. Any connotation of punishment they might occasionally have carried was too slight to matter. The case of Ch'iu Yüeh-hsiu in the winter of 1758–59 indicates that some further explanation was needed to give *mien* a punitive significance: in Ch'iu's case, *I-shih mien* (because of his involvement in a troublesome affair, his participation in imperial audiences as a grand councillor was stopped). I have put Ch'iu's case in the category of dishonorable departure. Another such example is Ying-ho's departure in the winter of 1820–21: "Because he violated the imperial will in his words and actions, his participation in imperial audiences as a grand councillor was stopped." To gather and check out data on the persons listed as removed punitively, I have used standard biographical sources, mainly Hummel and *Ch'ing-shih lieh-chuan.* My discussion of dishonorable exits differs from Fu Tsung-mao, p. 217, in differentiating not only between criminal and administrative punishments but also between final exits and exits followed by resumption of service on the Grand Council. Fu Tsung-mao counts 139 men as grand councillors, while I count 146. Our difference is largely or entirely due to the fact that Fu has excluded (pp. 146, 167) persons appointed to the Council on an explicitly temporary basis, while I have included them. For my purposes at least, temporary appointments are much the same as very short regular appointments, which Fu includes. However, I have followed Fu in excluding Fang Wei-tien, whom the *Ch'ing-shih* lists as being on the Council in Chia-ch'ing 16, since Fang never took up his post, instead returning home to care for his ill mother, as *Ch'ing-shih,* IV:2499, says. If I had followed Fu's figure of 139, my average length of tenure would have been slightly longer, but my percentage of grand councillors receiving criminal punishments would have been slightly higher. There is an arithmetical difficulty with Fu's table on p. 217, which deals with 130 grand councillors (it excludes the 9 members from the imperial family). Fu counts 130 exits. If he includes only final exits, however, then his figure of 25 men leaving with a demotion or dismissal is wrong; only 19 did. If he wants to count all exits, including those followed by reappointment to the Council, then there were more than 130, since some men served more than once on the Council.

Bibliography

Included are only the works which have directly played a role in the preparation of this study, not all works relevant to the themes discussed. Some works cited only once or twice in the footnotes are omitted here.

Almond, G. A. and G. B. Powell, Jr. *Comparative Politics*. Boston and Toronto, Little, Brown, 1966.

Balazs, Étienne. *Chinese Civilization and Bureaucracy*, tr. H. M. Wright. New Haven, Yale University Press, 1964.

———, tr. *Le Traité juridique du "Souei-chou."* Leiden, E. J. Brill, 1954.

Barnard, Chester I. *The Functions of the Executive*. Cambridge, Mass., Harvard University Press, 1962.

Beasley, W. G., and E. G. Pulleyblank, eds. *Historians of China and Japan*. London, Oxford University Press, 1961.

Bendix, Reinhard, ed. *State and Society*. Boston, Little, Brown, 1968.

——— and Seymour Martin Lipset, eds. *Class, Status, and Power*. New York, Free Press, 1964.

Bodde, Derk, and Clarence Morris. *Law in Imperial China*. Cambridge, Mass., Harvard University Press, 1967.

Brunnert, H. S., and V. V. Hagelstrom. *Present Day Political Organization of China*, tr. A. Beltchenko and E. E. Moran. Recent unidentified Taiwan reprint of copy with 1911 translators' preface.

CFTL, see *Ch'in-ting ch'ung-hsiu liu-pu ch'u-fen tse-li* (1887).

Chan Wing-tsit, tr. and comp. *A Source Book in Chinese Philosophy*. Princeton, N. J., Princeton University Press, 1963.

Chang Chin-chien 張金鑑. *Chung-kuo wen-kuan chih-tu-shih* 中國文官制度史 (A history of China's civil service). Taipei, Chung-hua wen-hua ch'u-pan shih-yeh wei-yüan-hui 中華文化出版事業委員會, 1955.

Chang Chung-li. *The Chinese Gentry*. Seattle, University of Washington Press, 1955.

——— *The Income of the Chinese Gentry*. Seattle, University of Washington Press, 1962.

Chang Te-ch'ang 張德昌. *Ch'ing-chi i-ko ching-kuan-te sheng-huo* 清季一個京官的生活 (The life of a capital official in late Ch'ing times). Hong Kong, Chinese University of Hong Kong, 1970.

Ch'en Ku-yüan 陳顧遠. *Chung-kuo fa-chih-shih* 中國法制史 (A history of China's legal institutions). Shanghai, Commercial Press, 1934.

Cheng Ching-i 鄭競毅, and P'eng Shih 彭時. *Fa-lü ta-tz'u-shu* 法律大辭書 (Large dictionary on law). 3 vols. Shanghai, Commercial Press, 1936.

Ch'eng Shu-te 程樹德. *Chung-kuo fa-chih-shih* 中國法制史 (A history of China's legal institutions). Shanghai, Hua-t'ung shu-chü 華通書局, 1931.

——— *Chiu-ch'ao lü-k'ao* 九朝律考 (A study of the penal statutes of nine dynasties). 2 vols. Taipei, The Commercial Press of Taiwan, 1965.

Chiang Shang-hsien 姜尚賢. *Hsün-tzu ssu-hsiang t'i-hsi* 荀子思想體系 (The structure of Hsün-tzu's thought). Tainan, published by Chiang Shang-hsien, 1966.

Ch'ien Mu 錢穆. *Chung-kuo chin-san-pai-nien hsüeh-shu shih* 中國近三百年學術史 (A history of Chinese thought during the last three centuries). Shanghai, Commercial Press, 1937.

——— *Kuo-shih ta-kang* 國史大綱 (A basic outline of our national history). 2 vols. Shanghai, Commercial Press, 1948.

Ch'in-ting ch'ung-hsiu liu-pu ch'u-fen tse-li 欽定重修六部處分則例 (Imperially endorsed and revised regulations on administrative punishment for affairs categorized according to the six boards). 52 chüan. 1887.

Ch'in-ting hsin-tsuan liu-pu ch'u-fen tse-li 欽定新纂六部處分則例 (Imperially endorsed, newly compiled regulations on administrative punishment relative to affairs categorized according to the six boards). 52 chüan. 1828.

Ch'in-ting hu-pu ts'ao-yün ch'üan-shu 欽定戶部漕運全書 (The board of revenue's imperially endorsed complete book on the grain tribute). 92 chüan. 1845.

Ch'in-ting hu-pu tse-li 欽定戶部則例 (Imperially endorsed regulations of the board of revenue). 15 chüan. 1838.

Ch'in-ting hu-pu tse-li 欽定戶部則例 (Imperially endorsed regulations of the board of revenue). 99 chüan. 1851.

Ch'in-ting hu-pu tse-li 欽定戶部則例 (Imperially endorsed regulations of the board of revenue). 100 chüan. 1865.

Ch'in-ting li-pu tse-li 欽定吏部則例 (Imperially endorsed regulations of the board of civil officials). 20 ts'e. 1843.

Ch'in-ting li-pu tse-li 欽定禮部則例 (Imperially endorsed regulations of the board of rites). 202 chüan. 1845.

Ch'in-ting wang-kung ch'u-fen tse-li 欽定王公處分則例 (Imperially endorsed regulations on the administrative punishment of princes). 4 chüan, 6 ts'e. Published no earlier than 1845.

Ch'ing-ch'ao hsü wen-hsien t'ung-k'ao 清朝續文獻通考 (A supplement dealing with the Ch'ing dynasty of the comprehensive historical study based on documents and more recent discourses), comp. Liu Chin-tsao 劉錦藻. 4 vols. Commercial Press. Preface, 1915.

Ch'ing-kuo hsing-cheng fa 清國行政法 (Administrative laws of the Ch'ing state), a translation by Ch'en Yü-nien 陳與年 *et al.* of part of *Shinkoku gyōseihō* (see below). Shanghai, Kuang-chih shu-chü 廣智書局, 1906.

Ch'ing-shih 清史 (History of the Ch'ing dynasty), comp. Ch'ing-shih pien-tsuan wei-yüan-hui 清史編纂委員會 (Commission for the compilation of the history of the Ch'ing dynasty). 8 vols. Taipei, Kuo-fang yen-chiu-yüan 國防研究院, 1961.

Ch'ing-shih-kao 清史稿 (Draft history of the Ch'ing dynasty), comp. Chao Erh-hsün 趙爾巽 *et al.* 2 vols. Lien-ho shu-tien 聯合書店, 1942.

Ch'ing-shih-kao hsing-fa-chih chu-chieh 清史稿刑法志註解 (The monograph on penal law of the draft history of the Ch'ing dynasty, annotated), comp. Kuo-wu-yüan fa-chih-chü fa-chih-shih yen-chiu-shih 國務院法制局法制史研究室 (Council of state, bureau of legal affairs, department for research into legal history). Peking, Fa-lü ch'u-pan-she 法律出版社, 1957.

Ch'ing-shih lieh-chuan 清史列傳 (Biographies of persons prominent in the history of the Ch'ing dynasty), comp. and pub. by Chung-hua shu-chü 中華書局. 10 vols. Taipei, 1962.

Ch'ing-shih-lu ching-chi tzu-liao chi-yao 清實錄經濟資料輯要 (Essential economic materials from the veritable records of the Ch'ing dynasty), comp. Nan-k'ai ta-hsüeh li-shih-hsi 南開大學歷史系 (History department of Nankai university). Peking, Chung-hua shu-chü 中華書局, 1959.

Ch'ing-tai wen-chi p'ien-mu fen-lei so-yin 清代文集篇目分類索引 (Categorized index of the Ch'ing dynasty's collections of an author's writings), comp. Kuo-li Pei-p'ing t'u-shu-kuan 國立北平圖書館 (National Peiping library). Peking, 1935.

Chou Chin-sheng 周金聲. *Chung-kuo ching-chi ssu-hsiang-shih* 中國經濟思想史 (A history of Chinese economic thought). 4 vols. Taipei, published by Chou Chin-sheng, 1965.

Chou Tao-chi 周道濟. *Han-T'ang tsai-hsiang chih-tu* 漢唐宰相制度 (The institution of the prime office in the Han and T'ang dynasties). Taipei, Cultural Foundation of the Chia-hsin Cement Co., 1964.

Chu Ch'uan-yü 朱傳譽. *Sung-tai hsin-wen-shih* 宋代新聞史 (A history of the flow of news in the Sung dynasty). Taipei, Chung-kuo hsüeh-shu chu-tso chiang-chu wei-yüan-hui 中國學術著作獎助委員會, 1967.

Chu-tzu chi-ch'eng 諸子集成 (A complete collection of the works of the ancient scholars), comp. by Chung-hua shu-chü 中華書局 on the basis of an earlier collection published by Shih-chieh shu-chü 世界書局. 8 vols. Peking, Chung-hua shu-chü, 1959. Vol. 2 consists of an edition of *Hsün-tzu* 荀子 annotated by Wang Hsien-ch'ien 王先謙, which is the edition used in this book.

Ch'u-fen tse-li t'u-yao 處分則例圖要 (Essentials in tabular form of the regulations on administrative punishment). 6 chüan. 1872. Part of a book totaling 6 ts'e, the rest of which is a similar digest of the penal code.

Chung-kuo cheng-chih ssu-hsiang yü cheng-chih chih-tu-shih lun-chi 中國政治思想與政治制度史論集 (Collected articles on the history of Chinese political thought and institutions), ed. Chang Ch'i-yün 張其昀. 3 vols. Taipei, Chung-hua wen-hua ch'u-pan shih-yeh wei-yüan-hui 中華文化出版事業委員會, 1955.

Chung-kuo chin-tai ching-chi ssu-hsiang yü ching-chi cheng-ts'e tzu-liao hsüan-chi 中國近代經濟思想與經濟政策資料選輯 (Selected materials on China's economic thought and economic policy in modern times), ed. Wu Pao-san 巫寶三 *et al.* 2 vols. Peking, K'o-hsüeh ch'u-pan-she 科學出版社, 1954.

Chung-kuo ts'ung-shu tsung-lu 中國叢書綜錄 (Index to China's collections of varied writings), comp. Shang-hai t'u-shu-kuan 上海圖書館 (The Shanghai library). 3 vols. Peking, Chung-hua shu-chü 中華書局, 1959-1962.

Chüeh-chih ch'üan-shu, see *Ta-Ch'ing chin-shen ch'üan-shu*.

Ch'ü T'ung-tsu. *Law and Society in Traditional China*. Paris and The Hague, Mouton, 1961.

——— *Local Government in China under the Ch'ing*. Cambridge, Mass., Harvard University Press, 1962.

Cohen, Jerome A. "New Developments in Western Studies of Chinese Law: A Symposium Introduction," *Journal of Asian Studies* 27.3: 475–483 (May 1968).

Creel, H. G. "The *Fa-chia*: 'Legalists' or 'Administrators'?" *Bulletin of the Institute of History and Philology, Academia Sinica*, extra Vol. 4, part 2, 607–636 (Taipei, 1961).

——— *The Origins of Statecraft in China*. Vol. 1, *The Western Chou Empire*. Chicago, University of Chicago Press, 1970.

Eberhard, Wolfram. *Guilt and Sin in Traditional China*. Berkeley, University of California Press, 1967.

Eisenstadt, S. N. *The Political Systems of Empires*. New York, Free Press of Glencoe, 1963.

——— *Essays on Comparative Institutions*. New York, J. Wiley, 1965.

———, ed. *The Protestant Ethic and Modernization; A Comparative View*. New York, Basic Books, 1968.

Escarra, Jean. *Le Droit chinois*. Peking, Henri Vetch, 1936. In Gertrude R. Browne, tr., *Chinese Law*. Works Progress Administration, W. P. 2799, Seattle, University of Washington, 1936. Reprinted (xerox), Cambridge, Mass., Harvard University Law School and East Asian Research Center, 1961.

Etzioni, Amitai. *A Comparative Analysis of Complex Organizations*. New York, Free Press of Glencoe, 1961.

———, ed. *A Sociological Reader on Complex Organizations*. New York, Holt, Rinehart and Winston, 1969.

Fairbank, John K. *Ch'ing Documents: An Introductory Syllabus*. 2 vols. Cambridge, Mass., Harvard University Press, 1965.

——— and Kwang-Ching Liu. *Modern China—A Bibliographical Guide to Chinese Works, 1898–1937*. Cambridge, Mass., Harvard University Press, 1950.

——— and Masataka Banno. *Japanese Studies of Modern China*. Rutland and Tokyo, Charles E. Tuttle, 1955.

——— and Ssu-yü Teng. *Ch'ing Administration: Three Studies*. Cambridge, Mass., Harvard University Press, 1961.

———, Edwin O. Reischauer, and Albert M. Craig. *East Asia—The Modern Transformation*. Boston, Houghton Mifflin, 1965.

Fang Hao 方豪. *Sung-shih* 宋史 (History of the Sung dynasty). 2 vols. Taipei, Chung-kuo wen-hua ch'u-pan shih-yeh wei-yüan hui 中國文化出版事業委員會, 1954.

Feng Yu-lan 馮友蘭. *Chung-kuo che-hsüeh-shih-pu* 中國哲學史補 (Supplement to a history of Chinese philosophy). Shanghai, Commercial Press, 1936.

Feuerwerker, Albert, and S. Cheng. *Chinese Communist Studies of Modern Chinese History*. Cambridge, Mass., East Asian Research Center, Harvard University, 1961.

Feuerwerker, A. *et al.*, eds. *Approaches to Modern Chinese History*. Berkeley, University of California Press, 1967.

Folsom, Kenneth E. *Friends, Guests, and Colleagues: The Mu-fu System in the Late Ch'ing Period*. Berkeley, University of California Press, 1968.

Fortes, M., and E. E. Evans-Pritchard, eds. *African Political Systems*. London, Oxford University Press, 1958.

Franke, Wolfgang. *An Introduction to the Sources of Ming History*. Singapore, University of Malaya Press, 1968.

Fromm, Erich. *Escape from Freedom.* New York, Farrar and Rinehart, 1941.

Fu Tsung-mao 傅宗懋. *Ch'ing-tai tu-fu chih-tu* 清代督撫制度 (The institution of the governor-general and the governor in the Ch'ing dynasty). Taipei district, National Chengchi University, 1963.

——— *Ch'ing-tai chün-chi-ch'u tsu-chih chi chih-chang chih yen-chiu* 清代軍機處組織及職掌 (A study of the functions and organization of the grand council of the Ch'ing dynasty). Taipei, Cultural Foundation of the Chia-hsin Cement Co., 1967.

Fujii Hiroshi 藤井宏. "*Kaichū* no imi oyobi kigen" 開中の意義及び起源 (The meaning and origin of *kaichū*), in *Katō Hakase kanreki kinen Tōyōshi shūsetsu* 加藤博士還暦記念東洋史集説 (Collected articles on oriental history in honor of Dr. Katō's sixty-first birthday). Tokyo, 1941.

——— "Mindai enshō no ikkosatsu" 明代鹽商の一考察 (A study of the salt merchants of the Ming dynasty); *Shigaku zasshi* 中學雜誌 (The journal of history) 54.5: 506–555; 54.6: 627–666; 54.7: 693–735 (1943).

Fuller, Lon L. *The Morality of Law.* New Haven, Conn., Yale University Press, 1964.

Goodrich, L. C. *The Literary Inquisition of Ch'ien-lung.* Baltimore, Md., Waverley Press, Inc., 1935.

HCCSWP, see *Huang-ch'ao ching-shih wen-pien.*

HPTL, see *Ch'in-ting hu-pu tse-li* (1851).

Han Fei-tzu 韓非子. Ssu-pu ts'ung-k'an 四部叢刊 edition. Shanghai, Commercial Press, 1929.

Han Yu-shan. *Elements of Chinese Historiography.* Hollywood, W. H. Hawley, 1955.

Han Yü 韓愈. *Han Ch'ang-li ch'üan-chi* 韓昌黎全集 (The complete writings of Han Yü). Shanghai, Shih-chieh shu-chü 世界書局, 1935.

Hightower, John R. *Topics in Chinese Literature.* Cambridge, Mass., Harvard University Press, 1965.

Ho Ping-ti. *Studies on the Population of China, 1368–1953.* Cambridge, Mass., Harvard University Press, 1959.

——— *The Ladder of Success in Imperial China.* New York, Columbia University Press, 1962.

——— 何炳棣. *Chung-kuo hui-kuan shih-lun* 中國會館史論 (A historical discussion of *Landsmannschaften* in China). Taipei, Hsüeh-sheng shu-chü 學生書局, 1966.

——— and Tang Tsou, eds. *China's Heritage and the Communist Political System*, Vol. 1, Book 1 of *China in Crisis.* Chicago, University of Chicago Press, 1968.

Ho Wei-ning 何維凝. *Chung-kuo yen-cheng-shih* 中國鹽政史 (A history of China's salt administration). 2 vols. Taipei, Ho Lung Li-fen 何龍澧芬, 1966.

Hou Wai-lu 侯外廬 *et al. Chung-kuo ssu-hsiang t'ung-shih* 中國思想通史 (A general history of Chinese thought). 5 vols. Peking, Jen-min ch'u-pan-she 人民出版社, 1957–1960.

Hsia Chün-yü 夏君虞. *Sung-hsüeh kai-yao* 宋學概要 (Essentials of Sung thought). Shanghai, Commercial Press, 1937.

Hsiao I-shan 蕭一山. *Ch'ing-tai t'ung-shih* 清代通史 (A general history of the Ch'ing dynasty). 5 vols. Taipei, Commercial Press, 1967.

Hsiao Kung-ch'üan. *Rural China: Imperial Control in the Nineteenth Century.* Seattle, University of Washington Press, 1960.

——— 蕭公權. *Chung-kuo cheng-chih ssu-hsiang shih* 中國政治思想史 (A history of China's political thought). 6 vols. Taipei, Chung-hua ta-tien pien-yin-hui 中華大典編印會, 1966.

Hsieh Pao Chao. *The Government of China (1644–1911)*. Baltimore, Md., Johns Hopkins University Press, 1925.

Hsin-hsiu Ch'ang-lu yen-fa-chih 新修長蘆鹽法志 (Newly revised salt laws gazetteer of the Ch'ang-lu zone). 16 chüan. Preface, 1726.

Hsing-an hui-lan 刑案滙覽 (Conspectus of penal cases), comp. Pao Shu-yün 鮑書芸 *et al.* 60 chüan plus 2 ts'e. Preface, 1834.

Hsü, Immanuel C. Y. *The Rise of Modern China*. New York, Oxford University Press, 1970.

Hsü Ta-ling 許大齡. *Ch'ing-tai chüan-na chih-tu* 淸代捐納制度 (The system of purchasing offices and official titles during the Ch'ing dynasty). Peking, Harvard Yenching Institute, 1950.

Hsü Tao-lin 徐道鄰. *Chung-kuo fa-chih-shih lun-lüeh* 中國法制史論略 (An outline history of China's legal institutions). Taipei, Cheng-chung shu-chü 正中書局, 1953.

Hsüeh Yün-sheng 薛允升. *Tu-li ts'un-i* 讀例存疑 (Questions on reading the penal regulations). 54 chüan. 1905.

Hsün-tzu, see *Chu-tzu chi-ch'eng.*

Hu Chi-ch'uang 胡寄窗. *Chung-kuo ching-chi ssu-hsiang-shih* 中國經濟思想史 (A history of Chinese economic thought). 2 vols. Shanghai, Shang-hai jen-min ch'u-pan-she 上海人民出版社, 1962–.

Huan K'uan 桓寬. *Yen-t'ieh-lun chiao-chu cha-chi* 鹽鐵論校注札記 (Discourses on salt and iron with two sets of notes). Taipei, Shih-chieh shu-chü 世界書局, 1962.

Huang-ch'ao cheng-tien lei-tsuan 皇朝政典類纂 (Our august dynasty's administrative institutions, arranged by category). 500 chüan. Shanghai, 1903.

Huang-ch'ao ching-shih wen-pien 皇朝經世文編 (Our august dynasty's writings on statecraft), comp. Ho Ch'ang-ling 賀長齡. 8 vols. Taipei, Shih-chieh shu-chü 世界書局, 1964.

Huang-Ming ching-shih wen-pien 皇明經世文編 (The august Ming dynasty's writings on statecraft), comp. Ch'en Tzu-lung 陳子龍 *et al.* 30 vols. Taipei, Kuo-lien t'u-shu ch'u-pan yu-hsien kung-ssu 國聯圖書出版有限公司, 1964. Reprint of an edition printed around 1635.

Huang Nai-lung 黃乃隆. *Wang An-shih pien-fa-te ts'ai-ching cheng-ts'e shu-p'ing* 王安石變法的財經政策述評 (An evaluation of the fiscal and economic policies in Wang An-shih's reform). Taichung, 1968.

Huang Pei. "Aspects of Ch'ing Autocracy: An Institutional Study, 1644–1735," *Tsing Hua Journal of Chinese Studies* 6.1–2: 105–148 (December 1967).

Hucker, Charles O. "On Confucianism and the Chinese Censorial System," in David S. Nivison and Arthur F. Wright, eds., *Confucianism in Action*. Stanford, Calif., Stanford University Press, 1959.

——— *The Censorial System of Ming China*. Stanford, Calif., Stanford University Press, 1966.

———, ed. *Chinese Government in Ming Times: Seven Studies*. Stanford, Calif., Stanford University Press, 1969.

Hulsewé, A. F. P. *Remnants of Han Law*, Vol. 1. Leiden, E. J. Brill, 1955.

Hummel, A. W., ed. *Eminent Chinese of the Ch'ing Period*. Taipei, Literature House, Ltd., 1964. Reprint of a 1943–44 ed. by United States Government Printing Office, Washington, D. C.

Juan K'uei-sheng 阮葵生. *Ch'a-yü k'o-hua* 茶餘客話 (Talk with guests over tea), in *Pi-chi hsiao-shuo ta-kuan* 筆記小說大觀 (Assorted stories and collection of notes).

554 ts'e. Shanghai, Chin-pu shu-chü 進步書局, published after 1911. Juan K'uei-sheng was an official who died in 1789.

Jui Ho-cheng 芮和蒸. *Hsi-Han yü-shih chih-tu* 西漢御史制度 (The system of the censorate in the Western Han dynasty). Taipei, Cultural Foundation of the Chia-hsin Cement Co., 1964.

Jung Chao-tsu 容肇祖. *Ming-tai ssu-hsiang-shih* 明代思想史 (A history of thought during the Ming dynasty). Taipei, Tai-wan k'ai-ming shu-tien 臺灣開明書店, 1969.

K'ang-hsi tzu-tien 康熙字典 (The K'ang-hsi dictionary). Shanghai, Commercial Press. Emperor's preface, 1716.

Katō Shigeshi 加藤繁. "*Ch'üeh* no imi ni tsuite" 榷の意義について (The meaning of *ch'üeh*), *Tōyō gakuhō* 東洋學報 (Reports of the investigations of the oriental society) 10.3: 122–129 (September 1920).

——— "Shindai no empō ni tsuite" 清代の鹽法について (Concerning the salt system of the Ch'ing dynasty), *Shichō* 史潮 (Historical trends) 7.1: 1–13 (February 1937).

Keisei bumpen sō-mokuroku 經世文編總目錄 (General index to editions of writings on statecraft), comp. Kindai Chūgoku kenkyū iinkai 近代中國硏究委員會 (Committee on research into modern China). 3 vols. Tokyo, 1956.

Kracke, E. A., Jr. *Civil Service in Early Sung China—960–1067.* Cambridge, Mass., Harvard University Press, 1953.

——— "Sung Society: Change within Tradition," *Far Eastern Quarterly* 14: 479–488 (1954–1955).

Ku-chin t'u-shu chi-ch'eng 古今圖書集成 (A complete collection of writings, pictures, tables, and maps from the past and present). Shanghai, 1884. Preface, 1726.

Ku-T'ang-lü shu-i 故唐律疏義 (The penal code of the T'ang dynasty with commentary). Ssu-pu ts'ung-k'an 四部叢刊 ed. 30 chüan plus supplementary material. Shanghai, Commercial Press, 1936. Some scholars say this book was compiled by Chang-sun Wu-chi 長孫無忌 *et al.* and promulgated in 653 A.D., while others hold that this book is a version of the T'ang code issued in 737.

Ku Yen-wu 顧炎武. *Jih-chih-lu chi-shih* 日知錄集釋 (Record of knowledge gained day by day with collected explanations). 36 chüan. Hupei, 1872.

Kuan-tzu 管子. Ssu-pu ts'ung-k'an 四部叢刊 ed. 24 chüan. Shanghai, Commercial Press.

Kung Lo-ch'ün 龔樂羣. *Meng Hsün i-t'ung* 孟荀異同 (Differences and similarities in the thought of Mencius and Hsün-tzu). Feng-shan, Taiwan, Huang-pu ch'u-pan-she 黃埔出版社, 1968.

Kuo-ch'ao ch'i-hsien lei-cheng ch'u-pien 國朝耆獻類徵初編 (The initial compilation of categorized Ch'ing biographies as transmitted by aged men of distinction), comp. Li Huan 李桓. 496 chüan. 1890.

LHYFC, see *Liang-huai yen-fa-chih* (1806).

La Palombara, Joseph, ed. *Bureaucracy and Political Development.* Princeton, N. J., Princeton University Press, 1963.

Legge, James, tr. *The Chinese Classics*, 5 vols. Hong Kong, Hong Kong University Press, 1960.

——— *The Li Ki.* 2 vols. Vol. 27 and 28 in F. M. Müller, *Sacred Books of the Far East.* Oxford, Eng., Clarendon Press, 1885.

Levenson, Joseph R. *The Problem of Monarchical Decay.* Berkeley, University of California Press, 1964.

Li Ch'eng 李澄. *Huai-ts'o pei-yao* 淮鹺備要 (Essentials of Liang-huai salt affairs). 5 chüan. Foreword, 1823.

Li-chi, see *Shih-san-ching shu-chu.*

Li-chi chu-shu 禮記注疏 (The Li-chi with commentary and subcommentary). Ssu-pu pei-yao 四部備要 ed. Shanghai, Chung-hua shu-chü 中華書局, 1933.

Li Chien-nung 李劍農. *Hsien-Ch'in liang-Han ching-chi shih-kao* 先秦兩漢經濟史稿 (Draft economic history of pre-Ch'in and Han times). Peking, Chung-hua shu-chü 中華書局, 1962.

——— *Sung Yüan Ming ching-chi shih-kao* 宋元明經濟史稿 (Draft economic history of the Sung, Yüan, and Ming periods). Peking, Sheng-huo tu-shu hsin-chih san-lien shu-tien 生活讀書新知三聯書店, 1957.

Li Kou 李覯. *Li Kan-chiang hsien-sheng ch'üan-chi* 李盱江先生全集 (Complete works of Li Kou). 37 chüan. 1893.

Li Tsung-t'ung 李宗侗. "Ch'ing-tai chung-yang cheng-ch'üan hsing-t'ai-te yen-pien" 清代中央政權形態的演變 (Changes in the pattern of central political power in the Ch'ing dynasty), *Bulletin of the Institute of History and Philology, Academia Sinica* 31.1: 79–158 (March 1967).

Liang-che yen-fa-chih 兩浙鹽法志 (Salt laws gazetteer of the Liang-che zone). 3 vols. Taipei, Hsüeh-sheng shu-chü 學生書局, 1966. Reprint of a 1792 reprint of an edition with a preface written in the winter of 1728–29.

Liang Ch'i-ch'ao 梁啓超. *Hsien-Ch'in cheng-chih ssu-hsiang-shih* 先秦政治思想史 (A history of political thought in China up to the Ch'in empire). Taipei, Chung-hua shu-chü 中華書局, 1956.

——— *Kuan-tzu-chuan* 管子傳 (A biography of Kuan-tzu). Taipei, Chung-hua shu-chü 中華書局, 1963.

Liang-huai yen-fa-chih 兩淮鹽法志 (Salt laws gazetteer of the Liang-huai zone). 4 vols. Taipei, Hsüeh-sheng shu-chü 學生書局, 1966. Reprint of a 1693 edition.

Liang-huai yen-fa-chih. 56 chüan. Yangchow, 1870. Reprint of a work completed in 1806.

Liang-huai yen-fa-chih. 160 chüan. Preface, 1904.

Lin Fu-shun. *Chinese Law Past and Present.* New York, The East Asian Institute, Columbia University, 1966.

Lin Yung-jung 林咏榮. *Chung-kuo fa-chih-shih* 中國法制史 (A history of China's legal institutions). Taipei, published by Lin Yung-jung, 1960.

Lipset, S. M. *Political Man: The Social Bases of Politics.* Garden City, N. Y., Anchor Books, Doubleday, 1963.

Liu, James T. C. *Ou-yang Hsiu, An Eleventh-Century Neo-Confucianist.* Stanford, Calif., Stanford University Press, 1967.

Liu-pu ch'eng-yü chu-chieh, see *Rikubu seigo chūkai.*

Liu Shao-fu 劉紹輔. *Chung-kuo ching-chi ssu-hsiang-shih* 中國經濟思想史 (A history of Chinese economic thought). Taichung, Chung-yang shu-chü 中央書局, 1960.

Liu Tsung-yüan 柳宗元. *Liu Ho-tung ch'üan-chi* 柳河東全集 (The complete works of Liu Tsung-yüan). Shanghai, Shih-chieh shu-chü 世界書局, 1935.

Lü-shih ch'un-ch'iu 呂氏春秋. Ssu-pu ts'ung-k'an 四部叢刊 ed. 26 chüan. Shanghai, Commercial Press, 1929.

Ma Feng-ch'en 馬奉琛. *Ch'ing-tai hsing-cheng chih-tu yen-chiu ts'an-k'ao shu-mu* 清代行政制度研究參考書目 (Annotated bibliography for research into the administrative institutions of the Ch'ing dynasty). Peking, Peking University, 1935.

March, James G., ed. *Handbook of Organizations.* Chicago, Rand McNally, 1965.

Marsh, Robert M. *The Mandarins*. Glencoe, Ill., Free Press, 1961.
Merton, Robert K. *Social Theory and Social Structure*. Glencoe, Ill., Free Press, 1962.
——— *et al.*, eds. *Reader in Bureaucracy*. Glencoe, Ill., Free Press, 1960.
Metzger, Thomas. "The State and Commerce in Imperial China," in *Asian and African Studies* (Annual of the Israel Oriental Society) 6 (1970).
——— "The Organizational Capabilities of the Ch'ing State in the Field of Commerce," in W. E. Willmott, ed., *Economic Organization in Chinese Society*. Stanford, Calif., Stanford University Press, 1972.
Miao Ch'üan-chi 繆全吉. *Ming-tai hsü-li* 明代胥吏 (Clerks in the Ming dynasty). Taipei, Cultural Foundation of the Chia-hsin Cement Co., 1969.
Mindaishi kenkyū bunken mokuroku 明代史研究文獻目錄 (An index to the literature on the history of the Ming dynasty), comp. Yamane Yukio 山根幸夫. Tokyo, Tōyō Bunko, 1960.
Ming-Ch'ing she-hui ching-chi hsing-t'ai-te yen-chiu 明淸社會經濟形態的硏究 (Studies in the form of the society and economy of Ming and Ch'ing times), comp. Chung-kuo jen-min ta-hsüeh chung-kuo li-shih chiao-yen-shih 中國人民大學中國歷史教硏室 (Chinese People's University, Institute for Teaching and Research in Chinese History). Shanghai, Shang-hai jen-min chu-pan-she 上海人民出版社, 1957.
Ming lü chi-chieh fu-li 明律集解附例 (The penal statutes of the Ming dynasty, annotated, with the regulations included). 30 chüan. 1908 reprint of an edition printed in 1610. Preface by Shen Chia-pen 沈家本.
Moore, Charles A., ed. *The Chinese Mind*. Honolulu, East-West Center Press, 1967.
Morohashi Tetsuji 諸橋轍次. *Dai Kan-Wa jiten* 大漢和辭典 (Great Chinese-Japanese dictionary). 12 vols. Tokyo, published by Suzuki Ippei 鈴木一平, 1955–1960.
Mote, F. W. "The Growth of Chinese Despotism," *Oriens Extremus* 8.1: 1–41 (August 1961).
Mu-ling-shu chi-yao 牧令書輯要 (Essentials from the book for departmental and district magistrates). 10 chüan. 1868.
Naitō Kenkichi 內藤乾吉. *Chūgoku hōsei kōshō* 中國法制考證 (Studies in Chinese law). Kyoto, Yūhikaku 有斐閣, 1963.
Nivison, D. S. *The Life and Thought of Chang Hsüeh-ch'eng (1738–1801)*. Stanford, Calif., Stanford University Press, 1966.
Pa-ch'ao sheng-hsün 八朝聖訓 (The instructions of the ruling sage over eight reigns). 457 chüan. Latest preface, 1856.
Po-hu t'ung-te-lun 白虎通德論. Ascribed to Pan Ku 班固. Ssu-pu ts'ung-k'an 四部叢刊 ed. 10 chüan. Shanghai, Commercial Press, 1929.
Pan Ku 班固. *Han-shu pu-chu* 漢書補注 (The history of the Former Han dynasty, with added explanations [by Wang Hsien-ch'ien 王先謙]). 8 vols. Peking, Commercial Press, 1959.
Pao-ching-t'ang ts'ung-shu 抱經堂叢書. Peking, 1923.
Pao Shih-ch'en 包世臣. *An-wu ssu-chung* 安吳四種. 36 chüan. 1846.
Parsons, Talcott. *The Structure of Social Action*. New York and London, McGraw-Hill, 1937.
——— *The Social System*. New York, Free Press, 1968.
———, *et al.*, eds. *Theories of Society*. 2 vols. New York, Free Press of Glencoe, 1961.
——— *Societies: Evolutionary and Comparative Perspectives*. Englewood Cliffs, N. J., Prentice-Hall, 1966.
P'eng Hsin-wei彭信威. *Chung-kuo huo-pi-shih* 中國貨幣史 (A history of Chinese money). 2 vols. Shanghai, Ch'ün-lien chu-pan-she 羣聯出版社, 1954.

Pfiffner, John M., and Frank P. Sherwood. *Administrative Organization*. Englewood Cliffs, N. J., Prentice-Hall, 1960.

Philastre, P. -L. -F. *Le Code annamite*. 2 vols. Taipei, Ch'eng-wen Publishing Co., 1967.

Pye, Lucian W. *The Spirit of Chinese Politics*. Cambridge, Mass., M. I. T. Press, 1968.

Reischauer, Edwin O., and John K. Fairbank. *East Asia—The Great Tradition*. Boston, Houghton Mifflin, 1958, 1960.

Rheinstein, Max, tr. *Max Weber on Law in Economy and Society*. Cambridge, Mass., Harvard University Press, 1954.

Rickett, W. A. *Kuan-tzu*. Hong Kong, Hong Kong University Press, 1965.

Rikubu seigo chūkai 六部成語註解 (Terminology of the six boards, annotated), ed. Naitō Kenkichi 内藤乾吉. Kyoto, published by Naitō Kenkichi, 1940.

Sa Meng-wu 薩孟武. *Chung-kuo she-hui cheng-chih-shih* 中國社會政治史 (A social and political history of China). 4 vols. Taipei, published by Sa Meng-wu, 1965–66.

Saeki Tomi 佐伯富. *Shindai ensei no kenkyū* 清代鹽政の研究 (A study of the salt administration of the Ch'ing dynasty). Kyoto, Tōyōshi kenkyūkai 東洋史研究會, 1956.

Schwartz, Benjamin I. "Some Polarities in Confucian Thought," in David S. Nivison and Arthur F. Wright, eds., *Confucianism in Action*. Stanford, Calif., Stanford University Press, 1959.

Shen Ming-chang 沈明璋. *Ming-tai cheng-chih-shih* 明代政治史 (A political history of the Ming dynasty). Taipei, Shen Ming-chang, 1967.

Shih-san-ching chu-shu 十三經注疏 (The thirteen classics, with commentary and subcommentary). Based on annotated edition prepared by Juan Yüan 阮元 (1764-1849). 2 vols. Shanghai, Shih-chieh shu-chü 世界書局, 1935.

Shinkoku gyōseihō 清國行政法 (Administrative laws of the Ch'ing state), comp. Rinji Taiwan kyūkan chōsakai 臨時臺灣舊慣調查會 (Temporary commission of the Taiwan government-general for the study of old Chinese customs). 5 vols. Tokyo, 1905–1911.

Shryock, John K. *The Origin and Development of the State Cult of Confucius*. New York, Paragon Book, 1966.

Solomon, Richard H. *Mao's Revolution and the Chinese Political Culture*. Berkeley, University of California Press, 1971.

Ssu-ch'uan yen-fa-chih 四川鹽法志 (Salt laws gazetteer of the Szechwan zone). 40 chüan. Completed about 1883.

Ssu-k'u ch'üan-shu tsung-mu t'i-yao 四庫全書總目提要 (Annotated list of works in the complete collection of writings from the four categories). 4 vols. Shanghai, Commercial Press, 1933.

Su chou-chih 宿州志 (Su department gazetteer). 36 chüan. 1889.

Sui-ning hsien-chih 睢寧縣志 (Suining district gazetteer). 18 chüan. 1886.

Sun E-tu Zen. *Ch'ing Administrative Terms*. Cambridge, Mass., Harvard University Press, 1961.

——— "The Board of Revenue in Nineteenth-century China," *Harvard Journal of Asiatic Studies* 24: 175–228 (1962–1963).

Sun K'ai (Chieh?) 孫楷. *Ch'in hui-yao* 秦會要 (Collection of essentials regarding the Ch'in dynasty). Taipei, Chung-hua ts'ung-shu wei-yüan-hui 中華叢書委員會, 1956.

Sung Hsi 宋晞. *Sung-shih yen-chiu lun-ts'ung* 宋史研究論叢 (Studies in Sung history). Taipei, Kuo-fang yen-chiu-yüan 國防研究院, 1962.

Sung-shih yen-chiu-chi 宋史研究集 (Collection of studies in Sung history), comp. Sung-shih tso-t'an-hui 宋史座談會 (Symposium on Sung history). Taipei, Chung-hua ts'ung-shu pien-shen wei-yüan-hui 中華叢書編審委員會, 1966.

TCHT, see *Ta-Ch'ing hui-tien* (1899).

TCHTSL, see *Ta-Ch'ing hui-tien shih-li* (1899).

TCLL, see *Ta-Ch'ing lü-li* (1870).

TLti, see Hsüeh Yün-sheng, *Tu-li ts'un-i*.

TWI, see *T'ao Wen-i kung ch'üan-chi*.

TYCS, see *Ch'in-ting hu-pu ts'ao-yün ch'üan-shu*.

TYT, see *T'ao Yün-t'ing hsien-sheng tsou-shu*.

Ta-Ch'ing chin-shin ch'üan-shu 大清搢紳全書 (Complete book of current information about persons with governmental status of the great Ch'ing dynasty). Many issues published privately over many years of the Ch'ing period, the rule being four issues a year. Similar books with different titles were also issued, such as *Chüeh-chih ch'üan-shu* 爵秩全書 (Complete book of persons with official rank).

Ta-Ch'ing hui-tien 大清會典 (Collected statutes of the great Ch'ing dynasty). 100 chüan. 1899. Earlier editions: 80 chüan, 1818; 100 chüan, 1763; 200 chüan, 1733; 162 chüan, 1690.

Ta-Ch'ing hui-tien shih-li 大清會典事例 (Precedents and regulations supplementary to the collected statutes of the great Ch'ing dynasty). 1,220 chüan, 1899; 920 chüan, 1818.

Ta-Ch'ing hui-tien tse-li 大清會典則例 (Precedents and regulations supplementary to the collected statutes of the great Ch'ing dynasty). 180 chüan. 1763.

Ta-Ch'ing li-ch'ao shih-lu 大清歷朝實錄 (The veritable records of the successive reigns of the great Ch'ing dynasty). 4,485 chüan. Dai Manshū teikoku kokumu-in 大滿洲帝國國務院, 1937–38.

Ta-Ch'ing lü-li 大清律例 (Penal statutes and regulations of the great Ch'ing dynasty). 39 chüan. 1870.

Ta-Ch'ing lü-li t'ung-k'ao 大清律例通考 (The penal statutes and regulations of the great Ch'ing dynasty, entirely annotated), compiled by Wu T'an 吳壇 no earlier than 1778. 40 chüan. 1886.

Ta-Ming hui-tien 大明會典 (Collected statutes of the great Ming dynasty). 5 vols. Taipei, Tung-nan shu-pao-she 東南書報社, 1963. Reprint of the 1587 ed.

Tai Yen-hui 戴炎輝. *Chung-kuo fa-chih-shih kai-yao* 中國法制史概要 (Essentials of the history of China's legal institutions). Taipei, Tai-wan lien-ho shu-chü 臺灣聯合書局, 1960.

——— *T'ang-lü t'ung-lun* 唐律通論 (A comprehensive discussion of the T'ang penal code). Taipei, Cheng-chung shu-chü 正中書局, 1965.

Takigawa, Kametarō 瀧川龜太郎, comp. *Shiki kaichū kōshō* 史記會注考證 (The records of the historian by Ssu-ma Ch'ien, with collected commentaries and textual notes). 10 vols. Tokyo, Tōhō bunka gaku-in, Tōkyō kenkyū-jo 東方文化學院東京研究所, 1932–1934.

T'ao Hsi-sheng 陶希聖. *Chung-kuo cheng-chih ssu-hsiang-shih* 中國政治思想史 (A history of political thought in China). 4 vols. Taipei, Tai-wan lien-ho shu-chü 臺灣聯合書局, 1964.

T'ao Wen-i kung ch'üan-chi 陶文毅公全集 (The complete writings of the master T'ao Chu). 66 chüan, including two unnumbered ones. Preface, 1840.

T'ao Yün-t'ing hsien-sheng tsou-shu 陶雲汀先生奏疏 (The memorials of the master T'ao Chu). 52 chüan. Printed after 1833.

Teng Ssu-yü 鄧嗣禹. *Chung-kuo k'ao-shih chih-tu-shih* 中國考試制度史 (A history of

China's examination system). Taipei, Hsüeh-sheng shu-chü 學生書局, 1967.

——— and Knight Biggerstaff. *An Annotated Bibliography of Selected Chinese Reference Works*. Cambridge, Mass., Harvard University Press, 1950.

Tōyōshi [*Tōyōgaku*] *kenkyū bunken ruiboku* 東洋史〔學〕研究文獻類目 (Annual bibliography of oriental studies), comp. Kyōto daigaku jimbun kagaku kenkyūjo 京都大學人文科學研究所 (Research institute for humanistic studies of Kyoto university). The latest edition, published in 1969, covers the 1967 literature. Previous editions cover all years back to at least 1935.

Tseng Fan-k'ang 曾繁康. *Chung-kuo cheng-chih ssu-hsiang-shih* 中國政治思想史 (A history of political thought in China). Taipei, Ta Chung-kuo t'u-shu yu-hsien kung-ssu大中國圖書有限公司, 1959.

Tseng-ting tse-li t'u-yao pien-lan 增訂則例圖要便覽 (The enlarged regulations [on administrative punishment]: essentials in tabular form, a digest to facilitate scrutiny), comp. Wang Yin-t'ing 王蔭庭 and Ch'en Ko-t'ang 陳哿堂. 40 chüan. 1792.

Tu K'uei-ying 杜奎英. *Chung-kuo li-tai cheng-chih fu-hao* 中國歷代政治符號 (The political symbols of China over successive dynasties). Taipei district, National Chengchi University, 1963.

Tung-hua ch'üan-lu 東華全錄 (The complete Tung-hua records), ed. Wang Hsien-ch'ien 王先謙. Peking, 1887.

Twitchett, Denis C. "The Fragment of the T'ang Ordinances of the Department of Waterways Discovered at Tun-huang," *Asia Major* 6: 23–79 (1957–58).

Tz'u-hai 辭海 (Ocean of terms), comp. Shu Hsin-ch'eng 舒新城 *et al.* Shanghai, Chung-hua shu-chü 中華書局, 1951.

Van der Sprenkel, Sybille. *Legal Institutions in Manchu China*. London, Athlone Press, 1962.

Wang Ch'ing-yün 王慶雲. *Shih-ch'ü yü-chi* 石渠餘紀. 6 chüan. 1890. Also known as *Hsi-ch'ao chi-cheng* 熙朝紀政.

Wang Shou-chi 王守基. "Yen-fa i-lüeh" 鹽法議略 (An outline of the salt system), in *P'ang-hsi-chai ts'ung-shu* 滂喜齋叢書. 1872.

Wang Shou-nan 王壽南. *T'ang-tai fan-chen yü chung-yang kuan-hsi chih yen-chiu* 唐代藩鎮與中央關係之研究 (A study of the relations between the regional commanders and the central government during the T'ang dynasty). Taipei, Cultural Foundation of the Chia-hsin Cement Co., 1969.

Watson, Burton, tr. *Hsün Tzu*. New York, Columbia University Press, 1969.

Weber, Max. *The Protestant Ethic and the Spirit of Capitalism*, tr. Talcott Parsons. New York, Scribner, 1958.

——— *The Religion of China*, tr. and ed. H. H. Gerth. Glencoe, Ill., Free Press, 1962.

——— *The Theory of Social and Economic Organization*, tr. A. M. Henderson and T. Parsons. Glencoe, Ill., Free Press, 1947.

Wittfogel, Karl A. *Oriental Despotism*. New Haven, Conn., Yale University Press, 1959.

Wu Che-fu 吳哲夫. *Ch'ing-tai chin-hui shu-mu yen-chiu* 清代禁燬書目研究 (A study of the movement to ban and burn books during the Ch'ing dynasty). Taipei, Cultural Foundation of the Chia-hsin Cement Co., 1969.

Wu, Silas Hsiu-liang. "The Memorial Systems of the Ch'ing Dynasty," *Harvard Journal of Asiatic Studies* 27: 7–75 (1967).

——— *Communication and Imperial Control in China*. Cambridge, Mass., Harvard University Press, 1970.

Yang Hung-lieh 楊鴻烈. *Chung-kuo fa-lü ssu-hsiang-shih* 中國法律思想史 (A history of Chinese legal thought). Taipei, Taiwan Commercial Press, 1964.

Yang Lien-sheng. "Government Control of Urban Merchants." Unpublished manuscript.

——— *Studies in Chinese Institutional History*. Cambridge, Mass., Harvard University Press, 1961.

——— *Les aspects économiques des travaux publics dans la Chine impériale; quatre conférences*. Paris, Collège de France, 1964.

——— 楊聯陞. "Ch'ao-tai-chien-te pi-sai" 朝代間的比賽 (Dynastic comparison and dynastic competition) in *Ch'ing-chu Li Chi hsien-sheng ch'i-shih-sui lun-wen-chi* 慶祝李濟先生七十歲論文集 (Symposium in honor of Dr. Li Chi on his seventieth birthday), Vol. 1. Taipei, Ch'ing-hua hsüeh-pao-she 清華學報社, 1965.

——— *Excursions in Sinology*. Cambridge, Mass., Harvard University Press, 1969.

Yeh Shih-ch'ang 葉世昌. *Ya-p'ien chan-cheng ch'ien-hou wo-kuo-te huo-pi hsüeh-shuo* 鴉片戰爭前後我國的貨幣學說 (Our country's monetary theories around the time of the Opium War). Shanghai, Shang-hai jen-min ch'u-pan-she 上海人民出版社, 1963.

Yen Chung-p'ing 嚴中平. *Ch'ing-tai Yün-nan t'ung-cheng-k'ao* 淸代雲南銅政考 (A study of the administration of copper affairs in Yunnan during the Ch'ing dynasty). Peking, Chung-hua shu-chü 中華書局, 1957.

Yen Keng-wang 嚴耕望. *Chung-kuo ti-fang hsing-cheng chih-tu-shih—chüan shang: Ch'in Han ti-fang hsing-cheng chih-tu* 中國地方行政制度史一卷上：秦漢地方行政制度 (A history of regional and local administration in China—part one: the Ch'in and Han periods). 2 vols. Taipei, Academia Sinica, The Institute of History and Philology, 1961.

——— "Lüeh-lun T'ang-liu-tien chih hsing-chih yü shih-hsing wen-t'i" 略論唐六典之性質與施行問題 (On problems concerning the nature and the realization in practice of the *Six Divisions of Administration of the T'ang Dynasty*), *Bulletin of the Institute of History and Philology, Academia Sinica* 24: 69–76 (1953).

Yen-t'ieh lun, see Huan K'uan, *Yen-t'ieh lun chiao-chu cha-chi.*

Yin Hai-kuang 殷海光. *Chung-kuo wen-hua-te chan-wang* 中國文化的展望 (An appraisal of Chinese culture and its prospects). 2 vols. Taipei, Wen-hsing shu-tien 文星書店, 1966.

Yü Ping-ch'üan 余秉權. *Chung-kuo shih-hsüeh lun-wen yin-te* 中國史學論文引得 (Chinese history: index to learned articles). Hong Kong, Hong Kong East Asia Institute, 1963.

Yüeh-tung sheng-li hsin-tsuan 粤東省例新纂 (Newly compiled provincial regulations of Kwangtung). 8 chüan. 1846.

Glossary and Terminological Index

Translations are given here for those expressions the meanings of which are not obvious and which have special significance within the context of this book. When such expressions have more than one meaning, usually just that one meaning relevant to the contents of this book is given. Also omitted are names and titles given in the bibliography, reign titles, the names of emperors and some exceptionally famous men, and most place names. Where a translation in the glossary differs slightly from one in the main body of the text, it is the former which has the more general significance transcending particular contexts.

ai-min 愛民 259
an 案 (administrative case, rule), 194–196, 202–203
an-chien 案件 (administrative case), 194
an-chüan 案卷 (office records), 112
an-tu 案牘 same as an-chüan, 112

cha 札 (order [sent by a superior official to a subordinate official]), 179
cha-tzu 劄子, 174
ch'a 查(to carry out an adjudicative inquiry), 116
ch'a-fa 茶法 222
ch'a-hsün 查訊 (to carry out an adjudicative inquiry), 116
ch'a-i 察議 (examine and advise in the case of impeachments calling for relatively mild sentences), 115
ch'a-ts'an 查參 (examine into and impeach), 115
ch'a-ts'ang yü-shih 查倉御史 (granary censor), 147n
ch'ai-wei 差委 (to commission an official to carry out a particular administrative mission [in some contexts, ch'ai is used for commissioning by the emperor, wei, by an official]), 296
chan 佔 (to move funds orginally reserved for one expenditure account into another), 114
chan-ai 佔礙 same as chan, 114
chan-chuan no-tien 輾轉挪墊 (to move funds a number of times from one expenditure account to another under difficult or illegal conditions but still in order to meet public needs), 114

Chan-shih 詹事 (Supervisorate of imperial instruction), 424
chan-ts'an 展參 (temporally extended impeachment), 301
chan-yung 佔用 same as chan, 114
chang 丈 375
chang-ch'eng 章程 (laws, rules), 38, 39, 196–197
Chang Chih-tung 張之洞 73n
Chang Ching 張井 374
Chang Chü-cheng 張居正 41n, 45n
Chang Heng-ch'ü 張橫渠 77
Chang Hsin-yüan 張心淵 376
Chang Hsüeh-ch'eng 張學誠 70
Chang Hui-yen 張惠言 68n
Chang P'eng-chan 張鵬展 310, 408
Chang T'ing-yü 張廷玉 47n
ch'ang 場 (salt production yard), 197n
ch'ang 常 28
ch'ang-she so-pu-yüan 常赦所不原 (criminals excluded from regular amnesties), 265n
ch'ang-ta-shih 場大使 (salt yard supervisor), 37
ch'ang-tao 常道 (unchanging true way), 28
chao 詔 176n
chao 著 (let), 181
chao chao-so-ch'ing hsing 著照所請行 (let action proceed according to what has been requested), 179
chao-chun 著准 (let), 181
Chao I 趙翼 47, 124n, 258, 259
chao-lü ch'u-fen 照律處分 (to carry out administrative punishment according to the penal code), 125n
ch'ao 朝 158
che-chia 折價 (tax in money paid in lieu of the value of the salt previously collected as a tax), 190
che-p'ien 摺片 (memorial postscript), 420
che-tsou 摺奏 (palace memorial), 419
che-tzu 摺子 same as che-tsou, 419
ch'e-chih 掣摯 (to pull out a salt bag as a sample for inspection), 118
ch'e-jen 撤任 (to remove from office), 112, 299
ch'e-yen 掣驗 (to inspect salt shipments by pulling out a salt bag as a sample), 118
Ch'en Hsien-chang 陳獻章 253
Ch'en Hung-mou 陳宏謀 24n, 73
Ch'en Liang 陳亮 67
Ch'en Tsu-fan 陳祖范 35n
cheng-shu 政書 (books on governmental institutions), 213n
cheng-t'i 政體 (fundamental structure of administration), 38, 39, 59, 159
cheng-t'iao 正條 (article of law directly applicable to a particular offense), 202n
cheng-yin shu-mu 徵引書目 (list of books used for verification), 228
ch'eng 承 (receive responsibility to carry out an administrative task), 294
ch'eng-an 成案 (established case), 196–197, 204
ch'eng-chien 成見 (closed, prejudiced viewpoint), 57
Ch'eng Chin-fang 程晉芳 70, 75
ch'eng-fa 成法 (established laws), 59
Ch'eng Hao 程顥 67
ch'eng-hsiang 承相 (prime minister), 243
ch'eng-hsien 成憲 (established laws), 81
Ch'eng I 程頤 328n
ch'eng-li 成例 (established regulations and precedents), 160, 198
ch'eng-lü 成律 (the penal code), 426
ch'eng-shu 成書 (established book of law), 81–88
chi 計 385
chi-ch'a 稽查 (to examine the affairs of another office), 295
chi-chu 輯註 307
Chi-feng-t'ing 稽俸廳 (Office for examining regular salaries), 321
chi-kung 記功 (merits), 298–299
chi-kuo 記過 (demerits), 298–299
chi-lu 紀錄 (commendation), 113n, 124
chi-lu erh tz'u 紀錄二次 (two commendations), 125
chi-sheng 卽升 (to be promoted as soon as possible), 314n
chi-ta-kuo 記大過 (major demerit), 299
Chi Yün 紀昀 27n
ch'i 氣 (spirited determination, morale), 327

ch'i 緝 (to arrest), 116
ch'i-chieh 氣節 (high morale and integrity), 413
ch'i-ch'ing 乞請 (to request [from the emperor]), 433
Chia I 賈誼 68, 255
chia-tai 夾帶 (smuggled within some legal unit of transport), 61
chia-tai 加帶 (legally added to carry along), 61
chiang 降 114n
chiang-chi liu-jen 降級留任 (demotion in subgrade with retention of duties), 300
chiang-chih 降職 300
chiang-chüan 降捐 (to be restored to a lower office by making a financial contribution), 303, 315
chiang-fa 降罰 (demotions and salary fines), 354
chiang-feng 降俸 (reduction in regular salary without reduction in subgrade), 301
chiao-tui 校對 (to check one manuscript against another), 133
chieh-ch'i-li 竭其力 48
chieh-hsien-jen pieh-hsü 解見任別敘 (to be removed from one's current post and appointed to another), 113n
chieh-tien 借墊 (to advance funds from one expenditure account to another), 114
chieh-ts'an 揭參 (to reveal the name of an offender and impeach him), 115
chieh-yung 節用 108
chien-ch'a yü-shih 監察御史 270
chien-ch'ung 兼充 (to fill another office in addition to one's regular one), 296
chien-ch'üeh 簡缺 (post with little administrative business), 49n
chien-kuan 兼管 (to take charge of certain administrative matters in addition to the regular duties of one's office), 296
chien-kuan pu-wu 兼管部務 (to direct the head officials of a board in addition to meeting the regular responsibilities of one's office), 123n
chien-ming 簡明 97
chien-pu-wu 兼部務 same as chien-kuan pu-wu, 123n
chien-sheng 監生 362
chien-tsuan 監纂 (editorial director), 133
ch'ien-chi 鈐記 179n
ch'ien-hsi 遷徙 429
ch'ien-hu 千戶 427
ch'ien-liang hu-hsiang chüeh-ch'a 錢糧互相覺察 (officials and other personnel assigned to granaries and treasuries are mutually to watch each other), 156
Ch'ien Ta-hsin 錢大昕 27n
Ch'ien Wei-ch'eng 錢維城 43
chih 質 47
chih 旨 (rescript), 367
chih 職 same as chih-chang, 212n
chih 志 204
chih-chang 職掌 (the function or duties of an office), 212n
chih-chih 職制 (institutions of office), 350
chih-fa 制法 (laws and fundamental order), 38
chih-kuan yu-fan 職官有犯 (when officials commit an offense), 277n
chih-ming ts'an-tsou 指名參奏 (to impeach in a memorial, naming the offender), 115
chih-ming yen-ts'an 指名嚴參 (to impeach calling for severe administrative punishment and naming the offender), 115
chih-shu 志書 (gazetteer), 225
chih-shu 制書 (imperial pronouncement), 176, 431
chih-tsui 治罪 (to sentence by inflicting a criminal punishment), 208
chih-ts'an 指參 (to impeach someone, naming him), 115
chih-tu 制度 (fundamental order and standards of government), 38
chih-t'ung 治統 (the line of transmission of imperial authority through the ages), 414
ch'ih 敕 210
ch'ih 飭 (to order), 181
ch'ih 恥 266
chin-hsin so-shih jen-lao jen-yüan 盡心所事任勞任怨 267

chin-ling 禁令 (prohibitions and laws), 169
chin-shih 進士 152n
ching-ch'a 京察 (capital inspection), 126, 368
ching-ch'a t'ung-li 京察統例 (general regulations of the capital inspection), 302n
ching-ch'eng 經承 (head clerk), 133
ching-chi 經濟 423
ching-li 經理 (to direct the management of certain official affairs), 53
ching-pan 經辦 same as ching-li, 53
ching-shih 經世 25–27
ching-shou 經手 (head clerk), 133
ch'ing-tan 清單 108
Chiu-ch'ing 九鄉 (Nine ministries)
chiu-ts'an 究參 (to examine into and impeach), 115
chiu-ts'an 糾參 (to impeach), 115
Ch'iu Chün 丘濬 59n
Ch'iu Yüeh-hsiu 裘日修 436
cho-i 卓異 (standing out above others), 314
cho-ku chun-chin 酌古準今 72n
ch'o-chi 戳記 179n
Chou Chen-yeh 周振業 326
Chou Kao (Hao?) 周鎬 266, 416
chu-chih 住支 (to stop disbursement), 345n
chu-feng 住俸 (stoppage of regular salary), 301
Chu Hsi 朱熹 30, 46, 67
Chu Mao-li 朱毛理 370
chu-p'i 硃批 (vermillion comment), 199, 419
chu-shih 主事 154
chu-tzu chi-li yü cheng-t'i fei i 銖錙計利亦於政體非宜 108
ch'u-chih 黜陟 (demotion or dismissal and promotion), 247
Ch'u Fang-ch'ing 儲方慶 261n, 366n
ch'u-fen 處分 (to dispose of, to carry out administrative punishment, administrative punishment), 125
ch'u-fen-li 處分例 (regulations on administrative punishment), 103
ch'u-fen tsa-li 處分雜例 (miscellaneous regulations on administrative punishment), 351
ch'u-li 出力 48
ch'u-mien 除免 (temporary dismissal from office), 272
ch'u-ming 除名 (reduction to the status of commoner), 272, 302
ch'u-ming tang-ch'ai 除名當差 (removal of name from status registers and assumption of responsibility for labor services), 359n
ch'u-na 出納 (expenditures and intake), 119
ch'u-shen 出身 (basis of eligibility to obtain the status of official), 393
ch'u-shih hsiao-yü 出示曉諭 (to make an order publicly known), 180
chuan-an t'i-pen 專案題本 (a t'i-pen memorial dealing exclusively with one matter), 390
chuan-che 專摺 (a separate memorial dealing exclusively with the subject at hand), 82, 83
chuan-t'i 專題 same as chuan-an t'i-pen, 390
chuan-tse 專責 123
ch'uan 傳 116
ch'uan-hsün 傳訊 (to summon an official and question him), 116
ch'uan-wen 傳問 same as ch'uan-hsün, 116
ch'uang-chü chang-ch'eng 創舉章程 190
chui 追 338
chun 准 180
chun ch'i-so-ch'ing 准其所請 (what is requested is authorized), 179
chun-chin cho-ku 準今酌古 73
chun-ku cho-chin 準古酌今 73
chung 中 120n
chung-ch'üeh 中缺 (post with a medium burden of administration), 49n
chung-jen 中人 256
chung-pao 中飽 71n
chung-ts'ai 中才 261
ch'ung 衝 49n
ch'ung-fu 重複 195
ch'ung-hsiao 銃銷 188n
chü-ho 舉劾 (recommending and impeaching), 355
chü-jen 舉人 362

chü-lien 聚斂 108
chü-t'i 具題 (to present a t'i-pen memorial), 117n
chü-tsou 具奏 (to memorialize), 117n
chü-wai ch'uan-wen 局外傳聞 58
ch'ü 取 (to arrest), 116
ch'ü-ch'u 區處 (to sentence according to the distinctions involved in the case), 113n
ch'ü-wen 取問 (to arrest and try criminally) 116
chüan 蠲 (to cancel a tax collection), 117
chüan 卷 101
chüan-an 卷案 same as an-chüan, 112
chüan-fu 捐復 (to be restored to office by making a financial contribution), 303, 308, 315
chüan-huan 蠲緩 (to postpone a tax collection), 117
chüan-mien 蠲免 (to cancel a tax collection), 117
chüan-na chi-lu 捐納紀錄 (commendations obtained by making a financial contribution), 313
chüan-na chia-chi 捐納加級 (added subgrades obtained by making a financial contribution), 307, 313
chüan-shu 捐贖 307
chüan-tu 卷牘 same as an-chüan, 112
ch'üan-liang 權量 218n
ch'üan pu ho-fu 全不合符 96
ch'üeh-wen 闕文 264n
ch'üeh-yu-pa-wo 確有把握 75
chün 君 399
chün-ch'en 君臣 271
chün-hsien 郡縣 66
chün-min chiao-tui 軍民交兌 34n
chün-tzu 君子 252
chün-yu pi-i 均有裨益 55

en 恩 381
en-chi-wei 恩騎尉 339

fa 發 114n
fa 法 78
fa-chih 法治 161
fa-chih 法制 (laws and fundamental order), 38, 39
fa-feng 罰俸 (cancellation of regular salary as a fine), 300
fa-li 法例 127n, 186n
fa-ssu 法司 135n
fa-ssu-kuan 法司官 (officials at the offices of law), 135
fa-wang 發往 (to be dispatched [to a place of punishment]), 302
fan 犯 266
fan 凡 185
fan 繁 49n
fan-chen 藩鎮 10, 11
Fan Chung-yen 范仲淹 77, 253
fan-li 凡例 180n
fan-pen 反本 31
fan-shih-yin 飯食銀 323
fan-so 繁瑣 97
fan-yin 飯銀 139
Fang Wei-tien 方維甸 436
fei jen-li-so-chih 非人力所致 279
fen 分 349
fen-fa 分發 (respectively dispatched), 151, 296
fen-pieh i-ch'u chih-tsui 分別議處治罪 (distinguishing between the two procedures, advise on administrative punishment and/or determine a criminal sentence), 113n
feng 俸 (regular salary), 111
feng-chiang ta-li 封疆大吏 (great regional officials), 126
feng-chien 封建 66
feng-hua 風化 43
feng-po 封駁 (to seal and return an imperial order, rejecting it as improper), 160n, 175n
fu-chun 覆准 (imperially approved reply), 182
fu-chun 俯准 (graciously authorize), 181
fu-p'ien 附片 (memorial postscript), 420
fu-tsou 附奏 (memorial postscript), 420

Hai Jui 海瑞 259
Han Yü 韓愈 44n
Ho-shen 和珅 244
hou-hsüan 候選 345
hou-pu 候補 334, 345
hou-wang 後王 63
hsi-shu 細數 108
hsia 轄 (to have authority over), 122

hsiang 詳 (report by a subordinate to a superior official), 179
hsiang-chih 相制 329
hsiang-chun 詳准 (proposal of a subordinate official approved by a superior official), 182
hsiang-fan 相反 33
hsiang-hsing 祥刑 423
hsiang-kuo 相國 173n
hsiang-yüan 鄉愿 406
Hsiao Ho 蕭何 32n
hsiao-hsiu 小修 (minor revision), 84, 87, 132
hsiao-jen 小人 255
hsiao-li shu-tsui 效力贖罪 (to expiate one's guilt by exertion in the performance of duties), 265
hsiao-shih 小事 (minor administrative matters), 420
Hsiao T'ung 蕭統 48n
hsieh-en 謝恩 433
hsien-hsing 現行 (currently in force), 216
hsien-hsing tse-li 現行則例 (regulations currently in effect), 216, 425
hsien-jen-kuan 現任官 (officials currently holding office), 357
hsien-li 賢吏 254
hsin 信 67
hsin-shou 信守 131
hsin-ting chih shu 新定之書 (newly authorized books of law), 81
hsing 刑 (criminal punishments), 78
hsing-ming 刑名 127n
hsing-pu 刑部 423
Hsing-pu lü-li 刑部律例 (The penal code), 118
Hsing-pu lü-li ch'üan-shu 刑部律例全書 (The penal code), 118
Hsing-pu t'ung-hsing chang-ch'eng 刑部通行章程 (Generally circulated rules of the board of punishments)
hsing-shu 行署 (mobile or temporary office), 55
hsing-tsou 行走 (carrying out government business in an office-like setting but outside the framework of a regular official post), 296, 301
hsiu-chih 休致 (to retire from office), 111, 125
hsiu-chin 修今 73n
hsiu-shen 修身 409
hsü 序 120n
hsü-feng 虛俸 (regular salary which was never received but which is owed on account of salary fines), 322n
Hsü Hsü-ling 徐旭齡 254n
Hsü Kuang-chin 徐廣縉 58, 76
Hsü Yüan-wen 徐元文 325
hsüeh-shu 學術 254
hsün 訊 (to carry out an adjudicative inquiry), 116
hsün-fang 巡方 366n
hsün-shou 巡狩 257
Hsün Yüeh 荀悅 255
hu-li 護理 (to take charge of an office on a short-term basis), 296
Hu-lü tse-li 戶律則例 198n
Huai-nan-tzu 淮南子 282
huan 緩 (to postpone a tax collection), 117
Huang Ju-ch'eng 黃汝成 70
huang-ts'e 黃冊 (yellow copy), 141
Huang Tsung-hsi 黃宗羲 75
hui-i 會議 (conference), 183
hui-pi 迴避 (avoidance), 37
hui-t'i 彙題 (a t'i-pen memorial dealing with a group of matters), 390
Hui-tien-kuan 會典館 (Bureau for compiling the collected statutes)
huo 獲 (to arrest), 116
huo 豁 same as huo-ch'u, 117
huo-ch'u 豁除 (to cancel a tax collection), 117
huo-huan 豁緩 117
huo-mien 豁免 same as huo-ch'u, 117

I-cheng 儀徵 357
I-cheng-wang 議政王 (princes with the authority to deliberate on governmental matters), 183
I chiang-kai-yüan-teng ying-te ch'u-fen tsou-shang 宜將該員等應得處分奏上 125n
i-chin kung-tsui 溢觔公罪 358
i-chu 挹注 54n
i-ch'u 議處 (to advise on administrative punishment), 115

i-chun 議准 (imperially approved proposal), 182
i-chü liang-pien 一舉兩便 56
i-chü liang-te 一舉兩得 56
i-hsü 議敍 (to advise on administrative honors), 359
I-i ch'in-tz'u 依議欽此 178
i-i kuan-t'ung 義意貫通 96
i-ku chun-chin 以古準今 72
i-kung tai-chen 以工代賑 55
i-li ch'ü-kuan 以理去官 (officials who have left office for a valid reason), 360
i-shih-mien 以事免 (because of involvement in a troublesome matter, participation in the grand council is stopped), 436
i-tai chih chang-ch'eng 一代之章程 (the laws of a dynasty), 38
i-tai chih tien-ts'e 一代之典冊 (the records of a dynasty's laws), 201
i-ting 議定 same as i-chun, 183
i-tsou 議奏 (to advise in a memorial), 183
i tzu ch'ien-hun 易滋牽混 99

Jan-ming 然明 260
jang 讓 71n
jen 人 253
jen 仁 78
Jen An任安 256
Jen Ch'i-yün 任啓運 68n
jen-chih 人治 161
jen chung 任重 48
jen-li 人力 48
jen-shih pu-yung 任事不勇 332
Jen Yüan-hsiang 任源祥 81, 153n
Juan Yüan 阮元 27n
jung-hsiao 融銷 (selling salt by shifting shipments to wherever the market is best), 54

kai-chih 改制 63
kai-chüan 改捐 (to be restored to a different office by making a financial contribution), 315
k'ai-chung-fa 開中法 119
k'ai-ch'üeh 開缺 (to vacate a post), 111
k'ai-fu 開復 (to be reappointed to an office), 300
k'an-shou 看守 (to keep under custody), 299
kang 綱 100
kang-fa 綱法 120
kang-shih chih fa 綱食之法 120
kao-an 稿案 (administrative case), 21n
kao-chia 告假 (to announce a leave of absence), 111
kao-ch'ih 誥勅 (title patent), 302
kao-t'ui 告退 (to announce retirement from office), 111
Kao-yu hsien-chih 高郵縣志
kao-yü 告諭 (to make an order publicly known), 180
k'ao-ch'eng 考成 (examination of administrative results), 49n, 125, 290, 367
k'ao-chi 考績 (examination of meritorious acts), 247
k'ao-yü 考語 (personnel evaluation), 314, 368
ko 格 209
ko-chih 革職 (dismissal from office), 112, 300
ko-chih fa-shen 革職發審 (dismiss from office and dispatch to be tried), 277
ko-chih liu-jen 革職留任 (dismissal from office with retention of duties), 300
ko-chih tai-tsui liu-jen 革職帶罪留任 (dismissal from office with retention of duties while carrying along one's guilt), 265
ko-chih wei-min 革職爲民 (dismissed from office and reduced to the status of commoner), 302n
ko-pu-yüan t'ang-chu-shih 各部院堂主事 (secretaries of the head officials at the boards and various other capital offices), 132n
ko-wai shih-en 格外施恩 (to bestow extraordinary favors), 40
k'o-ch'eng 課程 (rates of taxes on goods), 119
k'o-ju 課入 (tax intake), 119
k'o-shih liang-hsüan 課食兩懸 56
kou 勾 (to arrest), 116
kou-wen 勾問 (to arrest and try criminally), 116
Ku Yen-wu 顧炎武 27n

k'u-p'ing wen-yin 庫平紋銀 107n
kuan 官 212n
Kuan Chung 官仲 68
kuan-fang 關防 refers to certain metal seals of office, 179n
kuan-hsia 管轄 (have jurisdiction over), 123
kuan-li 管理 same as kuan-li shih-wu, 133n
kuan-li shih-wu 管理事務 (to be placed over the officials regularly in charge of a function), 123n
kuan-shou kuan-tui 官收官兌 34n
kuan-ssu 官司 (office), 212n
kuan-ssu so-shou 官司所守 (the duties of offices), 212n
kuan-tang 官當 (removal of one or more ranks as a substitute for criminal punishment), 272
kuan-yüan chiang-fa ti-hsiao 官員降罰抵銷 (canceling administrative honors in lieu of carrying out demotions and salary fines), 387n
kuan-yüan chiang-ko 官員降革 (the dismissal and demotion of officials), 303n
kuan-yüan fa-feng 官員罰俸 (salary fines of officials), 289n
kuan-yüan k'ai-fu 官員開復 (restoring officials to office), 265n
Kuang Ch'ien 光謙 376
kuei 規 (regulations), 226
kuei-pu 歸補 114
k'uei-sung chu-t'o 餽送囑託 (to give presents, asking for favors), 323n
k'uei-tseng 餽贈 (gift-giving), 322
kung 公 9, 28
kung 供 (to testify), 371
kung-li 功利 65
kung-ling chih shu 功令之書 (books of law), 169
Kung-pu chün-ch'i tse-li 工部軍器則例 199
kung-sheng 貢生 338n
kung-shih 供事 (clerk), 133
kung-shih 公式 (general rules, regulations), 226
kung-shih shih-ts'o 公事失錯 (mistakes in public matters), 276, 359n
kung-tsuan ch'eng-li 恭纂成例 (respectfully compile as tse-li), 115n
kung-tsuan wei-li 恭纂為例 same as kung-tsuan ch'eng-li, 115n
kung-tsui 公罪 (public offense), 268, 281–285
K'ung-tzu chia-yü 孔子家語 256n
K'ung Ying-ta 孔穎達 264n
kuo 國 71n
kuo-chi min-sheng 國計民生 56
kuo-t'i 國體 (proper order and dignity of the state), 82, 278

lang-chung 郎中 100
le-ling hsiu-chih 勒令休致 (forced retirement), 112
lei 類 185
leng-shu 冷署 50n
li 里 193
li 理 43
li 利 57
li 力 48
li 例 83, 86
li 禮 65
li-an 立案 197
li-an pu-hsing 立案不行 396
li-cheng 吏政 327
li-chih 吏治 415
Li Chih-fang 李之芳 310
li-ch'u chi-hsi 力除積習 53
Li Chung-fu 李中孚 27n
li-fa 立法 53, 261
Li Fu 李紱 153, 285, 309, 310, 317, 328
Li Hung-chang 李鴻章 80
li-jen 離任 (to leave office) 112
Li Kou 李覯 67, 103n
li-nien shih-li 歷年事例 265n
li-tien 吏典 357
Li T'ing-hsi 李廷錫 420
li-ts'ai 理財 108
Li Tz'u-ming 李慈銘 322
li-yen 例言 169n
liang 兩 107
Liang Ch'i-ch'ao 梁啓超 71
Liang Ch'ing-piao 梁清標 298n, 326
Lin Shih-chün 林士俊 153–154
Lin Tse-hsü 林則徐 26n, 60, 204, 208
ling 令 161, 169n, 176, 210–211
ling kung ssu liang pien 令公私兩便 281
Ling T'ing-k'an 凌廷堪 27n

ling yu chih ch'in tz'u 另有旨欽此 178
liu 流 302
liu-fa 六法 368, 395
Liu Ho-tung ch'üan-chi 柳河東全集 258n
Liu Hsiang 劉向 251n
Liu Hsin 劉歆 63
liu-jen 留任 (retention of official duties), 112
liu-jen tai-tsui 留任戴罪 (retention of official duties while carrying along one's guilt), 117
Liu-pu ch'eng-yü chu-chieh 六部成語註解 124–126, 393
liu-tien 六典 211
Liu-Tsung-yüan 柳宗元 46, 258
Lo 洛 253n
Lu Chiu-yüan 陸九淵 43
Lu Hsi-chin 盧錫晉 266n, 327
Lu Lung-chi (ch'i?) 陸隴其 325, 327
Lu Shih-i 陸世儀 27n, 76, 77n
Lu Shou-ming 陸壽名 37, 258n
Lu Wen-ch'ao 盧文弨 27n
lü 律 (penal statute), 84–86
lü-shüeh 律學 (study of penal law), 426
lü-li 律例 usually refers to penal code, 118, 150n
lü-li 履歷 (curriculum vitae), 369, 393
Lü-li ch'üan-shu 律例全書 (Penal code), 118
Lü-li-kuan 律例館 (Bureau for compiling the penal code), 87, 130, 135n
lü-ling 律令 (tse-li, tse-li dealing with punishments, laws), 120
lü-shu 律書 can refer to penal code as a whole, 426
lü-wen 律文 can refer to penal code as a whole, 425

Ma-p'eng-wan 馬棚灣 375
Ma Tuan-lin 馬端臨 32
mei-pao ti-an shou-chia 每包抵岸售價 106
mi 密 76, 416
mien 免 same as mien-chih, 436
mien-chih 免直 (participation in imperial audiences as a grand councillor is stopped), 436
min 民 71n
ming 名 126n
ming-fu 命婦 (an official's female relative possessing an honorary title derived from his title patent), 361
ming-hsi 明晰 97
ming-li 名例 (principles of sentencing), 126
mo 末 30
mou 畝 299
mu 目 101

na 拏 (to arrest), 116
nan 難 49n
nan i chien-yüeh 難以檢閱 99
nei 內 34
nei-p'i 內批 (inner court instructions), 175n
nei-ti 內地 302
nei-wai k'ao-ch'a kuan-yüan ch'eng-pien 內外考察官員呈辯 (the lodging of complaints by capital and regional officials arguing about their grading in the triannual evaluations), 396n
Nei-wu-fu 內務府 (Imperial household), 108
neng-li 能吏 254
no-i 挪移 (to use public funds or goods for public purposes but illegally), 284
no-i tien-yung 挪移墊用 (to advance funds from one expenditure account to another under difficult or illegal circumstances), 114
no-tien 挪墊 same as no-i tien-yung, 114

o-ch'üeh 額缺 (regular post), 296
o-wai ssu-yüan 額外司員 (departmental officials outside the regular quota of officials), 137, 151
Ou-yang Hsiu 歐陽修 73, 175

pa 霸 (hegemon), 66
pa-chih 罷職 113n
pa-i 八議 (eight conditions for consideration), 360n
p'ai-wang 派往 same as fa-wang, 303
pan 頒 same as pan-chiang, 115n
pan-chiang 頒降 (promulgate), 115n
pan-fa 頒發 same as pan-chang, 115n
pan-li 辦理 same as ching-li, 53
pan-shih kuei-t'iao 辦事規條 185

P'an Shih-en 潘世恩 137
pao-chü 包擧 97
pao-chün 暴君 75
pao-pen fan-shih 報本反始 31
pei-ho jen-yüan hsieh-ssu pao-fu 被劾人員挾私報復 (impeached officials who, harboring personal grudges, seek revenge), 396n
pei-le 貝勒 (prince of the third rank), 183
p'ei 賠 (making payments as restitution), 301
p'ei-ko 配割 (counted as part of another yin [fiscal unit of salt]), 60–61
pen 本 30, 31
pen-chang 本章 generic for memorials, covering t'i-pen and tsou-pen or tsou-che, 117n
pen-chi chieh-jang hui-pi 本籍接壤迴避 (avoiding office-holding in one's native district and adjacent areas, including some in neighboring provinces), 37n
pi 比 185
pi-chao 比照 196
Pi Yüan 畢沅 27n
p'i 批 (comment, authorization), 179, 181
p'i 疲 50n
p'i-yen-so ta-shih 批驗所大使 (inspection station supervisor), 118
pien 變 23
pien-chung hai-chih 邊中海支 119
pien-fa 變法 29, 54
pien-t'ung 變通 40
ping-chia 病假 (sick leave), 112
p'ing 平 9, 318
po 駁 180
po-hu 百戶 427
pu 捕 (to arrest), 116
pu-chih t'o-lou 不致脫漏 98
pu-chün 不均 44n
pu-i chih ching 不易之經 39
Pu-lan-t'ai 布蘭泰 317–319
pu-li 不力 48, 289
pu-tung-hsin 不動心 413
pu-yüan 部院 (boards and various other capital offices), 132n
pu-yüan ch'eng-shen shih-chien 部院承審事件 (matters connected to trials held by one or more of the pu-yüan), 132n
pu-yüan shih-chien hsien-ch'i 部院事件限期 (deadlines in the handling of pu-yüan affairs), 132n
p'u 蒲 60

san-fu 三輔 421
san-kung 三公 172
Shan Chuang-t'u 單壯圖 267
Shang-chün-shu 商君書 71n
shang-sheng 上聖 36
she-li yen-an 舍例言案 (disregard tse-li and cite cases), 202
shen 審 (to carry out an adjudicative inquiry), 116, 372
Shen Chia-pen 沈家本 424
Shen Chiao-sheng 沈椒生 354
Shen-chien 申鑒 256n
Shen Han 申韓 248n
shen-hsün 審訊 (to hold a criminal trial), 116
shen-li 審理 same as shen-hsün, 116
shen-pan 審辦 same as shen-hsün, 116
Shen Pu-hai 申不害 247n, 248
sheng 聖 36
sheng-chih 聖制 (order of the emperor), 175
Sheng Fu-sheng 盛符升 424
sheng-hsüan 陞選 (promotions and appointments), 355
sheng-hsün 聖訓 206
sheng-li 省例 (provincial regulations), 204
Sheng-yü shih-liu-t'iao fu-lü i-chieh 聖諭十六條附律易解 428
sheng-yüan 生員 362
shih 史 217
shih 士 264
shih 事 212n, 409
shih 矢 (oath), 371
shih 式 (ordinance), 186n
shih 勢 43
shih-an 食岸 120
shih-ch'a ch'in-tao 失察侵盜 (lack of vigilance leading to embezzlement and theft), 155
Shih Chieh 石介 29n
shih-chien 事件 194

shih-chih 世職 same as shih-chüeh, 339
Shih Chung-yin 石中隱 352n
shih-chüeh 世爵 (hereditary rank), 339
shih-li 事例 (tse-li, precedents of minor significance, laws), 121, 198
shih-li feng-hsing 實力奉行 (carry out orders energetically), 53
shih-lu 實錄 206
shih-tien 實墊 (truly to advance funds from one expenditure account to another), 114
shih-wei-chü-wen 視爲具文 (to regard an order as a mere piece of paper), 20
shih-yung 試用 (probationary), 296
shu 署 55
shu 書 204
Shu 蜀 253n
shu 屬 (to be under the authority of), 122
shu 疏 77
shu-chang 疏章 (memorials), 117n
shu-chih 述職 257
Shu-hsiang 叔向 429
shu-hsing 贖刑 (redemption of criminal punishments), 304n
shu-jen kuan-yüan yang-lien 署任官員養廉 (acting officials' payments to nourish integrity), 345n
shu-li 署理 (to be in charge of an office on an acting basis), 296
Shu-li ch'eng-pien 疏理成編 157
Shu-sun T'ung 叔孫通 63n
shun-min 順民 71n
Shuo 朔 253n
shuo-t'ieh 說帖 (memorandum), 231
so 所 118
ssu 私 28
ssu 死 251n
ssu-kuan 司官 (departmental official), 99n
Ssu-ma Kuang 司馬光 29n, 32, 67
Ssu-ma T'an 司馬談 65
ssu-tsui 私罪 (private offense), 269, 281–287
su 俗 77
Su Tung-p'o 蘇東坡 36n, 46, 77, 258
Sun Mei-shan 孫眉山 354
Sun Ting-ch'en 孫鼎臣 44

ta-ch'en 大臣 183
ta-chi 大計 (triannual evaluation in the provinces), 309, 368
ta-chi t'ung-li 大計統例 (general regulations of the triannual evaluation in the provinces), 368n
Ta-Ch'ing-lü 大淸律 (The penal code of the great Ch'ing dynasty), 118
Ta-Ch'ing lü chi-chieh fu-li 大淸律集解附例 118
ta-hsiu 大修 (major revision), 87, 132
Ta-hsüeh yen-i-pu 大學衍義補 59n
ta-i-t'ung 大一統 (the great rule of all by one king), 30
Ta-Ming-ling 大明令 431
tai-ch'ai tai-hsing 代拆代行 (breaking open the seals of communications and acting on behalf of another official), 55
tai-cheng chüan-huan ch'ien-liang 帶徵蠲緩錢糧 (collecting temporarily remitted taxes along with current ones), 117
tai-hsiao 代銷 (to sell salt at place x on behalf of the sales quota at place y), 54
tai-tsou 代奏 (to memorialize on behalf of another), 433
tai-tsui liu-jen 帶罪留任 (retention of duties while carrying along one's guilt), 117
t'an-tsang 貪贓 (greedy, illegal appropriation of wealth by officials), 305, 318
tang-an 檔案 same as an-chüan, 112
tang-ts'e 檔册 same as an-chüan, 112
t'ang-kuan 堂官 (head officials in capital offices), 299, 316
T'ang liu-tien 唐六典 211
t'ang-t'ieh 堂帖 174
tao 道 28, 29
tao-t'ung 道統 414
T'ao Cheng-ching 陶正靖 50n
T'ao Chu 陶澍 25, 26n
t'ao-shu 桃樹 26n
te 德 379
te-shih 得失 217
t'e-chih 特旨 (special rescript), 194
t'e-li tu-hsing 特立獨行 327
t'eng-huang 謄黃 (yellow poster), 163n
ti-hsiao 抵銷 (cancel in lieu of, i.e.,

cancel an administrative honor in lieu of inflicting an administrative punishment), 313
ti-huan 遞緩 (cancel immediate collection of a tax and stagger collection over a number of years), 117
ti-pen 底本 (basic or original manuscript), 120n
ti-ting 地丁 124, 128
t'i 體 34
t'i 提 (to arrest), 116
t'i-chih 體制 (fundamental structure of institutions), 38, 39
t'i-chun 題准 (imperially approved proposal in a t'i-pen memorial), 182
t'i-hsü 體恤 360
t'i-hsün 提訊 (arrest and try criminally), 116
t'i-li 體例 (organizational principles of a piece of writing), 211
t'i-pen 題本 (memorial for routine public matters), 419
t'i-tiao-kuan 提調官 (editorial supervisor), 133
t'i-ts'ai 體裁 (the format and style appropriate to a particular kind of writing), 108
t'i-ts'an 題參 (to impeach in a t'i-pen memorial), 115
t'i-tu 提督 434
t'i-wei . . . shih 題爲…事 110
t'i-wen 提問 (arrest and try criminally), 116
t'i-yao 體要 (essential structure), 38
tiao-yung 調用 (demotion in subgrade with transfer out of one's post), 300
t'iao 條 101, 121
t'iao-li 條例 (penal regulations or "substatutes"), 197
t'iao-tsou 條奏 (to memorialize), 117n
tien 典 (fundamental statute, institution), 39, 121, 205–206
tien 墊 same as tien-fa, 114
tien-chan 墊佔 (to move funds between one expenditure account and another), 114
tien-chang 典章 (fundamental statutes and laws), 38
tien-chieh 墊解 (to advance funds from one expenditure account to another in another office), 114
tien-chih 墊支 (to advance funds from one expenditure account into another in the same office), 114
tien-fa 墊發 (to advance funds from one expenditure account into another),114
tien-ts'e 典冊 39
tien-yung 墊用 same as tien-fa, 114
ting 定 201
ting-chih 定制 (fixed order of the state), 38, 39
ting-li 定例 usually same as tse-li, 159, 198, 202n, 210n
ting-lü 定律 425
Ting Pao-chen 丁寶楨 40
ting-to 定奪 178n
t'ing 廳 148
t'ing-ch'en 廷臣 135
t'ing-i 廷議 134
t'ing-nien-ko 停年格 (deciding promotion on the basis of seniority and merit), 326n
t'ing-sheng 停升 (temporary ineligibility for promotion), 301n
to-k'ai t'iao-k'uan 多開條款 96
tsa-fan ssu-tsui 雜犯死罪 (nominal death sentence commuted to a term of penal servitude), 304
tsai-hsiang 宰相 (prime office), 10, 172–176
tsai-jen shou-chih 在任守制 (observing mourning obligations while holding office), 41
Ts'ai Fang-ping 蔡方炳 288n
ts'ai-li 才吏 262
ts'an 參 (impeach), 115
ts'an-ch'e shih-ch'eng 參撤示懲 (remove from office through impeachment, warning others by the use of punishment), 116
ts'an-ch'eng 參懲 (impeach and call for punishment), 115
ts'an-ch'u 參處 (impeach and advise on administrative punishment), 115
ts'an-ho 參劾 (impeach), 115
ts'an-ko fa-shen 參革發審 (impeached, dismissed from office, and dispatched to be criminally tried), 372

ts'an-pan 參辦 (impeach), 115
ts'an-tsou 參奏 (to impeach in a memorial), 115
ts'an-yin 殘引 120n
tsang-tsui 贓罪 (the crime of illegally obtaining money or goods), 260
ts'ang-ch'ang chien-tu 倉場監督 147n
ts'ang-ch'ang shih-lang 倉場侍郎 143
ts'ao-pen 草本 139
Ts'ao Shen 曹參 32n
tse 責 177
tse-li 則例 (fully established precedents and regulation of capital offices, regulations), 197–205
Tse-li t'u-yao 則例圖要 353
ts'e 冊 95, 112, 117
ts'e-chi 冊籍 117
ts'en-tz'u i-t'ung 參差異同 96
tso-liang-t'ing 坐粮廳 147n
tso-tsa 佐雜 179n
tsou 奏 (to memorialize), 177
tsou-chang 奏章 (memorials), 117n
tsou-che 奏摺 same as che-tsou, 419
tsou-ch'en 奏陳 (to memorialize), 117n
tsou-chun 奏准 (imperially approved proposal in a tsou-pen or tsou-che memorial), 182
Tsou Hsi-ch'un 鄒錫淳 267
tsou-hsiao 奏銷 (memorialize on fiscal items to be checked and closed as correct), 367
tsou-i 奏議 (memorials), 117n
tsou-kao 奏藁 (memorials), 117n
tsou-ming 奏明 (to memorialize), 117n
tsou-pen 奏本 (memorial to be used largely for matters, like promotions, involving one's personal career in the bureaucracy), 419
tsou-shu 奏疏 (memorials), 84n
tsou-ts'an 奏參 (to memorialize calling for impeachment), 117n
tsou-wei . . . shih 奏爲…事, 110
Tsou Yen 鄒衍 45
tsu-chih 祖制 32
tsu-yung-tiao 租庸調 44
tsuan-hsiu 纂修 (compiler), 133
tsuan-ju tse-li 纂入則例 (compile as tse-li), 115n
tsuan wei ting-li 纂爲定例 same as tsuan-ju tse-li, 115n
tsui 罪 266
tsui-yao 最要 (post with an extremely heavy burden of administration), 49n
ts'ui 催 (press for payment of taxes), 338
tsun 尊 250
tsun-chün i-ch'en 尊君抑臣 250, 251n
tsun-chün pei-ch'en ch'ung-shang i-hsia 尊君卑臣崇上抑下 251n
tsun ku-fa cho shih-i 遵古法酌時宜 72
tsung-ping 總兵 433
tsung-shih 宗室 (imperial house), 339
tsung-shih wang-kung 宗室王公 433
tsung-shu 總數 108
tsung-ts'ai 總裁 (editorial director), 133
tsung-tsuan 總纂 (head compiler), 133
ts'ung-chih 從之 (the emperor followed the suggestion presented to him), 179
ts'ung-yen ts'an-pan 從嚴參辦 (to impeach calling for severe administrative punishment), 115
tu 督 (to supervise), 294
tu 蠹 (corruption), 304
tu-chih 度支 (matters of state finance), 54
tu-chih 度制 (fundamental state institutions), 38
Tu Huan-ch'en 堵煥辰 354, 356
tu-pan 督辦 53
Tu Yu 杜佑 37, 46, 172
t'u 徒 (penal servitude), 308
Tuan Yü-ts'ai 段玉裁 27n
t'ui 推 (arrest), 116
t'ui-hsieh 推卸 267
t'ui-kuan 推官 366n
t'ui-wen 推問 (arrest and try criminally), 116
Tung Chung-shu 董仲舒 31n, 64n, 258
t'ung-hsia 統轄 (have anthority over), 122
t'ung-hsing t'iao-li 通行條例 (generally circulated regulations), 204
t'ung-liao fan kung-tsui 同僚犯公罪 (if a public offense is committed in affairs carried out jointly by official personnel), 359n
t'ung-p'an 通判 394
T'ung-tien 通典 217
Tzu-ch'an 子產 64n, 259–260

tzu-chi 字寄 (court letter), 419
tzu-hsin 自新 265
tzu-wen 咨文 148n
Tz'u-hai 辭海 185
tz'u-i ch'ung-fu 詞意重複 96
tz'u-shih 刺史 258

wai 外 34
wai-pan chang-ch'eng 外辦章程 (provincial administrative rules), 197
wang 王 66
Wang An-shih 王安石 29n, 32, 64n, 67, 262
Wang Ch'ang 王昶 27n
wang-chih 往支 345n
Wang Chih-i 汪志伊 291, 309
Wang Chin 汪縉 67
Wang Chung 汪中 27n
Wang Ch'üan-chih 王泉之 369
Wang Fu-chih 王夫之 45
Wang Hsin-ching 王心敬 422
Wang Hui-tsu 王輝祖 35n, 149, 311
Wang Liu 王鎏 57n, 59
Wang Lun 王倫 175
Wang Mang 王莽 64n
Wang Ming-sheng 王鳴盛 27n
Wang Su 王肅 256n
Wang Tseng (Ts'eng?) 王曾 173
Wang Yang-ming 王陽明 72n
wang-yen 妄言 76
wei 衛 148
wei-chih 違制 (violate an imperial order), 312
wei-ho 未合 96
wei-hsien kung-tsui 違限公罪 (the public offense of violating the time limit), 358
wei-hsin 維新 23
wei-li 違例 (violate the laws), 40
wei-min 爲民 (be reduced to the status of commoner), 302
wei-yüan 委員 (commissioned official), 315
wen 問 (hold an adjudicative inquiry), 116
wen 文 47
wen-chien i-kai 文簡義賅 97
wen-chüan 文卷 same as an-chüan, 112
Wen-hsien t'ung-k'ao 文獻通考 125n
wen-hsing ya-men 問刑衙門 (offices in charge of handling criminal cases), 147
Wen-hsüan 文選 48n
wen-li 文理 110
wen-shu 文書 113
wen-ts'e 文册 same as an-chüan, 112
wen-wu-kuan fan kung-tsui 文武官犯公罪 (when civil or military officials commit a public offense), 273n
wen-wu-kuan fan ssu-tsui 文武官犯私罪 (when civil or military officials commit a private offense), 273n
wu-kuan fan-tsui 無官犯罪 (if the offense was committed before taking office), 359n
wu-she 無涉 96
Wu T'an 吳壇 424
Wu Tzu-feng 吳紫峯 424
wu-wei 無爲 48, 66
Wu-ying-tien 武英殿 144

ya-cheng 壓徵 126
Yang-ho t'ing 揚河廳 376
Yang-ho ying 揚河營 376
yang-lien 養廉 (payment to nourish integrity), 281, 301n, 320, 321n
yang-pen 樣本 145
Yang Sheng-wu 楊繩武 33n
Yang Yen 楊炎 32
yao-ch'üeh 要缺 (post with a heavy administrative burden), 49n
Yeh Shih 葉適 75
yen 研 (carry out an adjudicative inquiry), 116
yen-cheng 鹽政 26n
yen-chia i-ch'u 嚴加議處 (advise on severe administrative punishment), 115
yen-chia ts'an-ch'u 嚴加參處 (impeach calling for severe administrative punishment), 115
yen-chieh 研詰 (carry out an adjudicative inquiry), 116
Yen-fa-k'ao 鹽法考 157
Yen Fu 嚴復 14n
yen-hsing ts'an-pan 嚴行參辦 same as yen-chia ts'an-ch'u, 115
Yen Jo-ch'ü 閻若璩 62, 291
Yen-liao-k'u 顏料庫 140

Yen-p'u tsa-chi 簷曝雜記 124n
yen-shih 言事 433
yen-ts'an ch'eng-pan 嚴參懲辦 same as yen-chia ts'an-ch'u, 115
yen-ts'an chiu-pan 嚴參究辦 same as yen-chia ts'an-ch'u, 115
yen-yin 鹽引 117
yen-yün-shih 鹽運使 50
yin 因 290
yin 引 (fiscal weight unit, master license in salt monopoly), 61
yin 印 179n
Yin Chia-ch'üan 尹嘉銓 173
yin-chieh-yin 印結銀 (guarantee silver), 323–324
yin-chien 引見 (to lead an official into an imperial audience), 126
yin-hsin 印信 refers to certain metal seals of office, 179n
yin-hsün 因循 57
Yin-k'u 銀庫 139
yin-mu 引目 117
yin-sheng 廕生 361
yin-shih kua-wu 因事詿誤 (to be pressed by circumstances into a transgression), 276
yin-yung lü-li 引用律例 (citing the law in punitive cases), 385n
Ying-ho 英和 436
ying shih-chih-pien 應事之變 34, 413
yu-li 有力 305
yu-shou yu-wei 有守有爲 57
yu-t'i yu-yung 有體有用 56
yu-wei 有爲 66
yung 用 34
Yung-an-hsün 永安汛 376
yung-fa 用法 261
yung pu hsü-yung 永不敘用 (never to be reappointed), 300
yung-yüan chien-chin 永遠監禁 (imprisonment for life), 263
yü 欲 402
yü 諭 194
yü-k'o pien-min 裕課便民 56
yü-ling 諭令 210
yü-tsui 餘罪 (leftover guilt), 276
yüan 援 (to adduce), 185
yüan-i 冤抑 (to wrong and oppress), 391
Yüan Shih-chen 袁世振 32n, 62n
Yüan-tao 原道 44n
yüan-tsou 原奏 142
yüan-wei-li 援爲例 (adduce as precdent), 196
Yün Ching 惲敬 36n, 44n
yün-chun 允准 (authorize), 181
yün-hsing 允行 (authorize), 180
yün-shang 運商 187
yün-shih 運使 132

General Index

Harvard Studies in East Asian Law

1. *Law in Imperial China: Exemplified by 190 Ch'ing Dynasty Cases (translated from the* Hsing-an hui-lan*) with Historical, Social, and Juridical Commentaries.* By Derk Bodde and Clarence Morris. 1967

2. *The Criminal Process in the People's Republic of China, 1949–1963: An Introduction.* By Jerome Alan Cohen. 1968

3. *Agreements of the People's Republic of China, 1949–1967: A Calendar.* By Douglas M. Johnston and Hungdah Chiu. 1968

4. *Contemporary Chinese Law: Research Problems and Perspectives.* Edited by Jerome Alan Cohen. 1970

5. *The People's Republic of China and the Law of Treaties.* By Hungdah Chiu. 1972.

6. *China's Practice of International Law: Some Case Studies.* Edited by Jerome Alan Cohen. 1972

7. *The Internal Organization of Ch'ing Bureaucracy: Legal, Normative, and Communication Aspects.* By Thomas A. Metzger. 1973

Bei Fragen zur Produktsicherheit wenden Sie sich bitte an:
If you have any questions regarding product safety,
please contact:

Walter de Gruyter GmbH
Genthiner Straße 13
10785 Berlin
productsafety@degruyterbrill.com